Instructional Media

Instructional

AND THE NEW TECHNOLOGIES OF INSTRUCTION

Robert Heinich
Indiana University

Michael Molenda
Indiana University

James D. Russell
Purdue University

Media

THIRD EDITION

Macmillan Publishing Company
New York

Collier Macmillan Publishers
London

Cover Photo: Geoffrey Gove
Cover and Text Design: Kenny Beck

Macmillan Publishing Company
866 Third Avenue, New York, New York 10022

Collier Macmillan Canada, Inc.

Library of Congress Cataloging-in-Publication Data

Heinich, Robert.
    Instructional media and the new technologies of instruction
    Robert Heinich, Michael Molenda, James D. Russell.—3rd ed.
        p. cm.
        Includes index.
        ISBN 0-02-353020-0
        1. Educational technology.   2. Audio-visual education.
    I. Molenda, Michael.   II. Russell, James D.   III. Title.
    LB1028.3.H45 1989   88-12921
    371.3'07'8—dc19   CIP

Printing: 4 5 6 7   Year: 0 1 2 3 4 5

PREFACE

From the Publisher

Macmillan Publishing Company is pleased to have acquired the publication rights to *Instructional Media and the New Technologies of Instruction*. In a surprisingly short period of time, this award-winning book has become the most widely used textbook for college and university courses on instructional media. The book's leading position as an introductory text in the field of instructional technology is continuing evidence of its excellence. Its popular acceptance mirrors the very favorable reviews it has received in professional journals.

The first award recognition of the text came from Graphic Design U.S.A. The layout, special features, typography, graphics, use of color, and distinctive cover were recognized in the "Desi" award conferred in 1982. Early in 1983 *Instructional Media* won the James W. Brown Publication Award from the Association for Educational Communications and Technology (AECT). Later that year the National Society for Performance and Instruction (NSPI) honored the book with its Communication of the Year award over stiff competition. These awards confirm the judgment of the many individual instructors who chose this book to introduce their students to the world of instructional technology.

We wish to thank the many instructors who contributed to *Instructional Media*'s success. Through their reviews, formal responses to market research, and informal advice, they have helped shape the book to meet the needs of students and teachers in the field of instructional media. With their input, we believe that this expanded and updated third edition will continue its standard of excellence.

From the Authors

In the preface to the first edition, we related how the decision to write this book grew out of a survey of instructors of basic media utilization courses. The results of that survey and subsequent ones have helped in determining the scope of the book. Reviews of the draft manuscript by knowledgeable people in the field have helped us fine tune the manuscript.

A number of adopters have been asked to critique the book chapter by chapter. Thanks to all those who responded, we discovered what worked well and what needed revision.

Many of our readers have given us their reactions on aspects of the book. We take such comments very seriously. We are particularly pleased to hear that students enjoy reading the book.

A number of instructors have taken advantage of the offer we made in the *Instructors Guide* to engage in a telelecture with their students. This has been an invaluable way for us to maintain contact with readers in a wide variety of settings.

When we were preparing the first edition, we class tested each chapter with our own classes at Indiana University and Purdue University. We continue to solicit feedback from our own students as we develop new material. We are determined to maintain the reputation of the text as one that is classroom tested.

Basic Assumptions

For readers not familiar with the previous editions, we repeat our original convictions: (1) a rapprochement can be reached between the so-called humanist and technological traditions in the field of education; (2) a proper introduction to this field must involve not only technical skills but also understanding of the pedagogical rationales underlying the use of media/technology; and (3) to be comprehensive, a textbook such as this must encompass not only the traditional audiovisual media and the newer electronic media but also the non-hardware psychological technologies.

Special Features

This third edition maintains the special features introduced in the first two editions and adds one new feature. Adopting instructors indicate that these features aroused interest and contributed to better retention of media knowledge and skills among their students. The features are:

- **Outlines.** Each chapter begins with a broad outline of the contents, thus providing a quick advance organizer.
- **Objectives.** A detailed list of performance objectives precedes the text of each chapter.
- **Lexicon.** A short list of new or specialized vocabulary terms is introduced at the beginning of each chapter. This alerts readers to watch for these terms in the chapter, where they are discussed in context.
- **Close-Ups.** These serve as miniature case studies of media applications; many of the vignettes are drawn from business/industry settings.
- **Media Files.** Actual materials in different media formats are highlighted. The materials shown have been selected as *typical* of a given class, not as *exemplary.* No endorsement— nor even commercial availability—is implied.
- **How To . . .** Various media production and operation procedures are spelled out with clear, illustrated, step-by-step instructions. Each is boxed for easy reference.
- **Appraisal Checklists.** New checklists have been developed for appraising each media format. Users have permission to photocopy these lists for personal use. This makes it easy to preview materials systematically and to preserve the previews for later reference.

- **AV Showmanship.** This feature gives specific tips on delivering media presentations with flair and dramatic effect.
- **Flashbacks.** These are brief histories that lend a sense of perspective and often provide fascinating behind-the-scenes glimpses of historic developments.
- **Blueprints.** This new feature appears in several chapters. Each blueprint details how the ASSURE model applies to the use of specific instructional media. We believe these examples will enable students to apply the ASSURE model more readily in their own instructional planning.

Appendices

Appendix A contains suggested sources for the various types of materials discussed in the chapters. It has been thoroughly updated and revised for this edition. **Appendix B** has lists of sources of free and inexpensive materials. **Appendix C** deals with the issues of copyright law as they pertain to users of instructional media. Recent legal interpretations are discussed. Our point of view is that an informed approach to the spirit as well as the letter of the law can result in giving the instructor more "elbow room" than generally has been considered possible. The **Lexicon** terms and many other specialized terms are gathered into a revised **Glossary,** given at the end of the book as **Appendix D.**

What's New

In addition to the "Blueprints" just mentioned, the following changes have been made to the indicated chapters. In all chapters and appendices, references have been brought up to date.

Chapter 1 opens with descriptions of media utilization in nine widely varying situations. Eight methods of instruction that may incorporate media are introduced in this chapter, along with the psychological basis for using instructional media, including schemata and assimilation. There is a new "Flashback" on the history of media and technology in instruction. Recent patterns of the use of media in education and training are described. A new matrix showing the dimensions of the technologies of instruction (media, pedagogy, and management) is presented.

Most of the changes in Chapter 2 are meant to enhance the usefulness of the ASSURE model as a practical guide to integrating media into instruction. The "ABCD" format for writing performance objectives provides, we hope, a mnemonic guide to simplify this task. The organizational scheme for the cognitive domain now follows the taxonomy of Gagné rather than of Bloom; this reflects the trend in the field of instructional design.

The title of Chapter 3 has been changed from "Visual Literacy" to "Visual Design." A section on the use of visuals with adult learners has been added. Other additions include three "How To" boxes on designing printed materials, designing computer screens, and sketching. At the request of readers, the information on photography has been expanded. A "Blueprint" on applying the ASSURE model to high school Spanish appears at the end of Chapter 3.

Additions to Chapter 4 on "Nonprojected Visuals" include field trips and dioramas. There is a new "How To" on conducting a field trip. An "AV Showmanship" for still pictures and graphics has been included. The "Blueprint" at the end of the chapter features a training application from a small assembly plant.

The basic organization of Chapter 5 has not been altered. The content has been updated to reflect changes in technology, particularly in computer generation of visuals and the projection of computer images. New "Media File" boxes reflect recent trends in commercially produced transparencies.

The compact disc (CD) already has had considerable impact on home music listening and will eventually have one on educational uses of audio. The data-storing capability of the compact disc, CD-ROM, has made its influence felt in a remarkably short period of time. The CD is discussed in Chapter 6. We have added a "Flashback" on the history of sound recording. The "Flashback" not only presents the evolution of recording but also documents how an inventor goes about his work.

Chapter 7 reflects new developments in interactive video and its applications to instruction. The discussion of modules has been moved to this chapter and expanded. Advantages, limitations, and applications for all multimedia systems are included. Two new "Media File" boxes contain a description of IBM's Info-Window and the Principle of the Alphabet Literacy System. The evolution from interactive 8-mm film to interactive video is discussed in a new "Flashback." In the "Blueprint" we present an elementary science unit on the solar system for use in a learning center.

Chapters 8 and 9 have been thoroughly reorganized. Chapter 8 now encompasses both film and video in their roles as formats for displaying moving images in the classroom. Television in its role as a distribution system is dis-

cussed in Chapter 9. Chapter 8 has updated treatments of instructional video uses in schools, higher education, and business/industry training. Chapter 9 features new descriptions and utilization examples for radio, teleconferencing, and teletext/videotex. The changes in these chapters illustrate vividly the rapid proliferation of new electronic media forms and the equally rapid converging of these technologies.

Safety in handling audiovisual equipment has become an important issue in the field. Chapter 10 now includes safety tips, including ways equipment carts should be moved and a caution on recharging batteries.

Recent work in cognitive psychology has made significant contributions to our understanding of how people learn and process information. In Chapter 11, we show how current research in cognitive psychology can make technologies of instruction more flexible as well as more effective.

The structure of Chaper 12 has not been changed. The treatment of simulation and games has been updated in general. There are new examples of the use of these technologies both in schools and in corporate settings.

The chapter with the greatest expansion and updating is Chapter 13. It reflects the changes in computer technology and applications of computers to instruction. New sections of the chapter include computer graphics, databases, computer networks, and computer-based instructional design. The application of the ASSURE model to computer-based materials is described in detail with a new "Appraisal Checklist" and the utilization of a single computer with an entire class. In the new "Flashback" we discuss the early days of the PLATO system at the University of

Illinois. The hardware portion of the chapter has been significantly updated and expanded with a section on printers and new "Media File" boxes on the IBM Personal System/2 computers, the Apple Macintosh II, and the Tandy 1000 family of computers. The chapter concludes with a "Blueprint" on the use of a computer simulation in high school biology.

Information technology has made tremendous strides in the last few years in ways that will affect our lives for some time to come. We take a look at some of the implications of new technologies of data consolidation and distribution in Chapter 14. The professions in the field of instructional technology are changing, too. New professional organizations always follow in the wake of new technology, and we discuss those in Chapter 14.

For Instructors

If you are an instructor using this text, send your name and address to James D. Russell, School of Education, Purdue University, West Lafayette, IN 47907.

We offer the following services to instructors to assist them in putting together an outstanding course in instructional media.

- **Instructor's Guide.** Ask your Macmillan representative, or write to Macmillan directly, for a copy of this comprehensive guide. Additional content, suggestions for different ways to organize the course, test items for each chapter, and overhead transparency masters on perforated pages are features of the *Instructor's Guide*.
- **Telelecture.** We offer a free lecture by telephone to adopters of our text. Arrange the telelecture by calling any one of us in advance to be sure of

availability. Some instructors use the telelecture as part of the study of Chapter 9. Others use it to discuss the future directions of the field or of the profession. Whatever your purpose, give one of us a call. Our phone numbers are in the *Instructor's Guide*.

- **Newsletter.** When the second edition of the text came out, we decided to keep in touch with our adopters by distributing a newsletter several times a year. The newsletter keeps instructors informed about developments and activities of interest. You'll receive it free of charge if you send your name and address to Jim Russell.
- **Workshops.** At the time the first edition was published, we realized that the annual convention of AECT did not provide a forum for teachers of media courses to exchange ideas and techniques. We decided to create such a forum by offering a preconvention workshop on methods of teaching a basic media course. We have conducted workshops at each AECT convention since 1982. These exchanges have been helpful both to the participants and to us. We have become better acquainted with the problems of teachers of media courses in a wide variety of institutions. The participants benefit not only from the activities of the workshops but also from the sharing of course outlines and materials through the network created by the workshop. We believe that their courses are better as a result of this experience, and we know that our efforts have improved significantly.

We continue to welcome comments about the book. Please send suggestions to us so that we can keep future editions responsive to the demands of the times. Send the comments to Michael Molenda, Department of Instructional Systems Technology, School of Education, Indiana University, Bloomington, IN 47405.

Robert Heinich
Michael Molenda
James D. Russell

ACKNOWLEDGMENTS

We wish to thank a number of instructors who critiqued the third edition of *Instructional Media* as a whole and chapter by chapter: Larry M. Albertson, University of Nebraska at Omaha; Richard A. Cornell, University of Central Florida; Robert A. Schwartz, Kean College; Robert A. Senour, California State University at San Bernardino; and John Wedman, University of Missouri at Columbia. Their helpful suggestions were greatly appreciated.

Drafts of previous editions were reviewed by Ted Cobun, East Tennessee State University; Arni Dunathan, University of Missouri; Terry Holcomb, North Texas State University; Robert Hunyard, Northern Illinois University; Barbara Martin, Kent State University; Donna McGrady, Logan-Hocking (OH) Public Schools; Bruce Petty, Oklahoma State University; William Winn, University of Washington.

The editorial, design, and production staffs at Macmillan faced the formidable task of making an award-winning book even better. The high standard set by the first two editions made the complex job of collaboration even more difficult. The team at Macmillan met the challenge.

Kristine Brancolini of Indiana University continued her valuable assistance in compiling the bibliographies for each chapter and shaping up the glossary with her keen eye and deep understanding of the subject matter. Carl Stafford of Purdue University has provided continuing expertise to Chapter 10. John Soudah of the Northwest Indiana Educational Service Center and Andy McGuire of Indiana University contributed excellent photographs under considerable pressure of deadlines. The good work of Michael Neff, Deane Dayton of Intergraph Corporation, Danny Callison of Indiana University, Jim Owens of Asbury College, and Doris Brodeur of Illinois State University evidenced in the previous editions has been carried into the third. We thank the media publishers and manufacturers who supplied photographs and gave us permission to use them.

Carole Bagley of Mankato State University helped us with Chapter 13, "Computer-Based Instruction," and made innumerable contributions to the content of the chapter and to the source lists appearing in Appendix A.

Colleagues from other universities mentioned here provided valuable suggestions at various points in the development of this text:

Earl E. Adreani
Boston University

Larry M. Albertson
University of Nebraska at Omaha

Philip J. Brody
St. Louis Public Schools

J. Gordon Coleman
University of Alabama

Keith Collins
Northern Illinois University

Richard A. Cornell
University of Central Florida

Wallace Draper
Ball State University

Lester Elsie
University of Toledo

Gary Ferrington
University of Oregon

Jack Garber
University of Wisconsin— Eau Claire

Robert A. Gray
Baylor University

David Gueulette
Northern Illinois University

Kathryn Holland
Kutztown University

Charles E. Jaquith
Central Michigan University

Doreen Keable
St. Cloud State University

Robert B. Krueger
University of Wisconsin— River Falls

David Redmond
West Chester State College

Russell Reis
West Chester State College

Rhonda S. Robinson
Northern Illinois University

Clair Rood
University of Wisconsin— La Crosse

Charles F. Roth, Jr.
University of Michigan—Flint

Tony Schulzetenberg
St. Cloud State University

Eleanor E. Schwartz
Kean College of New Jersey

Robert A. Senour
*California State University,
San Bernadino*

James A. Shuff
Henderson State University

Don C. Smellie
Utah State University

Ross C. Snyder
Missouri Southern State College

Charles Vance
Ithaca College

Nancy H. Vick
Longwood College

Robert Ward
Bridgewater State College

John Wedman
*University of Missouri—
Columbia*

E. J. Zeimet
*University of Wisconsin—
La Crosse*

We are grateful to our colleagues from our own universities for their many and valued forms of support.

Finally, we thank our families whose continued support made this third edition possible.

R.H.
M.M.
J.D.R.

CONTENTS

SPECIAL FEATURES

1

Media and Instruction

Objectives

After studying this chapter, you should be able to:

1. Diagram and explain a communication model (Shannon-Weaver, Shannon-Schramm, or one of your own design).

2. Analyze a given instructional situation in terms of one of the communication models.

3. Describe the transactional nature of communication.

4. Distinguish among *message, method,* and *medium.*

5. Define *medium* and name five basic categories of media.

6. Identify eight different instructional methods and describe a specific example of each.

7. Explain the "concrete-to-abstract continuum" as presented in the text, indicating how it can be used to aid in the selection of media.

8. Relate Dale's Cone of Experience to the concrete–abstract continuum.

9. Discuss four roles or purposes of media in the instructional process. Your discussion should include an example of media in each of these roles.

10. Discuss the current uses of instructional media in both education and training programs.

11. Identify five findings and/or implications from research about media.

12. Define or describe *technologies of instruction* and cite an example.

13. Discuss the relationship between humanism and instructional technology in the classroom.

14. Describe four types of instructional situations in which media could be used. Your discussion should include specific examples of media in each of the situations.

Lexicon

communication model

medium/media

message

method

schemata

assimilation

accommodation

concrete–abstract continuum

digital representation

iconic representation

technology

technology of instruction

The technical terms listed in this section are discussed in the book and are defined in the Appendix D Glossary.

The Pervasiveness of Instructional Media

Some call the present an age of media. The pervasiveness of mass media in our lives as forms of *entertainment* is obvious. Not so obvious, but nearly as pervasive, are the uses of media for *learning*. Consider these vignettes.

1. As he heads for work, a pharmaceutical salesman plugs into his car stereo the new cassette from the company sales training center. It introduces him to the distinctive features of Banvex, the new drug for respiratory infections.

2. In a quiet corner just off the shop floor at Regent Industries, Jean views a videocassette that shows the proper operation and safety features of the machine that she will be operating during her shift. Jean "floats" among jobs as needed from day to day.

3. Flash cards are used by the therapist to teach word recognition to a mentally handicapped child at the rehabilitation center. The cards have a word on one side and a picture on the other; the "repeat" stack grows smaller as Stephanie masters each word.

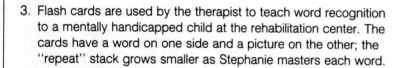

4. The junior high school age Samaritan Club members are studying the meanings of the parables. They compete as teams during the after-school program at their local church. Matching the facts of the stories with the accepted interpretation is the purpose of the game.

5. Anne, a graduate student in veterinary medicine, uses an interactive video system in the university's learning center to practice responding to animal owners in stressful situations. The scenarios present situations Anne is likely to face in actual veterinary practice.

6. As he unobtrusively photographs housing conditions in the inner city, Steve, a high school senior, reflects upon what brought him here. He had volunteered to do a slide-tape report on urban problems for his social studies class.

7. A pair of fourth graders eagerly "boot" (start up) the "Exploratorium" disc on their classroom microcomputer. They want to continue where they left off yesterday in a detective story. It challenges their logical reasoning skills in solving the mystery.

8. To learn how to take their blood pressure at home, Thelma and Harold listen to the nurse at the hospital as she guides the retired couple through a structured tutoring package. The nurse patiently answers any questions they have.

9. Dinner over, the Carter family settles into the family room to watch "This Old House." They are intrigued with the notion of buying and restoring an older house, and this television series provides them with valuable tips.

Here and now, in school and out, at home and at work, children and adults are enjoying the benefits of learning through media and the new technologies of instruction.

The goal of this book is to help put *you* into this picture.

INSTRUCTIONAL COMMUNICATION

INSTRUCTION is the arrangement of information to produce learning. The *transfer* of information from a source to a destination is called communication. Because new learning usually depends on taking in new information, effective instruction cannot take place unless communication takes place. It is, therefore, helpful to know something about the communication process in order to use instructional media effectively.

Communication Models

One of the first models of the communication process was developed by Claude E. Shannon of the Bell Telephone Laboratories. Because of his background and job, Shannon was interested solely in the technical aspects of communication. However, Warren Weaver collaborated with Shannon to develop a broader application of this model to other communication problems.* The Shannon-Weaver model (see Figure 1.1) can be used to analyze instructional situations.

_____

* Claude E. Shannon and Warren Weaver. *The Mathematical Theory of Communication.* Champaign, Ill.: University of Illinois Press, 1949, p. 7.

A message, such as the structure of the human heart, is selected by an information source. That message is then incorporated by the transmitter into a signal. The signal could be spoken words, a drawing on a chalkboard, or printed materials. The signal is then received by the receiver's ears and/or eyes and transformed into a message reaching the destination, for example, a student's mind. Acting on the signal as it is being transmitted are various distorting factors that Shannon called "noise." In our example, noise could be background sounds or glare on the chalkboard.

It is important to keep in mind that "meaning" per se cannot be transmitted. What are actually transmitted are *symbols* of meaning, such as words and pictures. As authors of this book, for example, we cannot directly transfer to you the personal "meanings" we have built up in our own minds about instructional media. (We even have trouble doing so among ourselves!) The most we can do is to transmit verbal and graphic symbols from which you can evoke your own "meanings." The most we can hope for is that our skills and knowledge will enable us to encode our messages in such a manner that your skills and knowledge can be used to decode and interpret them correctly.

Field of Experience

One major purpose of instructional communication is to broaden and extend the field of experience of the learner.

For instructional purposes, however, the meaning of the message and how the message is interpreted are of paramount importance. The Schramm* adaptation of the Shannon model incorporates Shannon's concern with the technical aspects of communication, but its central concern is with communication, reception, and interpretation of meaningful symbols. This is at the heart of instruction (Figure 1.2).

As a classroom teacher, for example, you would prepare your students for an instructional film (through a preliminary discussion of the topic, an overview of content, etc.), and you would design follow-up activities to reinforce and extend the range of what has been learned from the film.

Ideally, material presented to a student should be sufficiently within his or her field of experience so that he or she can learn what needs to be learned, but

_____

* Wilbur Schramm. "Procedures and Effects of Mass Communication." In Nelson B. Henry, ed., *Mass Media and Education.* Fifty-Third Yearbook of the National Society for the Study of Education. Part II. Chicago: University of Chicago Press, 1954, p. 116.

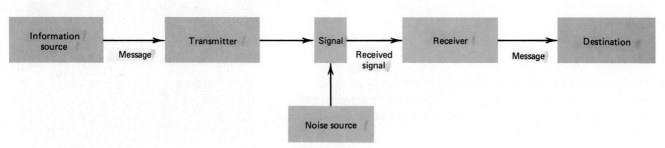

▲ *Figure 1.1*
The Shannon-Weaver communication model

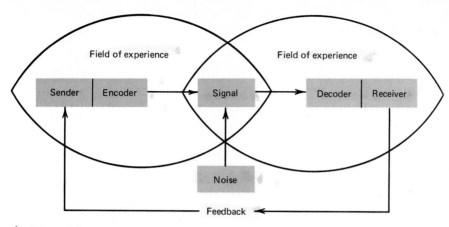

▲ *Figure 1.2*
Schramm's adaptation of the Shannon model emphasizes that only when the sender's and the receiver's field of experience overlap is there communication.

enough outside the field of experience to challenge and extend that field. How far the instruction can extend beyond the student's field of experience before confusion sets in depends on many factors. Perhaps the most important of these is the ability of the student. Able students can assume more of the responsibility for extending their own fields of experience than less able students. Slower students will need instructional content closer to their field of experience in order to be successful. Most retarded learners will require instruction that is almost entirely within their relatively limited field of experience. In Chapter 2, we will discuss the determination of "specific entry competencies," with particular attention to identifying the student's field of experience as he or she enters a lesson.

There will be times when the learning task (message) may not be within the field of experience of the *instructor*. When this occurs, both instructor and student seek to extend their respective fields of experience, and the instructor should not feel peculiar about being in this position. Some of the most effective learning takes place when instructor and

student must seek the answers together.

Another very important distinction between film (or any other medium) as a communication medium and as an instructional medium involves feedback from the receiver (see Figure 1.3). We usually think of feedback as some form of test, but many other techniques are available to indicate to the teacher how students are receiving instruction. Facial expressions, body language, dis-

cussion responses, student conferences, homework, responses on short daily quizzes, etc., are all forms of feedback. Not only does feedback help us to ascertain whether instruction has been successful or unsuccessful, but it also tends to take the burden off the student and place it where it more appropriately belongs—on the sender of the message (the instructor). Instructors are frequently tempted to blame the student when instruction is not successful. The real problem may be that the instruction has not been designed or delivered appropriately.

If "noise" unduly interfered with your signal, you can repeat instruction under more favorable conditions. If you made an error in appraising your students' field of experience, you may need to identify a more appropriate entry level for your particular group. If the message was not encoded properly, you may need to identify more suitable materials, or you can adjust your utilization of the materials to produce more effective instruction.

▲ *Figure 1.3*
In the classroom, feedback from the learners informs the instructor whether or not the point is being communicated.

TRANSACTIONAL NATURE OF COMMUNICATION

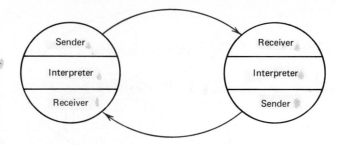

▲ *Figure 1.4*
A transactional model of communication shows the changing roles of the individuals.

W E emphasize that communication is an interpretive transaction between or among individuals. As noted previously, the sender of a message encodes it according to his or her skill and knowledge (field of experience), and the receiver decodes it according to his or her field of experience. In the feedback process, however, the receiver (student) does more than decode the message. He or she must also encode his or her interpretation of the signal for relay back to the sender (teacher), who, in turn, must decode it. In effect, receiver becomes sender and sender becomes receiver. And both interpret the message according to their fields of experience (Figure 1.4).*

This is an extremely important point to keep in mind. You must decode your students' feedback signals according to *their* interpretation of instructional content,

---

* Schramm, "Procedures and Effects," p. 119.

which may or may not be the same as yours, and which will very likely differ, at least in detail, from student to student. For example, instructional information about the labor movement in the United States may be interpreted one way by the child of a business executive and another way by the child of a union member. Black students and white students may interpret a film on slavery quite differently. The limited sensory abilities of some handicapped students may lead them to interpret instructional content differently from nonhandicapped children. Students raised in other countries will bring their cultural assumptions with them. For exam-

ple, in the United States, the owl is often used as a symbol of wisdom, but in one region of Nigeria, it is an omen of evil. As an instructor, you must always be sensitive to the fact that student response to a communication signal is a product of student experience.

MEDIA, MESSAGES, AND METHODS

A *medium* is a channel of communication. Derived from the Latin word for "between," the term refers "to anything that carries information between a source and a receiver."

▲ *Figure 1.5*
The head on the right *appears* to be larger than the one on the left.

▲ *Figure 1.6*
The heads are actually the same size, but the shape of the room and size of the windows have been manipulated.

Examples of media are film, television, diagrams, printed materials, computers, and instructors. These are considered instructional media when they carry messages with an instructional purpose. The purpose of media is to facilitate communication.

Instructional Media

The various instructional media described in this book cover a wide range of types appropriate for learners of all ages and backgrounds and for a wide variety of settings, formal and nonformal—from schools to colleges to businesses to homes . . . and places in between!

Nonprojected visuals such as photographs, diagrams, displays, models, and real objects are discussed in Chapter 4. In Chapter 5 projected media such as slides, filmstrips, and overhead transparencies are described. The following chapter deals with sound-slide sets, multimedia kits, and other such media combinations. Film and video and other varied electronic distribution systems are covered in chapters 8 and 9. Chapters 11 through 13 focus on the new technologies of instruction; these, too, often incorporate various audio and visual types of media.

Messages

In any instructional situation there is a message to be communicated. The message is usually subject-matter content, but it may be directions to the learners, questions about the content, feedback on the appropriateness of responses, or other information (see Figure 1.8).

Methods

Traditionally, instructional methods have been described as "presentation forms" such as lecture

▲ *Figure 1.7*
Listeners with different cultural backgrounds may derive different meanings from the same message.

and discussion. In this text we will differentiate between instructional *methods* and instructional *media*. *Methods* are the procedures of instruction that are selected to help learners achieve the objectives or to internalize the content or message. *Media* (medium, singular) are carriers of information between a source and a receiver. Such vehicles are considered *instructional media* when they are used to carry messages intended to change behavior.

The eight methods described here are applicable to learners of all ages. They are presentation, demonstration, drill-and-practice, tutorial, gaming, simulation, discovery, and problem solving. Vir-

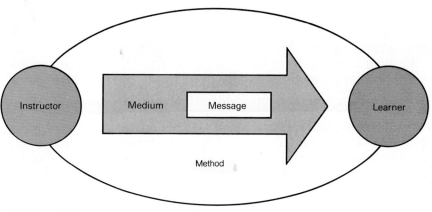

▲ *Figure 1.8*
In the relationship between message and medium, the medium carries the message.

tually any of the media described later can be used to implement virtually any of these methods.

Presentation. In the presentation method a source tells, dramatizes, or otherwise disseminates information to learners. It is a one-way communication controlled by the source, with no immediate response from or interaction with the learners. The source may be a textbook, an audiotape, a videotape, a film, an instructor, and so forth. Reading a book, listening to an audiotape, viewing a film or videotape, and attending a lecture are examples of the presentation method.

For example, as part of your visit to a museum, you check out a cassette tape and player with private headphones. The audiotape and accompanying map guide you through the museum and present information about each of the exhibits and displays.

Demonstration. In this method of instruction the learner views a real or lifelike example of the skill or procedure to be learned. Demonstrations may be recorded and played back by means of media such as video or film. If two-way interaction or learner practice with feedback is desired, a live instructor or a tutor is needed.

The objective may be for the learner to imitate a physical performance, such as swinging a golf club or changing the oil in a car, or to adopt the attitudes or values exemplified by someone who serves as a model. In some cases the point is simply to illustrate how something works, such as the effect of heat on a copper strip. On-the-job training often takes the form of one-to-one demonstration, with the experienced worker showing the new one how to perform a procedure, such as

▲ *Figure 1.9*
Demonstrations show a process to be learned or the way something works.

operating a packaging machine. This arrangement allows questions and answers to correct any errors or misperceptions.

Drill-And-Practice. In drill-and-practice the learner is led through a series of practice exercises designed to increase fluency of a new skill or to refresh an existing one. Use of the method assumes that the learner has previously received some instruction on the concept, principle, or procedure that is to be practiced. To be effective, the drill-and-practice exercises should include feedback to correct and remediate errors that the learner might make along the way.

Drill-and-practice is commonly used for such tasks as math facts, foreign language learning, and vocabulary building. Certain media formats and delivery systems lend themselves particularly well to student drill-and-practice exercises. For example, learning-laboratory instruction and programmed instruction are well suited to these purposes. Audio-

tapes can be used effectively for drill-and-practice in spelling, arithmetic, and language instruction.

Tutorial. A tutor—in the form of a person, computer, or special printed materials—presents the content, poses a question or problem, requests a learner response, analyzes the response, supplies appropriate feedback, and provides practice until the learner demonstrates a predetermined level of competency. Tutoring is most often done on a one-to-one basis and is frequently used to teach basic skills, such as reading and arithmetic.

Tutorial arrangements include instructor-to-learner (e.g., Socratic dialog), learner-to-learner, (e.g., tutoring or programmed tutoring), computer-to-learner (e.g., computer-assisted tutorial software), and print-to-learner (e.g., branching programmed instruction). These formats are discussed further in Chapter 11. The computer is especially well suited to play the role of tutor because of

◀ *Figure 1.10*
Tutorials are one of the most effective, but also one of the most expensive, methods of instruction.

◀ *Figure 1.11*
Games require active involvement on the part of each player.

its ability to deliver speedily a complex menu of responses to different learner inputs.

Gaming. Gaming provides a "playful" environment in which the learners follow prescribed rules as they strive to attain a challenging goal. It is a highly motivating method, especially for tedious and repetitive content. The game may involve one learner (e.g., solitaire) or a group of learners. Gaming often requires learners to use problem-solving skills and/or demonstrate mastery of specific content demanding a high degree of accuracy and efficiency (see Chapter 12).

A common type of instructional game is the business game. Participants form management teams making decisions regarding a mythical corporation. The winning team is the one reaping the highest corporate profits.

Simulation. Using this method, the learner confronts a scaled-down approximation of a real-life situation. It allows realistic practice without the expense or risks otherwise involved. The simulation may involve participant dialog, manipulation of materials and equipment, or interaction with a computer (see Chapter 12).

Interpersonal skills and laboratory experiments in the physical sciences are popular subjects for simulations. In some simulations the learner manipulates mathematical models to determine the effect of changing certain variables, such as controlling a nuclear power plant. Role playing is another common example of the simulation method. In *Participative Decision Making,* preservice teachers learn about allocating school budgets. Students assume the roles of a teacher representing the union, a principal, a school board member, a member of the PTA, a taxpayer with no children in school, and a student representing the student council.

Discovery. The discovery method uses an inductive, or inquiry, approach to learning; that is, presenting problems to be solved through trial and error. The aim of the discovery method is to foster a deeper understanding of the content through involvement with it. The rule or procedure that the learner "discovers" may be derived from previous experience, based upon information in reference books, or stored in a computer database.

Instructional media can help promote discovery or inquiry. For example, films may be used for discovery teaching in the physical sciences. Students study the films to perceive the relationships represented in the visuals and then go on to discover the principles that explain those relationships. For example, by viewing something as simple as a balloon being weighed before and after being filled with air, the student discovers that air has weight.

Problem Solving. In this method the learner uses previ-

▲ *Figure 1.12*
Discovery learning requires extra time but usually results in better retention.

ously mastered skills to reach a resolution of a challenging problem. The learner must define the problem more clearly, perhaps state a hypothesis, examine data (possibly with the aid of a computer), and generate a solution. Through this process the learner can be expected to arrive at a higher level of understanding of the phenomena under study.

One commonly used example of problem solving is the case study. For example, students in a business class are given information about a situation at a small manufacturing firm and are asked to design a solution to the problem of low production. One of the early decisions is to gather data from the case and to determine whether the solution is training or, instead, changing the environment or attitudes of the workers.

In any instructional situation a variety of methods may and should be used. Most of these methods can be used to teach any content to any group of learners.

However, some methods may be better for the specific content to be taught to certain learners. Experience and trying the various methods with actual students will determine which method or combination of methods is most effective. Consider a variety of methods for increased interest.

WHY USE INSTRUCTIONAL MEDIA?

Too frequently instructors use media without any reference to guiding principles of how the experiences contained in those media will be used by the learners. Without a good conceptual rationale, use of specific materials may become simply mechanical, with the hope that what is presented to the learners will eventually become meaningful to them. Instructors can develop conceptual and theoretical bases on which to choose specific materials and methods by knowing the

▲ *Figure 1.13*
Jean Piaget

relationships between media, learning, and instruction.

Instructional media can be used to facilitate, and in some cases provide for, intellectual development. Three concepts, as outlined by Jean Piaget*, are helpful in explaining how mental development occurs. They are schema (plural, schemata), assimilation, and accommodation.

Schemata

Schemata are the mental structures by which individuals organize their perceived environment. These adapt or change during mental development and learning. These schemata are used to identify, process, and store incoming information. Schemata can be thought of as categories into which individuals classify and store specific information and experiences.

Very young children learn to distinguish between mother and father. They soon separate dogs from cats and later become aware of different varieties of dogs. These differentiations based on experience lead to the develop-

---

* Jean Piaget. *The Development of Thought: Elaboration of Cognitive Structures.* New York: Viking Press, 1977.

ment of schemata; that is, the development of the ability to classify objects by their characteristics.

Schemata as structures of cognitive development change by the processes of assimilation and accommodation, so during instruction these changes should be encouraged. Adult learners have greater numbers and more elaborate schemata than children.

Assimilation

Assimilation is the cognitive process by which a learner integrates new information and experiences into existing schemata. Piaget borrowed the term from biology. It is the process by which an organism eats food, digests it, and then assimilates or changes it into a usable form.

During learning, assimilation results from experience. With new experiences, the schema expands in size, but does not change its basic structure. The process of assimilation attempts to place new concepts into existing schemata.

These experiences may come from real-life experiences. Rather than waiting for experiences to happen naturally, instructors cause experiences to happen through use of media and the new technologies of instruction.

Accommodation

Schemata change with experience, thus adult learners have a broader range of schemata than children. The process of modifying existing schemata or creating new schemata is accommodation.

When dealing with a new concept or experience, the learner attempts to assimilate it into existing schemata. When it does not fit, there are two possibilities: (1) the learner can create a new

schema into which the new stimulus is placed, or (2) the existing schema can be modified so that the new stimulus will fit. Both of these processes are forms of accommodation.

As instructors, we are responsible for providing learning experiences that will result in the creation of new schemata as well as the modification of existing schemata. Schemata develop over time with learning experiences. The role of instructional media is to provide many of those experiences.

The Concrete–Abstract Continuum

The psychologist Jerome Bruner, in developing a "theory of instruction," proposes that the instruction provided to a learner should proceed from direct experience (enactive), through iconic representations of experience (as in pictures, films, etc.), through symbolic, or digital, representation (as in words).† He further states that "the sequence in which a learner encounters materials" has a direct effect on achievement of mastery of the task.†† Bruner points out that this applies to *all* learners, not just children. When a learning task is presented to adults who have no relevant experiences on which to draw, learning is facilitated for them when instruction follows a sequence from actual experience through iconic, to symbolic representations.§ As we will discuss later, an important first step in instruction is to determine the nature of any learner's current level of experience. Concrete experiences

---

† Jerome S. Bruner. *Toward a Theory of Instruction.* Cambridge: Harvard University Press, 1966, p. 49.
†† Ibid.
§ See Flashback, page 13.

facilitate learning *and* the acquisition, retention, and usability of abstract symbols.

Instructional media not only provide the necessary concrete experiences but also help students integrate prior experiences. Many students have watched various aspects of the construction of a highway or a street. They have seen the machine that lays the asphalt down, they have seen graders at work, and they have seen a number of other stages of road building. However, they need to have all these experiences integrated into a generalized notion of what it means to build a highway. A film that can show all of these processes in relation to each other is an ideal way to integrate their various experiences into a meaningful abstraction.

Historically, improving the balance between concrete and abstract learning experiences was a key reason for using instructional media. However, current researchers question the nature of the distinctions between media made by earlier authors. The relative concreteness and abstractness of various media and methods and their comparative effectiveness in learning is not as clearcut as we once believed. Most instructional materials use a combination of presentation forms that vary in their degree of realism; for example, films (motion pictures) or filmstrips (still pictures) may be captioned or narrated (verbal symbols). In certain circumstances, line drawings (visual symbols) have been shown to be more effective than realistic photographs (still pictures). It now seems clear that a second key to effectiveness is learner response—the mental processing or overt practice conducted in response to the audiovisual stimuli. Regardless of the appeal of a method of presentation, the ultimate test is learner response and performance.

Decisions regarding trade-offs between concreteness of a learning experience and time constraints have to be made continually by the instructor. In general, as you move up Dale's Cone (see Flashback, p. 13) toward the more abstract media, more information can be compressed into a shorter period of time. It takes more time for students to engage in a direct purposeful experience, a contrived experience, or a dramatized experience than it does to present the same information in a motion picture, a recording, a series of visual symbols, or a series of verbal symbols. For example, a field trip can provide a learning experience relatively high in concreteness, but it also takes up a good deal of instructional time. A motion picture depicting the same experiences as the field trip could be presented to the students in a much shorter period of time and with much less effort. Similarly, a simulation (a contrived experience) such as the game "Ghetto" can help students relate to new situations and solve new problems, but such a simulation game does take more time than a more abstract learning experience such as watching a brief television documentary about ghetto life. In such cases, the instructor must decide whether the particular nature of the experience is worth the extra time it may take. As discussed later in this chapter, researchers have found that training directors consider contrived experiences (role playing, simulations) well worth the time they take. They often use filmed or videotaped simulations to take advantage of both "reality" and time compression.

The instructor must also decide whether or not the learning experience is appropriate to the experiential background of the student. The greatest amount of information can be presented in the least amount of time through printed or spoken words (the top of the concrete-to-abstract continuum and cone). But if the student does not have the requisite experiential background and knowledge to handle these verbal symbols, time saved in presentation will be time lost in learning. As mentioned before, the instructor finds out if the right match has been made by relying on what is perhaps *the* basic principle of instruction: learning means appropriate change in response, or performance. Because of this, emphasis in contemporary instructional research is placed on analysis of learner response as the key to choosing appropriate instructional experiences.

As Dale has pointed out, a model such as his Cone of Experience, although a simplification of complex relationships, is, nonetheless, a practical guide to analyzing the characteristics of instructional media and methods and how these media may be useful.

THE ROLES OF MEDIA IN INSTRUCTION

MEDIA can serve many roles in instruction. The instruction may be dependent upon the presence of a teacher, referred to as *instructor-based*. Even in this situation, media may be heavily used by the teacher. On the other hand, the instruction may not require a teacher when the student is learning, referred to as *instructor-independent*. This type of instruction is often called "self-instruction" even though it is guided by whoever designed the media.

In one of the first textbooks written about the use of audiovisual materials in schools, Hoban, Hoban, and Zissman stated that the value of audiovisual materials is a function of their degree of realism. In developing this concept, the authors arranged various teaching methods in a hierarchy of greater and greater abstraction, beginning with what they referred to as ''the total situation'' and culminating with ''words'' at the top of the hierarchy.[a]

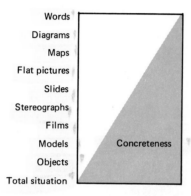

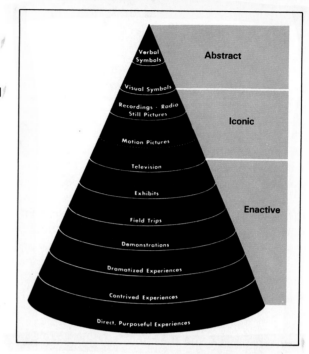

Dale's Cone of Experience. From *Audio-Visual Methods in Teaching,* Third Edition, by Edgar Dale. Copyright 1946, 1954, © 1969 by Holt, Rinehart and Winston. Reprinted by permission of Holt, Rinehart and Winston, p. 108.

In 1946, Edgar Dale took the same construct and developed what he referred to as the ''Cone of Experience.''[b] In the Cone of Experience, we start with the learner as participant in the actual experience, then move to the learner as observer of the actual event, to the learner as observer of a mediated event (an event presented through some medium), and finally to the learner observing symbols that represent an event. Dale contended that learners could make profitable use of more abstract

instructional activities to the extent that they had built up a stock of more concrete experiences to give meaning to the more abstract representations of reality.

It is interesting that psychologist Jerome Bruner, working from a different direction, devised a descriptive scheme for labelling instructional activities that parallels Dale's. As shown here, Bruner's concepts of enactive, iconic, and abstract learning may be superimposed on Dale's Cone. Bruner, though, intended to emphasize the nature of the mental operations of the learner rather than the nature of the stimuli presented to the learner.[c]

[a] Charles F. Hoban, Sr., Charles F. Hoban, Jr., and Samuel B. Zissman. *Visualizing the Curriculum.* New York: Dryden, 1937, p. 39.
[b] Edgar Dale. *Audio-Visual Methods in Teaching.* New York: Holt, Rinehart & Winston, 1969, p. 108. From *Audio-Visual Methods in Teaching,* Third Edition, by Edgar Dale. Copyright 1946, 1954 © 1969 by Holt, Rinehart & Winston. Reprinted by permission of Holt, Rinehart and Winston CBS College Publishing.

[c] Bruner, loc. cit.

Instructor-Based Instruction

The most common use of media in the instructional situation is for supplemental support of the instructor. Certainly there can be no doubt that properly designed instructional media can enhance and promote learning and support teacher-based instruction. But their effectiveness depends on the instructor (as will be made clear in the chapters that follow).

Research has long indicated the importance of the instructor's role in effective use of instructional media. For example, early studies

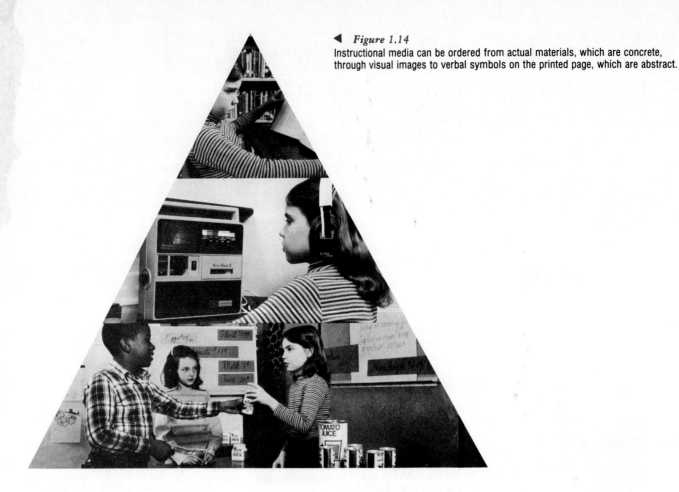

◀ *Figure 1.14*
Instructional media can be ordered from actual materials, which are concrete, through visual images to verbal symbols on the printed page, which are abstract.

showed that when teachers introduced films, relating them to learning objectives, the amount of information students gained from films increased.* Later research confirmed and expanded upon these original findings. Ausubel, for example, developed the concept of "advance organizers" as aids to effective instruction.† An advance organizer may take the form of an overview of or an introduction to lesson content, a statement of principles contained in the information to be presented, a statement of learning objectives, etc. Whatever the form, it is intended to create a "mind-set" for reception of instruction.

Advance organizers can be effective instruments for ensuring that media play their proper role as supplemental supporters of instruction. Many commercially produced instructional materials today have built-in advance organizers, which may be used as is or adapted by the instructor for specific educational purposes.

Instructor-Independent Instruction

Media can be effectively used in formal education situations where a teacher is not available or is working with other students. In nonformal education, media such as videocassettes and computer-based media can be used by trainees at the work site or at home. In some instances an instructor may be available for consultation via telephone.

The use of self-instructional materials allows teachers to spend more of their time diagnosing and correcting student problems, consulting with individual students, and teaching on a one-to-one and small-group basis (Figure 1.16).

How much time the teacher can spend on such activities will depend on the extent of the instructional role assigned to the media. Indeed, under certain circumstances, the entire instructional task may be left to the media. Experimental programs have demonstrated, for example, that an entire course in high school physics can be successfully

* Walter A. Wittich and J. G. Fowlkes. *Audio-visual Paths to Learning.* New York: Harper & Bros., 1946.
† David Ausubel. *Educational Psychology.* New York: Holt, Rinehart and Winston, 1968.

▲ *Figure 1.15*
The instructor's skill in weaving audiovisual media into the lesson is the single most important determinant of successful learning from media.

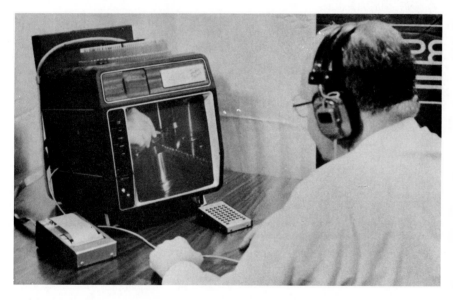

▲ *Figure 1.16*
Synchronized sound-slide presentations can be coupled with programmed instruction techniques for effective individualized instruction.

taught through use of films and workbooks without direct classroom intervention by the teacher. Successful programmed courses in calculus have been developed for use by able students whose high schools have no such course.

This is not to say, of course, that instructional technology can or should replace the teacher, but rather, that media can help teachers become creative managers of the learning experience rather than merely dispensers of information.

Distance Education

Distance education is a rapidly developing approach to instruction throughout the world. The approach has been widely used by business, industrial, and medical organizations. For many years doctors, veterinarians, pharmacists, engineers, and lawyers have used it to continue their professional education. These individuals are often too busy to interrupt their practice and participate in classroom-based education. Recently, academic institutions have been using distance education to reach a more diverse and geographically dispersed audience not accessible through traditional classroom instruction.

The distinguishing characteristic of distance education is the separation of the instructor and student(s) during the learning process. The communication of the subject matter is primarily to individuals rather than groups. As a consequence, the course content must be delivered by instructional media.

The media may be primarily print (books and paper-and-pencil tests), as in the case of traditional correspondence courses. Today, a wide variety of media are used. Audiocassettes, videotapes, videodiscs, computer-based instruction, and interactive video courses can be sent to individual students. In addition, radio, broadcast television, telelectures, and teleconferences are utilized for "live" distance education. The latter two delivery systems allow for interactive instruction between the instructor and the students.

Special Education

Another role of media is evident in work with special students. Handicapped children in particular need special instructional treatment. Mentally retarded children need highly structured learning situations because (referring back to our communication diagram) they lack the necessary field of experience and the ability

▲ *Figure 1.17*
Students can learn effectively from instructors at a distance via television and other electronic distribution systems.

Although severely handicapped students need to be helped through special education classes and courses, the trend today is to "mainstream" students whose disabilities do not preclude them from profiting from exposure to regular classroom activities. Instructional media specifically designed for such students and/or classroom adaptation of media to compensate for physical and mental disabilities can contribute enormously to effective instruction of handicapped students and can help prevent their unwarranted (albeit unintentional) neglect by the busy regular-classroom teacher.

MEDIA IN EDUCATION AND TRAINING

S INCE the turn of the century, teachers have used various types of audio and visual aids to help them teach (see Flashback). Recently, teachers have expanded their repertoire of materials and procedures to include the new technologies of instruction. The newer techniques include the use of microcomputers, compact discs, videodiscs, and satellite communications.

▲ *Figure 1.18*
For the benefit of the hearing impaired, the Public Broadcasting Service (PBS) and the commercial networks transmit many of their programs with "closed captions," visible only on television sets with special decoders.

▲ *Figure 1.19*
The Kurzweil reading machine allows those with impaired sight to "read" printed material. The device scans a printed page, analyzes letter combinations through a computer, and speaks the words by means of a voice synthesizer.

Pattern of Media Use in Education

to incorporate messages within their constructs. They need much more of the message placed within the context of their field of experience in order to expand that field of experience at all. Students who have impaired hearing or impaired vision require different kinds of learning materials; more emphasis should be placed on audio for visually impaired stu-

dents than for normally sighted individuals. Talking books, for example, are available for visually impaired students to use in special education programs and in the home. Adjusting instruction to all of these groups requires a heavy reliance on media and materials and the appropriate selection of these materials to fit specific purposes.

Teachers, particularly at the elementary school level, tend to use the "traditional media"—films, slides, overhead transparencies, and audiotapes—rather than "innovative media" such as computers and video programs. In general, elementary teachers utilize media more frequently than do their colleagues in junior high or high school. In a recent study by Seidman, 545 public school teachers in the Fort Worth, Texas, public school system completed a

TABLE 1.1 Ranking of Media Utilization by Fort Worth Public Schoolteachers*

Medium	Level	Mean**	Medium	Level	Mean**
Overhead Transparencies	Elem.	3.18	Motion Pictures	Elem.	1.78
	Mid./Jun.	3.14		Mid./Jun.	1.08
	High	2.84		High	1.47
	All	3.07		All	1.48
Pictures from Books and Magazines	Elem.	3.50	Audiotapes	Elem.	1.79
	Mid./Jun.	2.46		Mid./Jun.	1.11
	High	2.43		High	1.13
	All	2.87		All	1.40
Games and Simulations	Elem.	3.77	Computer Programs	Elem.	.80
	Mid./Jun.	1.98		Mid./Jun.	1.14
	High	1.84		High	1.23
	All	2.67		All	1.03
Phonograph Records	Elem.	3.98	Videotapes	Elem.	.73
	Mid./Jun.	.83		Mid./Jun.	.69
	High	1.22		High	1.18
	All	2.23		All	.85
Models	Elem.	2.32	35-mm Slides	Elem.	.50
	Mid./Jun.	1.84		Mid./Jun.	.45
	High	2.05		High	.72
	All	2.10		All	.55
Filmstrips	Elem.	2.29			
	Mid./Jun.	1.38			
	High	1.60			
	All	2.10			

N = 545

* *Source:* Steven A. Seidman. ''A Survey of Schoolteachers' Utilization of Media.'' *Educational Technology* (October 1986), pp. 19–23.

** Means based upon the following usage patterns:

- 6 = Every day
- 5 = A few times a week
- 4 = Once a week
- 3 = A few times a month
- 2 = Once a month or less
- 1 = A few times a year or less
- 0 = Never

media utilization inventory. The inventory measured the frequency of use of eleven different media. Overall, overhead transparencies were the most utilized materials, with pictures from books and magazines second, and games and simulations third. Table 1.1 contains a summary of the results of Seidman's study. Note the differences among elementary, middle/junior high, and high school teachers' utilization rates. If you were a media specialist at the ele-mentary level, which media would you build up your support for? Why? If you were a junior high media specialist? High school media specialist? Use of which media increases from elementary school to high school? Why do you think so? Use of which media decreases? Why? Which rates of use stay the same? Why?

In a similar study, Carter and Schmidt examined the production and utilization of instructional media by student teachers. Bulletin boards, posters, and overhead transparencies were the most commonly used. The complete results are shown in Table 1.2.

Pattern of Media Use in Training

As one might expect, the media and methods preferred by training directors are often different from those used by educators. One of the major reasons for this is that

Instructional media were originally referred to as "audiovisual aids." That phrase accurately describes their first role in elementary and secondary classrooms—that of serving as aids for the teacher. During the first decade of the twentieth century, school museums were created to house artifacts and exhibits for instructional purposes. The primary function of educational museums was to supplement and enrich the instructional programs of the school system. The first was the St. Louis Educational Museum, established in 1905. Horse-drawn wagons delivered instructional materials including charts, colored photographs, stereoscopic pictures, lantern slides, and maps to the schools.

Educational use of film began about the same time. Most films used for instructional purposes were theatrical, industrial, or government films. One of the early film projectors was developed by Bell and Howell in 1907. Like other media at the time, instructional films were considered aids to teaching rather than self-contained sequences of instruction.

During the first quarter of this century, the use of these materials was referred to as "visual instruction" or "visual education." Recorded sound on film was not available until the late twenties. Radio broadcasting developed during the same period, as sound recording and visual instruction quickly became audiovisual instruction.

The growth of instructional radio occurred primarily during the decade from 1925 to 1935. By the late 1930s radio education had begun its decline. Today it is easier to find a television set than a radio in most schools. Today school systems that operate their own radio stations typically do so to teach broadcasting skills and provide primarily entertainment programming.

During World War II, the use of media in American schools declined drastically because of the lack of equipment and materials. Conversely, a period of expansion began in the industrial and military sectors. During this time, the United States government purchased 55,000 film projectors and produced 457 training films at a cost of over a billion dollars.[a]

Viewgraph, the name of the first company to produce overhead projectors, is the term that some military and industrial personnel still use to describe all overhead projection equipment. During the war, "viewgraphs" were developed by the Navy for map briefings and instruction.[b] This early version of the overhead projector replaced the clumsy opaque projector, because notes could be made directly on the material during use. Today the overhead is the most widely used piece of audiovisual equipment.

Following World War II there was a period of expansion in audiovisual instruction due in large part to its successful use during the war. At the same time, audiovisual research programs emerged with the hope of identifying principles of learning that could be used in the design of audiovisual materials. However, educational practices were not greatly affected by these research programs, because many practitioners either ignored or were not aware of the findings.[c]

During the early 1950s many leaders in the audiovisual movement became interested in various theories or models of communication. These models focused on the communication process. The authors of these models indicated that during planning for instruction it was necessary to consider all of the elements of the communication process and not focus on just the medium, as many in the audiovisual field tended to do.

Instructional television experienced tremendous growth during the 1950s. In 1952 the Federal Communications Commission set aside 242 television channels for educational purposes. At the same time the Ford Foundation provided extensive funding for educational television. Credit and noncredit courses were offered on open- and closed-circuit television. Programs of wide educational and cultural interest have been offered on educational television stations. Today most educational television is offered via videotape, with the exception of the airing of news events as they take place. The television screen has begun to replace the movie screen

[a] J. R. Olsen and V. B. Bass. "The Application of Performance Technology in the Military." *Performance and Instruction* 21, no. 6 (July/August 1982), pp. 32–36.

[b] W. Wittich and C. Schuller. *Audio-Visual Materials: Their Nature and Use.* New York: Harper & Row, 1953, p. 351.
[c] Robert A. Reiser. "Instructional Technology: A History" in R. M. Gagne, ed. *Instructional Technology: Foundations.* Hillsdale, N.J.: Lawrence Erlbaum, 1987, pp. 11–48.

for the viewing of prepared materials. Many educational films are now available in either 16-mm or videotape format.

Programmed instruction can be traced to the work of psychologist B. F. Skinner in the mid-1950s. (See Chapter 11 for more details.) Whereas the other media we have been discussing are really presentation devices, programmed instruction utilizes principles of human learning and was the first of the new technologies of instruction. Skinner focused attention on a device called the "teaching machine." Later that device was replaced by books called "programmed texts." The programmed instruction movement reached its peak during the 1960s and paved the way for other technologies of instruction—audio-tutorial systems, personalized systems of instruction, and programmed tutoring in the 1970s. Computer-based instruction of the late 1970s and 1980s is based upon the principles of learning used in programmed instruction.[d]

Programmed instruction and other self-instructional approaches are fading from the formal education scene and are being replaced by computer-based instruction, which incorporates many of the same learning principles. In 1988 there was one computer for every thirty-six students in American public schools.[e] Even though the purchase of computers is still on the rise, the rate of increase is declining.

Textbooks are still the most commonly used instructional resource. Overhead projectors are readily available and are used as a presentation aid by many teachers. Commercially produced videocassettes are gradually replacing films as the most widely used form of projected media because of their relatively low cost and ease of use. Filmstrips and commercially prepared slides, along with audiotapes and printed study guides, are providing the basis for self-instruction in learning carrels and media centers (libraries).

Today, media and technologies of instruction are providing direct educational experiences for students rather than being used just as teachers' aids.

[d] For a thorough discussion of the history of media see Paul Saettler's *A History of Instructional Technology* (New York: McGraw-Hill, 1968).

[e] *Electronic Learning* (Nov./Dec. 1987), p. 12.

the curricula of the schools are fairly uniform, whereas training programs are often industry specific. Formats of media that lend themselves to local production are preferred by training directors. For example, slides are used more frequently than filmstrips; in schools the reverse is true. Videotape is employed more often than films in training, whereas in the schools many more films than videotaped programs are circulated.

Another difference arises from the fact that training directors are dealing with adults rather than children and adolescents. Role playing, games, and simulations are used much more frequently in training programs, particularly with management, supervisory, and sales personnel. These people's jobs require a great deal of interaction with people, and the types of training methods that develop relevant skills are given high priority. The trainees will have to call on those skills immediately after the training session and are more likely to become impatient with methods more abstract than the situation demands.

Refer back to Table 1.1 (page 17) and think about your education. In your experience, where are training and education similar and where are they different in regard to methods and media?

A survey conducted in 1987 indicated that video-based instruction had actually overtaken the lecture as the most commonly used format for corporate training and development. According to the *Training* magazine survey, 83.2 percent of all corporations with more than fifty employees used video, and 82.5 percent of such businesses used lectures.* A full rundown of the extent of use

_____
* Chris Lee. "Where the Training Dollars Go." *Training* (October 1987), pp. 51–65.

TABLE 1.2 **Percentage of Student Teachers Using and Producing Instructional Media***

Instructional Media	Using		Producing	
	Elementary	**Secondary**	**Elementary**	**Secondary**
Bulletin Boards	90%	51%	93%	40%
Posters	69	42	66	21
Transparencies	66	43	59	44
Photographs	55	27	24	4
Filmstrips	52	36	NA	NA
Models	41	23	NA	NA
Felt Boards	41	2	0	28
Flip Charts	28	4	3	0
Slides	24	29	10	11
16-mm Films	24	27	NA	NA
8-mm Films	17	17	0	0
Videotape	14	23	3	6

N = 29 elementary   NA = Not Applicable
      47 secondary

* *Source:* Adapted from Alex Carter and Kenneth C. Schmidt. "An Assessment of the Production and Utilization of Instructional Media by Student Teachers." *Educational Technology* (November 1985), p. 31.

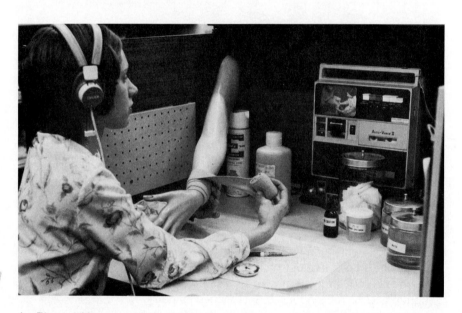

▲ *Figure 1.20*
An audiovisual learning station incorporating a filmstrip and audiocassette with real materials and a model arm provides training in nursing skills.

of the various media and methods is shown in Table 1.3. The listing indicates that media and technology play a very key role in this arena, with slides, films, simulations, games, role plays, self-study modules, and teleconferencing arrangements all heavily represented. Other media, such as overhead transparencies, are also widely used—usually in conjunction with lectures or other methods—although not separately reported in this table.

▲ *Figure 1.21*
Because institutional training often requires materials custom-made for specific settings, video recording is a primary source of materials.

TABLE 1.3 **Instructional Methods***
(of all organizations with 50 or more employees)

Media and Methods	Percentage Using These Media and Methods for Employee Training
Videotapes	83.2%
Lectures	82.5
One-on-one instruction	73.2
Role plays	52.9
Slides	46.8
Films	44.9
Case studies	42.8
Games & simulations	40.6
Self-assessment/self-testing instruments	35.7
Noncomputerized self-study programs	31.5
Teleconferencing (audio/video)	20.3
Teleconferencing (audio only)	10.5
Computer conferencing	5.3

* *Source:* From *Training* (October 1987), p. 60.

Growth of Training Programs

Business, industrial, and financial institutions have today become major settings for instruction. The development of sophisticated instructional media and our growing knowledge of how to use these media for effective learning have opened up instructional options not only for students in formal educational institutions but also for learners outside such institutions. Today, virtually any institutional setting can become a classroom with the aid of, and sometimes even near-total dependence upon, instructional technology.

According to a recent study sponsored by the Carnegie Foundation, corporations spend over $40 billion a year on employee training. That figure is a conservative estimate and does not include trainee salaries. The study also shows that as many students go through "corporate classrooms" in a year as go through U.S. colleges and universities. Examples of the types of training include management, technical, clerical, customer relations, sales, and safety.

As the economy becomes even more information oriented, the amount of money spent on training will increase correspondingly. According to *Training* magazine, of all organizations with fifty or more employees 78.5 percent provide management skills training, and 65 percent provide technical skills training.* These percentages will most likely increase in the future. Expenditures for training purposes are currently around $40 billion. The costs of custom-designed training by outside agencies and use of outside consultants and services are around $7 billion. At $40 billion, the training market is more attractive than the education market to producers of instructional products.†

The federal government began supporting training programs directly with the Jobs Training Partnership Act of 1983. The act stipulates that 70 percent of the $3.6 billion allocated must be spent on training. Private Industry Councils decide where the money will be spent, and most of it is expected to be allocated to on-the-job training. Significantly, the Department of Labor, not the

---

* *Training* (October 1987), p. 62.
† Ibid.

▲ *Figure 1.22*
Management trainees often participate in role-playing exercises to gain experience in dealing with people.

Department of Education, administers the act. Congress may have been indicating that it had lost faith in education and was willing to shift federal money to training.

Many of the nation's labor unions operate extensive training programs for their members, and some even include funding for membership education in their contract negotiations. Hospitals and other social welfare institutions have developed educational facilities to help keep their personnel abreast of current techniques and professional practices. Libraries, museums, and community centers of all types are likely to be organized centers of out-of-school education; and, of course, both national and local government agencies have contributed greatly to the trend toward instruction outside the formal educational setting.

The implications of this growing phenomenon are clear. In view of the increasing diffusion of instruction in our society, formal educational institutions now must be viewed as just one among many settings for education. As more and more instruction moves outside the school setting, more and more reliance will be placed on instructional media to meet diverse learning objectives.

APPLYING RESEARCH TO PRACTICE

P EOPLE who are just beginning study in the field of instructional media typically hold the misconception that this is a very young field, one in which formal research probably began around the 1950s or perhaps the 1960s. In fact, well-conceived psychological studies of learning from films were being conducted as early as 1919, when Lashley and Watson investigated the adaptation of World War I training films to civilian use.

A large-scale study of the instructional uses of films in the Chicago public schools was reported by Freeman in 1924.* The Lashley-Watson studies† and the Chicago school studies yielded considerable insight into the instructional potentials of film and arrived at surprisingly sophisticated conclusions about the role of media in the classroom. Many of their findings seem to have

---

* Frank N. Freeman. *Visual Education.* Chicago: University of Chicago Press, 1924, p. 79.
† K. S. Lashley and J. B. Watson. *A Psychological Study of Motion Pictures in Relation to Venereal Disease Campaigns.* Washington, D.C.: U.S. Interdepartmental Social Hygiene Board, 1922, p. 3.

been rediscovered by researchers studying the "new medium" of each succeeding generation. In the following quotations from the Chicago school studies, try substituting the term *television, computer-assisted instruction,* or *videodisc* whenever the term *film* or *visual media* is mentioned:

> *The relative effectiveness of verbal instruction as contrasted with the various forms of concrete or realistic material in visual media depends on the nature of the instruction to be given and the character of the learner's previous experience with objective materials.*
>
> *The peculiar value of a film lies not in its generally stimulating effect, but in its ability to furnish a particular type of experience.*
>
> *Films should be so designed as to furnish to the teacher otherwise inaccessible raw material for instruction but should leave the organization of the complete teaching unit largely to the teacher.*
>
> *The teacher has been found superior to all visual media in gaining and sustaining attention.*
>
> *Each of the so-called conventional forms of instruction that employ visual media has some advantage and some disadvantage, and there are circumstances under which each is the best form to use.*††

Media Comparison Studies

However, these promising beginnings were largely abandoned in favor of experimental designs in which one group of learners (the experimental group) is exposed

---

†† Paul Saettler. "Design and Selection Factors." *Review of Educational Research* 38, no. 2 (April 1968), p. 116.

to an audiovisual presentation of some sort while a similar group (the control group) receives "conventional instruction"—often a lecture. All are given the same final test, the results of which are used to indicate the effectiveness of the experimental version. Sometimes two media forms are compared, for instance, film versus slide/tape. This type of study is known as a media comparison study.

Reviewers of media comparison studies regularly point out that a majority of the studies find that there is "no statistically significant difference" in learning between the experimental treatment and the control treatment. Does this mean that audiovisual presentations are equivalent to lectures or that films are equivalent to slides/tapes in their impact on the audience?

Critics have pointed out a number of major faults in the very conception of media comparison studies that cast doubt on their utility as guides for making real-life decisions. First, what was compared with what? In some cases the "media" treatment was nothing more than a filmed or videotaped lecture, to ensure that the two treatments had the same content and method, differing only in delivery system. The film or videotape chosen in the study may or may not have made use of color, motion, or other special visual possibilities of the medium. Furthermore, the test items used to measure achievement often were drawn largely from the verbal information in the soundtrack, not from the visual content. On the other side of the coin, the "conventional instruction" treatment varied greatly from study to study, consisting of whatever was considered to be the traditional method in that setting—e.g., a lecture, a lecture plus discussion,

textbook reading, or any combination of these or other methods.

It is no wonder that the cumulative results of these media comparison studies are difficult to interpret. As one critic has put it, it is like trying to compare "can-of-worms A" with "can-of-worms B."

Unfortunately, the more successful the researchers were in controlling the conditions of the "media" treatment, the less it resembled what would be normal good practice in media utilization. For example, in order to control as many extraneous variables as possible, the "media" treatment ordinarily excluded such normal practices as introductory and follow-up discussion of the media presentation. What was needed to meet laboratory standards of purity bore little resemblance to what creative instructors do with either media *or* conventional instruction.

Analysis of the *content* treated in these studies reveals another bias—a bias toward cognitive subject matter, as opposed to attitudinal, interpersonal, or motor skill objectives. Further, attainment of the objectives was usually measured by ordinary paper-and-pencil verbal tests. Thus, the experiments typically revolved around highly verbal content being measured by highly verbal instruments (often using college students as subjects—an unusually verbally adept sector of the general population). This may help explain why lecture and textbook treatments—being highly verbal—yielded comparable results to the "media" treatments.

Implications for Practice

For the practitioner, a major question arises: If the conclusion from a majority of studies is that there is no statistically significant differ-

ence in learning between the media treatment and conventional instruction, does this mean that audiovisual presentations are approximately equivalent to lectures in terms of instructional usefulness? Not necessarily. At most, it means that when certain audiovisual materials are used in the same way as a lecture is used, for the same purposes as a lecture (e.g., verbal recall), with a random sample of learners, and *all other conditions are held constant,* outcomes measured by specific tests will be similar. But the qualifications listed here are assumptions that good instructors specifically *reject* in actual practice. They do not use audiovisual materials in the same way as print or lecture materials. They select media that suit particular *objectives;* audiovisual presentations can be powerful, for example, in conveying a historical period's feel, in building empathy with others, or in showing a role model in action. They also integrate media with the *methods* (e.g., tutorial, drill-and-practice, discovery) that are best suited to stimulating the cognitive processes connected with achieving given objectives. Good instructors select media for those learners who can profit from them. And they *evaluate* effectiveness not just on the basis of immediate verbal recall but also on the basis of what impact the experience had on the imagination, feelings, and long-term comprehension of the viewer.

Select Materials Based on Their Attributes. An insight derived from the errors made in media comparison research is that one cannot generalize findings about one film to all films, or one video lesson to all video lessons. Each material has its own set of attributes. One videotape may make full use of the potentials of the medium—graphics, animation, drama, etc.—whereas another may be no more than a recording of a "talking head." Each would have an entirely different impact on the imagination, feelings, and long-term comprehension of the viewer (despite the fact that each might yield the same score on an immediate posttest of verbal recall).

Materials must be examined in light of the specific objectives of the lesson and the specific needs and interests of learners. Does *this* filmstrip supply the needed realistic pictures of everyday life in ancient Roman times? Does *this* computer-assisted instruction module provide practice in making the kinds of decisions that loan officers make? Does *this* videocassette show a close-up view of a proper weld? In short, what attributes are needed for proper communication of the idea involved, and does *this* specific material have those attributes?

Utilize Material for Maximum Impact. If nothing else, research and practical experience have shown that much of the effectiveness of media depends on *how* they are integrated into the larger scheme. Wilbur Schramm, one of the most respected contemporary communication researchers, summarized it well:

> *Motivated students learn from any medium if it is competently used and adapted to their needs. Within its physical limits, any medium can perform any educational task. Whether a student learns more from one medium than from another is at least as likely to depend on how the medium is used as on what medium is used.**

---

* Wilbur Schramm. *Big Media, Little Media.* Beverly Hills, Calif.: Sage Publications, 1977, p. iv.

The user of the material can help increase the impact of any audiovisual material by applying sound utilization techniques: having selected material with appropriate attributes, introduce it to learners by relating it to prior learning and indicating how it relates to today's objectives, present it under the best possible environmental conditions, elicit a response from viewers, review the content, and evaluate its impact.

The ASSURE model described in Chapter 2 was developed as a planning aid to help assure that media are used to their maximum advantage, not just as interchangeable substitutes for printed or oral messages. Contrary to the requirements of research, the requirements of practice demand that the conditions surrounding the materials *not* be held constant. Indeed, one of the most important roles of media is to serve as a catalyst for change in the whole instructional environment. The effective use of media demands that instructors be better organized in advance, that they think through their objectives, that they alter the everyday classroom routine, and that they evaluate broadly to determine impacts on mental abilities, feelings, values, interpersonal skills, and motor skills.

TECHNOLOGIES OF INSTRUCTION

U P to this point we have been discussing ways in which audiovisual media and methods can help improve communication and thereby improve instruction. The emphasis has been on the "things" of instruction—the *products* of technology. But instruction is more than communication alone, and technology *as a process* is a powerful tool for analyz-

ing and solving instructional problems.

The principal definition of *technology* used in this book refers to "the systematic application of scientific or other organized knowledge to practical tasks."† Adapting this definition to instruction, we may define *instructional technology* as the application of our scientific knowledge about human learning to the practical tasks of teaching and learning. A *technology of instruction,* thus, is a particular, systematic arrangement of teaching/learning events designed to put our knowledge of learning into practice in a predictable, effective manner to attain specific learning objectives.

Over the years, many such arrangements have been devised, including programmed instruction, computer-based instruction, audio-tutorial systems, modular instruction, and simulation/gaming. Some technologies of instruction incorporate audiovisual media, others do not. Some employ electronic or mechanical devices, but others, such as programmed texts and simulation games, may involve no such devices. (Specific technologies of instruction are discussed in detail in Chapter 11.) However, they all have one thing in common: they focus on the learner and on scientific principles of human learning.

The Dimensions of Technology

In recent years it has become popular to describe applications of technology as "high technology" versus "low technology." And the usual implication is that "high" is better than "low." Looking at the items referred to as high technology, we find that the

---

† John Kenneth Galbraith. *The New Industrial State.* Boston: Houghton Mifflin, 1967, p. 12.

▲ *Figure 1.23*
The "teaching machine" was one of the first outgrowths of programmed instruction. The learner makes an overt response and checks the correctness of that response before proceeding to the next item.

label derives from the sophistication of the *hardware* entailed. Focusing on the media delivery vehicles is understandable; that's the most visible feature. But from an instructional viewpoint, the hardware is seldom the source of the success of a new system.

Looking beyond the obvious dimension of hardware, we find that any new technology of instruction has a second dimension—the *pedagogical*. That is, to what extent does the system embody sophisticated methods of instruction? For example, old-fashioned "educational" films and television programs, like old-fashioned textbooks, exemplify a primitive pedagogical view—that

pouring forth masses of information is an effective means of instruction. One step higher would be a video program incorporating interesting questions and pauses to allow time for the viewer to answer them.

There is a third dimension to any technological system—the simplicity or sophistication of its *management* function. On the high end would be a system with tightly structured rules and procedures organized to adapt flexibly to different users. An example of this would be a computer-assisted tutorial program that guides a medical student through the diagnosis of an illness in a simulated patient. On the low end would be

a traditional lecture, which starts when the lecturer is ready, presents a standard chunk of content at the lecturer's preferred pace, and stops when he or she is finished. There is no adaptation to individual listeners' needs.

The three dimensions of technology are illustrated by the cube in Figure 1.24. The point of this diagram is that any given system can be "high tech" on one dimension but low on the others and that its instructional value does not depend solely or primarily on its *media* sophistication. Let's look at some examples. How about a system that rates only a "1" on each dimension—a 1-1-1 system—such as a loose, rambling lecture. The teacher gives an extemporaneous talk about the causes and events of the War of 1812; only his voice is heard; no audiovisual media are used, not even the listing of key names and dates on the chalkboard. Pedagogically, we see no particular attempt to aid the learning process: no effort by the instructor to highlight key ideas, raise provocative questions, provide a summary, or involve students. The management, too, is primitive: no way for students to change the pace of delivery, review difficult concepts, or get answers to questions that occur to them intermittently throughout the lecture.

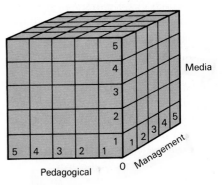

▲ *Figure 1.24*
The dimensions of the technology of instruction model include media, pedagogy, and management.

We can imagine the same situation with more sophisticated media, for instance, a 3-1-1 (media-pedagogical-management). Now the teacher shows a slide-tape presentation that illustrates scenes from the war and portraits of key individuals, and he uses the overhead projector to present important names and dates. This approach remains low on the pedagogical dimension because it is still basically a one-way message with little involvement and few opportunities for learners to practice their new knowledge. There is still no adaptation to individual differences nor any special structure to the learning episode beyond the structure of the lecture itself—a primitive management system.

What might a 5-5-5 technology of instruction look like? Imagine an interactive video setup employing high-resolution TV linked to a computer. It controls a simulation program that is used by pairs of students. Together they play the role of Andrew Jackson on the eve of the Battle of New Orleans in 1815. The video program shows the scene and pauses to provide historical data about the military, political, and economic conditions. It asks the users to decide whether to engage in battle or to await news of the peace talks going on in Ghent. The results of the decision are shown visually and in the form of new political and economic data. And the process continues. Such a program exemplifies a pedagogical design that is interesting, clear, challenging, involving, discovery oriented, and collaborative. The management system is self-paced, adaptive to different student learning strategies, responsive to different choices, and modular. It could also incorporate tests to determine student mastery, sending the student forward only after she demonstrates mastery.

The point of this diagram is that the pedagogical strength and the management flexibility of a technological system are at least as important as—and usually more important than—the glitter of the media component. The intelligent evaluator of the various instructional products on the market will want to be discriminating on *all* of these dimensions. Helping users be discriminating is a major goal of this book.

STRUCTURE AND FLEXIBILITY

RECENT research lends considerable support to the principle that the amount of time students spend on the instructional task is directly and positively related to achievement.* Media-directed instruction concentrates student time on task. For example, television teachers have frequently commented that their televised instruction is more concentrated and has fewer diversions than their classroom instruction. The learning laboratory has the effect of increasing the time spent directly on task.

Students achieve more when instruction has some degree of structure, when they know what is expected of them, and when the instructional environment is arranged to facilitate achievement of instructional objectives.† For example, if inquiry skills are the goal of instruction, then the obligation of the teacher is to be sure the environment is arranged to facilitate the necessary gathering of data from which inferences can be made by the student. Both the *kind* and *degree* of structure vary with instructional objectives.

Structure gives students confidence because it reduces ambiguity about objectives and purposes of learning. This is as true of adults in training programs as it is of students in schools and colleges. Acquisition of the skills necessary to do the job contributes more to a feeling of confidence than do motivational or inspirational sessions, concluded researchers at DCW Research Associates from a study of sales managers. Their findings "suggest that trainers concerned with motivational programs to enhance self-confidence in job performance might do well to look at task-oriented programs designed to assist individuals to get greater control of the elements of their jobs that tend to affect job performance."††

Structure, however, does not rule out flexibility. Even in a structured situation, accommodation should be made to individual needs and interests. Structured instruction need not be *excessively* task-oriented. Nor does it rule out exploration, creativity, and self-direction.§

The correct blend of structure and flexibility to best meet your instructional objectives will depend on a variety of factors, including the subject matter under study and the learning characteristics of your students— that is, their age and general level of intelligence and their specific knowledge about and attitude toward the topic at hand.

Drill-and-practice exercises are likely to be more structured than,

---

* N. L. Gage. *The Scientific Basis of the Art of Teaching.* New York: Teachers College Press, 1978, pp. 34–40.
† David L. Clark, Linda S. Lotto, and Martha M. McCarthy. "Factors Associated with Success in Urban Elementary Schools." *Phi Delta Kappan* (March 1980), pp. 467–470. Also Gage, op. cit., pp. 31–33.

---

†† *Training* (October 1983), p. 16.
§ Gage, op. cit., p. 40.

▲ *Figure 1.25*
In Montessori schools, carefully structured activities stimulate and channel children's curiosity.

▲ *Figure 1.26*
Audiovisual materials provide a springboard for small-group discussion—an alternative to the lecture and textbook.

say, a discovery lesson in geography. We would also expect a mathematics lesson on fractions to be more structured than a social science lesson on contemporary urban problems.

In general, younger children respond well to, and indeed need, a high degree of lesson structure. The Montessori method for teaching very young children, for example, is highly structured, and its success depends on a carefully worked out sequence of instruction and materials utilization. Yet the uninformed visitor to a Montessori-type classroom might think the children are simply playing and having fun (Figure 1.25).

In general, lower-ability students prefer fairly well structured lessons, primarily because they do not have a high degree of confidence in their ability to work independently, nor in their ability to pull together what are to them unrelated strands of subject matter. Higher-ability students respond well to a more flexible approach, because they have

more confidence in their abilities (provided, of course, they are not students with high anxiety levels or ones who prefer structured situations).

Motivation influences the tolerance students have toward a structured or flexible learning situation. Students who are highly motivated will be able to tolerate a very wide range of degree of structure. Students with little motivation will do better in learning situations that guide them to specific instructional ends. If given too much flexibility or too much independence in a learning situation, students with relatively low motivation will tend to lose direction along the way and not arrive at the specific goals that were set in the learning situation or to abandon the pursuit of those goals completely during the course of instruction.

Keep in mind that by *structure* we mean the extent to which the management system leads the student step-by-step to the specific objectives set by the program. Structure has nothing to do with

difficulty. In the case of students with low motivation, we are not suggesting that the material be difficult or present difficult problems, but that a structured learning situation can gently lead students toward instructional goals and instill a degree of confidence they would not pick up in a situation that was extremely flexible or that placed a great deal of the responsibility to learn on their shoulders.

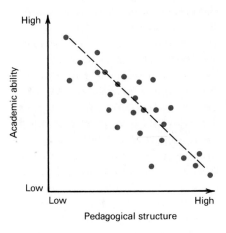

▲ *Figure 1.27*
Learners of high academic ability tend to prefer less strecture.

The role of media in allowing flexibility in learning is clear: materials—print and audiovisual—are attractive alternatives to the routine of the lecture. Materials that are relatively open-ended can be adapted to a variety of teaching/learning styles and situations. Self-instructional materials make possible such flexible arrangements as independent study and small-group work. Flexibility is enhanced when alternatives to "teacher talk" are available.

Whatever blend of structure and flexibility you choose, instructional media can help you achieve your goals. Media and media systems can be structured toward specific learning objectives, or they can easily be made open-ended and adapted to creative independent study and instructional flexibility.

rights, privileges, and motivations of their own, they will treat them as such, with or without the use of instructional media. In other words, it is not technology that tends to mechanize people but the uses to which people put technology.

One of our most thoughtful observers of life in the classroom is Philip Jackson of the University of Chicago. He has been concerned about the quality of life in American classrooms, which he has found somewhat impoverished. Perhaps it will be easier to visualize a humanistic classroom by looking at the traits of a mechanistic classroom. In the book *The Teacher and the Machine,* Jackson states that "the greatest intellectual challenge of our time is not how to design machines that behave more and more like humans, but rather, how to pro-

tect humans from being treated more and more like machines."* He goes on to clarify what he means by human mechanization: "the process by which people are treated mechanically; that is without giving thought to what is going on inside them." It is interesting that his illustrations of human mechanization in schools show how student attention, assignments, learning tasks, and discussion are mechanized with means as simple as the human voice and the teacher's right to turn students on and off.

The question is not so much what is used in the classroom as how are students treated. A corollary of this statement is that it is

———————
* Philip W. Jackson. *The Teacher and the Machine.* Pittsburgh: University of Pittsburgh, 1968, p. 66.

TECHNOLOGY AND HUMANISM

More than a few observers of the educational scene have argued that the widespread use of instructional technology in the classroom must lead to treating students as if they too are machines rather than human beings—that is, that technology dehumanizes the teaching/learning process. It is, on the contrary, a major theme of this book that, properly used, modern instructional media can individualize and thus humanize the teaching/learning process to a degree hitherto undreamed of. The danger of dehumanization lies not in the use of instructional media but in the way in which teachers perceive their students. If teachers perceive learners as machines, they will treat them as such, with or without the use of instructional media. If teachers perceive their students as human beings with

▲ *Figure 1.28*
Lecture-style instruction may or may not lead to humanistic ends. Are individual differences being cared for? Are students actively "processing" the information?

▲ *Figure 1.29*
Technology, in the form of audiovisual or print materials, can help free the teacher for one-to-one interaction—doing what humans do best.

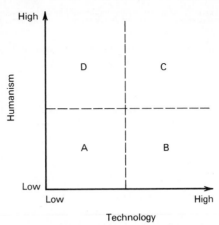

▲ *Figure 1.30*
Technology and humanism are not opposite ends of a single scale, but two different variables, either of which can be high or low.

mance objectives, materials to be used to complete objectives, and a self-evaluation test
C. The same as B, except that students choose modules based on counseling sessions with an instructor and meet periodically to discuss the content of the modules
D. A group that meets on a regular basis to discuss common reading assignments

not so much *what* a teacher teaches but *how* a teacher teaches. For example, many teachers, particularly in English and social studies, consider themselves "humanists" but may be anything but humanistic to their students. They may treat those students in the way in which Jackson said people can be treated mechanistically (Figure 1.29).

To reinforce this point, consider a case in which the introduction of machinery can make the instructional situation more humanistic. As research has indicated, students who have a high level of anxiety are prone to make mistakes and to learn less efficiently when under considerable pressure. Many teachers exert too much pressure on high-anxiety students, thereby making the instructional situation not only disagreeable but prone to error. Given the same sequence of instruction mediated through a machine that will continue only at the command of the student, the student can reduce the pressure simply by not responding. In other words, the machine awaits the command of the student to begin, whereas an overbearing teacher waits for no such command.

Contrary to what some educators believe, technology and humanism can work together or go their separate ways. Figure 1.30 suggests four basic mixes of technology and humanism.

Let's look at four examples of a mix of technology and humanism to see where each falls in Figure 1.30:

A. A college lecture with little or no interaction between professor and student
B. A course consisting of a required series of modules, each composed of perfor-

▼ *Figure 1.31*

These examples are overly simplified and only illustrative, but they serve as a basis for analyzing the relationship between humanism and technology. They illustrate that training/instruction can be low in both humanism and technology, just as it can be high in both.

To reiterate, instructional technology does not preclude a humane teaching/learning environment. On the contrary, instructional media can help provide a learning atmosphere in which students actively participate, as individual human beings, in the learning process. When instructional media are used properly and creatively in the classroom, it is the machines that are turned on and off at will—not the students.

"I like educational toys. I like educational TV. I like educational reading material. It's education I don't like."

References

Print References

Asimov, Isaac. "His Own Particular Drummer." *Phi Delta Kappan* (September 1976), pp. 99–103.

Barnouw, Eric. *Tube of Plenty.* (New York: Oxford University Press, 1975).

Culkin, John. "A Schoolman's Guide to Marshall McLuhan." *Saturday Review* (March 18, 1967), pp. 51–53, 70–72.

Ellson, Douglas G. *Improving the Productivity of Teaching: 125 Exhibits.* (Bloomington, Ind.: *Phi Delta Kappa,* 1986).

Fiske, John. *Introduction to Communication Studies.* (New York: Methuen, 1982).

Fleming, Malcolm L., and Hutton, Deane W., eds. *Mental Imagery and Learning.* (Englewood Cliffs, N.J.: Educational Technology Publications, 1983).

Fox, G. T., and DeVault, M. V. "Technology and Humanism in the Classroom: Frontiers of Educational Practice." *Educational Technology* (October 1974), pp. 7–13.

Gagne, Robert M., ed. *Instructional Technology: Foundations.* (Hillsdale, N.J.: Lawrence Erlbaum, 1987).

Hatcher, Barbara, ed. *Learning Opportunities beyond the School.* (Wheaton, Md.: Association for Childhood Education International, 1987).

Heinich, Robert, ed. *Educating All Handicapped Children.* (Englewood Cliffs, N.J.: Educational Technology Publications, 1979).

Hoban, Charles F. "Educational Technology and Human Values." *AV Communication Review* (Fall 1977), pp. 221–242.

Hooten, David E. "Educational Technology and the Adult Learner." *Educational Technology* (October 1976), pp. 20–25.

Johnston, Jerome. *Electronic Learning: From Audiotape to Videodisc.* (Hillsdale, N.J.: Lawrence Erlbaum, 1987).

Kaye, Anthony, and Keith, Harry, eds. *Using the Media for Adult Basic Education.* (Totowa, N.J.: Biblio Distribution Center, 1982).

Kolesnik, W. B. *Humanism and/or Behaviorism in Education.* (Boston: Allyn & Bacon, 1975).

Marlow, Eugene. *Managing the Corporate Media Center.* (White Plains, N.Y.: Knowledge Industry, 1981).

Marsh, Patrick. *Messages That Work: A Guide to Communication.* (Englewood Cliffs, N.J.: Educational Technology Publications, 1983).

"Media in Health Care Education." *Instructional Innovator* (January 1982), pp. 20–35.

Petrie, Joyce. *Mainstreaming in the Media Center.* (Phoenix, Az.: Oryx Press, 1982).

Pillon, Nancy Bach, ed. *Reaching Young People through Media.* (Littleton, Colo.: Libraries Unlimited, 1983).

Programming to Help Children Use Media Creatively. (Chicago: American Library Association, 1983).

Proulx, R. "The Dialectics of Andragogy and Instructional Technology." *NSPI Journal* (July 1980), pp. 3–4.

Reigeluth, Charles., ed. *Instructional Theories in Action.* (Hillsdale, N.J.: Lawrence Erlbaum, 1987).

Rice, Ronald E. *The New Media: Communication, Research, and Technology.* (Beverly Hills, Calif.: Sage, 1984).

Salomon, Gavriel. *Communication and Education: Social and Psychological Interactions.* (Beverly Hills, Calif.: Sage, 1981).

Severin, Werner, and Tankard, James W., Jr. *Communication Theories: Origins, Methods, Uses.* (New York: Hastings House, 1979).

Sigda, Robert B. "Using Media to Teach Science." *Instructional Innovator,* (September 1983), pp. 27–29.

Stakenas, Robert G., and Kaufman, Roger. *Technology in Education: Its Human Potential.* Fastback #163. (Bloomington, Ind.: Phi Delta Kappa Educational Foundation, 1981).

Thomas, James L., ed. *Nonprint in the Elementary Curriculum: Readings for Reference.* (Littleton, Colo.: Libraries Unlimited, 1982).

———. *Nonprint in the Secondary Curriculum: Readings for Reference.* (Littleton, Colo.: Libraries Unlimited, 1982).

Wadsworth, Barry J. *Piaget for the Classroom Teacher.* (White Plains, N.Y.: Longman, 1978).

———. *Piaget's Theory of Cognitive and Affective Development.* (White Plains, N.Y.: 1984).

Wiley, Ann L. *Sources of Information for Instructional Technology.* (Syracuse, N.Y.: ERIC Clearinghouse on Information Resources, 1981).

Wilkinson, Gene L. *Media in Instruction: 60 Years of Research.* (Washington, D.C.: AECT, 1980).

Audiovisual References

Case Studies in Communication. Salenger Educational Media, 1982. 16-mm film. 18 minutes.

The Child of the Future: How He Might Learn. Montreal: National Film Board of Canada, 1965. 16-mm film. 60 minutes.

Communication Feedback. Rockville, Md.: BNA Film, 1965. 16-mm film. 21 minutes.

A Communication Model. Bloomington, Ind.: Indiana University Audio-Visual Center, 1967. 16-mm film. 30 minutes.

Communication: The Name of the Game. Roundtable Film and Video, n.d. videocassette. 28 minutes.

Communications and Media. Learning Corporation of America, 1982. 16-mm film or videocassette. 20 minutes.

Communications Primer. Classroom Film Distributor, 1954. 16-mm film. 22 minutes.

Media for Presentations. Bloomington, Ind.: Indiana University Audio-Visual Center, 1978. 16-mm film. 20 minutes.

Perception and Communication. Columbus: Ohio State University, 1967. 16-mm film. 32 minutes.

This Is Marshall McLuhan: The Medium Is the Massage. New York: McGraw-Hill, 1968. 16-mm film. 53 minutes.

To Help Them Learn. Washington, D.C.: Association for Educational Communications and Technology, 1978. 16-mm film. 21 minutes.

Understanding Educational Technology. Washington, D.C.: Association for Educational Communications and Technology, 1977. Sound filmstrip with cassette.

Possible Projects

1-A. Read one of the books cited in the chapter or a book relating to a topic in the chapter and write or record on audiotape a report. The report should be approximately two and one-half double-spaced, typed pages or five minutes in length.

1-B. React to any of the topics or ideas presented in the chapter. Your reaction and comments may be written or recorded (approximately five double-spaced, typed pages or ten minutes in length).

1-C. Analyze an instructional situation (either real or hypothetical) and identify the elements of the communication process and their interrelationship.

1-D. Prepare a "position paper" (approximately five double-spaced typed pages) on a topic such as the role of humanism versus technology in education, or structure versus flexibility in teaching.

1-E. Describe an actual use of instructional media in an out-of-school setting based upon your experiences or readings.

2 Systematic Planning for the Use of Media

Objectives

After studying this chapter, you should be able to:

1. Describe six procedures (steps) in the systematic planning for the use of media (the ASSURE model).

2. List two general characteristics of learners and two types of specific competencies that could affect media selection.

3. Discuss the rationale for stating objectives for instruction. Your discussion should include three purposes or uses of objectives.

4. Write objectives that include the audience, behavioral outcome, conditions (if appropriate), and degree of mastery.

5. Classify given objectives into cognitive, affective, motor skill, and interpersonal skills domains; and locate them within each domain.

6. Describe the basic procedures for selecting, modifying, and designing materials, and indicate when each procedure is appropriate.

7. Explain how learner characteristics affect the selection of media.

8. State two examples of situational constraints on the selection of mediated materials.

9. Describe two ways of modifying materials without actually altering the original materials.

10. List and give examples of the five basic steps in utilizing instructional materials.

11. Identify general showmanship techniques in reference to strong and weak sectors of the classroom "stage," body positions, and movements.

12. Describe several methods for eliciting student response during and after using media.

13. Justify the need for requiring learner response when using media.

14. Compare and contrast the techniques for evaluating student achievement and the techniques for evaluating media and methods.

Lexicon

performance objective
criterion
cognitive domain
cognitive strategies
affective domain
internalization
characterization
motor skill domain
articulation
interpersonal skills
covert/overt response
showmanship

THE ASSURE MODEL

ALL effective instruction requires careful planning. Teaching with instructional media is certainly no exception to this educational truism. This chapter examines how to plan systematically for the effective use of instructional media. We have constructed a procedural model to which we have given the acronym ASSURE, because it is intended to

ASSURE effective use of media in instruction.

The ASSURE model, a procedural guide for planning and delivering instruction that incorporates media, assumes that training or instruction really is required (e.g., students don't know how to use the new laboratory microscopes, or assembly line workers must learn to handle safely the toxic materials they work with).

Unneeded or redundant instruction may be regarded as a fairly trivial nuisance in academic settings, but in business/industry training it is recognized as a major waste of time and money. Nevertheless, such instruction sometimes occurs, because training is the most obvious solution to performance problems. For example, the sales force of Amalgamated Houseware Industries is falling short of its target in sales of dust-

---

A Model to Help ASSURE Learning

A   S   S

Analyze Learners

The first step in planning is to identify the learners. Your learners may be students, trainees, or members of an organization such as a Sunday school, civic club, youth group, or fraternal organization. You must know your students to select the "best" medium to meet the objectives. The audience can be analyzed in terms of (1) general characteristics and (2) specific entry competencies—knowledge, skills, and attitudes about the topic.

State Objectives

The next step is to state the objectives as specifically as possible. The objectives may be derived from a needs assessment or a course syllabus, stated in a textbook, taken from a curriculum guide, or developed by the instructor. Wherever they come from, they should be stated in terms of what the learner (*audience*) will be able to do as a result of instruction (*behavior*). The *conditions* under which the student or trainee is going to perform and the *degree* of acceptable performance should be included.

Select Media and Materials

Once you have identified your audience and stated your objectives, you have established the beginning (audience's present knowledge, skills, and attitudes) and the ending points (objectives) of instruction. Your task now is to build a "bridge" between these two points. There are three options: (1) select available materials, (2) modify existing materials, or (3) design new materials.

pans. So the marketing vice-president suggests that the training department develop a self-instructional motivational videocassette on "Dynamic Dustpan Sales Techniques." In reality, it may be that the salespeople already *know* how to sell dustpans, but that Amalgamated dustpans are notoriously poorly engineered, or that the whole market for dustpans is depressed, or that higher commissions can be earned on other products in the Amalgamated line. If the cause of the problem is not a lack of knowledge, training will not solve the problem. Techniques for properly diagnosing learning needs or the sources of performance problems include needs assessment and front-end analysis (i.e., analysis prior to a commitment to design instruction).

The ASSURE model focuses on planning surrounding the actual classroom *use* of media. It is less ambitious than models of *instructional development,* which intend to guide the entire process of designing instructional systems. Such models include the processes of needs analysis, subject-matter analysis, product design, prototype tryout, system implementation, and the like. These larger-scale instructional development procedures typically involve teams of specialists and require

U R E

Utilize Materials

Having either selected, modified, or designed your materials, you then must plan how the materials will be used and how much time will be spent using them. Next, prepare the class and ready the necessary equipment and facilities. Then present the material using the "showmanship" techniques and suggestions described in the chapters of this text.

Require Learner Performance

Learners must practice what they are expected to learn and should be reinforced for the correct response. The first time they are expected to perform the behavior called for in the objectives should *not* be on the examination. Instead, there should be activities within the lesson that allow learners to respond and to receive feedback on the appropriateness of their performance or response.

Evaluate/Revise

After instruction, it is necessary to evaluate its impact and effectiveness. To get the total picture, you must evaluate the entire instructional process. Did the learners meet the objectives? Did the media assist the trainees in reaching the objectives? Could all students use the materials properly?

Wherever there are discrepancies between what you intended and what you attained, you will want to revise the plan for the next attempt.

major commitments of time and money. (Further information about instructional development can be found under that heading in the print references cited at the end of this chapter.) The ASSURE model, on the other hand, is meant for use by the individual instructor for planning everyday classroom use of media.

ANALYZE LEARNERS

I F instructional media are to be used effectively, there must be a match between the characteristics of the learner and the content of the lesson and its presentation. The first step in the ASSURE model, therefore, should be analysis of your audience.

It is not feasible to analyze every psychological or educational trait of your audience. There are, however, several factors about your learners that are critical for making good media and method decisions. First, in the category of *general characteristics* are broad identifying descriptors such as age, grade level, job/position, and cultural or socioeconomic factors. General characteristics are factors that are not related to the content of the lesson. These factors help you to determine the level of the lesson and to select examples that will be meaningful to the given audience.

Under the heading of *specific entry competencies* you should think about content-related qualities that will more directly affect your decisions about media and methods: prerequisite skills (Do learners have the knowledge base required to enter the lesson, such as the technical vocabulary?), target skills (Have learners already mastered some of the skills you are planning to teach?), and attitudes (Are there biases or misconceptions about the subject?).

A third factor, *learning style,* refers to the whole spectrum of psychological traits that affect how we perceive and respond to different stimuli, such as anxiety, aptitude, visual/auditory preference, and so on. The issue of what constitutes learning style, how it can be measured, and how it can be factored into educational decision making is still very much open. Because it is still such an innovative issue, we discuss it in depth among other emerging trends in Chapter 14.

General Characteristics

Even a superficial analysis of learner characteristics can provide helpful leads in selecting instructional methods and media. For example, students with substandard reading skills may be reached more effectively with nonprint media. If you are dealing with a particular ethnic or cultural subgroup, you might want to give high priority to considerations of ethnic/cultural identity in selecting particular materials.

If learner apathy toward the subject matter is a particular problem, consider using a highly stimulating instructional approach, such as a dramatic videotape or a simulation game. If you have a group diverging widely in background, consider self-instructional materials to allow self-pacing and other aspects of individualization.

Learners entering a new conceptual area for the first time will need more direct, concrete kinds of experiences (e.g., field trips, role playing). The more advanced have a sufficient base for using audiovisual or even verbal materials.

Heterogeneous groups including learners varying widely in their conceptual sophistication or in their amount of firsthand experience with the topic can profit especially from an audiovisual experience like a film or videotape. The media presentations provide a common experiential base that can serve as an important point of reference for subsequent group discussion and individual study.

For instructors dealing with a familiar audience, analysis of general characteristics will be something of a given. At times, however, audience analysis may be more difficult. Perhaps your students are new to you, and you have had little time to observe and record their characteristics. Perhaps your learners are a more heterogeneous group than is ordinarily found in the classroom—business trainees, for example, or a civic club, a youth group, or a fraternal organization—thus making it more difficult to ascertain if all or even a majority of your learners are ready for the media and method of instruction you are considering. In such cases, academic and other records may be helpful, as may direct questioning of and conversation with learners and group leaders.

Specific Entry Competencies

When you begin to plan any lesson, your opening assumption is that the learners *lack* the knowledge or skills you are about to teach and that they *possess* the knowledge or skills needed to understand and learn from the lesson. In reality, these assumptions are often mistaken. For example, a life insurance company used to routinely bring all its new sales associates back to the home office in Hartford, Connecticut at the end of their first year for a course on setting sales priorities. Puzzled by the cool reception given by the agents, the trainer decided to give a pretest, which revealed that a majority of the trainees already knew perfectly well how to set sales priorities. The company shifted to a less expensive and more productive strategy of giving incentives to field representatives who sent in acceptable sales plans showing their priorities.

The second assumption—that learners have the prerequisite knowledge or skill to begin the lesson—can seldom be accepted casually in school settings. Teachers of mixed-ability classes routinely anticipate that some students will need remedial help before they are ready to begin a particular new unit of instruction. Further, researchers studying the impact of different psychological traits on learning have reached the unexpected conclusion that a student's *prior knowledge* of a particular subject influences how and what he or she can learn more than does any psychological trait. For example, students approaching a subject new to them learn best from *structured* presentations (even if they have a learning style that would otherwise indicate more open-ended, unstructured methods).

These realizations underline the importance of verifying assumptions about entry competencies through informal means, such as in-class questioning or out-of-class interviews, or more formal means, such as testing with standardized or teacher-made tests. *Entry tests* refer to assessments, both formal and informal, that determine whether or not the student possesses the necessary prerequisites (entry skills). *Prerequisites* are those competencies that the learner must possess in order to benefit from the instruction, but that you or the media are not going to teach. For example,

▲ *Figure 2.1*
Entry tests help prevent the frustration students experience when placed in work too far above or below their ability level.

you may be teaching an apprentice lathe operator to read blueprints and assume that he or she has the ability to make metric conversions—and hence not teach this. Such previously acquired skills are properly referred to as prerequisites and should be assessed before instruction by use of an entry test.

Pretests are also given before instruction but are used to measure the content to be taught. If the learners have already mastered what you plan to teach, you are wasting your time and theirs by "teaching" it.

STATE OBJECTIVES

THE second step in the ASSURE model for using instructional media is to state the objectives of instruction. What learning goal is each learner expected to reach? More precisely, what new *capability* should the learner possess at the completion of instruction? Thus, an objective is a statement not of what the instructor plans to *put into* the lesson but of what the learner ought to *get out of* the lesson.

Your statement of objectives should be as specific as possible.

For example, "My students will improve their mathematical skills" is far too general to qualify as a specific lesson objective. It does, however, qualify as a "goal"—that is, a broad statement of purpose. Such a goal might serve as the umbrella for a number of specific objectives, such as "The second-grade students will be able to solve correctly any single-digit addition problem."

Why should you state instructional objectives? In the first place, you must know your objectives in order to make the correct selection of media and methods. Your objectives will, in a sense, dictate your choice of media and your sequence of learning activities. Knowing your objectives will also force you to create a learning environment in which the objectives *can* be reached. For example, if the objective of a unit of a driver's training course is "to be able to change a flat tire within fifteen minutes," the learning environment must include a car with a flat tire. If, on the other hand, the unit objective is "to be able to name and describe the tools necessary to change a flat tire," a driver's manual or textbook would probably suffice.

Another basic reason for stating your instructional objectives is to help assure proper evaluation. You won't know if your learners have achieved an objective unless you are absolutely sure what that objective is. For information on deriving test items from objectives, see pages 57–58. Particularly note the box titled "Test Items: General."

Without explicit objectives your students won't know what is expected of them. If objectives are clearly and specifically stated, learning and teaching become objective-oriented. Indeed, a statement of objectives may be viewed as a type of contract between teacher and learner: "Here is the objective. My responsibility as the instructor is to provide learning activities suitable for your attaining the objective. Your responsibility as the learner is to participate conscientiously in those learning activities."

The ABCDs of Well-Stated Objectives

A well-stated objective starts by naming the *Audience* of learners for whom the objective is intended. It then specifies the *Behavior* or capability to be learned and the *Conditions* under which the capability would be observed. Finally, it specifies the *Degree* to which the new skill must be mastered—the standard by which the capability can be judged. Writing useful objectives can be as easy as ABCD!

Audience. A major premise of systematic instruction is to focus on what the *learner* is doing, not on what the teacher is doing. Learning is most likely to take place when the learner is active— mentally processing an idea or physically practicing a skill. Because accomplishment of the objective depends on what the learner does, not what the teacher does, the objective begins by stating *whose* capability is going to be changed—e.g., "Ninth-grade algebra students" or "Newly hired sales representatives." Of course, if you are repeating the objective in material written for student use, the informal "you" is preferable to the formal "the ninth-grade algebra student."

Behavior. The heart of the objective is the verb describing the new capability that the audience will have after instruction. This verb is most likely to com-

To be sure of hitting the target,

shoot first

and whatever you hit, call it the target.

▲ *Figure 2.2*
Some archers may adopt this philosophy, but is it appropriate for designing instruction?

The Helpful Hundred: Suggested Behavioral Terms

Add	Defend	Kick	Reduce
Alphabetize	Define	Label	Remove
Analyze	Demonstrate	Locate	Revise
Apply	Derive	Make	Select
Arrange	Describe	Manipulate	Sketch
Assemble	Design	Match	Ski
Attend	Designate	Measure	Solve
Bisect	Diagram	Modify	Sort
Build	Distinguish	Multiply	Specify
Carve	Drill	Name	Square
Categorize	Estimate	Operate	State
Choose	Evaluate	Order	Subtract
Classify	Explain	Organize	Suggest
Color	Extrapolate	Outline	Swing
Compare	Fit	Pack	Tabulate
Complete	Generate	Paint	Throw
Compose	Graph	Plot	Time
Compute	Grasp (hold)	Position	Translate
Conduct	Grind	Predict	Type
Construct	Hit	Prepare	Underline
Contrast	Hold	Present	Verbalize
Convert	Identify	Produce	Verify
Correct	Illustrate	Pronounce	Weave
Cut	Indicate	Read	Weigh
Deduce	Install	Reconstruct	Write

municate your intent clearly if it is stated as an *observable behavior*. What will the learner be able to *do* after completing instruction? Vague terms such as *know*, *understand*, and *appreciate* do not communicate your aim clearly. Better are *define*, *categorize*, and *demonstrate*, which denote observable performance. The Helpful Hundred list (page 38) contains suggested verbs that highlight performance.

Ideally, the behavior stated in the objective will reflect the real-world capability actually needed by the learner, not some artificial test performance. As a surgical patient, do you want a surgeon who "is able to perform an appendectomy" or one who "is able to select the correct answers on a multiple-choice test on appendectomies"?

Although the exact format of the objective is not critical, it is recommended that the behavior be stated in this form: "The learner will be able to . . ." The use of the future tense is a reminder that you are referring to the new capability that will exist after instruction. The use of "be able to" forces you to phrase the objective in performance terms. In your own notes you may abbreviate this phrase to WBAT (will be able to) to avoid having to write it out each time. If you have a list of several objectives pertaining to a given unit of instruction, you may just state WBAT once and then list the performance terms. For example, "After completing Sociology 101, the entering Sociology major WBAT:

1. Define *sociology*.
2. Describe three significant events that shaped the development of sociology as a discipline.
3. Analyze the results of a sociological study and state appropriate conclusions.
4. State and defend a position on the issue of the biological basis of socialization."

Conditions. A statement of objectives should include the conditions under which performance is to be observed, if such conditions are relevant. For example, may the student use notes in describing the consequences of excessive use of alcohol? If the objective of a particular lesson is for the student to be able to identify birds, will identification be made from color representations or black/white photographs? What tools or equipment will the student be allowed to use in demonstrating mastery of the objective? What resources will the student *not* be allowed to use? Thus, for example, "*Given a political map of Europe*, you will be able to mark the major coal-producing areas."; "*Without notes, textbook, or any library materials*, you will be able to write an essay on the

---

CHECK YOURSELF: BEHAVIORS

Are the following statements written in *behavioral (performance) terms*? (Complete and then check your answers below.)

YES	NO	
____	____	1. The labor negotiations trainee will grasp the true significance of the Taft-Hartley Act.
____	____	2. The carpentry vocational trainees will learn the common tools in the woodworking shop.
____	____	3. The first-year medical student will be able to name all the bones in the hand.
____	____	4. The high school debate club member will include ten supporting facts in a written paragraph on "The Value of National Health Insurance."
____	____	5. The junior high school student will list on the chalkboard three major causes of the American Civil War.
____	____	6. The kindergarten student will sit straight and quietly in his or her seat while the teacher is talking.
____	____	7. The high school sophomore will show a favorable regard for volleyball by joining an intramural volleyball team.
____	____	8. The Anthropology 101 student will develop a sense of the cultural unity of humankind.
____	____	9. By the end of their orientation, new employees will appreciate the importance of productivity within the corporation.
____	____	10. The elementary school student will demonstrate a desire for a clean environment by voluntarily picking up litter in the classroom and on the playground.

Answers

1. No 2. No 3. Yes 4. Yes 5. Yes 6. Yes 7. Yes 8. No 9. No 10. Yes

relationship of nutrition to learning."

Degree. The final requirement of a well-stated objective is to indicate the standard by which acceptable performance will be judged. What *degree* of accuracy or proficiency must the learner display? Whether the criteria are stated in qualitative or quantitative terms, they should be based on some real-world requirement: How well must the machinist be able to operate a lathe in order to be a productive employee? What degree of mastery of French grammar is essential to pass on to the next unit?

Time and accuracy are meaningful dimensions for many objectives. How quickly must the observable behavior be performed—for example, to solve five quadratic equations in five minutes, or to run a mile in less than eight minutes? How accurate must the results be—to the nearest whole number or within one-sixteenth of an inch or plus or minus 1 mm? If the learning activity is archery, criteria for performance acceptability might be stated, as follows: "The student will be able to shoot ten arrows from fifty yards within five minutes and hit a three-foot-diameter target with at least seven of the arrows."

Quantitative criteria for judging acceptable performance may sometimes be difficult to define. How, for example, can an industrial arts teacher specify how smoothly a piece of wood must be sanded? How can an English instructor state quantitative criteria for an essay or short story? Here performance is qualitative. Your task is more difficult in such cases, but not impossible. The industrial arts teacher, for example, might stipulate that the wood be comparable to a given example or be judged satisfactory by the teacher or a peer. The English instructor might stipulate that the student's work will be scored for development of theme, characterization, originality, or the like. Again, a model story might be used as an exemplar. A quantitative criterion for the English instructor might be that more than five spelling and punctuation errors will be unacceptable. Whether quantitative or qualitative criteria are used, they should be as appropriate and as specific as you can make them (see Appraisal Checklist, p. 42).

Do the following statements include a properly stated *degree or criterion of acceptable performance*? (Complete and then check your answers below.)

YES NO

___ ___ 1. On a questionnaire at the end of the course, each management trainee will write at least two favorable comments about the course.

___ ___ 2. The machine shop trainee will be able to operate properly the Model 63-9 metal lathe.

___ ___ 3. In a controlled situation without access to any references, the college student of romantic poetry will be able to write an essay on the three themes in Shelley's poetry.

___ ___ 4. During a nature hike, the youth camper will be able to identify correctly at least three different geological formations.

___ ___ 5. The basketball squad member will be able to sink 75 percent of her free throws in a single practice session.

___ ___ 6. The vocational education student in basic electricity will operate a potentiometer to determine the resistance of resistors.

___ ___ 7. In a ballet practice session, each new dance company member will display proper form.

___ ___ 8. While being observed without his or her knowledge, the high school chemistry student will demonstrate all the safety precautions listed on the chart in the laboratory.

___ ___ 9. The football team member will be able to name correctly the formations illustrated by each of twelve diagrams.

___ ___ 10. Given a list of authors, the junior high school student will match the names of each with titles of their works.

Answers

1. Yes 2. No 3. No 4. Yes 5. Yes 6. No 7. No 8. Yes 9. Yes 10. Yes

The important consideration in appraising your objectives is whether the intent of the objectives, regardless of their format, is communicated to the user. If your objectives meet all the criteria in the Appraisal Checklist but still do not communicate accurately your intentions to your colleagues and students, they are inadequate. The final judgment on any objectives must be determined by their usefulness to you and your learners.

CLASSIFICATION OF OBJECTIVES

Classifying objectives is much more than an academic exercise for educational psychologists. It has practical value because the selection of instructional methods and media depends on what type of objective is being pursued, and so does the choice of evaluation instruments. An objective may be classified according to the *primary* type of learning outcome at which it is aimed. Although there is a range of opinion on the best way to describe and organize the subsets, three categories, or "domains," of learning are widely accepted: cognitive, affective, and motor skills. To these we add a fourth—interpersonal skills—which addresses important skills neglected in the other domains.

Cognitive learning involves the whole array of intellectual capabilities, from simple factual recall to the generation of new theories.

Affective learning involves feelings and values. Objectives in the affective domain may range from stimulating interest in a school subject to encouraging healthy social attitudes to adopting a set of ethical standards.

Motor skill learning involves athletic, manual, and other such physical skills. Objectives in the motor skill domain include capabilities ranging from simple mechanical operations to those entailing sophisticated neuromuscular coordination and strategy, as in competitive sports.

Interpersonal skills learning involves interaction among people. These are people-centered skills that involve the ability to relate effectively with others. Examples include teamwork, counseling techniques, administrative skills, salesmanship, discussion activities, and customer relations.

Most learned capabilities actually contain elements of all domains inasmuch as they entail voluntary display (affective) of some observable action (motor skill) that indicates possession of

Appraisal Checklist: Objectives Statements

	Very Well Stated		Weak		Missing

Audience

Specifies the learner(s) for whom the objective is intended □ □ □ □ □

Behavior (action verb)

Describes the *capability* expected of the learner following instruction □ □ □ □ □
   —stated as a *learner* performance
   —stated as *observable* behavior
   —describes a real-world *skill* (versus mere test performance)

Conditions (materials and/or environment)

Describes the *conditions* under which the performance is to be □ □ □ □ □
   demonstrated
   —equipment, tools, aids, or references the learner may or may not
   use
   —special environmental conditions in which the learner has to
   perform

Degree (criterion)

States, where applicable, the *standard* for acceptable performance □ □ □ □ □
   —time limit
   —accuracy tolerances
   —proportion of correct responses required
   —qualitative standards

---

some mental skill (cognitive). Nevertheless, the *primary* emphasis in the mind of the instructor can usually be stated as cognitive, affective, motor skill, or interpersonal. For example, the objective of having students perform a somersault on a trampoline requires their knowledge of the correct sequence of actions (cognitive) and willingness to perform the maneuver (affective), but the emphasis clearly is on the mastery of the *physical* ability; hence, it would be classified as a motor skill objective.

Take, as another example, the objective in an elementary school of developing the children's eagerness to clean up classroom litter voluntarily. It has a cognitive element—knowing the reasons why a clean classroom is better, distinguishing litter from intentional decorations, and the like. It also incorporates the physical skills of picking up, sweeping, and throwing into a trash can, among others. But the primary emphasis here is on changing the children's *attitudes* toward litter, making it an affective objective.

The Cognitive Domain

The original classification scheme for the cognitive domain proposed by Bloom* envisioned a rather orderly progression from simple to complex mental abilities. Research over the past three decades suggests that the cognitive domain incorporates at least three qualitatively different types

---

* Benjamin S. Bloom, ed. *Taxonomy of Educational Objectives, Handbook I: Cognitive Domain.* New York: David McKay, 1956.

of capabilities, not a single simple-to-complex continuum. Gagne's* categories are widely accepted among instructional designers:

1. *Verbal/visual information:* factual knowledge stored verbally or visually in memory; it consists of single images, facts, labels, memorized sequences, and organized information. Examples: To be able to recall that Mackenzie King served as prime minister of Canada three times between 1921 and 1948; To be able to recite the first paragraph of John F. Kennedy's inaugural address. This category also includes the somewhat higher level skill of comprehending—understanding the meaning of a fact. Example: To be able to summarize in your own words the contributions of President Kennedy to the civil rights movement.

2. *Intellectual skills:* the ability to use symbols to organize and manipulate the environment. The two most basic forms of symbols, words and numbers, allow us to read, write, and compute. These abilities underlie the continuum of capabilities that form the intellectual skill category:
   a. Discrimination: to be able to distinguish between two different stimuli, that is, to see the difference between physically similar objects. Example: To be able to distinguish between a turbo-prop and a turbofan jet engine.
   b. Concept learning: classify-ing things or ideas into categories on the basis of some shared attributes. Example: To be able to identify a bat as a mammal.
   c. Rule using: applying principles to a variety of situations. Using mathematical equations or following the rules of grammar to construct sentences in a foreign language are rule-using capabilities.

3. *Cognitive Strategies:* the internal "control processes" that govern the learner's ability to visualize, think about, and solve problems. The sophistication of our cognitive strategies determines how creatively, fluently, or critically we will be able to think. Example: To resolve logical contradictions by questioning the assumptions behind each.

The Affective Domain†

The affective domain is organized according to the degree of *internalization*—the degree to which the attitude or value has become part of the individual:

1. *Receiving:* being aware of and willing to pay attention to a stimulus (listen or look) (e.g., The student will sit quietly while the teacher reads Longfellow's *Paul Revere's Ride.*).
2. *Responding:* actively participating, reacting in some way (e.g., The student will ask questions relating to *Paul Revere's Ride.*).
3. *Valuing:* voluntarily displaying an attitude, showing an interest (e.g., The student will ask to read another story or poem about Paul Revere.).
4. *Characterization:* demonstrating an internally consistent value system, developing a characteristic lifestyle based upon a value or value system (e.g., The student will devote a percentage of his or her free time to studying American history.).

The Motor Skill Domain††

The motor skill domain may be seen as a progression in the degree of *coordination* required:

1. *Imitation:* repeating the action shown (e.g., After viewing the film on the backhand tennis swing, you will demonstrate the swing with reasonable accuracy.).
2. *Manipulation:* performing independently (e.g., Following a practice period, you will demonstrate the backhand tennis swing, scoring seven of the ten points on the performance checklist.).
3. *Precision:* performing with accuracy (e.g., You will demonstrate an acceptable backhand tennis swing, returning successfully at least 75 percent of practice serves to the backhand.).
4. *Articulation:* performing unconsciously, efficiently, and harmoniously, incorporating coordination of skills (e.g., During a tennis match, you will execute the backhand stroke effectively against your opponent, returning nine out of ten of all types of shots hit to the backhand side.).

---

* Robert Gagne, Leslie Briggs, and Walter Wager. *Principles of Instructional Design.* 3d ed. New York: Holt, Rinehart & Winston, 1988, p. 44.

† Adapted from David R. Krathwohl et al. *Taxonomy of Educational Objectives, Handbook II: Affective Domain.* New York: David McKay, 1964.

†† Adaptation based upon published works of E. Simpson (University of Illinois) and R. H. Dave (National Institute of Education, New Delhi, India).

© 1971 United Feature Syndicate, Inc.

▲ *Figure 2.3*
The fruits of a lesson aimed at some affective objectives that are poorly specified.

work rule against a colleague's attack.).

6. *Summarizing:* restating in a compact form the content of previous discussions or considerations (e.g., Before giving your comments in a departmental meeting you will summarize the arguments that have been presented.).

Types of Interpersonal Skills Learning*

The types of interpersonal skills can be classified into six categories:

1. *Seeking/giving information:* asking for/offering facts, opinions, or clarification from/to another individual or individuals (e.g., You will ask your supervisor about the meaning of a new work rule.).
2. *Proposing:* putting forward a new concept, suggestion, or course of action (e.g., You will make a job enrichment suggestion to your supervisor.).
3. *Building and supporting:* extending, developing, enhancing another person, his or her proposal, or concepts (e.g., In a departmental meeting you will suggest an amendment to someone's motion.).
4. *Shutting out/bringing in:* excluding/involving another group member from/into a conversation or discussion

(e.g., In a departmental meeting you will ask a quiet member to give his or her ideas.).

5. *Disagreeing:* providing a conscious, direct declaration of difference of opinion, or criticism of another person's concepts (e.g., During a lunchroom discussion you will defend a new

Objectives and Individual Differences

Objectives in any of the domains just discussed may, of course, be adapted to the abilities of individual learners. The stated philosophy of most schools and colleges is to help students fulfill *their* full potential, not to produce clone-like replications of a standard mold. In a physical education class with students of mixed ability, for instance, the midsemester goal might be for all students to be able to complete a run of 100 meters outdoors; but the time

▲ *Figure 2.4*
In a group that includes handicapped learners there may be as many different standards for each objective as there are individuals.

---

* Adapted from Neil Rackham and Terry Morgan. *Behaviour Analysis in Training.* London: McGraw-Hill, 1977.

Ralph Tyler, a professor at Ohio State University, is generally considered to be the father of performance objectives as we know them today. Tyler's original interest was in test-item construction. His main contribution was to point out the importance of constructing test items based on behaviorally stated objectives that could be determined by analyzing the curriculum content.[a]

However, it was those in the programmed instruction movement, and particularly Robert Mager, who popularized the use of objectives by educators. Mager was a research scientist at Fort Bliss, Texas, working on a study to compare an experimental version of a course with an ongoing army course. He drafted the objectives for the course and insisted that they be signed by the proper authorities before instruction began. Later, while employed by Varian Associates in Palo Alto, California, he was involved in designing a one-day session on programmed instruction for school administrators. In order to teach them to discriminate between properly written and poorly written programmed instruction, Mager decided to write a branching program with a variety of instructional errors:

Robert F. Mager

But what topic to write on? I couldn't think of one. I stared at the typewriter, counted the leaves on the tree outside the window, and checked my fingernails. Nothing. Finally, while thinking about the nature of the target population (audience), I had a flash! I'll fix you, I said to myself. I'll write about a topic that will get you so emotionally aroused that you won't be able to see programming from the subject matter. And I began to type out a dogmatic (error-filled) branching program called "How to Write Objectives." In addition to such pedagogical niceties as branching the reader to pages that didn't exist, I berated them on the wrong answer pages with comments such as "How can you sit there and SAY a thing like that. You're lying and you know it." And "Now look here! I don't want to have any trouble with you. So read the little gem: 'How do YOU know? Have you ever tried seriously to specify exact objectives for an academic course? Or are you upset simply because what is being suggested sounds like work?' "[b]

Mager's initial program on writing objectives was duplicated, and it generated a great deal of discussion and provided practice in spotting good and bad characteristics in an instructional program. In Mager's words, "The day was a huge success."[c]

Later Mager learned that at least two professors at local colleges were using his error-laden practice program as a text in their education courses, so he modified the original program and published *Preparing Objectives for Programmed Instruction*[d] in 1961. He and others quickly realized that his objectives could be applied to much more than just programmed learning, so the following year the book was rereleased with the title *Preparing Instructional Objectives*.[e] The book is a classic in the field of education; now in its revised second edition, it has sold over two million copies. As Mager says, "If you're not sure where you're going, you're liable to end up someplace else—and not even know it."

---

[a] Ralph Tyler. "The Construction of Examinations in Botany and Zoology." *Service Studies in Higher Education.* Bureau of Educational Research Monograph, no. 15. Columbus: Ohio State University, 1932.

[b] Robert F. Mager, "Why I Wrote . . ." *NSPI Journal* (October 1976), p. 4

[c] Ibid.

[d] Robert F. Mager. *Preparing Objectives for Programmed Instruction.* Palo Alto, Calif.: Fearon Publishers, 1961.

[e] See references at end of this chapter.

standards may vary. For some, twelve seconds might be attainable; for many others, sixteen seconds; and for some, twenty might be realistic. For a physically handicapped student, it might be a major victory to move ten meters in a minute.

Objectives are not intended to *limit* what a student learns. They are intended only to provide a minimum level of expected achievement. Serendipitous or incidental learning should be expected to occur (and be encouraged) as students progress toward an objective. Each learner has a different field of experience (as discussed in Chapter 1), and each has different characteristics (as discussed earlier in this chapter). Because of such individual differences, incidental learning takes different forms with different students. Class discussions and other kinds of student involvement in the instructional situation, therefore, should rarely be rigidly limited to a specific objective. Student involvement should allow for incidental learning to be shared and reinforced. Indeed, in order to foster incidental learning and provide for individual differences, it is sometimes advisable to have the students specify some of their own objectives.

In nonacademic organizations, such as the military or industry, the philosophy behind the training program may be quite different. Here the purpose is to operate the organization as efficiently as possible, and individuals are trained for roles in the organization. Objectives are written to reflect the actual demands of given jobs; individuals are trained and/or selected for those jobs based on their ability to meet those standards stated in the objectives.

SELECT MEDIA AND MATERIALS p.34

A systematic plan for *using* media certainly demands that the media be *selected* systematically in the first place. The selection process will be presented here in two stages: (1) choosing an appropriate media format and (2) selecting, modifying, or designing the specific materials within that format.

Choosing a Media Format

Choosing a media format can be a very complex task, considering the vast array of media available, the infinite variety among learners, and the objectives to be pursued. Over the years many different formulas have been proposed for simplifying the task. They are referred to as media selection models, and they usually take the form of flowcharts or checklists.

Within most media selection models the instructional situation or *setting* (e.g., large-group, small-group, or self-instruction), *learner* variables (e.g., reader, nonreader, or auditory preference), and the nature of the *objective* (e.g., cognitive, affective, motor skill, or interpersonal) must be considered against the *presentational capabilities* of each of the media formats (e.g., presenting still visuals, motion visuals, printed words, or spoken words). Some models also take into consideration the capability of each format to give *feedback* to the learner. One of the most recent and comprehensive models is that of Reiser and Gagne.* The user is first asked to specify the instructional *setting,* which

---

* Robert M. Reiser and Robert M. Gagne. *Selecting Media for Instruction.* Englewood Cliffs, N.J.: Educational Technology, 1983.

includes both the grouping arrangement and one major learner variable—reader versus nonreader. The choices of setting are as follows: instructor with readers, instructor with nonreaders, self-instruction with nonreaders, and central broadcast. Within each of these settings the user then specifies what *objective* is being pursued. This decision leads to a short list of "candidate" media. Figure 2.5 illustrates one of Reiser and Gagne's flowcharts—for the setting of "instructor with readers."

The limitation of any such media selection model is the trade-off between simplicity and comprehensiveness: reducing the process to a short checklist forces one to ignore some possibly important considerations. For example, the Reiser and Gagne model ignores all learner characteristics except reading ability; it ignores such settings as tutorial and small group; it ignores or downplays such media formats as simulation, gaming, manipulative materials (tactile), and direct immersion experiences (kinesthetic).

Our approach in this book is to give you the tools to construct your own schema for selecting appropriate media formats. We accept the desirability of comparing the demands of the setting, learner characteristics, and objectives against the attributes of the various media formats. But only *you* can decide how to weight these considerations: what options you have in terms of setting, which learner characteristics are most critical, and what elements of your objectives are most important in your own situation. You will have to make your own trade-off between simplicity and comprehensiveness of the schema you will employ.

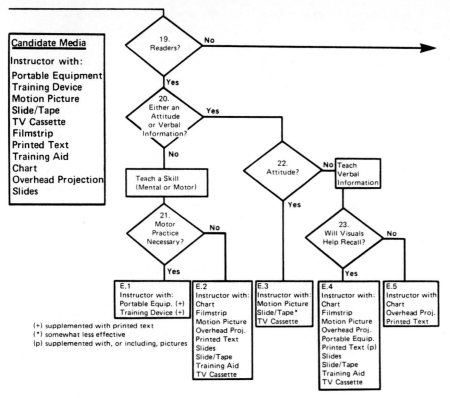

Candidate Media

Instructor with:
Portable Equipment
Training Device
Motion Picture
Slide/Tape
TV Cassette
Filmstrip
Printed Text
Training Aid
Chart
Overhead Projection
Slides

19. Readers?

No →

Yes ↓

20. Either an Attitude or Verbal Information?

Yes →

No ↓

Teach a Skill (Mental or Motor)

21. Motor Practice Necessary?

No →

Yes ↓

22. Attitude?

No → Teach Verbal Information

Yes ↓

23. Will Visuals Help Recall?

No →

Yes ↓

E.1 Instructor with: Portable Equip. (+) Training Device (+)

E.2 Instructor with: Chart Filmstrip Motion Picture Overhead Proj. Printed Text Slides Slide/Tape Training Aid TV Cassette

E.3 Instructor with: Motion Picture Slide/Tape * TV Cassette

E.4 Instructor with: Chart Filmstrip Motion Picture Overhead Proj. Portable Equip. Printed Text (p) Slides Slide/Tape Training Aid TV Cassette

E.5 Instructor with Chart Overhead Proj. Printed Text

(+) supplemented with printed text
(*) somewhat less effective
(p) supplemented with, or including, pictures

▲ *Figure 2.5*

Example of one of the flowcharts from Robert Reiser and Robert Gagne, *Selecting Media for Instruction*, Englewood Cliffs, N.J.: Educational Technology Publications, 1983.

Obtaining Specific Materials: Select, Modify, or Design?

Having decided what media format suits your immediate instructional objective, you face the problem of finding specific materials to convey the lesson. This is certainly one of the most important problems that instructors face, given the research finding that on the average 90 to 95 percent of instructional class time is spent on activities based on the use of instructional materials.*

---

* P. Kenneth Komoski, "How Can the Evaluation of Instructional Materials Help Improve Classroom Instruction Received by Handicapped Learners?" In R. Heinich, ed., *Educating All Handicapped Children*. Englewood Cliffs, N.J.: Educational Technology Publications, 1979, pp. 189–191.

Obtaining appropriate materials will generally involve one of three alternatives: (1) selecting available materials, (2) modifying existing materials, or (3) designing new materials. Obviously, if materials are already available that will allow your students to meet your objectives, these materials should be used to save both time and money. When the media and materials available do not match your objectives or are not suitable for your audience, an alternate approach is to modify the materials. If this is not feasible, the final alternative is to design your own materials. Even though this is a more expensive and time-consuming process, it does allow you to prepare materials to serve your audience precisely and meet your objectives.

Selecting Available Materials

The majority of instructional materials used by teachers and trainers are "off the shelf"—that is, ready-made and available from school, district, or company collections or other easily accessible sources. How do you go about making an appropriate choice from available materials?

Survey of Sources. Your first step might be to survey some of the published media reference guides to get a general idea of what is available. Unfortunately, no single comprehensive guide exists to all audiovisual materials available in all media formats in all subjects; you may have to consult several sources for a given problem.

One of the more comprehensive sources is the set of indexes published by NICEM (National Information Center for Educational Media). The NICEM indexes are arranged according to

▲ *Figure 2.6*

The NICEM indexes list commercially produced materials available in various media formats.

media format—e.g., slides, film-strips, overhead transparencies, and 16-mm films. In addition, there are several indexes devoted to specific topics, cutting across multiple media formats—e.g., environmental studies, health and safety, psychology, and vocational/technical education. These indexes do not include evaluations.

There also is a separate data bank for information and materials on special education: NICSEM (National Information Center for Special Education Materials). NICSEM publications provide information on the content of materials and their applicability to specific handicapping conditions. This information is intended to help in preparing individualized education plans for handicapped learners. (See Appendix A for details about NICEM and NICSEM.)

If you are working in elementary or secondary education, there are several additional sources that cover a broad range of media formats; for example, *Core Media Collection for Elementary Schools* and *Core Media Collection for Secondary Schools*. These books recommend specific audiovisual titles as core materials for elementary and secondary school library collections.

For general and adult audiences, a major reference source is the *Reference List of Audiovisual Materials Produced by the United States Government*. It describes all the training and educational materials produced by the armed forces and other government agencies that are available for general purchase. (See Appendix A for further details on all the reference sources discussed here.)

Beyond the sources just described, you will have to turn to the more specialized guides and indexes that are limited to spe-cific media formats or specific subjects. These are too many and too diverse to list here, but some are mentioned in the individual chapters dealing with different media formats, and others are gathered under the heading of "Specialized Information Sources" in Appendix A. Also, see Appendix B for sources of free and inexpensive materials.

Selection Criteria. The actual decision about whether to use a particular piece of instructional material depends on several factors. Among the major questions to ask are the following:

- Do the objectives of the material match my own?
- Do my learners have the required entry capabilities (reading ability and vocabulary level are often important)?
- Is the information accurate and up-to-date?
- Is the presentation likely to arouse and maintain interest?
- Does it promote active involvement of learners?
- Is the technical quality acceptable?
- Has the producer provided evidence of effectiveness, such as results of field tests?
- Is it free from objectionable bias?

Over the years scholars have debated over what should be *the* criteria applied in selecting materials. Studies have been conducted to try to quantify and validate various criteria. The net result is an understanding that different criteria are suitable for different situations. For example, a remedial reading teacher might decide to use a particular filmstrip primarily because its vocabulary level is just right, regardless of any other qualities. On the other hand, an elementary school teacher with a class that is very diverse ethnically might sort through materials with a special sensitivity to racial and ethnic portrayals.

Further, different media formats raise different issues. Film and video materials, for example, raise the issue of the pace of presentation, whereas this would not be relevant for overhead transparencies. In examining computer-assisted instruction courseware, one would look for relevant practice and remedial feedback, but these would not be expected in a filmstrip. To account for these differences this book provides a separate Appraisal Checklist for each media format. You will notice that certain criteria appear consistently in each checklist (they are all listed in the table of contents). These are the criteria that we feel have the securest basis in research and real-life experience. The Appraisal Checklists have been provided to give you a systematic procedure for judging the qualities of specific materials. But it's up to you to decide which criteria are most important to you in your own instructional setting.

The Instructor's Personal File. Every instructor should develop a file of media references and appraisals for personal use. This personal file card need not be as detailed as the appraisal form. What you are primarily interested in recording is instructional strengths and weaknesses. Figure 2.7 illustrates a suggested personal file form that is relatively simple and will fit on a 4-by-6-inch card. Under "synopsis," you can note the overall content of the item. Under "utilization pointers and problems," you might note information about vocabulary used in the material, lack or inclusion of opportunities for student response, timeliness of the con-

tent, inclusion of sensitive topics, and so on.

Modifying Available Materials

If you cannot locate entirely suitable materials and media off the shelf, you might be able to modify what is available. This can be both challenging and creative. In terms of time and cost, it is a more efficient procedure than designing your own materials, although type and extent of necessary modification will, of course, vary.

Perhaps the only visual available showing a piece of equipment being used in a junior high woodworking class is from a repair manual and contains too much detail and complex terminology. A possible solution to the problem would be to use the picture but modify the caption and simplify or omit some of the names of the labelled parts.

In a business or industry new employee orientation program, you may be using a slide set developed by corporate headquarters. Where possible and appropriate, you can replace existing slides with slides showing local facilities and local personnel.

Or perhaps there is just one film available that shows a needed visual sequence, but the audio

Title: _____ Format: _____

Length: _____ Source: _____ Technical data: _____

Synopsis:

Utilization pointers and problems (e.g., new vocabulary):

▲ *Figure 2.7*
Your personal file cards will provide an informal record of your own notes regarding particular materials.

▲ *Figure 2.8*
The most basic way of "modifying" material such as a film or video program is to show segments of the program interspersed with group discussion.

portion of the film is inappropriate because it is at too high or too low a conceptual level or discusses inappropriate points. In such a case, a simple solution would be to show the film with the sound turned off and provide the narration yourself. Another modification technique, which many instructors overlook, is to show just a portion of a film, stop the projector, discuss what has been presented, then continue with another short segment followed by additional discussion. A similar approach may be used for

sound filmstrips with audiotape. You can rerecord the narration and use the appropriate vocabulary level for your audience—and even change the emphasis of the visual material. If a transcript of the original narration is available, you probably will want to refer to it as you compose your own narration.

Modification also can be made in the audio portion of foreign language materials (or English language materials used in a bilingual classroom). Narrations can be changed from one language to another or from a more advanced rendition of a foreign language to a simpler one.

Videocassette recorders now provide teachers with the opportunity to modify television programs that previously were available only as shown on the air. With video playback units available in most schools, many producers now distribute programs having educational potential in videotape format. Programs may also be recorded off the air for replay on playback units.* Procedures and practices for modification of videotape are much the same as for film (as noted previously). Videocassette recorders also, of course, give the teacher much more flexibility in using television programs for instructional purposes. Programs can be shown at whatever time best suits the instructional situation and to whatever student group or groups that can best profit from viewing them.

One frequently modified media format is a set of slides with an audiotape. If the visuals are appropriate but the language is

---

* Broadcast materials vary in their recording restrictions. See Appendix C for general guidelines; consult a media specialist regarding specific programs.

not, it is possible to change the language. It also is possible to change the *emphasis* of the narration. For example, an original audiotape might emphasize oceans as part of an ecosystem, whereas the teacher may want to use the slides to show various types of fish found in oceans. By rewriting the narration, the teacher could adapt the material to his or her purpose while using the same slides. Redoing the tape can also change the *level* of the presentation. A slide-tape presentation produced to introduce a new product could have three different audiotapes. One tape could be directed toward the customer, another could be prepared for the sales staff, and the third for the service personnel.

Instructional games can be readily modified to meet particular instructional needs. It is possible to use a given game format and change the rules of play in order to increase or decrease the level of sophistication. Many instructional games require the players to answer questions. It is relatively easy for the teacher to prepare a new set of questions at a different level of difficulty or even on a new topic.

If you try out modified materials while they are still in more or less rough form, you can then make further modifications in response to student reaction until your materials meet your exact needs.

A word of caution about modifying commercially produced materials (and, indeed, about use of commercial products in general): be sure your handling and use of such materials does not violate copyright laws and restrictions. If in doubt, check with your school administrator or legal advisor. (Copyright laws and guidelines are discussed in Appendix C.)

Designing New Materials

It is easier and less costly to use available materials, with or without modification, than to start from scratch. There is seldom justification for reinventing the wheel. However, there may be times when your only recourse is to design your own materials. As is the case with selecting from available materials, certain basic considerations must be taken into account when designing new materials. For example:

Objectives—What do you want your students to learn?

Audience—What are the characteristics of your learners? Do they have the prerequisite knowledge and skills to use and/or learn from the materials?

Cost—Is sufficient money available in your budget to meet the cost of supplies (film, audiotapes, etc.) you will need to prepare the materials?

Technical expertise—Do you have the necessary expertise to design and produce the kind of materials you wish to use? If not, will the necessary technical assistance be available to you? (Try to keep your design within the range of your own capabilities. Don't waste time and money trying to produce slick professional materials when simple inexpensive products will get the job done.)

Equipment—Do you have available the necessary equipment to produce and/or use the materials you intend to design?

Facilities—If your design calls for use of special facilities for preparation and/or use of your materials, are such facilities available?

Time—Can you afford to spend whatever time may be necessary

to design and produce the kind of materials you have in mind?

UTILIZE MATERIALS p. 34

THE next step in the ASSURE model is the one that all the other steps lead up to and away from: the presentation itself. To get maximum learning impact from your presentation, you must follow certain utilization procedures identified in formal research stretching back to U.S. military training in World War II and the practical experience of several generations of teachers: in short, preview the materials, practice the presentation, prepare the environment, prepare the audience, and present.

Preview the Materials

No instructional materials should be used blind. During the selection process you should have determined that the materials are appropriate for your audience and objectives. Published reviews, reports of field tests, distributors'

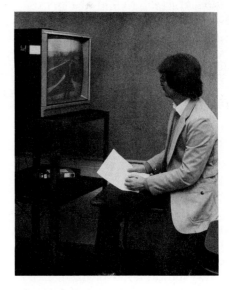

▲ *Figure 2.9*
Preview the material.

blurbs, and colleagues' appraisals all add evidence. However, the prudent instructor will insist on previewing the materials. Only such detailed familiarity with the contents can enable you to wrap the lesson around the audiovisual material properly.

For example, an industrial trainer ordered a videotape on fraction-to-decimal conversions. The information describing the videotape indicated that the content was exactly what many of the company employees needed. The videotape arrived ten days before the presentation, but the trainer did not take time to preview it. When the videotape was shown, it met with giggles and laughs; although the content was appropriate, the videotape was addressed to an elementary school audience. The adults were understandably distracted by the level of the narration and the examples used.

In addition, sensitive content may need to be eliminated or at least discussed prior to showing to prevent student embarrassment and/or impediment of learning. In one case, an elementary teacher and her young students were horrified to find that an unpreviewed and ostensibly unobjectionable film on Canada's fur seals contained a sequence showing baby seals being cold-bloodedly clubbed to death by hunters.

Practice the Presentation

After previewing the materials, you should practice your portion of the presentation. It is advisable to go through the presentation at least once well in advance and then to review your notes immediately before the presentation. However, do not overpractice, or the presentation will sound "canned."

Some presenters prefer to practice before a mirror; others like to have a colleague or friend present to provide feedback. Media can be used to provide a "replay" of your practice. An audiotape recording will let you hear how you sounded—what you said and how you said it. If you are concerned about how you look, how you handle manipulable objects, or whether or not you have any distracting mannerisms, you should use a video recording. The camera and recorder can be set up in the rear of the room, turned on, and allowed to operate while you go through the presentation.

The newness of the material, the importance of the presentation, and the amount of time available will determine how many times you practice and the type of "mirror" you use—a real mirror, a friend, an audiotape recorder, or a videotape recorder. The importance of practice cannot be overstated. Don't just "walk through it" in your mind; actually stand up and perform as you will in front of your group.

Prepare the Environment

Wherever the presentation is to take place—classroom, auditorium, meeting room, or whatever—the facilities will have to be put in order. Certain factors are taken for granted for any instructional situation—comfortable seating, adequate ventilation, climate control, suitable lighting, and the like. Utilization of many media requires a darkened room, a convenient power supply, and access to light switches. At the least the instructor should check that the equipment is in working order and should arrange the facilities so that all the audience can see and hear properly. More specific details on audiovisual setups are found in Chapter 10.

▲ *Figure 2.10*
Practice the presentation.

▲ *Figure 2.11*
Prepare the environment.

Prepare the Audience

Research on learning tells us very clearly that what is learned from a presentation depends highly on how the learners are *prepared* for the presentation. In everyday life we notice that entertainers are obsessed with having the audi-

▲ *Figure 2.12*
Prepare the audience.

ence properly warmed up. Nobody wants to come after "a hard act to follow" or to come on "cold." The same applies to media.

Proper *warm-up,* from an instructional point of view, will generally consist of an introduction including a broad overview of the content of the presentation, a rationale of how it relates to the topic being studied, a motivation (creating a "need to know"—how the learner will profit from paying attention), and cues directing attention to specific aspects of the presentation.

Several of these functions— directing attention, arousing motivation, providing a rationale— may be served simply by informing the viewers of the specific objectives.

In certain cases, other steps will be called for. For example, unfamiliar vocabulary may need to be introduced, or special visual effects, such as time-lapse photography, may need explanation. Other preparation steps relevant to particular media will be discussed in later chapters.

Present the Material

This is what you've been preparing for, so you will want to make the most of it. Our term for this is *showmanship.* Just as an actor or actress must control the attention of an audience, so must an instructor be able to direct attention in the classroom. The later chapters on individual media point out "showmanship" techniques relevant to each specific media format. General showmanship tips for all types of presentations are given in this chapter.

REQUIRE LEARNER PERFORMANCE   p. 34

T HE fifth step in the ASSURE model is to provide opportunities for learners to practice the capability being taught. Educators have long realized that participation in the learning process by the learner enhances learning. In the early 1900s, John Dewey urged reorganization of the curriculum and instruction to make student participation a central part of the process. Later, behavioral psychol-

ogists such as B. F. Skinner demonstrated that instruction providing for constant reinforcement of desired behaviors is more effective than instruction in which responses are not reinforced.

More recently, cognitive theories of learning, which focus on the internal mental processes, have also supported the principle that effective learning demands active manipulation of information by learners. Gagne* has concluded that there are several necessary "conditions" for effective learning of each type of objective; the one condition that pertains to *all* objectives is *practice* of the desired skill.

The implication for designers and instructors is clear. The most effective learning situations are those that require learner performance of activities that build toward the objective. The form of the participation may range from repetitive drill of new spelling or vocabulary words, to solving math problems on a worksheet, to

---

* Robert M. Gagne. *The Conditions of Learning*—4th ed. New York: Holt, Rinehart & Winston, 1985.

▲ *Figure 2.13*
Group discussion stimulated by a video sequence is a form of overt response.

● **You are a medium.**

Most audiovisual presentations include some sort of live performance by the instructor, perhaps as narrator or actor, perhaps as both. As a performer, you become an important component of the medium. Indeed, in a sense, you yourself become a medium, one that must perform effectively if your presentation is to be successful.

Be natural. Your audience will quickly sense affectation. Do not try to be someone or something you are not. But, by all means be enthusiastic! Successful actors know that their "energy level" directly affects audience response.

Avoid distracting mannerisms. Do you have an annoying habitual mannerism—smoothing your hair, twisting your watch, clicking a ballpoint pen— or a "verbal tic" such as inserting "um" or "you know" at every pause? Such mannerisms can become very annoying to an audience. The listener stops hearing the message and begins concentrating on the mannerism. The first step toward controlling such distractors is to become aware of them. Videotaping yourself in action can be an effective aid to discovering and correcting them.

● **Your classroom is a stage.**

When you are making a presentation from the front of a classroom, you are functioning like an actor on the stage. Your impact on the audience can be strengthened by observing a few of the basic principles of stagecraft.

Strong Areas. The front of the classroom, the "stage," can be divided into six sections, as shown in Figure A. Note that the front (near the audience) is generally stronger than the back, and that the center is stronger than either side. Of the two sides, the left (as seen by the audience) is stronger than the right.

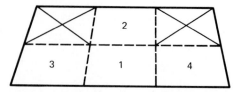

Figure A. The sectors of the "stage" vary in strength, with the front center strongest and the rear corners weakest.

The audiovisual presenter can use these strengths and weaknesses to good psychological advantage by using position to feature the dominant points of a presentation. See, for example, Figures B, C, and D.

Figure B. In this example the screen, because of its placement in the center, has dominance over the presenter.

Figure C. Here the presenter, situated at the front center, has more dominant placement.

Figure D. Here the presenter is in a moderately strong location, but the display table, at the front center, takes precedence.

Body Position. Facing the audience full-front is the strongest position. Three-quarters full-front is weaker; profile is weaker yet. Weakest is the one-quarter view, with the back nearly turned toward the audience. The use of chalkboards or charts will push you toward the weak position unless you consciously avoid it. (See Figures E, F, G and H.)

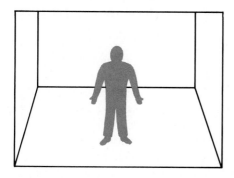

Figure E. The full-front body position is the strongest one.

Figure F. Three-quarters full front is the second strongest body position.

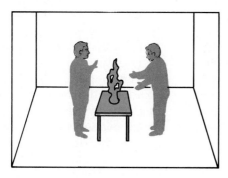

Figure G. Standing in profile, these figures are in a rather weak body position.

Movement. Given a static scene, any movement attracts the eye. This is one reason that nervous gestures are objectionable; they may distract attention from a point to be made. But movement can also be used positively to underscore important points. Experienced speakers often signal the beginning of a new topic by pausing and shifting their position, possibly walking to a different part of the room. But some movements are definitely stronger than others. As illustrated in Figure I, the strongest movement is toward the front center of the "stage" from one of the weaker areas. Conversely, the weakest movement is away from the front center, especially toward a corner.

In Figure G, if the speaker leaves the lectern to approach the display table, he or she will be executing a very strong movement that will add dramatic emphasis to the presentation.

- **Keep it light.**

A relaxed environment has been shown to increase suggestibility, a state conducive to rapid, effective learning. Humor can be very effective in establish-

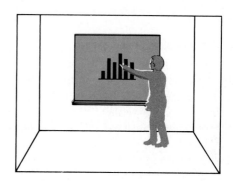

Figure H. A one-quarter view is the weakest body position.

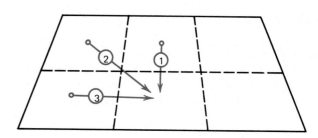

Figure I. The three stage movements shown here give the greatest emphasis to the presenter (in the order indicated by the numbers).

ing a relaxed environment, no matter what the age of the audience or the seriousness of the study. A joke, a humorous aside, or a comment poking fun at yourself can help build receptiveness. Obviously, humor should flow naturally from the instructional situation and should never be forced. Negative humor, such as sarcasm or ethnic jokes, has a high likelihood of offending your audience and should not be used.

● **Keep a surprise in store.**
Don't be afraid to surprise your audience. Unexpected conclusions and surprising visuals can add dramatic emphasis to your presentation.

● **Control attention.**
Eye contact with your audience is extremely helpful in controlling attention. One of the great advantages of the overhead projector is that it allows you to maintain eye contact with your audience during presentation, because you are at the front of the room and the room is lighted. Eye contact is more difficult with slides and filmstrips.

Keep in mind that attention naturally gravitates toward the brightest light in a given area. If you want your viewers to shift their attention from a lighted screen back to you, turn off the projector. Users of overhead projectors sometimes forget this simple rule. They leave a visual on the screen after they are finished with it or leave the projector on after the lesson segment is completed. When they then move on to a new topic, audience attention remains focused on the lighted screen rather than on the instructor.

● **Keep sight and sound synchronized.**
One sure way to confuse (and madden) your audience is to fail to synchronize sound and visuals. Careful scripting will help you avoid this serious pitfall. If a projectionist is advancing your visuals, provide a copy of the script containing clearly marked directions. If no such script is available, arrange ahead of time for signals that will alert the projectionist when to advance visuals. A nod of the head or an unobtrusive wave of the hand will suffice. A trumpeted "Next slide please!" is distracting and not at all necessary.

---

rehearsal of a basketball play, to construction of a product such as a term paper. Responses may be overt (outwardly observable) or covert (internal, not observable). An overt performance would be, for example, manipulating task cards illustrating the stages of mitosis. A covert performance could be silent repetition of phrases heard on a French language tape.

Some media formats lend themselves to participation more than others—at least on the surface. For example, student response to projected still pictures is easier to manage than response to a motion picture. Learners can read or elaborate on captions in filmstrips, discuss what is on the screen, or refer to other materials while the image is held on the screen. (Substitution of sound filmstrips for silent ones tends to weaken this advantage.) However, learners can also participate in and respond to the showing of a film. For example, May and Lumsdaine demonstrated that overt responses (vocalized verbal responses) during a film improved learning. The same authors cited research demonstrating that psychomotor skills are learned better if practiced while the skills are being performed in a film.* Overt written responses during the showing of a film (or any other fixed-pace medium) have been shown to facilitate learning, unless the responses are so involved that students are prevented from watching the film.

Immediate confirmation of a *correct* response is particularly important when working with students of lower-than-average abilities. For such students, evidence of immediate success can be a strong motivating force for further learning.

Discussions, short quizzes, and application exercises can provide opportunities for response and reinforcement during instruction.

Follow-up activities can provide further opportunities. Teacher guides and manuals written to accompany instructional materials often contain suggested techniques and activities for eliciting and reinforcing student response.

Research on the internationally renowned television series "Sesame Street" and "Electric Com-

---

* Mark A. May and A. A. Lumsdaine. *Learning from Films.* New Haven: Yale University Press, 1958.

▲ *Figure 2.14*
Audiovisual modules provide practice and feedback on an individual basis.

pany" demonstrates impressively the importance of following up a media presentation with practice activities. Research on "Sesame Street" showed that frequent viewers not only learned the specific skills aimed at but also had higher scores on a test of verbal IQ and more positive attitudes about school. Johnston* pointed out, though, that "parental encouragement and supplementary materials were essential to achieving the effects observed." In the case of "Electric Company," children with low reading ability who watched the programs *in school* under teacher supervision showed significant reading improvement. Johnston concluded that "learning definitely did occur when viewing was insured, and when teachers supplied additional learning materi-

---

* Jerome Johnston. *Electronic Learning: From Audiotape to Videodisc.* Hillsdale, N.J.: Lawrence Erlbaum, 1987.

als and helped the children to rehearse the material presented on television."

EVALUATE/REVISE p. 34

The final component of our ASSURE model for effective learning is evaluation. The most frequently thought of type of evaluation is the paper-and-pencil test; the most frequently thought of purpose, to measure student achievement. There are, however, many purposes of evaluation. Three that we will discuss here are evaluation of learner achievement, evaluation of media and methods, and evaluation of the instructional process.

Evaluation of Learner Achievement

The ultimate question in the instructional process is whether or not the students have learned what they were supposed to learn. Can they display the capabilities specified in the original statement of objectives? The first step in answering this question was taken back near the beginning of the ASSURE process, when you formulated your objectives, including in that statement of objectives a *degree* or *criterion* of acceptable performance. You now want to assess whether the learner's new skill meets that criterion.

The method of evaluating achievement depends on the nature of the objective. Some objectives call for relatively simple cognitive skills; for example, recalling Ohm's law, distinguishing adjectives from adverbs, describing a company's absence policy, or summarizing the purposes of the European Common Market. Objectives such as these lend themselves to conventional written tests or oral examinations.

Other objectives may call for process-type behaviors (for example, conducting an orchestra, performing a forward roll on a balance beam, operating a metal lathe, or solving quadratic equations), the creation of products (a sculpture, a written composition, a window display, or an account ledger), or the holding of attitudes (tolerating divergent political opinions, appreciating expressionist painting, observing safety procedures while on the assembly line, or contributing money to community charities).

The evaluation procedures should be directly correlated with the objectives stated earlier in the ASSURE model. See the box titled "Test Items: General" for examples.

Capabilities of the process, product, or attitude type could be assessed to some extent by means of written or oral tests. But test results would be indirect and weak evidence of how well the learner has mastered the objective. More direct and stronger evidence would be provided by observing the behavior *in action*. This implies setting up a situation in which the learner can demonstrate the new skill and the instructor can observe and judge it.

In the case of process skills, a performance checklist can be an effective, objective way of recording your observations, as shown with the checklist for driving skills. Other types of activities that can be properly evaluated through performance checklists are sales techniques, telephone-answering skills, and face-to-face customer relations. During the instructional process these types of activities may need to be evaluated in a simulated situation, with other learners, or with the instructor role playing the customer/client.

Test Items: General

Assume the objective is "Given a diagram of the human trachea, the student nurse will explain a bronchocele, describing cause and treatment." A possible test item would be "What is a bronchocele? Describe the cause and treatment in your answer."

In broadcaster training the objective might be "Given the pertinent information, facts, and figures, the student shall write a twenty-second and a thirty-second broadcast news story using correct broadcast style." The evaluation could be "Using the information provided, compose a twenty-second radio news story using the correct broadcast style."

For military training an objective could be "With the aid of a topographic map, the officer shall call for field artillery fire using the four essential items of information in prescribed military sequence." The written test could call for "How would you call for artillery fire upon point X on the accompanying topographic map?"

Performance Checklist: Driving Skills

Name _____ Class _____

Directions: Check yes or no with an X in the
             proper space.

Did the student: Yes | No
1. Fasten seat belt before starting car?
2. Use the nine o'clock and three o'clock
   hand position on steering wheel?
3. Drive with the flow of traffic yet stay within
   the speed limit?
4. Come to full and complete stops at stop
   signs?
5. Keep at least a two-second interval behind
   the vehicle ahead?
6. Stay in the proper driving lane—not cross
   center line?
7. Obey all traffic signs and signals?
8. Negotiate all turns properly (according to
   driving manual)?
9. Avoid excessive conversation with
   passengers?
10. Display courtesy to other drivers?

Instructor's name_____ Date_____

For product skills, a product rating checklist can guide your evaluation of critical subskills and make qualitative judgments more objective, as in the accompanying example regarding welding. Other types of products that lend themselves to evaluation by a rating scale include pastry from a bakery, compositions in an English course, and computer programs.

Attitudes are admittedly difficult to evaluate. For some attitudinal objectives, long-term observation may be required to determine if the goal has really been attained. In day-to-day instruction we usually have to rely on what we can observe here and now, however limited that may be. A commonly used technique for making attitudes more visible is the attitude scale, an example of which is shown regarding biology. A number of other suggestions for attitude measurement can be found in Robert Mager's *Developing Attitude Toward Learning.**

_____

* See references at end of this chapter.

▲ *Figure 2.15*
A performance-type skill should be judged by observation of the performance itself.

Evaluation of Media and Methods

Evaluation, as previously noted, also includes assessment of instructional media and methods. Were your instructional materials effective? Could they be improved? Were they cost effective in terms of student achievement? Did your presentation take more time than it was really worth? Particularly after first use, instructional materials need to be evaluated to determine if future use, with or without modification, is warranted. The results of your evaluation should be entered on your personal file form. Did the

▶ *Figure 2.16*
The ability to create a product should be evaluated by the quality of the product itself; a rating checklist is helpful for calling attention to the most critical qualities of the work.

Product Rating Checklist: Welding

Name _____ Date _____

Directions: Rate the welded product by checking the appropriate boxes. Add comments if you wish.

Base metal(s)_____ Filler metal(s)_____

Profile:	Excellent	Very Good	Good	Fair	Poor	**Workmanship:**	Excellent	Very Good	Good	Fair	Poor
Convexity (1/32-inch maximum)	☐	☐	☐	☐	☐	uniform appearance	☐	☐	☐	☐	☐
Fusion on toe	☐	☐	☐	☐	☐	arc strikes	☐	☐	☐	☐	☐
Overlap	☐	☐	☐	☐	☐	bead width	☐	☐	☐	☐	☐
Amount of fill	☐	☐	☐	☐	☐	bead start	☐	☐	☐	☐	☐
						bead tie-in	☐	☐	☐	☐	☐
						bead termination	☐	☐	☐	☐	☐
Overall evaluation:						penetration	☐	☐	☐	☐	☐
Evaluator comments:						amount of spatter	☐	☐	☐	☐	☐

Attitude Scale: Biology

Each of the statements below expresses a feeling toward biology. Please rate each statement on the extent to which you agree. For each, you may: (A) strongly agree, (B) agree, (C) be undecided, (D) disagree, or (E) strongly disagree.

A	B	C	D	E
strongly agree	agree	undecided	disagree	strongly disagree

_____ 1. Biology is very interesting to me.

_____ 2. I *don't* like biology, and it scares me to have to take it.

_____ 3. I am always under a terrible strain in a biology class.

_____ 4. Biology is fascinating and fun.

_____ 5. Biology makes me feel secure, and at the same time it is stimulating.

_____ 6. Biology makes me feel uncomfortable, restless, irritable, and impatient.

_____ 7. In general, I have a good feeling toward biology.

_____ 8. When I hear the word *biology*, I have a feeling of dislike.

_____ 9. I approach biology with a feeling of hesitation.

_____ 10. I really like biology.

_____ 11. I have always enjoyed studying biology in school.

_____ 12. It makes me nervous to even think about doing a biology experiment.

_____ 13. I feel at ease in biology and like it very much.

_____ 14. I feel a definite positive reaction to biology; it's enjoyable.

media assist the students in meeting the objectives? Were they effective in arousing student interest? Did they provide meaningful student participation?

Class discussions, individual interviews, and observation of student behavior should be used to sound out evaluation of instructional media and methods. Failure to attain objectives is, of course, a clear indication that something is wrong with the instruction. But student reaction to your instructional unit can be helpful in more subtle ways. Student–teacher discussion may indicate that your audience would have preferred independent study to your choice of group presentation. Or perhaps viewers didn't like your selection of overhead transparencies and feel they would have learned more if a film had been shown. Your students may let you know, subtly or not so subtly, that your own performance left something to be desired.

You may solicit learner input on the effectiveness of specific media such as a film or videotape. You may design your own form or use one similar to the "Module Appraisal Form."

Evaluation of the Instructional Process

Although ultimate evaluation must await completion of the instructional unit, evaluation is an ongoing process. Evaluations are made before, during, and after instruction; for example, before instruction, learner characteristics are measured to ensure that there is a fit between student skills and the methods and materials you

◀ *Figure 2.17*
The analysis of student reaction to lessons is an integral part of the total process of instruction.

Module Appraisal Form

User _____   Date _____

1. The objectives of this module were:

   Clear   Unclear
   7   6   5   4   3   2   1

2. The learning activities were:

   Very Interesting   Dull
   7   6   5   4   3   2   1

3. The scope (coverage) was:

   Adequate   Inadequate
   7   6   5   4   3   2   1

4. The module was:

   Difficult   Easy
   7   6   5   4   3   2   1

5. Overall, I consider this module:

   Excellent   Poor
   7   6   5   4   3   2   1

---

intend to use. In addition, materials should be appraised prior to use, as noted earlier in this chapter. During instruction, evaluation may take the form of student practice of a desired skill, or it may consist of a short quiz or self-evaluation. Evaluation during instruction usually has a diagnostic purpose—that is, it is designed to detect and correct learning/teaching problems and difficulties in the instructional process which may threaten attainment of objectives.

Evaluation is not the end of instruction. It is the starting point of the next and continuing cycle of our systematic ASSURE model for effective use of instructional media.

Revision

The final step of the instructional cycle is to sit back and look at the results of your evaluation data gathering. Where are there discrepancies between what you

intended to happen and what did happen? Did the student achievement fall short on one or more of the objectives? How did students react to your instructional methods and media? Are you satisfied with the value of the materials you selected? If your evaluation data indicate shortcomings in any of these areas, now is the time to go back to the faulty part of the plan and revise it. The model works, but only if you *use* it to upgrade the quality of your instruction constantly.

References

Print References

Allen, Sylvia. *A Manager's Guide to Audiovisuals.* (New York: McGraw-Hill, 1979).

Anderson, R. H. *Selecting and Developing Media for Instruction.* 2d ed. (New York: Van Nostrand Reinhold, 1983).

Bloom, Benjamin S., et al. *Taxonomy of Educational Objectives: Book 1: Cognitive Domain.* (White Plains, N.Y.: Longman, 1977).

Burbank, Lucille, and Pett, Dennis. "Designing Printed Instructional Materials." *Performance and Instruction* (October 1986), pp. 5–9.

Davies, Ivor K. *Objectives in Curriculum Design.* (Maidenhead, England: McGraw-Hill, 1976).

Dewey, John. *Democracy and Education.* (New York: Macmillan, 1916).

Fortune, Jim C., and Hutson, Barbara A. "Does Your Program Work? Strategies for Measuring Change." *Educational Technology* (April 1983), pp. 38–41.

Frederick, Peter J. "The Lively Lecture—8 Variations." *College Teaching* (Spring 1986), pp. 43–50.

Gagne, Robert M. *Instructional Technology: Foundations.* (Hillsdale, N.J.: Lawrence Erlbaum, 1987).

Gerlach, Vernon S., and Ely, Donald P. *Teaching and Media: A Systematic Approach.* 2d ed. (Englewood Cliffs, N.J.: Prentice-Hall, 1980).

Gronlund, Norman E. *Stating Behavioral Objectives for Classroom Instruction.* (New York: Macmillan, 1970).

Haladyna, Thomas M., and Roid, Gale H. "Reviewing Criterion-Referenced Test Items." *Educational Technology* (August 1983), pp. 35–38.

Kenny, Michael. *Presenting Yourself: A Kodak How-to Book.* (New York: Wiley, 1982).

Koroluk, Lorne E. "Using Instructional Resource Cards." *Educational Technology* (March 1983), pp. 24–25.

Krathwohl, David R., et al. *Taxonomy of Educational Objectives: Handbook 2: Affective Domain.* (White Plains, N.Y.: Longman, 1969).

Kurfiss, J. "Linking Psychological Theory and Instructional Technology." *International Journal of Instructional Media* (1981–1982), pp. 3–10.

Lanese, Lorena D. "Applying Principles of Learning to Adult Training Programs." *Educational Technology* (March 1983), pp. 15–17.

Mager, Robert F. *Developing Attitude Toward Learning.* 2d ed. (Belmont, Calif.: David S. Lake, 1984).

———. *Goal Analysis.* 2d ed. (Belmont, Calif.: David S. Lake, 1984).

———. *Making Instruction Work.* (Belmont, Calif.: David S. Lake, 1988).

———. *Measuring Instructional Results.* 2d ed. (Belmont, Calif.: David S. Lake, 1984).

———. *Preparing Instructional Objectives.* Revised 2d ed. (Belmont, Calif.: David S. Lake, 1984).

———, and Pipe, Peter. *Analyzing Performance Problems.* 2d ed. (Belmont, Calif.: David S. Lake, 1984).

Martinetz, Charles F. "A Checklist for Course Evaluation." *Performance and Instruction* (June–July 1986), pp. 12–19.

Pett, Dennis. "Effective Presentations." *NSPI Journal* (April 1980), pp. 11–14.

Ragan, Tillman J. "The Oldest Medium." *Educational Technology* (May 1982), pp. 28–29.

Reiser, Robert A., and Gagne, Robert M. *Selecting Media for Instruction.* (Englewood Cliffs, N.J.: Educational Technology Publications, 1983).

Renner, P. *The Instructor's Survival Kit: A Handbook for Teachers of Adults.* (Vancouver, B.C.: Training Associates, Ltd., 1983).

Rosmiszowski, A. J. *The Selection and Use of Instructional Media.* 2d ed. (New York: Nichols, 1987).

Thiagarajan, Sivasailam. "Alternatives: 25 Ways to Improve Any Lecture." *Performance and Instruction* (December–January 1985–1986), pp. 22–24.

Timpson, W. M., and Tobin, D. N. *Teaching as Performing: A Guide to Energizing Your Public Presentation.* (Englewood Cliffs, N.J.: Prentice-Hall, 1982).

Tyler, Ralph. "The Construction of Examinations in Botany and Zoology." *Service Studies in Higher Education.* Bureau of Educational Research Monographs, No. 15. (Columbus, Ohio: Ohio State University, 1932).

Instructional Development

Clark, Ruth Colvin, et al. "Training Content Experts to Design Instruction." *Performance and Instruction* (September 1983), pp. 10–15.

Dick, Walter, and Carey, Lou. *The Systematic Design of Instruction.* 2d ed. (New York: Scott Foresman, 1985).

Gagne, Robert M., et al. *Principles of Instructional Design.* 3d ed. (New York: Holt, Rinehart, & Winston, 1987).

Kemp, Jerrold E. *The Instructional Design Process.* (New York: Harper & Row, 1985).

Nadler, Leonard. *Designing Training Programs: The Critical Events Model.* (Reading, Mass.: Addison-Wesley, 1982).

Rosmiszowski, A. J. *Designing Instructional Systems.* (New York: Nichols, 1981).

——. *Developing Auto-Instructional Materials.* (New York: Nichols, 1987).

——. *Producing Instructional Systems.* (New York: Nichols, 1986).

Audiovisual References

Audiovisual Spectrum of the 80's. National Audiovisual Association, 1982. Sound filmstrip.

Can We Please Have That the Right Way Round? Northbrook, Ill.: Video Arts, n.d. 16-mm film or videocassette. 22 minutes.

Individualizing Instruction. Beacon Films, 1983. Videocassette. 27 minutes.

Making Your Case. Northbrook, Ill.: Video Arts, n.d. 16-mm film or videocassette. 25 minutes.

Media Utilization. Norwood, Mass.: Beacon Films, 1983. Videocassette. 29 minutes.

Non-Verbal Communication. Santa Monica, Calif.: Salenger Educational Media, 1982. 16-mm film. 17 minutes.

Novel Techniques for Evaluating Media. Boulder, Colo.: University of Colorado, 1982. Audiocassette.

Patterns for Instruction. Beverly Hills, Calif.: Roundtable Films, 1981. Videocassette and leader's guide. 21 minutes.

Principles for Learning and Instruction. Norwood, Mass.: Beacon Films, 1983. Videocassette. 29 minutes.

Teaching and Testing for Results. Columbia, S.C.: Educational Program Service, 1983. Videocassette. 30 minutes.

Teaching to Objectives, Parts I and II. Columbia, S.C.: Educational Program Service, 1983. Videocassettes. 30 minutes each.

Possible Projects

2-A. Plan a presentation using the procedures described in this chapter. Your description must include:
1. Description of learners:
   a. General characteristics.
   b. Specific competencies: knowledge, skills, and attitudes.
2. Objectives for the presentation.
3. Description of how you selected, modified, or designed instructional materials.
4. Procedures for the use of the materials.
5. Plans for learner involvement and reinforcement.
6. Evaluation procedures.

2-B. Classify a set of objectives into the cognitive, affective, motor skill, or interpersonal skills domain.

2-C. Write at least five objectives for a lesson you might actually teach; cover as many domains and levels as possible.

2-D. Select a chapter from a textbook of interest to you and derive a set of objectives that you feel are intended by the author.

2-E. Select a lesson you might teach, such as a chapter from a textbook, and develop a set of evaluation instruments (not necessarily all paper-and-pencil test items).

2-F. Compare all of the Appraisal Checklists in this book. Compile a list of the criteria that appear in *all* of the Appraisal Checklists.

3

Visual Design

Objectives

After studying this chapter, you should be able to:

1. Describe the function of a visual in the communication process.

2. Discuss the relationship between the degree of realism in a visual and the amount of learning from it.

3. Describe the relationship between people's preferences for visuals and the amount of learning from these preferred visuals.

4. Discuss briefly the effect of developmental age and cultural background on learning from visuals.

5. Identify three techniques for learning from making visuals.

6. Define *visual literacy*.

7. List three important findings of eye movement research and explain how they can be used in designing effective visuals.

8. Describe three categories of visuals and identify how each type should be used with adult learners.

9. Recognize and apply the principles of visual design related to unity, line, shape, form, arrangement, balance, color, and interaction.

10. State guidelines for legibility and color contrast in adding lettering to a visual.

11. Discuss four duplicating methods, including the relative costs, advantages, and limitations of each method.

12. Explain the basic principles of photography, including the elements of light, subject, camera, and film.

13. Describe the function(s) of the following camera parts: lens opening, shutter, view finder, focus, and film advance.

14. Discuss and apply the rules for effective composition when taking photographs.

Lexicon
referent
iconic
decoding
encoding
visual literacy
arrangement
balance
shutter
view finder
composition
rule of thirds

THE USE OF VISUALS

WE are a visual society, one that has experienced an increasing production and distribution of visual messages in recent years. Television comes immediately to mind, but images are all around us. New technologies of printing and reproduction have also contributed to the flood of visual messages in books, periodicals, and newspapers as never before. We are surrounded by visual messages on billboards and posters. Advertising of all kinds has become increasingly visual. Product instructions are becoming less verbal and more illustrative. Highway signs (especially international driving signs) are almost totally visual. Even T-shirt makers have gotten into the act!

From an instructional point of view, we know that most people are visually oriented. They learn about 10 percent from listening, but over 80 percent from what they see. More importantly, they remember only about 20 percent of what they hear, but over 50 percent of what they see and hear.

The wealth of visual messages and the amount of learning that takes place through visuals necessitate the proper design and use of visuals in instruction. Most of the media discussed later in the text have a visual component—overhead transparencies, slides, films, television, and even computer software.

This chapter contains a description of the characteristics of instructionally effective visuals, the concept of visual literacy, how people look at visuals, and how to design and use effective visuals. In addition, there are sections on photography, the layout of printed materials, cartooning, sketching, drawing, bulletin board displays, and computer screen design.

VISUALS AS REFERENTS TO MEANING

THE primary function of a visual as a communication device is to serve as a more concrete *referent* to meaning than the spoken or written word. Words are arbitrary symbols. They don't look or sound (usually) like the thing they represent. Visuals, however, are *iconic*. They normally resemble the thing they represent. As such, they serve as concrete clues to meaning. It is a general principle of human communication that the likelihood of successful communication is increased when a concrete referent is present. When the thing being discussed is not at hand, the next best referent is a visual representation of it.

One fundamental difference among visuals is their degree of realism. No media form, of course, is totally realistic. The real

▲ *Figure 3.1*
Visuals surround us in our everyday lives.

▲ *Figure 3.2*
"Frank & Ernest" illustrate the frailties of verbal communication.

▲ *Figure 3.3*
The graphic symbol, cartoon, line drawing, and photograph represent a continuum of realism in visuals.

object or event will always have aspects that cannot be captured pictorially, even in a three-dimensional color motion picture. The various visual media can, however, be arranged from highly abstract to relatively realistic, as indicated in Figure 3.3.

One might naturally conclude that effective communication is always best served by the use of the most realistic visual available. After all, the more realistic a visual is, the closer it is to the original. This, however, is not necessarily so. There is ample research evidence that under certain circumstances realism can actually interfere with the communication and learning process. For example, the ability to sort out the relevant from the irrelevant in a pictorial representation grows with age and experience. So, for younger children, and for older learners who are encountering an idea for the first time, the

wealth of detail found in a realistic visual may increase the likelihood of the learner's being distracted by irrelevant elements of the visual.

As Dwyer notes in his review of visual research, "The arbitrary addition of stimuli in visuals makes it difficult for learners to identify the essential learning cues from among the more realistic background stimuli."* Dwyer concludes that rather than being a simple yes-or-no issue, the amount of realism desired has a curvilinear relationship to learning. That is, either too much or too little realism may affect achievement adversely (Figure 3.4).

PICTURE PREFERENCES OF LEARNERS

We need to make a distinction between the pictures people *prefer* to look at and those from which they learn the most. People do not necessarily learn best from the kinds of pictures they prefer. For example, research on picture preferences indicates that children in upper elementary school tend to:

1. prefer color to black and white.
2. choose photographs over drawings.

---

* Francis M. Dwyer. *Strategies for Improving Visual Learning.* State College, Penn.: Learning Services, 1978, p. 33.

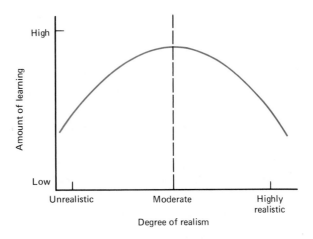

▲ *Figure 3.4*
Visuals tend to become less useful for instruction as they approach the extremes of very abstract or very realistic.

3. choose realism in form and color.
4. (younger children) prefer simple over complex illustrations.
5. (older children) prefer complex over simple illustrations.*

Teachers have to make appropriate choices between *effective* illustrations and *preferred* illustrations.

Most learners prefer colored visuals over black-and-white visuals. However, there is no significant difference in the amount of learning *except* where color is an essential part of the content to be learned. For example, when workers must learn to assemble electrical components with different colored wires, the presence of color is essential. Photographs are preferred over line drawings by most learners, even though in many situations drawings are more effective for learning. Drawings can highlight the important details. As indicated in the previous section, even though many learners prefer very realistic visuals over abstract representations, moderation tends to be the guideline for instructional purposes. Young learners prefer simple visuals, whereas older students and adults prefer more complex visuals. Nevertheless, simpler visuals are usually more effective, whatever the age group.

USING VISUALS IN INSTRUCTION

STUDENTS can learn from visuals in two ways. First, they must be able to "read" visuals accurately, understand the elements of visuals, and translate the visuals into verbal messages. This skill is referred to as *decoding*. Second, they should be able to create visuals as a tool to communicate effectively with others and be able to express themselves through visuals. This skill is called *encoding*. The development of both decoding and encoding skills requires practice.

Decoding: Learning from Visuals

Seeing a visual does not automatically ensure learning from it. Learners must be guided toward correct decoding of visuals. How a learner decodes a visual may be affected by many variables.

Prior to the age of twelve, children tend to interpret visuals section by section rather than as a whole. In reporting what they "see" in a picture, they are likely to single out specific elements within the scene. Students who are older, however, tend to summarize the whole scene and report a conclusion about the "meaning" of the picture. Hence, abstract symbols or a series of still pictures whose relationship is not clearly spelled out may fail to communicate as intended with younger viewers. We have already noted that realistic visuals may distract younger children. However, Dwyer notes, "As a child

gets older, he becomes more capable of attending selectively to those features of an instructional presentation that have the greatest potential for enhancing his learning of desired information."†

In teaching, we must keep in mind that decoding visuals may be affected by the viewer's cultural background. Different cultural groups may perceive visual materials in different ways. In a sense, this variable might be subsumed under prior learning experience, as discussed in Chapter 2. But these differences are more difficult to appraise. Cultural background has a strong influence on learning experience. For example, let us say your instruction includes use of visuals depicting scenes typical of the home life and street life of inner-city children. It is almost certain that students who live in such an area will decode these visuals differently than will students whose cultural (and socioeconomic) backgrounds do not include first-hand knowledge of inner-city lifestyles. Similarly, scenes depicting life in the Old West might be interpreted quite differently by an American Indian child than they would be by, say, a black, white, or Mexican American child (Figure 3.6).

The symbolic connotations of color and color preference may also be culturally biased. Cultures vary widely as to how the color spectrum is perceived. Westerners see red, orange, yellow, green, blue, and violet as more or less distinct and equidistant points along a spectrum. But this kind of color perception is by no means universal. Even less universal are the symbolic values given to various colors. Black, for example, is generally accepted in Western

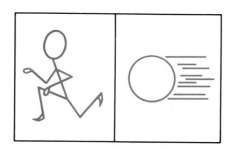

▲ *Figure 3.5*
An active posture, as in the figure on the left, communicates movement more reliably than arbitrary graphic conventions such as speed lines, as in the figure on the right.

* Barbara Myatt and Juliet Mason Carter. "Picture Preferences of Children and Young Adults." *Educational Communication and Technology* (Spring 1979), p. 47.

† Dwyer, op cit., p. 229.

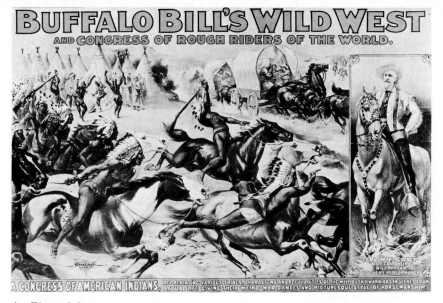

▲ *Figure 3.6*
The cultural biases of a communicator, although unspoken, may be perceived vividly by viewers having a different cultural background.

countries as the color of mourning. In some Eastern countries, however, the color of mourning is white.

Although you cannot eliminate all misconceptions in decoding arising out of differences in cultural background, you should always be cautious about using visuals that may, without prior explanation, cause confusion in some of your students.*

Encoding: Learning from Making Visuals

One of the best ways to develop encoding skills is to encourage students to present their message through a pictorial medium. Most older students have access to a camera. Slide film may be purchased to produce slides. They should be encouraged to present

reports to the class by means of well-thought-through sets of slides. The 35-mm slide is also a medium for students to use to develop their aesthetic talents. Portable videotape equipment can be used even by elementary children and is an excellent way of giving students the opportunity to present ideas and events pictorially.

One skill nearly always included in visual education curricula is that of *sequencing*. Reading specialists have long known that the ability to sequence—that is, to arrange ideas in logical order—is an extremely important factor in verbal literacy, especially in the ability to communicate in writing.

Children who have grown up exposed constantly to movies and television may expect the visuals they encounter in school to be similarly prepackaged and sequenced. They may need practice in arranging visuals into logical sequence as this is a learned skill, like the verbal sequencing of reading and writing. For this reason, many visual education programs, especially for primary school children, emphasize creative activities in arranging and making visuals. A popular set of instructional materials for this purpose is the *Photo-Story Discovery Kit* series developed in the 1960s by Eastman Kodak Company and now distributed by the Association for Educational Communications and Technology (AECT). Some sample cards from

* A discussion of cultural differences in interpreting visuals and how to deal with them, is found in James Mangan. "Cultural Conventions of Pictorial Representations." *Educational Communication and Technology* (Fall 1978), pp. 245–267.

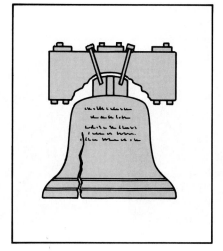 

▲ *Figure 3.7*
Symbolic images may be interpreted differently depending on cultural background.

a more recent commercially developed set are shown in the accompanying "Media File."

THE CONCEPT OF VISUAL LITERACY

U NTIL recently, the concept of literacy was applied almost exclusively to the ability to read and write. In the mid-1960s, how- ever, we began to hear of a differ- ent kind of literacy, "visual liter- acy." This new concept of literacy came in response to the realiza- tion that specific skills are needed to "read" and "write" visual mes- sages, just as they are needed to read and write printed ones.

Visual literacy is the learned ability to *interpret* visual mes- sages accurately and to *create* such messages. Thus, interpreta-

▲ *Figure 3.8*
Reading in print literacy parallels interpreting (decoding) in visual literacy.

▲ *Figure 3.9*
Writing in print literacy parallels creating (encoding) in visual literacy.

MEDIA FILE:
Story Sequencing Card Sets

Beginning or remedial readers can improve comprehension and logic skills by arrang- ing story cards in proper sequence. Each set of cards tells a story in comic strip form. Clues to proper sequence are given in the pictures and text on each card. Shape and size of the cards give additional hints. Five different sets are available, each emphasizing a particular comprehension skill: sequencing, cause and effect, main ideas, drawing conclusions, and predicting outcomes.

Source: Educational Insights

▲ *Figure 3.10*
Viewing and interpreting visuals represent just one aspect of visual literacy.

▲ *Figure 3.11*
Learning to interpret visuals without learning to create them is like learning to read but not learning to write.

tion and creation in visual literacy may be said to parallel reading and writing in print literacy.

Visual literacy has also become a "movement" within the field of education. The movement now has its own professional association—the International Visual Literacy Association—with its own periodicals.

The importance of visual literacy in today's society can scarcely be overstressed. Teachers of young children have a special responsibility to see that students do not leave their classrooms visually illiterate. Visual literacy may even be seen as an essential survival skill. As one observer puts it:

There is no easy way to develop visual literacy, but it is as vital to our teaching of the modern media as reading and writing was to print. It may, indeed, be the crucial component of all channels of communication now and in the future.*

HOW PEOPLE LOOK AT VISUALS

ALL instructors ought to be concerned about *how* people look at pictorial and graphic materials and what they see in them because these factors determine considerably what people get out of the materials. There are basically two ways to determine what people notice: (1) make inferences based on what individuals have learned from pictorial material and (2) determine the pattern of eye movements as they look at the same pictorial material.

If the ways in which people view and interpret pictures and

———

* Donis A. Dondis. *A Primer of Visual Literacy.* Cambridge, Mass.: MIT Press, 1973.

graphics can be guided, then people will learn more because attention will be directed to relevant content and not misdirected by irrelevant cues.

As a corollary, we can also say that the more we know about perceptual "sets" of students, the better we will be able to design visuals to take advantage of those sets or to overcome perceptual obstacles. For example, research on eye movement of people looking at still photographs indicates that viewers tend to look first at the upper-left-hand portion of a picture. The picture area in Figure 3.12 has been divided into thirds. The percentage at each intersection represents the frequency with which people first look at that part of the picture area. If upper and lower figures are combined, we see that observers tend to look first at the left-hand side of a picture two out of three times. It has been said that this is

---

CLOSE-UP:
Visual Literacy Education

An exemplary visual literacy education program was developed at an elementary school in a midwestern state. By producing visual materials themselves, the children manipulate colors, shapes, symbols, and spatial relationships. They develop perceptual skills and expressive abilities. Practice in drawing inferences from pictorial sequences leads to better critical viewing skills: distinguishing fantasy, persuasion, and propaganda from facts.

Student visual production projects are integrated into the basic curriculum. For example, experimentation with simple animation by drawing directly onto 16-mm film is a good chance to put math skills to work by calculating the number of frames needed to produce the desired action.

The visual literacy program spans the entire kindergarten through sixth-grade curriculum. More complex projects entail storyboarding and production planning. This contributes to growth of problem-solving ability.

In-service teacher training and parent involvement are integral elements of this program. A major role of parents is to participate in their children's home TV viewing—to encourage wholesome viewing habits and critical viewing skills.

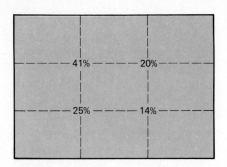

▲ *Figure 3.12*
Research in the United States indicates a tendency for viewers to begin reading a picture in the upper left and to focus attention at the intersections suggested by the "rule of thirds."

a culturally determined perceptual set because people from Western cultures learn to read and write from left to right. If so, then those people who learn to read from right to left, such as readers of Arabic and Hebrew, might be expected to look first at the upper-right area.

This information is relevant not only to your decision about where you should place important content in a picture area but also to how people will interpret certain graphic representations.

When designing visuals, we can take advantage of this research by placing at least the start of our main message where the eye first strikes the area. The research does not mean that *all* important information should be located in the upper-left area or even in the left half of a picture. But it does indicate that if the message is required (by the nature of the content) to be in the lower right, the eye of the observer will have to be *led* there. This can be achieved by use of such pictorial elements as color, composition, and texture. The important point is that the tendency of people *not* to look first in the lower right must be compensated for if the message is located there.

One of the most important of several findings in eye movement

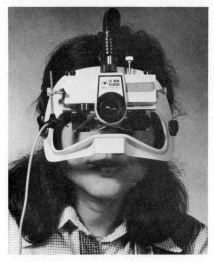

▲ *Figure 3.13*
Eye movement research is facilitated by automatic monitoring devices that record the movements of the pupils as they scan a visual.

studies concerns eye fixation on relevant cues.* For example, during a science telecast, the eyes of many of the students frequently strayed to an irrelevant micro-

———
* Egon Guba et al. "Eye Movements and TV-Viewing in Children." *AV Communication Review* 12, no. 4 (1964), pp. 386–401.

scope visible over the instructor's shoulder. In another sequence, the eyes of the viewers watched the lips of the instructor rather than what he was demonstrating. When only his hands and the object were shown on the screen, the viewers fixated on the demonstration. The lesson to be learned here is that distractors must be kept out of the frame of the image.

Another important finding demonstrates the importance of movement. When the picture on the screen is static, viewers "tune out" after a while. When the image is changed by introducing motion or changing the picture, the viewers "tune in" again. Changes in the image help keep students' attention on the visual.

VISUALS AND ADULT LEARNING

W E often think that pictures are for use with young children. However, visuals can play an important part in adult learn-

▲ *Figure 3.14*
Visuals are effective and in some cases required for adult learning.

▲ *Figure 3.15*
The photo is a representational visual.

ing as well. Dwyer* and his associates have conducted over 100 studies involving several thousand adult learners since 1965. In their research they have found that pictures generally facilitate adult learning. Adults who read a verbal passage supplemented with visuals remember more than adults

who only read the passage. Visuals can be classified into three categories: representational, analogic, and arbitrary.

Representational visuals are those that resemble the object or concept under study. They are realistic, highly concrete, and detailed. For example, a color photograph of an automobile engine would be representational.

Analogic visuals convey a concept or topic by showing some-

thing else and implying a similarity. Teaching about electricity flow by showing water flowing in series and parallel pipes illustrates the use of analogic visuals. An analogy of white blood cells fighting off infection would be an army attacking a stronghold. This type of visual helps the adult learner interpret new information in light of prior knowledge and thereby facilitates learning. Researchers have found that visual analogies can facilitate adult learning.†

Arbitrary pictures or nonrepresentational visuals are visuals such as flowcharts, graphs, maps, schematics, and classification charts. (See Chapter 4 for details on types of charts and graphs.) Graphic organizers can serve to structure the main points or concepts in textual material. This type of visual helps communicate the organization of the content (see Figure 3.17).

Researchers have found that adult learners may also benefit from drawing their own pictures. A number of studies have been conducted to investigate the

* Francis M. Dwyer. *Strategies for Improving Visual Learning.* State College, Penn.: Learning Services, 1978.

† K. L. Alesandrini. "Pictures and Adult Learning." *Instructional Science* 13 (1984), pp. 63–77.

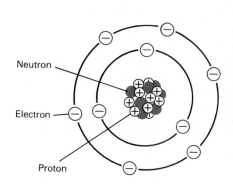

▲ *Figure 3.16*
The solar system is often used as a visual *analogy* to explain the composition of an atom.

adjective	+	suffix	=	adverb
quick		-ly		quickly
bad		-ly		badly
cool		-ly		coolly
gracious		-ly		graciously

▲ *Figure 3.17*
A chart using textual material presents a concept in a nonrepresentational manner.

One day in the late 1640s, Massachusett's Cotton Mather, ever zealous to make Puritan New England the cultural center of the New World, noted in his journal his disappointment that a certain "incomparable Moravian" was not, after all, to become an American by accepting the presidency of Harvard College:

> *That brave old man, Johannes Amos Comenius, the fame of whose worth has been trumpeted as far as more than three languages could carry it, was indeed agreed . . . to come over to New England, and illuminate their Colledge and Country, in the quality of a President, which was now become vacant. But the solicitation of the Swedish Ambassador diverting him another way, that incomparable Moravian became not an American.*

Who was this Johannes (John) Amos Comenius? Why had his fame as an educator spread all the way from Europe to Mather's Massachusetts Bay Colony?

Comenius was born in 1592 in Moravia (now part of Czechoslovakia). He was a clergyman of the United Brethren, an evangelical Protestant reform sect known popularly today as the Moravian church. At the time of his consideration for the presidency of Harvard, he was living in exile in Sweden. Indeed, the religious persecutions of the Thirty Years War and its aftermath had forced Comenius to live most of his life away from his native Moravia.

Despite this and the deprivations of war, Comenius achieved fame throughout Europe as an educational reformer and writer of innovative textbooks and other educational works. His *Janua Linguarum Reserata* (*The Gate of Language Unlocked*) was a Latin language textbook that taught a basic vocabulary of 8,000 carefully selected words and the principal points of Latin grammar. The instructional strategy of the *Janua* consisted of Latin sentences about a variety of topics, forming a kind of encyclopedia of basic human knowledge of that time. Comenius also argued that the teaching of languages should be divided into stages parallel to four human developmental stages. For this insight, Piaget acknowledged Comenius as a forerunner of genetic psychology.[a] The *Janua* became one of the great pedagogical best-sellers of all time, and it

---

[a] Jean Piaget. *J. A. Comenius*, *Pages Choisies*. Paris: UNESCO, 1957.

IOHAN - AMOS COMENIVS,
MORAVVS. A° ÆTAT 50: 1642
Crole sculpsit

influenced—wittingly or unwittingly—virtually all later scholars of language instruction.

Comenius was, in addition, one of the earliest and certainly the most renowned champions of what we call visual literacy and visual education. The last fourteen years of his life were spent in Amsterdam. It was from his haven there that Comenius oversaw the publication in 1657 in Nuremberg of the work for which he is today best known and on which he had been working for years: *Orbis Sensualium Pictus* (*The Visible World Pictured*).

Orbis Sensualium Pictus was the first illustrated textbook specifically designed for use by children in an instructional setting. (It was not the first children's picture book. The English printer Caxton, for example, had produced an illustrated edition of Aesop's *Fables* as early as 1484.) The design and illustrations of Comenius's text were expressly intended to enhance learning. The 150 woodcut drawings were learning and teaching devices, not mere decoration. The text embodied application of educational theories espoused by the author over a period of forty years. It is interesting to note, for example, that Comenius chose Aristotle's observation *Nihil est in intellectu, quod non prius fuit in sensu* (there is nothing in the mind which was not first in the senses), to adorn his title page. The primacy of this principle has been supported increasingly by modern psychological research.

Orbis Sensualium Pictus is truly remarkable for having incorporated, more than 300 years ago, so many educational concepts that seem thoroughly modern. Underlying Comenius's use of visuals was a theory of perception based on the idea that we learn through our senses and that this learning "imprints" a mental image which leads to understanding. A real object is preferable for this process, but visuals may be used in the learning environment as substitutes for the real thing.

The design and illustrations of *Orbis Sensualium Pictus*, he tells us in his preface, were intended "to entice witty children to it, that they may not conceit a torment to be in the school, but dainty fare. For it is apparent, that children (even from their infancy almost) are delighted with Pictures, and willingly please their eyes with these sights." His pedagogical aim, he tells us, was that children "may be furnished with the knowledge of the prime things that are in the world, by sport and merry pastime."

The idea that learning should be a "merry pastime" rather than a burdensome chore is startlingly modern. Indeed, centuries were to pass before this basic educational philosophy became what it is today—the common wisdom. Aptly called "that incomparable Moravian" in his own time, Johannes Amos Comenius may still be called so in ours.

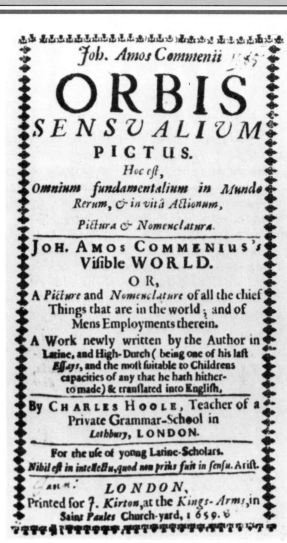

(104)

LI.

Piscatio.

Fishing.

(105)

The Fisher-man 1. catcheth fish,
   either on the shoar,
with an Hook, 2.
which hangeth by a line
from the angling-rod,
and on which
the bait sticketh;
   or with a
Cleek-Net, 3.
which hanging
on a Pole, 4.
is put into the water;
   or in a Boat, 5.
with a Trammel-Net 6.
   or with a Weel, 7.
which is laid in
the water by Night.

Piscator 1.
captat pisces,
   sive, in littore,
Hamo, 2.
qui ab *arundine*
filo pendet,
& cui inhæret
Esca ;
   sive
Fundâ, 3.
quæ pendens
Perticâ, 4.
aquæ immittitur ;
   sive, in *Cymba,* 5.
Reti, 6.
   sive *Nassâ,* 7.
quæ per Noctem
demergitur.

effects of training learners to generate their own graphic organizers for textual material. Typically, the learners have been asked to draw the organization of the content or material. In one study some adults were given the text, others read and were given a graphic organizer, and others read and generated their own graphic organizer. In this case the latter group learned the most. Findings from such research* suggest that a graphic organizer may not be very helpful unless the learners generate it themselves or manipulate it in some way.

Visuals can facilitate problem-solving activities. When given a word problem in math, learners should be encouraged to draw the situation before trying to solve the problem. By allowing the learner to "picture" the problem, visuals facilitate understanding of the situation presented.

Flowcharts improve the learner's speed in performing procedures and reduce the number of errors made. Flowcharts can also improve the comprehension of directions when compared with directions given in a verbal format.

Alesandrini† provides a succinct review of the effect of visuals on adult learning. Research suggests a possible sequence for using visuals with adults:

1. Begin with analogical visuals to relate the new information to prior learning.
2. Follow with arbitrary pictures to convey the essence of the new information and distinguish it from the analogous information.

---

* D. A. Norman and D. E. Rumelhart. *Explorations in Cognition*. San Francisco: Freeman, 1975.
† K. L. Alesandrini. "Pictures and Adult Learning." *Instructional Science* 13 (1984), pp. 63–77.

3. Conclude with representational pictures that serve to further define and distinguish the new information.

DESIGNING VISUALS

WELL-DESIGNED visuals—charts, posters, graphics for slides or television, bulletin board displays, and the like—not only promote learning of the subject matter but also provide aesthetic models for students' own creative growth.

When one is creating visuals, important design considerations are best faced by starting with a preliminary sketch of the intended visual. In commercial art this "blueprint" of the finished work is referred to as a rough layout. At the rough layout stage little attention is paid to rendering the artistic details, but careful consideration is given to choosing the right words and images, arranging them for best effect, selecting a lettering style, and choosing colors.

There is no magic recipe to achieve good visual design. You must develop creative and imaginative techniques through practice and exposure to good design methods. There are some general interrelated principles that apply to all forms of design. Together they form a foundation on which you can begin to design creative and educational visual materials. The principles relate to unity, line, shape, form, arrangement, balance, color, and interaction.

Unity

Unity is the relationship among the elements of a visual so that they function together. It concerns not only the verbal content but also the visual materials used to emphasize the main point. A mistake frequently made is to

▲ *Figure 3.18*
Visuals should present a single idea for effective communication as shown by this billboard.

crowd too much into one space. Eliminate every element that is not *essential* to the communication of your idea (see Figure 3.18). Only present *one* idea at a time!

Your message may require an orderly approach in which unity prevails. Sometimes, however, disorder is needed to convey a mood, such as that associated with the destructive force of natural or man-made disasters. How you arrange your visual elements depends upon your objective.

Line

The line is a one-dimensional structural device that attracts attention by moving the eye around or to a specific area. Lines suggest action, direction, and movement. Lines can also divide and then tie things back together when used as a structure on which to build.

- Horizontal lines give a feeling of stability and rest.
- Vertical lines imply strength; they draw the eye upward; they can be barriers in a visual field

because the normal "reading" pattern is horizontal.

- Diagonal lines strongly imply movement, action, and dynamism. Crossed diagonals give a sense of conflict. Curved lines also give a feeling of motion. These factors help explain the popularity of rounded patterns and S and Z patterns as basic arrangements for visuals.

Shape

A line closed upon itself becomes a shape. Shapes are two-dimensional and can form the outline of objects. Shapes can work together to create a meaningful whole. Some shapes communicate just from their silhouette without any internal detail (e.g., an apple, a cross, or a heart).

Form

Most visuals are two-dimensional with lines and shapes. However, a third dimension of form can be added with the use of textured or actual materials. Texture is the characteristic of three-dimensional objects and materials. It creates a definite feeling in the viewer—a visual image of the sense of touch. Texture can be used to give emphasis, to provide separation, or to enhance unity. For example, cotton can be used to represent clouds. Real objects such as book jackets can add interest and dimension to a bulletin board. Company products can be incorporated into a display. Correct and defective components can be shown with drawings and lettering for emphasis.

Arrangement

The visual and verbal elements of the layout should be arranged in a pattern that captures the viewer's attention and directs it toward the important details. Line, space, and

◀ *Figure 3.19*
Horizontal lines suggest tranquility.

◀ *Figure 3.20*
Vertical lines attract our attention against a commonly horizontal background.

◀ *Figure 3.21*
Diagonal lines imply movement and action.

◀ *Figure 3.22*
Three-dimensional objects in a display provide texture and form.

form are the designer's primary tools to be manipulated. The arrangement should be clear enough to attract and focus attention quickly. A regular geometric shape (e.g., oval, rectangle, triangle) provides a convenient framework to build on because its pattern is predictable to most viewers. Arrangements that approximate certain letters of the alphabet have the same virtue. The letters C, O, S, Z, L, T, and U are frequently used as underlying patterns in display layouts. Of course, the words used in the layout, as well as the pictures, form part of the arrangement.

Besides this basic underlying shape, one other principle should guide your arrangement. The "rule of thirds," mentioned earlier in regard to how people look at visuals (pages 71–72), also applies to graphic layout. Elements arranged along any of the one-third dividing lines take on a liveliness, a possibility of movement. The most dominant and dynamic position is at any of the intersections of the one-third dividing lines (especially the upper-left intersection). The most stable and least interesting point on the grid is dead center. Obviously, items placed in the corners or around the edges tend to create an unbalanced, uncomfortable feeling.

Balance

A psychological sense of equilibrium, or *balance,* is achieved when the "weight" of the elements in a display is equally distributed on each side of the axis—either horizontally, vertically, or both. When the design is repeated on both sides, the balance is symmetrical, or *formal.*

In most cases, though, for visuals that will catch the eye and serve an informational purpose

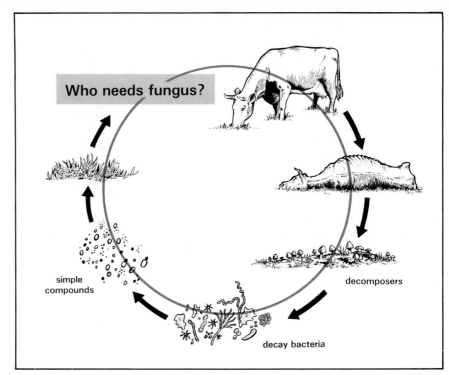

▲ *Figure 3.23*
Arrangement should follow an overall pattern such as the letter *O* shown here.

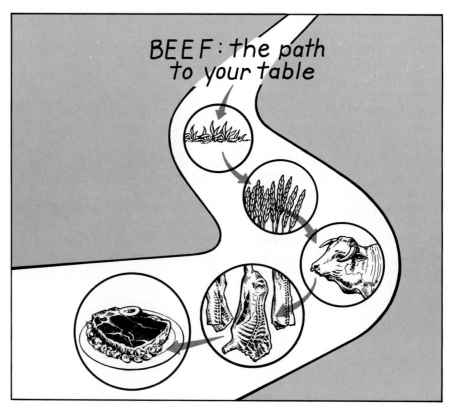

▲ *Figure 3.24*
An *S* arrangement provides flow and leads the viewer's eye from top to bottom.

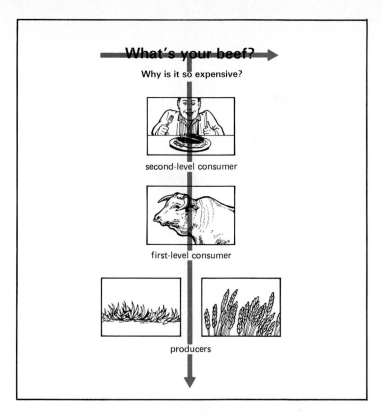

▲ *Figure 3.25*
A *T* pattern provides stability and formal balance.

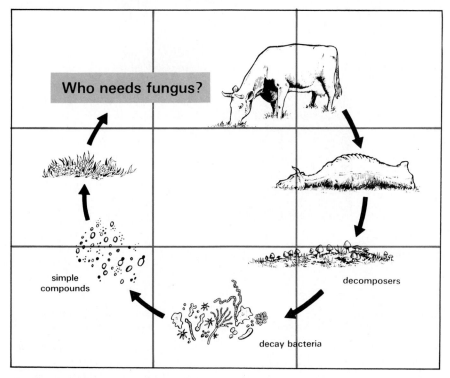

▲ *Figure 3.26*
The "rule of thirds" suggests that the most important elements of a visual should be placed near the intersections of lines dividing the visual into thirds.

the designer aims to achieve an asymmetrical or *informal* balance. Here, there is rough equivalence of weight, but with different elements used on each side; e.g., one large open square on one side, three small dark circles on the other. Informal balance is preferred because it is more dynamic and more interesting. Arrangements such as the C, S, Z, and the like are frequently used as frameworks because they supply precast molds for asymmetrical layouts.

Imbalance—having distinctly disproportionate weight distribution—ordinarily should be avoided as it tends to be psychologically jarring.

Color

Color can not only enhance and enrich your visual designs but also influence moods and indicate movement. Color commands attention and gives visual impact. Some of the other functions of colors in a visual are (1) to heighten the realism of the image by depicting the actual colors, (2) to point out similarities and differences, (3) to highlight important information and details, and (4) to create a particular emotional response.

Artists have long appreciated that blue, green, and violet are perceived as "cool," whereas red and orange are considered "hot." It is now understood that a physiological basis for this perception exists, the manner in which colors are focused in the human eye. The warmer colors appear to be approaching the viewer; the cooler colors seem to be receding from the viewer. The designer can capitalize on this tendency by highlighting important cues in red and orange, thus helping them leap toward the viewer.

Color choice is a very personal

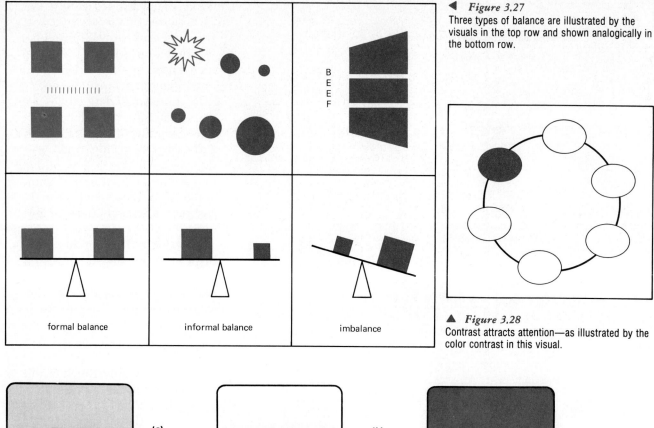

◀ *Figure 3.27*
Three types of balance are illustrated by the visuals in the top row and shown analogically in the bottom row.

formal balance   informal balance   imbalance

▲ *Figure 3.28*
Contrast attracts attention—as illustrated by the color contrast in this visual.

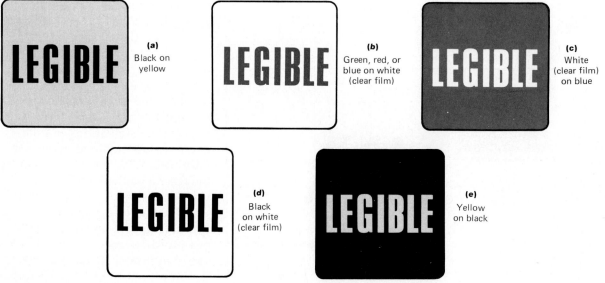

(a)
Black on yellow

(b)
Green, red, or blue on white (clear film)

(c)
White (clear film) on blue

(d)
Black on white (clear film)

(e)
Yellow on black

▲ *Figure 3.29*
Suggested colors for visuals. Most legible is black on yellow (example *a*) and so on in descending order of legibility.

thing. Dare to invent your own color combinations. You can also use contrast to emphasize points, create a mood, or provide visual interest. Color is important in visuals. Use it wisely, but do not overuse it!

Interaction

Particularly effective visuals may provide for learner interaction with the visual or manipulation of materials on the visual. Answer cards to math facts may be moved

into the correct position by the student. The teacher or learners may move dials on a weather display to indicate the forecast for the day or the actual weather outside the classroom.

In a manufacturing plant the

▲ Figure 3.30
Students learn more when they are involved and interacting with instructional media.

Gothic sans-serif

Aa Bb Cc Dd Ee Ff Gg Hh Ii Jj Kk Ll Mm Nn Oo Pp etc.

Roman sans-serif

Aa Bb Cc Dd Ee Ff Gg Hh Ii Jj Kk Ll Mm Nn

▲ Figure 3.31
These types of lettering are most readable.

visual display may be modified each day to indicate the number of accident-free hours worked by the employees. Workers may also be asked to manipulate materials on a display in the break room.

The *R* of the ASSURE model applies to all forms of media. Viewers can be asked to *respond* to visual displays by actually getting involved with them. The interaction should be for the purpose of increasing learning or enhancing awareness.

We have introduced some general design principles. Design is around you all the time. Professional designers are paid well to lay out newspaper ads, billboards, magazines, and commercial displays. Use their expertise as ideas for layout of your own visuals, but be aware that even some professionally produced designs are not effective for their intended purpose. Learn to observe carefully and remember what you have seen. Sharpen your senses, and then make practical applications of the good designs you find.

LETTERING VISUALS

Most visuals incorporate some type of lettering. The style of the lettering should be consistent and should harmonize with the "feel" of the visual as a whole. If your visual has primarily an aesthetic or motivational objective, one of the more ornate lettering styles might be appropriate; but for straightforward informational or instructional purposes a simple lettering style is recommended. The gothic or roman sans serif (without serifs) style is most readable. Equally important, these alphabets are easily reproducible by hand lettering (see Figure 3.31).

For best legibility, use lowercase letters, adding capitals only where normally required. Short headlines may be written in all capitals, but phrases of more than a half dozen words and full sentences should follow the rule of lowercase lettering.

The color of the lettering should contrast with the background color both for the sake of simple legibility and for the sake of emphasis in cases where you want to call particular attention to the verbal message. Legibility depends mainly on difference in contrast between the lettering color and the background color.

Size of Lettering. Displays such as bulletin boards and posters are often meant to be viewed by people situated thirty, forty, or more feet away. In these cases the size of the lettering is crucial in legibility. A common rule of thumb

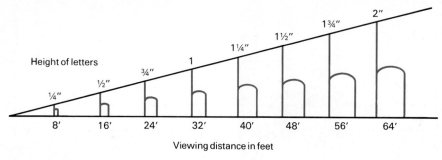

Height of letters

¼"   ½"   ¾"   1   1¼"   1½"   1¾"   2"

8'   16'   24'   32'   40'   48'   56'   64'

Viewing distance in feet

▲ *Figure 3.32*
Minimum heights of letters for visibility at increasing distances.

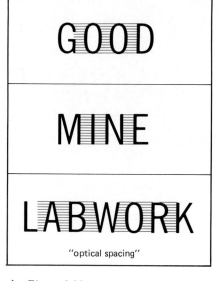

GOOD

MINE

LABWORK

"optical spacing"

▲ *Figure 3.33*
Irregular combinations of letters require estimating equal amounts of white space between each pair of letters. The technique is called "optical spacing."

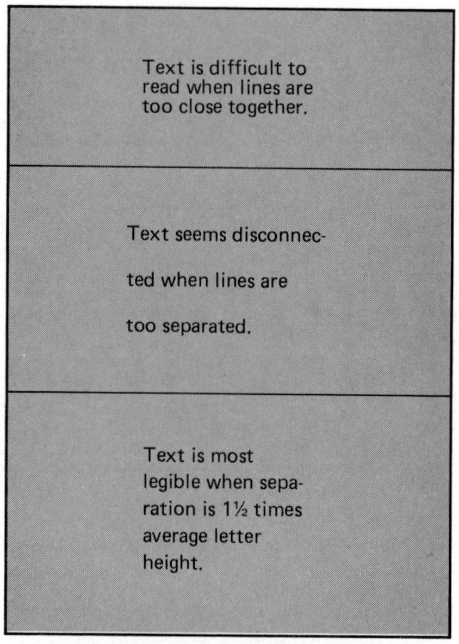

suggests that the lettering be ¼-inch high for each eight feet of viewer distance. This means, for example, that to be legible to a student seated in the last seat of a thirty-two-foot-long classroom, the lettering would have to be at least one inch in height. Figure 3.32 contains an illustration of these minimum specifications for lettering height.

Spacing of Lettering. The distance between the letters of the individual words must be judged by experience rather than on a mechanical basis. This is because some letters (e.g., capital A, K, W, and X) are quite irregular in shape compared to the rectangular letters (e.g., capital H, M, N, and S) and circular letters (e.g., capital C, G, O, and Q). When the rectangular letters or circular letters are combined with each other, there are rather regular patterns of white space between letters. But when irregular letters are combined with others, the patterns of white space can be very uneven. The only way to overcome this potentially distracting unevenness is to space all your letters by "optical spacing." What appears "even" to the eye is spacing in which the total amount of white space between each pair of letters is equal.

The vertical spacing between lines of printed material is also important for legibility. If the lines are too close together, they

will tend to blur together at a distance; if they are too far apart, they will seem disjointed, not part of the same unit. For a happy medium, the distance between the lines should be slightly less than the average height of the letters. To achieve this, use a ruler to draw lines lightly on your rough layout; separate the lines by about one-and-one-half times the height of your average lowercase letters.

Types of Lettering. A wide variety of lettering techniques for visuals exist. The simplest is freehand lettering with markers and felt-tip pens, which come in an array of colors and sizes.

Letters can be cut from construction paper or other materials. Precut letters are also available in stationery and office-supply stores. The letters are easy to use, because most come with an adhesive backing; however, they are rather expensive.

An alternative is dry-transfer lettering. These sticky letters, numbers, and symbols are attached to a large sheet and are transferred to the visual by rubbing them with a burnishing tool or other smooth, hard device (see Figure 3.35). Dry-transfer letters are available in numerous sizes and colors.

Many media centers and graphic production units in business and industry now use mechanical lettering devices such

Text is difficult to read when lines are too close together.

Text seems disconnec-

ted when lines are

too separated.

Text is most legible when separation is 1½ times average letter height.

▲ *Figure 3.34*
Various text separations illustrate the appropriate vertical spacing between lines.

as the Kroy 88 shown in Figure 3.36. The style and size of the letters are determined by the interchangeable large plastic wheels. The letters are "printed" on strips of clear plastic or colored film. Once the backing has been removed, the letters can be adhered to most surfaces.

Appraisal Checklist: Visuals

Title _____   Format _____

Producer _____   Date _____

Audience/Grade Level _____

Objectives (stated or implied):

Brief Description:

Rating	High		Medium		Low	Comments
Unity: limited to a single main idea	☐	☐	☐	☐	☐	
Line: suggests action, direction, and movement	☐	☐	☐	☐	☐	
Shape: easily interpreted; contributes to meaning or effect	☐	☐	☐	☐	☐	
Form: enhances interest or effect of visual	☐	☐	☐	☐	☐	
Arrangement: geometric shapes or letters as frameworks; ''rule of thirds''	☐	☐	☐	☐	☐	
Balance: elements equally distributed on each side	☐	☐	☐	☐	☐	
Color: simple; analogous; contrast for emphasis and legibility	☐	☐	☐	☐	☐	
Interaction: gets learners involved	☐	☐	☐	☐	☐	
Lettering: simple style; color contrast with background; $\frac{1}{4}$ inch per eight feet of viewer distance; optical spacing	☐	☐	☐	☐	☐	

Strong Points

Weak Points

Reviewer _____

Recommended action _____   Position _____

Date _____

When preparing printed instructional materials such as handouts, worksheets, and study guides, there are a number of factors to consider. They include headings, writing style, page layout, type style/mechanics, visuals, and highlighting. Here are a number of principles to guide the design of printed materials.

Headings

- Label all text so readers can locate the information they need.
- Provide headings to allow learners to skim for an overview and to retrieve information later.
- Use headings to show the organization of the content (e.g., start each new page with main heading).
- Use side heads (words in left margin) to call attention to important concepts.
- Use different type style for headings.

Writing Style

- State main idea/theme at the beginning of text.
- Put topic sentences at beginning of each paragraph.
- Use simple sentences and writing style.
- Use active voice where possible.
- Include technical terms with definitions so they won't be misconstrued or misspelled.

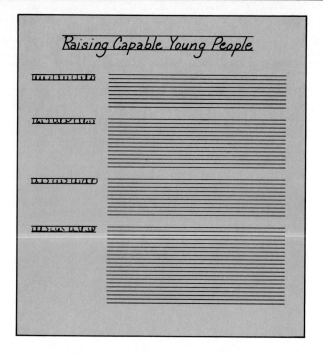

◀ *Figure 3.35*
Dry-transfer letters are easy to apply.

Page Layout

- Provide ample white space (use wide margins and uncrowded format) to facilitate initial comprehension, note taking, and location of information for review.
- Use unjustified right margins (justification adds to expense and production time with no effect on reading rate or comprehension—the only value is cosmetic).
- Increase the space between lines in a note-taking handout to increase the number of words noted.
- Be clear and consistent in page layout (use the same type of text in the same typeface, size, and layout).

Type Style/Mechanics

- Choose typeface styles with simple designs (such as gothic or roman sans serif).
- Use a space and a half between lines if material is typed for ease of reading.
- Avoid the breaking of words with hyphens at the end of lines.
- Limit the number of words per line to approximately the learner's age for preteenagers.

Visuals

- Keep visuals simple (avoid too much realism in visuals).
- Direct attention to visuals through questions and activities.
- Place visuals as near the related text as possible.
- Use larger visuals if more detail is required.

Highlighting

Highlighting techniques for printed materials include color, size of type, italics, and boldfacing.

- Highlight important ideas, thus limiting the demands on the learner to locate key points and ideas.
- Do not use capitals for highlighting because they are difficult to read within text (capitals are okay for headings).
- Avoid author-provided underlining because it has little or no effect on retention of content (underlining can be used to highlight negatives, e.g. *not* and *except*).

Sources: James Hartley. *Designing Instructional Text.* New York: Nichols, 1978. Also David H. Jonassen, ed. *The Technology of Text: Principles of Structuring, Designing, and Displaying Text.* Englewood Cliffs, N.J.: Educational Technology Publications. Vol. I, 1982 and Vol. II, 1985.

◄ *Figure 3.36*
Mechanical lettering machines produce professional results.

DRAWING, SKETCHING, AND CARTOONING

As described in Chapter 4, drawings, sketches, and cartoons are nonprojected visuals that can greatly enhance learning. There are many sources of these in magazines, textbooks, and advertisements. One often overlooked source is *you*. You don't have to be an artist to draw. There are some basic guidelines and many how-to books that can help you communicate effectively using these graphic media.

With a little practice, you may be surprised by how well you can draw. Simple drawings can enhance chalkboard presentations, class handouts, bulletin boards, and overhead transparencies. For ideas on getting started, see the "How To" on page 87 and the references at the end of this chapter.

INSTRUCTOR-DUPLICATED MATERIALS

On occasion you may want to distribute your own printed materials to students. These materials may be handouts, viewing notes for videotapes, outlines for presentations, study guides for mediated materials, or tests. With the availability of graphics and text programs for personal computers, the idea of "desk-top publishing" has emerged. You essentially develop materials at your desk rather than sending them away to be published. With word processing you can write, edit, and check your spelling at the computer. Graphics can be added from clip art or from your own sketches, as described earlier in this chapter.

Once your materials have been completed, they need to be duplicated. There are several duplica-

tion processes. Schools tend to use spirit duplication, mimeograph machines, and some photocopying, whereas businesses rely heavily on photocopying and offset. The characteristics and approximate costs of each of these processes are described in Table 3.1.

PHOTOGRAPHY FOR INSTRUCTION

Principles of Photography

All cameras, regardless of their size, shape, or type, operate on the same basic principles. There are four elements required for photography: light, a subject, a camera, and film. Light (sunlight or flash) is reflected from the subject and passes through the lens to form an invisible image on the film called an exposure.

TABLE 3.1 **Summary of Duplicating Processes**

Method	Principle	Materials and Approximate Cost	Evaluation
Spirit (for example, Ditto brand spirit duplicator)	Carbon impression on master transferred to paper with alcohol	Master: $0.08 Paper: $3.00/ream	Master easily prepared; operation simple; good for up to 150 copies in multicolor
Stencil (mimeograph)	Ink passes through openings in waxlike stencil and is picked up by paper in contact with stencil	Stencil: $0.30 Paper: $3.00/ream	Care needed in making master; machine more complex than spirit; each color requires separate operation; quality slightly better than spirit; clean-up takes time
Electrostatic (for example, Xerox brand plain paper copier)	Negatively charged ink powder is on a positively charged metal plate, from which it is transferred to paper by electrostatic attraction	Copy: $0.02–$0.05 Machine costs vary	Can copy anything; fair to good quality; machine cost high; operation simple after adjustments
Offset	Ink adheres to image on plate; transferred to blanket and then to paper	Master: $0.40–$0.70 Copies: $1.00/100	Inexpensive plates and preparation of plates of some types; quality excellent; operation requires technician; clean-up time lengthy

Faces: Use an oval and add a minimum of lines to indicate features and expressions.

- Start with a circle or oval.
- Add ears in the middle on each side.
- Draw a nose between the ears.
- Place the eyes near the top of the nose.
- Draw the mouth halfway between the nose and chin.
- Add hair and other features.

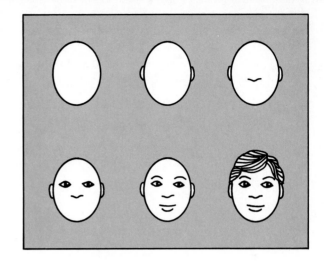

Body: Begin with stick figures, which can show action. With practice, add detail to your characters.

1.

2.

3.

4.

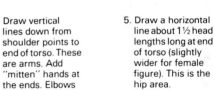

5.

1. Determine the head size and draw

2. Draw a straight line down from that head which is an *additional* 3 heads long. This is the torso.

3. Just below the head draw a *horizontal* line about 2 head lengths long. This is the shoulder line.

4. Draw vertical lines down from shoulder points to end of torso. These are arms. Add "mitten" hands at the ends. Elbows would fall midway on these lines.

5. Draw a horizontal line about 1½ head lengths long at end of torso (slightly wider for female figure). This is the hip area.

6.

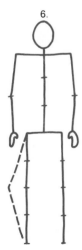

6. Draw vertical lines down from hip "joints" 4 head lengths long. Leg length comprises *half* of entire body length. Knees would fall about halfway or 2 head lengths down.

7.

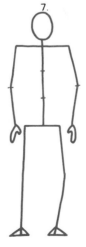

7. Superimpose simple triangular feet on the legs at the bottom.

When preparing instructional materials for use on computer screens, there are a number of factors to consider. They include titles, instructions, text, highlighting, and graphics. Here are a number of principles to guide the design of computer screens:

Titles

- Use short, concise, meaningful titles; avoid unnecessary words.
- Center titles at the top of the screen or place at the left margin.
- Spell out all words; do not use abbreviations or contractions.
- Describe the purpose or content of the screen in the title.
- Limit the title to not more than three lines.
- Place at least one blank line between the title and the text.
- Put title in boldface letters.

Instructions

- Use short sentences (not more than seven words).
- Provide step-by-step instructions.
- State instructions in a positive manner, except for serious warnings and cautions.
- State instructions in the active voice.
- Use clear wording in instructions; avoid highly technical terms or abbreviations.

Text

- Write in simple, uncluttered, and clear sentences.
- Use both upper- and lowercase letters to enhance readability.
- Use single screens under learner control for advancing (i.e., do not advance screens automatically).
- Provide double space within paragraphs.
- Put a period at the end of each sentence.
- Include only one paragraph per screen when possible.
- Use left justification (margins that are aligned) only.
- Break the lines of text at natural phrasing points (especially for poor readers).
- Avoid splitting words at the end of a line.

Highlighting

Highlighting techniques draw attention to words, text, or graphics and include color, size of type, underlining, boxes, asterisks, intensity, blinking or flashing elements (which may be the strongest attention getter), inverse images, and a cursor for pointing.

- Use italicization, if possible, to emphasize text without decreasing readability.
- Leave an extra space before and after any word displayed in reverse video (inverse text).
- Use blinking or flashing only for very important messages, then return to normal or alternative highlighting after getting the learner's attention.
- Avoid using blinking or flashing in two locations on the same screen.
- Avoid "hot" colors such as pink and magenta, because they appear to pulsate.
- Use sound, if available, to signify that user action is needed.
- Limit the use of highlighting; overuse may let design techniques upstage the content.

Graphics

- Avoid excessive detail or realism.
- Break down complex graphics into simpler parts.
- Present graphics simultaneously with corresponding text.
- Use color to focus attention on important components.
- Limit the number of colors on the screen at any one time (no more than four).
- Use effective combinations of color (avoid red and green, blue and yellow, green and blue, and red and blue).
- Use color as a redundant cue (i.e., should be effective on monochrome screen, too).

Sources: Wilbert O. Galitz. *Handbook of Screen Format Design.* 2d ed.Wellesley Hills, Mass.: QED Information Sciences, 1985. Also Jesse M. Heines. *Screen Design Strategies for Computer-Assisted Instruction.* Bedford, Mass.: Digital Press, 1984.

1. *Decide upon an objective.* Limit the display to one topic or objective. More than one idea usually results in confusion on the part of the viewers.
2. *Generate a theme and incorporate it into a headline.* It is a challenge to work out a catchy theme that will entice the viewer into further examination. Wording should be simple, couched in the viewer's language, and visually integrated into the arrangement of the display.
3. *Work out a rough layout.* Guidelines for literate visuals are discussed in this chapter. The blueprint you develop here should reflect those guidelines.
4. *Gather the materials.* Obtain or make the illustrations, photographs, or other visual materials.

Select a background material; e.g., cloth, wrapping paper, aluminum foil, colored construction paper, or shelf paper. Lines on the display can be made from ribbon, yarn, string, wire, or paper strips. Lettering may be freehand, drawn using a lettering guide, pressed on with dry-transfer type, or cut from construction paper; preformed plastic and ceramic letters are also available.
5. *Put up the display.* Setting up the display should be easy if all the preceding steps have been carried out. Step back and appraise it from a technical standpoint, and observe student reactions to evaluate its instructional effectiveness.

One especially handy application of opaque and overhead projectors is to enlarge visuals for classroom display. You can make your own enlargement of any original picture that you want to display on the chalkboard or to use as part of a bulletin board.

Using Opaque
- Place printed material to be copied in the projector.

Using Overhead
- Using an overhead pen, trace the figure on a clear sheet of acetate, and place on projector.

Then, in either case,

- Dim the lights.
- Tape a sheet of paper or cardboard to a wall or tack to a bulletin board.
- Direct the projected image onto the surface where you want to draw the image (paper, cardboard, or chalkboard).
- Adjust the distance of the projector from the wall to enlarge (or reduce) the image to the size desired. Move the projector farther back to enlarge (or closer to reduce).
- Trace over the projected image in whatever detail you wish.

Your students will be impressed with your "artistic ability," and maybe you will be, too.

Let's look at the four elements in more detail.

Light: may be from natural sources (i.e., sunlight) or from artificial sources (light bulbs or camera flash units). The film must be "exposed" to the proper amount of light. Too little exposure, and the picture will be dark; too much, and the picture will be too light. Controlling the amount of light that enters the camera is discussed in greater detail later.

Subject: should be interesting and imaginative. The subject should be "composed" in the picture properly. (See "How To . . . Compose Better Pictures" on pages 94–95.)

Camera: is a light-tight box with a lens to collect the light from the subject and to focus the light on the film. The amount of light getting into the camera is controlled by the lens opening and the shutter speed.

Film: is a light-sensitive material that records the image. The image becomes visible after it is processed by chemicals. With Polaroid film, the chemicals are part of the film "package."

Parts of a Camera

Cameras have many parts, but the most important parts common to all cameras are the lens opening (aperture), the shutter, the view finder, the lens, and the film advance.

Lens Opening: regulates the amount of light that enters the camera. On some cameras the size of the opening is fixed, and on other cameras there are two or three possible settings for the lens opening. On many cameras, however, the size of the lens opening is adjustable over a broad range.

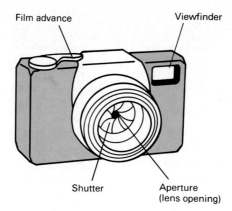

▲ *Figure 3.37*
Components of a typical camera

Shutter: controls the length of time that light enters the camera and reaches the film. Again, there is only one shutter speed on simple cameras but several on more complex cameras. The shutter speed refers to the period of time that light is allowed to enter the camera. On cameras the shutter speed is usually given as a whole number such as 250, 125, or 30. However, these numbers refer to fractions of a second (i.e., 1/250 of a second, 1/125 of a second, and 1/30 of a second). The higher the number, the shorter the time that the shutter is open. The very fast shutter speeds (with the shutter open only a very short period of time) allow you to photograph moving objects, such as race cars, because they do not move far while the shutter is open.

View Finder: allows you to see what the film will "see" when the shutter is opened. In some cameras, such as Kodak's Instamatic, the view finder is near the top of the camera and you look parallel to the lens opening. Consequently, you may not see exactly what will appear in the photograph. Except at very close range, the discrepancy is negligible. With a single lens

reflex camera, a movable mirror allows you to view directly through the lens. The mirror is moved out of the way when a photograph is taken.

Focus: is the setting of the lens that determines the sharpness of the image. Inexpensive cameras often cannot be focused and have just one setting which is usually good for objects from five feet to infinity. Other cameras have a full range of focus from three feet to infinity. The focus may be determined by a distance scale (to the subject) and is indicated in feet and/or meters. Other cameras have a range finder with a double image or a split image.

Film Advance: moves the exposed image and positions unexposed film in place for the next photograph. In older cameras it was possible to get a double exposure if the film was not advanced by the photographer. Most of today's cameras will not allow you to push the shutter release until the film has been advanced. The typical film advance mechanism is a lever mounted on the upper-right-hand side of the camera. Some cameras have an attachment for rapid advance, which allows you to take many pictures in a few seconds. This feature is not necessary for most educational applications. Many of the newer cameras have automatic film advance along with automatic focus.

Selecting a Camera

The type of camera you choose depends on the kinds of pictures you find useful for instruction. If you do not take extreme close-ups and do not have use for telephoto and other special lenses, then you may prefer a range-

◀ *Figure 3.38*
A 35-mm view finder camera

◀ *Figure 3.39*
A 35-mm single-lens reflex camera

finder camera for portability, reliability, and simplicity (Figure 3.38). The quality of the image taken with a moderately priced range-finder camera is very good.

If, however, you need to take extreme close-ups, have a use for a variety of lenses (wide angle, telephoto), and do a lot of copying, then a single lens reflex (SLR) camera is what you want. Although it is bulkier and more awkward to use, the SLR is more flexible than a range-finder camera (Figure 3.39).

Both types of cameras are available in models with automatic and semiautomatic exposure controls. Before the incorporation of photocells and microprocessors into cameras, even amateur photographers had to know the relationships between film speed, lens opening (f/stop), and shutter speed. Today's picture taker need learn only a few simple steps from the instruction manual to achieve a proper exposure on the film. Sometimes unusual lighting situations call for modifications of camera-determined settings. A little experience with the camera will guide such modifications. Relieved of the necessity to determine exposure, the photographer can concentrate on composing the picture (see Figure 3.40).

Let's discuss some of the more recent innovations in camera technology brought about by advancements in electronics and optics. For example, the 35-mm camera has long been associated with professional photography and sophisticated equipment. However, since the late 1970s there have been 35-mm cameras readily available that are as small and compact as the "Instamatics" of earlier years.

▲ *Figure 3.40*
Automatic features allow the amateur photographer to concentrate on composing the desired picture.

In addition, recent advances in miniaturization of microprocessors (computers) have made possible the development of a camera that not only contains an apparatus that sets the light controls automatically but also includes a pair of sensors that measure the distance from your subject, analyze the information, and automatically set the focus.

For strictly amateur picture taking, the 110- and disc-format cameras have become widely accepted. Both are very simple to use, and their compactness makes them easy to carry around. Some of the features of better 35-mm cameras have been built into the 110 cameras, considerably improving their flexibility and image quality. But both formats have limitations that make them less than ideal for instructional purposes. According to tests by Consumers Union, prints made from 110 negatives were judged by a panel of viewers to be significantly poorer in quality than ones made from 35-mm, and prints from disc negatives were poorer

than 110 prints.* If your picture taking is limited to snapshots of class activities, the 110—and disc—formats are adequate. For instructional purposes, the 126 Instamatic and, preferably, 35-mm are the formats of choice.

Most instructors in education and training use slides far more often than they do prints. Unless you can afford the luxury of two cameras—and don't mind carrying them around—you will probably be better off keeping slide film in your camera. If you find later that you need prints, very satisfactory ones can be made from slides. If very large photographs are required (8 by 10 inches or larger), laser technology can make prints of remarkable quality from slides. However, if you prefer using print film, slides can be made from your color negatives. Eastman Kodak, among other companies, provides this service.

Having chosen a camera and type of film, you will find guidelines for taking instructionally useful photos in "How To . . . Compose Better Pictures."

For hints on planning a slide or slide-tape presentation, see "How To . . . Develop a Sound-Slide Presentation" in Chapter 7. Further technical information on photography and suggestions for working with student photography will be found in the items listed in the audiovisual references at the end of this chapter.

APPLICATION OF THE ASSURE MODEL TO VISUALS

A̲FTER having analyzed the audience and content as described in Chapter 2, you must

_____
* *Consumer Reports* (November 1982), pp. 554–555.

state your objectives. If the objective indicates the need for visuals in instruction, you next select, modify, or design visuals to meet this need. The "Appraisal Checklist: Visuals" on page 83 can be very helpful in the selection process. If you need to modify the visuals selected, the sections of this chapter on lettering visuals and drawing, sketching, and cartooning should be good references. These same sections are valuable if you need to design your own visuals for instruction. In addition, refer to the section on designing visuals. If the visual will be part of a bulletin board, the "How To . . . Develop a Bulletin Board Display" contains some guidelines.

Following the selection, modification, or design of visuals, you will want to utilize them properly. The section of this chapter beginning on page 68, "Using Visuals in Instruction," has guidelines on how to assist learners in decoding (reading) and encoding (making) visuals. In the next two chapters on nonprojected and projected visuals there are six "Showmanship" sections which provide suggestions for the use of visuals.

When selecting, modifying, or designing visuals as well as deciding how you plan to use them, you should consider how you will require learner response from the visuals. As discussed, one of the sets of principles to be considered in designing visuals is interaction (page 80). Interaction provides for learner response and increased learning. Finally, the instruction involving visuals must be evaluated in terms of student learning and overall effectiveness, as discussed in Chapter 2. If you follow the ASSURE model in your use of visuals, your chances of successful instruction are increased.

Analyze Learners

General Characteristics. The high school students are in their first-year Spanish course. They attend the only high school in a small town in the southeastern United States. Consequently, the class members represent diverse socioeconomic backgrounds. Their grade levels range from freshman to senior, and their ages from fourteen to eighteen. The grade point averages go from a D average to an A average. The class members are highly motivated, because the course is an elective. None of the students have physical or emotional handicaps.

Entry Competencies. Some of the students have learned common words and phrases on their own. In the course the teacher has taught about 100 words, so all the students have a limited reading and speaking vocabulary.

The students have a very positive attitude toward learning to read and to speak Spanish. Some hope to travel in Spanish-speaking countries. The teacher usually takes a small group of students to Mexico during the spring break. Others plan to take a second course in Spanish while still in high school. A few plan to continue their study of Spanish in college.

State Objectives

The objectives for the Spanish vocabulary lesson are as follows:

1. Given an example of or the English word for a common color, the first-year Spanish student will pronounce correctly and write correctly the name of that color 90 percent of the time.
2. Given a visual showing or the English word for a common object, the first-year Spanish student will pronounce correctly and write correctly the name of that object 90 percent of the time.

Select, Modify, or Design Materials

In looking for materials to teach Spanish words for colors and objects, the teacher was unable to find anything other than the textbook. Realizing that the students learned from practice and interaction, the teacher wanted to incorporate these into the lesson. Upon further consideration, none of the materials could be modified to meet adequately the objectives of the lesson and the characteristics of the students, so the teacher decided to design an original bulletin board.

The bulletin board was titled "Color de Objetos." The teacher selected visuals of a dozen colorful objects—e.g., a green chair, a red box, a blue boat, and a brown horse—and mounted the pictures on the bulletin board. Next to each visual were its color and name in Spanish. These were covered by a large index card with a question mark on it.

Utilize the Materials

The materials were actually used by the students and not the teacher. Worksheets were distributed by the teacher with the numbers one through twelve and a place to write the color and name of the object.

Individually or in small groups the students were to look at the visuals, write the Spanish words on the worksheet, then lift the flap (index card) to reveal the correct color and name in Spanish.

Require Learner Response

The teacher designed interaction into the bulletin board. The students were to construct their Spanish words and then check their answers under the flaps. They were immediately given feedback as to the correctness of their responses.

An additional form of interaction resulted from the students' talking while at the bulletin board—challenging each other to get the correct answers, speaking the words in Spanish, and correcting each other's written and spoken answers. The result was a dynamic, interactive learning session.

Evaluate

The teacher evaluated the effectiveness of the bulletin board by watching the students' responses to it and listening to their positive comments about it. In addition, the students were given a weekly quiz each Friday covering the words that had been on the bulletin board that week. The bulletin board provided self-evaluation for the students as they learned while practicing the words for that week.

Taking better pictures means making the *subject* most prominent and *composing* the elements of the picture.

Subject. How you place your subject in the frame is critical in taking effective pictures.

- Zero in on your real subject. Cut out the unnecessary elements in a picture, even if it's yourself.
- Scale indications are important, particularly if the object being photographed is not common.
- Eliminate distracting backgrounds that may also cause poor exposure; e.g., make sure blinds or draperies are closed if you are shooting toward them.
- If you are photographing a moving object, put more space in front of the object than in back of it.
- Be cautious about possible distortion when taking dramatic angle shots. When taking pictures of a building, get as high as you can to reduce the angle of a shot. This is where a telephoto lens comes in handy.
- If a feeling of depth is important, place an object in the foreground—but not so that it is distracting.

Composition. In addition to the preceding comments, the following will help you frame your pictures for a more pleasing appearance and instructional clarity.

- Use the "rule of thirds." Divide a picture area in thirds both vertically and horizontally. The center of interest should be near one of the intersections of the lines.

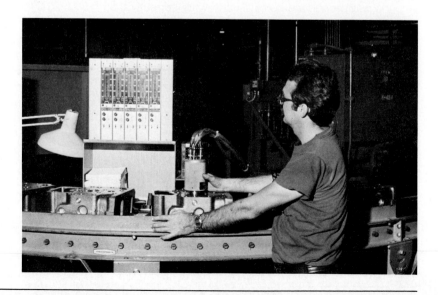

- Avoid splitting a picture exactly in half with a horizontal line. It is tempting to do so in photos that include beach and sea or the horizon.

- When taking a scenery shot or one of a building, framing the scene with something in the foreground often improves the picture in terms of interest and perspective.

- Learn to control depth of field— the region of sharp focus in front of and behind your subject. Shallow depth can often make a subject more dramatic. On the other hand, extreme depth can make scenery more striking. Depth of field can be controlled by varying the distance between you and your subject, the lens used, and the f/stop selected.

You will notice your photographs steadily improving as you master the composition of your subject.

References

Print References

Bloomer, Carolyn M. *Principles of Visual Perception.* (New York: Van Nostrand Reinhold, 1976).

Braden, Roberts, and Hortin, John A. "Identifying the Theoretical Foundations of Visual Literacy." *Journal of Visual Verbal Languaging,* 2, no. 2 (1983), pp. 37–42, 58–66.

Cassidy, Michael, and Knowlton, James Q. "Visual Literacy: A Failed Metaphor?" *Educational Communications and Technology* (Summer 1983), pp. 68–90.

Debes, John. "Some Foundations for Visual Literacy." *Audiovisual Instruction* (November 1968), pp. 961–964.

Do You See What I Mean? Learning through Charts, Graphs, Maps, and Diagrams. (Dickson, Australia: Curriculum Development Centre, 1980).

Doelker, Christian. "Audio-Video Language—Verbal and Visual Codes." *Educational Media International* (March 1980), pp. 3–4.

Dondis, Donis A. *A Primer of Visual Literacy.* (Cambridge, Mass.: MIT Press, 1973).

Donoho, Grace. "Measures of Audiovisual Production Activities with Students." *Drexel Library Quarterly* (Spring 1985), pp. 91–104.

Dwyer, Francis M., ed. *Enhancing Visualized Instruction.* (State College, Penn.: Learning Services, 1987).

Eckhardt, Ned. "The Learning Potential of Picture Taking." *Media and Methods* (January 1977), pp. 48–50, 53.

Fleming, Malcolm. "Characteristics of Effective Instructional Presentation: What We Know and What We Need to Know." *Educational Technology* (July 1981), pp. 33–38.

Hortin, John A. "A Need for a Theory of Visual Literacy." *Reading Improvement* (Winter 1982), pp. 257–267.

———. "Instructional Design and Visualization." *Performance and Instruction* (September 1983), pp. 20–21.

———. "Research for Teachers on Visual Thinking to Solve Verbal Problems." *Journal of Educational Technology Systems* (1984–1985), pp. 299–303.

———. "Visual Literacy and Visual Thinking." In L. J. Ausburn, ed., *Australian Society of Educational Technology National Yearbook, 1981.* (Hawthorn, Australia: ASET, 1982).

Kemp, Jerrold E., and Dayton, Deane K. *Planning and Producing Instructional Media.* 5th ed. (New York: Harper & Row, 1985).

McKim, Robert. *Experience in Visual Thinking.* 2d ed. Monterey, Calif.: Brooks/Cole, 1980.

Pictures of Ideas: Learning through Visual Comparison and Analogy. (Dickson, Australia: Curriculum Development Centre, 1980).

Simonson, Michael R., and Volker, Roger P. *Media Planning and Production.* (Columbus: Merrill, 1984).

Sless, David. *Learning and Visual Communication.* (New York: Wiley, 1981).

Thomas, James L. *Nonprint Production for Students, Teachers, and Media Specialists: A Step-by-Step Guide.* (Littleton, Colo.: Libraries Unlimited, 1982).

Walker, David A. *Understanding Pictures: A Study in the Design of Appropriate Visual Materials for Education in Developing Countries.* (David A. Walker, 1979).

What a Picture! Learning from Photographs. (Dickson, Australia: Curriculum Development Centre, 1981).

Williams, Catherine. *Learning from Pictures.* 2d ed. (Washington, D.C.: AECT, 1968).

Audiovisual References

Art Elements: An Introduction. Santa Monica, Calif.: BFA Educational Media, 1981. 16-mm film, 18 minutes.

Audiovisual Production Techniques. Indiana University Audio-Visual Center, 1982. Sound slide series (6 series). Series titles: "Designing Visuals That Communicate" (4 sets); "Fundamentals of Photography" (3 sets); "Lettering for Instructional Materials" (5 sets); "Visuals for Projection" (3 sets); "Audio Principles" (3 sets); "Duplication" (2 sets); and "Electricity and the Media Specialist" (1 set).

Bring Your Message into Focus. Eastman Kodak Co., 1982. Kit (dissolve slide program). 20 minutes.

Experiencing Design. Burbank, Calif.: Encore Visual Education, 1975. Four sound filmstrips, 58 frames.

How Does a Picture Mean? Washington, D.C.: Association for Educational Communications and Technology, 1967. Filmstrip, 76 frames.

How to Take Better Pictures. Media Tree, 1982. Slide set with audiocassette.

Learning to See and Understand: Developing Visual Literacy. White Plains, N.Y.: Center for the Humanities, 1973. Sound slide, 160 slides, 42 minutes.

Making Sense Visually. Washington, D.C.: Association for Educational Communications and Technology, 1969. Sound filmstrip, 76 frames.

Oh, C. Y. *Introduction to the Preparation of Instructional Materials.* 32 slide-tape sets, textbook, and student manual. Edmonton, Canada: Avent Media, 1980.

Photography: How It Works. Rochester, N.Y.: Kodak, 1979. 16-mm film, 12 minutes.

The Simple Camera. Washington, D.C.: Association for Educational Communications and Technology. 12 filmstrips.

A Visual Fable. Washington, D.C.: Association for Educational Communications and Technology, 1973. Sound filmstrip, with record or cassette. 18 minutes.

Possible Projects

3-A. Select a visual and classify it using the three types given in this chapter.

3-B. Design some instructional activities to improve visual literacy skills of learners you now work with or might in the future. Your description of the lesson should include the materials (or a description of the materials), the role/activities of the students, and the role of the instructor.

3-C. Select a series of photographs from your own collection and criticize them in terms of composition.

3-D. Select a visual or a display and appraise it in terms of intended audience, objectives, arrangement, balance, and color.

3-E. Design a rough layout of a display related to your interests. Appraise it in terms of arrangement, balance, and color.

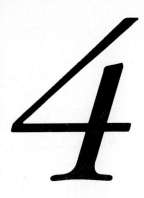

Nonprojected Visuals

Objectives

After studying this chapter, you should be able to:

1. Define *realia*.

2. Discuss the special advantages of models and/or realia for instruction.

3. Discuss five purposes of and the procedures for conducting a field trip.

4. List five attributes (advantages and/or limitations) of nonprojected still pictures.

5. Describe at least three classroom applications of still pictures.

6. Identify five criteria for selecting still pictures and apply the "Appraisal Checklist: Still Pictures" to actual materials.

7. Demonstrate at least three techniques (showmanship tips) to enhance the use of still pictures with a group.

8. Define *graphic material* and describe three types of graphics.

9. Describe five applications for graphic materials in your teaching.

10. Apply the "Appraisal Checklist: Graphic Materials" to actual materials.

11. Identify two methods of preserving nonprojected visuals and state three reasons for doing so.

12. Compare the advantages/limitations of rubber cement mounting with the advantages/limitations of dry mounting.

13. Describe five formats or devices for displaying visuals.

14. Demonstrate at least three techniques (showmanship tips) for improving your utilization of chalkboards.

15. State a major advantage that cloth boards and magnetic boards have over chalkboards.

16. Demonstrate five techniques (showmanship tips) to enhance the use of flip charts.

17. Discuss three purposes for exhibits and dioramas.

Lexicon
realia
study print
graphics
bar graph
line graph
circle graph
pictorial graph
dry mounting
lamination
multipurpose board
flip chart
exhibit
diorama

Many of the instructional materials discussed in this chapter are so common that instructors are inclined to underestimate their pedagogical value. Materials don't have to be exotic or expensive to be useful. Small can indeed be beautiful, and inexpensive can be effective! In fact, in some situations—for instance, with lack of electricity, isolation, a low budget, or small class size—these simpler materials may be the only media available.

Even though the focus in this chapter is on nonprojected visuals, the discussion includes some topics that technically might not be classified as visuals. These include real objects, models, field trips, and the devices used to display visuals—chalkboards, cloth boards, magnetic boards, and flip charts.

The discussion in this chapter begins with real objects and models, then moves to field trips, still pictures, and graphic materials, as well as techniques and methods for displaying all of these materials.

REALIA

Realia—real things: objects such as coins, tools, artifacts, plants, animals, etc.—are some of the most accessible, intriguing, and involving materials in educational use. The gerbils that draw a crowd in the kindergarten, the terrarium that introduces middle schoolers to the concept of ecology, the collection of Revolutionary era coins, the frogs dissected in the college biology laboratory, the real baby being bathed in the parenting class . . . just a few examples of the potentials of realia for elucidating the obscure and stimulating the imagination.

Being, by definition, concrete objects, realia are the instructional aids most closely associated with the bottom of Dale's Cone of Experience: direct purposeful experience (see Chapter 1). As such, they are ideal media for introducing learners to a new subject. Used as part of concept learning, they supply flesh-and-blood mental images, giving meaning to otherwise merely abstract words.

Realia may be used as is or modified to enhance instructional utility. Examples of modification include:

- Cutaways—devices such as machines with one wall cut away to allow close observation of the inner workings.
- Specimens—actual plants, animals, or parts thereof preserved for convenient inspection.
- Realia exhibits—collections of artifacts, often of a scientific or historical nature, brought together with printed information to illustrate a point.

Besides their obvious virtues as means of presenting information, raising questions, and giving hands-on learning experiences, realia also can play a valuable role in the evaluation phase of instruction. Real objects can be displayed in a central location with learners directed to identify them, classify them, describe their func-

▲ *Figure 4.1*
Nonprojected visuals are the most widely used media in many isolated, rural areas around the world.

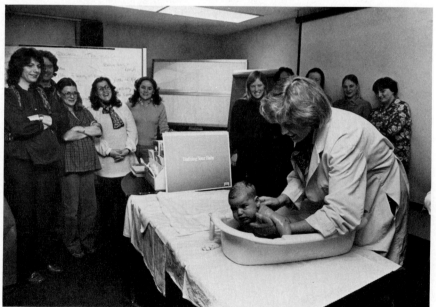

▲ *Figure 4.2*
There is no substitute for the real thing when learning some tasks.

tioning, discuss their utility, or compare and contrast them. Such a testing situation emphasizes the real-world application of the topic of study, aids transfer of training, and helps transcend the merely verbal level of learning.

MODELS

*M*ODELS are *three-dimensional representations of a real thing.* A model may be larger, smaller, or the same size as the object it represents. It may be complete in detail or simplified for instructional purposes. Indeed, models may provide learning experiences real things cannot provide. Important details can, for example, be accented by color. Some models can be disassembled to provide interior views not possible with the real thing.

Models of almost anything, from insects to airplanes, can be purchased for classroom use. A wide variety of plastic model kits are also available for assembly by you and/or your students. Assembly itself can be instructional. Classroom construction of plastic model kits appeals to children of all ages (and, indeed, to adults) and can stimulate inquiry and discovery. Assembly activities help sharpen both cognitive and psychomotor skills.

Familiarize yourself with your model before using it in classroom instruction. Practice your presentation. If your model is a working one, be sure you know just how it works. Be sure your audience does not get the wrong impression of the size, shape, or color of the real object if the model differs from it in these respects. Whenever feasible, encourage your students to handle and manipulate the model. It is a good idea to store models out of sight when not being used for

▲ *Figure 4.3*
A cutaway of a machine reveals the hidden components.

▲ *Figure 4.4*
Cultural artifacts come to life when presented in a well-designed exhibit.

instruction. Left standing around, they are likely to take students' attention from other classroom activities.

Mock-ups—simplified representations of complex devices or processes—are prevalent in industrial training. By highlighting essential elements and eliminating distracting details, mock-ups clarify the complex. They are sometimes constructed as working models to illustrate the basic operations of a real device. This allows individuals or small groups to manipulate the mock-up at their own convenience, working with the concept until they comprehend it. The most sophisticated type of mock-up, the simulator, is discussed in Chapter 12.

Models and realia are the recommended media when realism is essential to learning: three-dimensional concepts; tasks that require identification by size, shape, or color; hands-on or laboratory practice.

When considering students' learning styles, teachers often give models and realia a high priority. Most learners—including adults—when given a choice express a preference for hands-on experiences rather than passive listening. "Please touch" is a most welcomed invitation.

FIELD TRIPS

T HE *field trip—an excursion outside the classroom to study real processes, people, and objects*—often grows out of student needs for firsthand experience. It makes possible the utilization of phenomena that cannot be brought into the classroom for observation and study. Field trips may include a trip of a few minutes into the school yard to observe a tree, a trek across the street to see construction work, or perhaps a longer trip of several days to tour historical locations. Popular field-trip sites include zoos, museums, public buildings, and parks.

Real-life experiences such as field trips are particularly valuable

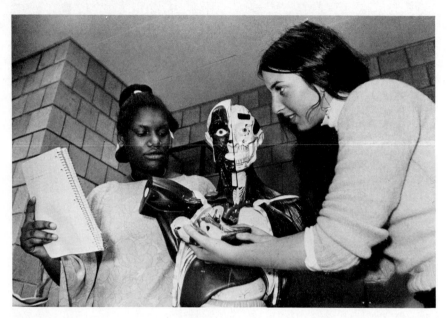

▲ *Figure 4.5*
An anatomical model, being three-dimensional, is a more concrete referent than a photograph, drawing, or even a motion picture.

▲ *Figure 4.6*
A mock-up of an engine provides the trainee a full-scale working model with only distracting details deleted.

▲ *Figure 4.7*
Field trips provide students with opportunities for firsthand observations.

for learners who have a "kinesthetic" perceptual strength; that is, a preference for bodily involvement. This preference is very common among young children, of course. As they grow older, they tend to develop a stronger ability to learn from other sensory channels—seeing and listening. But even adults enjoy and profit from field experiences. In fact, Dunn found that 70 percent of the adults studied preferred learning from real-life experiences versus 5 percent for reading and 26 percent for seeing or reading.*

For a field trip to be justified, it should grow out of and be directly related to the regular course of study. Objectives should be developed for the field trip. There should be lead-in as well as follow-up activities. The lead-in prepares the students for the field trip; the follow-up helps the pupils get the most from the field trip.

A field trip can serve many pedagogical purposes:

- Provide a source of enrichment for factual information read in textbooks and make words on the printed page meaningful
- Improve attitudes, expand understanding, and increase skills
- Provide firsthand experiences with objects, places, situations, and human relationships that cannot be provided in the classroom
- Sharpen awareness of the students' environment
- Expose students to careers that they might want to pursue

* Kenneth J. Dunn. "Measuring the Productivity Preferences of Adults" in *Student Learning Styles and Brain Behavior*. Reston, Va.: National Association of Secondary School Principals, 1982.

- Blend the classroom, the immediate community, and the larger world into a more meaningful whole.

The evaluation, or follow-up, is an equally vital aspect of a field trip. If the purpose for making the trip is to get additional factual information, the evaluation will be more formal. If the objectives are the formation of attitudes and appreciations, follow-up activities might include discussion, role playing, or creative art projects. Whatever form it takes, the follow-up activity should be used to assess the success of the trip. Both the content covered and possible ways to improve future trips should be addressed.

STILL PICTURES

*S*TILL *pictures* are *photographic (or photographlike) representations of people, places, and things.* The still pictures most commonly used in instruction are photographs, postcards, illustrations from books, periodicals, catalogs, etc., and *study prints (oversized illustrations* commercially prepared to accompany specific instructional units).

Advantages

Nonprojected still pictures can translate abstract ideas into a more realistic format. They allow instruction to move down from the level of verbal symbols in Dale's Cone of Experience to the more concrete level of still pictures.

They are readily available in books (including textbooks), magazines, newspapers, catalogs, and calendars. In addition, you may purchase large study prints for use with groups of students from educational supply companies, or you may obtain them from your media center or library.

Still pictures are easy to use because they do not require any equipment. They are relatively inexpensive. Many can be obtained at little or no cost. Still pictures can be used in many ways at all levels of instruction and in all disciplines.

▲ *Figure 4.8*
Nonprojected visuals include models, photographs, maps, and charts.

Planning

A. Have a clear picture of the purpose and objectives of the trip.
B. Have a clear overview of the content of the trip. Preview the trip yourself.
C. Make arrangements with the school principal, the host, and other teachers (if they are involved). Secure consent of the parents for pupils to make the trip.
D. Arrange transportation.
E. Provide sufficient supervision. Emphasize appropriate dress. Set up safety precautions and ground rules.

Preparing

A. Clarify the purpose of the trip with the entire group. Build interest in the trip through preparatory activities such as
   Class discussion
   Stories
   Reports
   Films
   Teacher–pupil planning
B. Give explicit directions to the pupils regarding
   What to look for
   Questions to ask
   Information to be gathered
   Notes to be made
   Individual and/or committee assignments

Conducting

A. Arrive promptly at the field-trip site.
B. Encourage students to observe carefully and to ask questions.
C. Obtain available materials that can be used later.
D. Account for all pupils before starting the return trip.

Follow-Up

A. Conduct follow-up of the field trip with
   A discussion of how the trip related to the purpose
   Reports
   Projects
   Demonstrations
   Creative writing
   Independent individual research
   Exhibits of pictures, maps, charts, graphs, drawings, etc.
B. Write a thank-you letter to the host, guides, parent chaperones, drivers, and others who were instrumental in conducting the field trip. Notes written by the class or a student committee are most appreciated.

Limitations

Some photographs are simply too small for use before a group. It is possible to enlarge any picture, but that can be an expensive process; however, the opaque projector (described in Chapter 5) can be used to project an enlarged image before a group.

Still pictures are two-dimensional. The lack of three-dimensionality in a picture can be compensated for by providing a series of pictures of the same object or scene from several different angles or positions. They do not show motion. However, a series of sequential still pictures can suggest motion (Figure 4.10).

Applications

There are numerous applications of nonprojected still pictures. Photographs may be used in a variety of ways. Teacher-made and/or student-made photographs may be used to illustrate and to help teach specific lesson topics. Photographs of local architecture, for example, can illustrate a unit on architectural styles. (In this case, the students' skill in "reading" a visual could be reinforced by the instructor's pointing out that merely looking at the buildings in our environment is not the same as really "seeing" them.) Photographs taken on field trips can be valuable sources of information for classroom follow-up activities.

Students can and should understand that textbook pictures are not decorations, but are intended to be study aids and should be used as such. Students should be encouraged to "read" them as aids to learning. Skill in decoding

▲ *Figure 4.9*
The smaller flash cards show details of the larger picture.

ences. In geography they may help illustrate relationships between peoples and their environments that, because of space limitations, could not easily be depicted in textbook pictures.

All types of nonprojected still pictures may be used in testing and evaluation. They are particularly helpful with objectives requiring identification of people, places, or things.

Nonprojected still pictures may also be used to stimulate creative expression such as the telling or writing of stories or the composing of poetry.

GRAPHIC MATERIALS

O UR second major category of nonprojected visuals is graphic materials, often referred to simply as graphics. *Graphics are nonphotographic, two-dimensional materials designed specifically to communicate a message to the viewer.* They often include verbal as well as symbolic visual cues.

As a group, graphics demand special caution in use by instructors. Because the images are visually symbolic rather than fully

textbook pictures may also be included in instructional objectives to motivate the learners to use them for study purposes. The quality and quantity of illustrations are, of course, important factors in textbook choice. See "Appraisal Checklist: Still Pictures," p. 106. Pictures from newspapers and periodicals may be used in similar ways.

Study prints—photographic enlargements printed in a durable form for individual use—also have many applications in the instructional setting. They are especially helpful in the study of processes—the production of iron or paper, for example, or the operation of the internal combustion engine. They are also very useful in teaching the social sci-

▲ *Figure 4.10*
A series of still pictures can approximate the impression of a motion picture sequence.

Appraisal Checklist: Still Pictures

Title (or content of picture) * _____

Series Title (if applicable) _____

Source _____ Date _____ Cost _____

Subject area _____

Intended audience _____

Objectives (stated or implied):

Brief Description:

Entry Capabilities Required:

- Prior subject-matter knowledge/vocabulary
- Reading ability
- Other:

Rating	High		Medium		Low	Comments
Relevance to objectives	☐	☐	☐	☐	☐	
Authenticity/accuracy of picture	☐	☐	☐	☐	☐	
Clarity (uncluttered by irrelevant distracting elements)	☐	☐	☐	☐	☐	
Timeliness; avoids out-of-date elements, such as dress	☐	☐	☐	☐	☐	
Clarity of scale (familiar objects imply size of unfamiliar)	☐	☐	☐	☐	☐	
Legibility for classroom use	☐	☐	☐	☐	☐	
Technical quality	☐	☐	☐	☐	☐	

Strong Points:

Weak Points:

Recommended action _____

Reviewer _____

Position _____

Date _____

In a psychology course, for the unit on experimental methods, the students use the photographs in their textbook as study aids, since they are excellent illustrations of the mazes and other experimental apparatus described in the text. During the class, the teacher draws attention to the photographs in the text and later asks various students to relate the pictures to the corresponding printed material. The teacher has also written the objectives for the course in a way that requires students to use the illustrations during their study.

Study prints are used by a fifth-grade teacher to show techniques for vegetable gardening. The teacher works with the children in small groups. While some of the students are working on other activities in the classroom and in the media center, the teacher gathers ten to twelve students around her to discuss the study prints. Her objective is for the students to be able to describe the proper method of spacing tomato plants. The students are shown the study prints and then are asked to describe what they see in terms of recommended procedures for measuring, planting, etc.

representational, they leave more room for viewers to misinterpret the intended meaning. This phenomenon was discussed in Chapter 3. As one example, research on newspaper readers' interpretations of editorial cartoons indicates that a large proportion of viewers may draw conclusions that are the *opposite* of what the artist intended. Psychologists find that people tend to "project" their own hopes, fears, and preconceptions into images or verbal messages that are ambiguous. This is the basis of the Rorschach or "inkblot" diagnostic test. The younger or less visually literate the audience, the more guidance the instructor will have to provide to ensure that the intended message is conveyed.

Let us explore five types of graphics commonly found in the classroom situation: drawings (including sketches and diagrams), charts, graphs, posters, and cartoons.

Drawings

Drawings, sketches, and diagrams *employ graphic arrangement of lines to represent persons, places, things, and concepts.* Drawings are, in general, more finished and representational than sketches, which are likely to lack detail. Stick figures, for example, may be said to be sketches. Diagrams are usually intended to show relationships or to help explain processes, such as how something works or how it is constructed (Figure 4.11).

Use of drawings may be similar to use of photographic still pictures. Drawings are readily found in textbooks and other classroom materials. They can be used in all phases of instruction, from introduction of the topic through evaluation. Because they are likely to be less detailed and more to the instructional point than photographic materials, they are easily understood by students of all ages.

Teacher-made drawings can be very effective teaching and learning devices. They can be drawn on the chalkboard (or some other appropriate surface) to coincide with specific aspects of the instructional unit. They can also be used as substitutes for or adjuncts to still pictures. For example, stick figures can be quickly and easily drawn to show motion in an otherwise static representation.

Charts

Charts are *graphic representations of abstract relationships such as chronologies, quantities, and hierarchies.* They appear fre-

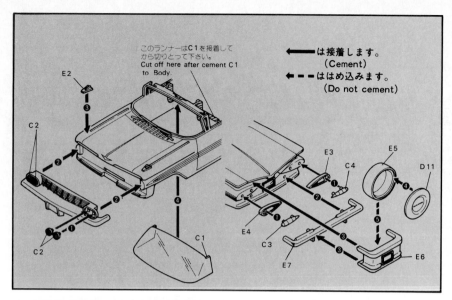

▲ *Figure 4.11*
The use of visual symbols reduces drastically the need for words in this multilingual diagram for assembling a scale-model plastic automobile.

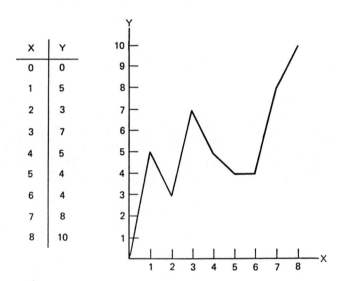

X	Y
0	0
1	5
2	3
3	7
4	5
5	4
6	4
7	8
8	10

▲ *Figure 4.12*
A line graph can make a table of data much easier to interpret.

most important thing to keep in mind is "keep it simple."

A well-designed chart should communicate its message primarily through the visual channel. The verbal material should supplement the visual, not the reverse.

Graphs

Graphs provide a *visual representation of numerical data.* They also illustrate *relationships between units of the data and trends in the data.* Many tabular charts can be converted into graphs, as shown in Figure 4.12. Data can generally be interpreted more quickly in graph form than in tabular form. Graphs are also more visually interesting. There are four major types of graphs: bar, pictorial, circle, and line. The type you choose to use will largely depend on the complexity of the information you wish to present and the graph-interpretation skills of your audience.

Posters

Posters incorporate *visual combinations of images, lines, color, and words* and are intended to catch and hold attention at least long enough to *communicate a brief message,* usually a persuasive one. To be effective, posters must be colorful and dynamic. They must grab attention and communicate their message quickly. One drawback in using posters is that their message is quickly blunted by familiarity. Consequently, they should not be left on display for too long a time. Commercial billboards are an example of posters on a very large scale.

Posters can be used effectively in numerous learning situations. They can stimulate interest in a new topic, a special class, or a school event. They may be employed for motivation—luring

quently in textbooks and training manuals as tables and flowcharts. They also are published as wall charts for group viewing in the form of organization charts, classification charts (e.g., periodic table), and time lines.

A chart should have a clear, well-defined instructional purpose. In general (especially for younger students), it should

express only one major concept or configuration of concepts. If you are developing your own charts, be sure they contain the minimum of visual and verbal information needed for understanding. A cluttered chart is a confusing chart. If you have a lot of information to convey, develop a series of simple charts rather than a single complex one. The

Types of Charts

Organization charts show the relationship or "chain of command" in an organization such as a company, corporation, civic group, or government department. Usually they deal with the interrelationship of personnel or departments.

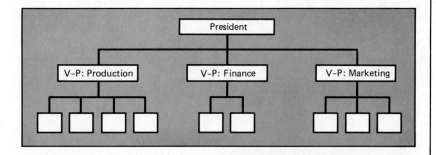

Classification charts are similar to organization charts but are used chiefly to classify or categorize objects, events, or species. A common type of classification chart is one showing the taxonomy of animals and plants according to natural characteristics.

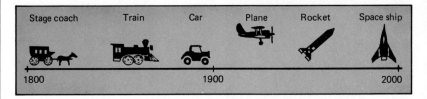

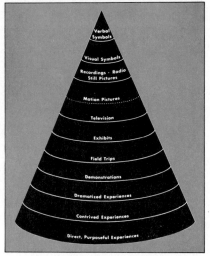

Time lines illustrate chronological relationships between events. They are most often used to show time relationships of historical events or the relationship of famous people and these events. Pictures or drawings can be added to the time line to illustrate important concepts. Time lines are very helpful for summarizing the time sequence of a series of events.

Flowcharts (or process charts) show a sequence, a procedure, or, as the name implies, the flow of a process. Flowcharts are usually drawn horizontally and show how different activities, ingredients, or procedures merge into a whole.

Tabular charts (or tables) contain numerical information, or data. They are also convenient for showing time information when the data are presented in columns, as in timetables for railroads and airlines.

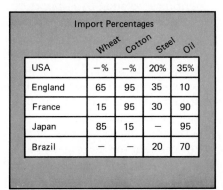

Import Percentages				
	Wheat	Cotton	Steel	Oil
USA	−%	−%	20%	35%
England	65	95	35	10
France	15	95	30	90
Japan	85	15	−	95
Brazil	−	−	20	70

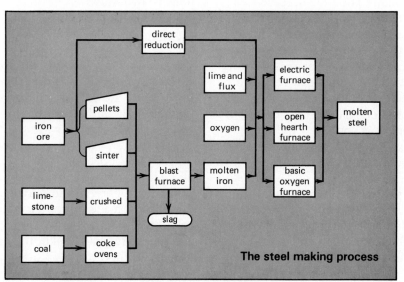

The steel making process

students to a school meeting or to the media center, for example, or encouraging them to read more. In industrial education courses, science laboratories, and other situations where danger may be involved, posters can be used to remind students of safety factors ("Always wear your safety glasses."). Posters can be used to promote good health practices ("Don't Smoke!"). An effective teaching and learning technique is to have students design posters as part of a class project—during fire prevention week or dental health month, etc.

Posters may be obtained from a variety of sources. Commercial poster companies publish catalogs containing pictures of their wares. Other companies and advertising organizations have posters available without cost to teachers for use in their classrooms. Two of the most common sources of posters are airlines and travel agen-

cies. Movie posters and political posters are also available. Stores and supermarkets are often willing to give posters (and other display materials) to teachers when they are no longer needed. And, of course, you can make your own posters.

Appendix B gives further guidance on obtaining free and inexpensive materials.

Cartoons

Cartoons, line drawings that are rough caricatures of real people and events, are perhaps the most popular and familiar graphic format. They appear in a wide variety of print media—newspapers, periodicals, textbooks, etc.—and range from comic strips intended primarily to entertain to drawings intended to make important social or political comments. Humor and satire are mainstays of the cartoonist's skill.

Cartoons are easily and quickly read and appeal to children and adults alike. The best of them contain wisdom as well as wit. Thus, they can often be used by the teacher to make or reinforce a point of instruction. As discussed earlier, appreciation and interpretation may depend on the experience and sophistication of the viewer. Research studies consistently have found that people tend to project their own feelings and prejudices into editorial cartoons. For example, a politician shown slinging mud at his opponent may be seen by supporters as a hero punishing the "wicked." Further, because they usually refer to contemporary characters dealing with current issues and events, editorial cartoons quickly become dated. Today's immediately recognized caricature becomes tomorrow's nonentity. Be sure that the cartoons you use for instructional purposes are

Types of Graphs

Bar graphs are easy to read and can be used with elementary age students. The height of the bar is the measure of the quantity being represented. The width of all bars should be the same to avoid confusion. A single bar can be divided to show parts of a whole. It is best to limit the quantities being compared to eight or less; otherwise the graph becomes cluttered and confusing. The bar graph, a one-scale graph, is particularly appropriate for comparing similar items at different times or different items at the same time; for example, the height of one plant over time or the heights of several students at any given time. The bar graph shows variation in only one dimension.

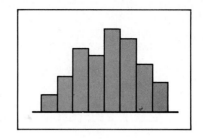

Pictorial graphs are an alternate form of the bar graph, in which a series of simple drawings is used to represent the value. Pictorial graphs are visually interesting and appeal to a wide audience, especially young students. However, they are slightly more difficult to read than bar graphs. Since pictorial symbols are used to represent a specific quantity, partial symbols are used to depict fractional quantities. To help avoid confusion in such cases, print values below or to the right of each line of figures.

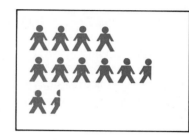

Circle (or pie) graphs are relatively easy to interpret. In this type of graph, a circle or "pie" is divided into segments, each representing a part or percentage of the whole. One typical use of the circle graph is to depict tax-dollar allocations. The combined segments of a circle graph should, of course, equal 100 percent. Areas of special interest may be shown separately from the others, just as a piece of pie can be illustrated separately from a whole pie.

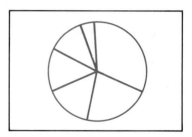

Line graphs are the most precise and complex of all graphs. Line graphs are based on two scales at right angles. Each point has a value on the vertical scale and a value on the horizontal scale. Lines (or curves) are drawn to connect the points. Line graphs show variations in *two* dimensions—how two or more groups of quantities changed over time. For example, a graph can show the relation between pressure and temperature when the volume of a gas is held constant. Because line graphs are precise, they are very useful in plotting trends. They can also help simplify a mass of complex information.

within the experiential and intellectual range of your students.

PRESERVING NONPROJECTED VISUALS

ONE drawback in using nonprojected visuals in the classroom is that they are easily soiled or otherwise damaged as they are passed from student to student. Repeated display, storage, and retrieval can also add to wear and tear. Mounting and laminating are the two most effective preservation techniques, and they can contribute to the instructional effectiveness of nonprojected visuals.

Mounting Nonprojected Visuals

Mount nonprojected visuals on construction paper, cardboard, or other such materials of sufficient durability. The color of the mounting material should not draw attention away from the visual. It is generally a good idea

Appraisal Checklist: Graphic Materials

FORMAT

Title (or content of graphic) _____

Series Title (if applicable) _____

Source _____

Date _____   Cost _____

Subject area _____

Intended audience _____

☐ drawing
☐ chart
☐ graph
☐ poster
☐ cartoon

Objectives (stated or implied):

Brief Description:

Entry Capabilities Required:
- Prior subject-matter knowledge/vocabulary
- Reading ability
- Mathematical ability
- Other:

Rating	High		Medium		Low	Comments
Relevance to objectives	☐	☐	☐	☐	☐	
Accuracy of information	☐	☐	☐	☐	☐	
Likely to arouse/maintain interest	☐	☐	☐	☐	☐	
Likely to be comprehended clearly	☐	☐	☐	☐	☐	
Technical quality	☐	☐	☐	☐	☐	
Legibility for use (size and clarity)	☐	☐	☐	☐	☐	
Simplicity (clear, unified design)	☐	☐	☐	☐	☐	
Appropriate use of color	☐	☐	☐	☐	☐	
Appropriateness of accompanying verbal information	☐	☐	☐	☐	☐	
Provisions for discussion	☐	☐	☐	☐	☐	

Strong Points:

Weak Points:

Recommended action _____

Reviewer _____
Position _____
Date _____

- **U**se large visuals that everyone can see simultaneously. (If visuals are not large enough for all to see, use one of the projection techniques described in Chapter 5.)

- Use simple materials.

- Hold visuals steady when showing them to a group by resting them against a desk or table or by putting them on an easel.

- Limit the number of pictures used in a given period of time. It is better to use a few visuals well than to overwhelm your audience with an overabundance of underexplained visuals.

- Use just one picture at a time except for purposes of comparison. Lay one picture flat before going on to the next.
- Keep your audience's attention and help them learn from a visual by asking direct questions about it.
- Teach your audience to interpret visuals. See the visual literacy techniques in Chapter 3.
- Display questions pertaining to each visual alongside it. Cover the answers with flaps of paper. Have each student immediately check his or her own response for accuracy.
- Provide written or verbal cues to highlight important information contained in the visuals.

to use pastel or neutral tones rather than brilliant or primary colors. Using one of the minor colors in the visual as the color for the mounting can enhance harmony. The total effect of your mounting should be neat and pleasing to the eye. Borders, for example, should be evenly cut, with side borders of equal width and the bottom border slightly wider than the top.

A variety of glues, cements, and pastes are available for mounting purposes. When used according to directions, almost all of them are effective. Some white glues, however, are likely to cause wrinkles in the picture when the adhesive dries, especially if used full strength. If you run into this problem, dilute the glue; for example, use four parts Elmer's glue to one part of water. Cover the entire back of the visual evenly with the adhesive before placing it on the mounting board. If excess adhesive seeps out around the edges, wipe it off with a damp cloth or sponge.

Glue sticks, marketed under names such as Stix-A-Lot and Pritt, may be used in place of liquid glues. They have the advantage of

▲ *Figure 4.15*
Glue sticks are convenient and effective for doing paste-ups and mounting small visuals.

not running out around the edges of the material. Rubber cement can eventually damage and discolor photographs. Glue sticks are less likely to do so (Figure 4.15).

Rubber Cement Mounting. One of the most commonly used adhesives for mounting purposes is rubber cement. It is designed specifically for use with paper products. It is easy to use and less

messy than many other liquid glues. Excess cement can easily be wiped away, and it is inexpensive. Rubber cement does, however, have two disadvantages. When the container is left uncovered for any length of time, the adhesive tends to dry out and thicken. Periodic doses of thinner (available commercially) may be necessary to keep the cement serviceable. A second disadvantage is

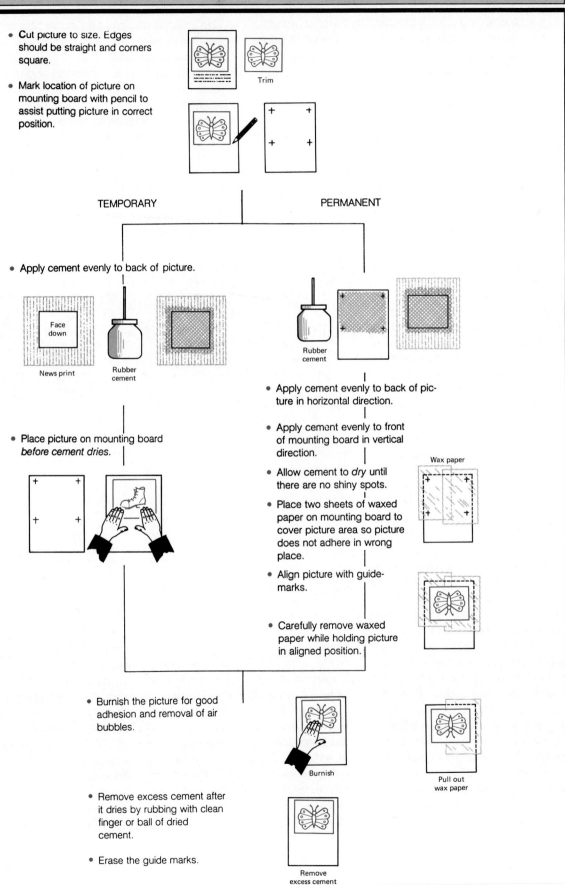

- Cut picture to size. Edges should be straight and corners square.
- Mark location of picture on mounting board with pencil to assist putting picture in correct position.

Trim

TEMPORARY   PERMANENT

- Apply cement evenly to back of picture.

Face down

News print

Rubber cement

Rubber cement

- Place picture on mounting board *before cement dries.*

- Apply cement evenly to back of picture in horizontal direction.

- Apply cement evenly to front of mounting board in vertical direction.

- Allow cement to *dry* until there are no shiny spots.

- Place two sheets of waxed paper on mounting board to cover picture area so picture does not adhere in wrong place.

- Align picture with guide-marks.

- Carefully remove waxed paper while holding picture in aligned position.

Wax paper

- Burnish the picture for good adhesion and removal of air bubbles.

Burnish

Pull out wax paper

- Remove excess cement after it dries by rubbing with clean finger or ball of dried cement.

- Erase the guide marks.

Remove excess cement

that the adhesive quality of rubber cement tends to diminish over a period of time. Constant exposure to dry air may eventually cause it to lose its grip. This disadvantage may be compensated for with special precautions as noted for permanent rubber cement mountings. However, even these will not last indefinitely.

Dry Mounting. Dry mounting employs a specially prepared paper impregnated with heat-sensitive adhesive. The paper is available in sheets and in rolls and is marketed under such names as Fusion-4000 and MT-5. The dry-mounting tissue bonds the backing material to the back of the visual. A dry-mount press is used to supply the heat and pressure necessary to activate the tissue's adhesive. The process is rapid and clean and results in permanent high-quality mounting.

One disadvantage of dry mounting is that it is relatively expensive. However, it is possible to dry mount visuals without a dry-mount press by using an ordinary household iron (see the "How To . . ." box on page 117).

Laminating Nonprojected Visuals

Lamination provides visuals with protection from wear and tear by covering them with clear plastic or plasticlike surfaces. Lamination helps to protect visuals against tears, scratches, and sticky fingers. Soiled surfaces can be wiped clean with a damp cloth.

Lamination also allows you to write on your visuals with a grease pencil or water-soluble ink for instructional purposes. The writing can be easily erased later with a damp cloth or sponge. A teacher of mathematics, for example, might write percentage figures on a laminated illustration of

a pizza or a pie in order to help teach the concept of fractions. You can also have students write on laminated materials to facilitate learner responses. When the lesson is completed, the markings can be erased and the material made ready for further teaching. Classroom materials other than nonprojected visuals (e.g., workbook pages) may also be laminated to add extra durability and to allow for erasable writing by teacher and students.

The simplest but also least effective technique for laminating visuals is to spray them with plastic from a can. More effective and durable procedures involve using sheets of clear plastic cut to size. Rubber cement may be used for adhesion. Apply the rubber cement to the face of the visual and to one side of the plastic sheet. Allow the adhesives to dry and then carefully press the plastic over the surface of the visual.

Clear plastic sheets with adhesive backing (such as Con-Tact shelf paper) are also available for laminating purposes. Remove the backing cover to expose the adhesive and carefully press the clear plastic sheet on the visual. Any portions of the plastic sheet that extend beyond the edges of the visual can be cut off or doubled back for additional protection.

Rolls of laminating film for use with a dry-mount press are available from commercial sources.

Filing and Storing Nonprojected Visuals

You will find it handy to have a system for filing, storing, and retrieving your nonprojected visuals. The nature of the filing system that you use will depend upon the number of nonprojected visuals in your collection and how you intend to use them. The simplest filing system usually

involves grouping them according to the teaching units in which they are used. Elementary teachers often categorize them by subject or curriculum area (e.g., math, science, language arts, social studies) and then subdivide them (e.g., seasons, foreign countries, jobs, addition, subtraction, place value, telling time). Some instructors, especially those who teach just one subject, set up their filing system according to the chapters in their textbook, the topics they cover, or objectives. Teachers who use just a few visuals sometimes file them with their other teaching materials for each lesson.

Noting the size of the visuals will help you determine the most appropriate storage container. Many teachers store their pictures in file folders or large mailing envelopes. If the pictures are slightly larger than the mailing envelopes, you can open the envelopes on two adjacent sides, and the envelope will serve as a useful pocket. If the pictures are considerably larger than the 9-by-11-inch file folders or the envelopes you have available, you can

▲ *Figure 4.16*
Large-format mounted visuals can be stored conveniently in an artist's portfolio.

Dry the mounting board and picture before trimming picture by placing in dry-mount press for about one minute at 225°F. Close press, but do *not* lock.

Place a sheet (either side up) of dry-mounting tissue over the *back* of the *untrimmed* picture, with sheet overlapping edges.

Attach the tissue to the back center of the picture with tip of a tacking iron set on "medium."

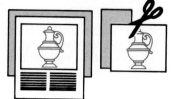

Turn picture and tissue over and trim both simultaneously to desired size. (A paper cutter works best, but razor knife with metal straight edge or scissors may be used.)

Place the picture and dry-mounting tissue on the mounting board and align in proper position.

Tack the tissue to the mounting board at two *opposite* corners.

Tacking iron

Cover mounting board and picture with clean paper on both sides.

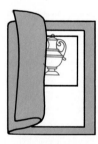

Place in dry-mount press preheated to 225°F for about one minute.

Remove from dry-mount press and allow the materials to cool. (Placing the cooling materials under a metal weight will help prevent curling.)

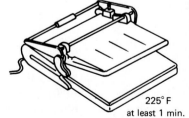

225° F
at least 1 min.

- **S**et the iron on "silk" or "rayon." Do *not* use steam.
- Follow the procedures described in "How to . . . Dry Mount Pictures." The tip of the household iron can be used in place of a tacking iron.
- Tack the tissue to the picture and the tissue to the mounting board as described.
- Place a sheet of clean paper over the top of the picture, dry-mounting tissue, and mounting-board combination.

- Holding the materials in position, carefully and slowly move the iron over them while applying pressure (see the accompanying pictures).
- Remove the paper and allow the mounting to cool. If the picture is not completely adhered to the mounting board, cover again and apply more heat and pressure.

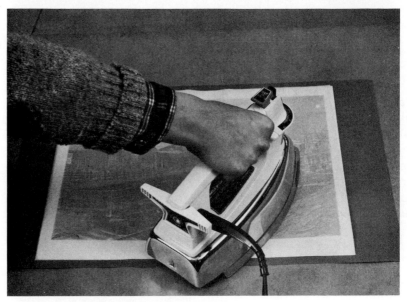

use artists' portfolios, which are available in various sizes up to 36 by 48 inches.

In addition to a workable filing system and proper size storage containers, you should have a clean, out-of-the-way place to store your visuals when they are not in use. The storage location can range from elaborate built-in drawers or filing cabinets to simple cardboard storage cartons. There is no problem in using cardboard cartons to store files of pictures and other visuals if you have a clean and dry location to place the cartons. Of course, the cartons should be readily accessible when you need them. Some teachers use the tops of closets in their classrooms or a corner of a supply room as storage spaces.

DISPLAY FORMATS

I F you are going to use nonprojected visuals, such as photographs, drawings, charts, graphs, or posters, you need a way to dis-

- **T**he dry-mount press should be heated to 225°F. If you live in an area with high humidity, you may get better results if you preheat the visual (to remove excess moisture) in the press for about one minute. Close the press but do not lock it.
- Cover the picture to be laminated with a piece of laminating film slightly larger than the picture. The inside of the roll (dull side) contains the heat-sensitive adhesive and should be toward the visual. Press the film onto the picture with your hands. Static electricity should cause the film to stay in place.
- Put the picture and laminating film in a cover of clean paper to protect the visual and to prevent the adhesive from getting onto the surfaces of the dry-mount press.
- Insert the material in the press for one minute. Remove it; if the adhesion is not complete, put it back into the press for another minute. It may be helpful to put a magazine or a $\frac{1}{4}$-inch stack of paper on top of the picture to increase the pressure and improve adhesion between the picture and the laminating film.

play them. Nonprojected visuals may be displayed in the classroom in a wide variety of ways, ranging from simply holding up a single visual in your hand to constructing elaborate exhibits for permanent display. Classroom items commonly used for display of nonprojected visuals include chalkboards, multipurpose boards, pegboards, bulletin boards, cloth boards, and magnetic boards. Flip charts may also be used for display of visuals. Exhibits, a display format incorporating a variety of materials such as realia and models along with visuals, are also common. How you display your visuals will depend upon a number of factors, including the nature of your audience, the nature of your visuals, the instructional setting, your lesson objectives, and, of course, the availability of the various display formats.

▲ *Figure 4.17*
The chalkboard is universally recognized as a flexible and economical display format.

Chalkboards

The most common display surface in the classroom is, of course, the chalkboard. Once called black-boards, they, like chalk, now come in a variety of colors. Although the chalkboard is most commonly used as a medium of verbal communication, it can be

- **P**ut extensive drawing or writing on the chalk-board before class. Taking too much time to write or draw creates restlessness and may lead to discipline problems.

- Organize in advance *what* you plan to write on the chalkboard and *where* you plan to write it.

- Cover material such as a test or extensive lesson materials with wrapping paper, newspaper, or a pull-down map until you are ready to use it.

- Eye contact with students is important! Face the class when you are talking. Do not talk to the board. Do not turn your back to the class any more than absolutely necessary.

- Vary your presentation techniques. Do not over-use or rely entirely on the chalkboard. Use hand-outs, the overhead projector, flip charts, and other media during instruction when appropriate.

- Print neatly rather than using script. For a 32-foot-long classroom, the letters should be 2- to $2\frac{1}{2}$-inches high and the lines forming the letters should be $\frac{1}{4}$-inch thick.

- Check the visibility of chalkboard from several positions around the room to be sure there is no glare on the board. In case of glare, move the board (if portable), or pull the window shades.

- If your printing normally runs uphill or downhill, use water soluble felt-tip pen markings as tempo-rary guidelines for straighter printing. The guide-lines will not be wiped off by a chalk eraser but may be washed off when no longer needed.

- Hold the chalk so that it does not make scratch-ing noises.

- Use colored chalk for emphasis, but don't over-use it.

- Move around so you do not block what you have written on the chalkboard. Do not stand in front of what you have written.

- Use chalkboard drawing aids such as rulers, chalkboard stencils, and templates (patterns) to save time and improve the quality of your drawings.

- For frequently drawn shapes, use a template cut from wood or heavy cardboard. A dresser drawer knob or empty thread spool mounted on the tem-plate makes it easier to hold in position while tracing around it.

- Outline your drawings with barely visible lines before class and then fill them in with bold lines in front of the class. Your audience wil think you are an artist!

---

used as a surface upon which to draw visuals (or pictures can be fastened to the molding above the chalkboard or placed in the chalk tray) to help illustrate instruc-tional units and serve as adjuncts to verbal communication. Graph-ics, such as sketches and dia-grams, or charts and graphs, may be drawn on the chalkboard for display to the class.

A chalkboard is such a com-monplace classroom item that instructors often neglect to give it the attention and respect it deserves as an instructional device. Using a chalkboard effec-tively requires conscious effort.

Multipurpose Boards

Some newer classrooms are equipped with multipurpose boards instead of chalkboards. As the name implies, they can be used for more than one purpose. They have a smooth white plastic surface and use special marking pens rather than chalk. They are cleaned with a damp cloth or spe-cial felt eraser. Sometimes called visual aid panels, they usually have a steel backing and can be used as a magnetic board for dis-play of visuals (Figure 4.18). The white nonglare surface is also suitable for projection of films, slides, and overhead transparen-cies. Materials (figures, letters, etc.) cut from thin plastic will adhere to the surface when rubbed in place.

Pegboards

Another popular display surface is the pegboard. It is particularly useful for displaying heavy

▲ *Figure 4.18*
Multipurpose boards are replacing chalkboards in business and industrial training classrooms and in some educational institutions.

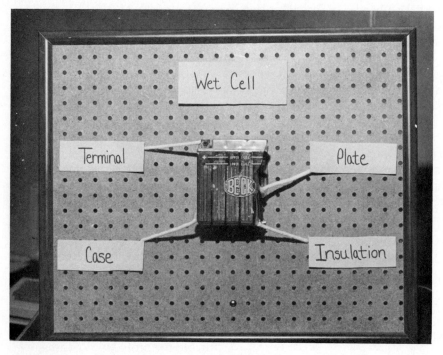

▲ *Figure 4.19*
Pegboards are especially useful for displaying heavy objects.

objects, three-dimensional materials, and visuals.

Pegboards are made of tempered masonite with $\frac{1}{8}$-inch holes drilled 1 inch apart. Pegboard material is usually $\frac{1}{8}$-inch thick and comes in 4-by-8-foot sheets which can be cut to any size. Special metal hooks and holders can be inserted into the pegboard to hold books, papers, and other objects. A variety of these special hooks are available in most hardware stores. Golf tees can also be inserted into the holes for holding lightweight materials such as posters and visuals mounted on cardboard. For a background effect, the entire pegboard surface can be covered with cloth or colored paper. Golf tees or the special hooks can then be inserted through the cloth or paper.

Bulletin Board Displays

The name *bulletin board* implies an area in which bulletins—brief news announcements of urgent interest—are posted for public notice. This may have been the original purpose and it may still be true in some cases, but it does not describe the most general use of these display spaces. Physically, a bulletin board is a *surface of variable size and shape made of a material that holds pins, thumbtacks, and other sharp fasteners without damage to the board.* In practice, bulletin board displays tend to serve three broad purposes: (1) decorative, (2) motivational, or (3) instructional.

The decorative bulletin board is probably the most common, certainly in schools. Its function would seem to be to lend visual stimulation to an environment that otherwise would be rather sterile. Thus, it could contribute to youngsters' aesthetic development. More often, though, it offers a tired, predictable cliché, typically based on a seasonal motif: September—autumn leaves; October—witches and pumpkins; November—pilgrims and Indians; December—Santa Claus, reindeer, and Christmas trees; January—snowflakes; February—Valentine hearts and presidential silhouettes; March—kites and shamrocks; April—showers; May—flowers. Do students tire of the predictability of such displays? No one seems to have asked. Perhaps the best justification for such

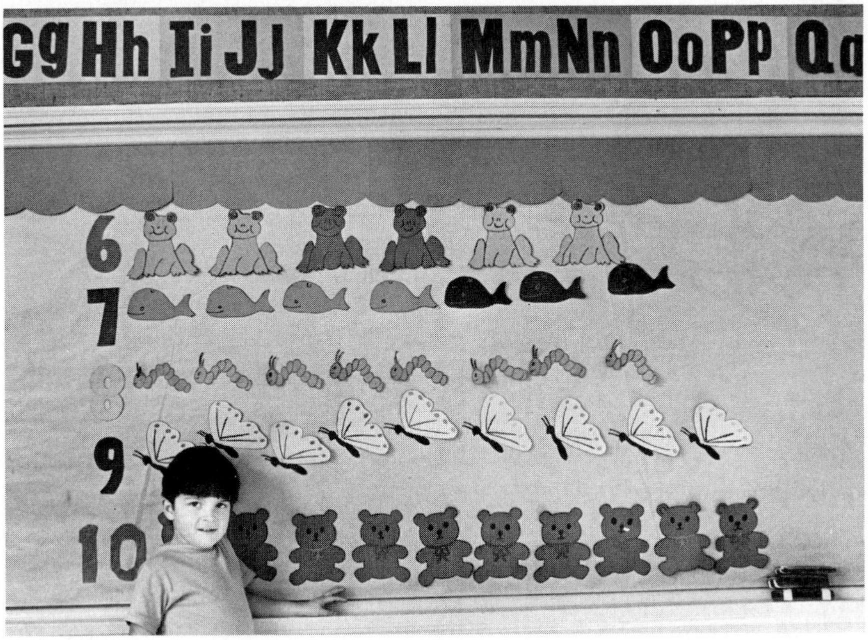

▲ *Figure 4.20*
Bulletin boards, long a standard in elementary classrooms, are now used increasingly in higher education and corporate settings.

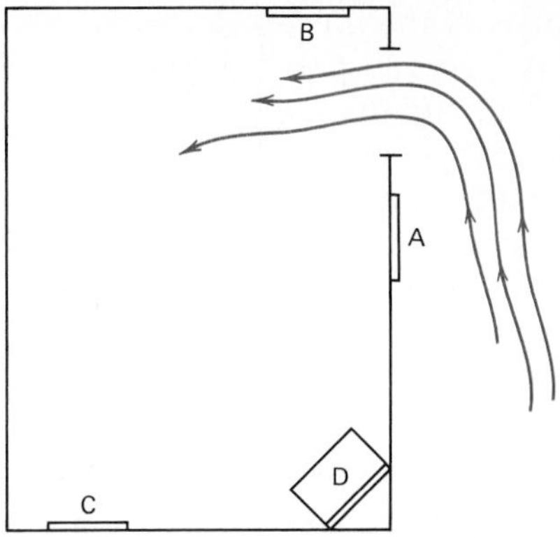

▲ *Figure 4.21*
The location of a display depends on its intended use. High-traffic locations (such as *A* and *B*) are most suitable for motivational messages and short announcements. Quiet corners (such as *C*) and individual learning centers (such as *D*) are appropriate for displays to be studied in some detail.

seasonal flourishes is the preservation of deeply ingrained cultural traditions.

Displaying student work exemplifies the motivational use of the bulletin board. The public recognition offered by such displays seems to play an important role in the life of the classroom. It fosters pride in achievement, reinforcing students' efforts to do a good job. It is also a relatively effortless display for the teacher to put together. The display of student work lends itself to combination with the decorative motif.

The third broad purpose is instructional, complementing the educational or training objectives being pursued within the formal curriculum. Rather than merely presenting static informational messages, many creative instructors design displays that actively invite participation. Such displays ask questions and give viewers some means of manipulating parts of the display to verify their

answers—flaps, pockets, dials, movable parts, and the like.

Another form of learner participation is to take part in the actual construction of the display. There are many fervent testimonials from teachers affirming the value of such activities to their students. For example, one language arts

teacher approached a unit on the family by requiring each student to cut out or draw a picture concerning the family (but it could not be an actual picture of a family). These pictures were combined into a montage that served as the centerpiece for a lively discussion of the symbolic signifi-

▲ *Figure 4.22*
The placement of a display should vary according to the average height of the intended viewers. A useful rule of thumb is to match the middle of the display with the viewer's eye level.

cance of the images depicted. Posting news photographs is a way of stimulating discussion of current events.

Bulletin boards need not always be attached permanently to the wall. Portable boards may be set on an easel for temporary display purposes or integrated into a learning center. The possible proliferation of such boards leads to a cautionary note: beware of clutter—too many competing visual messages will tend to drown them all out.

Cloth Boards

Cloth boards are constructed of *cloth stretched over a sturdy backing material such as plywood, Masonite, or heavy cardboard.* The cloth used for the board may be of various types, including flannel, felt, or hook-and-loop material.

Flannel is inexpensive and readily available. Pieces of flannel stick together when gentle pressure is applied. Visuals cut from flannel can be drawn on with felt-tip markers and put on the flannel board. You can also back still pictures and graphics with flannel. Coarse sandpaper sticks to flannel and can also be used to back visuals for attachment to the board. Pipe cleaners, available in a variety of colors, and fuzzy yarns stick to the flannel and can be used for drawing lines and letters. Felt, slightly more expensive than flannel, has the same properties. With flannel and felt, durability of adhesion is less than could be desired, so slant the board slightly to help prevent materials from slipping or falling off.

The best cloth board, and the most expensive, is made from hook-and-loop materials (Velcro and Teazlegraph). The hook-and-loop board has a fine but fuzzy surface composed of tiny, strong nylon loops. The material used for backing visuals and other items to be attached to the board has a coarse, hooklike texture. When pressed together, the two surfaces stick firmly. The hooklike material can be purchased in rolls or strips. One great advantage of the hook-and-loop board is that it can support large and heavy visuals, even entire books and three-dimensional objects. One square inch of the cloth can support up to ten pounds of properly backed visual material.

Cloth boards are particularly useful for instruction requiring that visuals be easily moved around to illustrate a process or sequence. They can also be easily removed from the board.

Teachers of reading and other creative activities often use the cloth board to illustrate stories, poems, and other reading materials. Visuals depicting characters and scenes in a story, for example, can be placed on the board and moved around as the story unfolds. Creativity may be further encouraged by allowing the children to manipulate cloth-board materials. Shy children may particularly profit from this kind of activity. It encourages them to speak through the visual representations of story characters as they manipulate illustrations on the board.

Be sure you have proper storage space for your cloth board and cloth-board visuals when not

▲ *Figure 4.23*
Cloth boards are often used to involve students in storytelling.

The base of the cloth board can be a piece of plywood, particle board, or heavy cardboard of whatever size you desire. Tan or gray materials make a good background. Cut the cloth material several inches larger than the board. Stretch the cloth tightly over the edges of the board and fasten it with small nails, thumbtacks, staples, or tape. Covering the face of the board with white glue (Elmer's glue) before covering it will help the cloth to adhere to the board. Do not put the glue on too heavily, or it will soak through the cloth and appear unsightly, even though it dries clear.

A two-sided cloth board can be made by sewing two pieces of cloth together in the form of a bag. Two different colors of cloth can be used and give you a choice of backgrounds. The wood base or heavy cardboard is then inserted into the bag and the open end sewn or pinned in place. Pinning it in place allows you to remove the cloth in order to clean it.

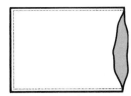

Make a bag by sewing three sides of the cloth.

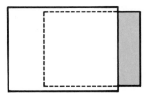

Turn it inside out and insert a stiff backing

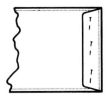

Pin the open end in place.

◀ *Figure 4.24*
Magnetic boards allow quick manipulation of materials.

in use. Proper storage will help keep them clean and prevent them from being bent or torn. If possible, store your materials on a flat surface rather than stacking them up against a wall. If you use sandpaper backing on your visuals, put paper between them during storage. Sandpaper can scratch the surface of visuals.

Magnetic Boards

Magnetic boards serve much the same purpose as cloth boards, but their adhesion is due to magne-

◀ *Figure 4.25*
Flip charts are standard equipment in the sales and marketing classrooms at AT&T Communications.

tism. Visuals are backed with magnets and then placed on the metal surface of the board. Magnetic boards, magnets, and flexible strips of magnetic materials for use in backing are available commercially. Plastic lettering with magnetic backing is available from supply stores and can be used for captioning visuals.

Any metal surface in the classroom that a magnet is attracted to can serve as a magnetic board. For example, some chalkboards are backed with steel and will thus attract magnet-backed visuals. Chalk can be used on such chalkboards for captioning or to depict lines of association between visuals. Steel cabinets and metal walls and doors can be used as magnetic boards.

You can make your own magnetic board from a thin sheet of galvanized iron, a cookie sheet, a lap tray, or any similar thin sheet of metal. Paint the sheets in the color of your choice with paint designed for use on metal surfaces or cover with Con-Tact paper. Unpainted surfaces are likely to be unattractive and to

cause glare. Another alternative is to fasten steel screening to a non-metal surface (plywood, perhaps) and cover it with a piece of cloth.

The major advantage of magnetic boards is that they provide for easier and quicker maneuverability of visuals than even cloth boards do. For example, magnetic boards are often used by physical education instructors to demonstrate rapid changes in player positions. Magnetic boards also provide greater adhesive quality. Visuals displayed on a magnetic board are not likely to slip or fall. They move only when you *want* to move them.

Flip Charts

A *flip chart* usually refers to a *pad of large-sized paper fastened together at the top and mounted on a wooden or metal easel.* The individual sheets each hold a limited verbal/visual message and are arranged for sequential presentation to a small group. The messages can be written extemporaneously while the presenter is talking or can be prepared ahead

of time and revealed one at a time. Commercially produced materials are also available in this format; they are especially prevalent in reading and science instruction and military training. Pre-prepared visual sequences are especially useful for instruction involving sequential steps in a process. Each sheet can be displayed and discussed before flipping it over and moving on to the next one. The diagrams or words can serve as cues, reminding the presenter of the next point in the presentation.

The most common use of flip charts, though, is for the extemporaneous drawing of key illustrations and key words to supplement a stand-up presentation. Therefore, it is an extremely versatile, convenient, and inexpensive media format. The flip chart requires no electrical power, has no moving parts to wear out, can be used in a wide range of lighting conditions, is portable, and requires only a marking pen as peripheral equipment. Next to the chalkboard it is the most "user-friendly" audiovisual tool.

- **D**etermine the number of pages you wish to use and stack them evenly.
- Fasten them together with staples or by some other means to assure they will remain in position. If there is a likelihood you will want to change the sequence of the pages for instructional purposes, use removable fastening pins.
- Fasten a cover of heavy paper or light cardboard to the sheets. Two thicknesses of covering may be used for extra durability.
- Hinge the cover and sheets together at the top.
- For even more rigidity, the assembled flip chart may be mounted on light wood or heavy cardboard. The sheets can be held in place by putting a strip of cardboard or light wood on the face of the chart through which bolts can be inserted to make contact with the backing. Use wing nuts to fasten the bolts. If the backing is cardboard, heavy tape, such as duct tape or bookbinding tape, can be used to secure the sheets to the backing.
- The inside covers of the flip chart may be treated with special "blackboard paint," thus giving you a small portable chalkboard to work with in your presentation. You can also convert the inside covers into miniature display boards by lining them with cloth or metal.

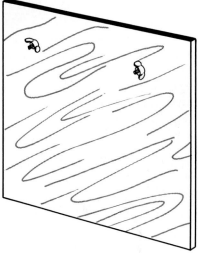

- **K**eep the lettering and visuals simple but large enough for everyone to see.

- Use marking pens that provide sharp contrast but will not bleed through to the next sheet.

- Talk to the audience, not to the flip chart.

- Avoid blocking students' view of the flip chart.

- Be sure your materials are in proper sequence.

- Reveal sheets only when you are ready to discuss them, not before.

- Print rather than using cursive lettering.

- Be sure the flip chart is securely fastened so it will not fall apart during your presentation. (The sudden collapse of your flip chart may get a laugh, but not the kind of laugh you may want.)

- Put summary points on a separate sheet rather than paging back as you make your summary.

◀ *Figure 4.26*
A complex exhibit such as this one at the
Lowell, Massachusetts National Historical Park
may bring together realia, still pictures and other
visuals with verbal information.

Audience members, too, seem to regard the flip chart in friendly terms. It seems casual and comfortable, a pleasing change of pace in an increasingly high-technology world. It is an exceptionally valuable aid to any group discussion process. Ideas contributed by group members can be recorded in a way visible to all participants. Comments and corrections can be made and the results can be preserved. Finished sheets can be torn off the pad and taped to walls or windows for later reference. Flip charts are available in a variety of sizes for large-group use, and others, often referred to as travel easels, are designed for portability.

Exhibits

Exhibits are *displays of various types of nonprojected visuals designed to form an integrated whole for instructional purposes.* These are sometimes referred to as minimuseums. Any of the visuals discussed in this chapter, including models and realia, may be included in an exhibit. Any of the display methods discussed may be used to contribute to it.

Exhibits may be used for much the same instructional purposes and in much the same ways as their individual components are used. Techniques for using them in the instructional situation are also similar.

Exhibit locations are readily available in most classrooms. Simple exhibits can be set up on a table, shelf, or desk. More complex exhibits may require considerable floor space and special constructions (a booth, for example).

Student assembly of an exhibit can be a motivating learning

experience and can foster both retention of subject matter and sharpening of visual skills. For a lesson in transportation, one sixth-grade teacher had each student bring in a replica of a vehicle. Some students made their own vehicles from construction paper. Others brought in toys from home or contributed vehicles assembled from hobby kits (boats, cars, trucks, trains, space ships, etc.). The teacher placed tables and other classroom furniture along a wall to provide the children with a shelf on which to arrange and display their three-dimensional visuals. On the wall above this makeshift exhibit surface, the teacher placed a long sheet of paper containing a time line. The time line illustrated vehicles of transportation from early time (humans and beasts), through the present (trains, cars, planes, etc.), and on into the future (space vehicles from *Star Wars* and *Star Trek*). The exhibit was a great success with the children and with the teacher.

Dioramas

Dioramas are *static displays consisting of a three-dimensional foreground and a flat background to create a realistic effect.* The foreground is usually a landscape of some sort with models of people, animals, vehicles, equipment, or buildings. The naturalistic background of the horizon or a city scene may be a photograph, drawing, or painting. The diorama is usually contained within a box, with the sides of the box providing the side of the scene. The rear corners or the entire back may be rounded to provide an illusion of depth, and lights can be added for special effects.

Dioramas are designed to reproduce reality of the past or present or depict future events. Examples in museums are often life-size, whereas those used in classrooms are usually on a smaller scale.

Teachers construct dioramas to illustrate their lessons or to introduce major topics. Students can be asked to design their own dioramas as a follow-up activity to instruction. In industry, dioramas can be constructed to show company products in use. Scenes from

▲ *Figure 4.27*
A simple teacher-made exhibit may consist of a few artifacts and a brief verbal explanation or question.

▲ *Figure 4.28*
Dioramas can depict current scenes, historical (even prehistorical) events, or future possibilities.

history, particularly battles, are often portrayed with model figures. Animals can be shown in their natural habitats for a biology class. Scenes including towns and landscapes from various parts of the world make stimulating dioramas for geography instruction. Prehistoric landscapes and geologic formations are also popular topics for dioramas.

APPLICATION OF THE ASSURE MODEL TO NONPROJECTED VISUALS

THE ASSURE model discussed in Chapter 2 applies to nonprojected visuals as well as to all other media. However, because of the diversity of formats and countless uses of nonprojected visuals, it is difficult to provide a concise set of principles and procedures for them.

First, you must analyze your audience and determine its nature and characteristics. Find out what its members already know about the topic. Then state your objectives in terms of what you want your audience to be able to do after viewing the presentation of visuals, real objects, models, or exhibits.

When selecting, modifying, or designing visuals, you should decide upon visuals or materials that will best communicate your instructional message under the conditions in which you will be using them. Keep them simple! Be certain that all titles, lettering, figures, and the visuals themselves are large enough to be seen from the intended viewing distance.

Many utilization techniques are included in the showmanship tips presented in this chapter. Plan your presentation or display carefully. Start where the audience is (as determined from your audi-

ence analysis). Organize the presentation in a logical sequence. Practice your presentation before a mirror or colleague.

Build learner activity and response into the use of the visuals or display. Involve the viewers as much as possible. Repetition and emphasis will help your audience remember key points. Watch them to see if they are following the presentation. Use questions and dialogue to keep them interested and to provide opportunities for learner response.

Finally, as recommended in the ASSURE model, evaluate your visuals and associated presentation. Through formal and informal evaluation, determine if most of your audience was able to meet your objectives. Determine which parts of the presentation were received best—and worst. Solicit feedback from your audience, and then make the necessary revisions.

Analyze Learners

General Characteristics. The assembly line workers at the Reliable Furnace Company manufacture small gas furnaces. They range in age from eighteen to sixty-eight, both males and females. All are high school graduates, but most have low reading abilities (the average is ninth grade, with a range from sixth to fourteenth).

Because of attrition and shifts of workers to different jobs on the assembly line, a burner-box assembler needs to be trained about once each week. The assembler's job requires manual dexterity and mobility. Because various colored wires are soldered to different locations, the trainee cannot be color blind.

Entry Competencies. The chief requirements are the ability to follow assembly instructions (which may be committed to memory after several weeks on the job) and to solder. Because soldering is required for other jobs within the company and is a skill many of the workers already know, it will not be taught as part of the lesson. A separate module on soldering techniques is available for those who need it.

Employees who have worked for the company less than four months are highly motivated to be successful and want to please the supervisor. This is especially true of the younger workers (less than twenty-five years old). The more mature individuals and those with more than a year's seniority generally just want to get by with as little effort as possible.

State Objectives

Upon completion of the burner-box assembly unit, the worker will be able to:

1. Assemble the burner box for a small gas furnace according to company specifications within seven minutes when given the necessary components and appropriate tools. Subobjectives include:
   a. Solder the control wires onto the correct terminals with a solder joint that will conduct current and withstand a five-pound pull.
   b. Position the top and side panels on the base and attach with metal screws. Panels must be in proper position and all screws must be firmly seated.

There are several other subobjectives including this affective objective.

2. Wear safety goggles and work gloves during the entire assembly process. (The workers know they should do this, but don't always do so.)

Select, Modify, or Design Material

After checking through catalogs of industrial training materials and talking with training directors from other furnace-manufacturing firms, Jan Smith, the training coordinator, concluded that there were no "off-the-shelf" materials available for use or for modification. Consequently, she decided to develop a set of drawings and photographs to be incorporated into a small (9-by-12-inch) flip chart for use by the trainee. Because of the need for hands-on practice and training (approximately one per week), a self-instructional unit will be developed with actual burner components, the flip chart, and an audiotape. Humor will be incorporated to enhance motivation for those employees who are not motivated.

Utilize the Materials

The trainee will be allowed to practice the assembly as many times as necessary in the training room. A trainer will be available to answer questions and to evaluate the completed burner boxes.

When the trainee is satisfied that the task has been mastered, an experienced employee will provide additional on-the-job training (OJT) at the assembly line. The experienced worker will demonstrate the task under actual working conditions with the assembly line running. Then the trainee will take over, with the experienced worker providing guidance and encouragement until the trainee is competent and confident.

Evaluate

The trainee and the training will be evaluated based on a number of factors. The number of defective or inoperative burner boxes identified by quality control or during installation is one criterion. Periodically the line supervisor will observe the workers for safety procedures (gloves and goggles) and assembly sequence. Accident and injury reports will also be sent to the training department.

References

Print References

Nonprojected Visuals

Alesandrini, K. L. "Pictures and Adult Learning." *Instructional Science* (May 1984), pp. 63–77.

Bullough, Robert. *Creating Instructional Materials*. 3d ed. (Columbus: Merrill, 1978).

Center for Vocational Education. *Prepare Teacher-Made Instructional Materials*. (Athens, Ga.: American Association for Vocational Instructional Materials, 1987).

————. *Present Information with Models, Real Objects, and Flannel Boards*. (Athens, Ga.: American Association for Vocational Instructional Materials, 1977).

Coplan, Kate. *Poster Ideas and Bulletin Board Techniques for Libraries and Schools*. 2d ed. (New York: Oceana Publications, 1980).

Do You See What I Mean? Learning through Charts, Graphs, Maps, and Diagrams. (Dickson, Australia: Curriculum Development Centre, 1980).

Hollister, Bernard C. "Using Picture Books in the Classroom." *Media and Methods* (January 1977), pp. 22–25.

Hynes, Michael C. "Selection Criteria." *Arithmetic Teacher* (February 1986), pp. 11–13.

Jones, Colin. "Cartoons in the Classroom." *Visual Education* (November 1976), pp. 21–22.

Kemp, Jerrold E., and Dayton, Deane K., *Planning and Producing Instructional Media*. 5th ed. (New York: Harper & Row, 1985).

Kohn, Rita. *Experiencing Displays*. (Metuchen, N.J.: Scarecrow Press, 1982).

Krulek, Stephen, and Welderman, Ann M. "The Chalkboard—More Than Just for Chalk." *Audiovisual Instruction* (September 1976), p. 41.

Marino, George. "A Do-It-Yourself 3-D Graph." *Mathematics Teacher* (May 1977), pp. 428–429.

Minor, Ed. *Handbook for Preparing Visual Media*. 2d ed. (New York: McGraw-Hill, 1978).

————, and Frye, Harvey R. *Techniques for Producing Visual Instructional Media*. 2d ed. (New York: McGraw-Hill, 1977).

Satterthwait, Les. *Graphics: Skills, Media and Materials*. 3d ed. (Dubuque, Ia.: Kendall-Hunt, 1977).

Scheer, Janet K. "Manipulatives Make Math Meaningful for Middle Schoolers." *Childhood Education* (November–December 1985), pp. 115–121.

Smith, Judson. "Choosing and Using Easels, Display Boards, and Visual Control Systems." *Training* (May 1979), pp. 51, 53–56.

Sumey, Violet, and Wade, Saundra. *Library Displays*. (Minneapolis: T. S. Denison, 1982).

Trimblay, Roger. "Using Magazine Pictures in the Second-Language Classroom." *Canadian Modern Language Review* (October 1978), pp. 82–86.

Waller, Robert H. W. "Four Aspects of Graphic Communication: An Introduction to This Issue." *Instructional Science* (September 1979), pp. 213–222.

Bulletin Boards

Alsin, Mary Lou. "Bulletin Board Standouts." *Early Years* (September 1977), pp. 66–69.

Carney, Loretta J. "No Comment: Eloquent Dissent." *Social Education* (November 1976), pp. 586–587.

Center for Vocational Education. *Prepare Bulletin Boards and Exhibits*. (Athens, Ga.: American Association for Vocational Instructional Materials, 1977).

"Hands-on Bulletin Boards." *Instructor* (January 1984), pp. 34–37.

Kelley, Marjorie. *Classroom-Tested Bulletin Boards*. (Belmont, Calif.: Fearon Publishers, 1961).

Kincheloe, Joe L. "No More Turkey-Lurkeys!" *Instructional Innovator* (September 1982), pp. 24–25.

Koskey, Thomas. *Baited Bulletin Boards*. (Belmont, Calif.: Fearon Publishers, 1954).

Prizzi, Elaine, and Hoffman, Jeanne. *Teaching off the Wall: Interactive Bulletin Boards That Teach with You*. (Belmont, Calif.: Pitman Learning, 1981).

Ruby, Doris. *4-D Bulletin Boards That Teach*. (Belmont, Calif.: Pitman Learning, 1960).

————, and Ruby, Grant. *Bulletin Boards for the Middle Grades*. (Belmont, Calif.: Pitman Learning, 1964).

Audiovisual References

Display and Presentation Boards. Chicago: International Film Bureau, 1971. 16-mm film or videocassette. 15 minutes.

Dry Mounting with Heat Press. Salt Lake City, Utah: Media Systems, Inc., 1975. Filmstrip or slides, 40 frames.

Heat Laminating. Salt Lake City, Utah: Media Systems, Inc., 1975. Filmstrip or slides, 40 frames.

Lettering: A Creative Approach to Basics. Stamford, Conn.: Educational Dimensions Group, 1978. 2 sound filmstrips with audiocassettes.

Production Techniques for Instructional Graphic Materials. Columbus: Charles E. Merrill, 1977. 27 filmstrips in basic series, 12 filmstrips in advanced series, 18 audiocassettes.

Tables and Graphs. Weekly Reader Filmstrips. Guidance Associates, 1981. 4 filmstrips with audiocassettes. Grades 3–6.

Three-Dimensional Displays. Burbank, Calif.: Encore Visual Education, 1975. 4 sound filmstrips with audiocassettes.

Suppliers of Materials and Equipment

Graphics, Mounting, Laminating, Lettering

Dick Blick
Box 1267
Galesburg, Illinois 61401

Demco Educational Corp.
P.O. Box 1488
Madison, Wisconsin 53701

Chartpak
One River Road
Leeds, Massachusetts 01053

Seal, Inc.
251 Roosevelt Drive
Derby, Connecticut 06418

Cloth Boards

Ohio Flock-Cote Co.
14500 Industrial Avenue N.
Maple Heights, Ohio 44137

Instructo Corporation
1635 North 55th Street
Paoli, Pennsylvania 19301

Charles Mayer Studios
168 East Market Street
Akron, Ohio 44308

Maharam Fabric Co.
420 New Orleans Street
Chicago, Illinois 60610

Bulletin Boards and Magnetic Boards

Bangor Cork Co.
William and D Streets
Pen Argyl, Pennsylvania 18072

Bulletin Boards and Directory Products
724 Broadway
New York, New York 10003

Charles Mayer Studios
168 East Market Street
Akron, Ohio 44308

Eberhard Faber, Inc.
Crestwood
Wilkes-Barre, Pennsylvania 18701

Weber-Costello Company
1900 Narragansett Avenue
Chicago, Illinois 60639

Possible Projects

4-A. Select three pictures and mount one with temporary rubber cement, one with permanent rubber cement, and a third with dry-mount tissue.

4-B. Select several pictures that are approximately 8½-by-11 inches and laminate them utilizing the cold or heat process.

4-C. Select a set of still pictures you might use in your teaching. Then appraise them using the "Appraisal Checklist: Still Pictures." Turn in the pictures and appraisal forms.

4-D. Plan a lesson in which you use a set of still pictures. Within this lesson show evidence that you have followed the utilization principles suggested. Submit pictures with lesson.

4-E. Devise for your subject field one graph (line, bar, circle, pictorial) and one chart (organization, classification, time line, tabular chart, flow chart). Each of these should be prepared on a separate sheet. Evaluation will be based on the "Appraisal Checklist: Graphic Materials."

4-F. Make a list of ten possible posters students could make to depict aspects of your teaching area. Prepare *one* yourself to serve as a model or motivational device. The poster should be at least 12-by-14 inches.

4-G. Review Chapter 3 or examine books on bulletin board displays. Prepare rough layouts for two displays pertinent to your subject area. Construct one of these.

4-H. Obtain an example of a real object or model that you could use for instruction. Submit the object or model and a description of how you would use it, including an objective.

4-I. Prepare a cloth board, magnetic board, flip chart, or exhibit. Submit the material, a description of the intended audience, the objectives, how it will be used, and how it will be evaluated.

5

Projected Visuals

Objectives

After studying this chapter, you should be able to:

1. Define projected visuals.

2. Describe the characteristics and operation of overhead transparency projection systems including three advantages and three limitations.

3. Discuss two applications of the overhead in your teaching field.

4. Describe three utilization techniques to enhance your use of the overhead projector.

5. Describe the following techniques for overhead transparency production: write-on, thermal film method, electrostatic method, and spirit duplication.

6. Describe three design guidelines that can enhance the effectiveness of overhead transparencies in instructional situations.

7. Describe the characteristics of slides including three advantages and three limitations.

8. Synthesize an instructional situation in which you might use a series of locally produced slides.

9. Describe the basic operation of a Kodak Visualmaker.

10. Demonstrate the correct technique for thumb spotting slides.

11. Describe two utilization techniques that enhance your use of slides.

12. Describe the characteristics of filmstrips, including three advantages and limitations.

13. Synthesize an instructional situation in which you might use a commercially produced filmstrip.

14. Describe two utilization techniques to enhance your use of filmstrips.

15. Describe the characteristics and operation of opaque projection systems, including two advantages and three limitations.

16. Discuss two applications of opaque projection in your teaching field.

17. Describe three utilization techniques to enhance the effectiveness of opaque projection in instructional situations.

Lexicon

projected visual
fresnel lens
transparency
thermal film
electrostatic copying
  (xerography)
spirit duplication
slide
filmstrip
opaque projection
overhead projection

B ECAUSE an illuminated screen in a darkened room tends to rivet the attention of viewers, projected visuals have long been popular as a medium of instruction as well as of entertainment. The lighted screen is a silent shout—a shout likely to be heard and heeded even by the most reluctant learners.

It is not too fanciful to conjecture that some of this attraction is due to the aura of magic that seems to surround such presentations. The room lights are dimmed; the viewers grow quiet in expectation; a switch is thrown and (presto!) a large, bright image appears on the screen. You have their attention. They are ready to receive your message. Exploit this readiness by selecting materials that will maintain the viewers' attention and by using them in a way that *involves* viewers actively in the learning process.

Projected visuals refer to *media formats in which still images are enlarged and displayed on a screen.* Such projection is usually achieved by passing a strong light through transparent film (overhead transparencies, slides, and filmstrips), magnifying the image through a series of lenses, and casting this image onto a reflective surface. Opaque projection is also included in this category. In opaque projection, light is cast onto an opaque image (one that does not allow light to pass through), such as a magazine picture or printed page. The light is reflected from the material onto mirrors, which transmit the reflection through a series of lenses onto a screen.

The focus of this chapter is on the characteristics and applications of overhead projection, slides, filmstrips, and opaque projection—the most widely accepted means of providing projected visuals in education and training settings.

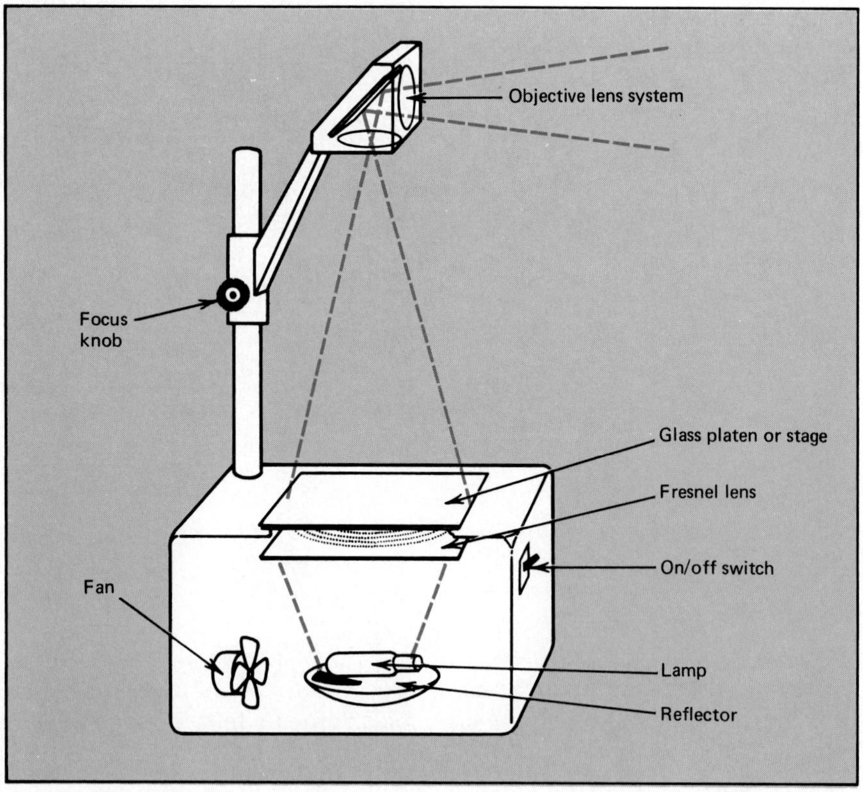

OVERHEAD PROJECTION

B ECAUSE of its many virtues, the overhead projection system has advanced rapidly in the past several decades to become the most widely used audiovisual device in North American classrooms.

The typical overhead projector is a very simple device (Figure 5.1). Basically, it is a box with a large aperture or "stage" at the top. Light from a powerful lamp inside the box is condensed by a special type of lens, known as a *fresnel lens*, and passes through a transparency (approximately 8 by 10 inches) placed on the stage. A lens-and-mirror system mounted on a bracket above the box turns the light beam 90 degrees and projects the image back over the shoulder of the presenter.

Because of the widespread familiarity of overhead projection, the general term *transparency* has taken on, in the instructional setting, the specific meaning of the large-format 8-by-10-inch film used with the overhead projector. Transparencies may be composed of photographic film, clear acetate, or any of a number of other transparent materials capable of being imprinted with an image by means of chemical or heat processes.

Transparencies may be used individually or may be made into a series of images consisting of a base visual with one or more "overlays" attached to the base with hinges. Complex topics can be explained step-by-step by flip-

▲ *Figure 5.1*
Overhead projector, cutaway view

- Objective lens system
- Focus knob
- Glass platen or stage
- Fresnel lens
- On/off switch
- Fan
- Lamp
- Reflector

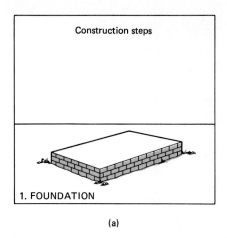

Construction steps

1. FOUNDATION

(a)

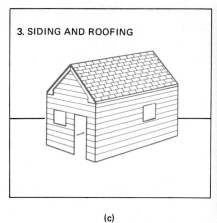

3. SIDING AND ROOFING

(c)

▲ *Figure 5.3*
With the overhead projector, the presenter maintains eye contact with viewers.

2. FRAME

(b)

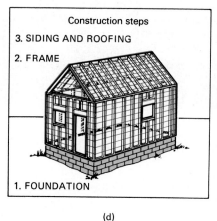

Construction steps

3. SIDING AND ROOFING

2. FRAME

1. FOUNDATION

(d)

▲ *Figure 5.2*
By means of overlays, complex visuals can be built up step by step.

▲ *Figure 5.4*
Some overhead projectors can be collapsed into a compact carrying case for true portability.

ping on a series of overlays one at a time that add additional features to a diagram (Figure 5.2).

Advantages

The overhead projection system has a number of unique features that give it the tremendous versatility for which it is acclaimed by so many instructors.

Its bright lamp and efficient optical system generate so much light on the screen that the overhead can be used in *normal room lighting*.

The projector is operated from the front of the room with the presenter *facing the audience,* allowing direct eye contact to be maintained.

Most overhead projectors are lightweight and easily portable. All are *simple to operate*.

A *variety of materials* can be projected, including cutout silhouettes, small opaque objects, and many types of transparencies.

Projected materials can be *manipulated* by the presenter. You can point to important items, highlight them with colored pens, add details during the lesson (notes, diagrams, etc.) by marking on the transparency with a marking pen, or cover part of the mes-

sage and progressively reveal information in a step-by-step procedure. As noted previously, complex visuals can be presented in a series of overlays.

Commercially produced transparencies are available covering a broad range of curricular areas. A major directory of commercially available overhead transparencies is published by the National Information Center for Educational Media (NICEM)—*Index to*

▲ *Figure 5.5*
In business meetings, projected images help focus attention, channel discussion, and facilitate establishment of a consensus.

Educational Overhead Transparencies. See Appendix A for details and other sources.

Instructors can easily prepare their own transparencies (several common methods of production are explained later in this chapter).

Information that might otherwise have to be placed on a chalkboard during a class session (lesson outlines, for example) may be prepared in advance for presentation at the proper time. Research indicates that retention of main points improves significantly when visual outlines are presented.

A recent study indicates that the use of overhead transparencies also has positive attitudinal effects in business meetings. In a study by the Wharton Applied Research Center, candidates for master's degrees in business administration participated in a business simulation that included group meetings to decide whether or not to introduce a new product. The findings showed that

• More individuals decided to act on the recommendations of presenters who used overheads than on the recommendations of presenters who did not.
• Presenters who used overheads were perceived as better prepared, more professional, more persuasive, more credible, and more interesting.
• Groups in which presenters used overheads were more likely to reach consensus on their decisions than groups where no overheads were employed.*

Another study suggests that teachers who use the overhead projector tend to be more organized than teachers who rely on notes or printed outlines. Students in this study participated more frequently in discussions in the classes where the overhead was used.[†]

Limitations

The effectiveness of overhead projection presentations is heavily dependent on the presenter. The overhead projector cannot be programmed to display visual sequences by itself, nor is an audio accompaniment provided.

The overhead system does not lend itself to independent study.

* *A Study of the Effects of the Use of Overhead Transparencies on Business Meetings.* Philadelphia: Wharton Applied Research Center, The Wharton School, University of Pennsylvania, 1981.

[†] James Cabeceiras. "Observed Differences in Teacher Verbal Behavior When Using and Not Using the Overhead Projector." *AV Communication Review* (Fall 1972), pp. 271–280.

The projection system is designed for large-group presentation. Of course, an individual student could look at a transparency by holding it up to the light or laying it on a light table; but because captions or audio tracks are not a part of this format, the material would ordinarily not be self-instructional.

Printed materials and other nontransparent items, such as magazine illustrations, cannot be projected immediately, as is possible with the opaque projector. To use the overhead system such materials have to be made into transparencies by means of some production process.

Distortion of images is more prevalent with the overhead than with other projection systems. The projector is commonly placed at desktop level to facilitate the instructor's writing on transparencies. The screen, on the other hand, needs to be placed on a higher level for unobstructed audience sight lines. This discrepancy in levels causes a distortion referred to as the "keystone effect." (This problem and its solution are discussed in Chapter 10.)

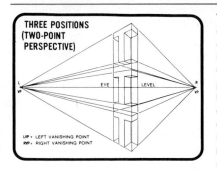

MEDIA FILE:
"The ABCs of Drafting" Overhead Transparencies

This set of overhead transparencies covers an entire course in drafting. Although designed for grades six through eight, it has been used successfully in high school. One of the advantages of overhead transparencies is that the basic illustrations can be adapted to different age levels. The set consists of thirty-six well-drawn illustrations on sturdy transparency material. The instructor's guide comes complete with reproductions of all the transparencies and step-by-step instructions for the most effective use.

Source: DCA Educational Products Inc.

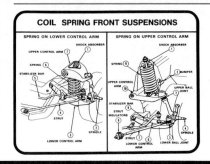

MEDIA FILE:
"Automotive Technology: Engine Systems" Overhead Transparencies

This is a comprehensive set of sixty transparencies designed for a high school or area vocational school course in automotive repair. Many of the transparencies have overlays. The instructor's guide has descriptions of each transparency. The descriptions give the order in which the overlays are to be used. The transparencies are printed on sturdy stock.

Source: DCA Educational Products Inc.

Applications

As indicated by its ubiquitous presence in the classroom, the overhead system has a myriad of group-instruction applications, too numerous to list here.

One indication of the breadth of applications is the fact that commercial distributors of transparencies have made available materials for virtually all curricular areas, from kindergarten through college levels and in business and industry. These materials range from single, simple transparencies to elaborate sets replete with multiple overlays, masking devices and other teaching aids. Transparent plastic devices such as clocks, engines, slide rules, and the like are available. These can be manipulated by the instructor to demonstrate how the parts interact as they are displayed on the screen.

Projection of Computer Displays. Anyone who has ever sought to demonstrate use of a computer program to a group has needed to display an image larger than the monitor screen. A video projector serves the purpose but is very expensive. A much less expensive solution is a liquid-crystal display screen that fits on the stage of an overhead projector. The screen is plugged into the output of the computer, and whatever appears on the computer monitor is also projected by the overhead so that all may easily follow the demonstration (see Figure 5.6).

Creating Overhead Transparencies

As previously noted, one of the major advantages of the overhead system is that instructors—and students—can easily prepare their own transparencies. Beginning with simple hand drawing on clear acetate sheets, numerous other methods of preparing trans-

in mediaware section

In addition to the general utilization practices, here are some hints specifically related to overhead projection:

- Start by projecting an *outline* to show learners what will be presented.

- *Avoid* diminishing the possible impact of overhead projection by using the projector as a doodle pad. For *random notes* or *verbal* cues, use the chalkboard.

- Shift the audience's attention back to you by *switching off* the projector during changes of transparencies and, especially, when you have finished referring to a particular transparency.

- Plan ways to *add meaningful details* to the transparency during projection; this infuses an element of spontaneity. If the basic transparency is a valuable one which will be reused, cover it with a blank acetate before drawing.

- Place your *notes* (key words) on the frame of the transparency. Do not try to read from a prepared script.

- Use *dual projectors* to retain the outline while covering secondary issues on a second projector. Dual projection is also helpful in difficult to read presentations.

Direct viewer attention to parts of the transparency by using the following techniques:

- *Point* to specific portions, using a pencil as a pointer. Lay the pencil directly on the transparency, because any elevation will put the pencil out of focus and any slight hand movement will be greatly exaggerated on the screen. Avoid pointing to the screen.

- *Reveal* information one line at a time to control pace and audience attention by placing a sheet of paper under the transparency.

- *Mask* unwanted portions by covering them with a sheet of paper or using cardboard "windows" to reveal one section at a time.

- *Overlay* new information one step at a time. Build up a complex idea by superimposing transparencies one at a time. Up to four overlays can be used successfully.

---

parencies have evolved over the years. We will look closely at only the processes most commonly used at the classroom production level—direct drawing, thermal film process, and electrostatic film process (xerography).

▲ *Figure 5.6*
Devices are available that permit computer output to be projected from the stage of the overhead projector.

Direct Drawing Method. The most obvious way of quickly preparing a transparency is simply to draw directly on a transparent sheet with some sort of marking pen. Clear acetate of five to ten mils (.005–.010 inches) thickness is recommended. Other types of plastic can be used, even household food wrap and dry-cleaning bags. Although some of these alternatives may be a great deal cheaper than the thicker acetate, some of them also impose limitations in terms of durability, ease of handling, and ability to accept different inks (i.e., disintegrating completely under alcohol-based inks). If available, blue-tinted acetate is preferred because it

reduces the glare of the projected image.

Although the glass platen or stage of the overhead projector generally measures about 10 by 10 inches, your drawing and lettering should be restricted to a rectangular "message area" of about $7\frac{1}{2}$ by $9\frac{1}{2}$ inches. This fits the dimensions of acetate sheets, which are commonly cut into rectangles of 8 by 10 inches or $8\frac{1}{2}$ by 11 inches.

Some overhead projectors come equipped with a pair of roll attachments made to carry long rolls of plastic which can be advanced or reversed by a small hand crank. This assures a steady supply of transparency material

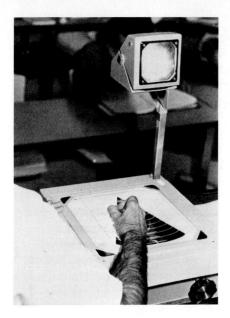

▲ *Figure 5.7*
Most overhead projector users like to draw directly on the transparency, in this case to add significant details to a previously prepared visual.

▲ *Figure 5.8*
Plastic erasers will remove permanent ink, at least that of the same manufacturer.

light transmitted through the film, thereby decreasing legibility. In addition, typewritten letters are usually too small to be readable for the whole group. If a larger typeface is available (such as Primary or IBM's Orator), typing on frosted sheets may be acceptable if you do not have access to a thermal-process machine (see next section). If an enlarging photocopy machine is available, a standard typeface can be enlarged and then made into a thermal film transparency. Frosted sheets should be used only as a last resort.

for extemporaneous use. It also allows a series of images to be prepared in advance in proper sequence. Such rolls can be saved for later reuse.

In addition to the transparency, you will need a writing instrument. Felt-tipped marking pens are the handiest for this purpose. They come in two general types—*water-soluble* and *permanent ink*. Within these two types a wide variety of pens are available. Not all are suitable for overhead transparencies. Here are some important cautions to keep in mind:

- Markers with *water-soluble* ink generally will not adhere well to acetate; the ink tends to bead up and disappear as the water evaporates. A label stating "for overhead marking" means it *will adhere* to acetate and project in color. Such special pens can be erased readily with a damp cloth. This allows you to reuse the acetate sheet—a con-

siderable advantage in view of the escalating cost of acetate, which is a petroleum product.
- Virtually all the permanent-ink felt-tipped pens will adhere to acetate, but only those labelled "for overhead marking" are sure to project *in color*. Otherwise, the ink itself may be opaque and project only in black.
- Permanent inks really are permanent. They can be removed only with special plastic erasers.

Less frequently used but very serviceable are *wax-based* pencils, often referred to as grease pencils. Unless otherwise marked, they will project black. The great advantage of wax-based pencils is that they can be erased from acetate with any soft, dry cloth.

Finally, there are some specially treated ("frosted") acetate sheets made to be typed on directly by a typewriter or written on with a pencil. However, the frosting reduces the amount of

Thermal Film Process. In the thermal film process infrared light passes through a specially treated acetate film onto a prepared master underneath. The artwork and lettering on the master are done with a heat-absorbing material such as India ink, ordinary lead pencil, or other substance containing carbon. An image is "burned into" the film wherever it contacts such carbonaceous marking.

Depending on the film used, a number of different color patterns are possible. The most common pattern is color or black print on a clear or pastel background, analogous to positive film. Clear or colored lines can also be put on a black background, analogous to negative film.

Another option is the use of printed, commercially prepared transparency masters. Thermal film producers and other audiovisual publishers offer a broad range of printed masters—many thousands of individual titles covering virtually all curricular areas. Some publishers offer sets of masters specifically correlated with the leading textbooks in language arts, reading, math, social studies, and science.

First prepare the master. Any ordinary white paper may be used. Draw the artwork by hand or paste illustrations from other sources (magazine illustrations, photocopies, etc.) onto the master. Lettering, added by hand, by mechanical lettering guide, or by paste-up of existing lettering, must consist of a carbonaceous substance. An alternative is to create the visual using any types of materials and then electrostatically copy it and use the copy as the master. (Note that some electrostatic copies work better than others. Experiment with what is available to you.)

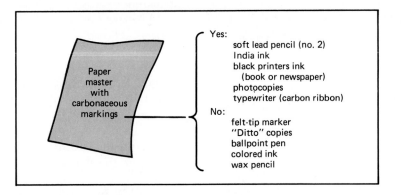

Paper master with carbonaceous markings

Yes:
soft lead pencil (no. 2)
India ink
black printers ink
   (book or newspaper)
photocopies
typewriter (carbon ribbon)

No:
felt-tip marker
"Ditto" copies
ballpoint pen
colored ink
wax pencil

Second, place a sheet of thermal acetate over the master. Most brands of acetate have a notch in one corner of the film to ensure that is put on correctly. The notch should always be placed at the upper right-hand corner of the master.

Thermal film

THERMAL COPIER

Third, feed the two sets into a thermal copy machine, using the dial setting recommended by the manufacturer. Transfer of the image to the acetate requires only a few seconds. Then separate the two sheets. The film is ready for projection! The master is not affected in the production process and may be reused to make additional copies of the transparency.

To use commercially prepared thermal masters, simply remove one from the book or folder in which it is packaged, lay the thermal film on it with the notch in the upper-right corner, and run both through the copier. Commercial masters may, of course, be altered by the instructor to better suit the needs of a particular audience.

Electrostatic Film Process (Xerography). The rapidly evolving technology of xerography provides another method of producing transparencies. All plain paper copying machines that operate by the electrostatic process can now be used to prepare black-and-white transparencies. Some models, such as the Xerox 6500, can produce high-quality full-color transparencies from originals on paper or from slides, but these costly machines are not widely available.

Similar to the thermal process, this process requires a paper master and specially treated film. In this case the film is electrically charged and light sensitive (rather than heat sensitive). The steps just outlined for thermal film are essentially the same as those needed to produce an electrostatic film transparency. However, because the xerographic process responds to darkness of the image rather than carbon content, it is not necessary to confine the artwork to carbonaceous images. Any substance that yields a good opaque mark can be used.

Spirit-Duplication Process. If you are already planning to make a spirit-duplicator master (often referred to by the brand name, Ditto), it is just one simple extra step to make a transparency from that master.

After you have prepared a regular spirit-duplicator master and

Harvey Frye, the developer of many visual production techniques, accidentally discovered a process for "lifting" colored photographs from magazines and projecting them with the overhead. He recalled,

One evening, I was teaching rubber cement mounting in my basic production course. As is usually the case, students spilled rubber cement on the table top. This particular evening a student forgot and applied rubber cement to the face of the picture instead of the back side. Realizing what he had done, he threw the picture face down on the table where some rubber cement had been spilled. When the two surfaces of rubber cement touched, there was instant adhesion. It was left there until the end of class.

As always, I washed the tables with water to clean the surfaces for the next morning's class. As I washed the table, water ran over the picture. When I reached the end of the table where the picture was stuck, I pulled the wet page from the table surface. To my amazement and joy, I found a beautiful ink image on the table. There was a white chalky residue floating on the wet table surface which I later learned was the clay coating on the paper. The clay coating was the important element in making the transfer process possible.

This accident gave me a clue to a possible approach to transfer printed ink images from paper to acetate. Rubber cement is not water-soluble so it will remain stable while the clay coating, solvent in water, will break down, permitting the ink image to remain on the rubber cement surface. Thus, the first picture lift was made by applying rubber cement to an acetate surface and to the front of a picture printed on clay-surfaced paper such as Life *and* Time *magazines.*

During the mid-1950s Harvey Frye and his assistants at Indiana University experimented and tried to find variations in the process. For simplicity, they found that Frisket film used by airbrush artists as a mask was transparent and had a rubber cement–

Harvey Frye (center)

type adhesive on one side. By pressing this down tightly on the picture surface, it would lift an image quite successfully. For a short time, this process was referred to as the "Fryeon" process in honor of its discoverer.

Harvey Frye continued to experiment with additional processes for making transparencies. His experimentation led him to use a piece of acetate that would withstand heat, spraying it with several coats of acrylic spray. After it dried, he placed a picture on the sprayed side and placed the combination in a mounting press. The process worked. The idea was introduced to Seal, Incorporated, who manufacture dry-mount presses. After additional research they developed Transpara-Film. This product permitted the production of good, heavyweight, colored transparencies using heat.

Since Harvey Frye's experimentation in the 1950s, a variety of methods for "lifting" have appeared using both hot and cold techniques. The hot processes include the use of clear laminating film with a dry-mount press. The cold processes can use a variety of products such as clear Con-Tact paper. Unfortunately, in recent years publishers have modified their printing processes for "slick" clay-coated magazines and now spray them with a clear plastic film, so the "lifting" processes do not work on as many magazines as they did when accidentally discovered by Frye in the early 1950s.

How To... DESIGN OVERHEAD TRANSPARENCIES

Whatever production process you choose for preparing your transparencies, keep in mind these design guidelines based on research and practical experience:

YES   NO

- *Horizontal* format covers projected viewing area best. Screens are frequently rectangular and better fit the horizontal format. On a square screen, the audience has difficulty seeing the bottom fourth of a vertical-format transparency.

- *Visual* ideas should be used for overheads. Diagrams, graphs, and charts should be incorporated. If not, consider using chalkboard or print to convey verbal information.

- A *single concept* should be expressed in simple, uncluttered visuals. In general, not more than three or four images per transparency.

- *Minimum verbiage* should be included, with not more than six words per line and six or fewer lines per transparency.

- *Key words* help the audience remember each point. These are usually most effective as "headlines" at the top of the visual.

- *Legibility* is important. One quick way to check it is to lay the transparency on the floor over a white piece of paper. If you can read it from a standing position, your audience should be able to read it when projected. Use letters at least $\frac{3}{16}$-inch high.

- *Overlays* can explain complex ideas by adding information sequentially to the base transparency.

mounted it on the duplicating machine, feed in a sheet of frosted acetate with the etched side up. If greater permanence is desired, the resulting transparency can be sprayed with a clear plastic spray, such as Krylon, which will remove the matte effect and protect the ink image from smearing.

An advantage of this process is that it allows you to use a master you may have prepared for another purpose to produce a transparency. Your students may then refer to their own copies of the visual while you project an image of it. A disadvantage is that the process requires some special materials—the frosted acetate and plastic spray.

Computer-Generated Masters. Software packages that can combine graphics with varying sizes of print are available for most microcomputers on the market. The printed masters produced by such programs can then be used to make the overhead transparencies. If a laser printer is available, professional-quality masters can be made very easily. Microcomputers are becoming so commonplace in schools and offices that production of high-quality overhead masters by software programs will likely render obsolete some of the other methods mentioned in this section.

SLIDES

THE term *slide* refers to a *small-format photographic transparency individually mounted for one-at-a-time projection.*

The size of slides most frequently encountered in educational use is 2 by 2 inches (metric equivalency either 50 by 50 millimeters or 5 by 5 centimeters)

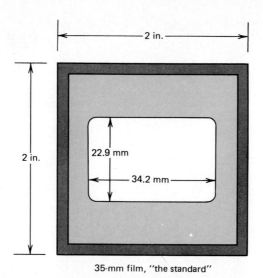

35-mm film, "the standard"

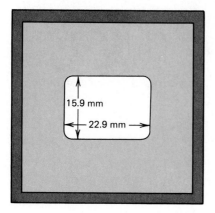

35 mm
"half-frame" film

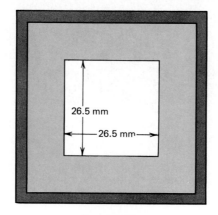

Type 126 film
"Instamatic"

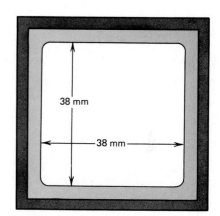

Type 127 film
"Super-slide"

measured by the outer dimensions of the slide mount. When 35-mm and other popular types of slide film are sent out to be processed, they are usually returned mounted in 2 by 2-inch mounts. The actual dimensions of the *image* itself will vary with the type of film (Figure 5.9).

Advantages

Because slides can be arranged and rearranged into many different sequences, they are more flexible than filmstrips or other fixed-sequence materials.

As photographic equipment is continually refined and simplified, more and more amateurs are able to produce their own slides. Auto-

matic exposure controls, easy focusing, and high-speed color films have contributed to this trend. High-quality color slides

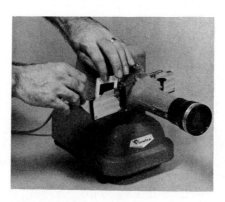

▲ *Figure 5.10*
Originally, slides were fed into the projector one at a time, and manual-feed projectors are still in use.

can be taken by any amateur photographer.

The assembly of slide programs is facilitated by today's automatic projectors, which hold sets of slides in trays and feed them into place in sequence. Most automatic projectors also offer the convenience of remote control advancing of slides, allowing the presenter to remain at the front of the room or off to a side while advancing the slides via a push-button unit connected by wire to the projector. Wireless remote control is also available. Certain models can be preset to advance automatically. This feature allows continuous showing in exhibits, display cases, and other automated situations.

▲ *Figure 5.11*
The Ektagraphic III is Kodak's latest updating of the Carousel line of slide projectors.

▶ *Figure 5.12*
The slide-tape format has been adapted for individual viewers.

General availability and ease of handling make it relatively easy to build up permanent collections of slides for specific instructional purposes. Instructors may collect and store their own collections, or the slides may be compiled and kept in a learning resource center. Such collections enable users to assemble presentations partially or wholly from existing pictures, thus reducing the expense required for new production.

Slides can be integrated into individualized instruction programs. Although slides have been developed primarily as a large-group medium, recent hardware innovations have made slides feasible for small-group and independent study as well. However, the complex nature of these new mechanisms makes them relatively expensive. Thus, slide-tape viewers for individual use are more likely to be found in learn-ing resource centers than in classrooms (Figure 5.12).

Limitations

Because slides, unlike filmstrips, come as individual units, they can easily become disorganized. Even when they are stored in trays, if the locking ring is loosened, the slides can come spilling out.

Slide mounts come in cardboard, plastic, and glass of varying thicknesses. This lack of standardization can lead to jamming of slides in the slide-changing mechanism: cardboard becomes dog-eared with the frayed edges getting caught in the mechanism; plastic mounts swell or warp in the heat of the lamp; glass mounts thicker than the aperture chamber fail to drop into showing position.

Slides that are not enclosed in glass covers are susceptible to accumulation of dust and finger-prints. Careless storage or handling can easily lead to permanent damage.

A final limitation of slides is their cost in comparison to filmstrips. The cost *per frame* of a commercially produced slide set may be two to three times the cost per frame of a filmstrip of equal length.

Applications

Like other forms of projected visuals, slides may be used at all grade levels and for instruction in all curricular areas. Many high-quality slides are available commercially, individually, and in sets. In general, the fine arts, geography, and the sciences are especially well represented with commercially distributed slides.

The following examples give some idea of the types of slide materials available through com-

- **T**here are eight possible ways a slide can be placed in a projector. *Seven of them are wrong* (e.g., upside-down, backwards, sideways, etc.). To avoid all seven mistakes a standardized procedure is recommended for placing a reminder spot on the slide.

- First, your slides should be arranged and numbered in the order in which they are to be shown.

- Then take each slide and hold it the way it is supposed to be seen on the screen, that is, right-side up with the lettering running left to right—just as it would be read. (If the slide lacks lettering or other orienting information, hold it so that the *emulsion* side is toward the screen.)

- Then simply place a spot on the bottom left-hand corner.

- This spot is referred to as a ''thumb spot'' because when the slide is turned upside-down to be placed in the projector, your thumb will grip the slide at the point of the thumb spot, as shown below.

- Before all the slides are put in the tray in proper order, some users like to run a felt-tip pen across the tops of the slide mounts in a diagonal line. This way if some slides later get out of order, they can be replaced just by following the line.

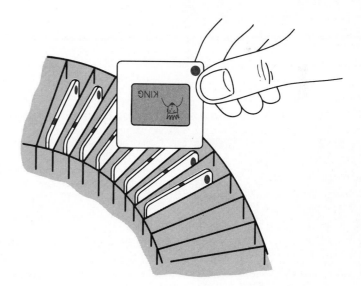

▲ *Figure 5.13*
Teacher-made slide sets are an effective way for the teacher to personalize instruction.

MEDIA FILE:
Harbrace "Science 700" Slides

"Science 700" consists of three sets of slide programs: Life Science, Earth Science, and Physical Science. All the slides are developed with dark backgrounds to allow projection on chalkboards in normal room lighting.

Source: Harcourt, Brace, Jovanovich.

MEDIA FILE:
"Contemporary Painting and Sculpture" Slides

A set of 480 slides illustrates contemporary works of painting and sculpture, including landscapes, figurative, still life, new realism, pop art, and surrealism.

Source: Art Now, Inc.

---

mercial channels. A major directory of commercially available slides is published by the National Information Center for Educational Media (NICEM)—*Index to Educational Slides.* See Appendix A for details and other sources.

Local Production of Slides

As noted earlier (Chapter 3), a major advantage of slides as an instructional device is the ease with which they can be produced by instructors—and students. Modern cameras are so simple to operate that even the most amateur of photographers can expect usable results. As with all locally produced materials, instructor- and student-made slides are likely to have an immediacy and a specificity lacking in commercially produced instructional materials. Further, such locally produced efforts gain credibility by depicting local people and conditions.

Among the myriad possibilities, here are some ideas of typical subjects for slide presentations:

* Providing a tour for new employees of a local business without walking through the plant.
* Making a visual history of your community, school, or organization.
* Demonstrating local operating and sales procedures for real estate agents.
* Documenting student activities, products of student work, and community problems (e.g., crime and pollution).
* Presenting a preoperative explanation about a surgical procedure personalized for a specific surgeon's patients.
* Showing people at work in various jobs, for career awareness.
* Illustrating the uses of a company's products throughout the world.

In addition to the general guidelines for audiovisual utilization discussed in Chapter 2, here are several specific practices that can add professionalism to your slide presentations:

- Use a remote control advance device; this will allow you to stand at the side of the room. From this position you can keep an eye on the slides while maintaining some eye contact with the audience.

- Make *very* certain your slides are in sequential order and right-side up. Disarrangement can be an embarrassment to you and an annoyance to your audience. Refer to the section entitled "How to . . . 'Thumb Spot' Slides," to find a foolproof method of avoiding this embarrassment.

- Employ visual variety. Mix the types of slides, using verbal title slides to help break the presentation into segments.

- Prepare a way to light up your script after the room lights are dimmed; a penlight or flashlight will serve this purpose.

- Limit your discussion of each slide—even a minute of narration can seem long to your audience unless there is a complex visual to be examined at the same time.

- Plan and rehearse your narration to accompany the slides if it is not already recorded on tape.

- If there is a "talky" section in the middle of your presentation, put a gray or black slide on rather than holding an irrelevant slide on the screen. (Gray slides can be produced locally or purchased from commercial sources. They let through enough light to allow the presenter to be seen, avoiding total darkening of the room during the "blackout.")

- Consider adding a musical accompaniment to your live or recorded narration. This can help to establish the desired mood and keep your audience attentive. But do not have music playing in the background when providing narration.

- Begin and end with a black slide. A white flash on the screen at the beginning and end is irritating to the eye and appears amateurish.

- Teaching a step-by-step process with close-ups of each operation.
- Simulating a field trip.
- Promoting public understanding of your school or organization.

Using the Kodak Visualmaker

Along with modern camera technology, a further boon to teacher/ student production of slides has been a device called the Kodak Ektagraphic Visualmaker. This device permits reproduction of flat visual materials—such as magazine illustrations, maps, charts, photographs, business forms, and the like—without the need for specialized photography skills.

The secret is in the Visualmaker hardware itself: a copy stand containing a built-in supplementary lens that is positioned and focused to allow easy picture taking with a Kodak Instamatic camera. This preset mechanism eliminates the need for extra lenses and specialized skills in proper framing of the picture (see "How To . . . Make Slides with the Visualmaker").

Computer-Generated Slides.
Computer programs that can generate complex graphic displays are now commonplace. Recently, however, special systems have been developed that permit anyone to construct a graphic on the monitor screen and then have a 2-by-2-inch slide made of the dis-

▲ *Figure 5.14*
Software packages make it easy to generate slides and overhead transparencies on the computer. The image shown on the monitor does not reflect the high resolution of the completed slide.

play. Slides made this way are superior in resolution and color quality to the image on the monitor. The special programs and associated equipment are too

The basic steps for making slides from visuals are simple and foolproof:

1. *Select a suitable visual.* Keep in mind that the flash unit will flood a lot of light onto the picture. If the picture is shiny, that light will reflect back in the form of glare. So avoid glossy photos and glass, acetate, and such surfaces. White backgrounds, too, should be avoided. Photographs, drawings, and tables from books, magazines, and other printed materials generally reproduce well.[a]

2. *Attach the Instamatic camera to one of the two copy stands included in the Visualmaker kit.* The Visualmaker kit is equipped with a copy stand with an 8-by-8-inch frame and a smaller one with a 3-by-3-inch frame. Choose the one that frames your visual best.

3. *Compose the shot.* If your visual is equal to or larger than the frame, keep in mind that its outer edges will be lost. Make sure that important visual information is no more than $7\frac{1}{2}$ inches square (for the large copystand) or $2\frac{3}{4}$ inches

square (for the small copystand). Keep critical information out of the "bleed" area around the border.

4. *Add lettering, if appropriate.* Lettering can be added to your visual with a typewriter if you are using the small copystand. Size and specifications are shown. However, if you are using the large copystand, you will need to use dry-transfer letters, cutouts, a "primary" or "bulletin board" typewriter, or some other special lettering method. The letters should be at least ⅜-inch high in order to be legible when projected on the screen.

```
TYPED LETTERING
FOR SLIDES SHOULD
BE ALL CAPITALS,
DOUBLE-SPACED,
AND NO MORE THAN
SEVEN LINES LONG.
```

5. *Mask the visual, if necessary.* If your visual is smaller than the frame, mask the extra space with dark construction paper or other such matte material as shown. Textured fabrics also make attractive backgrounds. Again, avoid white or shiny materials, to reduce possible glare.

6. *Snap the shutter and it's done!* The Visualmaker system is designed to provide adequate, even lighting by means of the flash unit supplied with the kit. The type of flash unit is determined by what vintage Visualmaker you are using. Two models are in common use: the Kodak Ektagraphic Visualmaker and the Kodak Ektagraphic EF Visualmaker. The former is the older model, distributed prior to 1979; it uses Magicubes as a lighting source. The EF model comes equipped with a special electronic flash unit (thereby doing away with the need to keep a stock of Magicubes on hand). Hold the camera down firmly with one hand while squeezing the shutter release with the other hand.

NOTE: Three-dimensional objects will photograph well if they are not too thick. With the large Visualmaker copystand, the sharp-focus area extends up to about $1\frac{1}{2}$ inches above the table top. With smaller copystand, ½-inch is approximately the thickness limit.

For more complete information, see the Kodak publication *Simple Copying Techniques with a Kodak Ektagraphic Visualmaker* (publication #S-40), available from audiovisual dealers or the Eastman Kodak Company, Rochester, NY 14650.

[a] Remember that published materials including illustrations are protected by the copyright laws. For an extensive discussion of an educator's rights and responsibilities refer to Appendix C.

expensive for individual purchase, but audiovisual production centers in many colleges and universities and in industry have made computer-generated slide services available to their staffs. Many custom audiovisual production shops make computer-generated slides from graphics submitted by customers who do not want to acquire the necessary program and equipment to produce their own.

Polaroid Instant Slides. At the 1987 COMMTEX (see Chapter 14), the Polaroid Corporation demonstrated a device that makes photographic prints or slides of any image from a videocassette recorder, video camera, videodisc player, or computer graphic work station. Polaroid calls this device Freeze Frame Video Image Recorder, or Freeze Frame for short. The Freeze Frame device plugs directly into the equipment generating the video image. Polaroid also makes an adapter for a 35-mm camera that makes instant slides from any exposure made.

▲ *Figure 5.15*
Polaroid's Freeze Frame Video Image Recorder can make a still photograph of any video image displayed on the screen.

FILMSTRIPS

A *filmstrip* is a *roll of 35-mm transparent film containing a series of related still pictures intended for showing one at a time.*

Various filmstrip formats have evolved since the advent of the filmstrip over a half century ago. The most widely used format today is the single-frame filmstrip. Note that in the single-frame format the images are printed *perpendicular* to the length of the film, whereas in the slide format the images are *parallel* to the length of the film. It is, in fact, the same size and configuration as the 35-mm slide before the slide is cut apart and mounted. Commercially produced filmstrips typically contain about twenty to sixty

images or "frames" and are stored rolled up in small plastic canisters.

Until the 1960s most filmstrips were silent; that is, there was no audio accompaniment. Narrative information was printed at the bottom of each frame. Since that time there has been a growing trend toward having recorded sound tracks accompany the filmstrip. Initially the narration, music, sound effects, and so on were recorded on phonograph records and were played on record players either separate from the projector or built into it. Currently, audiocassette tapes are the standard means for giving *sound filmstrips* their "voice." It should be noted that the sound track is not recorded on the filmstrip itself; rather, it comes on a separate cassette tape which is played back on a regular cassette recorder or on one built into the filmstrip projector unit.

For most sound filmstrips, the record or tape contains, besides the sound track, a second track carrying inaudible signals that automatically trigger the projector to advance to the next frame. Depending upon the capability of the projector, users generally have a choice of manually advancing the filmstrip according to audible beeps or setting the projector to

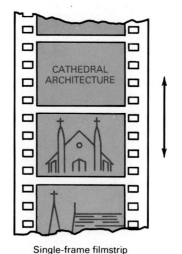

Single-frame filmstrip

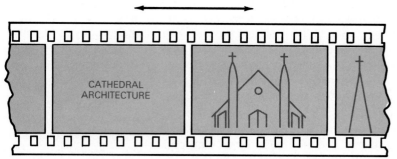

35-mm slide film

▲ *Figure 5.16*
Comparison of the single-frame filmstrip and the 35-mm slide format.

▲ *Figure 5.17*
A modern silent-filmstrip projector

▲ *Figure 5.19*
A sound filmstrip projector that uses
audiocassettes to advance the frames
automatically

▲ *Figure 5.20*
A compact tabletop viewer for silent filmstrips

▲ *Figure 5.18*
Filmstrip sets synchronized with audiocassettes
are a popular format.

run automatically according to the inaudible synchronization pulses.

Advantages

The filmstrip has gained considerable popularity because of its compactness, ease of handling, and relatively low cost. A filmstrip of sixty frames will fit comfortably in the palm of your hand and weighs only a few ounces. It is inserted easily into a simple projector. A commercially distributed filmstrip costs substantially less *per frame* than a set of slides or overhead transparencies purchased from commercial sources.

The sequential order of the frames can often be a teaching and learning advantage. A chronological or step-by-step process can be presented *exactly in order* without any fear of having any of the pictures out of sequence or upside-down, as can sometimes happen with slides.

In contrast with audio and motion media, the pace of viewing filmstrips can be controlled by the user. This capability is especially relevant for independent study but is also important for teacher-controlled group showings. A slow, deliberate examination of each frame might be suitable for the body of a lesson, whereas a quick runthrough might suffice for purposes of advance overview and review. Not only the pace but also the level of instruction can be controlled. Particularly with silent filmstrips, the vocabulary and/or level of narration supplied by the presenter can be adapted to audience abilities.

Filmstrips lend themselves well to independent study. Many types of tabletop viewers are made especially for individual or small-group use. Young children have no difficulty loading light, compact filmstrips into these viewers. The fixed sequence of the frames structures the learner's progress through the material; the captions or recorded narration add a verbal component to the visuals, creating a convenient self-contained learning "package." And because the user controls the rate of presentation, the filmstrip allows self-pacing when used for independent study.

Limitations

Having the frames permanently fixed in a certain sequence has disadvantages as well as advantages. The main drawback is that it is not possible to alter the sequence of pictures without destroying the filmstrip. Backtracking to an earlier picture or skipping over frames is cumbersome.

Because the filmstrip is pulled through its projector by means of toothed sprocket wheels, there is the constant possibility of tearing the sprocket holes and/or damaging the filmstrip. Improper threading or rough use can cause tears which are very difficult for you to repair, although, if you have a 35-mm splicing block, not impossible. (In cases where damage to the sprocket holes is extensive, the frames can be cut apart and mounted individually to be used as slides.)

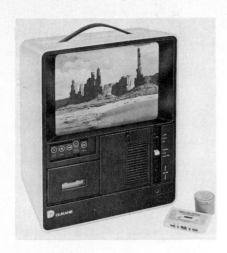

▲ *Figure 5.21*
The tabletop sound-filmstrip viewer can serve an individual or a small group, and it can be viewed in a fully lighted room.

Applications

Because they are simply packaged and easy to handle, filmstrips are well suited to independent-study use. They are popular items in study carrels and media centers. Students enjoy using filmstrips on their own to help prepare research reports to their classmates.

The major difference in application between slides and filmstrips is that slides lend themselves to teacher-made presentations, whereas filmstrips are better suited to mass production and distribution. Further, slide sets tend to be used in a more open-ended fashion than filmstrips. Nowadays filmstrips are usually packaged as self-contained kits. That is, the narration to accompany the pictures is provided either in the form of captions on the filmstrip, or a recorded sound track on record or cassette. Other teacher support materials may be integrated into the kit.

As with the other sorts of projected visuals discussed in this chapter, filmstrips find appropriate applications in a wide variety of subjects and grade levels. Their broad appeal is attested to by the constantly growing volume of commercial materials available. Tens of thousands of titles are already in distribution. Indeed, it would be difficult to identify an audiovisual medium offering a larger number of different titles in commercial distribution.

A small sample of the broad range of filmstrips on the market is illustrated by the following examples. A major directory of commercially available filmstrips is published by the National Information Center for Educational Media (NICEM)—*Index to 35-mm Filmstrips.* See Appendix A for details and other sources.

An innovation introduced in 1984 may foreshadow a future role for the filmstrip as an element in interactive video programs. The Society for Visual Education (SVE), a major commercial distributor of filmstrips, produced a single videodisc incorporating more than 30,000 still pictures. The videodisc player is connected to a microcomputer containing a computer-assisted instruction program. The computer program presents verbal instruction *and* controls the videodisc player, calling up particular pictures onto the display screen as needed. The

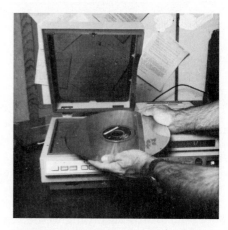

▲ *Figure 5.22*
A filmstrip library of 30,000 frames can be stored on a single videodisc.

AV Showmanship - FILMSTRIP

The general utilization guidelines discussed in Chapter 2 apply comprehensively to filmstrip use. There are several additional points, though, that pertain especially to filmstrips:

• Do not feel compelled to run the filmstrip all the way through without stopping. You can do this as a kind of *overview* and then go back and reshow it, pausing for discussion at key frames.

• Encourage *participation* by asking relevant questions during the presentation. You may want to ask the students to read the captions. This is a particularly good reading activity for elementary students.

• Use filmstrips to *test* visually the mastery of visual concepts. This can be done, for instance, by projecting individual frames without the caption or sound track and asking students to make an identification or discrimination.

entire videodisc—all 30,000 images—can be scanned in less than five seconds and the desired frame inserted in the lesson. As discussed in detail in Chapter 7, interactive video is usually thought of as combining moving images (television) with computer interaction, but in many learning situations only still pictures are needed. The SVE system could suit those purposes, eliminating television production costs and recycling vast libraries of existing pictures.

OPAQUE PROJECTION

*O*PAQUE *projection* is *a method of enlarging and displaying nontransparent material on a screen.* A very bright light is reflected from the material to be displayed rather than passed through it. The opaque projector was among the first audiovisual devices to come into widespread use and is still used because of its unique ability to project a magnified image of two-dimensional materials and some three-dimensional objects.

The opaque projector works by directing a very strong incandescent light (typically about 1,000 watts) down onto the material. This light is reflected upward to strike a mirror, which aims the light beam through a series of lenses onto a screen (Figure 5.23).

The process of reflected, or indirect, projection is optically less efficient than the direct projection process used for showing slides, filmstrips, and overhead transparencies. Consequently, the image on the screen is dimmer, and much more complete room darkening is required. Still, opaque projection makes such a wide range of visual materials available for group viewing that it

should not be overlooked as a valuable tool.

Advantages

Opaque projection allows on-the-spot projection of readily available classroom materials, such as maps, newspapers, and illustrations from books and magazines (Figure 5.24).

It permits group viewing and discussion of student work, such as drawings, student compositions, solutions to math problems, and the like.

Three-dimensional objects, especially relatively flat ones such

MEDIA FILE
"California: The Golden State" Filmstrip Set

This set of four filmstrips for intermediate grades comes with some uncommon features. Each filmstrip begins with a set of learning objectives, and each contains vocabulary frames to alert teachers and students to key words. A set of twenty-four "skill sheets" provides written exercises that reinforce the content of the filmstrips. The four filmstrips are titled (1) California's Geography; (2) California's Early History through the Gold Rush; (3) California: Statehood and After; and (4) California: Diversity, Challenge, and Change.

Source: Society for Visual Education

MEDIA FILE:
"The American Revolution: Who Was Right?" Filmstrip

The American Revolution would never have occurred if there had not been disagreement between England and her colonies. Both sides of the issues are revealed through visuals and spoken dialogue. One recording discusses the topic from the English point of view and the other recording gives the American interpretation using the same visuals. The categories have been carefully selected in order to present material that was not only relevant in 1776, but is still discussed and pertinent today.

Source: Current Affairs Multimedia

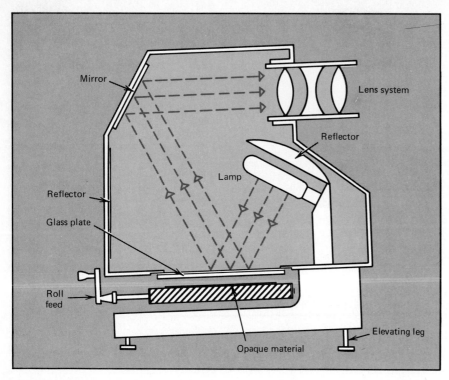

▲ *Figure 5.23*
Opaque projector, cutaway view

as coins, plant leaves, and insect specimens, can be magnified for close-up inspection.

Limitations

The relative dimness of the reflected image demands rather complete room darkening if the visual is to be clear enough for instructional purposes. Areas that cannot be sufficiently darkened are unsuitable for opaque projection.

The opaque projector is bulky, heavy, and cumbersome to move.

The high-wattage lamp generates a lot of heat, making parts of the projector unsafe to touch. The heat may also damage the materials being projected if they are exposed too long to the projector's light. If metal objects are being projected, they may rapidly become too hot to handle.

Applications

The opaque projector is useful for many small groups or classroom-size groups (up to about twenty) that need to view some printed or visual material together. Applications may be found in all curricular areas at all grade levels. Here are just a few typical examples:

All subjects: group critique of student work and review of test items.

Art: group discussion of reproductions of paintings and architectural details; study of advertising layouts.

Business: group work on business and accounting forms, organization charts, sales territory maps, parts of a product, and the like.

Home economics: group viewing of sewing patterns, textiles, recipes, close-up views of fabrics and weaving styles; and so forth.

Industry: projection of blueprints for group study; description of

▲ *Figure 5.24*
The opaque projector can be used to magnify small objects as well as print materials and pictures.

assembly line flow with production diagrams.

Language arts: group critique of student compositions, picture books, or reference books.

Other possible applications include the following:

Medical: group study of anatomical drawings; discussion of diabetic diets and food exchange charts.

Military: review of maps and official documents; illustration of flight plans.

Music: group reading of musical scores.

Religious education: Bible story illustrations; group examination of religious documents.

Science: magnification of specimens; group study of geologic maps, tables of random numbers, and the like.

Social studies: map study; viewing of artifacts from other cultures, postcards, and atlas illustrations.

One especially handy application of the opaque projector is for copying or adapting illustrations for classroom display. You can make your own enlargement of any original picture that you might want to display on the chalkboard or as part of a bulletin board. The procedure is easy. Place the material to be copied in the projector and dim the room lights. Adjust the projector to enlarge (or reduce) the image to the size you want, and direct the projected image onto the surface on which you are working. Then trace over the projected image in whatever detail you wish. Every line of the original can be reproduced, or just the outlines for a more stylized effect. Your students will be impressed with your "artistic ability," and maybe you will be too.

SELECTION CRITERIA FOR PROJECTED VISUALS

I N this chapter we have attempted to survey broadly the many similarities and differences among several major formats of projected visuals—overhead projection, slides, filmstrips, and opaque projection. You might have noticed that the differences are mainly logistical ones—small technical differences that lead to trade-offs in cost, portability, flexibility, and so on. Basically, projected visuals look very much alike on the screen. For the viewer/learner there is, in most cases, "no significant difference" among these formats in terms of learning impact. So it is appropriate that the chapter close by emphasizing the commonalities among the various types of projected visuals. The "Appraisal Checklist: Projected Visuals" is designed to apply equally to the various formats.

AV Showmanship - OPAQUE PROJECTION

In addition to the general principles of audiovisual utilization discussed in Chapter 2, there are several special techniques that apply particularly to opaque projection.

- Because the opaque projector requires near-total room darkening, be prepared to operate in the dark. A student should be stationed at the light switch to help you avoid tripping over students, cords, and other obstacles in getting to and from the projector in the dark. Although the projector does spill quite a bit of light around its sides, you may need to use a *flashlight* to follow any prepared notes or script.

- Most opaque projectors are equipped with a built-in optical *pointer*—a bright arrow that can be aimed at any point on the screen. Experiment ahead of time so that you will be able to aim the pointer effectively during the presentation. It can

be used to focus viewers' attention to particular words on a printed page, details of an art work, and so on.

- For some purposes (especially in teaching elementary school language arts) it is useful to arrange pictures on a long strip or roll of paper. In this way you can put a series of illustrations into a fixed sequence to tell a story or show steps in a process. This simulates the action of a filmstrip.

- The opaque projector will accept a wide range of picture sizes. When you are setting up the projector, be sure to use the *largest* of your illustrations to fill the screen area. If you use a smaller picture, the bigger one will extend beyond the edges of the screen when you get to it. This will force you to stop in the middle of the presentation (and thus distract your audience) to adjust for the big picture.

Appraisal Checklist: Projected Visuals

Title _____

Series title (if applicable) _____

Source _____

Length _____ frames _____ minutes (sound track)

Date _____ Cost_____

Subject area _____

Intended audience _____

Format
☐ overhead transparency
☐ slide
☐ sound/slide
☐ filmstrip
☐ sound filmstrip

Objectives (stated or implied):

Brief Description:

Entry Capabilities Required:

- Prior subject-matter knowledge/vocabulary
- Reading ability
- Mathematical ability
- Other

Rating	High		Medium		Low	Comments
Relevance to objectives	☐	☐	☐	☐	☐	
Accuracy of information	☐	☐	☐	☐	☐	
Likely to arouse/maintain interest	☐	☐	☐	☐	☐	
Likely to be comprehended clearly	☐	☐	☐	☐	☐	
Technical quality	☐	☐	☐	☐	☐	
Promotes participation/involvement	☐	☐	☐	☐	☐	
Evidence of effectiveness (e.g., field-test results)	☐	☐	☐	☐	☐	
Free from objectionable bias	☐	☐	☐	☐	☐	
Provisions for discussion/follow-up	☐	☐	☐	☐	☐	

Strong Points:

Weak Points:

Reviewer _____

Position _____

Recommended action _____ Date _____

References

Print References

Barman, C. "Some Ways to Improve Your Overhead Projection Transparencies." *American Biology Teacher* (March 1982), pp. 191–192.

Beatty, LaMond F. *Filmstrips.* (Englewood Cliffs, N.J.: Educational Technology Publications, 1981).

Bodner, George M. "Instructional Media: Resisting Technological Overkill—35-mm Slides as an Alternative to Videotape/Videodisk." *Journal of College Science Teaching* (February 1985), pp. 360–363.

Bohning, G. "Storytelling Using Overhead Visuals." *Reading Teacher* (March 1984), pp. 677–678.

Burton, D. "Slide Art." *School Arts* (February 1984), pp. 23–26.

Center for Vocational Education. *Present Information with Overhead and Opaque Materials.* (Athens, Ga.: American Association for Vocational Instructional Materials, 1977).

———. *Present Information with Filmstrips and Slides.* (Athens, Ga.: American Association for Vocational Instructional Materials, 1977).

Clark, Jean N. "Filmstrips: Versatility and Visual Impact." *Media and Methods* (January–February 1988), pp. 20–21.

DeChenne, J. "Effective Utilization of Overhead Projectors." *Media and Methods* (January 1982), pp. 6–7.

Effective Visual Presentations. (Rochester, N.Y.: Eastman Kodak, 1979).

Elliot, Floyd. *The Filmstrip—A Useful Teaching Aid.* (Montreal, Canada: National Film Board of Canada, 1963).

Gersmehl, Philip J. "One Commandment and Ten Suggestions: Teaching the Video Generation with Slides." *Journal of Geography* (January–February 1985), pp. 15–19.

Green, Lee. *501 Ways to Use the Overhead Projector.* (Littleton, Colo.: Libraries Unlimited, 1982).

Jones, J. Rhodri. "Getting the Most out of an Overhead Projector." *English Language Teaching Journal* (April 1978), pp. 194–201.

Kueter, Roger A., and Miller, Janeen. *Slides.* (Englewood Cliffs, N.J.: Educational Technology Publications, 1981).

Lefever, Margaret. "A Mother Lode of Images for Teaching History." *Social Education* (May 1987), p. 265.

McBride, Dennis. *How to Make Visual Presentations.* (New York: Art Direction Book Company, 1982).

May, Jill P. *Films and Filmstrips for Language Arts: An Annotated Bibliography.* (Urbana, Ill.: National Council of Teachers of English, 1981).

Perez, Fred. "Using Slides to Promote Intramurals." *Journal of Physical Education and Recreation* (May 1978), p. 63ff.

Radcliffe, Beverly. "Using the Overhead Projector for Homework Correction." *Foreign Language Annals* (April 1984), pp. 119–121.

Ring, Arthur. *Planning and Producing Handmade Slides and Filmstrips for the Classroom.* (Belmont, Calif.: David S. Lake, 1974).

Runte, Roseann. "Focusing in on the Slide—Its Practical Applications." *Canadian Modern Language Review* (March 1977), pp. 547–551.

Sheard, B. V. "They Love to Read Aloud from Filmstrips." *Teacher* (May 1973), p. 66ff.

Van Vliet, Lucille W. "Tackling Production Techniques: The Opaque, It's Great." *School Library Media Activities* (April 1986), pp. 36–37.

Warner, Linda A. "Consider Your Camera." *Science and Children* (April 1985), pp. 20–22.

White, Gene. "From Magic Lanterns to Microcomputers: The Evolution of the Visual Aid in the English Classroom." *English Journal* (March 1984), pp. 59–62.

Winters, Harold A. "Some Unconventional Uses of the Overhead Projector in Teaching Geography." *Journal of Geography* (November 1976), pp. 467–469.

Audiovisual References

"Color Lift" Transparencies. Salt Lake City, Utah: Media Systems, 1975. Filmstrip or slides, 40 frames, captioned.

Effective Projection, Photography for Audiovisual Production, and *The Impact of Visuals in the Speechmaking Process.* Eastman Kodak, 1982. 3 filmstrips with audiocassettes.

"I Like the Overhead Projector Because . . ." Washington, D.C.: National Audiovisual Center, 1977. Filmstrip with audiocassette, 12 minutes.

Thermofax (covers making thermal transparencies). Iowa City, Iowa: Audiovisual Center, University of Iowa, 1986. Videotape.

Use of the Overhead Projector and How to Make Do-It-Yourself Transparencies. Swan Pencil Co., n.d. 80 slides with cassette. 18 minutes.

Possible Projects

5-A. Take a series of slides for use in your teaching. Describe your objectives, the intended audience, and how the slides will be used.

5-B. Design a lesson around a commercially available filmstrip. Describe your objectives, the intended audience, how the filmstrip will be used, and how the lesson will be evaluated. (If possible, submit the filmstrip with the project.)

5-C. Prepare transparencies using both the write-on and thermal methods.

5-D. Prepare a set of visuals for use with an opaque projector.

5-E. Preview a set of slides or a filmstrip. Complete an appraisal sheet (from the text or one of your own design) on the materials.

5-F. Examine *two* of the selection sources for slides, filmstrips, or overheads and report on the kinds of materials you believe would be appropriate for your teaching situation.

6

Audio Media

Objectives

After studying this chapter, you
should be able to:

1. Distinguish between *hearing*
and *listening*.

2. Identify four areas of breakdown
in audio communication and specify
the causes of such breakdowns.

3. Describe four techniques for
improving listening skills.

4. Discuss ten attributes of audio
media, including five advantages and
five limitations.

5. Describe four types of audio media most often used for instruction. Include in your description the distinguishing characteristics and limitations.

6. List three characteristics of the compact disc that make it useful for data storage.

7. Describe one possible use of audio media in your teaching field. Include the subject area, the audience, objective(s), role of the student, and the evaluation techniques to be used.

8. Identify five criteria for appraising/selecting audio materials.

9. Discuss the techniques for making your own audiotapes, including guidelines for the recorder controls, the acoustics, microphone placement, tape content, and audio presentation.

10. Distinguish among the common types of microphones.

11. Describe two procedures for duplicating audiotapes.

12. Describe two procedures for editing audiotapes.

13. Identify the advantages of rate-controlled audio playback.

14. Select the best audio format for a given instructional situation and justify the selection of that format, stating advantages and/or disadvantages.

Lexicon

hearing
listening
open reel tape
cassette
compact disc
digital recording
audio card
oral history
acoustics
rate-controlled playback

If you were asked which learning activities consume the major portion of a student's classroom time, would you say reading instructional materials, answering questions, reciting what one has learned, or taking tests? Actually, typical elementary and secondary students spend about 50 percent of their school time just listening (or at least "hearing," which, as we shall see, is not the same as "listening"). College students are likely to spend nearly 90 percent of their time in class listening to lectures and seminar discussions. The importance, then, of audio media in the classroom should not be underestimated. By *audio media* we mean the various means of recording and transmitting the human voice and other sounds for instructional purposes. The audio devices most commonly found in the classroom are the phonograph or record player, the open reel tape recorder, the cassette tape recorder, and the audio card reader.

Before going on to discuss these audio formats in particular and audio media in general, let us examine the hearing/listening process itself, as it pertains to the communication of ideas and information and to the development of listening skills.

THE HEARING/LISTENING PROCESS

HEARING and listening are not the same thing, although they are, of course, interrelated. At the risk of some oversimplification, we might say that hearing is a *physiological* process, whereas listening is a *psychological* process.

Physiologically, *hearing* is a process in which sound waves entering the outer ear are transmitted to the eardrum, converted into mechanical vibrations in the middle ear, and changed in the inner ear into nerve impulses that travel to the brain (Figure 6.3).

The psychological process of *listening* begins with someone's awareness of and attention to sounds or speech patterns, proceeds through identification and recognition of specific auditory signals, and ends in comprehension.

The hearing/listening process is also a communication/learning process. As with visual communication and learning, a message is encoded by a sender and decoded by a receiver. The quality of the encoded message is affected by the ability of the sender to express the message clearly and logically. The quality of the decoded message is affected by the ability of the receiver to comprehend the message.

The efficiency of communication is also affected by the hearing/listening process as the message passes from sender to receiver. The message can be affected by physical problems such as impaired hearing mechanisms. It also can be affected by auditory fatigue. The brain has a remarkable capacity for filtering out sounds it doesn't want or need to hear. We have all had the experience of "tuning out" a boring conversationalist or gradually losing cognizance of noises (the ticking of a clock, traffic outside a window, etc.) that seemed obtrusive when we first encountered them. Nevertheless, in the classroom extraneous noise can cause auditory fatigue and make communication difficult. A monotonous tone or a droning voice can also reduce communication effi-

▲ *Figure 6.1*
Elementary/secondary students spend about half of their in-school time listening to others.

▲ *Figure 6.2*
At the college level, about 90 percent of class time is spent in listening.

ciency by contributing to auditory fatigue.

The message can also be affected by the receiver's listening skills or lack of them. The receiver must be able to direct and sustain concentration on a given series of sounds (the message). He or she must have the skill to "think ahead" as the message is being received (we think faster than we hear, just as we think faster than we read or write) and use this time differential to organize and internalize the information so that it can be comprehended.

Breakdowns in audio communications, then, can occur at any point in the process: encoding, hearing, listening, or decoding, as illustrated in Figure 6.4. Proper encoding of the message depends upon the sender's skill in organizing and presenting it. For example, the vocabulary level of the message must be within the vocabulary range of the receiver. And, of course, the message itself must be presented in such a way that it is within the receiver's experiential range. The transmission process can be affected if the sender speaks too loudly or too softly or if the receiver has hearing difficulties or auditory fatigue. Communication can be reduced by the listener's lack of attentiveness or lack of skill in auditory analysis. Finally, communication can break down because the receiver lacks the experiential background to internalize, and thus comprehend, the message.

DEVELOPING LISTENING SKILLS

In formal education, much attention is given to reading, a little to speaking, and essentially none to listening. Listening is a skill, and like all skills, it can be

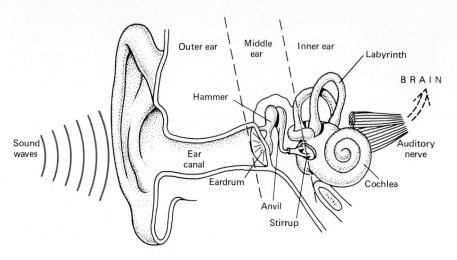

▲ *Figure 6.3*
The physiological process of human hearing

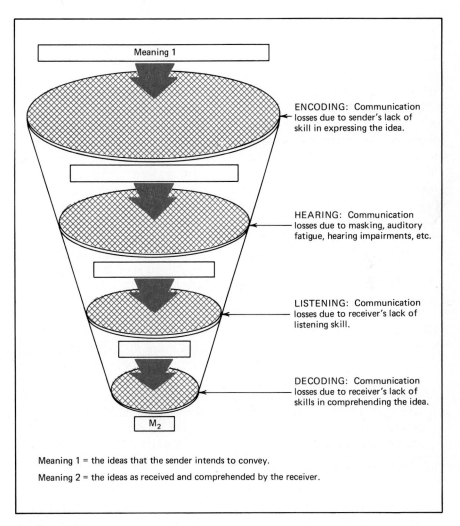

Meaning 1 = the ideas that the sender intends to convey.

Meaning 2 = the ideas as received and comprehended by the receiver.

▲ *Figure 6.4*
The hearing/listening process: impediments at each step act like filters, reducing the perceived meaning to a small fraction of the original intended meaning.

▲ *Figure 6.5*
Listening skills are being taught at all levels and form a major component of many management development programs.

improved with practice. You should first determine that all of your students can hear normally. Most school systems regularly request the services of speech and hearing therapists who administer audiometric hearing tests that provide the data you need. There are also standardized tests that measure students' listening abilities. These tests are often administered by the school district, so you should check to see if listening test scores are available.

There are a number of techniques the teacher can use to improve student listening abilities:

1. *Directed listening.* Before orally presenting a story or lesson, give the students some objectives or questions to guide their listening. Start with short passages and one or two objectives, then gradually increase the length of the passage and the number and complexity level of the objectives or questions.

2. *Following directions.* Give the students directions individually or as a group on audiotape and ask them to follow these instructions. You can evaluate the students' abilities to follow the audio instructions by examining worksheets or products of the activity. When giving directions orally, the "say it only once" rule should be observed so that a value is placed on both the teacher's and students' time and the incentive to listen is reinforced.

3. *Listening for main ideas, details, or inferences.* Keeping the age level of the students in mind, you can present an oral passage and ask the students to listen for the main idea and then write it down. A similar technique can be used with details of and inferences to be drawn from the passage.

4. *Using context in listening.* Younger students can learn to distinguish meanings in an auditory context by listening to

sentences with words missing and then supplying the appropriate words.

5. *Analyzing the structure of a presentation.* The students can be asked to outline (analyze and organize) an oral presentation. The teacher can then determine how well they were able to discern the main ideas and to identify the subtopics.

6. *Distinguishing between relevant and irrelevant information.* After listening to an oral presentation of information, the student can be asked to identify the main idea and then rate (from most to least relevant) all other ideas that are presented. A simpler technique for elementary students is to have them identify irrelevant words in sentences or irrelevant sentences in paragraphs.

CHARACTERISTICS OF AUDIO MEDIA

Advantages

AUDIO media have many desirable attributes. First and foremost, they tend to be inexpensive forms of instruction. In the case of audiotape, once the tapes and equipment have been purchased, there is no additional cost, because the tape can be erased after use and a new message recorded.

Audio materials are readily available and very simple to use. They can be adapted easily to any vocabulary level and can be used for group or individual instruction.

Students who cannot read can learn from audio media. For young nonreading students, audio can provide early language experiences.

Audio can present stimulating verbal messages more dramatically than can print. With a little imagination on the part of the teacher, audio can be very versatile.

Audiocassette recorders are very portable and can even be used "in the field" with battery power. Cassette recorders are ideal for home study. Many students already have their own cassette machines. Audiotapes are easily duplicated in whatever quantities are needed.

Limitations

As with all media, audio instructional devices have limitations. Audio tends to fix the sequence of a presentation even though it is possible to rewind the tape and hear a recorded segment again or advance the tape to an upcoming portion.

Without someone standing over them or speaking with them face-to-face, some students do not pay attention to the presentation. They may hear the presentation but not listen to and comprehend it.

The initial expense of playback and recording equipment may be a problem. Development of audio materials by the instructor is time-consuming. Determining the appropriate pace for presenting information can be difficult if your listeners have a wide range of listening skills and experiential backgrounds.

Storage and retrieval of audiotapes and phonograph records can also cause problems.

MEDIA FILE:
"Law: You, the Police, and Justice" Record

The impact of the spoken word is frequently greater than that of print, particularly when emotional atmosphere is of more importance than the literal meaning of conversations or arguments between people or the impassioned statements by participants in a real-life drama. This record is alive with the feelings of real people talking about the law in natural and unrehearsed settings. Included are youths, police officers, lawyers, a judge, and a boy and a girl in serious trouble with the law. The recordings were made in a bowling alley, on a city street, in a police station, in a jail for delinquent girls, and at an actual courtroom trial. The situations portrayed will raise many questions about relationships between youth and the apparatus of civil control and law.

Source: Scholastic Records

MEDIA FILE:
"Singing Games and Folk Dances" Record Series

Undoubtedly, the most frequently used piece of mediaware in the primary classroom is the phonograph. At this age level, learning experiences are frequently tied to physical activity. One of the favored ways of managing this type of instructional effort in a classroom of energetic youngsters is a carefully planned sequence of activities on a phonograph record. The teacher is free to lead the group in the action called for on the disc. A typical collection of such activities is included in this series.

Source: Bowmar Records.

AUDIO FORMATS

LET's examine the comparative strengths and weaknesses of the audio formats most often used for instructional purposes—phonograph records (disc recordings), the open reel tape, the cassette tape, the compact disc, and the audio card, plus a format more suited to home and office use, microcassettes.

Phonograph Records

The phonograph record (disc recording) has a number of attributes that make it an attractive instructional medium. Its frequency response is such that it can reproduce the audio spectrum even beyond the limits of human hearing. All types of communication, from the spoken word to the sounds of a hurricane, the mating call of the yellow-billed cuckoo,

▲ *Figure 6.6*
A wealth of recorded material is available on the common audio formats: records, cassettes, and compact discs.

amount of information recorded on them.

Audiotapes

The major advantage of magnetic audiotape over discs is that you can record your own tapes easily and economically, and when the material becomes outdated or no longer useful, you can erase the magnetic signal on the tape and reuse it. Tapes are not as easily damaged as discs, and they are easily stored. Unlike discs, broken tapes can be repaired.

Of course, there are some limitations to magnetic tape recordings. In the recording process background noises or a mechanical hum may sometimes be recorded along with the intended material. Even a relatively low-level noise can ruin an otherwise good recording. The fact that audiotapes can be erased easily can pose a problem as well. Just as you can quickly and easily erase tapes you no longer need, you can accidentally and just as quickly erase tapes you want to save. It is difficult to locate a specific segment on an audiotape. Counters on the recorder assist retrieval, but they are not very accurate. Audiotapes also tend to deteriorate in quality when stored for a long period of time.

Open Reel Tapes.

When magnetic tape recording was first introduced to the public in 1946, the tape was mounted on "open" reels, similar to 16-mm film. The tape had to be threaded through the tape recorder and the free end of the tape secured to an empty take-up reel. This is why this tape format is often referred to as reel-to-reel. The now familiar cassette was introduced at the Berlin Radio Show in 1963. Within a few years the convenience, flexibility, and portability of the new format made open reel tapes obsolete for

▲ *Figure 6.7*
"Exploded" view of an audio cassette: (1) the ⅛-inch tape, (2) styrene housing, (3) idler rollers, (4) lubricated liner, (5) pressure pad, (6) hub and clip, (7) metal shield, (8) clear index window, (9) screw (or other closure method)

virtually all education and training applications.

Cassette Tapes.

The cassette tape is in essence a self-contained reel-to-reel system with the two reels permanently installed in a rugged plastic case (Figure 6.7). The ⅛-inch-wide tape is permanently fastened to each of the reels. Cassette tapes are identified according to the amount of recording time they contain. For example, a C-60 cassette can record sixty minutes of sound using both sides (that is, thirty minutes on each side). A C-90 can record forty-five minutes on each side. Cassettes are available in C-15, C-30, C-60, C-90, and C-120 lengths, and other lengths can be specially ordered. The size of the plastic cassette containing the tape is the same in all cases, and all can be placed on any cassette machine.

The cassette is durable—virtually immune to shock and abrasion. It is the easiest of the tape formats to use because it requires no manual threading. It can be

and Beethoven's Ninth Symphony, are recorded on phonograph records. A major directory of commercially available records is published by the National Information Center for Educational Media (NICEM)—*Index to Educational Records*. See Appendix A for details and other sources.

Selections are separated by "bands," thereby making cuing of segments easier. The location or band of each segment of the recording is usually indicated on the label of the record and on its sleeve or dustcover. Because phonograph records are stamped from a master in a fairly high-speed process, they are relatively inexpensive.

Despite all the advantages of phonograph records, they are not without serious limitations from an instructional point of view. The most limiting is that you cannot economically prepare your own records. A record is easily damaged if someone drops the stylus (needle) on the disc or otherwise scratches the surface. Excess heat and improper storage may cause the disc to warp and make it difficult, if not impossible, to play. Storage can pose another problem in that records take up more space than either open reel or cassette tapes with the same

Audio Formats

		Speeds	Advantages	Limitations	Uses
Phonograph record (disc recording)	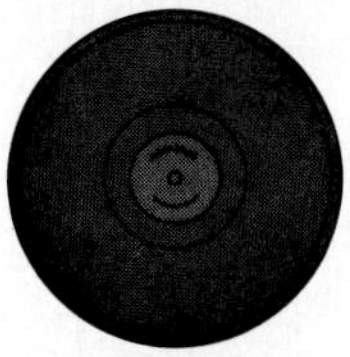 Diameters: 7, 10, 12 in.	78 rpm[a] 45 rpm 33⅓ rpm 16⅔ rpm	• Excellent frequency response • Compatibility of records and phonographs • Selection easily cued • Wide variety of selections • Inexpensive	• Impractical to prepare locally • Easily scratched • Can warp • Requires much storage space	• Music • Long narrations • Classroom listening • Historical speeches • Drama, poetry
Compact disc	Size: 4.72 in. 	Variable high speed	• Very durable • High fidelity • No background noise • Random search of data	• Playback only • Expensive	• Music • Drama • Data storage
Open Reel audiotape (reel-to-reel)	Reel sizes: 3, 5, 7 in.  Tape ¼ in. wide	7½ ips[b] 3¾ ips 1⅞ ips	• Can be prepared locally • Can be erased and used again • Not easily damaged • Easily stored • Broken tapes easily repaired • Excellent frequency response • Easily edited	• Accidental erasure • Difficult to use (threading) • Unlabelled or mislabelled tapes • Selections difficult to locate and cue	• Teacher-made recordings • Group listening • Self-evaluation
Cassette audiotape	Size: 2½ by 4 by ½ in.  Tape ⅛ in. wide	1⅞ ips	• Very portable (small and light) • Durable • Easy to use (no threading) • Can prevent accidental erasing • Requires little storage space	• Tape sometimes sticks or tangles • Noise and hiss • Poor fidelity (inexpensive models) • Broken tapes *not* easy to repair • Difficult to edit	• Listening "in the field" using battery power • Student-made recordings • Extended discussions • Individual listening
Microcassette	Size: 1⁵⁄₁₆ by 1³⁄₃₂ by ²¹⁄₆₄ in. 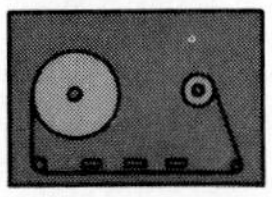 Tape ⅛ in. wide	¹⁵⁄₁₆ ips	• Very compact • Portable • Fits in pocket	• Not compatible with other cassettes • Poor fidelity	• Dictation by business executives • Amateur recording • LIMITED EDUCATIONAL USE
Audio card	3½ by 9 in. or 5½ by 11 in.  ¼ in. magnetic stripe	2¼ ips 1⅛ ips	• Sound with visual • Student can record response and compare with original • Designed for individual use • Participation; involvement	• Most cards less than 8 seconds • Time-consuming to prepare	• Vocabulary building • Concept learning • Associating sounds with visuals • Technical vocabulary

[a] rpm = revolutions per minute.

[b] ips = inches per second.

snapped into and out of a recorder in seconds. It is *not* necessary to rewind the tape before removing it from the machine. Accidental erasures can be avoided by breaking out the small plastic tabs on the edge of the cassette.

Storage is also convenient. A cassette collection can be stored in about one-third the space required for open reel tapes with the same amount of program material on them.

With all of these attributes you might wonder if there are any drawbacks. Unfortunately, longer cassette tapes, particularly C-120s, sometimes become stuck or tangled in the recorder due to the thinness of the tape. If this happens, and unless the content on the tape is one of a kind and of considerable value to you, you are best advised to throw the tape away. If it sticks or gets tangled in the machine once, it is likely to do so again. If a cassette tape

breaks, its smaller size and difficult access make it much more difficult to splice than the open reel tape. However, there are special cassette splicers that make the job easier. The frequency response and overall quality (fidelity) of cassette playback units are not as good as those of reel-to-reel machines or record players because of the small speakers in most portable cassette playback units. However, for most instructional uses the quality is more than adequate.

A major directory of commercially available audiotapes is published by the National Information Center for Educational Media (NICEM)—*Index to Educational Audio Tapes.* See Appendix A for details and other sources.

Compact Discs

Someone once commented that the more sophisticated technology becomes, the more it seems

like magic. That certainly is true of an audio format that was introduced in 1983—the compact disc (CD). Physically, the compact disc looks like a small, silver phonograph record without grooves. The digital code is in the form of tiny pits in clear plastic, protected by a thin covering of an acrylic resin (see Figure 6.8). The disc is only twelve centimeters (4.72 inches) in diameter. This small disc, rotating much faster than a phonograph record, stores an incredible amount of information. Some CDs contain as much as seventy-five minutes of music.

Until the compact disc was developed, all retail audio recordings were "analog" recordings. That is, they retained the essential wave form of the sound, whether as grooves in a phonograph record or as patterns of magnetized particles on audiotape. The recording on a CD is in digital form. Analog information, whether in the form of music, speech, or print, is transformed into a series of 1s and 0s, the same mathematical code used in computers. A powerful laser burns a microscopic pit into the plastic master for each 1 in the digital code. A blank space corresponds to 0. The laser moves in an ever-widening spiral from the center of the master to the edge, leaving on the disc hundreds of thousands of binary bits (1s and 0s). After a low-power laser beam in the playback unit picks up the pattern of pits and blank spaces, the beam is reflected back into the laser mechanism, and the digital code is transformed back into the original analog sound. The laser mechanism does not come in direct physical contact with the CD and can move independently of the disc, unlike the stylus in a record groove or a tape head. This means that the laser beam can scan the CD and quickly locate desired

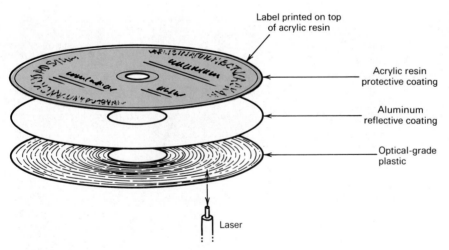

Label printed on top of acrylic resin

Acrylic resin protective coating

Aluminum reflective coating

Optical-grade plastic

Laser

▲ *Figure 6.8*
The compact disc, shown in one-half of actual size, is a three-layer sandwich. The digital code in the form of pits is on the top side of a clear, tough plastic very much like Plexiglas. A reflective coating of aluminum, or sometimes silver, is placed on top of the pitted plastic surface. A protective coating of an acrylic resin is "painted" on the top of the reflective surface. Label information is printed on top of the resin. This arrangement protects the program information from both the top and bottom of the disc. The laser beam reads the code through the clear plastic and is reflected back by the aluminum (or silver) layer. The manufacturing process must be carried out in an environment completely free of dust because of the almost microscopic size of the pits.
Unlike an LP, the recording on a CD begins near the center and ends at the outer rim. Also unlike an LP, the CD does not rotate at a constant speed. The speed varies from 500 rpm at the innermost track to 200 rpm at the outer edge.

information. In other words, the CD can be programmed so that the user can quickly access any part of the disc. CD players for the home indicate what track is playing, the sequence in which tracks will be played, how many more tracks are on the disc, and remaining playing time. Another characteristic of digital recording is the complete absence of background noise.

The technology of the CD makes it an attractive addition to education and training programs. Teachers can quickly locate selections on the disc and even program them to play in any desired sequence. Information can be selectively retrieved by trainees or programmed by the trainer. A major advantage of the CD is its resistance to damage. There are no grooves to scratch or tape to tangle and tear. Stains can be washed off, and ordinary scratches do not affect playback of the recording.

Compact disc technology has been accepted rapidly for use in the home. But the cost of a CD—almost twice that of a record or cassette—plus the need for a CD player will slow its acceptance in the education market. However, when prices eventually come down, the CD's advantages, especially its resistance to damage, will make it a standard format for using audio in education.

Digital Audiotape. When compact discs were introduced to the high fidelity market in 1983, many audio enthusiasts put pressure on equipment manufacturers to market digital tape recorders. Finally, the first digital cassette tape recorders became available in the fall of 1987. These machines make it possible for anyone to make a digital recording. The digital tape recorder is expensive. Although attractive to the home

market, the machine will be accepted slowly in education and training because of the cost.

The Compact Disc as Database: CD-ROM. Although the compact disc was originally developed for playing back music, its capability to access stored data quickly made the CD attractive as a means of storing print and visual information. A single CD can hold as many as 250,000 pages, and each of those pages can be accessed very quickly. Compact discs used for data banks are referred to as CD-ROM (for read-only-memory).

A number of data banks are now available. Perhaps the one most useful to educators is the complete Educational Resources Information Clearinghouse (ERIC) files with an update available to subscribers. But companies are making varied use of the CD-ROM capability. McGraw-Hill Publishing Company has put its scientific encyclopedia and dictionary on a single disc. A marketing information service has introduced a database containing demographic information for 250,000 neighborhoods in the

United States. The data can be used for marketing decisions, such as retail-store or restaurant site selection. Automobile manufacturers are putting their parts catalogs on disc for the convenience of their dealers. The first retail CD-ROM program, Microsoft Bookshelf, is designed as a reference tool for word processing. It contains a thesaurus, ZIP code directory, almanac, spelling checker, *Bartlett's Quotations,* and several other reference works. Anyone engaged in word processing can switch to the CD and access needed information quickly. Other companies are exploring ways of incorporating words, sounds, and images on compact disc. An encyclopedia entry on John F. Kennedy, for example, could include his voice as well as photographs and text.

Audio Cards

Another widely used audio instructional format is the audio card (Figure 6.9). An audio card is approximately the size of a business envelope. It contains a strip of magnetic recording tape near

▲ *Figure 6.9*
The audio-card reader allows individual or small-group practice of skills that can be broken into small steps. At 2¼ ips, about a dozen words can be recorded on a ten-inch card.

▲ *Figure 6.10*
Audiotronics "Tutorette" audio-card reader

▲ *Figure 6.11*
A "Talking Books" record player and disc recording

▲ *Figure 6.12*
In the language laboratory, audiotapes allow modeling of proper speech, student response, corrective feedback, and evaluation of mastery.

the bottom edge. The audio card is essentially a flashcard with sound. The card is inserted into a slot on a machine, such as the Bell and Howell Language Master or the Audiotronics Tutorette (Figure 6.10), and a transport mechanism moves the card through the slot. Up to fifteen seconds of sound can be played through the speaker (or headset for individual use). The audio card is used in a dual-track system that allows the student to record his or her own response on the card and then play it back for comparison with the prerecorded response. If the student's response is incorrect, it can be erased and rerecorded correctly by simply running the audio card through the machine again while depressing the record lever. Both the student's and the prerecorded response can be replayed as often as desired by just flipping a lever. The prerecorded message is protected from erasure by a switch on the back of the machine. The

teacher can use the switch to change the prerecorded message.

APPLICATIONS OF AUDIO MEDIA

T HE uses of audio media are limited only by the imagination of teachers and students. They can be used in all phases of instruction from introduction of a topic to evaluation of student learning. Perhaps the most rapidly growing general use of audio media today is in the area of self-paced instruction and in "mastery learning." The slow student can go back and repeat segments of instruction as often as necessary because the recorder/playback machine can serve as a *very* patient tutor. The accelerated student can skip ahead or increase the pace of his or her instruction.

Prerecorded audio materials are available in a wide variety of subjects. For music classes, records and tapes can be used to introduce new material or to provide musical accompaniment. The sounds of various musical instruments can be presented individually or in combinations. In preschool and primary grades, tapes and records can be used for developing rhythm, telling stories, playing games, and acting out stories, songs, etc. In social studies, the tape recorder can bring the voices of persons who have made history into the classroom. The sounds of current events can also be presented.

One special application of prerecorded audio media is "talking books" for blind or visually impaired students. A "Talking Books Program" has been set up by the American Printing House for the Blind to make as much material as possible available to the visually impaired. At present over 11,000 book titles are available, along with recordings of several current periodicals. The service is a cooperative effort of the Library of Congress and fifty-six regional libraries in the United States. The materials are provided on $8\frac{1}{3}$-rpm records which require special players.

Audiotapes can easily be prepared by teachers for specific instructional purposes. For example, in industrial arts, audiotapes can describe the steps in operating a machine or making a product. Recordings of class presentations by the teacher can be used for student makeup and review. One of the most common uses of audio materials is for drill work. For example, the student can practice spelling vocabulary words recorded by the teacher on tape using multiplication tables, taking dictation or typing from a prerecorded tape, or pronouncing a foreign language vocabulary.

History can come alive when students get involved in an *oral history* project. This entails the recording of interviews with living witnesses of the recent or more distant past.

Tape recorders can be used to record information gleaned from a field trip. Upon return to the classroom, the students can play back the tape for discussion and review. Many museums, observatories, and other public exhibit areas now supply visitors with prerecorded messages about various items on display, which may (with permission) be rerecorded for playback in the classroom.

Students can also record themselves reciting, presenting a speech, performing music, etc. They can then listen to the tape in private or have the performance critiqued by the teacher and/or other students. Initial efforts can be kept for comparison with later performances and for reinforcement of learning. Many small-

group projects can include recorded reports that can be presented to the rest of the class. Individual students can prepare oral book reports and term papers on tape for presentation to the class as a whole or one student at a time. One high school literature teacher maintains a file of taped book reports that students listen to before selecting books for their own reading. It is also possible for the students and teacher to bring interviews with local people or recordings of discussions of local events and concerns into the classroom.

An often overlooked use of audio materials is evaluation of student attainment of lesson objectives. For example, test questions may be prerecorded for members of the class to use individually. Students may be asked to identify sounds in a recording (to name the solo instrument being played in a particular musical movement or to identify the composer of a particular piece of music). Students in social studies classes could be asked to identify the historical person most likely to have made excerpted passages from famous speeches, or they

could be asked to identify the time period of excerpted passages from their content. Testing and evaluating in the audio mode is especially appropriate when teaching and learning have also been in that particular mode.

Cassette: The Constant Companion

A few years ago, the American Psychological Association surveyed a sample of its membership to determine their preferred medium for continuing professional development. The cassette won handily, beating out traditional standbys such as newsletters, workshops, and conferences. Like print, the cassette can go wherever the individual goes, and players are as common as telephones—more so when one considers that there are more cassette players than phones in cars!

American corporations are using cassettes most often as extensions of sales training and for personnel development. An executive of the Gillette Corporation estimates that the company's sales representatives in rural areas spend the equivalent of eighteen

---

MEDIA FILE:
"The Professional Guide to Career Success"
Cassette Tape/Workbook

Whether you're entering the job market for the first time or seeking to move up from where you are, help in making your job search more effective is always welcome. This new cassette/workbook program enables the job seeker to: identify and avail himself or herself of the unadvertised job market, where 80 to 85 percent of all job openings exist; ensure that the new job is economically and professionally rewarding; enhance job security in today's uncertain market. The package, consisting of six audio cassette tapes integrated with a workbook, lays out a step-by-step search strategy.

Source: Information Management Institute.

Prerecorded Audio Cards (Vocabulary Practice). In an elementary classroom, the teacher uses a set of audio cards for vocabulary building. They are used on an individual basis with children who are having difficulty grasping the meaning of words because they cannot attach the appropriate spoken word to the printed form of the word or to the object it represents. The audio cards provide simultaneous visual and auditory stimuli designed to increase a child's spoken vocabulary. The teacher shows the student how to use the machine and the cards, then lets the child work alone. Later, the teacher uses the same cards without the machine, holding them up one at a time and asking the child to say the word.

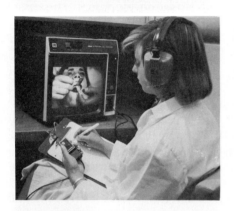

Teacher-Prepared Audiotapes (Direct Instruction). In a vocational-technical school, dental laboratory technology students are instructed on the procedures for constructing prosthetic devices such as partial plates and bridges by listening to an audiotape prepared by their instructor. To be efficient and effective in their work, these students must have both hands free and their eyes must be on their work, not on a textbook or manual. Audiotapes allow the students to move at their own pace, and the instructor is free to circulate around the laboratory and discuss each student's work individually.

Teacher-Prepared Audiotapes (Shorthand Practice). In a high school business education class, the students practice taking dictation by listening to audiotapes prepared by the teacher and other individuals in the school, such as the principal, guidance counselor, or shop instructor. The variety of voices on the tapes allows the students to practice dealing with different voices, different accents, and a variety of dictation speeds. The business teacher categorizes the tapes according to difficulty of transcription and word speed. The students begin with the easy tapes and then move to more difficult ones. The teacher is also experimenting with a variable-speed tape recorder, which will allow her to present the same tape to the students at a variety of speeds. Individually, the students use the variable-speed recorder to determine how fast they can take dictation and still maintain accuracy.

Prerecorded Audiocassette (Sales Information). The sales representative of a manufacturing company pops a cassette into the sound system of the car and, after a few seconds, a popular tune fills the air. The song fades away and the voice of the marketing manager comes in: "What's new at Marflap Manufacturing is a vastly improved system for . . ." Another song follows the information about the new system and, after that, more news about Marflap products. The cassette makes the automobile a learning environment, thereby making use of otherwise wasted time.

Teacher-Prepared Audiotapes (Listening Skills). A teacher of ninth-grade students with learning difficulties (but average intelligence) provides instruction on how to listen to lectures, speeches, and other oral presentations. The students practice their listening skills with tapes of recorded stories, poetry, and instructions. Commercially available tapes of speeches and narration are also used. After the students have practiced their listening skills under teacher direction, they are evaluated using a tape they have not heard before. The students listen to the five-minute tape without taking notes and then are given a series of questions dealing with important content of the passage.

Student-Prepared Audiotape (Gathering Oral History). One of the most exciting projects in a twelfth-grade social studies class is the oral history project. The students interview local senior citizens regarding the history of their community. Only one student interviews each senior citizen, but the interviewing task is rotated among the students, and the entire class assists in determining which questions should be asked. In preparation for this project, the students study both national and local history. All the tapes prepared during the interviews are kept in the school media center. Excerpts are duplicated and edited into programs for use with other social studies classes and for broadcast by the local radio station. This audiotape project serves the dual purpose of informing students and local residents about local history and collecting and preserving information that might otherwise be lost.

Student-Prepared Audiotapes (Oral Book Report). The tape recorder can be used for presenting book reports. Students may record their book reports during study time in the media center, or at home. The reports are evaluated by the teacher, and the best ones are kept on file in the media center. Other students are encouraged to listen to them before selecting books for leisure reading. Since the reports are limited to three minutes, the students are required to extract the main ideas from the book and to organize their thoughts carefully. During the taping, they practice their speaking skills. They are encouraged to make the report as exciting as possible in order to get other students to read the book.

Student-Prepared Audiotapes (Self-Evaluation). As part of a sales training program in a large insurance company, trainees learn sales presentation principles through taped examples and associated programmed booklets. They are then asked to prepare a series of their own sales presentations for different types of clients and for selling different types of insurance. The trainees outline their presentation, practice, and then record them on audiotape. For example, they role play making a presentation on group health insurance to the board of directors of a large corporation. After the simulated presentation they listen to the recording and evaluate their performance using a checklist provided in the teaching materials. If they are not satisfied with their performance, they can redo the tape. Since no instructor is present, the inexperienced salesperson is not embarrassed by mistakes made during a training period. Later the instructor will listen to and critique the tape for the individual trainee. The final step in the training program is a ''live'' presentation, with the other trainees role playing the clients.

Appraisal Checklist: Audio Materials

Title _____

Series title (if applicable) _____

Source _____

Date _____ Cost _____ Length _____ Minutes _____

Subject area _____

Intended audience _____

Format   **Speed**

☐ cassette   _____ ips

☐ open reel

☐ record   _____ rpm

☐ compact disc

Objectives (Stated or Implied):

Brief Description:

Entry Capabilities Required:

- Prior subject-matter knowledge/vocabulary
- Reading ability
- Mathematical ability
- Other:

Rating	High		Medium		Low	Comments
Relevance to objectives	☐	☐	☐	☐	☐	
Accuracy of information	☐	☐	☐	☐	☐	
Likely to arouse/maintain interest	☐	☐	☐	☐	☐	
Technical quality	☐	☐	☐	☐	☐	
Promotes participation/involvement	☐	☐	☐	☐	☐	
Evidence of effectiveness (e.g., field-test results)	☐	☐	☐	☐	☐	
Free from objectionable bias	☐	☐	☐	☐	☐	
Pacing appropriate for audience	☐	☐	☐	☐	☐	
Clarity of organization	☐	☐	☐	☐	☐	
Appropriate vocabulary level	☐	☐	☐	☐	☐	

Strong Points:

Weak Points:

Recommended action _____

Reviewer _____

Position _____

Date _____

to twenty-five weeks a year in their cars. During that time, they can be receiving product information, sales leads, and customer information.

Many companies and individuals have found cassette tapes extremely useful for personnel development. Usually the tapes are closely integrated with workbooks for two reasons: (1) requiring the user to go back and forth from tape to workbook means attention is more certain to be constant; and (2) overt response strengthens learning (R in the ASSURE model). Perhaps the most commonly used cassette programs are the ones that develop basic skills: reading improvement, writing skills development, listening skills. Motivation programs are also popular.

Some companies have exploited the dramatic capabilities of the audio medium in management training programs dealing with conflict resolution and stress management. The low price of cassettes compared to video or

a series of seminars plays an important part in the decision to use audiotape.

Sponsors of conferences and conventions frequently offer cassette recordings of sessions, thereby making important information more widely available. For example, the Association for Educational Communications and Technology, through a commercial company, makes cassettes of sessions available before the close of the convention as well as by mail.

Joggers and walkers are primarily responsible for the rapidly increasing number of literary works on cassettes. Many have found that those two-mile hikes and five-mile jogs lend themselves to catching up on the bestsellers they don't have time to read. As Carol Haubert, president of Caedmon Records, remarked, "We were the first company to put its entire backlist into cassette form. That was in 1974. We knew when the Sony Walkman came on the scene, that something big was

about to happen. It meant that well-performed literature could become portable—in the car, on the beach, jogging. [In addition] parents decided that they'd rather have a child play with his own cassette than with an expensive record player." Many publishers have followed Caedmon, long the leader in recorded literature, into the cassette market.

SELECTING AUDIO MATERIALS

I N selecting audio materials to use in your instruction, first determine what materials are available locally. If appropriate materials are not available, refer to the various directories of audio materials (see Appendix A). Materials both commercially and locally produced that seem appropriate should be previewed before introducing them to your students. The appraisal checklist can serve as a model for the sort of form you can use to guide your selection decisions.

MAKING YOUR OWN AUDIOTAPES

A s previously noted, a major advantage of audiotapes as instructional media is the ease with which they can be prepared by teacher and students. All that is needed is a blank audiotape, a tape recorder, and a bit of know-how.

The first order of business in making an audiotape is to familiarize yourself with the operation of the particular tape recorder you intend to use.

Recorder Controls

Most recorders have clearly marked knobs, dials, or levers for control of the recorder's mechanism: on/off, playback, tone, volume, etc. Experiment a bit. For volume control, try a moderate setting. A high setting expands the pickup range of the recorder's microphone, increasing its ability to pick up extraneous sounds and unwanted noises. A high setting also tends to distort the sounds you do wish the microphone to pick up. Newer recorders have *automatic volume control,* thus making it unnecessary for you to adjust volume while recording. While playing back the tape, experiment with the tone control until you find the tone level that will give you the most lifelike quality. A high treble setting generally plays back the human voice more faithfully.

Acoustics and Microphone Placement

Wherever you record—in the classroom, at home, on a field trip—you need to consider the area's acoustics. Sparsely furnished rooms with plaster walls and ceilings and bare cement or tile floors are likely to be excessively "live," with distracting sound reverberations interfering with the fidelity of the recording. Such areas can, of course, be improved by installation of acoustic tiles and carpeting. However, you will probably have to make do with more makeshift improvements—throw rugs, for example, or even heavy blankets or sheets of cardboard on the floor. Cardboard and blankets may also be used to cut down on bare-wall reverberations. Fabric-covered movable screens and drawn window shades and draperies may help. (The latter will also help eliminate unwanted noise from outside.)

Many recording problems can be traced to the microphone's inability to ignore sounds. Unlike the brain, which can concentrate on only meaningful sounds (your quiet conversation with a friend in a restaurant, for example) and ignore extraneous ones (the clink of dishes, doors opening and closing, the air conditioner, other conversations), the microphone picks up every sound within its range and transmits them all faithfully to the recording device. Thus, microphone placement becomes an artful compromise between maximum pickup of desired sounds and minimal pickup of extraneous ones.

Avoid placing the microphone close to any hard surface that might act as a sounding board. In a classroom, for instance, the recording setup should be at least six feet from the chalkboard, windows, or hard walls. Because many tape recorders themselves generate unwanted clicking, whirring, and humming noises, keep the microphone as far as possible from the recorder. Correct positioning will often require a bit of trial-and-error testing. As a rule of thumb, your mouth should remain about a foot away from the microphone. If you are much closer, "popping" of p's and b's and other "breathy" sounds may become annoying. Do not speak directly into the microphone, but rather, talk over it. Placing the microphone on a cloth or some other sound-absorbing material or on a stand will decrease the possibility of noise being transferred to the microphone from the desk or table. Avoid handling sheets of paper near the microphone. If possible, use index cards or some such materials and handle them quietly. For recording multiple sound-source performances (such as musical shows), other variables must also be taken into consideration. For instance, a greater sound-to-microphone distance might be needed in order to pick up the entire range and scope of sounds emanating from a musical ensemble.

Microphones

A wide variety of microphones are available; they vary in the type of generating element used in their construction, their sensitivity, their directionality, and in other technical features.

The basic function of any microphone is to convert sound waves into electrical energy. The major components of all microphones are similar. Sound waves enter the microphone to strike the diaphragm, which vibrates from the pressure of the sound waves. Connected to the diaphragm is a generating element that converts these vibrations into electrical impulses (Figure 6.13).

As noted, microphones differ with regard to their directionality, that is, the pattern of the area from which they can efficiently pick up the signal or "pickup pat-

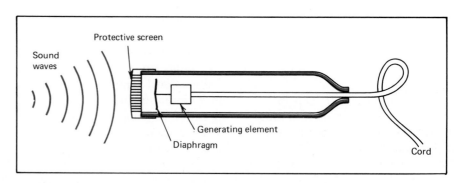

Sound waves

Protective screen

Generating element

Diaphragm

Cord

▲ *Figure 6.13*
The main components of a microphone, cutaway view

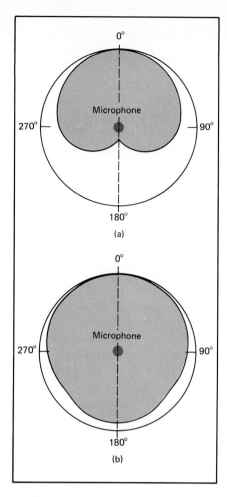

▲ *Figure 6.14*
Pickup patterns of two common types of microphones: (1) the unidirectional, or "cardioid," microphone and (2) the omnidirectional microphone

Microphone Types	Attributes
Crystal	• Simplest construction • Least expensive • Fragile • Sensitive to temperature and humidity • Can be used for speech
Ceramic	• Simple construction • Moderately expensive • Produces weak signal • More rugged than crystal • Not sensitive to temperature and humidity
Dynamic (moving coil)	• High quality • Good fidelity • Very rugged • Very reliable • Expensive
Condenser or electret	• Good frequency response • Sensitive to physical shock • Sensitive sound pickup • Not sensitive to mechanical vibration

tern.'' The microphones most commonly found in educational use these days are the two basic directional types—*unidirectional* and *omnidirectional.* The differences in their pickup patterns are illustrated in Figure 6.14.

AUDIO LESSON RECORDING

Tape Content and Audio Presentation Techniques

INTRODUCE the subject of the audiotape and other appropriate material ("This is Biology 101, Lesson 2, on plant function . . .") at the outset of your recording. Identifying the tape is particularly important if it is to be used for individual instruction.

Try to use conversational rather than pedantic or "textbook" diction. Of course, the normal rules of grammar and clarity of expression must be followed. Talk to the tape recorder as you would normally talk to a friend. Explore your subject with your listener. Do not lecture on it. In general, your presentation will come across as more natural if you work from informal notes. If you do feel you must work with a more formal script, remember that a good script requires special writing skills and skill in script reading.

Keep the tape short even if it is to be used only by adult students—twenty to twenty-five minutes for adults and even less for younger students.

Whenever appropriate for your learning objectives, involve your listener(s) in meaningful learning activities. You might, for example, supply a study guide or worksheet for use along with the tape. Such materials may contain lesson objectives, key information, diagrams or other visuals, questions

to be answered, or practice exercises. Try, also, to provide ample space for students to take notes while listening to the tape. These ancillary materials can also be used for review purposes after the lesson has been completed (Figure 6.15).

Note, however, that if you include student activities you may have to allow time on the tape for the listener to complete an activity. In addition, different students will take varying amounts of time to complete these activities. Rather than trying to guess how much quiet time to leave on the tape, you can provide a brief musical interlude (approximately ten seconds) as a signal for the student to turn off the tape and perform the activity or exercise. The student can then return to the tape, hear the music again, and know that nothing has been missed.

If your listeners are to use slides with your audio presentation, a nonvocal signal should be used to indicate when to advance the slides rather than continually repeating "Change to the next slide." There are electronic tone

Checklist for Instructor-Prepared Audiotapes

Sample page from a study guide to accompany an audio lesson.
OBJECTIVE 3:
Compute depreciation using the "straight-line method."

"Straight-Line" Method Summarized

Formula $\dfrac{\text{Cost of the Asset} - \text{Estimated Salvage Value}}{\text{Number of Accounting Periods in Productive Life}}$

Application $\dfrac{\$1250 \text{ Cost} - \$250 \text{ Salvage}}{5 \text{ Years of Productive Life}} = \$200$ to be DEPRECIATED Each Year

. . . .

TURN OFF TAPE AND COMPLETE ACTIVITY NO. 4

. . . .

Activity #4
A machine costs $2600 and was estimated to have a four-year service life and a $200 salvage value. Calculate the yearly depreciation using the straight-line method.

ANSWER _____

. . . .

TURN ON TAPE AND COMPLETE ACTIVITY
NO. 5 WHILE LISTENING.

. . . .

Activity #5
Advantages of the "units-of-production" method are:
1. _____
2. _____
3. _____
4. _____
Disadvantages of the "units-of-production" method are:
1. _____
2. _____

▲ *Figure 6.15*
Sample page from a study guide to accompany an audio lesson

Checklist for Instructor-Prepared Audiotapes

□ minimum extraneous background noise
□ constant volume level
□ voice quality and clarity
□ clarity of expression
□ conversational tone
□ listener involvement
□ coordination with worksheet or study guide, if used
□ content clear
□ duration not too long

devices available for this purpose, or a door chime can be used. A simple technique for producing your own signal is to tap a spoon on a glass partially filled with water.

When you are finished with the recording, give it a critical evaluation. As a guide, you might use a checklist such as the one shown below. It may also be helpful to have a colleague and/or students listen to the tape and give you their reactions to it.

DUPLICATING AUDIOTAPES

It is a relatively simple procedure to duplicate (or "dub") an audiotape. You can duplicate your tapes by one of three methods: the acoustic method, the electronic method, or the high-speed duplicator method.

The *acoustic* method does not require any special equipment, just two recorders (cassette, reel-to-reel, or one of each). One recorder plays the original tape, the sound of which is transferred via a microphone to blank tape on the other recorder. The drawback to this method is that fidelity is lessened as the sound travels through the air to the microphone, and the open microphone may pick up unwanted noise from the environment (Figure 6.16).

The *electronic* method avoids this problem. The signal travels from the original tape to the dubbing recorder via an inexpensive patch cord. The cord is attached to the output of the first machine and the "line" or auxiliary input of the second. It picks up the signals of the original tape and transfers them electronically to the duplicating tape (Figure 6.17).

If you use reel-to-reel recorders for both playing and recording, you can save half the normal duplicating time by playing $3\frac{3}{4}$-ips tapes at $7\frac{1}{2}$ ips. The speed of the machine doing the recording must also be set at $7\frac{1}{2}$ ips. The duplicated tape can then be played back at the $3\frac{3}{4}$-ips rate of the original tape.

The *high-speed duplicator* method requires a special machine. Master playback

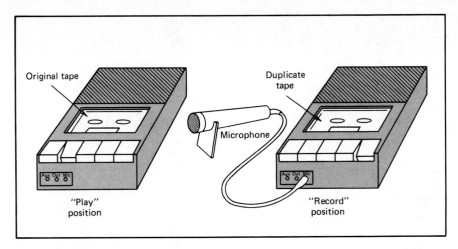

▲ *Figure 6.16*
Configuration for duplicating by the *acoustic* method

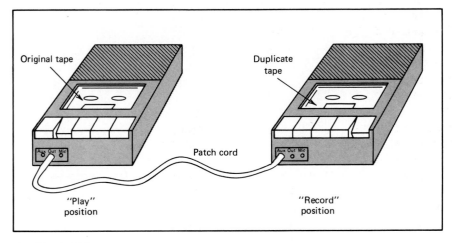

▲ *Figure 6.17*
Configuration for duplicating by the *electronic* method

machines have a series of up to ten "slave units," each of which can record a copy of the original tape at sixteen times its normal speed.

Multiple copies of a thirty-minute cassette tape can be duplicated in about one minute. Since the master and slave units are connected by a patch cord, fidelity is likely to be very good, and there is no danger of picking up background noise.

EDITING AUDIOTAPES

Y OU may wish to edit your audiotapes, either to remove errors and imperfections or to adapt a tape to a specific learning situation. There are two general methods for editing tapes: mechanical editing and electronic editing.

For *electronic editing,* set up two recorders as described for tape duplication and then record just the portion of the original tape that you want on the second tape. You can accomplish the same effects (deleting and resequencing) as with mechanical editing, but the results may not be as precise.

Mechanical editing (splicing) involves physically removing unwanted portions of the tape or changing the sequence of materials by reordering sections of the tape. If you plan to do mechanical editing, record your original tape on only one side and at the fastest speed possible. Open reel tapes can be mechanically edited more easily than cassette tapes because they are wider and more accessible. Splicing tape and splicing blocks are available for both open reel and cassette tape. Follow the specific instructions given for the equipment you are using.

RATE-CONTROLLED AUDIO PLAYBACK

A N important but little known piece of audio equipment is a cassette tape deck that can play back recorded speech either at a faster or slower rate than the rate at which it was recorded—but with no loss of voice quality or intelligibility.

Before this technological breakthrough, playing a tape back at a higher speed resulted in high-pitched distortion, as if the speaker were a chattering chipmunk. Slowing down the playback resulted in a low-pitched, unintelligible garble.

The pedagogical significance of this innovation lies in the fact that although the average person speaks at 100 to 150 words per minute, most of us can comprehend spoken information at the rate of 250 to 300 words per minute. Research has shown that most students learn as quickly and retain as much when spoken instruction is speeded up. On the other hand, slowing down recorded instruction also has instructional advantages, especially in working with slow learners or in special education situations and in foreign language instruction. It is also useful in ordinary circumstances for emphasizing a specific instructional point or for explaining a particularly difficult one.

Early speech compressors (technically, speeding up recorded speech is called "compressing") were costly and their

The technology of recorded sound has gone through several transformations since Edison recited "Mary had a little lamb" into the horn of the first phonograph and to his own astonishment heard his voice played back to him. That was in 1877.

Because Edison kept detailed notes on his pursuit of an idea and wrote comments on his method of inquiry, the invention of the phonograph affords us a rare insight into how a resourceful and imaginative technologist works. The ability to put seemingly unrelated events together to generate new knowledge and new devices is an important hallmark of both scientists and technologists. Edison once gave this advice to aspiring inventors, "When you are experimenting and come across anything you don't thoroughly understand, don't rest until you run it down; it may be the very thing you are looking for or it may be something far more important."

Early in 1877, Edison had invented a carbon transmitter for Bell's telephone, so transmission of sound was on his mind. At the same time, he was also trying to expand the usefulness of the telegraph. He was working on a device that could imprint on paper tape the Morse code coming over a telegraph line and then reproduce the message at any desired speed. A steel spring pressed against the paper helped keep the tape in a straight line. Edison noticed that when the tape was running at a high speed, the dots and dashes hitting the spring gave off a noise that Edison described as a "light musical, rhythmic sound, resembling human talk heard indistinctly." During his work on the carbon transmitter, Edison, who was already hard of hearing, had attached a needle to the diaphragm of the telephone receiver in order to judge the loudness of the sound. By holding his finger lightly to the needle, loudness could be judged by the strength of the vibration. Recalling this experience, and applying it to his interest in transmission of sound and his work with the telegraph, Edison set about determining if the needle vibrations could be impressed on a suitable material.

After experimenting with a number of materials, Edison, for reasons unknown, decided to use tinfoil wrapped around a cylinder as his recording medium with two needle-diaphragm units—one for recording and one for playback. In December 1877 he applied for a patent.

Edison's vision of the potential of sound record-

ing was amazingly prescient, but the first commercial exploitation of the invention was as a novelty. The Edison Speaking Phonograph Company, formed on January 24, 1878, and not under Edison's control, charged admission to demonstrations of the machine during which members of the audience were invited to come up to the stage to record their voices. But the novelty wore off, and Edison's attention was diverted to the challenge of electric lighting.

Alexander Graham Bell built a laboratory in Washington, D.C., to work on improving the phonograph. His work led to an improved cylinder which made the device useful for business dictation. Bell's efforts also made possible the first "juke box." Machines were manufactured that would play a recording when the customer dropped a nickel in the slot. But this novelty also wore off.

The next major advance was made in 1887 by a German immigrant, Emile Berliner, when he developed his idea of a stylus engraving lateral grooves as it moved across a disc coated with a pliant but firm material. The flat disc had a greater potential to be mass produced than did the cylinder. When he hit on the idea of making a metal master that could stamp out duplicates, the flat disc became the accepted format.

But recordings were still acoustic. Horns, not microphones, were used to gather and direct the sound waves that drove the recording diaphragm and needle. Playback was the same only in reverse. Quality was still poor and volume limited. Electricity, already employed in the telephone, was the answer. In 1920, two British inventors, Lionel Guest and H. R. Merriman, successfully recorded a ceremony in Westminster Abbey by transmitting the signals from their electric microphone over phone lines to their laboratory. A few years later, the vacuum tube amplifier made possible an all-electronic system. From then until the end of World War II, slow, steady improvements in recording technology made the 78-rpm record, in 10- and 12-inch sizes, the standard. However, only four minutes of sound could be accommodated on each side of the disc. Then the long-playing record and magnetic tape recording shook up the record industry.

In June 1948, Peter Goldmark of Columbia Records demonstrated the long-playing record (LP) that was destined to drive 78-rpm records from the home market. The record that he demonstrated contained twenty-three minutes of music on each side. Subsequent improvements increased the time to thirty or thirty-two minutes per side. The public responded positively and quickly to the new format. But magnetic tape recording would have an even more dramatic effect.

Until 1946 all recordings were made by cutting grooves in a disc surfaced with soft but firm material from which a metal master was made. This was a cumbersome, delicate process that was troublesome in the lab and infuriating on location. There were simply too many opportunities for Murphy's law to operate. Magnetic recording came along just at the right time to become the standard for making the recordings from which masters could be cut later under ideal conditions.

Magnetic recording was the direct cause of the proliferation of record companies that occurred after 1947. A relatively small investment in high-quality equipment enabled a small company to make tapes that could be marketed directly or sold to established record companies for distribution. For example, Caedmon Records was started by two young women who hired an engineer with the necessary equipment and set out to record authors reading from their works. Their first prize was Dylan Thomas, the Welsh poet, and from that beginning

they built the largest catalog of recorded literature in the industry.

The idea of recording sounds magnetically has been around since 1899 when a Danish inventor recorded sound on paper tape impregnated with iron oxide and also on magnetizable wire. However, the absence of electronic amplification stymied development. Other inventors experimented with magnetic recording, particularly in Germany, where a magnetic recorder for dictation was marketed in 1937. During World War II, British and American intelligence detected evidence that the Germans were using recordings of superior quality. Their suspicions were confirmed when, on September 11, 1944, the Allies captured Radio Luxemburg and found in the station a magnetic recorder that played 14-inch reels of tape at 30 inches per second with remarkable fidelity. Within a short period of time, American companies, capitalizing on the German developments, were marketing magnetic tape and recorders that could record and play back with unprecedented quality. Wire recorders also became available, but wire was not as reliable or as convenient a recording medium.

The idea of stereo recording also had been around for a long time, but there was no marketable medium until magnetic tape recordings were made available to the public. In 1955, stereo recordings on magnetic tape were marketed but on reel-to-reel tape, a format that the general public did not find congenial. Then in 1957, cutting a stereo groove in a master disc was perfected, and stereo discs soon flooded the market. LPs were the standard format for stereo until 1970, when advances in audiocassette technology, including the Dolby method of suppressing background noise, challenged the LP. Now both the LP and cassette are facing the formidable competition of the compact disc (CD).

In slightly more than 100 years recorded sound has progressed from the barely audible voice of Edison etched in an impermanent groove on tinfoil to the ability to record, for example, Mahler's Symphony of a Thousand with astounding clarity and richness on an almost indestructible compact disc.

This FLASHBACK is based primarily on Roland Gelatt, *The Fabulous Phonograph, 1877–1977*. N.Y.: Collier Books, 1977. The two Edison quotes are from that book.

How to . . . PREVENT ACCIDENTAL ERASURE OF CASSETTE TAPES

Cassette tapes provide protection against accidental erasure. At the rear corners of each cassette are small tabs which can be broken out. The tab on the left controls the top side of the tape. The tab on the right controls the bottom side. No machine will record a new sound on a side of a tape for which the appropriate tab has been broken out.

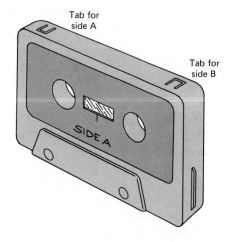

Tab for side A

Tab for side B

SIDE A

If you want to reuse the tape, carefully place some cellophane tape over the hole where the tab was removed. The tape can then be used for a new recording. Most prerecorded tapes come with both tabs already removed to prevent accidental erasure.

▲ *Figure 6.18*
This variable speech control compact recorder allows playback at up to twice the normal rate when the "speed control" and "pitch control" are moved together.

technology not very refined. The machines could only be set at certain fixed speeds, such as 200 words per minute. The entire recording had to be made and played back at this rate.

Newer compressors provide for variable speed rates. Recorders can now be equipped with rate-control devices that, using a tape recorded at normal speaking speed, are capable of providing variable rates of speech at the discretion of the listener, from half the normal speed to $2\frac{1}{2}$ times normal speed. Changing the rate during playback allows the listener to listen at his or her own pace, skimming over familiar material at a high rate, slowing down for material that may require more time for comprehension.

Research has shown that learning time can be cut (as much as 50 percent and an average of 32 percent) and comprehension increased (as much as 9.3 percent and an average of 4.2 percent) through use of compressed and variable-speed audiotapes.* One reason that comprehension increases with accelerated listening rate may be that the listener is forced to increase his or her concentration on the material and is also freed from the distractions that often accompany normal speech, such as pauses, throat clearing, and other extraneous sounds. A slow, monotonous speaking rate also allows listeners' minds to wander.

Research also indicates that variable-speed audiotapes can be very effective in increasing reading speed. One junior high school teacher prepared variable-speed tapes of printed material for his students to listen to as they read the material. The students' reading rate gradually increased with increase in their listening rate. The ear, it seems, helps train the eye.

---

* See the listings under Olsen, Hughes, and Short in the list of references.

References

Print References

Alley, Douglas. "Radio Tapes: A Resource for English Teachers." *English Journal* (October 1979), pp. 40–41.

Banerjee, Sumanta. *Audio Cassettes: The User Medium.* (Paris: UNESCO, 1977).

Bradtmueller, Weldon G. "Auditory Perception as an Aid to Learning in the Content Areas." *Journal of the Association for the Study of Perception* (Spring 1979), pp. 27–29.

Center for Vocational Education. *Present Information with Audio Recordings.* (Athens, Ga.: American Association for Vocational Instructional Materials, 1977).

Christenson, Peter G. "Children's Use of Audio Media." *Communication Research* (July 1985), pp. 327–343.

Clifford, Martin. *Microphones: How They Work and How to Use Them.* (Blue Ridge Summit, Pa.: TAB Books, 1977).

DeMuth, James E. "Audio Cassettes as a Means of Professional Continuing Education for Pharmacists." *Adult Education* (Summer 1979), pp. 242–251.

Gates, Ward M. "Recording Tips for Teachers." *Clearing House* (January 1976), pp. 229–230.

Gibbons, Jane. "Young Children's Recall and Reconstruction of Audio and Audiovisual Narratives." *Child Development* (August 1986), pp. 1014–1023.

Harnishfeger, L. *Basic Practice in Listening.* (Denver, Colo.: Love Publishing, 1977).

Hughes, Lawson H. "Developments in Rate-Controlled Speech." *NSPI Journal* (September 1976), pp. 10–11.

James, Charles J. "Are You Listening? The Practical Components of Listening Comprehension." *Foreign Language Annals* (April 1984), pp. 129–133.

Jones, Barry. "Le Jeu des Colis—An Exercise in Foreign Language Communication." *Audio-Visual Language Journal* (Winter 1979), pp. 159–167.

Kelly, Patrick, and Ryan, Steve. "Using Tutor Tapes to Support the Distance Learner." *International Council for Distance Education Bulletin* (September 1983), pp. 19–23.

Laaser, Wolfrom. "Some Didactic Aspects of Audio Cassettes in Distance Education." *Distance Education* (March 1986), pp. 143–152.

Olsen, Linda. "Technology Humanized—The Rate Controlled Tape Recorder." *Media and Methods* (January 1979), p. 67.

Postlethwait, S. N. "Audio Technology: Audio Tape for Programming Instruction." *Educational Broadcasting* (July–August 1976), pp. 17–19.

Short, Sarah H. "A Comparison of Variable Time-Compressed Speech and Normal Rate Speech Based on Time Spent and Performance in a Course Taught by Self-Instructional Methods." *British Journal of Educational Technology* (May 1977), pp. 146–156.

———. "The Use of Rate Controlled Speech to Save Time and Increase Learning in Self-Paced Instruction." *NSPI Journal* (May 1978), pp. 13–14.

Smith, Judson. "How to Buy Headsets and Listening Centers." *Training* (September 1977), pp. 92–95.

Ullom-Morse, Ann, et al. "The Use and Acceptance of Compressed Speech by Nursing Students." *NALLD Journal* (Winter 1979), pp. 20–27.

Wieder, Alan. "Oral History in the Classroom: An Exploratory Essay." *Social Studies* (March/April 1984), pp. 71–74.

Zimmerman, William. *How to Tape Instant Oral Biographies.* (New York: Guarionex Press Ltd., 1982).

Audiovisual References

Basic Audio. Alexandria, Va.: Smith-Mattingly Productions, 1979. Videocassette. 30 minutes.

Learning about Sound. Chicago: Encyclopedia Brittannica Educational Corporation, 1975. 16-mm film. 17 minutes.

Sound Recording and Reproduction. Salt Lake City, Utah: Media Systems, Inc., 1978. 6 filmstrips with audiocassettes.

Tape Recorders. Salt Lake City, Utah: Media Systems, Inc., 1978. Filmstrip with audiocassette.

Tips on Tapes for Teachers. Boulder, Colo.: National Center for Audio Tapes, 1972. Audiocassette.

Utilizing the Tape Recorder in Teaching. Salt Lake City, Utah: Media Systems, Inc., 1975. 2 filmstrips with audiocassette.

Possible Projects

6-A. Prepare an audiotape including your voice and some music. It will be evaluated using the criteria in the "Checklist for Instructor-Prepared Audiotapes." Include a description of how the tape will be used, along with its objective(s).

6-B. Obtain any commercially prepared audio materials and appraise them using a given set of criteria, such as "Appraisal Checklist: Audio Materials," or using your own criteria.

6-C. Do a short oral history of your school or organization by interviewing people associated with it for a long time. Edit your interviews into a five-minute presentation.

6-D. Prepare an outline for a short oral presentation. Deliver your presentation as if you were addressing the intended audience and record it. Critique your presentation for style as well as content. Revise and try again.

6-E. Practice editing by deliberately recording a paragraph from a news report or a literary work with the sentences out of order. Put the paragraph back in proper sequence by editing the recorded tape.

6-F. Develop a brief audio-tutorial lesson. Choose a basic skill, such as spelling or arithmetic, or a performance aid—e.g., how to make out a bank check or how to fill out an application form. Design the lesson with paper and pencil first, then record the tape. Try the lesson out on your fellow students.

7

Multimedia Systems

Objectives

After studying this chapter, you should be able to:

1. Define *multimedia* systems and state a rationale for the use of multimedia systems.

2. List five considerations when preparing, purchasing, and/or selecting multimedia kits.

3. Describe a multimedia kit that you could use in your teaching field. Your description should identify the topic, the audience, the overall objectives, and the contents of the kit.

4. Define *instructional module* and include six components of a module in your definition.

5. Describe the characteristics, advantages, limitations, and applications of classroom learning centers.

6. Identify three methods of providing learner feedback in a classroom learning center.

7. Discuss the teacher's role in learning-center management.

8. Identify three advantages of sound-slide programs.

9. Describe four combinations of projected visuals and audio materials, including three procedures for synchronizing them.

10. Describe an instructional situation in which you could use an audio plus projected visual presentation. Your description should include the topic, the audience, the objectives, and a rationale for using this media format.

11. Describe and/or apply the basic steps involved in the planning of a slide-tape presentation.

12. Discuss instructional applications of dissolve units and automatic programmers.

13. Describe an instructional situation in which you could use a multi-image presentation. Your description should include the topic, the audience, the objectives, and a rationale for using this media format.

14. Diagram the components of a typical interactive video system.

15. Identify five advantages, three limitations, and five instructional applications of interactive video.

Lexicon

multimedia systems
multimedia kit
module
learning center
carrel
storyboard
multi-image
multiscreen
dissolve unit
automatic programmer
interactive video

We have previously considered various audio and visual instructional media. We will now explore various combinations of these media and how these combinations can be used for instructional purposes. Media combinations are generally referred to as *multimedia systems*.

The multimedia concept involves more than using multiple media for a given instructional purpose. It involves integrating each medium and media format into a structured, systematic presentation. Each medium in a multimedia system is designed to complement the others so that, ideally, the whole multimedia system becomes greater than the sum of its parts.

The use of multimedia systems in the classroom and training center has received considerable impetus from the general trends toward individualization of learning and encouragement of active student participation in the learning process. Multimedia systems are especially adaptable to these current educational and training concepts.

Multimedia systems are also multisensory and thus stimulate

learning as it takes place in the world outside the classroom. Learning in the real world is indeed multimedia and multisensory learning. We are constantly learning via all our senses and via a multitude of stimuli—newspapers, books, radio, television, pictures, etc.

In this chapter we will discuss the major multimedia systems commonly used in the classroom:

multimedia kits, modules, learning centers, sound-slide combinations, multi-image systems, and interactive video.

MULTIMEDIA KITS

A *multimedia kit* is a collection of teaching/learning materials involving more than one type of medium and organized

▲ *Figure 7.1*
Multimedia kits can be used to teach a wide variety of skills, such as this one for basic reading.

▲ *Figure 7.2*
Like any other instructional approach, multimedia presentations can be overdone.

around a single topic. The kits may include filmstrips, slides, audiotapes, records, still pictures, study prints, overhead transparencies, maps, worksheets, charts, graphs, booklets, real objects, and models.

Some multimedia kits are designed for use by the teacher in classroom presentations. Others are designed for use by individual students or by small groups.

▲ *Figure 7.3*
Multimedia kits provide varied sensory experiences; they give the concrete referents needed to build a strong foundation for more abstract mental abilities.

Commercial Multimedia Kits

Commercial multimedia kits are available for a variety of educational subjects. For example, the Society for Visual Education markets a series of multimedia kits with titles such as *Beginning Math Concepts, Metric System, Communities in Nature* (an ecology unit), *Planning the Human Community, Initial Consonant, Vowel Sounds,* and *Threshold to Reading.*

These learning kits include sound filmstrips, cassette tapes, floor games, board games, posters, full-color photographs, activity cards, lotto cards, murals, wall charts, geometric shapes, flash cards, student workbooks, and a teacher's manual. Clearly defined objectives are stated and supported with suggested teaching strategies for using the materials in the kit.

Many other multimedia kits on a wide variety of topics are available from commercial sources, some of which contain, among other materials, transparencies, laboratory materials for science experiments, and even puppets to act out story concepts.

Teacher-made Multimedia Kits

Multimedia kits can also be prepared by teachers. First, you must decide if the kit is to be used by the students. You will also have to decide if you are going to prepare only one kit for student use or if you are going to duplicate the kit so that more than one student can have access to it at any given time. Another alternative might be to make a variety of kits and have the students take turns using them.

Availability and cost of materials will affect your choice of materials to be included in the kit. Cost is particularly important if duplicate kits are to be provided and if materials are not reusable. Remember too that if the kits are to be taken home for unsupervised individual use, allowance should probably be made for loss or damage to some items. Nevertheless, cost is not an insurmountable problem. Many simple but satisfactory resource materials are free. Multimedia kits need not be expensive to be effective.

It is important that the components of the kit be integrated— that is, each component contributes to attainment of your lesson objective. Multimedia activities should also be correlated with other relevant learning activities in the classroom.

The availability of equipment may also affect your selection of materials. If filmstrips or other projected visuals are included, for example, you will need a projector for group use. A hand-held viewer, however, might suffice for individual use. Audio materials will require playback machines.

Multimedia kits should be designed to teach specific knowledge and skills. They should involve the student in the learning process as he or she handles and manipulates the resource materials.

Advantages

Most important, multimedia kits are interesting to use, exciting to manipulate, and useful in making learning enjoyable. Contributing to these advantages is the fact that they are multisensory. Students like to learn using a variety of senses, particularly the sense of touch. Everyone likes to manipu-

▲ *Figure 7.4*
Multimedia kits frequently include raw materials for student inquiry into the phenomena of nature.

late objects and materials. At the same time, handling materials contributes to learning. These advantages go along with the *R* in the ASSURE model and provide for active participation on the part of the learners.

Because multimedia kits are so versatile in their content, range of media, and variety of applications, they can contribute to learning for a wide variety of learners in many subject areas.

In addition, multimedia kits can provide for individualized instruction for single students or a small group of learners with the same educational needs. As described earlier, multimedia kits can be used within the learning environment or taken to other locations including the student's home. The kits can be prescribed by the teacher to meet specific learning needs.

Limitations

The biggest disadvantage of multimedia kits is that components of

the kits get lost or damaged and significantly impair the effectiveness of the kit. In addition, multimedia kits can be expensive to purchase and time-consuming to make.

Applications

The instructional uses of teacher-made multimedia kits are limited only by teacher ingenuity. Following are a few examples.

Because such kits typically center on realia and other such concrete materials, they lend themselves especially well to *discovery* learning. Questions are used to guide students' exploration of the material and arrival at conclusions.

A multimedia kit on magnetic fields might include (among other materials) several types of magnets, such as permanent and electromagnets, and an assortment of metal objects that may or may not be attracted to them. For older students, iron filings might also be provided. A kit on aerodynam-

An elementary teacher developed a series of separate multimedia kits on science topics for use with her third-grade class. She incorporated real objects, such as magnets, small motors, rocks, harmless chemicals, and insect specimens in the kits. She also gathered pictures from magazines and old textbooks associated with each topic. A study guide, prepared for each unit, required the student to inquire into the topic, make hypotheses, and conduct investigations. Audiotapes were prepared for use at school and at home for those students who had access to cassette players.

The students enjoyed taking the kits home to work on the experiments. The response from parents was very positive. Several parents reported that they too learned by working through the activities with their children. Students often preferred to stay in at recess and work on the multimedia kits in the science corner.

ics might include paper or balsa along with patterns and instructions for constructing various types of aircraft. If proper safety precautions are taken, you might allow the students to fly their models and award prizes for the longest or highest flight.

Mathematical topics are especially suitable for multimedia kits. Such a kit could include a statement of the problem(s) the student must solve, suggestions for procedures to use, and materials needed. A kit on metric measurement, for example, could include a metric ruler or meter

▲ *Figure 7.5*
Modules may incorporate many types of media and involve a variety of instructional methods.

stick, various objects to be measured, and suggestions for taking metric measurements of various objects in the classroom.

MODULES

FOR generations teachers have spoken in terms of "lessons" and "units" when talking about the parts of a course of instruction, but the age of space travel and computer technology has given us a new way of looking at the basic building blocks of instruction: the concept of the module.

In order to create complex electronic systems, engineers had to think in terms of small interchangeable units that could be easily plugged into and detached from the total system. Thus, the concept of modules (as in "lunar module" and "modular designed TV") was born and popularized. Carried over into education, *instructional module* has become the generic name for free-standing instructional units. Modules

carry a wide variety of labels, including unipack, individualized learning package, and learning activity package.

Modules are usually designed as self-instructional units for independent study. However, group-based modules (for example, built around a simulation, a game, or a field experience) are also found. The Personalized System of Instruction (PSI) and Audio-Tutorial Systems, discussed in Chapter 11, are two types of course management systems that are designed around modules.

The reading materials used in a PSI course, for example, may be designed in the module format. If so, those modules become part of the PSI technology of instruction. However, it is also possible for modules to be designed in a conventional prose style and to be used in a conventional teaching method.

Components of Modules

There are many different formulas for designing instructional modules, but certain components are agreed upon:

1. *Rationale.* An overview of the content of the module and explanation of why the learner should study it.
2. *Objective.* What the learner is expected to gain from studying the module, stated in performance terms.
3. *Entry-Test.* To determine if the learner has the prerequisite skills needed to enter the module, and to check whether the learner already has mastered the skills to be taught.
4. *Multimedia Materials.* A wide variety of media formats to involve learners actively and to utilize a number of their senses. Most media formats lend themselves to use in modules.
5. *Learning Activities.* All of the methods described in Chapter 1 may be incorporated into modules. A variety of methods and media increase student interest and meet student needs.
6. *Self-Test.* A chance to review and check one's own progress.
7. *Posttest.* An examination to test whether the objectives of the module have been mastered.

Design of Modules

Modules should include an introduction to the topic and instructions or suggestions about how the various components of the module are to be used. If the module is to be used only under instructor supervision, oral instructions may suffice. In most cases, however, a printed study guide should be a part of the module. The guide should introduce the topic of the module and relate its media and activities to the objectives. It should give instructions for using the materials included with the module and

directions for the learning activities involved. Questions and space for responses may also be contained in the guide. The study guide should be as simple as possible, containing just the essential directions and relevant information. See "How to . . . Design Printed Materials" on page 84.

Some teachers prefer to put their study guide materials on audiotape or to use an audiotape in conjunction with a printed guide. Either of these procedures can be helpful for slow readers and may be essential for very poor readers and nonreaders. See "Making Your Own Audiotapes" on page 173.

It is important for the instructor to monitor each learner's progress in order to reward successes and to alleviate frustrations. At the conclusion of each module's use, the learner should discuss the activity with the teacher individually or in a small group. The teacher and the student(s) can go over the nature of the problem presented in the module, compare answers (if appropriate), and discuss the concepts learned from the module. The follow-up discussion can be used as an evaluative device in addition to or instead of a written quiz.

Specific guidelines on selection criteria, design steps, and utilization principles for instructional modules can be found in the references listed at the end of this chapter.

LEARNING CENTERS

T HE development of multimedia instructional technology and the growing interest in small-group and individualized instruction have led to the establishment of special learning environments generally called *classroom learning centers.* A learning center is an individualized environment

designed to encourage the student to use a variety of instructional media, to engage in diversified learning activities, and to assume major responsibility for his or her own learning.

Learning centers may be set up in any suitable and available classroom space. Or they may be set up outside the classroom, in a laboratory, for example, or even in a school corridor. They are also commonly found in libraries and media centers. Learning centers with many stations are found in business, industry, medical facilities, and the armed forces.

Learning center materials may include practically any or all of the media and multimedia formats mentioned in this text. Center materials may be purchased from commercial producers or may be teacher-made.

Carrels

Although simple learning center activities might be carried out at a student's desk or some other open space, it is advisable that learning centers be confined to a clearly identifiable area and that they be at least partially enclosed to aid concentration and avoid

▲ *Figure 7.6*
A "wet" carrel provides facilities for audiovisual media.

distraction. Learning carrels (booths), which may be purchased from commercial sources or made locally, will provide a clearly identifiable enclosure.

Carrels may be made by placing simple cardboard dividers on classroom tables, or freestanding commercially constructed carrels complete with electrical connections and rear projection screens may be purchased.

Carrels are often referred to as being either "wet" or "dry." A dry carrel provides private space for study or other learning activities but contains no electrical equipment. The typical library carrel is a dry carrel. A wet carrel, on the other hand, is equipped with or has outlets for audiovisual mechanisms such as cassette recorders, projection screens, television monitors, or computer terminals.

Advantages

Aside from exposing students to a variety of multimedia learning experiences, the advantages of learning centers are chiefly those that generally apply to individualized learning and teaching. Learning centers allow the teacher to move around the classroom and provide individual help to students when they need it. Centers encourage students to take responsibility for their own learning and allow them to learn at their own pace (thus minimizing the possibility of failure and maximizing the likelihood of success). They provide for student participation in the learning experience, for student response, and for immediate feedback to student response. Students tend to spend more time on the task of learning.

Limitations

On the other hand, learning centers do have some drawbacks. They can be costly. A great deal of time must be spent in planning and setting up centers and in collecting and arranging for center materials. The teacher who manages the learning center must be a very good classroom manager and organizer—and must avoid the temptation to let the learning center replace him or her.

Applications

Learning centers can be used for a number of basic instructional purposes and are often categorized according to their primary purpose.

As *teaching centers* they can be used to introduce new content or skills and to provide an environment for individual or small-group instruction in lieu of whole-class instruction. Teaching the basics of the "three Rs" lends itself quite well to the learning center instructional approach.

As *skill centers* they can provide the student with an opportunity to do additional practice or can reinforce a lesson that has previously been taught through other media or teaching techniques. For example, a skill center might be designed to reinforce skill in using prefixes for students who are learning to read.

As *interest centers* they can promote present interests or stimulate new interests and encourage creativity. For example, a get-acquainted center on insect life might be set up in the classroom before actually beginning a unit on specific insects.

As *remedial centers* they can be used to help students who need additional assistance with a particular concept or skill. A student who has difficulty determining the least common denominator of a group of fractions, for example, could be given the needed help in a remedial learning center.

As *enrichment centers* they can provide stimulating additional learning experiences for those students who have completed other center or classroom activities. Students who have completed their assigned math activities, for example, may be allowed to go to the center on "How Computers Work."

Design

Let us consider how you might go about planning and designing your own learning center according to the ASSURE model discussed in Chapter 2.

Analyze Learner Characteristics. Diagnosis of student characteristics is the key to placing your students in the learning center that best suits their abilities, needs, and interests.

State Objectives. Determine the learning objective(s) you wish your students to attain in the center. State these objectives in terms of student behavior. Be sure the center includes a statement of objectives for user reference. A statement of objectives might be included in the center's printed material, or it might be recorded on tape.

Select Media and Materials. Your selection of materials, of course, should be dictated by the abilities and instructional needs of your students and by the availability of slides, filmstrips, audiotapes, realia, multimedia kits, printed materials (worksheets and instruction sheets), and so forth. Ideas for materials to include in your center, either as is or adapted for your own specific purposes, may be gleaned from descriptions of commercially produced learning centers and from audiovisual periodicals and reference books. A list of the materials contained in your center should be included in the center for user reference.

Utilize Materials. Learning centers are designed for use by individual students or small groups. Grouping has the advantage of allowing the students to interact as they utilize center materials, thus learning from one another's efforts and mistakes and reinforcing correct responses. In either case, instructions for using center materials should be included in your center. They should be concise and as clear as possible, in print format or on audiotape.

The exact nature and order of learning activities within the center may be strictly controlled by the teacher or may be left in whole or in part up to the student. In most cases it is advisable to control activities at the outset and gradually increase students' freedom to choose activities as they demonstrate ability to assume responsibility for self-direction. Similarly, assignment to specific centers may be strictly controlled or left in whole or in part up to the students.

Be available to your students when they are using center materials. Many students, particularly younger children, need or can profit by frequent teacher contact as they use the materials and carry out the activities of the learning center. Circumstances may also warrant scheduling short one-to-one conferences with center users at periodic intervals.

Require Learner Performance. Learning centers should be designed to include opportunities for learners to respond to center materials and receive feedback to their responses. There are various ways of providing such opportunities. You might, for example, provide an answer key to printed or audiotaped questions. The key

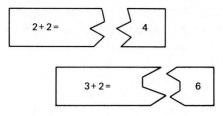

▲ *Figure 7.7*
Self-checking puzzles may be used for math drills.

might be included within the center or placed outside it, perhaps on a bulletin board. The latter option allows the student to get up and move around a bit, thus alleviating the sense of confinement some children may feel with prolonged center use. Answers might also be put on the back of an activity card. Puzzle pieces may also be used to provide for student responses and feedback. This device entails putting questions and answers on a piece of paper or cardboard and then separating questions from answers by zig-zag cuts. Only the correct answer portion of the paper will fit a given question, as shown in Figure 7.7. It is advisable to use a variety of techniques for providing feedback to learner response. In all cases, feedback to learner response should be as immediate as possible. Instant feedback has the distinct advantage of reinforcing correct responses and correcting wrong ones while material is fresh in the student's mind.

Evaluate/Revise. Attention to student response and the provision of feedback will have given you some opportunity to evaluate student progress toward attainment of your center's learning objectives. Further evaluations can be made through periodic testing while work is in progress and through individual conferences. When the learning center project is completed, student mas-

tery of the center's objectives can be tested by traditional end-of-lesson written tests, performance tests, or other appropriate techniques.

Now is the time, also, to evaluate the learning center itself. Did most of its users attain its learning objectives? If not, why not? Were your materials well chosen? Were they too difficult for your students to work with or manipulate, or too easy? Did your center provide the right learning environment? Was it too dark? Too bright? Too noisy? Were your objectives clearly understood? Were your instructions clear? Your own careful observations and solicitations of student comments and suggestions will help you evaluate your center and make appropriate revisions.

Management

There are a variety of learning center management strategies. A block of time can be set aside for use of each center, and students can be assigned to each one for certain periods. The length of the time block should be determined by the age of the students and the content of the center. The alternative of having the students move from center to center on their own is acceptable as long as they are held accountable for getting the "job" done. (See the film "Classroom Learning Centers," cited in the list of audiovisual references.)

In using learning centers, your role is not to teach one subject or to control the students from the front of the room. Instead, it is to move around and deal with students on an individual or small-group basis. As you circulate about the classroom, you can assist students who are having difficulty, while becoming actively involved in the learning process with the students and assessing the progress of each student.

With an hour class period, it is helpful to have ten or fifteen minutes at the end of the period for group discussion and wrap-up. Of course, follow-up activities may be available for the students when learning center projects are completed. Some instructors develop an "activities checklist." Students use the checklist to monitor their progress through the learning center environment.

▲ *Figure 7.8*
Learning centers offer opportunities for informal teacher–student interaction.

SOUND-SLIDE COMBINATIONS

COMBINING 2-by-2-inch slides with audiotape is the easiest multimedia system to produce locally, which is one reason for the increasing popularity of its use in the instructional setting. The system is also versatile, easy to use, and effective for both group instruction and independent study. A well-done sound-slide presentation can have significant dramatic impact, thus further enhancing the learning process. Filmstrips may also be combined with audiotape, to address the same general educational purposes as sound-slide presentations.

Sound-slide programs can be developed locally by teachers or students. In terms of emotional impact and instructional effectiveness, they may rival film or television productions, yet they can be produced for a fraction of the cost and effort. Indeed, sound-slide sets are produced frequently as prototypes of more elaborate film

CLOSE-UP:
"Indy 500" Learning Center

A fifth-grade teacher in Indianapolis capitalizes on local enthusiasm for the Indianapolis 500 car race by designing a math learning center based upon car numbers and speeds. Center material includes a variety of questions. "What is the difference in speed between Car 20 and Car 14?" "How many cars have even numbers?" "If an Indianapolis race car gets 1.8 miles per gallon, how many miles can it go on one tank of fuel (40 gallons)?" The center has colorful pictures and souvenir postcards of the cars and drivers. Each student draws, colors, and numbers his or her own race car, which goes in the "Victory Circle" when the lesson is completed. The students complete worksheets, for which they are awarded "completed laps" rather than numerical points. When they have completed their "500 miles," they have "finished the race" and receive a miniature checkered flag. The center is designed so that all students can eventually master its content and be rewarded by receiving a flag.

		VISUALS	
		Slides	Filmstrip
SOUND	Audio Tape	Local production	Commercial
	Phonograph record	Commercial	Commercial

▲ *Figure 7.9*
Sound-slide sets may consist of various combinations of audio and visual formats. The slide-audiotape combination is the only one that can be locally produced.

```
Sound   ||  |  | ||||   |||| | ||||||||||||   |||||| ||||| |  | | | | ||||||||| || | |||||||
Tone          •              •   •              •
```
Direction of play

▲ *Figure 7.10*
Synchronized sound-slide programs are controlled by inaudible tones put on one track of the tape.

or video projects, because they allow the presentation to be tried out and revised in its formative stages.

Sound-slide sets are available from commercial sources. However, mass distribution programs of this sort usually are converted to a filmstrip/audiotape format, because filmstrips require less storage space than slides and are less expensive. Some commercial programs are available with phonograph records instead of audiotapes. Major guides to identifying the many thousands of sound-slide and filmstrip sets available commercially are two National Information Center for Educational Media (NICEM) publications—*Index to Educational Slides* and *Index to 35mm Filmstrips.* See Appendix A for details and other sources.

The visuals in sound-slide programs may be advanced manually or automatically. In manual operation, the visual and audio components are usually on two separate machines. You begin by projecting the title slide or frame on the screen and then starting the sound track. An audible beep on the sound track signals you to advance the slides or filmstrip to the next visual. In manual operation, it is important that you test out at least the beginning of the program to make certain that you have sound and visuals in proper synchronization. Note also that some sound tracks do not contain a beep signal, in which case a

script containing instructions for advancing visuals must be used.

In automatic advancing of visuals with an audiotape, two sound tracks are used, one for the audible narration and one with inaudible tones that activate the advance mechanism on the slide or filmstrip projector, as shown in Figure 7.10.

Advantages

As just described, sound-slide combinations are easy and economical to produce locally with a simple camera and tape recorder. In addition, they lend themselves to student production.

These audiovisual presentations involve two senses and can have a very dramatic impact on learners. Sound-slide presentations can be used to inform or to change attitudes. They are applicable for both individual and group instruction with little or no modification. Combined with a printed study guide, sound-slide shows can actively involve the learners.

Limitations

One of the chief limitations is that the slides and audiotape may get out of synchronization. This may happen when showing the presentation to a group, but it occurs more commonly when an individual student is using the sound-slide combination. In addition, it is difficult to go back and reexamine a portion of the program

while keeping the slides in synchronization with the sound. This limitation can be overcome by putting the two-media combination on a single medium, namely videotape.

The videotape format also overcomes the limitation of requiring both a slide projector and an audio player. Some devices like the Kodak Caramate do combine both slide projection and tape playback into a single unit.

Applications

Sound-slide presentations may be used in almost any instructional setting and for instructional objectives involving the presentation of visual images to inform or to evoke an emotional response. They may be used for effect in group instruction, and they can be adapted to independent study in the classroom and in the media or learning center. This comparatively simple multimedia system is especially versatile as a learn-

▲ *Figure 7.11*
Sound-slide programs are readily adapted to individual use.

ing/teaching tool in that more than one narration can be prepared for a given set of visuals. For example, a single set of visuals might have one audio narrative suitable for introduction of and preliminary instruction in a study unit and another narrative for more detailed study. The narration could be on two or more vocabulary levels—one for regular students and another for educationally handicapped students. For foreign language instruction, one audiotape might be narrated in the student's native language and a matching narration recorded on another tape in the foreign language being taught. This technique can also be used in bilingual situations.

STORYBOARDING AND PLANNING SOUND-SLIDE PRESENTATIONS

WITH the use of more than one medium, it is very helpful to use a technique known as storyboarding. *Storyboarding,* an idea borrowed from film and television production, is a technique for helping you generate and organize your audiovisual materials. A sketch or some other simple representation of the visual you plan to use is put on a card or piece of paper along with production notes pertaining to production of the visual and verbal cues to its accompanying narration. After a series of such cards have been developed, they are placed in rough sequence on a flat surface or on a storyboard holder designed to keep them in place.

Index cards are commonly used for storyboarding because they are durable, inexpensive, and available in a variety of colors and sizes. Small pieces of paper can also be used. Recently the small sheets of paper with an adhesive backing (such as Post-It-Notes) are being used for storyboarding because they will stick to almost anything—cardboard, desks, walls, chalkboards, bulletin boards, and so on.

The individual storyboard cards can be divided into areas to accommodate the visual, the narration, and the production notes (Figure 7.13). The exact format of the storyboard card should fit your needs and purposes. Design a card that facilitates your working rather than constraining yourself to an existing or recommended format.

You can make a simple sketch or write a short description of the desired visual on the card. Polaroid pictures or visuals cut from magazines can also be used.

Some people like to use different-colored cards for different topics within the program, or various colors for objectives, content, and types of media (visuals, audio, films, etc.). Each component (slide, overhead, film sequence) should be on a separate card.

When a series of cards has been developed, the cards can be laid out on a table or placed on a storyboard holder. The cards are sequenced in tentative order, thus giving you an overview of the production. The storyboarding technique facilitates addition, deletion, replacement, revision, and refinement of the sequence, because the cards can easily be discarded, added to, or rearranged. The display of cards also allows others (teachers, students, production assistants) to look at the presentation in its planning stage. Number the cards in pencil; you may wish to change numbers as your planning progresses.

Several cards in sequence on a page can be photocopied for use

▲ *Figure 7.12*
The storyboard helps in visualizing the total presentation and rearranging parts within it.

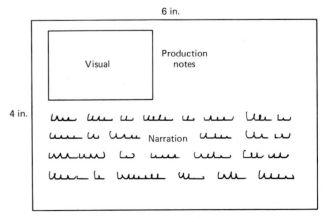
▲ *Figure 7.13*
The storyboard card contains a place for the visual, production notes, and the narration.

Here is a simple approach to developing your own sound-slide presentation:

Step 1. Analyze your audience both in terms of general characteristics and specific entry characteristics (as described in Chapter 2).
- Why are they viewing the presentation?
- What is their motivation toward your topic?
- How much do they already know about the subject?

Step 2. Specify your objectives (as described in Chapter 2).
- What do you want to accomplish with the presentation?
  —learning to be achieved
  —attitudes to be formed or changed
  —skills to be developed
- What should the viewers be able to *do* after the presentation?
  —activity or performance?
  —under what conditions?
  —with what degree of skill?

Step 3. Having completed your audience analysis and stated your objectives, you now have a much clearer idea of how your presentation will fit into your overall lesson plan, including what might precede it and follow it. Perhaps you will decide at this point that a sound-tape presentation is *not* really what you need to do after all.

If it is what you need to do, get a pack of planning cards (use index cards or cut some sheets of paper into 4-by-6-inch rectangles). Draw a large box in the upper left-hand corner of each card.

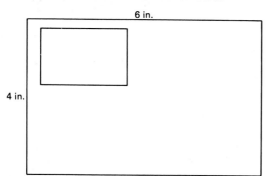

Step 4. Take a planning card. In the box draw a rough sketch of whatever image comes to your mind when you think about one of your major points.[a] You don't have to start with the *first* point, just whatever comes into your mind first. Your sketch may be a symbol, a diagram, a graph, a cartoon, or a photo of a person, place or thing, for example.

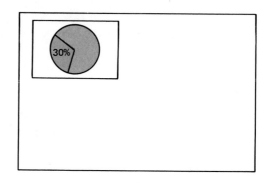

Step 5. Below your sketch, write a brief statement that captures the essence of the point you are trying to make. State it in as few words as needed to cue yourself to the thought. Some developers prefer to start with the visuals and then write the narration. Others prefer to do the narration first. Actually developing a sound-slide presentation is likely to be a dynamic process, with visual and narration evolving one from the other, separately and simultaneously. In some cases, of course, your narration will be already at hand—printed information, for example, or a story or poem—and all that remains is to develop the proper visuals to fit it. Or, the visuals may already be in hand—slides from a field trip, for example—and all you have to do is organize them and develop your script to accompany the visuals.

Step 6. Make a card for the thought that *leads into* the point you have just sketched. Then do another one about the thought that *follows* your first one. Continue like this, building a chain of ideas as you go along.

Step 7. When you run out of ideas in the chain, switch to one of the other major points that hasn't fallen into sequence yet.

Step 8. Arrange the cards in sequential and logical order. (This technique is called "storyboarding" and is described in more detail elsewhere in this chapter.)

Would some other arrangement liven up the beginning and the end of your presentation? Keep in mind the "psychology" of the situation as you thought it through in your audience analysis. The *beginning* and the *end* are generally the best places to make major points. Have you grabbed the viewer's attention right from the beginning?

How about pacing? Are any complicated ideas skimmed over too lightly? Do sections get bogged down in unnecessary detail? Add or subtract cards as needed.

You should have at least one slide on the screen for every point you make. Each slide should be on the screen long enough to support the point, but not so long that it gets tiresome to look at.

As a rule of thumb, you can estimate the number of slides you need by timing your presentation and multiplying the number of minutes by five or six. This means one slide change about every ten or twelve seconds. You may find that you need more slides in some instances, fewer in others. Don't be afraid to use "filler" slides to hold visual interest. They're perfectly acceptable as long as they relate to the topic.

Step 9. Edit your planning cards in terms of practicality. Be sure you have ready access to the artistic talent and/or photographic equipment needed to turn your sketches into slides.

Step 10. Use your notes to prepare an audio script.

Consider using two different voices for the narration, perhaps one male and one female for variety.

Would sound effects add impact to your presentation? How about actual sounds from the place where you will be shooting the pictures? You can take along a recorder and pick up background sounds and personal interviews while doing the photography.

Consider, too, adding music, especially as a finishing touch to the beginning and end. Be careful to keep it unobtrusive. Avoid highly recognizable tunes, trendy songs that will date your presentation, and music aimed at very specialized tastes.

Step 11. Rehearse your presentation, imagining that your cards are slides on the screen. Time your presentation and see if you need to shorten or lengthen it. To keep your audience's attention, limit your show to fifteen minutes. If you need more time than that, break it into two or more parts interspersed with audience activity.

Now you are ready to turn your sketches into slides! (To record your tape, see Chapter 6.)

[a]The visual organization hints given here are adapted from *How to Give a Better than Offhand Talk*. . . . Rochester, N.Y.: Eastman Kodak.

How To . . . MAKE A STORYBOARD HOLDER

You can construct an inexpensive storyboard holder from cardboard and strips of clear plastic. Obtain one or two pieces of cardboard about the size that you need to accommodate the number of cards which you will be using. About 18-by-24 inches is a convenient size if you plan to carry the storyboard holder with you.

If you use two pieces, they can be hinged in the middle (as shown above) with bookbinding tape or wide masking tape, giving you a usable surface measuring 36-by-24 inches when unfolded. If you do not plan to move the storyboard frequently, you could use a larger piece of cardboard (perhaps from a large appliance box such as a refrigerator carton) which could give you up to 6-by-4 feet of usable surface.

Staple or tape 1-inch-wide strips of clear plastic on the cardboard to hold the cards. If you are planning to use 3-by-5-inch index cards, the strips should be attached about 4 inches apart. One-inch strips of paper or light cardboard can be used to keep the card in place instead of the clear plastic, but this has the disadvantage of not allowing you to read the portion of the card that is behind the strip.

Left screen	Right screen	Narration

Left screen	Middle screen	Right screen	Narration

▲ *Figure 7.14*
Development charts, such as these, are used in planning multi-image or multiscreen presentations.

with the final script, thus avoiding duplication of effort and providing a convenient assemblage of visuals, narration, and production notes.

Your narration can be written from the notes on your storyboard cards. It is a good idea to triple space the typing of the final script for easy reading and last-minute changes. Marking pauses on the script with a slash (/) and underlining key words will help you record your narration effectively.

Having learned how to develop a single-screen presentation, you could choose as your next project a two-screen or even a three-screen presentation—although it should be pointed out that multiple-image presentations require even more planning and attention to detail. A two-screen presentation may require more than twice the time and effort needed to produce a single-screen one, and a three-screen display may require more than four times as much effort.

A "development chart" can help ease your extra burden. After you have storyboarded the sequence of your material, use the development chart for your production notes on the images to appear on each screen and for your notes on accompanying narration (see Figure 7.14).

Multi-image presentations must be carefully planned to fit your audience (multiple images may confuse younger students) and to meet your objectives. You should do a complete practice run-through prior to classroom presentation to be sure that the sequencing is correct and that equipment is operating the way you want it to operate.

Multi-image productions can incorporate short segments of film, overhead transparencies, slides, or a series of slides to simulate movement. They can also incorporate dissolve units.

Multi-image presentations can also be used very effectively for learning in the affective domain and for establishment of mood. For example, one could provide a visually dramatic background for listening to musical and choral works, plays, and readings.

MULTI-IMAGE SYSTEMS

THE multi-image presentation is another popular multimedia system. Whether you call the system multi-image or multiscreen depends primarily upon the way you display it. *Multi-image* refers to the use of two or more separate *images,* usually projected simultaneously in a presentation. (It does not usually refer to two images from a single source.) *Multiscreen* refers to the use of more than one screen in a single presentation. The two concepts usually go hand in hand, because the multiple images are often projected on adjacent multiple screens. Most often the images are projected from slides, but overhead transparencies, filmstrips, or motion pictures may also be used.

Dissolve Units

You can achieve dramatic effects in your slide/tape presentations by using a dissolve unit and two slide projectors. A dissolve unit has a mechanism for slowly turning one projector bulb off, causing one picture to fade out, while the other picture slowly appears on the same screen. The screen does not go black between pictures, but rather, one picture fades into the next. With a dissolve system you can gradually overlap images, blend or change directly from one visual to another, or blend one image into the other while the level of screen illumination remains constant. This provides a smooth visual presentation without any intervals of darkness on the screen between slides.

All dissolve units require at least two projectors focused to a single point on the screen so that the images will overlap. The projectors may be placed alongside each other or stacked one above the other (as shown in Figure 7.15).

You can achieve some very interesting effects by superimposing images from the two projectors. You can add elements to a particular visual or eliminate

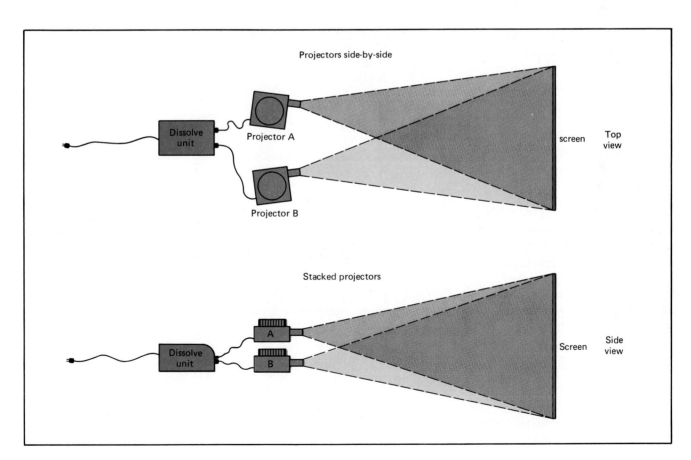

▲ *Figure 7.15*
When using a dissolve unit, the projectors may be aligned side-by-side or stacked one above the other.

unneeded ones. You can make an object appear to rotate, or make a head turn or a facial expression change in apparent response to a comment on the audiotape.

With the push of a button, you can control the speed and type of dissolve. A fast dissolve provides an instantaneous change from one visual to the next. A medium dissolve, lasting a couple of seconds, provides a visual blend between the slides. A slow dissolve allows one image to change more gradually into the next. The modes of changes available on most fade/dissolve units include:

Cut mode: the slide presentation switches from one projector to the other with instantaneous image change.

Dissolve mode: the first slide gradually fades in intensity as another slide from the second projector increases in intensity, creating a fading and overlapping effect as slides are changed.

Fade-out/fade-in mode: the slide gradually fades as light is reduced until there is total darkness on the screen; then a new image appears as light is gradually increased.

Automatic Programmers

There is a limit to the number of pieces of equipment you (with or without helpers) can operate and control directly. Fortunately, *automatic programmers* are available that can control a number of projectors. They can also be programmed to stop during your presentation for discussion or questions from the audience and then resume at the touch of a button.

There are two common types of programmers: magnetic tape and microcomputers. Magnetic tape programmers are increasing in

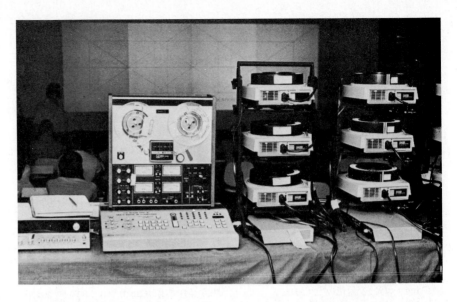

▲ *Figure 7.16*
A multi-image presentation controlled by an automatic programmer using magnetic tape

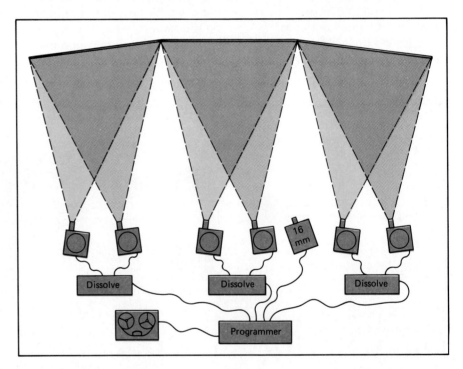

▲ *Figure 7.17*
Setup for a three-screen presentation using dissolve units and an automatic programmer

popularity and use and at the same time decreasing in cost. The newer microcomputers can also be used to control multi-image presentations. Microcomputers are very versatile and relatively easy to program for this function.

Automatic programmers enable you to operate motion pictures, filmstrips, and slide projectors together, separately, or in any combination with synchronized sound from an audiotape. A typical three-screen setup with dissolve control for each projector is shown in Figure 7.17.

Advantages

Multi-image systems have the advantage of incorporating a wide variety of media, such as slides, overhead transparencies, filmstrips, and motion pictures. They can show comparisons, time sequences, or wide-angle panoramic views (see the following discussion of applications).

With rapidly changing images, attention of the learners can be captured and held. Some very dramatic effects can be achieved by rapidly changing still pictures, which is possible with dissolve units and automatic programmers. Combined with appropriate music, multiple images can also set a mood.

Dissolve units can simulate motion through rapid sequential still pictures without the use of film or videotape. The production costs of multi-image presentations can be significantly less than that of film or video.

Limitations

Development of multi-image materials requires considerable time and expertise to plan (see the section on Storyboarding and Planning). Because a wide variety of materials are incorporated, the production time and costs can be high. Finally, additional time is required to program the presentation with the dissolve units and/or automatic programmers.

The time to set up the presentation and align the projectors can also be significant. The amount of equipment required for their presentation increases the cost of using multi-image systems.

Because multi-image presentations require several pieces of equipment, projectors, dissolve units, and programmers, the chances for problems increase.

Applications

Multi-image presentations can be used creatively in a variety of instructional situations. For example, one screen could be used to present an overview or long-range view of a visual while another

▲ *Figure 7.18*
Showing a broad panorama is a typical application of multi-image systems.

presents a close-up view or a detail of it. This technique might be used to show the relationship of a component of a system or process in its entirety, or to show a detail of a work of art in relationship to the complete piece. Two or more images could be projected side-by-side for students to compare and contrast different art forms, or art and architectural forms in different periods of history.

"Before-and-after" shots could be used in industrial arts classes, for example, to show the final results of a furniture-refinishing project; or they could be used in a social studies class to show the inroads of industrialization on an ecological system. In electronics instruction, schematic codes of circuit components could be shown next to visuals of the actual components. Similarly, line draw-ings of an object can be exhibited adjacent to its photograph, or a photograph can be displayed on one screen and data or questions about the picture presented on another. A map of an area might be shown on one screen, and a photograph or aerial view of the area presented in another.

Two or more screens may also be used to present wide-angle or panoramic views of a visual that might be impossible to present on a single screen. Multiple-screen images can also be used to show physical activities in more detailed sequence, such as swimming, diving, swinging a tennis racquet, or hitting a golf ball. They can also be used to present several views of the same object to achieve a three-dimensional effect or to allow viewers to see an object from different distances and angles.

INTERACTIVE VIDEO

INTERACTIVE video creates a multimedia learning environment that capitalizes on the features of both instructional television and computer-assisted instruction. It is an instructional delivery system in which recorded video material is presented under computer control to viewers who not only see and hear the pictures and sounds but also make active responses, with those responses affecting the pace and sequence of the presentation.

The video portion of interactive video is provided through videotape or videodisc. Videodiscs (see Chapter 8 for more detail) can provide color, motion, and sound. The images can be presented in slow motion, fast motion, frame-by-frame, or single frame—equivalent to a slide or filmstrip display. The audio portion of a videodisc may occupy two channels, making possible two different narrations with any specific motion sequence. Many of the features of videodiscs can be obtained with currently available videotape systems at a lower cost.

The "interactive" feature of interactive video is provided through a computer. Computers have very powerful decision-making abilities, which video players lack. Combining these technologies means the strengths of each can compensate for the limitations of the other to provide a rich educational environment for the learner. Interactive video is a powerful, practical method for individualizing and personalizing instruction.

A variety of levels of interactivity are available, ranging from essentially linear video to learner-directed sequencing of instruction. The goal of most developers of interactive video is to provide fully interactive response-depen-

▲ *Figure 7.19*
An interactive video setup using a videocassette as the picture source (see upper-left shelf)

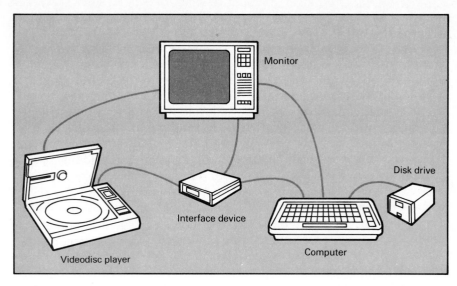

▲ *Figure 7.20*
The components of a typical interactive video system

System Components

The heart of an interactive video system is a computer. (See Figure 7.20.) The computer provides the "intelligence" and interactivity required for interactive video. The computer can command the video player to present audio and/or video information from the videotape or videodisc, wait for the learner's response, and branch to the appropriate point in the instructional program from that response.

The learner communicates with the instructional program by responding to audio, visual, or verbal stimuli displayed through the monitor. Input devices provide the means for these

dent instruction featuring embedded questions, response feedback, and branching within the lesson. In addition, student response histories can be used to affect instructional decisions.*

responses. They may include a keyboard, a touch-sensitive panel, a light pen, voice activation, or a three-dimensional simulator. (See "Close-up: CPR Computer/Videodisc Learning System," p. 207.)

The computer storage system is usually a diskette. The diskette holds the instructional program and may also store information such as student responses, response time, and accuracy of responses throughout the lesson.

The video player offers a sophisticated means of presenting visual and audio information. The videotape or videodisc can provide color, sound (two different audio tracks on videodisc), still visuals, or motion pictures.

The monitor is used to display the video signal and sound from the video player. It also provides the output from the computer program, usually in the form of printed verbal information, but graphics or sound is also possible. Some interactive video systems make it possible to overlay computer lettering or graphics on the video image. Some commercially available videodisc players have the computer, the memory, and input devices built into them.

The interface device provides the link between the computer and the video player. It allows the computer to communicate with the video player. Through the device, the computer can control which portion of the video is presented to the learner.

Advantages

One of the major advantages of interactive video is that it requires learner response (the *R* of the ASSURE model). Learners respond through typing on a keyboard, touching the screen, or manipulating objects connected to the system. By requiring frequent response, interactive video captures learners' attention and holds their interest to a greater extent than does videotape alone. The system allows the learner to participate actively in an educational video presentation that is thereby adapted to the learner's ability and knowledge level.

Another important feature of interactive video is its branching (nonlinear) capability. Depending upon the response of the learner, the computer can branch to another section of the video program to provide remedial instruction rather than simply repeating the original information. Or the system may branch to a new section of the video to provide enrichment material for the learner. When the learner has mastered the objective or already has knowledge of the subject matter or skill, the program can be branched to a new topic or more advanced treatment of the same topic. In some cases the student may choose what to study from a "menu."

As a result of its learner response and branching capabilities, interactive video can serve as an individualized, self-paced system capable of presenting infor-

* M. J. Hannafin and K. L. Peck. *The Design, Development, and Evaluation of Instructional Software.* New York: Macmillan, 1988.

mation in an order determined by and appropriate to a learner's responses and needs.

Two additional advantages of interactive video are its convenience and variety. A variety of media formats are included in one system. Text, audio, graphics, still pictures, motion pictures, and manipulation of objects can all be combined in one instructional system without requiring numerous projectors, tape recorders, and synchronization equipment. From the student's perspective the operation of the system is very simple, in many cases requiring only the use of a keyboard. A large amount of content and a variety of information are made available to the learner in a matter of seconds.

Multipurpose usage is another advantage. In the medical field a single interactive videodisc can be programmed to provide patients with the information they need for self-care, to train nurses in certain procedures, and to educate doctors in making diagnoses. In schools, one video program may be used with different computer programs at different grade levels or with different ability students.

According to research studies, students using interactive video may not learn more, but they learn faster and retain the information longer.* Learning a specific task can take from 30 to 35 percent less time with interactive video than with other methods.

Videodiscs provide very fast access to any of the 54,000 frames on one side of a twelve-inch constant angular velocity (CAV) laser videodisc. Another advantage of discs over videotape is the quality

of the freeze-frame images. Also, because nothing touches the videodiscs during operation, they are wear free and so have a very long life. Videotapes eventually wear out, lose quality, and twist or break in the machine during operation, particularly with a lot of fast-forwarding and rewinding.

The use of floppy discs with the computer component of interactive video provides an immense storage capacity for instructional programming and recording of student responses. Some content updating can be accomplished through programming of the floppy disk at much less cost than updating the videodisc.

From the instructor's point of view, a further advantage is the record-keeping ability of the system. The computer can be programmed to keep track of learner responses, for tracking the learner's progress, for determining where the learner will be directed next, and for assisting the instructor in revising the program. The system lends itself to the collection of research data on factors affecting student learning and the measurement of the effectiveness of various instructional techniques.

Limitations

The most significant limitation of interactive video is its cost. Expensive equipment—including a computer, video-playback unit, and monitor—is required. It is expensive to produce and update videotape and even more costly and difficult to produce and update a videodisc. However, once mastered, videodiscs are inexpensive to duplicate. Therefore, interactive video is not cost-effective for a few students. In addition, it should not be used if the visuals and learning materials

will change substantially within a short time.

Videodiscs can only be mastered by a limited number of companies at the present time. The complexity and high cost of developing and mastering videodiscs limit their use primarily to high-volume informational or training applications in business and industry. They currently are not in widespread use in formal education, beyond demonstration projects.

Videotape is less expensive than videodisc as a format for producing small numbers of copies, but it has the drawbacks of being slower in search time (to get from one frame to another) and less efficient in showing a particular single frame. Also, searching for a single frame is more difficult. Most videocassette machines lack slow motion and fast motion. Consequently, the user must trade off the more expensive costs of producing videodiscs for fewer capabilities and increased time required to access material on a videotape.

The limited research reported for interactive video is generally favorable. Hannafin points out that much of the support for interactive video has been derived from presumed inherent capabilities of the technology. Additional research is needed to verify many of these assumptions.*

Applications

Interactive video is a valuable learning device for tasks that must be shown rather than simply told. Some instruction cannot be adequately presented by printed materials. If the learner needs to

* Donald G. Ebner et al. "Videodiscs Can Improve Instructional Effectiveness." *Instructional Innovator* (September 1984), pp. 26–28.

* Michael J. Hannafin. "Empirical Issues in the Study of Computer-Assisted Interactive Video." *ECTJ* 33, no. 4 (Winter 1985), pp. 235–247.

A precursor to interactive video that combines a computer with videotape or videodisc was variable motion programming which utilized an audiocassette and an 8-mm film cartridge. In contrast to standard motion picture presentations, the sound and the picture in the 8-mm film–audiocassette system are separated into two individual packages. The audiotape moves at a constant speed, but the film can be programmed to move at variable speeds from still (stop action) up to twenty-four frames per second. The film cartridge contains fifty feet of Super-8-mm film and includes 3,600 frames (visuals) that can be shown individually or in rapid succession to simulate motion. The film and sound are synchronized by inaudible pulses recorded on the audiocassette. The systems provide "variable motion sound filmstrips" with the impact of motion pictures and the teaching effectiveness of still pictures.

Beseler's Cue/See ® variable motion system

The idea was conceived by the Philips Company in Holland in 1967. The following year the first unit was brought into the United States for evaluation. The Norelco Training and Education Systems Group of North American Philips added some new features and set up production facilities for the manufacture of the Personalized Individual Presentation (PIP) unit. The unit was distributed widely for about ten years to industry, educational institutions, and the government for training purposes. It was dropped from the market in the early 1980s.

A similar system was developed and marketed by Retention Communications Systems. The original Retention machine was replaced by Retention II. It, too, was dropped from the market in the mid-1980s.

The longest lasting of the variable motion programming machines was the Beseler Cue/See. It was introduced in 1971 and was discontinued in 1988.

These systems can intermix the equivalent of slides, filmstrips, and motion pictures along with narration or sound effects. Separate audiocassettes allow the user to choose which narration to use with a given film. The projection mechanism is essentially a variable speed projector with a built-in tape player and synchronization device. The machinery is light, weighing about twenty pounds, and thus is readily portable.

The speed at which the image changes on the screen can be determined by the nature of the material being presented. Separation of "sound track" from the film permits the film to be moved at variable speeds while the tape is moving at a constant speed. Just as pulses advance the frames of a filmstrip, pulses in this system advance the frames of the film slowly, to illustrate specific lesson points, or very rapidly, to create motion.

The machine has a built-in rear projection screen as well as a mirror and lens system for projecting the image on a screen, so it is suitable for individual or small-group use. It can show slow motion, time lapse, or stop action. The machines also incorporate a "skipped" frame mechanism that allows two, three, or even five frames at a time to be advanced at high speed without detection by the viewer, because each new frame is advanced in less than a hundredth of a second. This feature is particularly valuable when the same film is used with separate audiotapes for two different types of audiences.

All of the features of variable motion programming are available in interactive video systems— and more! Perhaps these additional capabilities, the decreasing cost of computers, and the increasing number of videodiscs all contributed to the demise of the machines that combine audiocassette tapes and 8-mm film cartridges. Of course, the 8-mm film cartridge is another rapidly dying media presentation format.

The techniques of variable motion programming live on in the newer interactive video delivery system.

interact with the instruction, interactive video is almost essential.

Interactive video systems are currently being used in a variety of instructional applications. Formal education demonstration projects cover a wide range, from physics instruction to teaching special education students to tell time. The programs can challenge a small group of gifted students or provide remedial instruction for slow learners. The materials can be used by individuals or an entire class. Most teachers feel that their greater effectiveness is with individuals.

These systems are for both instruction and information. In the latter case, they provide a large pictorial database. These information applications include point-of-purchase displays or public information kiosks in grocery stores and department stores. The videodisc and computer provide detailed consumer information to help a buyer make a purchase decision.

Interactive video systems are also used for remote shopping by presenting features of various items and responding to customer questions selected from a menu. Sales increases between 50 percent and 350 percent have been reported for products presented in stores and airports by an "intelligent" videodisc point-of-purchase system. These interactive information systems can also accept orders, make reservations, and sell tickets.

Army recruiters now provide significant decision-making information to potential recruits through a videodisc-based interactive system. The army's various job types and training opportunities are explained and visually demonstrated by the system in response to a potential recruit's questions. Recruiting offices using the videodisc system currently realize almost double the number of recruits compared to matched samples from offices without the system.

Now let's turn our attention to *instructional* applications of interactive video. In business and industry, these systems are being used to train automobile mechanics to troubleshoot electronic ignition systems, to improve communication skills for bank tellers, and to teach relaxation and stress management techniques to executives. One company reports reducing the training time of lift truck operators from three hours to one hour by replacing classroom training with interactive video training. (See "Close-up: Safety Training via Interactive Video.")

Technical repair skills also can be taught with interactive video. A program can teach the trainee to locate a faulty component and can visually demonstrate how to adjust or replace the component while oral instructions are provided through one of the two audio channels on the videodisc. Data collected regarding such a system indicate that mechanics using it did demonstrate mastery of the maintenance skills. Moreover, both training time and training costs for the interactive video group were less than half of those of the traditional on-the-job training group.

Interactive video programs are also being used to teach and reinforce interpersonal skills through intensive simulation. For example, welfare caseworkers and sales personnel can benefit through such programs. One of the "Big-Three" automakers uses videodiscs to train its sales personnel within the dealerships as well as to sell automobiles to customers. The same video sequences are used for both. One of the audio channels is directed to the customer, pointing out the important sales features of the various makes and models. The other audio channel is used by the sales staff to learn critical information concerning how their cars compare to the competition. Sales pointers are included as well.

One of the most widespread applications of interactive video is the teaching of cardiopulmonary resuscitation (CPR). (See "Close-up: CPR Computer/Videodisc Learning System.")

In the medical field interactive video systems are being used for patient education; e.g., on weight control and on diabetes. Doctors are receiving in-service education through a library of medical simulations on patient management, differential diagnosis of stomach pain, and various diagnostic techniques. For training nurses and doctors to handle badly injured people, a single videodisc can hold hundreds of different injury situations that might take months or even years for a learner to encounter on the job. The U.S. Navy's combat medicine simulation won the top Nebraska Videodisc Award in 1987.

The military is a big user of interactive video, for tasks such as Jeep mechanical maintenance, visual simulation of life inside a military tank, and simulation of the task of calling for artillery fire. In 1980 a course was developed around an interactive video system for troubleshooting the HAWK missile system. Evaluation of this training simulation provided impressive evidence of the power of interactive video. The videodisc simulation replaced equipment costing up to $4,000 per student hour and provided more opportunities for practice than could be possible with the

The Clark Equipment Company, manufacturer of fork lift trucks in Battle Creek, Michigan, has developed an operator safety refresher course using interactive video. The course was designed in response to supervisors who expressed concern that they didn't have time to do the refresher training. In addition, the supervisors were concerned about the time they wasted in retraining operators. The operators themselves didn't see the need to be retrained in order to learn about something they did every day. An interactive videotape system was selected for the safety training.

Training via interactive video was compared with training using conventional videotape. Studies involved Clark employees and operators in other companies that had purchased Clark fork lifts. The results indicated higher initial learning and retention of the content after twenty-four days that was almost 20 percent higher for the operators using the interactive video system. Training time for the operators was reduced, as well as time required by the supervisors to provide the training. Consequently, there was a significant reduction in the wages and overhead devoted to training.

Furthermore, the training system motivated operators to request other opportunities to learn using interactive video. In addition, there was no evidence in the interactive video group to indicate any effects of age or experience on an operator's score as there was in the group of operators learning from ordinary videotape.

Source: D. Wooldridge and Thomas Dargan. "Linear vs. Interactive Videotape Training." *International Television.* (August 1983), pp. 56–60.

actual equipment. All trainees attained 100 percent mastery after interactive video training and did so in less than half the time of trainees taught by conventional means. In the latter group, only 30 percent reached mastery.

Interactive videodiscs can also be used for testing. One state now uses an interactive videodisc driver's license test. The system both administers and scores the test. The system shows video sequences of realistic situations. The testee must then make the correct decision about the driving situations illustrated in order to pass the test. Other educational situations needing evaluation of motion sequences would lend themselves to videodisc testing.

The U.S. Army made a commitment to interactive video in 1987 when it installed about 2,000 units in its training schools. As many as 50,000 units may be in place by 1990. The Electronic Information Delivery System (EIDS) is geared primarily for training and serves as the accepted standard hardware delivery system for interactive video and computer-based instruction in the U.S. military. Much of the videodisc courseware has been developed by civilian contractors. Over 10,000 hours of videodisc and computer-based materials have been developed for the EIDS system. Industry experts predict that the sheer size of the military training and the development of the associated hardware and software will influence how schools and private industry develop and deliver multimedia instruction in the future.*

---

* "U.S. Army Makes New Commitment to Interactive Discs." *Interactive Discs Today* 1, no. 2 (January 12, 1987), pp. 32–35.

Cardiopulmonary resuscitation, or CPR, is currently being taught using interactive video. Developed by David Hon of the American Heart Association, the system incorporates a variety of media including an optical videodisc player, a monitor, a microcomputer, and a random access audio player. At the "heart" of the system is a mannequin wired with an array of sensors placed at key points in its lung system that monitor the depth and placement of CPR compressions.

As the trainee practices these compressions, he or she receives several different types of feedback: audiovisual "coaching" from the doctor on the screen, a visual readout on the computer monitor (indicating, for instance, that hand placement is too high or depth is too shallow), audio tones to indicate proper timing of each compression, and a graphic pattern on the computer detailing overall performance.

At various points during the program, the computer asks evaluative questions in "fill-in" or multiple-choice format. Using a light pen or typing in a response, the trainee actively participates in learning CPR. The computer monitors and displays learner progress throughout the course. Video segments can be accessed for review and for detailed explanations when necessary.

After the instructional segment of the program is completed, the student is ready for evaluation. The same computer/videodisc system with mannequin monitors the student's final "hands-on" performance for certification and "asks" questions about CPR.

Source: Biomedical Communications (September 1981).

In formal education there are a number of instructional applications of interactive video. There are numerous discs available for use in the schools and in adult education (see the accompanying "Media Files").

Interactive video may also be used for group instruction. The relatively high cost of interactive video equipment often precludes the purchase of enough units to implement self-study for each learner. The instructional program can be designed to allow the instructor to stop the program for discussion, skip ahead to new material, or repeat previous instruction. For example, a set of instructional video materials titled "Critical Incidents in Discipline" provides preservice and in-service teachers a sample of the discipline problems they might encounter in a classroom. The incident is presented vividly on video, and future sequences are shown based on the group's choice of action they would carry out if confronted with the situation. After each choice, the interactive video program shows the result of that action. The group can then be shown the results of their decision and be lead to another decision. The student teachers were able to try a number of different choices and see the results of each. One important consequence of this technique was the stimulation of class discussion which occurred after the students saw the results of each choice. Many students learn better in group instruction where interaction with others can be very stimulating.*

---

* William D. Milheim and Alan D. Evans. "Using Interactive Video for Group Instruction." *Educational Technology* (June 1987), pp. 35–37.

MEDIA FILE:
IBM InfoWindow System

In 1986 IBM introduced its InfoWindow System for interactive video applications. The system features the InfoWindow Display, a monitor with a touch-sensitive screen. It can be used with any IBM personal computer, such as the Personal System/2 Model 30, the XT or the AT. The computer and monitor can be used with a number of laser videodisc players.

Because the touch screen does not require learners to use a keyboard or to have any computer skills, the InfoWindow System decreases the "intimidation factor" for learners. It provides highly interactive text and graphics presentations.

IBM offers three different InfoWindow authoring and presentation systems to meet the individual instructor's development and presentation needs. The Presentation System Editor uses a spreadsheet divided into time segments to help an author select and position the elements of video, text, graphics, and sound. The Learning System/1 Authoring System includes built-in features for creating one-to-one tutorials. A less structured and more powerful authoring tool is available for experienced course developers.

Source: IBM

MEDIA FILE:
"Principle of the Alphabet Literacy System"

Officials estimate that about 15 percent of adults in America cannot read or write. Millions more are functionally illiterate. IBM's Principle of the Alphabet Literacy System (PALS) addresses this problem. The interactive video program uses the IBM Info-Window (see Media File above) to help adolescents and adults achieve higher levels of reading and writing skills. PALS uses a dramatized story to introduce learners to the alphabetic principle of how to combine the letters of the alphabet to form words. They learn to read and write by recognizing different phonemes (letter sounds). The system incorporates interactive video, separate microcomputers, typing manuals, work journals, teacher's manuals, and wall charts.

Source: IBM

Blueprint: THE SOLAR SYSTEM

Analyze Learners

General Characteristics. The first-grade students are six and seven years old. They have grown up in a middle to upper socioeconomic environment. Their intellectual aptitude is generally above average. They are more attentive to learning methods in which they actively participate than to those that require passive observation.

Entry Competencies. The concept of the solar system is relatively new to the students. They can differentiate between Earth and space. They are able to tell time and perform simple linear measurements. Some of the students have substandard reading skills.

State Objectives

Upon completion of the lesson, the students will be able to

1. Describe the concept of the solar system.
2. State the number of planets in the solar system.
3. Match the names of the planets with a visual showing the planets in the solar system configuration.
4. Compare and contrast the temperatures of the planets closer to the sun with those farther from the sun.
5. Demonstrate the travel of the planets in reference to the sun.
6. State the order of each planet in terms of distance from the sun.

Select Media and Materials

The teacher, Cathy Richardson, was not able to locate commercial materials other than printed materials that would meet her objectives, were appropriate for her students, and were within her budget. She wanted to utilize mediated materials containing individual or group activities to maintain student interest and to enhance student learning.

Because she had no appropriate materials in her classroom and did not locate any in the school media center, there was nothing to modify. Consequently, she decided to design her own learning center on the solar system. There were some things in her classroom, other items in the media center, and many ideas in books that she could incorporate within her center.

As part of her solar system learning center, Cathy used a portable, three-sided wooden carrel that could be placed on a table in the back of the room. She decorated the carrel with pictures from magazines and old textbooks showing the various planets.

For the basic instruction she prepared a slide-tape presentation using the Visualmaker to prepare slides from books and drawings. Cathy wrote the narration after the slides were developed. Stravinsky's "Rite of Spring" was selected as background music for the recording.

Finally, three activity packets were prepared for use in the carrel after the students had viewed the slide-tape. The packets were designed to involve the students actively in learning about the solar system.

Utilize the Materials

The students are scheduled individually or in pairs to go to the learning center at the rear of the classroom during a one-week period. They first view the slide-tape introduction using headphones, thereby not interrupting other classroom activities.

At least one of the activity packets is selected by the student for completion. Most students elect to complete all three packets. All packets are directed toward the objectives outline for the center.

Require Learner Performance

After learning the characteristics of the solar system from the teacher-designed slide-tape presentation, the students are actively involved in learning activities that provide practice and feedback. One activity asks the students to answer riddle cards related to the objectives. For students with reading problems, the questions and answers are read by a student with good reading skills.

Additional practice is provided by student activity sheets titled "Space Explorer." On these sheets the students practice labelling the planets on a diagram of the solar system. They also practice listing the planets in order from the sun. Several of the sheets have pictures to color.

A third learning activity folder describes the movement of the planets around the sun. Students use manipulative objects to demonstrate the circular motion of the planets.

Evaluate/Revise

Some of the learning-center activities use self-checks so that each student can check his or her work on an independent basis. The riddle cards serve this function. Students are encouraged to attend the center more than once if they are not successful with the self-checks.

Students also complete a sheet with five faces from smiling to frowning to indicate their personal response to the learning center. Their mastery of the objectives is determined by a paper-and-pencil test covering the objectives. For students with reading difficulties, the teacher administers the evaluation orally.

Source: Developed by Cathy Richardson, Lafayette, Ind.

References

Print References

Multimedia Systems

Benedict, Joel A., and Crane, Douglas A. *Producing Multi-Image Presentations.* (Tempe, Ariz.: Arizona State University, 1976).

Bretz, Rudy, with Schmidbauer, Michael. *Media for Interactive Communication.* (Beverly Hills, Calif.: Sage Publications, 1983).

Bullough, Robert V. *Multi-Image Media.* (Englewood Cliffs, N.J.: Educational Technology Publications, 1981).

Dunn, Rita, and Dunn, Kenneth. "Seeing, Hearing, Moving, Touching, Learning Packages." *Teacher* (May/June 1977), pp. 48–51.

Effective Visual Presentations. (Rochester, N.Y.: Eastman Kodak, 1979).

Goldstein, E. Bruce. "The Perception of Multiple Images." *AV Communication Review* (Spring 1975), pp. 34–68.

Green, Lee. *Creative Slide/Tape Programs.* (Littleton, Colo.: Libraries Unlimited, 1986).

Hitchens, Howard B. "The Production of Multimedia Kits." *Educational Media International* (March 1977), pp. 6–13.

Kenny, Michael F., and Schmitt, Raymond F. *Images, Images, Images: The Book of Programmed Multi-Image Production.* (Rochester, N.Y.: Kodak Motion Picture & Audiovisual Division, 1981).

McMeen, George R. "Toward the Development of Rhetoric and Content in the Communication of Meaningful Verbal Information in Multimedia Instructional Materials." *Educational Technology* (September 1983), pp. 22–25.

Perrin, Donald G. "A Theory of Multi-image Communication." *AV Communication Review* (Winter 1969), pp. 368–382.

Planning and Producing Slide Programs. (Rochester, N.Y.: Eastman Kodak, 1975).

Instructional Modules

Fisher, Kathleen M., and Mac-Whinney, Brian. "AV Autotutorial Instruction: A Review of Evaluative Research." *AV Communication Review* (February 1976), pp. 229–261.

Johnson, Rita B., and Johnson, Stuart R. *Toward Individualized Learning: A Developer's Guide to Self-Instruction.* (Reading, Mass.: Addison-Wesley, 1975).

Moore, David M. "Self-Instruction and Technology: A Review." *Journal of Educational Technology Systems,* no. 1 (1976–1977), pp. 51–56.

Radway, Bonnie, and Schroeder, Betty. "Modular Instruction Is the Way of the Future!" *Journal of Business Education* (March 1978), pp. 247, 249–250.

Russell, James D., and Johanningsmeier, Kathleen A. *Increasing Competence through Modular Instruction.* (Dubuque, Iowa: Kendall/Hunt, 1981).

Sussman, Miriam L. "Making Tracks with LAP's." *Florida Vocational Journal* (April 1978), pp. 17–19.

Thiagarajan, Sivasailam. *Groprograms.* Volume 8, Instructional Design Library. (Englewood Cliffs, N.J.: Educational Technology Publications, 1978).

Learning Centers

Beach, Don M. *Reaching Teenagers: Learning Centers for the Secondary Classroom.* (Santa Monica, Calif.: Goodyear Publishing, 1977).

Blake, Howard E. *Creating a Learning-Centered Classroom.* (New York: A & W Visual Library, 1977).

"Book Nooks and Classroom Crannies: How to Make a Classroom Anything but Ordinary." *Instructor* (August 1982), pp. 22–25.

Cooper, Arlene. "Learning Centers: What They Are and Aren't." *Academic Therapy* (May 1981), pp. 527–531.

Deal, Candace C. "Big Returns from Mini-Centers." *Momentum* (May 1984), pp. 34–35.

Evans, Richard M. "Troubleshooting Individualized Learning Centers." *Educational Technology* (April 1984) pp. 38–40.

Feldhusen, Hazel. "Teaching Gifted, Creative, and Talented Students in an Individualized Classroom." *Gifted Child Quarterly* (Summer 1981), pp. 108–111.

Gruendike, Janis L. "Centering on Sea Life in the Classroom." *Science and Children* (October 1982), pp. 26–27.

Hopkins, Jeri. "The Learning Center Classroom." *The Computing Teacher* (December/January 1985–1986) pp. 8–12.

Lutz, Charlene Howells, and Brills, Patricia. "Ten-Minute Super Centers." *Instructor* (September 1983), pp. 158–175.

Maxim, George W. *Learning Centers for Young Children.* (New York: Hart Publishing Co., 1977).

Nations, Jimmy E., ed. *Learning Centers in the Classroom.* (Washington, D.C.: National Education Association, 1976).

Orlich, Donald C., et al. "Science Learning Centers—An Aid to Instruction." *Science and Children* (September 1982), pp. 18–20.

Strauber, Sandra K. "Language Learning Stations." *Foreign Language Annals* (February 1981), pp. 31–36.

"Walk-in, Talk-in, Learn-in Labs." *Instructor* (August 1983), pp. 48–52.

Interactive Video

Brodeur, Doris R. "Interactive Video in Elementary and Secondary Education." *Illinois School Research and Development* (Winter 1986), pp. 52–59.

Daynes, R., and Buttler, B., eds. *The Videodisc Book: A Guide and Directory.* (New York: Wiley, 1984).

DeBloois, M. L., ed. *Videodisc/Microcomputer Courseware Design.* (Englewood Cliffs, N.J.: Educational Technology Publications, 1982).

DeLoughry, Thomas J. "Videodiscs Gain a New Role in Classrooms as Medium to Simulate Real-Life Situations." *Chronicle of Higher Education* (December 2, 1987), pp. A13, A16, and A17.

Hannafin, M. J., Phillips, T. L., and Tripp, S.D. "The Effects of Orienting, Processing, and Practicing Activities on Learning from Interactive Video." *Journal of Computer-Based Instruction* 13, pp. 134–139.

Hershberger, Linda. "How Interactive Training Affects Corporations." *Educational/Industrial Television* (January 1984), pp. 64–65.

Johnson, Kerry A. "Interactive Video: The Present and the Promise." *New Directions for Continuing Education* (Summer 1987), pp. 29–40.

Kearsley, G. P., and Frost, J. "Design Factors for Successful Videodisc-Based Instruction." *Educational Technology* 25, pp. 7–13.

Lehman, James D. "Biology Education with Interactive Videodiscs." *American Biology Teacher* (January 1985), pp. 34–37.

———. "Interactive Video: A Powerful New Tool for Science Teaching." *Journal of Computers in Science and Mathematics Teaching* (Spring 1986), pp. 24–29.

Salpeter, Judy. "Interactive Video: The Truth Behind the Promises." *Classroom Computer Learning* (November–December 1986), pp. 26–34.

Smith, Eric E. "Interactive Video: An Examination of Use and Effectiveness." *Journal of Instructional Development* 10 pp. 2–10.

Videodiscs for Education: A Directory. (St. Paul, Minn.: MECC, 1987.)

Audiovisual References

Classroom Learning Centers. Birmingham, Ala.: Promethean Films, 1976. 16-mm film.

Creating Slide-Tape Programs. Washington, D.C.: Association for Educational Communications and Technology, 1980. Filmstrip with audiocassette.

Development of a Slide-Tape Instructional Presentation. National Audio-Visual Center, 1979. Slides with cassette. 16 minutes.

Effective Visual Presentations. Rochester, N.Y.: Eastman Kodak, 1978. Slide set with audiocassette and 16-mm film.

How to Produce Better Sound/Slide Shows. Slide Images, 1980. Slides with cassette.

Series Ten. Viscom, 1979. 10 slide sets, 10 audiocassettes, and 10 guides.
Module 1: How to Write and Storyboard A.V. Programs
Module 2: Cures for the Ten Most Common Design Problems
Module 3: Producing Artwork for Slide Shows
Module 4: Photography for A.V. Shows
Module 5: Basic Special Effects
Module 6: Advanced Special Effects
Module 7: Animation and Movement
Module 8: Assembling and Programming A.V. Programs
Module 9: Producing Soundtracks for A.V. Programs
Module 10: Designing A.V. Facilities

Synchronizing a Slide/Tape Program. Rochester, N.Y.: Eastman Kodak, 1976. Slide set with audiocassette. 12 minutes.

Writing Learning Activity Packages. Educational Filmstrips, n.d. 2 filmstrips with cassettes.

Possible Projects

7-A. Plan a lesson in which you use a sound-slide set or sound filmstrip. With this lesson show evidence that you have followed the utilization principles suggested in Chapter 2 as well as other pertinent suggestions from this chapter. Include a brief description of the audience and your objectives.

7-B. Develop a set of storyboard cards for an instructional sound-slide presentation.

7-C. Locate and examine a multimedia kit in your field of interest. Prepare a written or oral report on the possible applications and relative merits of the kit.

7-D. Utilize an instructional module as though you were a student. Be sure to do all the activities and complete the exercises. Prepare an appraisal of the module from your point of view. Submit the module with your appraisal, if possible.

7-E. Design a classroom learning center. Describe the audience, the objectives, and the materials/media to be incorporated. Explain the roles of the students and the instructor in using the center. Evaluate its actual effectiveness if used or potential effectiveness if not used.

7-F. Locate and examine an interactive video program. Prepare a written or oral report on the possible applications and relative merits of the program for your instructional needs.

8

Film and Video

Objectives

After studying this chapter, you
should be able to:

1. Define *film*.
2. Describe how film creates an
illusion of motion.
3. Define *video*.
4. Identify the film formats most
common in instructional use.
5. Identify the video formats most
common in instructional use.
6. Contrast film and video on technical and psychological grounds.
7. Name at least two of the special
attributes shared by film and video.
8. Distinguish between time lapse
and slow motion in technical terms.

9. Define *documentary* and explain why a particular film selected from this chapter fits the definition.

10. Identify two film conventions that must be culturally learned.

11. Name at least five advantages of film and video as instructional resources.

12. Explain at least three limitations of film and video as instructional resources.

13. Characterize the status of video in the schools.

14. Characterize the status of video in higher education, in both on- and off-campus programs.

15. Characterize the utilization patterns of video in corporate training and development.

16. Recognize videocassettes and videodiscs as primary delivery systems for classroom video.

17. Describe the special capabilities of videodiscs compared to videocassettes.

18. Outline the process of selecting a particular film or video program for classroom use.

19. List at least five criteria that are important in the appraisal of film and video materials.

20. Generate at least four concrete suggestions for improving classroom utilization of film and video.

21. Visually diagram the setup for single-camera local video production.

22. Plan a lesson incorporating film or video materials.

Lexicon

persistence of vision
film
video
frame
optical sound track
videodisc
time lapse
slow motion
animation
documentary
film convention
zoom lens

THE MOVING IMAGE: FILM AND VIDEO

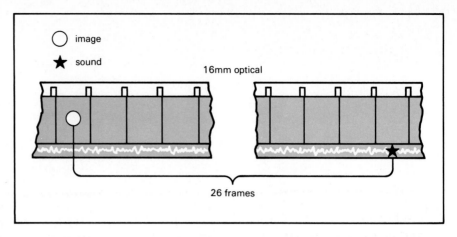

▲ *Figure 8.1*
In the 16-mm optical sound system, the sound accompanying a specific image is recorded on the film 26 frames ahead of the frame containing that image. The proper setting of the lower loop on the projector is critical for keeping the image and sound synchronized.

T HE instructional applications of film and video will be examined side-by-side in this chapter. Historically, the two technologies have been considered so different that their implications must be viewed separately. There is good justification for this viewpoint, but an alternative view is also possible. Our position, simply, is that *as they are used for instruction,* film and video share a great many of the same attributes, applications, advantages, and limitations. At heart, both technologies present the learner with moving images accompanied by a sound track. They differ in logistical considerations—cost and convenience— but not in pedagogical features. Trying to establish different utilization principles and selection criteria for film versus video is an artificial exercise.

This chapter focuses on what is done with the moving image *inside* the classroom. Chapter 9 deals with the many ways and means by which audio and video signals are transmitted *to* the classroom and the instructional implications of those delivery systems.

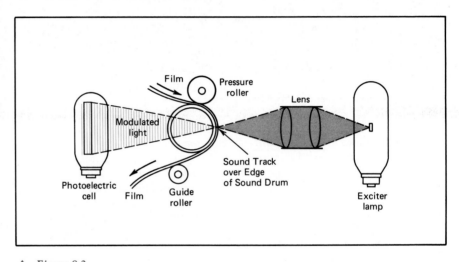

▲ *Figure 8.2*
In playing back an optical sound track, the light from the exciter lamp passes through the sound track, picking up the "image" of that recorded sound. This image is then focused on a photoelectric cell. These very weak signals are amplified and then converted back into sound waves by the speaker.

Film Defined

Film refers to the celluloid material on which a series of still images are chemically imprinted; this series of transparent images, when projected at twenty-four images (or "frames") per second, is perceived by humans as a moving image. The illusion of motion is caused by an optical phenomenon known as *persistence of vision:* the eye and brain retain an image cast upon the retina of the eye for a fraction of a second after that image is removed from view.

If a second image is presented before the trace of the previous image fades, the images blend together, creating the illusion of continuous motion.

In order to avoid the appearance of an incomprehensible blur on the screen, the film projector has a shutter that shuts out the light while the mechanism is actually moving the film from one frame to the next. Ironically, we *don't* see the actual movement of

the film, but our brain creates an illusion of movement from a series of still images projected on the screen.

The sound that accompanies a film is contained in a *sound track* that runs along one edge of the film (Figure 8.2). The most common type of sound track, the *optical* sound track, is actually a photographic image of sound recorded on the film as varying shades of dark and light.

Because the camera photographs a scene as a series of separate, discrete images, motion picture film consists of a sequence of slightly different still pictures called *frames*. When these frames are projected on a screen at a certain speed (at least twelve, usually twenty-four, frames per second), the images appear to be in continuous motion.

Each still picture (frame) is held stationary at the film aperture (1), as seen on the left side of the diagram. While it is stationary, the shutter (2) is open, permitting the light from the projection lamp to pass through the image, go through a focusing lens system (3), and display the picture on the screen. Then the shutter closes and a device like a claw (4) engages the sprocket holes and pulls the film down so that the next frame is in position, as shown in detail on the right side of the diagram. The claw withdraws, the shutter opens, and the next picture is projected on the screen.

Although the film moves past the aperture intermittently, the top sprocket wheel (5) pulls the film into the projector at a steady twenty-four frames per second (sound speed), and the bottom sprocket wheel (6) pulls the film out of the projector at the same steady rate of speed. If no slack were put into the film at upper and lower loops (7) and (8), the film would be torn apart. These two loops compensate for the two different motions the film must have. Because sound cannot be accurately recorded or reproduced on a film that is not moving smoothly, the intermittent movement of the film must be smoothed out by the bottom sprocket and an idler system before the film reaches the sound drum.

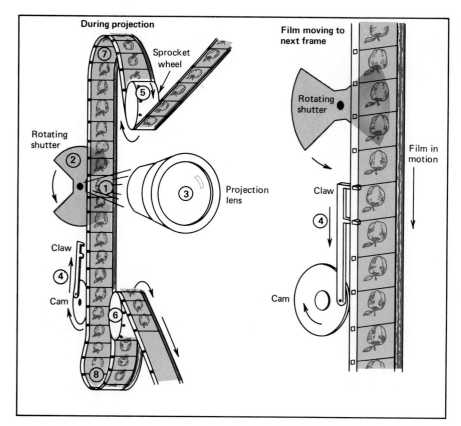

From Wyman, Raymond, *Mediaware: Selection, Operation, and Maintenance,* 2nd ed. Copyright ©1969, 1976. Wm. C. Brown, Dubuque, Iowa. Reprinted by permission.

Flip the pages of the text from here to page 237. If you flip them fast enough, the still pictures will appear to move, approximating $\frac{1}{2}$ second of screen action.

Thomas A. Edison, whose work in developing the kinetograph (a camera that used film rolls) and the kinetoscope (a peep-show device) contributed greatly to the development of motion pictures, had high hopes for the instructional value of this popular medium.

As depicted in the cartoon from *The Chicago Tribune* of 1923, he fully expected the motion picture to revolutionize education, give new life to curricular content, and provide students with new motivation for learning.

We all know that the history of the motion picture took a turn quite different from that anticipated by Edison. "Movies" were quickly and eagerly adopted as an entertainment medium, but in education the acceptance of film as a useful medium has been glacially slow. Part of the problem was technical. The standard size for film quickly became set at 35 mm, which meant that equipment for projection was bulky and expensive. Also, the film base that was used for many years, cellulose nitrate, was extremely flammable, and many state regulations required a film to be projected only from an enclosed booth and by a licensed projectionist. Thus, films were too expensive for schools to use for other than special occasions. There was also resistance on the part of the educational establishment to acknowledging the educational value of this "frivolous" new invention. Its very success as an entertainment medium automatically made it suspect as an educational tool.

The first extensive use of film as an educational medium occurred during World War I, outside the classroom, when psychologists working with the U.S. Army produced a series of training films on venereal disease.

After World War I, several prestigious organizations combined forces to produce a series of Amer-

Thomas A. Edison

ican history films that became known as the *Yale Chronicles of America Photoplays.* This series of films was the subject of extensive research and documented for the first time the effectiveness of films in direct instruction, even though the films were considerably handicapped because they were made in the "silent" era.

When sound on film finally did become a reality, many educators resisted its use in educational films. They felt that by putting a sound track on a film the producer was imposing external standards on every class in the country. They insisted that teachers should be free to narrate films according to principles and practices prescribed locally. Teacher narration of films, however, was favored by theorists and administrators but not by practitioners. (Anyone who has ever attempted to narrate a film knows what a difficult task it can be.) Some administrators also resisted the use of sound films in the classroom because this newer technology made existing inventories of silent-film projectors and silent films obsolete.

World War II gave an even greater impetus to the educational use of films. In a crash program to train Americans in the skills necessary to produce weapons, the Office of Education engaged in an extensive program of film production under the leadership of Floyde Brooker. Most of the films produced by the Office of Education were technical.

The armed forces also produced films during this period for training purposes, and their research indicated that films (and other audiovisual media) contributed significantly to the success of their training programs.

The success of instructional technology, including film, in achieving war-related instructional objectives created sentiment among educators and laypeople alike for more widespread use of this technology in the nation's schools.

The late 1950s witnessed the introduction of 8-mm film into education. Cartridged, looped 8-mm films quickly acquired the label "single-concept films" because they concentrated on presenting a single event or process for study. Because 8-mm

Floyde Brooker directing one of the wartime-training films of the U.S. Office of Education

cartridges were easily inserted in their projectors and the projectors were small, portable, and simple to use, they lent themselves particularly well to individual and small-group study and to incorporation into programs of individualized instruction. However, mechanical problems with the projectors and the vulnerability of the film itself discouraged use.

Television soon became the primary source of most filmed courses used in the instructional setting, and, with the rise of videotape technology, television itself, both educational and commercial, became a major force in the growing use of recorded moving images for instructional purposes.

Mr. Edison's dream of the immediate and overwhelming impact of the film on education may have been a little fuzzy around the edges—as dreams sometimes are—but it was not, after all, so far off the mark. It took a quarter century longer than the Wizard of Menlo Park had anticipated for the film to become an important factor in education and another quarter century for it to reach its present state of instructional prominence. His dream did come true, in its own time and in its more realistic way—as dreams sometimes do.

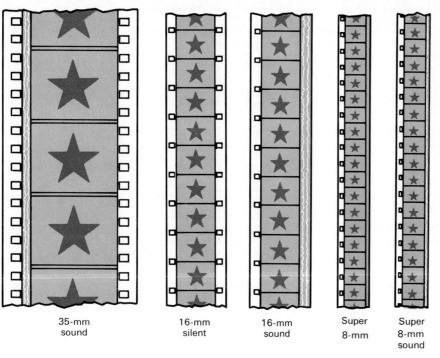

35-mm
sound

16-mm
silent

16-mm
sound

Super
8-mm

Super
8-mm
sound

▲ *Figure 8.3*
Common motion picture film formats

Video Defined

The primary meaning of *video* is the *display of pictures on a television-type screen* (the Latin word *video* literally means "I see"). Any media format that employs a cathode-ray screen to present the picture portion of the message can be referred to as video. Thus, we have videocassettes, videodiscs, interactive video, video games, and the like.

The phosphorescent images of video are composed of dots of varying intensity on the screen. Every thirtieth of a second 525 lines of dots are "sprayed" onto the back of the cathode-ray screen, creating one full screen or "frame." As with film, each frame is actually a still picture. As with film, the rapid succession of frames is perceived as a moving image because of persistence of vision.

The sound that accompanies the video image is recorded magnetically (in the case of video-

tape) on the videotape just as in audio recording, as explained in Chapter 6.

In colloquial speech we often hear people say that they are going to rent "a video" from the local videocassette rental store, referring to the cassette itself—the software—rather than the overall process of storage and display. Here we will avoid that colloquial usage and adhere to the more formal meaning of the term.

Originally video was synonymous with broadcast television, but the concept has expanded dramatically in recent years with the proliferation of new technologies that are connected to television sets—home computers, videocassette recorders, video games, electronic banking, specialized cable TV services, and many other hybrids that are still emerging. These new services continue to multiply because it tends to be cheaper and more efficient to transmit information electronically than to transport infor-

mation, goods, or people physically.

Film Formats

Motion picture film comes in various widths and image sizes. For theatrical films 35-mm film is most commonly used. For instructional films and other types of films made to be shown in schools, 16-mm film is the most common format. The most common format for "home movies" is 8-mm film. It is referred to as "Super-8" to distinguish it from an earlier version of 8-mm film having larger sprocket holes and smaller images. All these formats are compared in Figure 8.3.

Video Formats

The technology of video is still evolving rapidly. Currently, the most prominent formats are disc and tape, each packaged in forms that vary in size, shape, speed, and playback mechanism.

The most common type of *videodisc* is the reflective optical laser type. These discs resemble shiny, silver phonograph records. They are produced from a master videotape transferred to disc by imprinting microscopic pits to be "read" by a laser beam during play. The standard-size videodisc can hold up to thirty minutes of motion video images or up to 54,000 frames of still images. Any frame can be rapidly accessed without causing wear.

Videotape may be packaged in an open reel or enclosed in a cassette. Although varying widths of tape are used, the most common type in educational institutions is the 1-inch width. *Videocassettes* are found in at least three tape widths: $\frac{3}{4}$-inch, $\frac{1}{2}$-inch, and 8-mm. As the tape width narrows, the package becomes smaller, lighter, and cheaper, but visual quality

Formats	Speeds	Advantages	Limitations
Videodisc Diameter: 12 inches	(30 mins. per side)	• flexible storage capacity: can hold 54,000 images, still or motion, or audio • fast random access to specific frames • highly durable; no wear with use • inexpensive when mass produced	• not for local production • originals expensive to produce • limited acceptance in education so far, so software is limited
Open reel Tape width: one inch	9.6 ips (34–188 mins.)	• full broadcast quality; suitable for professional production	• requires professional handling; manual threading • bulky • found primarily in professional studios
Videocassette (U-matic) Tape width: ¾ inch	3.75 ips (10–60 mins.)	• self-contained and self-threading • compatible with all other U-Matics • superior video quality	• found more in corporate training and TV news field recording, not as common in education • quality deteriorates with use
Videocassette (Beta or VHS) Tape width: ½ inch	Beta = 1.57 ips VHS = 1.31 ips (30–180 mins. at standard speed)	• self-contained and self-threading • more compact than open reel or U-Matic • all VHS compatible with each other; same for Beta • abundant software available • easy local production	• video quality lower; not broadcast quality • two competing standards; VHS 10 times more popular than Beta • quality deteriorates with use
Videocassette (8-mm) Tape width: 8-mm (about ¼ inch)	(60–120 mins.)	• most compact format • full compatibility among all makes & models • easy local production	• video quality lower • limited acceptance in education so far; little software available

▲
Common video formats

▲ *Figure 8.5*

also tends to decline as the tape width narrows. The most common video formats are shown in Figure 8.4.

Differences between Film and Video

If you were seated in a darkened room facing two screens, one showing a film of a cowboy riding into the sunset and the other showing a video projection of a cowboy riding into the sunset, you might detect some differences, perhaps in clarity or in color quality. However, you would probably conclude that for practical, pedagogical purposes they were essentially equivalent. Media research indicates that displays having the same basic features—motion, color, and sound—have the same basic effects on cognitive and motor learning.

On the other hand, you would notice that the two images do differ in subtle ways, technically and psychologically. Technically, film allows a wider range of colors

than video; furthermore, the colors vary more in terms of hue and saturation. Film can portray a greater range of contrast than video.

Psychologically, the large, bright image of film holds our attention better than video. Because of our cultural experiences with broadcast television, we expect video to be showing a *reality* that is happening now. We approach film with the understanding that the images were carefully composed and *artificially* manipulated sometime in the past. Different styles of production have evolved in the two media because of these technical and psychological differences.

In sum, the two media forms differ enough in their artistic and emotional connotations that they will probably continue to coexist side by side, each serving a slightly different purpose. However, in most instructional situations we will choose between them on *logistical* grounds: which one can deliver the moving image most conveniently and inexpensively in our present situation?

SPECIAL ATTRIBUTES OF FILM AND VIDEO

Manipulation of Space

FILM and video permit us to view phenomena in microcosm and macrocosm—that is, at extremely close range or from a vast distance. Charles and Ray Eames made a film called *Powers of Ten* that within a few minutes takes us from a close-in observation of a man lying on a beach to views of the man as observed from distances expressed as increasing powers of ten until he disappears from sight. Perspective then changes quickly in the reverse direction and the film ends with a microscopic view of the man's skin. A similar effect can be seen in a National Film Board of Canada film titled *Cosmic Zoom*. This film starts with a microscopic examination of the skin of a man in a rowboat and then moves farther and farther away until we lose track of him entirely and, from some vantage point far from earth, see only the world of which he is a part. Both

▲ *Figure 8.6*
Cosmic Zoom

▲ *Figure 8.7*
Time lapse: A slow event is condensed into a short screen time by allowing several seconds to elapse between the shooting of each frame of the film.

films are extremely effective examples of how film can manipulate spatial perspective.

Multi-image presentations are often manipulations of space. For example, the film *A Place to Stand* persuades the viewer that Ontario, Canada, is a great place to live by showing exciting scenes from different parts of the province in split-image format. As many as six different images are on the screen at one time. The viewer gets the impression of being instantly transported around the province.

Manipulation of Time

Time Lapse. Film and video can compress the time that it takes for an event to occur. We have all seen films of flowers slowly opening right before our

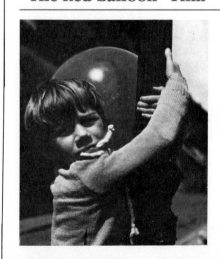
eyes. Simple arithmetic indicates that if a process normally takes four hours and we want to be able to see that process in one minute on the screen, then a single picture must be taken of that process every ten seconds. This technique has important instructional uses. For example, the process of a chrysalis turning into a butterfly is too slow for classroom observation. However, through time-lapse cinematography, the butterfly can

emerge from the chrysalis in a matter of minutes on the screen.

This attribute has particular value in education. For example, it would take an impossibly long time for students actually to witness a highway being constructed, but a carefully edited video presentation of the different activities that go into building a highway can recreate the essentials of such an event in a few minutes.

▲ *Figure 8.8*
Slow motion: A fast event is expanded into a longer screen time by shooting more than 24 frames (up to thousands) of film per second.

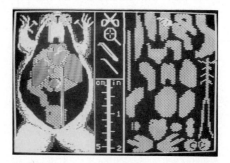

▲ *Figure 8.9*
Animation in film and video is becoming easier to produce with the aid of computer-generated animation.

Slow Motion. Time can also be *expanded* in film and video photography. Some events occur too fast to be seen by the naked eye. By photographing such events at extremely high speeds and then projecting the film at normal speed, we can observe what is happening. A chameleon catches an insect too rapidly for the naked eye to observe. High-speed cinematography can slow down the motion so that the process can be observed.

Motor skill tasks are often better analyzed if photographed at higher-than-normal speeds and studied at normal speed. Many training programs can be improved by this type of task analysis.

Animation

Time and space can also be manipulated in animated films. *Animation* is a technique whereby the film maker gives motion to otherwise inanimate objects. If such an object is photographed, then moved a very short distance and photographed on one frame of film, then moved

and photographed again, and so on, when the film is projected the object will look like it has been continuously moving through space.

With the continuing evolution of computer programs that can manipulate visual images adroitly, we are experiencing a rediscovery of the art of animation through the video display format. Computer-generated animation sequences are being used more and more in instructional video programs to depict complex or rapid processes in simplified form.

Documentaries as Social Commentaries

The documentary as a special genre of film and television has a long history of use as social commentary—*education* in the broader sense of the term. The *documentary* attempts to *depict essentially true stories about real-life situations and people.* Through the work of film makers such as Robert Flaherty in the United States and John Grierson in England, the documentary has

▲ *Figure 8.10*
Documentary film maker Robert Flaherty and crew on location

also acquired a reputation for artistic merit.

Grierson defined the documentary as "a creative treatment of actuality." He believed that the documentary should have a point of view, that it should be a vehicle for presenting and interpreting "human problems and their solutions in the spheres of economics, culture, and human relations." Thus, Grierson, Flaherty, and other like-minded film makers inaugurated the concept of the documentary as a socially significant film form rather than merely a vehicle for presentation of newsreel footage and "travelogue" material. Flaherty's film on the Eskimos of Hudson Bay, *Nanook of the North,* is generally credited with generating worldwide recognition of the documentary as a distinct film genre. By the late 1930s many countries had inaugurated documentary film units or were commissioning documentaries from independent producers. In the United States important and classic documentaries were produced both by government film units (e.g., *The River, Power and the Land*) and by independent film units (e.g., *The City, Valleytown, And So They Live*). In Great Britain, government units produced documentary classics such as *Night Mail* and *Song of Ceylon.* In Spain renowned feature film director Luis Buñuel made the striking film *Las Hurdes* (released in the United States as *Land without Bread*). In Belgium Henri Storck directed what is regarded by many as the classic film on slums and slum clearance, *Les Maisons de la Misére* (1937). In the Soviet Union the work of Dziga Vertov culminated in the technical and conceptual tour de force *Man with a Movie Camera* (1929). In Germany, the two controversial but classic films by Leni Riefen-

▲ *Figure 8.11*
Although not a true ethnographic film, *Nanook of the North,* made in 1922, portrayed vividly the impact of modernization on traditional Eskimo life-style.

▲ *Figure 8.12*
The City

▲ *Figure 8.13*
Frederick Wiseman's *High School* is an example of a "cinéma vérité" documentary, in which the unobtrusive camera catches an intimate view of real-life events.

stahl, *Triumph of the Will* (a film of the Nazi Party Congress of 1934) and *Olympia* (the 1936 Olympic games in Berlin), were prominent among a number of powerful documentaries.

Newsreels were a standard part of commercial movie programs in the 1930s and 1940s. Presented before the showing of the feature film, newsreels were little more than illustrated headlines depicting current news in segmented and superficial form. *The March of Time* (1934) took a different approach—a documentary approach. For an average length of eighteen minutes, *The March of Time* examined one topic in

223

▲ *Figure 8.14*
Le Duc Tho and Henry Kissinger, chief
negotiators at the Paris peace conference, as
shown in *Vietnam: A Television History*

MEDIA FILE:
"Citizen Kane" Videodisc

The Criterion Collection is a set of videodiscs aimed at students of film appreciation. Each contains not only the original
commercial film but also, on a separate
track, other supplementary material. In this
case the film is Orson Welles's masterpiece about the rise and fall of a newspaper magnate. It is supplemented with a
visual essay by Bob Carringer with over
100 photos and the original theatrical
"trailer."

Source: Voyager Company

reasonable depth and often with a
point of view. Today, many of *The
March of Times* films are still valuable as historical perspectives of
critical events and issues. For
example, the *March of Time* film
Palestine, made before the state
of Israel was formed, gives students an opportunity to examine a
current issue from a unique historical point of view.

During World War II, the documentary was widely used by all
combatants in training programs
and for propaganda purposes.
More than a few "propaganda"
documentaries, however, also had
lasting artistic and historical
merit—John Huston's *Let There
Be Light,* for example, and Hum-
phrey Jennings's *The Silent Village* and *Diary for Timothy.*

Today television has become
the prime influence on the continuing development of documentary films. The commercial networks, primarily through their
news departments, and the Public
Broadcasting System regularly
produce and broadcast significant
documentaries. Programs such as

*Vietnam: A Television History,
The Selling of the Pentagon, Yo
Soy Chicano,* and the Jacques
Cousteau and National Geo-
graphic specials are examples of
outstanding TV documentaries.

UNDERSTANDING FILM
CONVENTIONS

T HE devices and techniques
used in film making to
manipulate time and space are for
most of us readily accepted conventions. We understand that the
athlete whose jump is stopped in
midair is not actually frozen in
space, that the flashback is not an
actual reversal of our normal time
continuum, that the light bulb
does not really disintegrate slowly
enough for us to see that it
implodes rather than explodes.
Teachers of young children, however, must keep in mind that the
ability to make sense out of film
conventions is an acquired skill.
When do children learn to handle
flashbacks, dissolves, jump cuts,
and so on? Unfortunately, we

know very little about when and
how children learn to make sense
of filmic manipulation of reality,
and much research on the matter
remains to be done.

Some insight into the kind of
difficulties that may be encountered in the instructional situation
because of student inability to
handle film conventions can be
gleaned from the experiences of
film makers involved with adults
unfamiliar with standard film conventions.

After World War II, film crews
from the United States were sent
to various parts of the world to
make instructional films designed
to help the people better their
skills in farming, housing, sanita-
tion, and so forth. One crew
member working in rural Iran
noted that in the United States
film makers could have a man
walk out a door in lower Manhat-
tan and immediately pick him up
in another shot at Times Square.
In Iran this technique was not
possible. Viewers there would
insist that the man be shown making the journey to Times Square.

In other words, rural Iranians, because they were at that time unfamiliar with the conventions of time-space manipulations, could not accept this filmic view of reality.

John Wilson, another American film producer of the period, commented:

We found that the film is, as produced in the West, a very highly conventionalized piece of symbolism, although it looks very real. For instance, we found that if you were telling a story about two men to an African audience and one had finished his business and he went off the edge of the screen, they wanted to know what happened to him; they didn't accept that this was just the end of him and that he was of no more interest to the story. . . . We had to follow him along a street until he took a natural turn. . . . It was quite understandable that he could disappear around the turn. The action had to follow a natural course of events. . . .*

The film is not, of course, alone among media in its reliance upon accepted conventions for interpretation and appreciation. Flashback techniques are regularly used in literature and usually accepted by readers. The theatrical convention of the "aside" is readily accepted by playgoers. The following anecdote about Picasso illustrates how a new artistic convention may seem to the uninitiated to be merely a distortion of reality rather than, as intended, a particular and valid view of reality. It also illustrates how a convention (in this case a

convention of photography) can become so readily accepted and commonplace that we are amusingly surprised at being reminded it exists:

Picasso showed an American soldier through his villa one day, and on completion of the tour the young man felt compelled to confess that he didn't dig Picasso's weird way of painting, because nothing on the canvas looked the way it really is. Picasso turned the conversation to more acceptable matters by asking the soldier if he had a girl back in the States. The boy proudly pulled out a wallet photograph. As Picasso handed it back, he said "She's an attractive girl, but isn't she awfully small?"*

ADVANTAGES OF FILM AND VIDEO

THE special attributes just detailed suggest some of the ways that film and video lend themselves to educational applications. Some of their other instructional advantages are as follows:

Motion. Moving images have an obvious advantage over other visual media in portraying concepts (such as tying knots or operating a potter's wheel) in which motion is essential to mastery.

Processes. Operations, such as assembly line steps or science experiments, in which sequential movement is critical can be shown more effectively by means of motion media.

Safe Observation. Visual recordings allow learners to observe phenomena that might be dangerous to view directly—an

▲ *Figure 8.15*
Film is especially useful for observing complex motor skills that involve motion.

eclipse of the sun, a volcanic eruption, or warfare.

Skill Learning. Research indicates that mastery of physical skills requires repeated observation and practice; through the recorded media a performance can be viewed over and over again for emulation.

Dramatization. Dramatic recreations can bring historical events and personalities to life. In business or industry training they allow us to observe and analyze human relations problems.

Affective Learning. Because of their great potential for emotional impact, films can be useful in shaping personal and social attitudes. Documentary and propaganda films have often been found to have a measurable impact on audience attitudes.

Problem Solving. Open-ended dramatizations are frequently used to present unresolved confrontations, leaving it to the viewers to discuss various ways of dealing with the problem.

Cultural Understanding. We can develop a gut-level appreciation for other cultures by seeing film and video depictions of everyday life in other societies.

* Joan Rosengren Forsdale and Louis Forsdale. "Film Literacy." *The Teachers College Record.* (May 1966), p. 612.

* Ibid., p. 609.

▲ *Figure 8.17*
The video program *Face to Face* dramatizes a human relations problem which is left for viewers to solve through discussion.

▲ *Figure 8.16*
With film, history can come to life in dramatic recreations such as *The Pilgrims.*

The whole genre of *ethnographic films* can serve this purpose; some examples of feature-length ethnographic films are *The Hunters, The Tribe that Hides from Man, The Nuer,* and *River of Sand.*

Establishing Commonality. By viewing a film or video program together, a disparate group of people can build up a common base of experience to discuss an issue effectively.

LIMITATIONS OF FILM AND VIDEO

As with all other instructional media, there are limitations to the instructional applications of film and video. Here are some of the more obvious limitations.

Fixed Pace. Although projectors and video players can be stopped and sequences replayed, this is not usually done in group showings, nor would it be practical to try to cater to individual needs in this way. The program runs at a fixed pace; some viewers are likely to be falling behind while

others are waiting impatiently for the next point.

Still Phenomena. Although film and video are advantageous for concepts that involve motion, they may be unsuitable for other topics where detailed study of a single visual is involved, for

example, a map, a wiring diagram, or an organization chart.

Misinterpretation. Documentaries and dramatizations often present complex or sophisticated treatment of an issue. A scene intended as satire might be accepted literally by a young or

---

MEDIA FILE:
"AIDS—What Everyone Needs to Know" (Revised) Videocassette

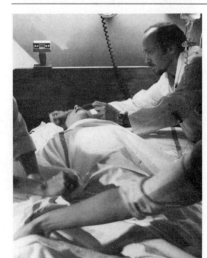

This updated revision of a highly rated film explains facts about AIDS: how the AIDS virus is spread and how it is not spread; what high-risk behaviors are and how to avoid them. Animation illustrates the body's immune system, showing how the AIDS virus disables it. Interviews with AIDS patients emphasize the importance of avoiding infection by the AIDS virus.

Source: Churchill Films

Training films can be competitive at film festivals as well as effective instructionally. This award-winning film demonstrates that good managers have the ability to focus on long-range goals as well as on immediate objectives. A case study, the subject of the film is a manager who changes from an overworked, compulsive problem solver to an effective, productive innovator. The system he develops draws attention from the public as well as the business community. Research has established that a film is more effective when the target audience can project itself into the roles portrayed on the screen. This film exemplifies that quality.

Source: CRM Films

▲ *Figure 8.18*
Images of Einstein, distributed by IBM, is a sponsored film, the content of which is unrelated to the sponsor.

naive viewer. A villain may be taken as a hero. For example, the film *Phoebe* uses a stream-of-consciousness approach as Phoebe fantasizes about what will be the reactions of her parents and her boyfriend to her announcement of her pregnancy. Some students (and parents) have misinterpreted the speculations of a troubled mind as being the attitude of the film maker toward all the characters in the story.

Cost. Film has become an expensive medium, both for the software and the hardware. Video-cassettes have begun to replace film partly for this reason. Instructors who make this substitution often face problems of visibility of the smaller television screen and give up the rich resources found in their local film library.

Logistics. Films must usually be ordered well in advance of their intended use. Elaborate arrangements may be needed to be sure that the right film arrives at the right place at the right time and that a projector is there and in running order. The complexity of the logistics discourages many instructors. In the case of video, the challenge is to adapt your les-

son to the broadcast schedule or arrange for someone to record a program off-air and get it to you in time to incorporate it in the lesson.

Sponsored Films. Private companies, associations, and government agencies sponsor films for a variety of reasons. Private companies may make films to promote their products or to enhance their public image. Associations and government agencies sponsor films to promote causes: better health habits, conservation of natural resources, proper use of park and recreation areas. Many of these sponsored films make worthwhile instructional materials. They also have the considerable advantage of being free.

A certain amount of caution, however, is called for in using sponsored films for instructional purposes. Some private-company films may be too flagrantly self-serving. Or they may deal with products not very suitable for certain instructional settings; for example, the making of alcoholic beverages or cigarettes. Some association and government films may contain a sizable dose of prop-

aganda or special pleading for pet causes along with their content. Ralph Nader's Center for the Study of Responsive Law has issued a report highly critical of instructional materials distributed free by industry.* It claims that many sponsored materials subtly influence the curriculum in socially undesirable ways. Certainly you must preview sponsored films.

Properly selected, many sponsored films can be valuable additions to classroom instruction. Modern Talking Picture Service is one of the major distributors of sponsored films. The best single source of information on sponsored films is the *Educator's Guide to Free Films.* Details on this and similar free and inexpensive sources are given in Appendix B.

---

* Sheila Harty. *Hucksters in the Classroom: A Review of Industry Propaganda in the Schools.* Washington, D.C.: Center for Study of Responsive Law, 1980.

227

INSTRUCTIONAL APPLICATIONS OF VIDEO

W E all know how television has permeated North American popular culture since it first leaped into visibility a scant forty years ago. How has it fared as an instructional tool in this same period of time—in the schools, higher education, nonformal education, and corporate training?

In referring to "instructional" applications of video we mean any planned use of video programs to promote learning, regardless of the audience, the source of the program (such as commercial broadcasts), the transmission system (such as cable TV), or the setting of use (such as a viewing room in an industrial plant).

Instructional Video in the Schools

Instructional video is alive and well and being used more than ever in American elementary and secondary schools. Its history goes back to the 1950s, but its visibility has waxed and waned over the years. Why is it shining more brightly today than ever? Undoubtedly the rapid spread of video recording equipment has been a major factor. Now that 90 percent of schools have videocassette recorders, teachers can easily "time shift" broadcast programs to make them fit better into the school schedule. Program quality has risen, too. The typical format has moved away from the "talking head" toward dramatic vignettes, animated sequences, and frequent graphic overlays. School programming has tended to follow the pattern of commercial programming, becoming slicker and more eye-catching.

Availability and Usage Rates.
According to the most recent comprehensive survey of the use of video in the schools, 97 percent of all teachers have access to television sets (most of which are color sets), and about 90 percent have access to video recording/ playback equipment.* As is shown in Figure 8.20, that equipment is often shared with many other teachers; the higher the grade level, the more thinly the equipment is spread.

The survey indicates that about half of those teachers who have access to video programming use it at some time; about 29 percent use video regularly, meaning that they use all or most of some particular program series. The students of the video users spend an average of one and three-quarters hours each week viewing these programs.

Content of Programs Used.
There are now programs available and used in every area of the curriculum. Producers try to provide programs that fill curricular gaps. The perception of a gap is often influenced by national or local interest groups campaigning on behalf of their favored subject. But there is perennial interest in the use of video to update knowledge in rapidly changing areas, such as science, and to stimulate student interest in subjects, such as literature, in which motivation is a problem. Figure 8.20 indicates the most popular content areas at each school level.

Patterns of Utilization. In its early days television was expected to spark a restructuring of classroom organization as video programs replaced teacher talk as the core of instruction. That revolution has not come to pass. Instead, video has fallen into place as a supplementary tool, adding enrichment to the classroom. In 1987 journalist Robert

---

* John A. Riccobono. *Availability, Use, and Support of Instructional Media, 1982–83. Summary Final Report of the School Utilization Study.* Washington, D.C.: Corporation for Public Broadcasting (CPB), 1984.

▲ *Figure 8.19*
Video is very much at home in schools throughout North America.

LEVEL	TV	VCR	SUBJECTS

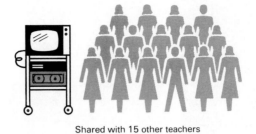

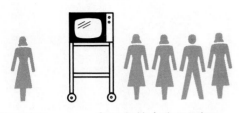

Elementary   Shared with 4 other teachers   Shared with 15 other teachers

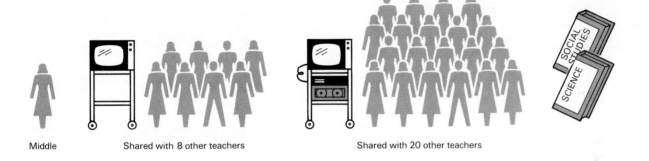

Middle   Shared with 8 other teachers   Shared with 20 other teachers

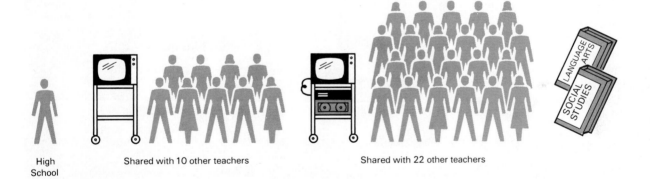

High School   Shared with 10 other teachers   Shared with 22 other teachers

Source: John A. Riccobono. *Availability, Use, and Support of Instructional Media, 1982–83.* Washington, D.C.: Corporation for Public Broadcasting, 1984.

▲ *Figure 8.20*
Patterns of video use in schools

Carlisle visited schools all across the United States, interviewing hundreds of teachers about their use of video. His report* provides

* Robert Carlisle. *Video at Work in American Schools.* Bloomington, Ind.: Agency for Instructional Technology, 1987.

a portrait of rich and endless variety in the ways teachers incorporate video into their daily lessons. Examples range from using programs on parenting to highlight certain points in a family life course, to using broadcast lessons on English as a second language

as the core of instruction for immigrant children, to bringing the Holocaust to life through videotaped interviews with survivors who live in the city.

The selective use of parts of series is definitely the predomi-

▲ *Figure 8.21*
In compiling his report, *Video at Work in American Schools,* author Robert Carlisle typically found video programs used as supplements to regular lessons.

▲ *Figure 8.22*
Jan O'Connor's comment, quoted in *Video at Work in American Schools,* typifies teachers' attitudes about videocassette use: "There's nothing hard about using it; all you have to do is shove in a cassette."

nant mode. This selectivity has been made possible by the diffusion of video recorders. In the infancy of television, all instructional video was live; nowadays most teachers use taped segments. There is an interesting countermovement, though, back toward live programs as two-way transmission technology becomes less expensive. With the two-way capability it's advantageous to have live programs so that viewing students can ask questions of the instructor and hold discussions with other students.

Specialists to Help Overcome Obstacles.

What inhibits teacher use of video? The barrier mentioned most often by teachers is having the programs available when needed. The next greatest hindrance is related—finding out about broadcast programs in advance. The increasing use of video recording is reducing both of these problems. Many schools are addressing these problems by

▲ *Figure 8.23*
Systematic integration of video into the curriculum requires constant planning and dissemination work, such as this workshop conducted for teachers by a fellow teacher.

appointing a professional in the building to be an instructional video coordinator, in most cases the school librarian or media specialist. Many public television stations and state or provincial departments of education have video utilization specialists who offer workshops to teachers and

disseminate information about their programs.

Instructional Video in Higher Education

On-Campus Programs.

Among colleges and universities the use of video for instruction is widespread and growing. According to a Corporation for Public Broadcasting (CPB) survey,* 80 percent of institutions nationwide reported using video at least for one-way presentation of instruction to students on campus. Usage is reportedly greater at four-year public institutions than at community colleges or at private colleges.

Applications of video vary widely; only 32 percent of all institutions polled in the CPB study offer full video telecourses. The majority of these telecourses are aimed at regular students taking courses on campus, although about half of the large public universities aim video telecourses at off-campus audiences. There are examples of colleges and universities where thousands of students engage in telecourses across many areas of study, but in the *typical* case, according to the CPB survey, twelve courses are offered, enrolling 442 students. This gives an average of only thirty-eight students in each video class.

Most students experience video courses as prerecorded programs broadcast over public TV stations or played back in the classroom on a videocassette recorder. In about one-quarter of the cases, though, students receive "real-time" programs in which a live instructor appears on television and the receiving students can interact with that instructor and other students by means of telephone talk-back systems.

---

* *Instructional Technology in Higher Education.* Washington, D.C.: Corporation for Public Broadcasting, 1986.

▶ *Figure 8.24*
In higher education, television is a valuable tool for bringing real-life events into the classroom for discussion.

MEDIA FILE:
"Reading Rainbow" Television Series

This fifty-program series was developed for summer viewing to highlight good books and encourage summer reading by children aged five to nine. Each episode enters into the world of one book through location photography, animation, and original music and dance. Actor LeVar Burton hosts the series. Surveys following the first season indicated that library and bookstore demand for books featured on "Reading Rainbow" increased substantially. An estimated eight million viewers watched at least one episode.

Source: The Corporation for Public Broadcasting, the nation's public television stations, the National Science Foundation, and the Carnegie Corporation of New York

MEDIA FILE:
"Global Geography" Video Series

This series attempts to capture the interest of middle and junior high school students with compelling problems related to the places in which people live and to the interactions of place, culture, people, movement, and change. Each program focuses on a specific world region. A story line dramatizes an issue important to a topic usually featured in geography textbooks.

Source: Agency for Instructional Technology

MEDIA FILE:
"The Mole Concept" Video Series

This six-program science series is aimed at the high school level. The programs clarify the reasoning behind the development of the mole concept (the "standard container" for directly comparing large numbers of atoms) and open the way to understanding chemical reactions at the molecular level. Each program uses animation of scientific concepts and analogies from daily life to illustrate the material.

Source: TV Ontario

Off-Campus Programs. During the 1970s and 1980s a shrinking college-age population led many two-year and four-year colleges to think seriously about ways of attracting new audiences. Television seemed to be an ideal mechanism for bringing the college to the student, particularly the working adult. Broadcasting college courses to home audiences could be mutually beneficial, offering higher education opportunities to the student and new audiences to the college.

Higher education institutions have experimented with a variety of delivery systems for these "distance education" programs. The success of the British Open University provided a model that was emulated by quite a number of experimental projects in North America, one of the more ambitious being the University of Mid-America. Most of these efforts faltered, however, lacking one or more of the critical elements for viability.

More recently the trend has been toward reducing the expense of distance education programs by pooling resources—sharing the costs of program production and distribution among a number of schools. The TAGER network in the Dallas region, for example, shares the resources of nine local colleges in telecasting courses to provide graduate engineering classes to employees at nearby industrial plants. The International Consortium for Telecommunications in Learning (IUC) provides another cooperative model. It is described in "Close-Up: Off-Campus Continuing Education via Television."

As the technological options for telecommunications expand—with cable, satellites, microwave, fiber-optics, and the like—more and more educational institutions are becoming linked into consor-

CLOSE-UP:
Off-Campus Continuing Education via Television

An organizational model that appears promising is the consortium. One of these, the International University Consortium for Telecommunications in Learning (IUC), headquartered in Maryland, has grown steadily, encompassing over twenty colleges and a like number of public television stations. The membership includes two Canadian distance education institutions—Athabasca University in Edmonton and the Open Learning Institute in Vancouver. Thanks to the cooperative sharing of telecourse materials, institutions such as these are able to offer broad enough arrays of courses to enable an adult to obtain a bachelor's degree at home by television. A typical student for such at-home television participation is female, the mother of children who are in school or just beyond school age, and someone anticipating reentry into the job market.

tiums for sharing programs. These networking arrangements are discussed in greater depth in Chapter 9.

A related problem, the shortage of high-quality instructional video programs worthy of mass distribution, has traditionally hindered the success of large-scale adult continuing education efforts. A significant breakthrough on this problem occurred in 1981 when publisher and philanthropist Walter H. Annenberg announced his intention to donate $150 million over a fifteen-year period toward the improvement of such programs. In 1984 the first wave of Annenberg-funded programs began to be distributed. One example is described in the accompanying "Media File: 'Congress: We the People.'"

Instructional Video in Corporate Training and Development

As already discussed in Chapter 1 (pp. 21–22), a great majority of American corporations report that they use video in some way in their training effort. In fact, among businesses with more than fifty employees more claim to be using video than lectures (83.2 percent to 82.5 percent). Thus, the impact of video in corporate training appears to be quite comparable to that in formal education, and the variety of utilization patterns is as broad.

Utilization Patterns. There are many reasons why organizations are willing to make the investment in video as a means of training; among them are the following:

- Orientation for new employees
- Training in job-related skills
- Development of interpersonal abilities for management

- Introduction of new products, policies, or markets
- Customer training
- Standardization of training among dispersed offices

▶ *Figure 8.25*
A typical video use in corporate training is to record and play back a simulation of interpersonal skills, such as sales presentations.

A moment's reflection will reveal that most of these purposes demand specifically tailored, customized materials. You can't explain *your* company's personnel policies with a *generic* film. Video is the logical medium for local production of custom materials. In addition to the demands of customization there is the factor of rapid change. Increasing competition and technological change also dictate an instructional medium that can turn out updated and modified programs rapidly.

Corporate use of video therefore contrasts sharply with school use in terms of the amount of locally produced material that is used. Most large corporate users maintain professional-quality production studios and facilities for in-the-field location shooting. There are, of course, a good number of corporate skills that *are* generic in nature (for example, supervisory skills, meeting management, stress management) and lend themselves to off-the-shelf media such as film.

Corporate Networks. Larger corporations with multiple office and plant locations have the problem of standardizing training among the different sites. Again, this is a purpose well suited to video. Hundreds of such corporations (for example, IBM, Ford

---

MEDIA FILE:
"Meetings, Bloody Meetings" Film/Videocassette

John Cleese, star of the Monty Python comedy troupe, plays the part of an inefficient chairman who dreams he is brought up before a judge for negligent conduct of business meetings. His past meetings are played back as evidence of his failures. The judge demonstrates how the techniques and logic of running a meeting parallel those of conducting a court case. The film provides a formula for making meetings shorter and more productive.

"Meetings, Bloody Meetings" has won a half dozen awards for its success in illustrating a serious point humorously. It's part of a series of some sixty films that are popular in corporate training and development. Each is accompanied by a leader's guide and viewer's booklet.

Source: Video Arts Inc.

CLOSE-UP:
Corporate Video at Allstate Insurance

Faced with increased competition and turbulent change in the industry, Allstate Insurance has built up a large corporate video operation to keep pace with its training needs. The audiovisual production unit produces dozens of programs each year using two professionally equipped studios and three mobile crews. Programs deal with updating Allstate agents on changes in the insurance industry, motivating agents to maintain good relationships with clients, and informing them of new products and new company policies.

Allstate recently began setting up "neighborhood offices" in areas where no Sears store exists. To assist agents in these offices the audiovisual unit produced a Neighborhood Office Agent Classroom Training Series dealing with such topics as setting up an office, advertising, and hiring help. The company also provides videotapes for customers to watch while waiting for service in one of their outlets.

Source: Eva J. Blinder, "New Shapes in Insurance Video." *E/ITV* (December 1987), pp. 18–25.

Motor Company, Coca-Cola, and many insurance companies) operate full-fledged video networks, many of them with fifty or more outlets. Together these corporate video networks produce and transmit many more programs than the commercial television networks combined, and they are still growing.

Interactive Video. The use of interactive video—videodisc or videotape controlled by a computer-assisted system—has a firmer foothold in corporate training than it does in formal education, but it has shown minimal growth up to the end of the 1980s. One industry survey* indicated that about 15 percent of all U.S. organizations with more than 50 employees used interactive video for training in some form. For companies with more than 10,000 employees the figure was up to 32 percent. An example of interactive video is the program used by Massachusetts Mutual Life Insurance Company to train its new recruits at the various field offices. The new agent sits at a terminal containing a touch-screen monitor and a laser disc player containing a variety of lessons on sales skills, office management, and client counseling. The user controls the path through the program by touching the screen as directed. The system also contains a video camera and tape player that allow the agent to practice his or her performance and review it on videotape.

The speculation is that such systems will become accepted at a faster rate when the hardware systems become more standardized and less expensive.

Other Organizations. Government agencies and some larger

* Chris Lee. "Where the Training Dollars Go." *Training.* (October 1987), p. 57.

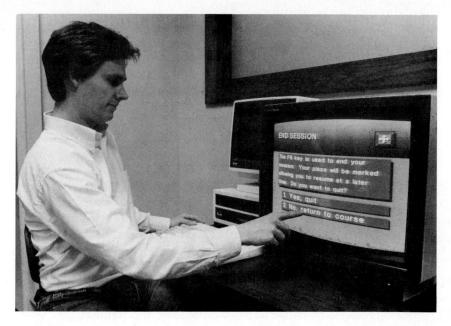

▲ *Figure 8.26*
The touch-screen is a convenient means of registering a trainee's responses to an interactive lesson.

private institutions, such as labor unions, foundations, and public interest groups, also produce instructional video programs for use within their organizations. Smaller agencies generally have been inhibited by the cost of producing and distributing video. The advent of inexpensive videocassette players and field recording units is spurring the use of video in these sectors. Further information on organizational use of video can be found in the Brush and Dranov listings under "Video in Adult and Higher Education" in the references at the end of this chapter.

CLASSROOM VIDEO DELIVERY SYSTEMS

T HERE are many ways of delivering video programs to students; with technological advances the options seem to multiply ever more rapidly. Chapter 9 deals with electronic distribution systems such as closed-circuit, cable, microwave, and satellite. This section focuses on

the several methods of playing back recorded video programs in the classroom—primarily tape and disc systems. These portable forms of delivery give instructors great flexibility in choosing what programs they want to use and when and where they want to use them. They even allow individual learners to pick up their own video programs and use them in a carrel or at home.

Videocassette

The conventional recording medium for video programs is magnetic tape similar to that used in audio recording. The tape may be used either in an open reel format or enclosed in a cassette. Open reel tape in the one-inch format is still popular for professional studio production and for broadcast transmission, but it is seldom used as a *classroom* delivery system so it will not be discussed at length here. Currently, the favored videocassette format for broadcast-quality educational/

235

industrial recording is that using $\frac{3}{4}$-inch tape, a format pioneered by Sony's U-Matic system in the early 1970s.

The success of the $\frac{3}{4}$-inch videocassette helped stimulate demand

▲ *Figure 8.27*
The $\frac{3}{4}$-inch videocassette format

▲ *Figure 8.28*
The $\frac{1}{2}$-inch videocassette format

▲ *Figure 8.29*
"I think it's an old VCR."

for a less expensive home version. The result is the $\frac{1}{2}$-inch videocassette which has rapidly risen to a dominant position both for home and school use.

There are two $\frac{1}{2}$-inch videocassette formats on the market: Sony's Beta and the VHS (Video Home System) offered by a number of competing Japanese manufacturers. Unfortunately, the two systems are incompatible, using different tape speeds and transport mechanisms. So recordings made for one system cannot be used with the other. However, the VHS system has gradually taken over a larger share of the market year by year, suggesting that it will become the standard.

The most recent addition to the videocassette family is the 8-mm videotape camera-recorder system introduced by Kodak in 1984. This miniature format features a single-unit camera and recorder weighing only five pounds. Based on a cassette format nearly as small as the audiocassette, it offers a "camcorder" and playback system lighter and more compact than others. So far it has made only a small impact on the videocassette market, primarily as a "home movie" consumer product. Kodak, the originator, has discontinued its support. The future of this system in education and training is still unclear.

Videodisc

As the name implies, in the videodisc format audiovisual information is recorded on plastic discs. The special attraction of the disc format is its ability to store massive amounts of audio and video messages in a compact and durable package.

Because videodiscs have slow-motion and stop-action capability, still pictures and even print can be stored as readily as television

▲ *Figure 8.30*
A videodisc and its player

programs. With a storage capacity of some 54,000 frames per side, one disc can hold an hour of color TV programming, about a thousand filmstrips, or several thousand pages of printed text. In addition, some videodisc players contain a microprocessor with a memory storage capability, allowing them to be programmed to present branching sequences of programmed instruction. (Interactive video is discussed in more detail in Chapter 7.)

As Cambre* points out, although the videodisc has been hailed primarily as a medium for individualized study, its real uniqueness is its speed and convenience in giving random access to visual materials. Hence, three special applications suggest themselves:

- As a group visual display device, like an overhead projector, but with thousands of images—still or motion—at the instructor's fingertips
- As a stimulus for small-group activities, such as cooperative problem-solving or projects
- As an individual instruction device presenting tutorials, drill-and-practice exercises, simulations, and the like.

---

* Marjorie A. Cambre. *A Reappraisal of Instructional Television.* Syracuse, N.Y.: ERIC Clearinghouse on Information Resources, 1987.

some discretionary control over selection of ITV materials, either as individual teachers or as members of a selection committee.

The development of sophisticated delivery systems and easy-to-use videotape recorders has stimulated an increase in the number and variety of available televised instructional materials. Program guides and directories can help keep you abreast of available materials in your areas of interest and guide you toward selection of materials best suited to your particular teaching needs. The most comprehensive listing of current educational video recordings is NICEM's *Film and Video Finder.* Other broad catalogs are *Videolog* and *Video Source Book.* These and other more specialized catalogs are described in Appendix A.

SELECTING FILM AND VIDEO MATERIALS

Locating Films

As just mentioned, because of the high cost of 16-mm films as well as the impracticality of local production, an individual school or small organization is unlikely to have its own film collection. So most instructors must acquire films on loan from an outside agency—the school district, state library, or rental library, for instance. A basic resource for you, then, is a collection of catalogs of those rental agencies you are most likely to turn to for films. To be more thorough in your search you will want *The Educational Film/Video Locator,* a comprehensive listing of the films that are available in various college and university rental collections. If you are just beginning your search you should consult the *Film and Video Finder,* the most comprehensive listing of currently available films; it provides listings by subject. Other more specialized film catalogs are mentioned in Appendix A.

Locating Video Materials

In some cases the instructor has no real control over the selection of ITV materials. A program or series may be administratively mandated as an integral part of the curriculum. In most cases, however, instructors do have

Appraising Film/Video Materials

After you have located some potentially useful films or video

▲ *Figure 8.31*
Dr. Curt Fuchs, director of media services in Columbia, Missouri, and a portion of that school district's videocassette collection

► From *Movement in Classical Dance,* Indiana University Audio-Visual Center.

Appraisal Checklist: Film and Video

Title _____

Series Title (if applicable) _____

Source _____

Date _____ Cost _____ Length _____ minutes_____

Subject area _____

Intended audience _____

Format

☐ 16-mm film

☐ other film:

☐ broadcast TV

☐ $\frac{3}{4}$-inch videocassette

☐ $\frac{1}{2}$-inch VHS videocassette

☐ $\frac{1}{2}$-inch Beta videocassette

☐ videodisc

☐ other video:

Objectives (stated or implied):

Brief Description:

Entry Capabilities Required:

- Prior subject-matter knowledge/vocabulary
- Reading ability
- Mathematical ability
- Other:

Rating	High		Medium		Low	Comments
Relevance to objectives	☐	☐	☐	☐	☐	
Accuracy of information	☐	☐	☐	☐	☐	
Likely to arouse/maintain interest	☐	☐	☐	☐	☐	
Technical quality	☐	☐	☐	☐	☐	
Promotes participation/involvement	☐	☐	☐	☐	☐	
Evidence of effectiveness (e.g., field test results)	☐	☐	☐	☐	☐	
Free from objectionable bias	☐	☐	☐	☐	☐	
Pacing appropriate for audience	☐	☐	☐	☐	☐	
Use of cognitive learning aids (e.g., overview, cues, summary)	☐	☐	☐	☐	☐	

Strong Points:

Weak Points:

Reviewer _____

Position _____

Recommended action _____ Date _____

programs, you will want to preview them and appraise them. Some schools and organizations have standard appraisal forms ready to use. Some of these are meticulously detailed, covering every possible factor; others are much more perfunctory. A good appraisal form is one that is brief enough that it is not intimidating but complete enough to help individuals choose materials that may be useful not only for now but for future applications. It should also stand as a public record that can be used to justify the purchase or rental of specific titles. The ''Appraisal Checklist: Film and Video'' on page 238 includes the most commonly used criteria, particularly those that research indicates really *do* make a difference. You may wish to use it as is or adapt it to your particular needs.

UTILIZING FILM AND VIDEO

T HE next step after selecting your materials is to put them into actual use in the classroom.

Preview. It is not always possible to view a TV program prior to use, but you can usually read about the program in a teacher's guide. Films and videocassettes should be previewed for appraisal and selection purposes, but they should also be checked after the material arrives at the classroom. Avoid potential embarrassment by making sure that the film on the reel is the one that you ordered and that it contains the subject matter and treatment that you expected.

Prepare the Environment.
Before students can learn from any media presentation, they first have to be able to see it and hear it! Provide proper lighting, seating, and volume control. These

elements are described in detail in Chapter 10.

Prepare the Audience.
Research in educational psychology as well as the practical experiences of thousands of teachers in all sorts of settings demonstrate

that learning is greatly enhanced when learners are *prepared* for the coming activity. No competent instructor would advocate approaching a TV lesson by suddenly stopping the regular lecture, switching on the TV set, and abandoning the classroom for a

▲ *Figure 8.32*
Preview the material.

▲ *Figure 8.33*
Prepare the environment.

▲ *Figure 8.34*
Prepare the audience.

coffee break. Yet we know that many instructors do just that.

To start the "warm-up" before the film/video lesson, create a mind-set by reviewing previous related study. Help students see how today's lesson fits into the total picture. Create a "need to know." Stimulate curiosity by asking questions, and evoke questions the *students would like answered* about this subject.

Clarify the objectives of the lesson. Mention cues—specific things to look for—in the presentation. It helps to list such cues on the chalkboard or on a handout so that students can refer to them as the lesson proceeds (and during the follow-up activities). If large amounts of new information are to be retained, give students some "advance organizers"—memory hooks on which they can hang the new ideas. Be sure to preview any new vocabulary needed.

AV Showmanship - FILM AND VIDEO

First, here are some generic tips that apply equally to the enhancement of film or video presentations:

- Check lighting, seating, and volume control to be sure that everyone can see and hear the presentation.
- Get students mentally prepared by briefly reviewing previous related study and evoking questions about today's topic.
- List on the chalkboard the main points to be covered in the presentation.
- Preview any new vocabulary.
- Most important, get involved in the program yourself. Watch attentively and respond when the presenter asks for a response. Be a good role model. Highlight major points by adding them to the chalkboard during the lesson.
- Support the presentation with meaningful follow-up activities.

Second, here are showmanship tips that apply specifically to *film* showings:

- Many classrooms have a wall-mounted screen in the front of the room. In some classrooms, unfortunately, the door is near the front of the room and often has a large window in it or a window area beside it. If light from the hall interferes with the brightness of the projected image, you may have to cover part or all of the window area with poster board or butcher paper. If this is not possible, move the projector closer to the screen to get a brighter picture. Remember that a smaller, brighter image is better than a larger, dimmer one.
- You should always set the focus and note the correct sound level before the class assembles; then turn the volume knob back down to zero and run the film back to the beginning. Some films have focus and sound-level adjustment footage before the start of the film. If so, you can properly set focus and sound before you reach the beginning of the film.
- It is *not* good showmanship to project the academy leader (the strip of film with the number sequence on it). The first image the audience should see is the title or opening scene of the film.
- When ready, start the projector, turn on the lamp, and turn the volume knob to the predetermined level (this is particularly important when the film has no introductory music). Fine adjust the focus and sound after you start the projector.
- Most projectors must run a few seconds before the sound system stabilizes. Therefore, if you stop the film to discuss a particular sequence, the viewers may miss a few seconds of narration or dialogue when you start the projector. If this is so, turn the volume knob down, back up the film a few feet, start the projector, turn on the lamp, and then turn up the sound.
- When the film is over, turn off the lamp, turn down the sound, and stop the projector. Run the rest of the film footage through after class. Rewind the film if you are going to show it again. If you are not showing it again, and if you used the same size reel the film came on, you need not rewind the film. The agency you got it from will rewind the film during routine inspection. Before putting the film back in the container, fasten down the end of the film with a piece of tape. The film normally arrives with the film held down with tape. Peel it off and stick it on the projection cart so that you can use it later to hold the end down. The film is better protected when this is done.

▲ *Figure 8.35*
Present the material.

Present the Material. A well-designed film/video presentation will call for frequent student participation. By responding yourself, you provide an example the students will follow. Learners are quick to detect and act according to your attitude toward the material. Many studies have indicated that the instructor's attitude—often conveyed nonverbally—significantly affects students' learning from media.

Situate yourself so that you can observe learner reactions. Watch for clues indicating difficulties or boredom. Note individual reactions for possible use in the follow-up discussion. Deal with individual discipline problems as quickly and unobtrusively as possible.

Require Learner Response

If active participation was not explicitly built into the film/video program it is all the more important to stimulate response after the presentation. The ability to generalize new knowledge and transfer it to real-life applications depends on learner practice under a variety of conditions. The possibilities for follow-up activities are virtually limitless. A few of the common techniques are:

• Discussion—question-and-answer sessions, buzz groups, panel discussions, debates.

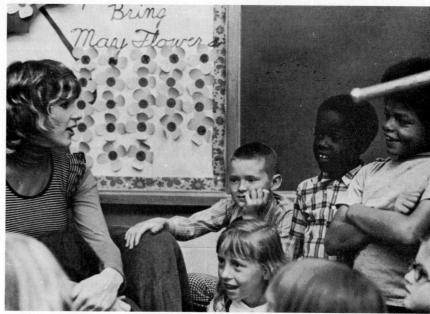

▲ *Figure 8.36*
Post-viewing discussion is an integral component of the total lesson, especially when using affectively oriented film and video materials.

• Dramatization—role playing, skits, oral presentations.
• Projects—experiments, reports, exhibits, models, demonstrations, drawings, story-writing, bulletin boards, media productions.

Evaluate

Assessment of student learning can be carried out informally by observing performance during the follow-up activities. Individual projects can be good indicators of successful learning. In many cases, though, more formal testing serves a valuable purpose. First, tests that are followed by feedback of correct answers can provide an efficient review and summary of the main points of the lesson. Second, objective tests can help pinpoint gaps that need to be followed up in the classroom, and, they can identify individuals who need remedial help. In this way, the instructor can complement the media compo-

nent by catering to individual differences in ways the media cannot.

LOCAL VIDEO DESIGN AND PRODUCTION

A feature that separates television from many of the other audiovisual media is that the instructor is not limited to off-the-shelf materials but can with reasonable ease prepare custom materials to fit local needs. "Do-it-yourself" television has become commonplace since the popularization of the battery-operated portable video recording systems—the "porta-pak." This technological advance has liberated ITV production from the confines of the engineer-dominated studio. More recently, the development of the "camcorder" (camera and recorder built into a single book-size unit) has increased the ease and portability of $\frac{1}{2}$-inch recording. It allows ITV production to

Components of the Single-Camera System:

Camera. The heart of the portable video camera is the pick-up tube, which is basically a vacuum tube that converts light rays into electronic signals that are transmitted through a cable to the video recorder. The camera may be a viewfinder type. The viewfinder camera is so named because it has built into it a small TV set that allows the operator to monitor the image being received by the pick-up tube. Even small hand-held cameras typically contain built-in viewfinders with 1-inch screens. The nonviewfinder camera costs several hundred dollars less since it lacks the built-in monitor. It may be used for fixed-camera purposes, however, and it can be used for other local production purposes if it is hooked up to a separate monitor, allowing the operator to aim and focus the camera according to the image shown in the monitor.

Microphone. Hand-held cameras usually come with a microphone built into the front of the camera. This microphone has "automatic level control," a feature that automatically adjusts the volume to keep the sound at an audible level. The camera, so to speak, "hears" as well as "sees." The problem is that these microphones amplify *all* sounds within their range, including shuffling feet, coughs, street noises, and equipment noise, along with sounds that are wanted. You may, therefore,

A hand-held-color TV camera

A compact-color TV camera complete with microphone and eyepiece/viewfinder

want to bypass the built-in microphone by plugging in a separate microphone better suited to your particular purpose.

In selecting a microphone, remember that television is more than pictures. Indeed, the audio track usually carries more critical information than the visual. (If you doubt this, try watching your favorite TV show with the sound turned off.) So the selection and handling of the microphone are of vital importance. The best advice is to think of your portable video system as an audio recorder plus a video recorder, and to make the same careful preparations as you would for an audio recording session.

The lavalier, or "neck mike,"

is a good choice when a single speaker is being recorded. It can be clipped to a tie or dress, hung around the neck, or even hidden under light clothing. A desk stand may be used to hold a microphone for a speaker or several discussants seated at a table. The microphone might be unidirectional or omnidirectional, depending on the number and seating arrangements of the speakers. For situations in which there is unwanted background noise or the speaker is moving, a highly directional microphone should be used, usually held by hand and pointed toward the sound source.

Monitor/Receiver. The final major component of the single-camera VTR system is the monitor/receiver, the device on which the recording is played back. The name is derived from the dual capabilities these units usually possess. Television signals may be sent through cables in the form of a "video signal," as in a closed-circuit TV studio. A "monitor" is a TV set built to pick up video signals; a "receiver" is a TV set built to pick up radio frequencies. A "monitor/receiver" is a unit especially adapted to receive both. The flick of a switch allows it to go from off-air pickup to playback of a VTR connected to it by cable.

Recording Setup for the Single-Camera System. Here are some tips for an effective arrangement for single-camera VTR recording:

Cameras used in this system usually are equipped with automatic light-level control enabling them to adjust automatically to the brightest light striking the lens. If there is a window in back of your subject, the camera will adjust to that light, thus throwing your subject into shadowy darkness. An important caution when recording outdoors: one of the greatest hazards to the pick-up tube in your camera is exposure to direct sunlight. Aiming at the sun can cause its image to be burned into the pick-up tube, possibly causing irreparable damage.

1. The monitor/receiver and recorder are set on a sturdy mobile cart. This allows easy movement of the equipment around the room. The cart can be swiveled around so that the monitor/receiver faces the camera operator (to allow monitoring when a nonviewfinder camera is being used). In most cases it is advisable to turn the monitor/receiver away from on-camera performers to avoid distracting them during recording. It can easily be swiveled back for later "instant replay" viewing.
2. The camera is mounted on a sturdy, wheeled tripod, maximizing mobility and stable support.
3. The camera is outfitted with a zoom lens, an expensive option, but one that adds great flexibility to the system. The zoom lens, having a variable focal length, can be adjusted to provide a wide-angle view, a medium view, or a close-up view with just a twist of the wrist. You should, however, resist the impulse to zoom in and out during a shot unless there is very good reason for doing so.
4. The camera and mobile cart are placed close to the wall. This arrangement helps reduce the likelihood of passersby tripping over the profusion of cables that connect all the components to each other and to the power source.
5. The camera is aimed away from the window (or other bright light source).
6. The subjects are well lighted. If natural light is insufficient, you may supplement it with incandescent or fluorescent lighting in the room. Today's pick-up tubes operate well with a normal level of artificial light.
7. The camera is positioned so that the faces of all subjects can be seen. A common mistake in taping a classroom scene is to place the camera at the back of the room. This provides a nice full-face view of the teacher, but makes reaction shots of the students nearly impossible to see. Placement of the camera at the side of the classroom is a reasonable compromise when recording classroom interaction.
8. A desk-stand microphone is used. This allows pickup of the voices of all subjects, while reducing the pickup of unwanted background noises.

Analyze Learners

General Characteristics. The class is a self-contained one with twenty-nine fifth-graders (sixteen girls, thirteen boys) in an urban elementary school. The average age is ten years; the average reading level is fourth grade.

The class is about half black; three students are Asian; the remainder are Caucasian. Seventeen come from single-parent families.

They are "lower middle class" in socioeconomic status. Motivation is usually a challenge with this class.

Entry Competencies. Regarding today's topic, the Panama Canal, awareness is low. In yesterday's discussion of Central America only Nicaragua and El Salvador were mentioned without prompting. There is an old barge canal on the north side of town, so many students were able to identify canals as man-made waterways but were vague about their purposes.

State Objectives

The fifth-grade social studies students will be able to

1. Locate the Panama Canal on a wall map of North and South America.
2. Explain the main advantage of the Panama Canal as a shortcut between the Atlantic and Pacific oceans.
3. Visually recognize a canal, distinguishing it from other waterways.
4. Discuss the Panama Canal's historic importance, citing at least its commercial and military advantages and the achievement of overcoming the obstacles to its construction.
5. Demonstrate that they value the sort of cooperative effort represented by the building of the Panama Canal by participating actively in a group project. (a general affective objective)

Select Media and Materials

The teacher surveys the *Film and Video Finder* under the topic of "Panama Canal" and finds four titles that look promising. Two of these are in the school district film library. After previewing both, she selects one because the content and vocabulary come closest to her class's. She notes that the political description of Panama is no longer accurate, so she prepares some comments to correct it.

Utilize Materials

Because motivating interest is predictably difficult, she begins to stimulate students' curiosity by rolling down the wall map of North and South America and asking how a traveler in the days before airplanes and automobiles might get from New York to San Francisco. What if you were a merchant who wanted to ship tools and work clothes to the miners of the gold rush in Alaska in 1898? What if you were an admiral needing to move his fleet rapidly from the Atlantic to the Pacific?

Having identified the *problem,* the teacher states that the film is going to show the solution developed early in the twentieth century. She lists several key questions on the overhead projector.

After reviewing the questions by having students take turns reading them, she asks them to look for the answers to these questions while viewing the film. She then shows the film.

Require Learner Performance

After showing the film, the teacher divides the students into groups of three to discuss the questions. Each group elects a recorder who will write the answers agreed to by the group.

After a few minutes of discussion the teacher brings the whole class back together in a large group and calls on two or three recorders to give their answers to question 1, with the whole class reacting to these. This process is repeated for the rest of the questions.

The teacher concludes by going back to question 3, focusing on how the builders of the canal succeeded because of their systematic plan and determination to overcome all obstacles. If *we* were going to construct a display to tell the story of the Panama Canal, what steps would we have to carry out? What ideas would we put into our display? With questions such as these the teacher builds interest in constructing a display, works out a time line, and organizes the students into project groups to carry out the assignment.

Evaluate/Revise

The teacher collects the recorders' written notes and checks to see how accurately the questions were answered. She makes note of test items keyed to the objectives to be included on the written test at the end of this unit. During carrying out of the display project she will be able to check the accuracy of the information being put into the display and, regarding the attitudinal objective, she will circulate among the work groups to assess the enthusiasm exhibited in their work.

▲ *Figure 8.37*
Local production by students is a major application of video in today's schools.

▲ *Figure 8.38*
The "microteaching" technique uses video to record and play back practice-teaching sessions involving four to six representative students.

be taken "into the field," wherever that might be: the science laboratory, the classroom, the counseling office, the athletic field, the factory assembly line, the hospital, the neighborhood, even the home. Equally important, the simplicity of the system has made it feasible for nonprofessionals, instructors and students alike, to create their own video materials.

Applications. Locally produced video could be used for virtually any of the purposes described earlier in relation to still pictures, audio, and film; but its unique capability is to capture sight and sound for immediate playback. So this medium would fit best with activities that are enhanced by immediate feedback: group-dynamics sessions, athletic practice, skills training, and interpersonal techniques (e.g., "micro-counseling" and "micro-teaching").

Other applications that emphasize the *local* aspect of local video production are

- Dramatization of student stories, songs, and poems.
- Student documentaries of school or neighborhood issues.
- Preservation of local folklore.
- Demonstrations, for example, of science experiments, eliminating delays and unanticipated foul-ups.
- Replays of field trips for in-class follow-up.
- Career information on local businesses via field recordings.

Of course, many organizations have more elaborate facilities than the simple single-camera field units that we are describing here. But closed-circuit TV studios and the like are the domain of the media specialist or engineer. Our focus is on the typical sort of system that instructors might expect to be using by themselves.

References

Print References

Film

Arwady, Joseph W. "The Oral Introduction to the Instructional Film: A Closer Look." *Educational Technology* (July 1980), pp. 18–22.

Beatty, LaMond F. *Motion Pictures.* (Englewood Cliffs, N.J.: Educational Technology Publications, 1981).

Blackaby, Linda; Georgakas, Don; and Margolis, Barbara. *In Focus: A Guide to Using Films.* (New York: New York Zoetrope, 1981).

Burmester, D. "Short Films Revisited." *English Journal* (January 1984), pp. 66–72.

Cassidy, J. M. "Lights, Camera, Animation!" *School Arts* (February 1984), pp. 36–38.

Downie, Robert, and Alexander, Lynne. "Films and Videotapes on Animal Development—A Check

List." *Journal of Biological Education* (Spring 1986), pp. 68–71.

Gaffney, Maureen, ed. *Films Kids Like.* (Chicago: American Library Association, 1973).

———. *More Films Kids Like.* (Chicago: American Library Association, 1977).

Gaffney, Maureen, and Laybourne, Gerry Bond. *What to Do When the Lights Go On: A Comprehensive Guide to 16-mm Films and Related Activities for Children.* (Phoenix, Az.: Oryx Press, 1981).

Gilkey, Richard W. "16mm Film, Videotape, Videodisc: Weighing the Differences." *Media and Methods* (March–April 1986), pp. 8–9.

Guide to Classroom Use of Film/Video. Compiled by Shirley A. Fitzgibbons. Edited by Deborah Davidson Boutchard. 2d ed. (Washington, D.C.: National Education Services, American Film Institute, 1981).

Jacobs, Lewis. *Documentary Tradition.* (New York: W. W. Norton, 1980).

Jones, Emily S., and Dratfield, Leo. "40 Years of Memorable Films." *Sightlines* (Fall–Winter 1983–1984), pp. 15–17.

Langer, J. "What Is a Documentary?" *Cinema Papers* (October 1982), pp. 442–445, 487, 489.

Limbacher, James L. "Feature Films to Teach Literature." *English Journal* (January 1981), pp. 86–88.

McDonald, Bruce, and Orsini, Leslie. *Basic Language Skills through Films: An Instructional Program for Secondary School Students.* (Littleton, Colo.: Libraries Unlimited, 1983).

Mercer, John. *The Information Film.* (Champaign, Ill.: Stipes, 1981).

Parlato, Salvatore, J., Jr. *Films Too Good for Words: A Directory of Non-Narrated 16-mm Films.* (New York: Bowker, 1973).

————. *Superfilms: An International Guide to Award-Winning Films.* (Metuchen, N.J.: Scarecrow Press, 1976).

Shemin, J. B. "Experimenting with Film as Art for Kids." *Film Library Quarterly* no. 1 (1982), pp. 15–19.

Street, Douglas, ed. *Children's Novels and the Movies.* (New York: Ungar, 1984).

Vick, Nancy H. "Freedom to View: Coping with Censorship, A Summary Report." *Sightlines* (Spring 1981), pp. 5–6.

Video

Abelman, R. "Children and TV: The ABC's of TV Literacy." *Childhood Education* (January–February 1984), pp. 200–205.

Adams, Dennis M., and Hamm, Mary. "Teaching Students Critical Viewing Skills." *Curriculum Review* (January–February 1987), pp. 29–31.

Bunyan, John A. *More Practical Video.* (White Plains, N.Y.: Knowledge Industry, 1984).

Cambre, Marjorie. *A Reappraisal of Instructional Television.* (Syracuse, N.Y.: ERIC Clearinghouse on Information Resources, 1987).

Carlisle, Robert D. B. *Video at Work in American Schools.* (Bloomington, Ind.: Agency for Instructional Technology, 1987).

Center for Vocational Education. *Present Information with Televised and Videotaped Materials.* (Athens, Ga.: American Association for Vocational Instructional Materials, 1977).

Choat, Ernest, and Griffin, Harry. "Young Children, Television and Learning: Part 1. The Effects of Children Watching a Continuous Off-Air Broadcast. Part 2. Comparison of the Effects of Reading and Story Telling by the Teacher and Television Story Viewing." *Journal of Educational Television* (1986), pp. 79–104.

Choat, Ernest; Griffin, Harry; and Hobart, Dorothy. "Educational Television and the Curriculum for Children Up to the Age of Seven Years." *British Journal of Educational Technology* (October 1986), pp. 164–173.

Combes, Peter, and Tiffin, John. *Television Production for Education.* (New York: Focal Press, 1978).

Cortes, Charlotte E., and Richardson, Elinor. "Why in the World: Using Television to Develop Critical Thinking Skills." *Phi Delta Kappan* (June 1983), pp. 715–716.

Doerken, Maurine. *Classroom Combat: Teaching and Television.* (Englewood Cliffs, N.J.: Educational Technology Publications, 1983).

Dorr, Aimee. *Television and Children: A Special Medium for a Special Audience.* (Beverly Hills, Calif.: Sage, 1986).

DuBey, Kenneth. "How to Videotape through a Microscope." *Audiovisual Instruction* (January 1978), p. 33.

Emmens, Carol A. "The Fourth Basic: Courses in Viewing Television Critically." *School Library Journal* (February 1982), p. 45.

Far West Laboratory for Educational Development. *Inside Television: A Guide to Critical Viewing.* (Palo Alto, Calif.: Science and Behavior Books, 1980).

Gothberg, Helen M. *Television and Video in Libraries and Schools.* (Hamden, Conn.: Shoe String Press, 1984).

Hanson, Janice. *Understanding Video: Applications, Impact and Theory.* (Newbury Park, Calif.: Sage, 1987).

Hilliard, Robert L., and Field, Hyman H. *Television and the Teacher: A Handbook for Classroom Use.* (New York: Hastings House, 1976).

Howe, M. J. A., ed. *Learning from Television: Psychological and Educational Research.* (New York: Academic Press, 1983).

Johnston, Jerome. *Electronic Learning: From Audiotape to Videodisc.* (Hillsdale, N.J.: Lawrence Erlbaum, 1987).

Kaplan, Don. *Television and the Classroom.* (White Plains, N.Y.: Knowledge Industry, 1986).

Lewis, Richard F. "Using Canadian *Sesame Street* Segments in Elementary Classrooms to Teach French." *Programmed Learning and Educational Technology* (August 1983), pp. 190–196.

Penman, Brian, et al. *Making Television Educational.* (Toronto, Can-

ada: Ontario Secondary School Teachers' Federation, 1976).

Post, Linda Williams. "Frankly, My Dear." *English Journal* (January 1987), pp. 28–30.

Reed, Sally, and Sautter, R. Craig. "Video Education: Taking a New Look at an Old Technology." *Electronic Learning* (November–December 1986), pp. 22–27.

Rockman, Saul. "If Not Now, When? The Rationale for Technology in the History/Social Science Classroom." *Social Studies Review* (Spring 1986), pp. 30–34.

Salomon, Gavriel. "Television Is 'Easy' and Print Is 'Tough': The Differential Investment of Mental Effort in Learning as a Function of Perceptions and Attributions." *Journal of Educational Psychology* (1984), pp. 647–658.

Schultz, Jill M., with Tobe Berkovitz. *A Teacher's Guide to Television Evaluation for Children.* (Springfield, Ill.: Charles C. Thomas, 1981).

Smith, Welby A. *Video Fundamentals.* (Englewood Cliffs, N.J.: Prentice-Hall, 1983).

Szumski, Richard. "How to Produce Your Own Instructional Video Tapes." *Social Studies Review* (Spring 1986), pp. 60–62.

Thompson, Margery. "Television May Be Just What's Needed to Teach the Basics." *American School Board Journal* (January 1978), pp. 41–42.

Williams, P. A.; Haertel, E.; Haertel, G.; and Walberg, H. "Impact of Leisure-Time Television on School Learning: A Research Synthesis." *American Educational Research Journal* (Spring 1982), pp. 19–50.

Withey, Stephen B., and Abeles, Ronald P., eds. *Television and Social Behavior: Beyond Violence and Children.* (Hillsdale, N.J.: Lawrence Erlbaum, 1980).

Video in Adult and Higher Education

Abel, John D., and Creswell, Kent W. "Study of Student Attitudes Concerning Instructional TV." *E-ITV* (October 1983), pp. 72–79.

Brush, Judith M., and Brush, Douglas. *Private Television Communications: New Directions.* (Cold Spring, N.Y.: HI Press of Cold Press, 1986).

Blythe, Hal, and Sweet, Charlie. "Using Media to Teach English." *Instructional Innovator* (September 1983), pp. 22–24.

Dranov, Paula; Moore, Louise; and Hickey, Adrienne. *Video in the 80's: Emerging Uses for Television in Business, Education, Medicine, and Government.* (White Plains, N.Y.: Knowledge Industry, 1980).

Eyster, George W. "ETV Utilization in Adult Education." *Adult Leadership* (December 1976), pp. 109–111.

"Guess What's on the Tube This Fall—Education." [Annenberg/CPB Project] *AGB Reports* (September–October 1984), pp. 29–30.

Gueulette, David G. "Television: The Hidden Curriculum of Lifelong Learning." *Lifelong Learning: The Adult Years* no. 5 (1980), pp. 4–7, 35.

Helmantoler, Michael C. "The Non-Traditional College Student and Public TV." *Community and Junior College Journal* (March 1978), pp. 13–15.

McInnes, James. *Video in Education and Training.* (New York: Focal Press, 1980).

McKinney, Fred, and Miller, David J. "Fifteen Years of Teaching General Psychology by Television." *Teaching of Psychology* (October 1977), pp. 120–123.

Zuber-Skeritt, Ortrun. *Video in Higher Education.* (New York: Nichols, 1984).

Audiovisual References

Film

And Yet It Moves. New York: Phoenix Films, 1981. 16-mm or videocassette. 8 minutes.

Animation (Set). Fountain Valley, Calif.: Warner Educational Productions, 1981. 2 filmstrips with cassettes. 59 frames and 65 frames. 14 minutes each.

Basic Film Terms: A Visual Dictionary. Santa Monica, Calif.: Pyramid Films, 1970. 16-mm film or videocassette. 15 minutes.

Basic Movie Making. Rochester, N.Y.: Eastman Kodak, 1973. 16-mm film. 14 minutes.

Claymation. Santa Monica, Calif.: Pyramid Films, 1980. 16-mm film. 8 minutes.

The Eye Hears and the Ear Sees. Montreal, Canada: National Film Board of Canada, 1970. 16-mm film. 59 minutes.

Facts about Film. 2d ed. Chicago, Ill.: International Film Bureau, 1975. 16-mm film or videocassette. 10 minutes.

Frame by Frame: The Art of Animation. Santa Monica, Calif.: Pyramid Films, 1973. 16-mm film or videocassette. 13 minutes.

Odette's Ordeal. Wilmette, Ill.: Films Incorporated, 1976. 16-mm film. 38 minutes.

Project the Right Image. Lincoln, Nebr.: Great Plains ITV Library, 1976. 16-mm film or videocassette. 14 minutes.

So You Wanna Make a Film. Lawrence, Kans.: Centron Films, 1980. 16-mm or videocassette. 9 minutes.

Teaching Basic Skills with Film. Mississauga, Ontario, Canada: Marlin Motion Pictures, 1981. Videocassette.

Video

Basic Television Terms: A Video Dictionary. Santa Monica, Calif.: Pyramid Films, 1977. 16-mm film or videocassette. 17 minutes.

Camera Techniques for Video. Great Falls, Mont.: Video International Publishers, 1980. Videocassette. 30 minutes.

Cost Effective Creative Video. Alexandria, Va.: Smith-Mattingly Productions, 1979. Videocassette. 30 minutes.

High Technology: How It Works. Stamford, Conn.: Educational Dimensions Group, 1983. Filmstrips: "Fiber Optics," 18 minutes; "Television," 21 minutes; and "Videodisc," 20 minutes.

How to Watch TV. Columbus, Ohio: Xerox Educational Publications, 1980. Four filmstrips with audiocassettes. 12 minutes each.

Introducing the Single-Camera VTR/VCR System. Alexandria, Va.: Smith-Mattingly Productions, 1979. Videocassette. 30 minutes.

Learn Video Via Video (series). New York, N.Y.: Imero Fiorentino Associates, 1981. Three videocassettes.

Learning from Film and Television. Norwood, Mass.: Beacon Films, 1983. Videocassette. 27 minutes.

Producing a Videotape. Great Falls, Mont.: Video International Publishers, 1980. Videocassette. 35 minutes.

TV: An Inside View. Salt Lake City, Utah: Media Systems, 1976. Three filmstrips with audiocassettes.

Television Viewing Skills. Austin, Tex.: Southwest Educational Development Laboratory, 1980. Multimedia kit.

Toward Improved Candid ITV (series). Atlanta, Ga.: AMCEE, 1982. Two videocassettes. 25 minutes each.

Utilizing Instructional Television. Salt Lake City, Utah: Media Systems, 1976. Two filmstrips with audiocassettes.

Video Encyclopedia of the 20th Century. New York: CEL Educational Resources, 1986. 75 videocassettes or 38 videodiscs, index, and four-volume reference set.

Videotape-Disc-Or . . . ? Columbia, S.C.: Educational Program Service, 1983. Videocassette. 30 minutes.

What Is Microteaching? London: British Council, 1980. 16-mm film. 20 minutes.

Possible Projects

8-A. Preview a film and appraise it using a form such as the "Appraisal Checklist: Film and Video" found in this chapter.

8-B. Observe a teacher using a film or video program in a classroom situation and critique the teacher's utilization practices.

8-C. Use one or more of the selection aids described in Appendix A to compile a list of films or video programs available on a topic of interest to you.

8-D. Plan a lesson in a subject area of your choice in which you will incorporate the use of a film or video program. Follow the outline shown in the "Blueprint."

8-E. Preview one of the documentary films described in this chapter. Prepare a review, either written (about 700 words) or recorded on audiotape (approximately five minutes long). Briefly summarize the content of the film and describe your reaction to it.

9

Electronic Distribution Systems

Objectives

After studying this chapter, you should be able to:

1. Contrast the current status of instructional radio in the developed and less developed countries.

2. Describe an "interactive" radio program format and justify its use.

3. Describe verbally or with a schematic drawing each of the following television delivery systems: (a) broadcast via commercial station, (b) broadcast via noncommercial station, (c) closed-circuit television, (d) cable television, (e) microwave transmission, and (f) satellite transmission.

4. Identify a major educational application of each of the delivery systems mentioned in objective 3.

5. Contrast the role of public television in at-home and in-school viewing.

6. Characterize the sorts of programs that are most frequently used for (a) school television and (b) college/university television.

7. Identify the educational potentials of closed-circuit television and cable television that are not shared with broadcast television.

8. Characterize the current role of ITFS in American education.

9. Differentiate among an audioconference, an audiographic conference, and a videoconference.

10. Describe verbally or with a schematic diagram a teleconference system.

11. Describe an advantageous educational application of teleconferencing for either elementary/secondary education, higher education, or business/industry training.

12. Name at least five important considerations in conducting successful teletraining.

13. Differentiate between teletext and videotex.

14. Describe an education/training situation for which videotex would be justified both pedagogically and economically.

Lexicon
"interactive" radio
public television
closed-circuit television
ITFS
geosynchronous satellite
teleconference
audioconference
audiographic conference
videoconference
uplink/downlink
ad hoc network
dedicated network
teletraining
teletext
videotex

A generation ago there were two popular means of electronic distribution of sounds and pictures—radio and television. "Radio" meant audio programs broadcast through the air to be picked up in real time by individual receiving sets. "Television" meant the same, with the addition of moving pictures to the audio programs. Gradually some broadcasting channels were devoted to programs of an educational nature. Schools wishing to make use of these audiovisual resources needed to be within range of an educational station, to have the properly equipped receivers, and to tune in to the educational station at the specified time.

Nowadays in North America and other technologically developed areas of the world there is a bewildering array of electronic distribution systems available, thanks to rapid advances in all areas of electronics. Audio resources in schools are no longer limited to "radio," nor are video resources limited to "televi-

sion." In this chapter we will explore some of the most common channels through which sound and picture resources can be conveyed into the classroom, emphasizing those that are communicated over a distance. (In Chapter 8 the emphasis is on media that are stored and used in the classroom.)

RADIO

L IKE broadcast television, radio programs broadcast through the air are being replaced by other forms of delivery (such as cassettes played in the classroom) that are more flexible and economical. Instructors resist media that have to be used according to someone else's schedule, and educational administrators want to avoid the big budget outlays needed to support broadcasting stations. As educators become more and more responsive to the needs of individual learners, there is less and less demand for pro-

grams that are aimed at mass audiences simultaneously.

Broadcast Radio

In the 1920s and 1930s many higher education institutions and school districts undertook operation of educational radio stations. By experimenting with different program formats and design procedures, the educational radio pioneers were laying the foundations for today's field of instructional development. The design and utilization principles worked out in those early days are now being rediscovered for application to video- and computer-based instruction.

Later in the 1930s and 1940s these school and college stations were linked into networks, usually of statewide scope, in order to share programming and to expand coverage of their "market." Ohio started a "School of the Air" in the early 1930s, and others followed in Wisconsin, Kansas, Michigan, Minnesota,

Generalized electronic distribution system

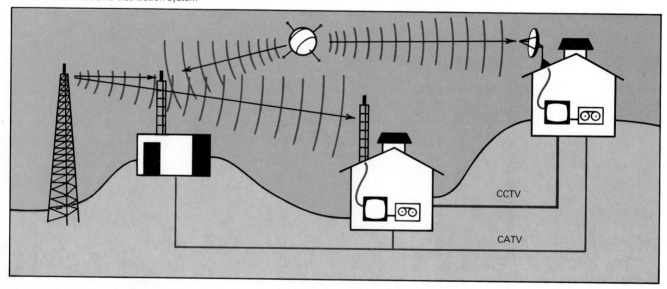

▲ *Figure 9.1*
Generalized electronic distribution system. You should be able to see at least seven different pathways a television signal could follow to get into a classroom.

Indiana, New York, and Texas. But by the 1950s school interest in radio was waning as television grew in popularity. Most school use of radio has receded from center stage. It persists now mainly in areas that are geographically or economically cut off from the newer technologies. This includes the less developed countries, which are making some very interesting uses of the broadcast radio medium.

"Interactive" Radio

In less developed countries, where large populations still reside in isolated villages, millions of children attend schools in which the learning resources begin and end with the teacher and chalkboard. In their search for a technology that could provide stimulating resources to schools scattered over vast geographic regions at low cost, educators have rediscovered broadcast radio. An experimental project begun in the late 1970s in Nicaragua demonstrated success in providing mathematics lessons over the radio. The key to success was a novel program format requiring fast-paced responses by the children to questions or other cues given in the broadcast program. In this format the radio lesson is organized around a drill-and-practice pattern: bits of new information or questions are presented, students respond vocally as a group, and the narrator gives the correct response (prerecorded, of course). A sample of a script is shown in "Close-Up: 'Interactive' Radio in Nicaragua."

The system is referred to as "interactive" radio by its designers, but here that term is used in quotation marks because the format only *simulates* true interaction. For a media format to be truly interactive, the student's

▲ *Figure 9.2*
In Kenya, "interactive" radio has proven to be a cost-effective method for learning English.

response must actually have some effect on the sequence of the following instruction. In this case there is no true feedback from the students to the (prerecorded) teacher. (See the definition of *interactive media* in the glossary.)

In any event, because of its great success in Nicaragua and in other field trials, this design format has been exported to several other countries, including Honduras, Bolivia, the Dominican Republic, Papua New Guinea, and Kenya. In Kenya "interactive" radio is being used for English language learning, reaching most of the schools in the country. One observer reported this scene in a dirt-floored, mud-walled school in a Kenyan village:

This radio classroom is not like any the observer has seen before. When the program starts, a rapid-fire dialogue between the radio and the children begins, punctuated by music and little dramas, with regular pauses for the children to answer and receive immedi- *ate reinforcement for their answers. The students are following the adventures of a boy, a girl, and their family. They are singing songs, and responding orally, physically, and in writing to the incessant, engaging pace of the radio. They are involved, they are enthusiastic, and they see immediate results from their work.**

Each half-hour broadcast teaches all four language skills: listening, speaking, reading, and writing. The lessons are not supplementary; they are the core of the English language curriculum. Research results have shown that students in the radio classrooms outperform students in the regular classrooms on measures of all four skills: listening, speaking, reading, and writing. The average control-group student would score at the fiftieth percentile, whereas the average radio-group student would score at the sixty-

* Peter Spain. "The Fourth R—(Interactive) Radio." *Development Communication Report* no. 49 (Spring 1985), p. 13.

CLOSE-UP:
"Interactive" Radio in Nicaragua

Between 1974 and 1979 Stanford University conducted a research and development project in Nicaragua under sponsorship of the U.S. Agency for International Development. Its purpose was to test whether radio could be used to teach mathematics skills efficiently and effectively. The highly positive results can be attributed in large part to the sophisticated pedagogical design of the radio math programs. The following is a sample of a script for a second-grade mathematics radio lesson. This particular lesson was the winner of the Japan Prize in 1977 for achievements in educational radio.

Music:	Theme music for notebook activity
Children:	*Hurrah . . . Hurrah . . . Rah, Rah, Rah!*
Monster:	To the notebooks, to the notebooks.
All:	Here we go.
Raymond:	Now we're going to do the exercises in Part One.
Lita:	Look at the first exercise. Read it out loud.
Children:	*One-third plus one-third.*
Raymond:	Tell me, one-third plus one-third . . . how much is that?
Children:	*Two-thirds.*
Lita:	Two-thirds.
Raymond:	Good. After the equal sign write two-thirds.
Music:	(eight seconds)
Lita:	Tell me, did you write two over three?
Children:	*Yes.*
Raymond:	Good. That's how we write two-thirds. Let's go to the next exercise. Tell me, what are you going to add?
Children:	*Two-fifths plus one-fifth.*
Lita:	And two-fifths plus one-fifth . . . how much is it?
Children:	*Three-fifths.*
Raymond:	Three-fifths. Next to the equal sign write three-fifths.
. . .	
Music:	Theme music for notebook activity
Lita:	Boys and girls, open your notebooks again.
Raymond:	Find an empty part because you are going to draw some marbles.
Lita:	Yes, you're going to draw marbles to solve some division problems.
Raymond:	First you are going to solve thirteen divided by five.
Lita:	Tell me, how many marbles are you going to draw?
Children:	*Thirteen.*
Raymond:	Thirteen. Draw them.
Music:	(fifteen seconds)
Lita:	The exercise is thirteen divided by five, so circle five marbles.
Music:	(eight seconds)
Raymond:	Circle another five marbles.
Music:	(eight seconds)
Lita:	Tell me, how many marbles are *not* circled?
Children:	*Three.*
Raymond:	Three. Now, tell me, how many groups did you make?
. . .	
Etc.	

Source: The Radio Mathematics Project: Introduction and Guide. Stanford, Calif.: Institute for Mathematical Studies in the Social Sciences, Stanford University, 1980.

ninth percentile . . . a dramatically superior performance rate for the radio group.*

---

* Maurice Imhoof and Philip Christensen, eds. *Teaching English by Radio.* Washington, D.C.: Academy for Educational Development, 1986.

TELEVISION

THERE are literally thousands of institutions and agencies, public and private, using video communications for instruction within formal and nonformal education settings. The overall impression is one of tremendous diversity. One way to organize a closer look at this panorama is to consider one by one each of the major TV "delivery systems," that is, the physical methods used to package and transmit programs to users: commercial and noncom-

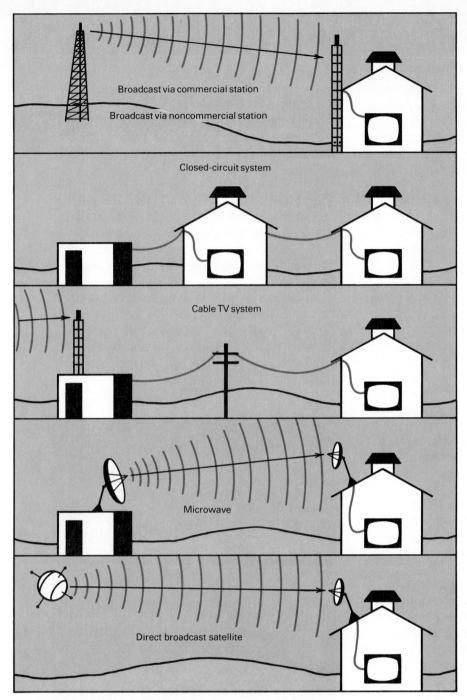

◀ *Figure 9.3*
The most common distribution systems for instructional television, shown individually. Compare with Figure 9.1.

Within the first image:
- Broadcast via commercial station
- Broadcast via noncommercial station
- Closed-circuit system
- Cable TV system
- Microwave
- Direct broadcast satellite

▲ *Figure 9.4*
"If school were as important as they say it is, we wouldn't have to go. It would be televised."

Classroom" (described in the accompanying Flashback).

Although the commercial networks soon dropped the idea of becoming major vehicles for instructional television, commercial broadcasting still plays a major role in instructional television in the United States. In fact, about one-quarter of the television programs used today in schools originate with *commercial* stations. Most of these programs are not designed with educational intents (although in some areas educational programs such as "Sesame Street" and "The Electric Company" are carried by commercial stations). They are, instead, programs intended to entertain and/or inform the general public, but which can be adapted to instructional purposes by classroom teachers. Such programs might include classic and contemporary dramas, dance and musical performances, science programs, dramas based on historical situations (such as *The Jesse Owens Story* and *The Day After*), documentaries, and in-depth coverage of current news events.

mercial broadcasting, closed-circuit TV, cable systems, microwave transmission, and satellites.

Broadcasting by Commercial Stations

Both entertainment and instructional TV trace their roots to the commercially licensed stations that began to make their impact as instruments of mass communication in the early 1950s. Early attempts to reach mass audiences with educational programming were made using commercial channels, including such pioneering efforts as NBC's "Continental

All things considered, Sputnik I has to get the credit for breathing life into this project, the NBC-TV series which had a five-year run from 1958 to 1963. Sometime after Sputnik spurted aloft on October 4, 1957, NBC's Director of Public Affairs and Education, Edward Stanley, was coming back from Europe. He read that New York State's Commissioner of Education, the late James Allen, was planning a refresher course for science teachers in the state. Probable cost: $600,000. Stanley thought that "for not a great deal more than that you could reach every science teacher in the country." And, he thought further, "we could do the whole damn thing."

While Sputnik may have catalyzed *Continental Classroom*, two people, more than any others, made it work. Ed Stanley had the institutional punch and the moxie to argue and lead, at a level essential for a venture of this scope. Then, Dorothy Culbertson, executive producer in the public affairs department, brought intelligence and important persuasiveness to both the critical fund raising and direct management of the project.

Assembling the series actually amounted to a kind of benevolent brokerage by Stanley and Culbertson. At his suggestion, she talked to the Fund for the Advancement of Education about using the NBC-TV network for college credit courses. They were "excited." At almost the same time, the American Association of Colleges for Teacher Education (AACTE) approached NBC tentatively. Would it put up $25,000 to study how TV could be used to improve teacher training? "I thought it was a helluva good idea," recalls Stanley. But his vision was broader: Would they be interested in something considerably bigger? Indeed they would, they said. This became vital in the funding arrangements that were to follow.

It seemed apparent that NBC alone could not float the concept. And so, after appeals to the Ford Foundation, it finally agreed to put in $500,000, a major share of the first year's expected cost. Then, following beguiling calls from Culbertson, added increments of $100,000 apiece came in from a number of large corporations. As a practical matter, the funds all went to AACTE, which thereupon paid NBC for its facilities, at cost.

By then, the apt series title had been locked up, as an outgrowth of a conversation between Stanley and noted educator Dr. James Killian, then Science Advisor to President Eisenhower. "What you'd have here," Stanley explained, "would be a continental classroom." Dr. Killian liked the idea, and the coinage stuck.

On October 6, 1958, the daily broadcasts began on the NBC network. That first year, the topic was "Atomic Age Physics," a college-level course 165 lessons long. Says Stanley: "Physics was the subject that was in trouble then. Many people teaching

In addition to such programs, commercial television may also provide what might be called incidental instructional opportunities. Popular programs regularly viewed by students at home may provide experiential background upon which the creative teacher can build learning experiences.

Television, as we know, has considerable potential in the area of attitude formation. Popular dramatic series (even situation comedies) often revolve around moral dilemmas: Should the doctor inform the parents of the unwed pregnant teenager about her condition, or should the girl's condi-

it had received their degrees before atomic energy was invented." And the man to teach these teachers was Dr. Harvey White, professor of physics at the University of California at Berkeley. Moving in to the NBC project, he lined up a veritable "Who's Who" of American scientists as guest lecturers. There's probably never been another national refresher course quite like it.

White and the other *Continental Classroom* teachers who were to follow had to do 130 lectures of their own in a year's time, five a week. They were under fantastic pressure. They would work from outlines, rather than from prepared scripts. NBC tried to let their talent go into the studio when they wanted. Largely, this meant afternoon sessions. A four-hour stretch of studio time allowed for camera-blocking, a dress rehearsal, and the tape-recording.

NBC's audience-research specialists estimated that 400,000 viewed "Physics," while 600,000 tuned in to "Chemistry," in the second year. But at no time over the five-year span of *Continental Classroom* did more than 5,000 sign up for actual credit in a course. Even so, to Lawrence McKune of Michigan State, that first series on physics was unique:

For the first time in the history of education, 4,905 students . . . in all parts of the United States, studied precisely the same course with the same teacher at the same hour, using the same outlines and the same texts.

In the second year, NBC repeated physics at 6 A.M., then ran its new chemistry course at 6:30. Physicists began watching chemistry, and the chemists brushed up on their physics, a neat refresher switch.

By 1960, the mathematicians were asking for a course. This time, a new approach was tried. The first half of the year was devoted to algebra; John Kelley of Berkeley taught three days a week, and

Julius Hlavaty took the Tuesday–Thursday pair. Then, in the second "term," Frederick Mosteller, chairman of statistics at Harvard, carried the main load on Probability and Statistics, while Paul Clifford of Montclair State College did the "applications" on Tuesday–Thursday. By that particular term, as many as 320 colleges and universities were granting credit for the course. Stanley notes that "few of them were giving probability in those days."

At that point, the Ford Foundation decided to cut off its financial support. And even though a number of corporate sponsors stuck with the project, Stanley began to feel a budget squeeze (a cutback to two TV cameras, instead of the normal three). Regardless, Stanley still managed to come up with a star performer for that fourth year, the late Peter Odegard, then chairman of the political science department at Berkeley and former president of Reed College.

Successful? Stanley says that Odegard's "American Government: Structure and Function" had an audience of 1.5 million. The League of Women Voters, he recalls, "were convinced we did this especially for them!"

But then *Continental Classroom* folded. Why? "Money," says Stanley. "The company did lose a little, and wasn't willing to take a chance on raising some money the next year." The series budget—it ran between $1.2 million and $1.5 million annually—was "not a helluva lot for a network, not really." But NBC must have thought so. "American Government" was rebroadcast in the fifth year, and *Continental Classroom* ended officially on May 17, 1963.

ªExcerpted from Robert D. B. Carlisle. *College Credit through TV: Old Idea, New Dimensions*. Lincoln, Neb.: Great Plains National Instructional Television Library, 1974.

tion be considered a private and confidential matter between doctor and patient? Is the policeman who knows that a brutal murderer will go unpunished justified in taking the law into his own hands by, say, planting false evidence against the murderer? More and more teachers are finding popular commercial programs a prime resource for discussion of moral and ethical issues.

Broadcasting by Noncommercial Stations

The 320-plus TV stations in the United States that hold noncommercial licenses are referred to

▲ *Figure 9.5*
"Big Bird," a main character on *Sesame Street,* after more than 20 years, still the most recognized series from Children's Television Workshop.

▲ *Figure 9.6*
Off-air reception from public TV stations is still common, but it has been replaced by in-classroom playback of videocassettes as the primary delivery system for instructional television.

In-School Instructional Programming.

Programs for direct classroom use to reach specific curricular objectives—*instructional television* (ITV)—are a mainstay of most public TV stations' daytime schedules. The average station transmits about forty elementary and twenty secondary series. There is also a rapidly growing trend toward distribution of programs by videocassette in addition to broadcast distribution by stations.

ITV programs tend to be about fifteen minutes (at the earlier grade levels) to thirty minutes long, and a single program is often repeated at different hours throughout the week to allow for flexibility in classroom scheduling. Contrary to the popular image, broadcast ITV programs usually do not present core instruction in basic subject areas. One leading researcher described ITV's contemporary role thusly:

1. To assist the classroom teachers in those subjects in which they often have the most difficulty (for example, art, music, "new" mathematics, science, and health);
2. To supplement the classroom instruction in subject areas in which limited classroom resources may prevent full examination of historical or international events; and
3. To bring outside stimulation in subject areas, such as literature, where teachers have difficulty exciting and motivating the students.*

Concerning the content of in-school programming, Table 9.1 contains data on the twenty most

---

* Saul Rockman. "Instructional Television Is Alive and Well." In Cater and Nyhan, eds., *The Future of Public Broadcasting.* New York: Praeger, 1976, p. 79.

collectively as *public television stations,* a term designating their common commitment to operate not for private gain but for the public benefit. Although these stations have various patterns of ownership, they tend to operate along roughly similar lines. Just as most commercial stations act as outlets for commercial network programming, most public television stations serve as outlets for the network programming of the Public Broadcasting Service (PBS). Their evening schedules feature PBS offerings and other programs aimed at home viewers in general, while during the daytime hours these stations typically carry instructional programs designed for specific school or college audiences.

Home Audience Programming.

Public television attempts to offer an alternative type of programming for viewers who are not well served by the mass audience programs of commercial broadcasting. In reaching out to selected subgroups, public TV programming does not usually attract viewers on a scale comparable to the commercial networks. However, well-produced series such as *Wall Street Week, Masterpiece Theatre,* and *Nova* have won critical acclaim and loyal audiences that in recent years have grown to a size comparable to those of their commercial rivals. On a more general plane, public opinion polls indicate that over 60 percent of American adults can name their local public TV channel and do watch such programs at least occasionally.

As mentioned in regard to commercial programs, the types of programs carried on public TV—documentaries, dramas, public affairs features, musical performances, science programs, and the like—are often useful as adjuncts to instruction in schools and colleges.

used instructional TV series, according to the most recent national survey. The most used series tended to be those intended for the primary and intermediate grade levels, although two of the three most popular series are aimed at high school and adult audiences and deal with science themes. In general, science, social studies, and language arts—in that order—are the most popular content areas for ITV.

At the college and university level there is less use of broadcast television. This is not surprising, because the prime audience for a college would be its own students on its own campus, who can easily be reached by means of a closed-circuit system. But colleges do also try to reach nonresident students, such as part-time students who live in the wider community or even in outlying areas. So noncommercial stations do sometimes carry programming aimed at postsecondary audiences. According to the most recent comprehensive survey of public television stations, there were a number of series broadcast for formal educational purposes by more than a handful of public television stations. The fifteen most frequently broadcast postsecondary TV series are shown in Table 9.2.

Closed-Circuit Television

The term *closed-circuit television* refers to a TV distribution system in which the sender and receiver are physically linked by wire. At its simplest, a connection between a single camera and a receiver within the same room (e.g., for image magnification in a science lab) constitutes closed-circuit TV (CCTV). Or several classrooms could be linked to a studio to form a building-wide

TABLE 9.1 Most Widely Used ITV Series

Rank	Series	Intended Grade Level	Total Teachers Using
1	Electric Company	Primary, intermediate	104,000
2	Nova	High school	94,400
3	National Geographic Specials	High school	77,500
4	Inside Out	Intermediate	74,600
5	All About You	Primary	72,500
6	Goodbody	Primary	69,000
7	Read All About It	Intermediate	55,300
8	Gather-Round	Primary	55,000
9	Mulligan Stew	Intermediate	46,400
10	Think About	Intermediate	46,000
11	It Figures	Intermediate	44,600
12	Stories of America	Primary	42,200
13	Sesame Street	Pre-school, primary	34,400
14	Book Bird	Primary, intermediate	33,900
15	Life on Earth	High school	32,900
16	Shakespeare	High school	27,500
17	Cover to Cover	Intermediate	25,300
18	Storybound	Primary	25,000
19	Zoo Zoo Zoo	Primary	24,700
20	After School Specials	Intermediate	24,200

Source: John A. Riccobono. *Availability, Use, and Support of Instructional Media, 1982–83. Summary Final Report of the School Utilization Study.* Washington, D.C.: Corporation for Public Broadcasting, 1984.

TABLE 9.2 Most Frequently Broadcast Formal Postsecondary Series

Rank	Series	Number of Stations Carrying	Percent of Stations
1	Understanding Human Behavior	70	53
2	Focus on Society	60	46
3	Personal Finance and Money Management	48	37
4	It's Everybody's Business	47	36
5	Making It Count	36	27
6	Contemporary Health Issues	36	27
7	American Government Survey	33	25
8	America: The Second Century	32	24
9	Art of Being Human	31	24
10	Oceanus	30	23
11	Growing Years	27	21
12	American Story	26	20
13	Business of Management	23	18
14	Writer's Workshop	18	14
15	Voyage	17	13

Source: Public Television Licensees' Educational Services, 1982–83. Washington, D.C.: Corporation for Public Broadcasting, 1984.

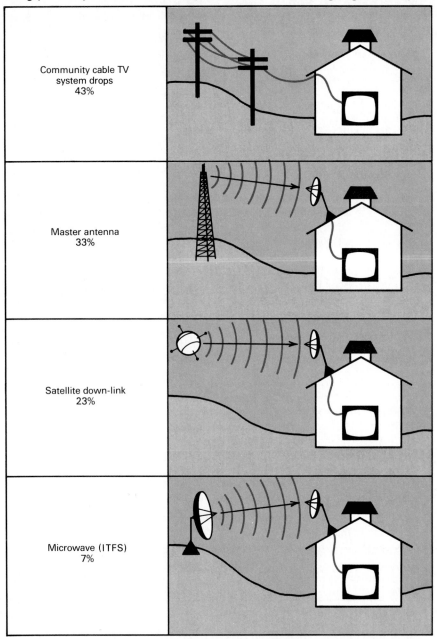

Community cable TV system drops 43%

Master antenna 33%

Satellite down-link 23%

Microwave (ITFS) 7%

Source: Instructional Technology in Higher Education: A National Study of the Educational Uses of Telecommunications Technology in American Colleges and Universities. Washington, D.C.: Corporation for Public Broadcasting, 1986.

CCTV system. Campus-wide and school-district-wide interconnections are also possible. In some areas, South Carolina and Indiana for example, one finds campus and district centers connected by state-wide CCTV linkages forming networks of impressive scope. For special purposes, transcontinental telephone lines can be leased to set up CCTV hookups of national scope. A common example is the showing of championship boxing matches projected on a large screen in theaters.

One of the principal advantages of CCTV is that such systems, because they do not operate through the airwaves controlled by government agencies, can be set up freely by anyone who has the money to do so. Although the cost tends to increase with the size of the coverage area (unlike through-the-air delivery systems), the freedom, privacy, and multi-channel capability of CCTV make it an attractive option for some educational purposes.

Because cost increases as geographic coverage increases, CCTV is not widely used in large school districts. It has, however, become the leading delivery system for ITV on college and university campuses.

Cable Television

The cable concept of television program delivery was first applied commercially in the 1950s in isolated towns where, due to interference from a mountain overshadowing the town, people were unable to receive a viewable signal from the nearest TV station. Local businessmen developed the idea of building a master antenna atop the mountain. There the weak signals were amplified and fed into a coaxial cable that ran down the mountain into the town. By paying an installation charge and a monthly subscription fee, a customer could have his or her home connected to the cable. This idea of having a single tall antenna to serve a whole community gave the process the name *community antenna television,* or CATV, now more commonly known as cable television.

Most CATV systems in operation today still basically resemble the original master antenna model, in which broadcast television signals are captured by a favorably situated high-mast antenna (see Figure 9.9). The signals are amplified and delivered to the head-end of the system, where they are processed, fed into a trunk line, and further amplified. The signals then proceed along feeder lines and eventually to smaller drop lines that enter individual homes and other buildings. The signal-carrying cables are installed underground in some systems (especially in congested urban areas), but ordinarily they are strung out along telephone poles, with a fee paid

▲ *Figure 9.8*
At all educational levels, student learning from television is heavily dependent on how the instructor *uses* the material.

Typical cable television distribution system

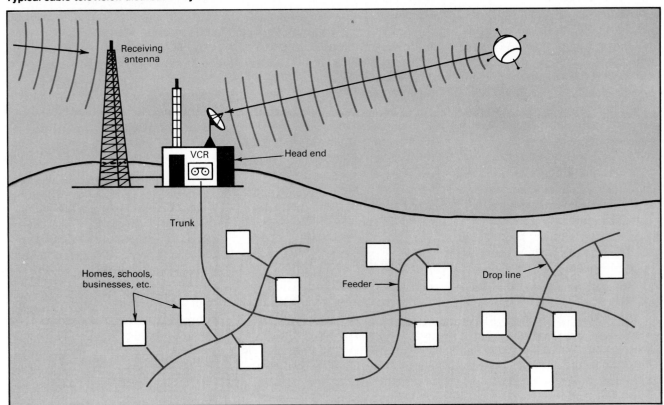

Receiving antenna

VCR

Head end

Trunk

Homes, schools, businesses, etc.

Feeder →

Drop line

▲ *Figure 9.9*

to the telephone company for this use of its property.

The growth of cable television has been slowed by the need to obtain legal rights to establish a system in each municipality and by the sheer expense of installing all the cable required to reach every home in the coverage area. Nevertheless, by 1988 over 60 percent of the households in the United States were within reach of a cable TV system, and about 50 percent of all homes were subscribers. The cable subscriber, besides getting a strong, clear video image on the screen, has access to more channels than are readily available over the air. Some of these channels are reserved for use by community groups; others are devoted to sports, music videos, special movies, news, weather, medical programs, and other specialized interests.

Innovative Educational Applications of CATV.
Thousands of educational institutions are now plugged into CATV systems, often without charge from the local cable operator. In many cases, schools and colleges are operating public access channels for their own institutional and/or instructional purposes.

The availability of multiple channels facilitates a number of special services: (1) transmission of several programs simultaneously and repetition of programs at different hours for more flexible matching with classroom schedules; (2) "narrowcasting"—the aiming of specialized programs at small subgroups, for example, those speaking foreign languages or having sight or hearing impairment; (3) retrieval of remotely stored libraries of video materials, allowing teachers—or individual students—access to materials on demand without the

logistic struggle often associated with instructional media use.

The Future. Actually, the number of channels available on many cable systems is still small—the average system supplying less than a dozen channels. Recent developments, however (such as fiber-optics as a replacement for coaxial cable and improvements in the system's other hardware components), foreshadow the development of CATV systems capable of supporting scores, even hundreds, of transmission channels.

But what has caused futurists among educators really to sit up and take notice is the characteristic of CATV that most distinguishes it from other television delivery systems: its ability to transmit signals not only from sender to receiver but also from the receiver back to sender. Although most cable systems today send signals only "downstream" to the home or school, the technology is available to permit return communications "upstream" back to the sender. These return signals can take the form of simple yes/no digital communications, audio signals alone, or full television images with accompanying sound. Each of these feedback possibilities evokes exciting prospects for converting ITV into a two-way, interactive medium of instructional communication.

Microwave Transmission

The only television delivery system in the United States set up exclusively for educational purposes is also the least well known. In 1963 the Federal Communications Commission established the *Instructional Television Fixed Service* (ITFS), setting aside channels in the microwave

band (2500–2690 MHz) for instructional use by educational institutions. Later rule changes allowed ITFS operators to expand into audio and hard-copy transmission and into two-way television systems.

The ITFS system has one major technical limitation: signals broadcast at these high microwave frequencies travel in a line-of-sight pattern. Consequently, coverage of ITFS is limited to areas in direct sightline of the transmission tower.

Nevertheless, this coverage is sufficient in many educational situations. Coverage can generally extend over areas about the size of a large school district, and, unlike closed-circuit television, no wiring is required for connection among classrooms. Like cable, ITFS allows transmission on multiple channels; the average licensee operates about six channels. This greatly expands the broadcasting possibilities in a given locale beyond what would exist merely with VHF and UHF outlets. Because the system operates on frequencies above those that can be received on ordinary sets without a converter, it offers a higher degree of audience selectivity and programming privacy than regular broadcasts. Also, cost of equipment and operation is lower than for regular broadcast television.

At the present time ITFS delivers less of the total ITV used in classrooms than any of the other delivery systems discussed here, but it has been growing slowly over the years. There are now over 100 licensees operating some 600 microwave channels, but geographic distribution is uneven. Twenty-three states and the metropolitan area of Washington, D.C., have no ITFS systems at all. On the other hand, in Milwaukee and Los Angeles, most of the

available ITFS channels are already being used by educational institutions. Most of the area channels in the New York and San Francisco area are also in use—not, however, by the city public school districts, but by suburban and parochial schools.

Catholic school systems, having largely missed out on the earlier allocation of VHF and UHF channels for educational purposes, have become prominent users of ITFS. The Catholic schools in New York City and Brooklyn operate some twenty-three channels; a newer system in Chicago has ten channels. Other sizable Catholic operations are centered in Milwaukee, San Francisco, Boston, and Miami.

Within higher education, ITFS is used predominantly for graduate and professional school extension purposes. Typical use connects engineering or medical schools (often with two-way links) with professionals out in the field who require continuing education updating. Some of the most sophisticated technical systems in all of ITV are found within this sector.

In short, ITFS is a delivery system with considerable potential. It may well come to play a more prominent role in the future as the available frequencies in the VHF and UHF bands become saturated and educators seek additional channels for distributing video materials.

Satellites

Communication satellites now carry most international telephone calls as well as most network television transmissions. Virtually all of today's satellites are placed in a *geosynchronous* orbit—an orbit synchronized with the speed of the earth's own rotation. By keeping pace with the spin of the earth, they appear to remain motionless above the same spot on the ground. Geosynchronous satellites operate as transmitting stations on top of an imaginary tower so tall (23,000 miles high) that they can "see" nearly half of the earth's surface at one time. Theoretically, three properly placed geosynchronous

Direct broadcast satellite reception

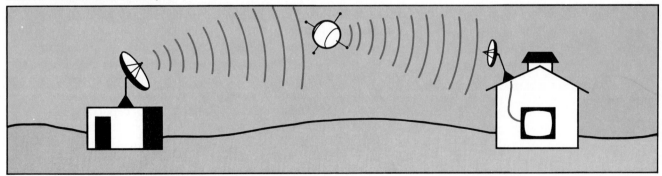

▲ *Figure 9.10*

satellites could cover the entire globe. However, because of the immense and growing amount of communications traffic, there are usually dozens of satellites in operation at any given time.

The trend in recent years has been to design larger, more complicated satellites and to put more transmission power up in the satellites. The great advantage of doing so is that reception equipment on the ground can be smaller and less complicated. For example, Telstar, launched in 1962, required an earth receiver with an eighty-five-foot dish. In 1974, the ATS-6 satellite, weighing a ton and a half itself, needed a dish only nine feet in diameter on the ground. Today's satellites permit transmission direct to home dish receivers only three feet across.

Direct Home/School Reception.

The technology for direct reception of satellite signals has become so simple and inexpensive that businesses, private individuals, and schools have been setting up their own dish antennas to tap directly into the non-stop stream of TV programming that is constantly being relayed to and from the great flock of "birds" that circle overhead. As costs have dropped, direct satellite reception at the home, school, and workplace has become an increasingly realistic alternative delivery system.

CLOSE-UP:
Satellite TV Network Solves Rural School Problem

Moran Independent School District in West Texas encompasses a vast area of 325 square miles. But its total school population is only 101 students, kindergarten through high school. Like other rural, isolated school districts, Moran found it difficult to attract teachers, especially specialists in subjects such as math, science, and foreign languages, in which teachers are scarce to begin with. Students faced an educationally impoverished future.

The answer came in the unconventional form of satellite television, specifically a network called TI-IN. Begun in 1985, TI-IN is a privately owned satellite network devoted exclusively to transmitting educational materials. For about $20,000 Moran was able to join the TI-IN network, receiving a satellite dish, reception device, TV monitor, videocassette recorder, and printer.

TI-IN classes are transmitted from San Antonio; the high school courses in linear algebra, physics, computer science, and French are taught by master teachers. They distribute handouts, tests, and homework assignments by means of the printer. Students in the receiving classes can interact with the teacher or with students at other sites by means of a cordless telephone in each classroom. An adult volunteer monitors the satellite classes.

The TI-IN system, which now reaches schools in twenty-five states, is also used after hours for staff development and administrative teleconferencing.

The satellite system has been a boon to educators and to taxpayers, who support the education system, but students love it too. They're having a chance to take courses that will enable some of them to go on to college, to interact with guest speakers, and even to meet students in other schools, expanding their social circle far beyond the old boundaries of their little towns.

Source: Sandra Gudat. "Satellite Network Helps Keep Rural Schools Open." *Phi Delta Kappan* (March 1988), pp. 533–534.

Satellite Networks. Faced with the dilemma of increasing demand for educational services and dwindling resources, several states operate instructional TV networks linked by satellite. Such special-purpose networks are especially common in states with many rural schools. Through satellite transmission they can provide high-quality, low-cost instruction to widely dispersed rural schools. One example is the TI-IN Network, a private, for-profit enterprise centered in Texas. Originally established in Texas to help small schools meet upgraded graduation requirements in for-

eign language and computer science, TI-IN now serves over 200 schools throughout the country. It offers high school classes in art and business as well as foreign language and computer science, broadcasting throughout the day on three channels. Programs are broadcast live via satellite; students can interact with the TV teacher by means of a cordless

▶ *Figure 9.11*
Satellite-reception dishes bring satellite signals directly into homes, hotels, schools, businesses—anywhere education or training is needed.

CLOSE-UP:
The University without a Campus

In the fast-paced world of high technology a corporation's knowledge base can become obsolete overnight. How can a nation keep its engineering talent updated? In the United States, instructional television lessons delivered by satellite are the answer. The National Technological University was formed in 1984 through the collaboration of more than a dozen large corporations, two dozen universities, and the federal government. It now operates as a private, nonprofit university offering its own master's degrees in computer engineering, manufacturing systems, and other fields.

The students of National Technological University (NTU) are engineers employed at cooperating businesses and government agencies. Each cooperating organization maintains classrooms and a satellite downlink. The employee students choose from among dozens of courses, which are broadcast twenty hours a day, six days a week on two channels. Most of these classes are videotaped and broadcast one-way via satellite, but about 30 percent of the classes are live and interactive with two-way audio feedback from the receiving sites.

Through NTU engineers can stay current in their fields and advance toward a master's degree without leaving their jobs or commuting long distances. Because the NTU involves many of the leading engineering universities in the nation, students have access to the top specialists in their fields of study.

NTU demonstrates vividly how technology can be harnessed to promote productivity.

Source: National Technological University, P.O. Box 700, Fort Collins, Colorado 80522.

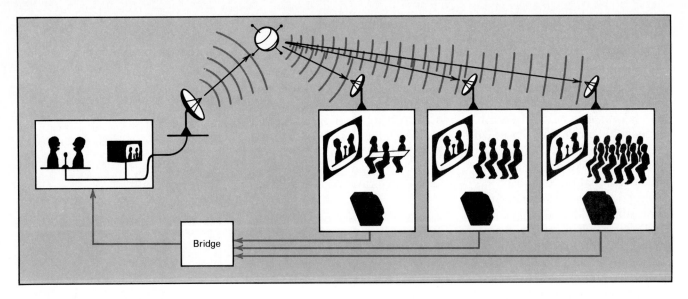

▲ *Figure 9.12*
A generalized teleconference system. Voice-only or voice-plus-picture may be sent out to receive sites; viewers respond by telephone, with calls from different sites screened at the "bridge."

telephone located in each receiving classroom.

TELECONFERENCE SYSTEMS

AFTER years of slow growth, teleconferencing has become one of the fastest-growing segments of the telecommunications industry as more and more corporate and educational institutions embrace the teleconference as an efficient means of informing and educating their constituents. Basically, a *teleconference* is *any live point-to-point electronically delivered two-way conversation, especially when involving groups at separate locations.* A teleconference resembles an ordinary telephone conference call except that there is usually a group of people gathered at either the sending site, the receiving site, or both. A major speaker may be shown on video, making it a videoconference, as discussed in a subsequent section. Other features, such as graphics or two-way video, may also be blended into the mix. The configuration depends on the purpose of the session and the expense that may be justified.

Types

The most common type of teleconference is the *audioconference,* which involves *transmission of voices only;* these are amplified at each end by a speaker system. By being limited to voices only, it can usually be handled over regular telephone lines rather than needing a satellite. Because it's the most cost-effective type, the great majority of all teleconferences are of this type. A typical instructional application would be using an audioconference to enable a class of students to listen to a famous author discuss his work; they would also be able to hold a conversation with the author and with students in any other classes that might be interconnected.

An *audiographic conference* employs *voice plus graphic display capability.* The most frequently used graphic supplement is a facsimile machine, which transmits electronically and reproduces at remote locations anything that can be printed on paper. Electronic blackboards and electronic tablets are other graphics options. The additional cost of such options is justified in cases, for example in engineering education, in which mathematical formulas and visual diagrams are critical to understanding.

In a *videoconference* a *television-type picture is transmitted and displayed along with the audio message.* The most common format is to send out a full motion video presentation, for example a featured speaker, and to receive back voice only from the reception sites, for example questions to the speaker. If full motion is not necessary to get the point across, "freeze-frame" video—consisting of single frames of the presentation—can

Ohio State University has been experimenting with telephone conversations as a supplement to self-paced foreign language courses. The program allows students from anywhere in the United States to call a toll-free number during specified hours throughout the week to talk, listen, and learn by means of conversations with a live instructor. The students are mainly college graduates enrolled on a noncredit basis; they have ranged in age from nine to sixty-seven. The core of their study is a self-instructional package consisting of textbooks and cassette tapes. To move on from one unit to the next they must pass tests administered live at local participating colleges.

The originator of the project was Leon Twarog, a professor of Slavic languages. The first languages tested were Russian, Polish, and Czech; but experiments with Arabic, Chinese, Japanese, Spanish, and French have also proven successful. The telephone conversations help overcome the feelings of isolation and decreasing motivation that often afflict distance education students.

be transmitted at much less expense.

How a Teleconference Works

Let's look at a videoconference with one-way video and two-way audio as an example of how a teleconference setup might work. At the origination site would be a studio with TV camera and microphone plus a telephone switchboard to receive incoming calls and a speaker system to amplify those voices. The studio could be a built-in locally owned facility or a modular portable unit rented for the occasion.

The voice and picture of the instructor in the studio would be sent up to a satellite by means of an *uplink—a transmitter sending signals from earth to a satellite.* The distribution system, whether telephone line or satellite based, could be owned by the teleconference originator (a *dedicated network*) or it could be rented for

▲ *Figure 9.13*
Video-teleconference participants often view the program on projection TV, giving feedback to the speaker via telephone.

one-time use (an *ad hoc network*).

At the reception site would be a *downlink—a satellite dish with a decoder to receive the signals,* a display screen, such as a video projector, and a telephone to

allow voice communication back to the origination site.

Advantages

Teleconferences are being used by both educational institutions

▲ *Figure 9.14*
Teletraining is used widely by AT&T for corporate training and development.

and corporations for group meetings and for instruction. When used for instruction the process is often referred to as *teletraining.* Some features that make teletraining especially appropriate are

- Teacher shortage: providing expert instructors to remote schools or offices
- Standardization: offering uniform, quality-controlled instruction to learners scattered over many sites or over a large area
- Interactivity: allowing learners at multiple locations to interact with the instructor and with each other
- Immediacy: giving large numbers of learners simultaneous access to fresh and accurate information
- Convenience: providing inservice updating without leaving the workplace

Limitations

Teleconferencing, still a young technology, entails some limiting factors; among them are

- Cost: Although costs are falling, purchasing or renting the needed hardware and paying the hourly rates for satellite or telephone lines are still expensive.
- Complexity: The complexity of the equipment involved raises many possibilities for disruptive technical malfunctions.
- Unfamiliarity: True dialog among the participants is impeded by the unfamiliar, often intimidating, technology.
- The "slickness syndrome": The audience expectation of broadcast-quality presentations often leads to productions that impress but don't instruct.

Applications

A corporate example of teletraining is provided by Allstate Insurance Company, which maintains a dedicated two-way video network between its headquarters and twenty-eight regional offices. Their philosophy is that virtually anything that can be taught in a live classroom can be taught via videoconferencing. A facsimile system is used to transmit paper information between sites. Trainees can ask questions by pressing a button on the console in the reception site; all calls are queued up automatically and are answered in turn by the instructor.

Since 1982 the National University Teleconferencing Network (NUTN) has been offering teleconferences of nationwide scope to the several hundred colleges and universities that subscribe. Their programs tend to be one-time updates on topics of current interest, two of the most popular having been "Microcomputer Software" and "A Passion for Excellence." It is becoming a major source for continuing professional education.

The accompanying "Close-Up: Sharing Teachers Via Videoconferencing," illustrates a potential use of two-way instructional television at the secondary school level.

TELETEXT/VIDEOTEX

RECENT years have seen a proliferation of methods for inputting, storing, and transmitting text and graphic information. Computers can store such information in digital form, and there are many channels for transmitting the data to users—telephone wire, cable, broadcasting, microwave, satellites, and so on. Each different combination of storage and transmission media may acquire a different name, either a generic one or a trade name. One cluster of such services can be referred to under the generic names of teletext and videotex.

Teletext refers to the *one-way broadcasting of text and graphic information for display on a modified television set.* The user, at home, office, or school, simply selects a given channel in order to view a "page" of information such as a weather forecast, stock market data, TV program listings,

CLOSE-UP:
Sharing Teachers Via Videoconferencing

How can small rural schools offer advanced courses in mathematics and foreign languages when no single school has a large enough enrollment to justify its own teacher? Four school districts in Carroll County, Illinois, have been experimenting with a simplified two-way videoconferencing system as an answer to this question. Each participating school has set up one classroom as a teleconference room, equipped with cameras, microphones, video recorder, monitors, and special effects generator/switcher. Classes are taught live at the school in which there is a qualified teacher; students in any of the other three schools may participate.

Students in the receiving schools watch and listen to the class. They can also be heard and seen by activating the camera and microphone in their own classroom. A camera mounted on top of the teacher's desk gives close-up views of visual materials.

Lessons can be videotaped for review by absent students. They can also be videotaped in advance when the instructor must be absent during usual class times.

Source: Peter C. West, Rhonda S. Robinson, and Keith Collins. "A Teaching and Telecommunications Partnership." *Educational Leadership* (March 1986), pp. 54–55.

How To . . . ORGANIZE AND CONDUCT SUCCESSFUL TELETRAINING

At the origination end:

- Be clear about audience needs and the purpose of the program.
- Plan and organize more intensively than you would for face-to-face training.
- Promote the session with attractive, humanized mailers and personal contacts with local coordinators.
- Provide printed supporting materials: points to react to, pre- and postviewing assignments.
- Stimulate active participation by setting up reaction panels, arranging buzz groups, and "planting" starter questions.
- Keep the presentation itself informal, personal, and narrowly focused; punctuate it with opportunities for questions or local discussions.

At the reception end:

- Arrange the classroom for comfort, easy viewing, and easy discussion among participants.
- If the session is a long one, plan for refreshment breaks or meals to break up the day.
- Check the setup the day before; then arrive early on the designated day and check again; monitor equipment functioning throughout the session itself.
- Introduce the session by familiarizing participants with the equipment, outlining objectives clearly, and explaining procedural details, especially the ground rules for questions or other feedback.
- Carry out postviewing activities, such as a local panel discussion or discussion groups.
- Collect evaluations; follow up on suggestions made or on any questions left unanswered.

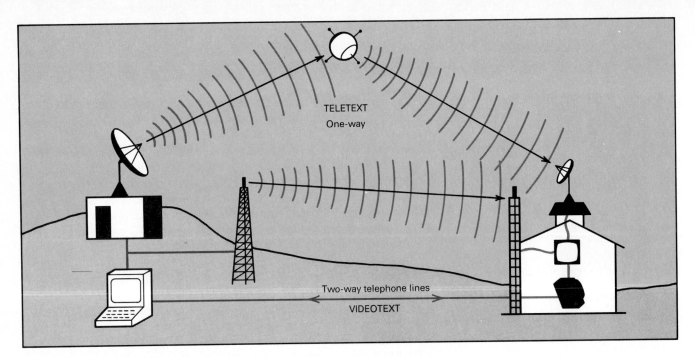

▲ *Figure 9.15*
A generalized teletext/videotex distribution system

▲ *Figure 9.16*
The heart of a teletext/videotex terminal is a television set.

local movie guide, or the like. An important distinction here is that the user does *not* communicate directly with the central computer in which the information is stored.

In *videotex* there is *two-way communication, usually through telephone lines, between a computer database and the user's terminal (typically a modified television set).* In this case the user can use a keypad to send a signal back to the originating computer, select items from a menu, and control the pace and sequence of

presentation of the desired text and graphics. Videotex services allow users to search databases and even to work through computer-assisted instruction lessons—all through a television set that might be only slightly modified from the ordinary home configuration.

Teletext/videotex services have developed more rapidly in Europe, Japan, Canada, and Australia than in the United States primarily because in those countries the central government has actively promoted their development. Promoting a unified national policy on telecommunications is more manageable when the broadcasting, telephone, and other communication services are owned and operated by the government. In France, for example, teletext has been promoted by means of free distribution of the necessary hardware as part of normal telephone service. In some regions the printed telephone directory has been replaced by a teletext system, requiring users to adapt to the newer technology for looking up a needed phone number.

Limitations

The principal limitation to videotex is the high cost of creating a network and linking the computers that are involved. In countries or regions where government or private enterprise has established the basic telecommunications network, start-up and maintenance costs for a school would be moderate, particularly if the school already has a computer system in place. In general though, videotex has grown slowly in the United States because of the high investment costs for the information provider, the need for users to invest in computers or decoders, relatively high user fees, limited services available, and low public awareness.

Applications

The major educational applications of videotex to date have been as an information source, a delivery medium, and as a computer-assisted instruction medium. As an information source, videotex can be used in the classroom to give students online access to information databases, library catalogs, newspaper articles, and job placement services. The novelty of using the new technology typically causes students to be much more enthusiastic about using such systems than conventional search tools.

In southern Australia the national videotex system, Viatel, has been used to deliver self-instructional learning packages to elementary school students living in isolated areas and receiving home education. In this case the text and graphic data are sent out by high-speed transmission, stored in the student's home microcomputer terminal, and used by the student, with responses transmitted back to the origination point. This use demonstrates the possibility of distributing instructional materials from central libraries through public communication channels, such as the telephone system.

Instructional applications are still mostly experimental. In Canada, for example, there is a nationally standardized videotex service, known as NAPLPS. At the University of Guelph this system was used to provide testing and feedback of students who were taking courses in the form of the Personalized System of Instruction (discussed in Chapter 11). In PSI courses students work individually and take frequent tests over each unit of the course. Ordinarily, a trained proctor sits down with each student to administer and review each test. Through Guelph's videotex system students were able to take their tests and receive personalized feedback by means of a central computer database, thereby reducing the amount of labor needed to operate the courses.

Experience has demonstrated that teletext/videotex services do work technologically, and there are legitimate instructional applications. Whether it makes sense to use this capability depends on the economics of a given situation. Does the necessary sending and receiving hardware already exist? Is the communication network—telephone or broadcasting system—already set up? What are the costs of competing methods of doing the same job, such as mailing printed material or sending out computer software in the form of disks? In cases where the costs favor electronic transmission, teletext and videotex can be feasible means of providing computer-assisted instruction, special services for homebound students, supplemental materials to accompany instructional TV programs, do-it-yourself instructions, and tutorial programs for literacy and job retraining.

References

Print References

Telecommunications

Brush, Judith M., and Brush, Douglas. *Private Television Communications: New Directions.* (Cold Spring, N.Y.: HI Press of Cold Spring, 1986).

Eilber, Carol B. *Cable Television: What Educators Need to Know.* (Kettering, Ohio: National Federation of Local Cable Programmers, 1981).

Hudspeth, Delayne, and Brey, Ronald. *Instructional Telecommunications.* (Westport, Conn.: Greenwood Press, Praeger, 1985).

Instructional Technology in Higher Education. Washington, D.C.: Corporation for Public Broadcasting, 1986.

Jones, Maxine H. *See, Hear, Interact: Beginning Developments in Two-Way Television.* (Metuchen, N.J.: Scarecrow Press, 1984).

Jordahl, Gregory. "The Television Classroom." *E-ITV* (October 1987), pp. 38–41.

Sang, Herb A. "T.V., Telephones, and Teachers Bring Homework Help to Kids." *Executive Educator* (November 1986), pp. 25–26.

Sokoloff, Michele, and Muskat, Linda. "Cable in the Classroom." *Media and Methods* (April 1983), pp. 10–15.

Stern, Claire M. "Teaching the Distance Learner Using New Technology." *Journal of Educational Technology Systems* 15, no. 4 (1986–1987), pp. 407–419.

Wacker, Katherine A., et al. "The Classroom . . . and the Library . . . That Cover Seven Counties." *Community and Junior College Libraries* (Summer 1985), pp. 23–32.

Wall, Milan. "Technological Options for Rural Schools." *Educational Leadership* (March 1986), pp. 50–52.

Wood, Donald N., and Wylie, Donald G. *Educational Telecommunications.* (Belmont, Calif.: Wadsworth, 1977).

Teleconferencing

Bell, Arthur H., and Housel, Tom. "Teleconferencing Comes of Age—Again." *T.H.E. Journal* (May 1986), pp. 71–73.

Dallmann, Christa A. "Teletraining in a Corporate Environment: Implementing Training through Teleconferencing Technology." *Media and Adult Learning* (Fall 1986), pp. 3–5.

Eastman, Susan Tyler. "Teleconferencing in Education and Business." *Feedback* (Summer 1985), pp. 8–11.

Hilton, Jack, and Jacobi, Peter. *Straight Talk about Video Teleconferencing.* (New York: Prentice Hall, 1986).

Knapp, Linda Roehrig. "Teleconferencing: A New Way of Communicating for Teachers and Kids." *Classroom Computer Learning* (March 1987), pp. 37–41.

Parker, Lorne A. *Teletraining Means Business.* (Madison, Wis.: Center for Interactive Programs, University of Wisconsin, 1984).

———, and Olgren, Christine H., eds. *Teleconferencing and Electronic Communications V.* (Madison, Wis.: Center for Interactive Programs, University of Wisconsin, 1986).

Robertson, Bill. "Audio Teleconferencing: Low-Cost Technology for External Studies Networking." *Distance Education* (March 1987), pp. 121–130.

Rosetti, Daniel K., and Surynt, Theodore J. "Video Teleconferencing and Performance." *Journal of Business Communication* (Fall 1985), pp. 25–31.

Wilson, Virginia S., et al. "Audio Teleconferencing as a Teaching Technique." *Social Education* (February 1986), pp. 90–92.

Winn, William, et al. "The Design and Application of a Distance Education System Using Teleconferencing and Computer Graphics." *Educational Technology* (January 1986), pp. 19–23.

Zemke, Ron. "The Rediscovery of Video Teleconferencing." *Training* (September 1986), pp. 28–34.

Teletext/Videotex

Carey, J. *Electronic Text and Higher Education: A Summary of Research Findings and Field Experiences.* (New York: Greystone Communications, 1984). ERIC Document No. ED 257 446.

Hammond, Morrison F. "The Use of Telecommunications in Australian Education." *T.H.E. Journal* (April 1986), pp. 74–76.

Hurly, Paul; Laucht, Matthias; and Hlynka, Denis. *The Videotex and Teletext Handbook.* (New York: Harper & Row, 1985).

Kerr, Stephen T. "Videotex and Education: Current Developments in Screen Design, Data Structure, and Access Control." *Machine-Mediated Learning* (1985), pp. 217–254.

Moore, George A. B. "The Development of VITAL: A Microcomputer-Based Videotex Teaching and Learning System for Education." *Canadian Journal of Educational Communications* 15, no. 2 (Spring 1986), pp. 105–116.

Tydeman, John, et al. *Teletext and Videotex in the United States.* (New York: McGraw-Hill, 1982).

Audiovisual References

Educational Communication via Satellite. Washington, D.C.: National Aeronautics and Space Administration, 1980. 16-mm film series.

Radio: The Interactive Teacher. Washington, D.C.: Academy for Educational Development, 1985. 16-mm film, $\frac{3}{4}$-inch videocassette, or $\frac{1}{2}$-inch videocassette. Available in English, French, and Spanish.

Organizations

Agency for Instructional Technology (AIT)
P.O. Box A
Bloomington, Indiana 47402-0120

AIT produces television programs and computer courseware as the coordinating agency of a consortium that includes most of the United States and the Canadian provinces. It serves as a national distribution center also. It publishes a newsletter and an annual catalog listing dozens of series incorporating several hundred separate programs. Emphasis is on the elementary/secondary levels.

Association for Educational Communications and Technology (AECT)
1126 Sixteenth Street, N.W.
Washington, DC 20036

AECT holds conferences, publishes journals and books related to instructional uses of media including TV, and represents the educational communication/technology profession. Its Division of Telecommunications provides a home for members who work in instructional TV and radio.

Corporation for Public Broadcasting (CPB)
1111 Sixteenth Street, N.W.
Washington, DC 20036

CPB is a nonprofit, private corporation established and funded in part by the federal government. It performs a broad coordinating function for the nation's public radio and television stations and supports the interests of public broadcasting in general. CPB carries out research on educational applications of television and coordinates the Annenberg Project, aimed at providing programming for higher education.

International Consortium for Telecommunications in Learning (IUC)
Center of Adult Education
Adelphi Road at University Blvd.
College Park, Maryland 20742

A cooperative organization consisting of some twenty colleges and universities and a corresponding number of public television stations in the United States and Canada. It aims to provide bachelor's level coursework to adults unable to enroll in full-time on-campus programs. IUC develops its own courses and adapts British Open University courses. Each member institution grants its own degrees.

International Television Association (ITVA)
6311 North O'Connor Road, Suite 110
Irving, Texas 75039

ITVA is an organization of non-broadcast television professionals in eight countries, primarily North America. It supports the use of television in the private sector—training, communications, and public relations—and sponsors regional and national conferences and an awards program.

Action for Children's Television
46 Austin Street
Newtonville, Massachusetts 02160

Annenberg/CPB Project
1111 Sixteenth Street, N.W.
Washington, DC 20036

Association for Media and Technology in Education in Canada (AMTEC)
500 Victoria Road North
Guelph, Ontario N1E 6K2

Bicultural Children's Television (BCTV)
155 Callan Avenue, Suite B
San Leandro, California 94577

Cable Television Information Center
1800 Kent Street, Suite 1007
Arlington, Virginia 22209

Children's Television Workshop
1 Lincoln Plaza
New York, New York 10023

Public Service Satellite Consortium (PSSC)
1660 L Street, N.W., Suite 907
Washington, DC 20036

Western Educational Society for Telecommunication (WEST)
c/o Station KAET
Arizona State University
Tempe, Arizona 85281

Possible Projects

9-A. Investigate the use of radio for instructional purposes in a local school or college. Check with your local public radio station to see if it supports any specifically instructional activities. Prepare a short written report (500–750 words) or audiocassette report (about five minutes).

9-B. Interview a teacher who regularly utilizes broadcast television programs in the classroom. Prepare a brief written or recorded report covering the objectives addressed, utilization techniques used, and problems encountered.

9-C. Invent a new telecommunications service by putting together an original (as far as you know) combination of features. An example might be an international pen-pals club using facsimile machines interconnected via satellite. Your service need not be economically practical, but it should serve some describable purpose.

9-D. Generate a list of interesting uses for teleconferencing in a course that you are currently enrolled in. Who might your class communicate with? For what purposes?

9-E. Prepare an abstract of a report of a research or demonstration project related to instructional telecommunications, for example, two schools sharing one teacher by means of one-way television and two-way telephone.

10 Mediaware and Media Setups

Objectives

After studying this chapter, you should be able to:

1. Operate each of the following pieces of equipment: cassette tape recorder, record player, overhead projector, slide projector, filmstrip projector, opaque projector, 16-mm film projector, and videotape recorder.

2. Indicate the basic care and maintenance procedures that ought to be observed with the pieces of equipment listed in objective 1.

3. Identify a possible remedy when given a potential problem with any of the pieces of equipment listed in objective 1.

4. Describe the safety precaution about recharging batteries.

5. Describe the consequences of using an improper stylus with a phonograph record.

6. Describe four general factors that should be taken into consideration when using audio equipment for group instruction. Your description should include volume and tone setting, speaker placement, type and size of speaker, and echo/feedback.

7. Relate speaker size to audience size.

8. Describe how to overcome the problem of audio feedback.

9. Identify and discuss the five variables that affect visual projection and describe how they would be applied in an example situation.

10. State and apply a general rule (the "2-by-6 rule") for matching screen dimensions and audience seating.

11. List the distinguishing characteristics of the four major types of screen surface and apply these variables to specific projection situations.

12. State and apply a general rule for determining the height of screen placement.

13. Name three types of projection lamps and identify special characteristics of each.

14. Describe the procedures for replacement of lamps, including types of lamps and handling procedures.

15. Relate lens focal length to image size.

16. Discuss four general features of projection carts and describe examples of each.

17. Demonstrate how to move an equipment cart safely.

18. Describe the "keystone effect" and state two ways to correct it.

19. Relate projector location to image size and shape.

20. Distinguish between the 1000 hertz system for slide synchronization and the 50 hertz system for filmstrip synchronization in terms of audiotape format and type of equipment needed.

21. Describe the "ideal" physical arrangements for class viewing of television. Your description must include the factors of seating, monitor placement, lighting, and volume with the minimum and maximum distances and angles.

Lexicon
stylus
feedback
2-by-6 rule
focal length
keystone effect
hertz (HZ)
automatic programmer

M OST media users are not— and do not expect to become—electronic wizards, but they do want to be able to use audiovisual media effectively. The most fundamental element of effective media use is simply keeping the equipment—the mediaware—running and being ready to cope with the snags that always seem to occur at the most inopportune times.

This chapter contains guidelines for the setup of projection equipment, screens, and speakers and then provides step-by-step operating procedures for the major types of mediaware. Included with each item are hints for the proper care of your mediaware and a troubleshooting checklist to help you cope with the most commonly occurring malfunctions.

Be aware that the equipment operation guides are not intended to be read straight through. They are meant to be *referred to* while you practice with actual AV equipment. Also, the operating instructions in the guides are necessarily somewhat general because they must cover a range of equipment models. If your own mediaware differs markedly from the descriptions given here, refer to the operating instructions provided by the manufacturer.

If you have the responsibility for recommending or actually purchasing mediaware, you should become familiar with *The Equipment Directory of Audio-Visual, Computer and Video Products* issued annually by the International Communications Industries Association (ICIA), and with the equipment evaluations published by the EPIE (Educational Products Information Exchange) Institute. These resources are described in the references section at the end of this chapter.

TAPE RECORDERS

T HE part of a tape recorder needing most frequent attention is the record/playback head. To get good-quality recording or playback, the tape must make full

---

How To . . . OPERATE A CASSETTE RECORDER

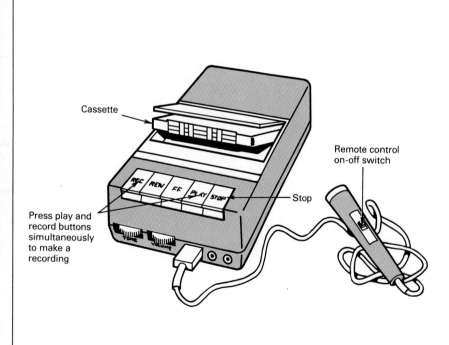

Cassette

Remote control on-off switch

Stop

Press play and record buttons simultaneously to make a recording

Set up
- Connect power cord to AC outlet.
- Press "stop" key.
- Insert cassette (full reel on left side).

Operate
- Press "play" key.
- Press "stop" key.

Record
- Connect microphone to recorder.
- Press "play" and "record" keys simultaneously.
- Record your voice.
- Rewind tape to starting point by pressing "rewind" key.
- Play tape.

Disassemble
- Rewind tape.
- Remove cassette.
- Restore to storage conformation.

---

contact with the record/playback head. Each time the tape passes across the head, small bits of debris are deposited on it. Eventually, this debris will interfere with proper contact between the tape and the head. Therefore, the record/playback head should be cleaned regularly. Most manufacturers recommend cleaning after five to ten hours of use. Of course, it should be done more frequently when the machine is used in dusty areas, such as in a machine shop, close to a woodworking area, or near a chalkboard.

For cleaning tape-recorder heads, you should use special head-cleaning fluid (available at most stores selling tape recorders or from audiovisual suppliers). Apply with a cotton swab. Do not use carbon tetrachloride, which can damage the heads, or alcohol, which can leave a residue of its

own on the head. Alcohol can also damage tapes if they are played immediately after cleaning. In addition, over a period of time, carbon tetrachloride and alcohol can cause rubber parts of the pressure rollers to deteriorate.

The entire tape path should be inspected for dirt or damage that might interfere with proper tape operation. Most importantly, follow the recommended maintenance procedures in the manual that accompanies the recorder. Do not oil any tape recorder unless the manufacturer specifically recommends doing so. Most tape recorders are designed so that they do not need lubrication.

Audio equipment in general is subject to buildup of carbon or other contaminants on the contacts inside the volume and tone controls. This buildup causes an annoying scratching sound whenever the control knob is turned.

Usually the problem can be resolved quickly and easily by spraying "tuner cleaner" (available at hi-fi and electronics supply stores) directly onto the shaft of the control. More stubborn fouling of the contacts might require some disassembly of equipment to get the spray closer to the source of the trouble.

BATTERY TIPS

Because of advances in lightweight motor design and solid state electronics, many types of equipment—for example, audiocassette recorders, portable video recorders, and cameras—operate on batteries. The advantages of portability, ease of handling, and freedom from extension cords have spurred sales of battery-operated equipment. But you need to be aware that batter-

Cassette Recorder Troubleshooting

Problem	Possible Remedy
Tape comes out of cassette and snarls around the capstan of recorder	1. Very thin tape, as found in longer-length cassettes (e.g., C-120) is especially prone to do this. Convert to shorter length (thicker) tapes. 2. The plastic hub of the take-up reel may be rubbing against the cassette. Try rotating the hub with a pencil to see if you can free it. 3. Mechanical problem: Take-up spindle is not pulling hard enough because of faulty clutch or belt. Have cassette repaired by qualified specialist.
"Record" button on cassette will not stay down	The "accidental erasure" tab on the back of the cassette has been broken out. Place tape over the gap left by the missing tab if you want to record something new on the cassette.
Hiss in background	Demagnetize the heads
No high frequencies	Head out of alignment or worn
Lack of high frequencies	Heads not aligned properly; heads worn. Have heads checked.
Low playback volume	Heads dirty; clean with head-cleaning fluid.

▲ *Figure 10.1*
A battery charger can be a money saver—but charge *only* rechargeable batteries.

ies and battery-operated equipment need special attention. Batteries should be removed from seldom-used equipment to prevent possible damage from leakage and corrosion. Batteries should also be removed from equipment if there is any danger of freezing or overheating.

If you operate a piece of equipment frequently, you may want to consider using rechargeable batteries for long-term savings. Rechargeable batteries are more expensive, but the extra cost can be more than recovered. However, *never* recharge batteries that are not specifically made to be recharged. Nonrechargeable batteries may explode if placed in a recharging unit.*

RECORD PLAYERS

THE component of a record player (phonograph) that is most likely to cause problems for the user is the stylus ("needle") assembly. Fortunately, most of these problems can be recognized

---

* Ralph Whiting and Roberta Kuchta. *Safety in the Library Media Program: A Handbook.* Wisconsin Educational Media Association, Manitowoc, Wis. 1987. This booklet is a comprehensive guide to safe handling of audiovisual equipment.

and remedied by even the most "nonexpert" of people.

Phonograph records come in three basic types, classified according to the speed at which they revolve on the turntable (rpm = revolutions per minute). Each type has a different groove width:

78 rpm: The original standard type, no longer being produced; it has the widest grooves.

45 rpm: Has grooves about one-half the width of those on 78 rpm records, allowing more recording time per inch.

$33\frac{1}{3}$ rpm: Often referred to as "microgroove" because its grooves are narrower than those of 78 and 45 rpm records.

Each of these basic record types requires a stylus whose tip diameter exactly matches the width of the record's grooves. If the tip of the stylus is too narrow for the record, it will ride on the bottom of the groove instead of along its sides (where the signal is encoded), thereby picking up the signal poorly and possibly damaging the groove itself. If the stylus tip is too wide, it will ride too high in the groove, thereby failing to pick up recorded sounds properly, possibly skipping out of the grooves entirely, and causing excessive wear on the grooves. (See Figure 10.2.) It is essential, therefore, that your stylus be one that fits the type of record you wish to play. Most styli today, however, are compatible with both $33\frac{1}{3}$ rpm and 45 rpm records.

Most modern styli have tips of diamond or sapphire and are thus extremely durable. They are not, however, damage proof. One frequent cause of damage to the stylus is allowing it to strike down hard upon a record or empty

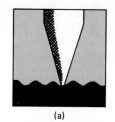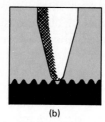

▲ *Figure 10.2*
Mismatch between stylus size and type of record

turntable. Do not move or carry the player around without first securely fastening the tone arm (which contains the stylus assembly). Continual playing of cracked or warped records can also damage the stylus, as can using it on the wrong type of record (too wide or too narrow a groove).

Keep the stylus clean of any dust it may pick up as it plays the records. If your phonograph does not have a cleaning brush attached to the tone arm, clean your stylus periodically with a quick flick of a soft brush from back to front. Do not use your fingertip for this purpose. You may damage the stylus by too heavy a touch. Further, your finger may leave a deposit of oil that will attract additional dust.

Even if your stylus is well cared for, it will gradually wear out and need to be replaced. If you think that a stylus might need changing, inspect it closely with a strong magnifying glass, or a stylus microscope, available at hi-fi shops. A worn stylus will show one or more flattened surfaces instead of a smoothly rounded tip. Removal of the stylus usually involves nothing more complex than removing the stylus from the cartridge. If in doubt, consult an audiovisual or hi-fi specialist about the selection of a proper stylus and its proper installation.

Set up
• Open case and connect power cord to AC outlet.

Operate
• Turn amplifier and turntable power "on."
• Set turntable speed control.
• Place record on turntable.
• Release tone arm from the locking screw or locking clip.
• Position tone arm on record.
• Adjust volume control.
• Adjust tone control.
• Turn amplifier and turntable power "off."

Disassemble
• Place turntable speed control in "neutral" (if possible).
• Lock the tone arm into place.
• Return to storage conformation.

Record Player Troubleshooting

Problem	Possible Remedy
Tone arm skates across record	1. Stylus may not be the proper one for the record. If the stylus does match the record speed, the tone arm may not be exerting sufficient pressure; if the machine has an adjustment to correct this, increase the pressure slightly, but only within the limits recommended for your phonograph—usually 2 to 7 g. In many cases the tracking pressure may already be too great, thus guaranteeing even faster wear on records and the stylus. 2. Check the stylus for excessive wear; replace if worn.
Sound is tinny, murky, distorted	1. Replace stylus if worn. 2. Cartridge may be cracked; if so, replace it.
No sound	1. Check to see if the volume is turned on. Sometimes it is a separate control from the on/off switch for the turntable. 2. Determine if wires to cartridge are broken.
Turntable revolves jerkily ("wow" sound) or too slowly	The idler wheel may have become flattened on one side or may have oil on it, causing it to make poor contact with the turntable rim. Consult an audiovisual specialist or repairperson to check the idler wheel.

Built-in Speaker Systems

Most audiovisual equipment intended for use in educational settings comes equipped with a built-in speaker system. The built-in speaker is usually a single-unit "piston" speaker. This kind of unit is suitable for many but not all instructional purposes. Small speakers built into the chassis of table-model recorders, phonographs, filmstrip projectors, and so on, often lack the fidelity necessary for audio clarity throughout a large audience area. Because built-in single-speaker units have a limited frequency response, sounds falling outside this range may become distorted—bass sounds, for example, may cause the speaker to vibrate.

Portable cassette recorders are particularly troublesome when used for playback in an average-size classroom. Even under the best conditions, the sound quality of portable cassettes is severely limited by their undersized speakers. If such a unit is used to play back material in which audio fidelity is essential (a musical composition, for example), an auxiliary speaker should be used. A high-efficiency speaker—for instance, one having a 6- or 8-inch diameter—may be plugged into the earphone or external-speaker jack of the cassette player to provide better fidelity.

Size alone, however, does not guarantee high quality in a speaker. If high fidelity audio is needed, two-way speakers (bass and treble speaker in one cabinet) or three-way speakers (bass plus midrange tweeter plus regular tweeter) are highly desirable. Such speakers may require an auxiliary amplifier when used in conjunction with AV equipment, but they are capable of reproduc-ing the complete frequency range audible to humans.

Another problem with built-in speakers is that they are often built into the side of the machine containing the controls. This is fine when the operator of the tape recorder or the phonograph is also the listener. But if the apparatus is placed on a table or desk and operated by an instructor for the benefit of an audience, the speaker will be aimed *away from* the audience (see Figures 10.3 and 10.4). A simple way to remedy this situation is to turn the machine around so that the speaker faces the audience and operate the controls from beside rather than in front of the machine.

In the case of film projectors with a built-in speaker, the prob-

▲ *Figure 10.3*
You have to be aware of the location of the built-in speaker when using audio equipment. Although this arrangement is comfortable for the operator, the speaker is facing away from the audience.

▲ *Figure 10.4*
This arrangement is much more satisfactory. The speaker is facing the audience.

lem is compounded by the fact that film projectors are usually set up near the back of the room. Thus, the speaker will be behind most, if not all, of the audience. The problem may be further aggravated by noise from the projector itself. This is a tolerable situation if you have a small audience. But an auxiliary speaker will be necessary if you have a large audience.

If you are operating in a lecture hall or auditorium that has a built-in public address system, you will want to plug your projector or player into that system. This might require an adapter to match up the output plug and input jack.

Detached Speaker Systems

The detachable speakers that accompany some film projectors and stereo tape recorders are generally large and sensitive enough to provide adequate quality sound throughout the instructional area if, as with other separate speaker systems, you give consideration to their individual placement.

Whenever possible, speakers should face toward the center of your audience. If reverberation is a problem, however, especially in long narrow rooms, the speaker may be aimed diagonally across the audience to help alleviate this situation (see Figure 10.5).

In the case of film projection, it is also important that the speaker be placed as close as possible to the screen. Psychologically, we are conditioned to expect sound to come directly from its source. We are, consequently, most comfortable with film sound when it appears to be coming directly from the screen image that constitutes its source.

Be sure nothing obstructs the sound waves as they travel from the speaker toward your audience.

◀ *Figure 10.5*
A suggested speaker placement: the detachable speaker is placed near the screen, raised to head level, and aimed toward the audience with no obstructions in the way.

Certainly you would not place the speaker behind an actual sound barrier, but even classroom furniture (desks, chairs) and the audience itself may present physical obstructions to sound. To avoid such interference, place the speaker on a table or some other kind of stand so that it is at or above the head level of your seated audience, as in Figure 10.5.

If you are using a stereophonic system, the speakers should be far enough apart so that the sound is appropriately balanced between the two. As a rule of thumb, the distance between the speakers should equal the distance from the speakers to the middle of the audience. Thus, in the typical twenty-two-by-thirty-foot classroom, stereo speakers would be placed about fifteen feet apart—nearly in the corners of the room.

Feedback

Feedback is the name given to that annoying squeal that so often

intrudes in public address systems or tape recorders being used as voice reinforcers. The usual cause is simple: The signal coming out of the speaker is fed back into the microphone. The most direct remedy is to make sure that the speakers are set up *in front* of the microphone. If the speakers cannot be moved, you may be able to stop the feedback by adjusting the tone and volume controls or even by moving the microphone. (Omnidirectional microphones are more likely to cause feedback problems than unidirectional microphones.)

Volume and Tone Setting

Because sound-wave intensity decreases rapidly over distance, achieving a comfortable sound volume for all listeners can be quite a challenge. This is particularly true in larger rooms, for it is difficult to reach the back of the room without generating a very loud sound at the front. This, of course, can cause considerable

discomfort to those seated near the speaker. An ideal solution would be to use several low-power sources rather than a single high-power one. But because this is usually not feasible, you can only strive to achieve a reasonable compromise through proper setting of the volume control. By moving around the room during the presentation (unobtrusively), you can get a feel for the best volume setting to suit your situation. The problem may be further alleviated by not seating students at the extreme front or back.

The tone control can be used to correct certain other acoustical problems. For instance, low-frequency (bass) sounds will reverberate annoyingly under certain conditions ("boominess"). This can be compensated for somewhat by turning the tone control of the film projector or tape recorder toward "treble." This also tends to improve the audibility of male speakers' low-pitched voices. Conversely, high-pitched sounds can be dampened with the tone control.

OVERHEAD PROJECTORS

I N terms of its mechanics and electronic components, the overhead projector is a very simple apparatus, with few components requiring special maintenance procedures. Reliable as it is, however, it should not be taken for granted. Take a few basic precautions to ensure that the projector keeps putting on a bright performance.

Keep the overhead projector as clean as possible. The horizontal stage tends to gather dust, fingerprint smudges, and marking-pen traces. It should be cleaned regularly with window spray or a mild solution of soap and water. The lens in the head assembly should

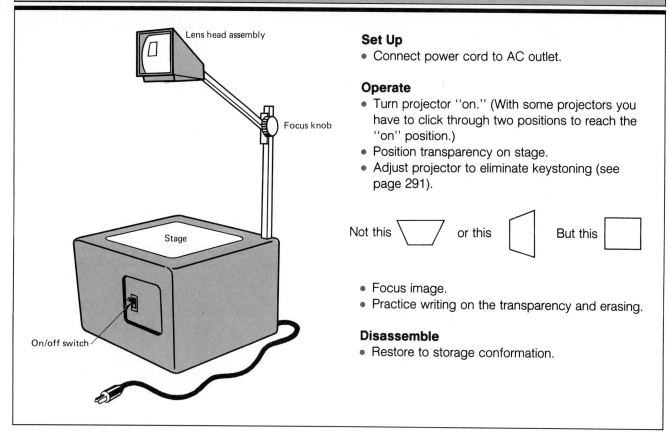

Lens head assembly

Focus knob

Stage

On/off switch

Set Up
● Connect power cord to AC outlet.

Operate
● Turn projector "on." (With some projectors you have to click through two positions to reach the "on" position.)
● Position transparency on stage.
● Adjust projector to eliminate keystoning (see page 291).

Not this   or this   But this

● Focus image.
● Practice writing on the transparency and erasing.

Disassemble
● Restore to storage conformation.

also be kept free of dust and smudges. Clean it periodically with lens tissue and a proper lens-cleansing solution. The fresnel lens under the stage may also need cleaning eventually, but this procedure is better left to the specialist. The lens is a precision optical element requiring special care. In addition, some disassembly of the unit may be required to get at the lens.

The best way to prolong the life of the expensive lamp in the overhead projector is to *allow it to cool before moving* the projector. Move the projector with care. Keep the projector on a cart that can be rolled from one location to another. When hand carrying the apparatus, hold on to the body of the projector, not the thin arm of the head assembly. The head

assembly arm is not intended to be a carrying handle. Used as such, it can easily be twisted out of alignment, thus distorting the projector's image.

SLIDE PROJECTORS

I N normal use, slide projectors require little special attention to keep working smoothly. The only regular maintenance required of the user is to clean the front element of the projection lens if it shows finger marks. More likely to cause difficulties are the slides themselves, which should always be stored away from heat and handled only by their mounts. The most frequent cause of foul-ups in slide presentations is a slide that jams because

it is warped or frayed ("dog-eared"). Remount slides that could cause jams.

The Kodak Ektagraphic III projector has a number of desirable features not found on earlier models. For example, the projection lamp can be changed from

▲ *Figure 10.6*
The Kodak slide projectors feature convenient controls.

Overhead Projector Troubleshooting

Problem	Possible Remedy
No light after flipping switch	1. Be sure projector is plugged into an electrical outlet. 2. Turn the switch all the way on. Many overheads have a three-position switch: off, fan, and on. 3. If lamp is burned out, switch to spare lamp within projector if it has this feature. Otherwise, you will need to replace the lamp. Be sure to use a lamp of the same wattage (too high a wattage can cause overheating). Do not handle the lamp while it is hot. Avoid touching the new lamp with bare fingers; this could shorten its life. 4. Switch may be defective. If so, replace it.
Dark edge with light in center of image	The fresnel lens is upside-down. Turn it over if you know how; if not, have a qualified specialist do it.
Dark spot on area of screen	The lamp socket within the projector needs adjustment. The task is best done by a trained audiovisual technician.
Dark spot on screen or failure of lens to focus despite all adjustment of focus	After determining that it is not simply a matter of dirt on the lens or improper use of the focus control, check for a warped fresnel lens. This lens is plastic and can become warped from excessive heat, usually caused by the fan not running properly. Have a qualified specialist repair the fan or thermostat and replace the fresnel lens.

the rear of the projector without having to turn the projector over. There is a quick release on the elevation stand so the projected image can be raised without having to turn the adjustment knob many times by hand. In addition, the "select" function allows the carousel tray to be turned when the power is off. Finally, the controls are on the side of the projector where the operator usually stands.

Even though some new projectors, such as the Ektagraphic III, do not project a distracting white "image" when there is not a slide in position, it is still recommended that you include a dark slide at the beginning and end of your presentation. Solid plastic slides work best.

▲ *Figure 10.7*
A proper carrying case prolongs the life of slide projectors that are moved frequently.

The purchase and use of a carrying case for your slide projector is highly recommended if the projector is to be moved from loca-

tion to location, especially from building to building. Slide projectors should only be moved on a projector cart or within a carrying case. The case provides a place to store the projector, tray, remote control unit, a spare lamp, and remote extension cords. The carrying case helps to keep all the accessories together, decreasing the chances for loss, as well as providing protection from damage and dust.

More serious damage can occur if the slide projector falls because it has been propped up precariously on top of a stack of books or on some other unstable base. This happens all too often because the projector's elevation leg seems never to be quite long enough to raise the image up to the top of

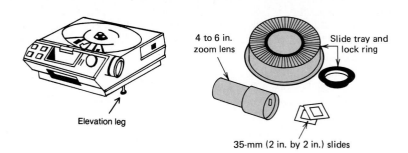

4 to 6 in. zoom lens

Slide tray and lock ring

Elevation leg

35-mm (2 in. by 2 in.) slides

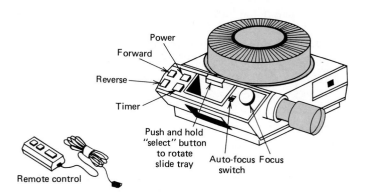

Power
Forward
Reverse
Timer

Push and hold "select" button to rotate slide tray

Auto-focus switch
Focus

Remote control

Set up

- Connect power cord to AC outlet (power cord is stored on the bottom of the projector).
- Plug in remote control cord with white dot on top.
- Insert lens.
- Check to see that bottom ring is locked on slide tray. If not, lock it or slides will drop out.
- Load slides into tray and tighten the locking ring on the tray.
- Seat slide tray on projector. *Note* the notch at "0."

Operate

- Set automatic timer at "m" (manual operation).
- Move on/off switch to "low" or "high" lamp setting.
- Position image on screen, making it smaller or larger by means of the lens barrel.
- Focus image with focus knob.
- Project slides using remote control or buttons on the forward side of the projector.

Disassemble

- Press and hold "select" button while turning the tray to "0." The "select" function will not operate when projector is off, except on the Ektagraphic III model.
- Remove slide tray.
- Allow lamp to cool before switching off.
- Remove slides from slide tray.
- Restore to storage conformation.

the screen. Better solutions are to use a higher projection table, to raise the whole projection table, or to raise the whole projector by placing it on a sturdy box or similar platform.

FILMSTRIP PROJECTORS

A filmstrip projector requires the same sort of care and handling as a slide projector. With the filmstrip projector, however, an additional concern is keeping the film gate clean. Lint and dirt in the gate may be seen around the edges of the projected image and are an annoyance to the viewer. The film gate can be

Slide Projector Troubleshooting

Problem	Possible Remedy
Can't find power cord	Look for a built-in storage compartment. On the Kodak Carousel, the power cord is wrapped around a recessed core on the bottom of the projector.
No power after plugging in	If you are sure the outlet is "live" (a fuse or circuit breaker may have killed all electrical power in the room), check the circuit breaker on the slide projector.
Fan runs but lamp does not light	Some projectors have separate switches for "Lamp" and "Fan" or a two-stage switch for these two functions. Make sure all switches are properly set. Then check for burned-out lamp. If neither of these is the problem, have technician check the projector.
Image not level	Most slide projectors have an adjustment knob on one of the rear feet. Use the knob to raise or lower that side.
Slide is distorted	The lenses may be out of alignment or broken. Often they can be adjusted easily by aligning them correctly in their slots.
Slide mounts begin to warp	For plastic black and white mounts, check to see that *white side* of mount is *facing* the lamp. If the dark side of mount is facing lamp, a build-up of heat can cause the mount to warp (or even melt, in the case of plastic mounts).
Slide image upside-down or backwards	Remove the slide and reverse it. (Improper loading can be avoided by "thumb-spotting" slides. See Chapter 5.)
Slide jams in gate	1. Manually remove the slide. On the Kodak Carousel, press the "select" button (power must be on). If the slide does not pop up, the tray will have to be removed. Turn off the power and use a coin to turn the screw in the center of the tray; this unlocks the tray, allowing it to be lifted off and giving access to the gate for manual removal of the slide.
	2. Jamming can be avoided by not placing bent slides in the tray. Plastic mounts have a tendency to warp; cardboard mounts fray; glass mounts may be too thick for the slide compartment of the tray. For this reason, jamming is more likely with *narrow* slide compartments, as are found in the 140-slide Carousel trays. Use the 80-slide tray whenever possible.

cleaned with a special aperture brush (also used with motion picture projectors) or with some other nonmetal, soft-bristle brush.

Filmstrip projectors that come in enclosed cases carry a warning to remove the projector from the case before operating it. This is to ensure that air can circulate freely to the cooling fan located on the underside of the projector. Any interference with the fan, such as a sheet of paper sucked up against the fan grid or an accumulation of dust adhering to the fan grid, can lead to overheating and damage to filmstrips.

OPAQUE PROJECTORS

THE opaque projector presents a few unique operating problems. Because of the aperture size and the focal length of the lens, the opaque projector will be placed ten to twelve feet from the screen. This, then, usually puts a very bulky piece of equipment in the middle of the audience. Consequently, the projector must be positioned below eye level so students can see over it, and the front elevated, causing keystoning. The noisy fan sound and the light that spills from the projector

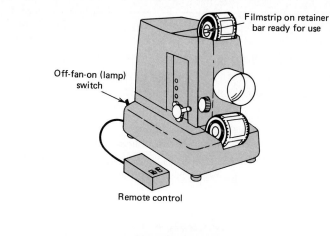

Filmstrip on retainer bar ready for use

Off-fan-on (lamp) switch

Remote control

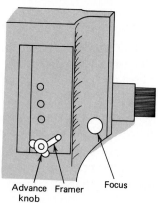

Advance knob   Framer   Focus

Set up
- Connect power cord to AC outlet.

Operate
- Turn projector "on."
- Place filmstrip on retainer bar.
- Thread filmstrip down into film slot. Be sure that "START" or "FOCUS" appears at head of filmstrip.
- Turn advance knob until "FOCUS" frame appears.
- Adjust framer so the full frame is projected when you click the advance knob.
- Turn projector "off."

Disassemble
- Return filmstrip to container. Do not pull the end of the filmstrip to tighten the roll. Start with a tight roll at the center and continue, holding the film by the edges.
- Restore to storage conformation.

also create distractions from the presentation.

One last point—a WARNING! Some of the older opaque projectors can transfer heat to paper. There have been instances of the paper becoming hot enough to burn. If you are using an opaque projector, keep an eye on the material, especially if the paper is old and dry. Should the paper begin to darken, remove it immediately!

PROJECTION SETUPS

ARRANGING a proper environment for viewing projected visuals involves several variables, including audience seating pattern, screen size, type of screen surface, screen placement, type of lens, and projector placement.

In most cases, the instructor only has to deal with a couple of these variables, probably seating pattern and projector placement. For everyday teaching situations the classroom often will be equipped with a screen of a certain type attached in a fixed position, and the projector will already have its own lens.

There may be times, however, when you will have to make decisions about any or all of these variables—for instance, setting up an in-service workshop in the school cafeteria or running a film showing at a youth group meeting in a church hall. Let us examine some guidelines for handling each of these variables by looking at a specific hypothetical case.

Seating Arrangement

Let us assume that the room you are to use for projecting visuals is twenty-two feet wide and thirty feet long, a fairly typical size both for formal and nonformal instructional settings. Let us further assume that you must arrange seating for between thirty and forty viewers, a fairly typical audience size. Figure 10.9 illustrates a conventional seating pattern for a group of this size (in this case,

Filmstrip Projector Troubleshooting

Problem	Possible Remedy
Dark areas or smudges projected on the screen	Cleans the lens.
Dirt/lint visible at edges of projected image	Foreign matter in the film gate. Clean with an aperture brush or other brush with no metal components.
Filmstrip is not properly framed.	Correct with framer knob.

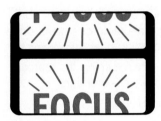

The frame appears first.	If this is the first frame you see, the filmstrip has been inserted tail-first. Withdraw it and insert the head end. (If the lettering appears backwards, you have threaded it with the wrong side facing the screen; reverse it. The ends of the strip should curl toward the screen.)

How To . . . OPERATE AN OPAQUE PROJECTOR

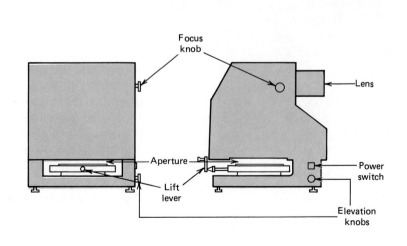

Set up
- Connect power cord to AC outlet.

Operate
- Turn projector "on."
- Use lift lever to open platen.
- Insert material.
- Close platen.
- Focus picture.
- Elevate projector.

Disassemble
- Remove material.
- Turn lens back into projector.
- Lower elevation.

Opaque Projector Troubleshooting

Problem	Possible Remedy
No light after flipping switch	1. Be sure projector is securely plugged into an electrical outlet. 2. Check lamp. If burned out, replace it. Since you must push down very hard on the lamp while twisting it, be sure to use a cloth. 3. Switch may be defective. If so, have a media technician replace it.
Line through picture	The piece of glass between the material and the lamp may be broken. Be sure to replace it with the manufacturer's glass since this glass has special properties for resisting heat and pressure.
Glass is broken	Someone applied too much pressure when loading the material. The material should be snug in the projector—not tight.
Brown spot appears within projected image	The material is beginning to burn. GET IT OUT!

▲ *Figure 10.8*
With proper attention to projection variables, even makeshift facilities can become learning environments.

set back somewhat from the desk area, where the screen is to be set up, so that front-row students will not be too close to the screen for comfortable viewing.

If the room is closer to a square in shape, you might want to consider placing the screen in the corner and seating the audience in diagonal rows. This possibility will be examined later in terms of screen placement.

Screen Size

A general rule of thumb (the "2-by-6 rule") accepted by most audiovisualists dictates that *no viewer should be seated closer to the screen than two screen widths or farther away than six screen widths*. This means that in our hypothetical case, in which the farthest viewer could be thirty feet from the front of the room, a screen about five feet wide (sixty inches) would be required to ensure that this farthest-away viewer is within six screen widths

thirty-six viewers). Note that the seats are arranged across the narrower room dimension. If the seats were turned to face the left or right side of the room and arranged across its thirty-foot length, viewers along either end of the rows would have a distorted view of the screen. Note too, that the first row of seats is

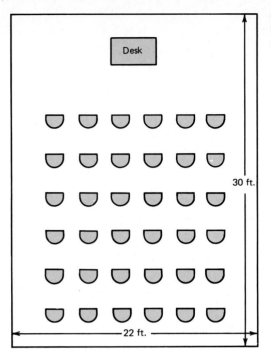

◀ *Figure 10.9*
Typical-size classroom
arranged to seat thirty-six

Desk

30 ft.

22 ft.

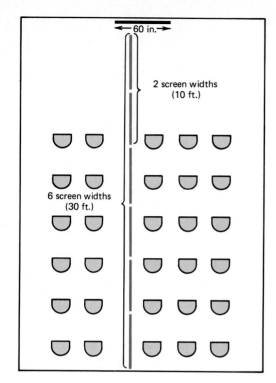

▶ *Figure 10.10*
Appropriate screen size for
the typical-size classroom
according to the "2-by-6
rule"

60 in.

2 screen widths
(10 ft.)

6 screen widths
(30 ft.)

of the screen (30 ÷ 6 = 5). A square screen is generally preferable, because it can be used to show rectangular images (film, slides, filmstrips, etc.) as well as square images (overhead and opaque projections). Thus, in this case a screen measuring sixty-by-sixty inches is recommended, as illustrated in Figure 10.10.

With a zoom lens on a carousel slide projector or a 16-mm projector, you can put the projector at the rear of any normal-size classroom and "fill" a seventy-inch screen.

Screen Surfaces

Projection screens vary in their surface treatments. Various surfaces have different reflectance qualities and offer different viewing-angle widths.

Matte White Surface. The matte screen has a smooth, nonshiny surface that has the lowest reflectance but provides a constant level of brightness over the widest viewing angle (more than forty-five degrees on either side of the center axis). It is durable and inexpensive. Matte white screens can be rolled up for storage or carrying. Because of these qualities the matte white screen is the one most commonly used in instructional settings. In addition, a matte white screen can be cleaned with an extra strength household cleaner such as Mr. Clean. None of the other surfaces can be cleaned.

Beaded Surface. The beaded screen is a white surface covered with small glass beads. Approximately two to four times more light is reflected from this surface than from the matte white surface. However, the beads tend to reflect light straight back toward the light source, narrowing the optimal viewing area. In fact, beyond twenty-five degrees on either side of the center axis the brightness is less than that of a matte white screen. Beaded screens are primarily recommended for long, narrow halls.

Lenticular Surface. The lenticular screen is made from a plastic material that has a pattern molded into the surface, usually a series of very narrow ridges running vertically up the screen. It represents a compromise between the beaded and the matte white surfaces, being nearly as reflective as the former and offering nearly the breadth of viewing angle of the latter. Like the beaded screen, the lenticular screen provides the brightest image within twenty-five degrees of the center axis and a dimmer image out to about forty-five degrees. It must be stretched tight to be effective. It is more expensive than the matte or beaded screen and is seldom used in schools.

Aluminum Foil Surface. Developed by Kodak under the trade name Ektalite, this is the brightest

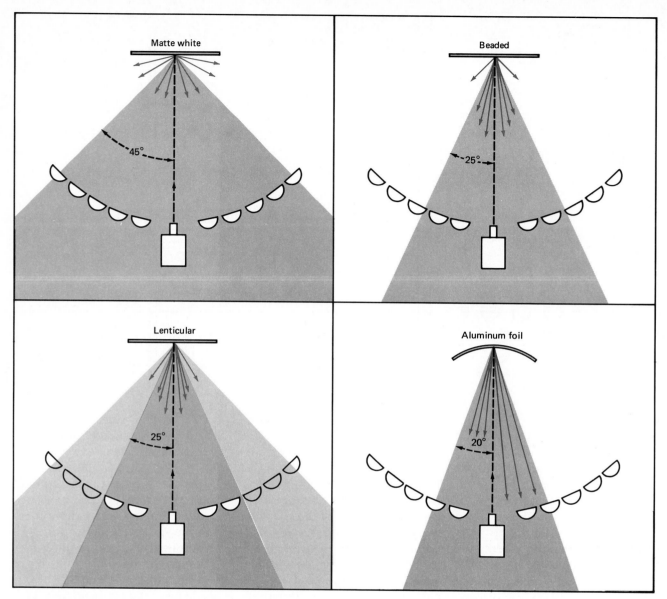

▲ *Figure 10.11*
Comparison of reflectance and recommended viewing angles for four different screen surfaces

surface available, about twenty times brighter than the matte white surface. However, it has a very narrow viewing angle, with visibility limited to about twenty degrees from the center axis. Screen size is also limited, forty-by-forty inches being the largest standard size. It is rigid and cannot be rolled up. Its greatest advantage is visibility in full room light. It is particularly recommended for small-group use in conditions of high ambient light.

The major features of these screen types are shown in comparison in Figure 10.11. Given the room dimensions and audience size in our hypothetical case, a matte white screen would be most suitable.

Screen Placement

In most cases, placement of the screen at the center of the front of the room will be satisfactory. In some cases, however, it may not

be. Perhaps light from a window that cannot be fully covered will wash out the projected image (sunlight is much brighter than any artificial light), or you might wish to use the chalkboard during your presentation and a screen positioned in the center front will make it difficult or impossible for you to do so. An alternative position is in a front corner of the room. Indeed, the screen should not be at "center stage" when there is danger that it will attract

MEDIAWARE AND MEDIA SETUPS

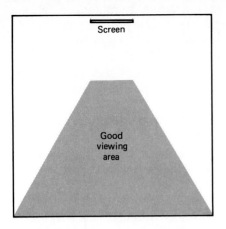 

▲ *Figure 10.12*
In a rather square room, placement of the screen in the corner creates a larger good-viewing area.

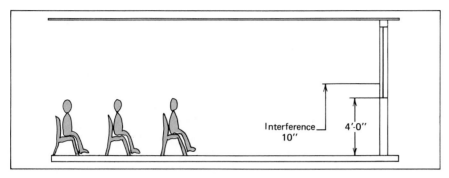

▲ *Figure 10.13*
The bottom of the screen should be above head level to avoid obstruction of the view.

unwanted attention while nonprojection activities are going on.

Corner placement is especially advantageous in a room that is square or nearly so. As illustrated by Figure 10.12, placing the screen in one corner allows more viewers to be seated in the good viewing area.

In any case, nowhere is it written in stone that the screen must be placed front and center. Position your screen wherever it will best suit your purpose.

The height of the screen should generally be adjusted so that the *bottom* of the screen is about level with the heads of the seated viewers. The bottom of the screen should be at least four feet above the floor to prevent excessive head interference as illustrated in

Figure 10.13. Other inhibiting factors aside, this arrangement will allow reasonably clear sight lines for the most viewers. In general, the higher the screen, the greater the optimal viewing area. Of course, care must be taken that the screen can be seen without viewers uncomfortably craning their necks.

Lamps

Types. There are three types of projection lamps: incandescent, tungsten halogen, and tungsten halogen with surrounding reflector. The incandescent lamps should be watched because they have a tendency to blister. Such blisters can become so big that the lamp cannot be removed

from the projector. If the lamp does blister to the extent that it must be broken for removal, an audiovisual technician should be contacted. In addition to the blistering problem, the incandescent lamps require more wattage for the same light output.

The first innovative response to incandescent blistering was the tungsten halogen lamp. These lamps do not blister as incandescent lamps do, but they do require the same high wattage and thus have the associated heat problems and fan noise.

The newest type of lamps is the tungsten halogen lamps with surrounding reflectors. These lamps generally operate at one-half the wattage of the incandescent or tungsten halogen lamps.

Coding. Projection lamps are labelled with a three-letter ANSI (American National Standard Institute) code. This code is printed on the lamp and on the box. In addition, many projectors now have stickers in the lamp housing of the projectors with the ANSI code stating which lamp should be used in that projector.

▲ *Figure 10.14*
Projection lamps come in a wide variety of sizes and shapes; when they burn out, they must be replaced with a matching type.

Replacement of Lamps. When replacing a lamp, the replacement should be a lamp with the same ANSI code or an authorized substitute. Substitutes can be found in replacement guides written by the lamp manufacturers. These guides are available from the manufacturers or from local audiovisual dealers. NOTE: Do *not* use higher wattage lamps than specified. You may burn the materials in the projector!

Handling a Lamp. When handling a lamp, *never* touch the clear glass bulb. The oils from your fingers can shorten the life of the lamp. The lamp should always be manipulated by its base. The incandescent lamps and the tungsten halogen lamp (without exterior reflector) are supplied with a piece of foam or paper around the lamp. This wrap or a cloth should be used to hold the lamp when it is inserted into the projector.

When removing a burned-out lamp, wait until the lamp has cooled to prevent injuring your fingers. It is wise to always use a cloth when removing a lamp. A word of caution—even a lamp that burns out when the projector is first turned on will be hot enough to burn. So use a cloth!

Expense. Lamps are expensive. They usually cost about twenty times the cost of a household light bulb. Because the average lamp life is fifty hours, projectors should be turned off when not in use. If the projector offers a low lamp setting, use it if possible to increase the life of the lamp. A projector should not be jarred when the lamp is on, as this can cause a premature burnout of the lamp. You should not leave the fan on for cooling after use unless the projector is going to be moved immediately, as this also will shorten the life of the bulb.

Lenses

For everyday media use you do not have to pay much attention to technicalities about lenses. Whatever lens your projector is equipped with is usually sufficient. However, understanding some basic ideas about lenses can help you cope with extraordinary situations.

First, lenses vary in focal length (measured in inches in the United States, in millimeters elsewhere). *The longer the focal length, the smaller the image* at a given distance. Your objective is to project an image that will fill the screen, so the shorter the projection throw, the shorter the lens (in terms of focal length) that will be needed to enlarge the projected image sufficiently. Fortunately, the actual length of most lenses corresponds roughly with their focal length; the longer of two lenses will have the longer focal length. Figure 10.16 illustrates the relationship of lens focal length to the size of its projected image.

One type of lens has a variable focal length—the zoom lens. It can, therefore, be adjusted to cast a larger or smaller picture without moving the projector or changing its lens. The most commonly encountered zoom lens (found on many slide projectors) has a focal-length range of four to six inches.

When precise specifications are needed in selecting lenses for particular conditions, media specialists use calculation devices prepared by manufacturers, such as the *Da-Lite Lens-Projection Screen Calculator* or Kodak's *Projection Calculator and Seating Guide.*

Projector Placement

The first requirement in projector placement is to align the projection lens perpendicular to the screen (that is, it must make a ninety-degree angle with the

▲ *Figure 10.15*
Avoid directly touching both burned out lamps (because they are hot) and replacement lamps (because the oil on your fingertips can shorten the life of a lamp and cause it to blister).

screen). Thus, the lens of the projector should be about level with the middle of the screen. If the projector is too high, too low, or off to either side, a distortion of the image will occur, referred to as the "*keystone effect.*" The effect takes its name from the typical shape of a keystoned image—wide at the top, narrower at the bottom, like a keystone. Figure 10.17 is an illustration of this problem and its remedy: Move either the projector or the screen to bring the two into a perpendicular relationship.

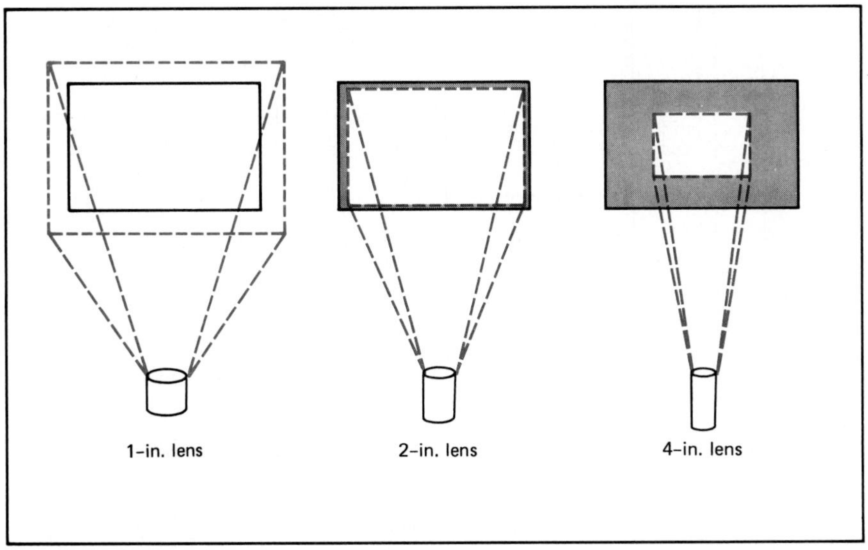

The keystone effect is especially prevalent with the overhead projector because it is ordinarily set up very close to the screen and far lower than the screen (to allow the instructor to write on its stage). For this reason, many screens used for overhead projection are equipped with a "keystone eliminator," a notched bar at the top that allows the screen to be tilted forward (see Figure 10.18).

Once you have properly aligned the projector and screen, consider the distance between projector and screen. If the distance is too long, the image will spill over the edges of the screen. If it is too short, the image will not fill the screen properly. Your goal is to fill the screen as fully as possible with the brightest image possible. The principle to remember here is that the image becomes *larger and less brilliant* with an increase in distance between projector and screen. If the projected image is too large for your screen, push the projector closer. If the image is too small, pull the projector back.

Positioning a projector at the proper distance from the screen need not be done solely by trial and error. Because classroom-type projectors usually are fitted with certain focal-length lenses, their proper placement can be estimated in advance. Figure 10.19 shows the placement of the overhead, slide, and 16-mm film projectors when they are equipped with their most typical lenses. However, it is best to place all projectors, except the overhead

▲ *Figure 10.16*
The longer the focal length of the lens, the smaller the image.

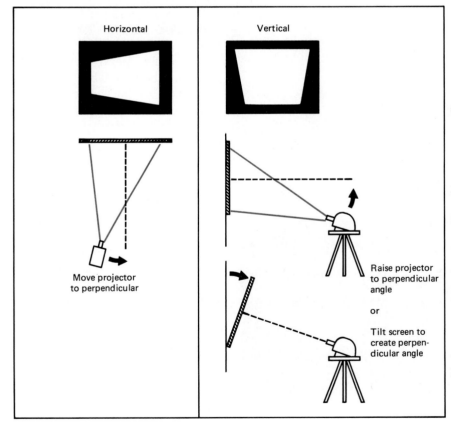

▲ *Figure 10.17*
The "keystone effect"—its causes and its remedies

and the opaque, behind the audience to prevent people from tripping over the power cords. For the same reason, extension cords should be used so that the power cords can be run along the wall to the outlet rather than across the center of the room.

The projection distances described here assume appropriate lighting conditions. Where the room light is so bright that it is washing out the screen image and it cannot be dimmed any further, you must move the projector forward. This will give you a brighter image, but also, unfortunately, a smaller one. In some cases, however, it may be possible to compensate for this reduction in image size by having your audience move closer to the screen.

Equipment Tables and Carts

Projection tables have legs and are meant to be used in one position. The portable projection table is designed to be folded up and moved to another location and reassembled. Its legs telescope so that the projector can be as high as five feet from the ground. When the table is folded up, the typical package dimension of 30 inches × 12 inches × 3 inches makes it easily transportable.

Carts come with wheels that allow the equipment to be set up and easily moved. The carts are designed both for inside-only use and inside/outside use. You take a great risk in moving equipment out of doors on a cart designed for inside use. The small wheels can catch in cracks in sidewalks and cause the cart to tip over. For this reason, even for exclusive indoor use it is wise to purchase carts with 5-inch casters.

Manufacturers normally offer power outlet cord assemblies for their carts. These are worthwhile investments. You plug your projector into the outlet on the cart and the cord on the cart into the

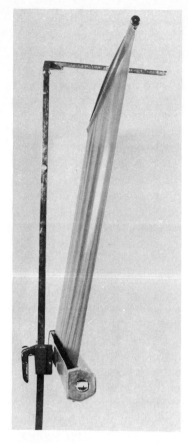

▲ *Figure 10.18*
Portable tripod screen with "keystone eliminator"

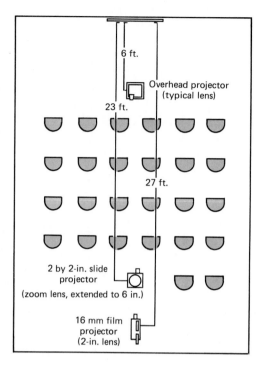

▲ *Figure 10.19*
Approximate placement of projectors when equipped with typical lenses

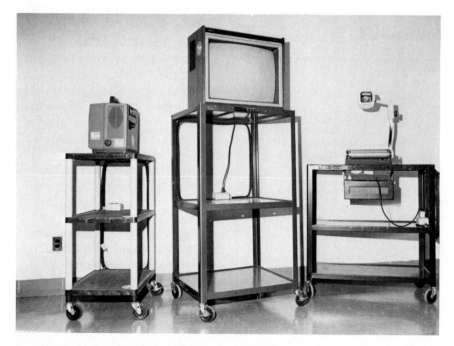

▲ *Figure 10.20*
The varied types of equipment carts are suited for different purposes.

Moving

- Do not allow young children to move loaded carts.
- Do not allow anyone to ride on a cart.
- Be sure to engage caster locks before loading.
- Place equipment on the lower shelves before moving.
- Make sure all power cords are disconnected from wall plugs and wrapped around equipment before moving cart.
- Disconnect VCR from TV monitor before moving units to lower shelves.
- Unlock all casters before moving cart.
- Make sure you can see where you are going.
- Always push the cart, applying force on the narrow dimension; never pull the cart.
- When entering or leaving an elevator, push the cart at an angle so that one caster at a time goes over the gap between building and elevator floors.
- If cart is to be moved up or down a ramp, use a strap to secure equipment to the cart.
- When moving cart over rough floors, proceed with extreme caution.

Using

- Always engage the caster locks as soon as the cart is in position.
- Make sure equipment is centered on the cart shelf.
- Keep power and speaker cords out of traffic lanes and use a lot of slack.
- If equipment power cord or extension is plugged directly into the wall, wrap the cord around the bottom of a leg of the cart so that if someone does trip on the cord, the cart, not the equipment, is pulled.

One of these junior high students, who has a clear view of the path, guides the cart while the other pushes.

- Do not use the cart as a stool or ladder.
- When finished, move the cart as previously described.

This HOW TO was adapted from guidelines published by the International Communications Industries Association (ICIA). Additional information, including stickers for carts (see Figure 10.21), is available from ICIA, 3150 Spring Street, Fairfax, VA 22031.

wall outlet. If someone should trip over the power cord, the cart moves but the projector does not crash to the floor. In addition, the cord on the cart is considerably longer than the typical power cord furnished with the projector. The longer cord can be laid on the floor along the wall, thereby reducing the risk that someone will trip over it.

Features of Carts. Carts have a number of possible features related to location of use, construction materials, degree of enclosure, and type of equipment with which the cart can be used.

We have already discussed the location of use—inside or outside.

Projection carts are constructed of both metal and plastic. A metal cart should be welded together instead of bolted. The nuts on the bolts will become loose over time, and the cart will become very unstable. Plastic carts, although not as stable as welded metal carts, have a number of advantages. They are much lighter and less expensive than metal carts. Some plastic carts can be disassembled and placed in the trunk of a car.

Projection carts have varying degrees of enclosure. The basic cart has no enclosed cabinets. Cabinets provide for security of materials and protection from dust during storage.

Some carts are designed for specific projectors. For example, overhead projector carts have adjustable-depth wells into which the projectors can be placed. They are 26 inches high for use in seated positions and 39 inches high to be used while standing. Low carts are to be used with opaque projectors. Carts 34 inches and 42 inches high are used with 16-mm, 8-mm, slide, and filmstrip projectors. Video equipment carts have heights of 39 inches, 42 inches, and 54 inches. The lower carts can be used as "mobile production centers" (recorder and monitor mounted on the cart) to be moved from one classroom to another. The 54-inch carts are used to hold large 19-inch, 21-inch, and 25-inch television monitors. Since these carts tend to be somewhat unstable, caution must be exercised when moving them.

Cart Safety Tips. The U.S. Consumer Product Safety Commission (CPSC) and the International Communications Industries Association (ICIA) have alerted schools to the hazards involved in moving TV and projection carts. CPSC has noted at least four deaths of children and four serious injuries resulting from tipped-over carts. Seven of the carts were loaded with a TV set on the top shelf, and the eighth had a 16-mm projector on the top. Particularly

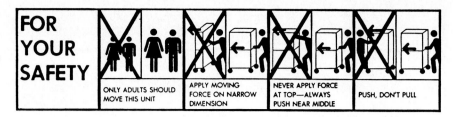

▲ *Figure 10.21*
This safety sticker, available from International Communications Industries Association, should be on all carts.

hazardous are carts 50 or more inches high. With many school districts switching from 16-mm film to video, there will be an increasing number of tall carts for transporting VCRs and TV sets.

The children involved in the accidents ranged in age from seven to eleven. Teachers have been warned *not to ask children to move carts with heavy equipment on them.* Adolescents and adults, although less likely to sustain serious injuries, must move carts with caution. The falling equipment will certainly be damaged, possibly beyond repair. Be sure to follow the instructions in the box "How to . . . Move and Use Equipment Carts."

SOUND SYNCHRONIZATION

CASSETTE player/recorders with sound-synchronizing capability allow you to play an audiotape that is coordinated with a set of slides or a filmstrip. As shown in Figure 10.23, the synchronizers designed primarily for use with slide projectors use two tracks on the audiotape, one for the narration and the other to synchronize the sound and picture. These units use a 1000 hertz signal for changing the slide and a 150 hertz signal to stop the playback of the cassette tape. A button must then be pushed to restart the tape.

The synchronization units designed to be used with filmstrip

▲ *Figure 10.22*
A typical sound-slide synchronization setup

projectors do not have the "pause" feature. They often are built into the filmstrip projector itself. This system uses an *inaudible* 50 hertz signal to trigger the change from one frame of the filmstrip to another. This signal is "buried" within the narration (see Figure 10.24). Thus, only one track on the tape is needed. Generally, the other track of the tape (which is reached by turning over the cassette) contains a recording of the audio material with an audible signal to tell you when to change to the next frame of the filmstrip if your filmstrip projector lacks an automatic advance mechanism. The tape will be labelled "inaudible signal" or "50 Hz signal" on one side and "audible signal" on the other.

Please note that the 1000 Hz system is NOT compatible with the 50 Hz system. To solve this problem, the manufacturers have produced cassette player/recorders that will record and play back the 1000 Hz system and only play

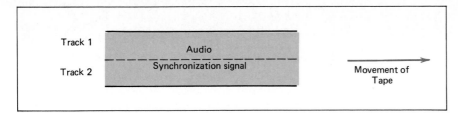

▲ *Figure 10.23*
Tape configuration for cassette sound-slide synchronization

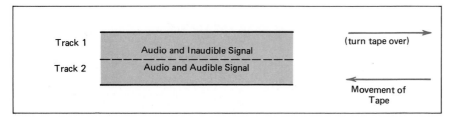

▲ *Figure 10.24*
Tape configuration for synchronized sound filmstrips

back the 50 Hz system. These units do not come as a single piece of equipment. You must have the appropriate cords to connect the cassette unit to your slide projector or to your filmstrip projector. Your audiovisual equipment dealer can supply the correct cords for your cassette unit with the appropriate plugs for your projectors.

Of course, your show can *stay* in the proper synchronization only if it *starts* in synchronization. Check to be sure the sequence starts on the correct frame.

Single-Unit Projectors

Most of the single-piece projectors with cassette player and filmstrip unit are for front projection. There are other units that have built-in rear screens for individual viewing. Some of these allow you to open a small door for front projection. Because these projectors have very short focal length lens, you must place the projector close to the screen. This means that the light and sound will

"spill" from the machine into the middle of your audience.

Single-piece units also are available for use with slides using the 1000 Hz system. Some units have dissolve-control devices built into them. They allow for a variable rate of dissolve to be used either through digital coding or altering the pitch of the synchronizing signal. Units from different manufacturers are generally not compatible.

Automatic Programmers

All of the aforementioned slide projector units allow for an external control signal to be "written" on the tape by a programmer. However, you do need a programmer or a "reader" to interpret the signals coming from the tape when you play it back. The programmer/reader causes projectors to advance/reverse and to dissolve at various rates, and causes auxiliary units to turn projectors or lights on and off. The programmers include independent units, units combined with a dissolve

unit, and units that use microcomputers. If you decide to get involved in this area of multi-image/multimedia, you should work with a media production specialist.

FILM PROJECTORS

Because film projectors and 16-mm films are comparatively expensive instruments of instruction (the typical half-hour educational film costs about $550), it is particularly important for instructors to prolong the life of these items by taking proper care of them.

The average life of an acetate-based film is approximately 100 showings. The newer mylar-based film has the potential for 1,000 showings. Mishandling, however, can greatly reduce this span of service. On the other hand, careful threading, inspection after each use, periodic lubrication of the film, and proper storage (at room temperature, 40 percent humidity) can lengthen the working life of the film.

Proper care of the projector can also help extend the service span of film. It is important to keep the projector's film path clean to pre-

▲ *Figure 10.25*
Slot threading greatly simplifies the use of 16-mm projectors.

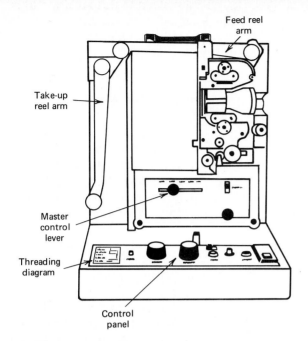

Feed reel arm

Take-up reel arm

Master control lever

Threading diagram

Control panel

Set up (refer to Figure 10.26)

- Unbuckle and separate speaker from projector.
- Swing *feed reel arm* up and into position.
- Raise *take-up reel arm* into position.
- Attach drive belt onto pulley on take-up reel arm.
- Place take-up *reel* on spindle and lock spindle.
- Plug power cord into AC outlet.
- Plug *speaker* or headphones into speaker jack.
- Place *film* on feed reel arm spindle and lock spindle.
- Unwind about 5 feet of film.

Threading

- Check to be sure that "rewind" lever is in raised position.
- Follow threading diagram printed on projector. On the Kodak Pageant projector, the steps are as follows:

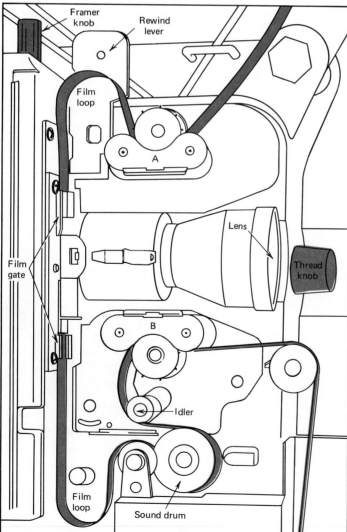

Framer knob

Rewind lever

Film loop

A

Lens

Thread knob

Film gate

B

Idler

Film loop

Sound drum

1. Open clamps around upper and lower drive sprockets. See (A) and (B) on diagram.
2. Turn thread knob until white line faces you.
3. Loop film under *upper sprocket* (A) and engage teeth with sprocket holes in film; then close clamp.
4. Open *film gate* and slide film into channel so that it is flat.
5. Close film gate by pressing in on clamp.
6. Form a loop to match red line on rewind lever or to the top of the lever.
7. Bring film around black *bottom* roller to form loop.
8. Thread film over *pressure roller* and around *sound drum*.
9. Thread film around idler and over lower sprocket (B).
10. Engage sprocket holes with teeth on sprocket (B) and close clamp.
11. Thread film around three remaining *idler rollers*—if more film is needed, turn master control briefly to "motor."
12. Insert end of film leader into slot of empty take-up reel.
13. Double check threading diagram to ensure that film is properly threaded.
14. Rotate threading knob clockwise to check film loops.

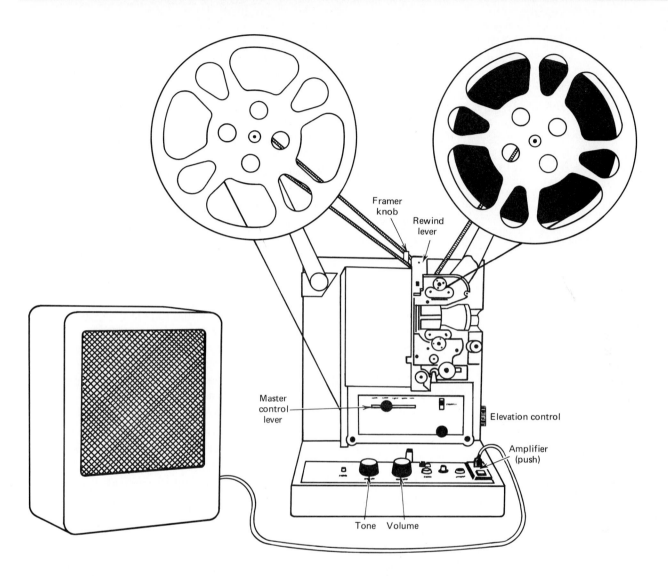

Operate
- Turn amplifier "on."
- Move *master control lever* to "motor," then to "lamp."
- Position image on screen by moving projector and adjusting the elevation control.
- *Focus* image by turning lens.
- Adjust volume and tone.
- Rotate *framer knob* if image is not framed properly.
- You may *reverse* film by pulling master control lever to "off," then "reverse."
- Run film *forward* until all film has run through projector.
- Turn master control lever to "off."

Rewind
- Secure end of film in slot of feed reel, and take up slack.
- Pull *rewind lever* down.
- Move master control to "rewind/forward" position, *not* "reverse."
- When film has been rewound onto feed reel, turn master control lever to "off" and lift rewind lever to "up" position.
- Turn amplifier "off."

Disassemble
- Push rear arm forward to remove belt.
- Lower feed reel arm.
- Press release lever and carefully lower take-up arm.
- Return projector and speaker to storage conformation.

Film Projector Troubleshooting

Problem	Possible Remedy
Projector runs but lamp doesn't light	First, be sure that you have turned the operation lever all the way on. It should be in the "Lamp" position. If the lamp doesn't light after being properly switched on, it is possible that it is burnt out and needs to be replaced.
Projector runs but there is no sound	1. Be sure that the "Amplifier" switch is turned on. 2. Be sure that the speaker is plugged in. 3. Check to see that the film is threaded properly around the sound drum. 4. Check the other switches, such as "Sound/Silent" and "Micro./Film." If there is still no sound after checking all the above steps, it is likely that the exciter lamp is burnt out and needs to be replaced.
Distorted sound	Make sure that the film is wound tightly around the sound drum.
Flowing blur instead of an image	The film is not properly engaged in the gate. Be sure that the sprockets are meshing with the sprocket holes and that the film gate is closed.
Fuzz around edges of projected image	Dirt and lint collect easily around the aperture (due to the static electricity created by moving film). The film gate should be cleaned with a brush before each showing. If dirt is causing distraction during a showing, it can be cleared away by blowing into the aperture area. That is not recommended as a routine cleaning practice (since the moisture in your breath can harm lenses and delicate metal parts), only as a "quick fix" in an emergency.
Projector chatters noisily	Lower loop has been lost. Stop the projector and reform the loop, or press down on the loop restorer while the projector continues running.
Film breaks	Stop the projector. If possible, determine and correct the cause. Then rethread the film. The broken end should be overlapped on the take-up reel. Mark the break by inserting a slip of paper into the reel at this point. Do *not* attempt to repair the break with tape, pins, paper clips, etc.
Voice not synchronized with image (lips)	The lower loop is either too tight or too loose, causing the sound track to pass over the sound drum either before or after the image is projected in the aperture. Adjust the lower loop.

vent undue wear on the film. An aperture brush or other soft-bristled, nonmetalic brush should be used regularly to clean the film path, the film gate, and the area around the sound drum.

The lens of the projector should be kept free of dust and smudges by periodic cleaning with lens tissue and cleaner. The projector's volume- and tone-control mechanisms sometimes

develop internal carbon buildup, causing crackling sounds when the knobs are turned to adjust audio. This debris can generally be eliminated simply by spraying around the external extensions of the control knobs with an aerosol tuner cleaner while turning the knobs.

Given the electromechanical complexity of the film projector, you should not go much beyond these routine cleaning procedures to help keep your projector in good working order.

VIDEOTAPE RECORDERS

V IDEO record/playback machines are highly sophisticated electronic instruments. Maintenance and repair, consequently, should generally be left to the specialist. In addition, videotape recording systems are far from standardized in their various mechanisms and modes of operation. You should, therefore, refer to the manufacturer's man-

ual for information about the operating principles and procedures of the particular system you happen to be using. The "Troubleshooting" guide included here is limited to general sorts of problems that may occur with virtually any video system and that can be remedied by the nonspecialist.

Physical Arrangements

Before students can learn from any instructional TV presentation, they first have to be able to see it and hear it! Provide proper lighting, seating, and volume control.

Seating and Monitor Placement. An ideal seating arrangement for

ITV may sometimes be difficult to achieve. Because of economic constraints, there are often not enough television sets available to give every student an adequate view. Ideally, one twenty-three-inch-screen TV set should serve no more than thirty students seated at desks in a classroom with aisles. If conditions are not ideal, the best you can do is do your best. If feasible, seats may be shared or moved closer together so that all may have at least an adequate view of the screen. If possible, stagger seats to help prevent view blockage.

Here are some basic rules of thumb for good seating arrangement (see Figure 10.26):

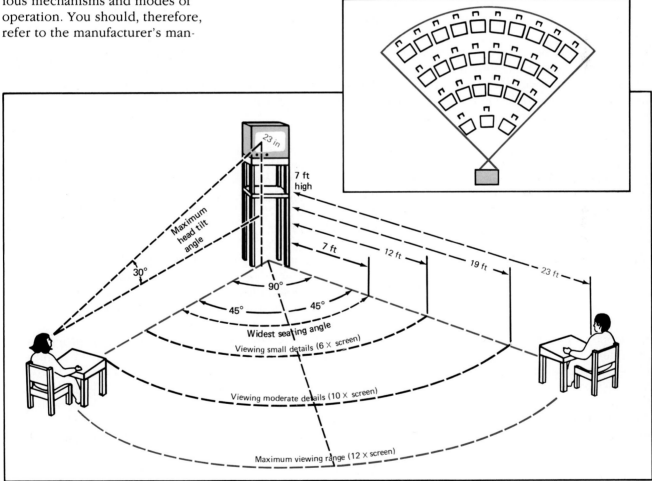

▲ *Figure 10.26*
Recommended monitor placement and seating distances for TV viewing

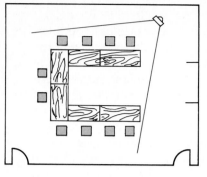

Small Conference Room

Classroom

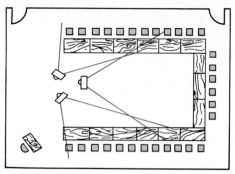

Large Training Room

▲ *Figure 10.27*
TV monitor placements for typical viewing situations

- Seat no one closer than seven feet from the receiver.
- Seat no one farther away (in feet) than the size of the TV screen (in inches).
- Seat no one more than forty-five degrees from the center axis of the screen.
- Place the TV set no more than thirty degrees above the normal eye level of any seated viewer to avoid having viewers crane their necks uncomfortably.

Monitor Placement. When locating television monitors for instructional viewing, you need to consider the amount of detail to be shown on the screen. As illustrated in Figure 10.26, a distance of no more than six times the size of the monitor is best if *small details* are important. Examples might include studying computer output, reading small captions, and televised viewing through a microscope using a high-resolution camera. For a 23-inch monitor, the acceptable viewing range would be from seven feet to twelve feet.

Viewers should be no further than ten times the monitor size away if *moderate details* are important.

If details are not critical, as in the case of people and landscapes, the farthest viewer can be back as far as twelve times the

monitor size. For a 23-inch monitor, the maximum range would be twenty-three feet (unless details are important).

Sample room arrangements indicating placement of television monitors are shown in Figure 10.27. In addition to the distance of the viewers from the monitor, you must also consider the height of the monitor. For group viewing a 54-inch-high stand or cart works best.

Lighting. Television should be viewed in normal or dim light, not darkness. Besides being more comfortable to the eye, normal illumination provides necessary light for student participative activities, for referring to handouts, and for occasional note taking.

The television receiver should be located so that harsh light from a window or light fixture cannot strike the screen and cause glare. Do not place the receiver in front of an unshaded window that will compete with light from the television screen and make viewing difficult.

Volume. For proper hearing, the volume of the receiver should be set loud enough to be heard clearly in the rear of the viewing area, but not so loud that it bowls over those in the front. Normally

▲ *Figure 10.28*
Periodically clean monitor and TV screens with a weak detergent solution.

this happy middle ground is not difficult to achieve—if your seating arrangement is within acceptable bounds and your receiver's speaker mechanism is functioning properly.

Obviously, volume should be kept low enough so as not to disturb neighboring classes. Unfortunately, contemporary "open plan" buildings with only movable room dividers as walls provide a poor environment for TV or other audiovisual presentations. Under such conditions cooperation is critical. Teachers in neighboring areas can mutually agree to lower their decibel level to minimize interference (better than escalating the problem by trying to drown each other out!). Sometimes the only alternative is to seek an enclosed room that can be reserved for audiovisual use.

Appraisal Checklist: Equipment

Type: _____   Price: _____

Make: _____ Model: _____

Audio

Speaker size: _____   Amplifier output: _____

Inputs	Outputs
_____	_____
_____	_____

Sound controls   Tape

_____   Size: _____ Tracks: _____

_____   Speeds: _____

Other features:

Projector

Lamp: _____ (wattage) _____)   Exciter lamp: _____

Power controls   Lamp level control

_____   _____

_____   _____

Lens: _____

Other features:

Rating	High		Medium		Low	Comments:
Sound quality	☐	☐	☐	☐	☐	
Picture quality	☐	☐	☐	☐	☐	
Ease of operation	☐	☐	☐	☐	☐	
Price range	☐	☐	☐	☐	☐	
Durability	☐	☐	☐	☐	☐	
Ease to maintain	☐	☐	☐	☐	☐	
Ease to repair	☐	☐	☐	☐	☐	

Strong Points:

Weak Points:

Reviewer _____

Position _____

Recommended action _____   Date _____

Videotape Recorder Troubleshooting

Problem	Possible Remedy
Recording. Videotape is running but there is no picture on the monitor	1. Check to see that all components are plugged in and turned on. Make sure the lens cap is off the camera and the lens aperture is open. 2. Check the monitor. Switch it to "TV" and try to tune in a broadcast channel; make sure the brightness and contrast controls are properly set. If you still fail to get a picture, check to see if there is a circuit breaker on the back of the monitor that needs to be reset. If you get a picture while switched to "TV" you should then check the connection between camera and monitor. 3. Check the cable connections from camera to recorder and from recorder to monitor. 4. Check the settings of the switches on the recorder. Is the input selector on "Camera?" Is the "Record" button depressed?
Playback. Videotape is running but there is no picture or sound on monitor	1. Make sure the monitor input selector is set at "VTR" and all units are plugged in. 2. Check connectors between playback unit and monitor (e.g., make sure "Video Out" from playback is connected to "Video In" on monitor). Wiggle the end of the cable to see if there is a loose connection. 3. Check switches on playback unit.
Fuzzy sound and/or snowy picture	1. Video and/or audio heads may be fouled. Clean with approved spray. 2. Brushes under head-drum cover may be fouled or damaged. Have a technician check this possibility.
Picture slants horizontally across screen (the audio may also sound offspeed)	If adjustment of the horizontal hold knob does not clear up the situation, you may have a tape or cassette that is incompatible with your playback unit. Obtain a playback machine that matches the format of the tape or cassette.

References

Print References

Alten, Stanley R. *Audio in Media.* (Belmont, Calif.: Wadsworth Publications, 1981).

Bullard, John R., and Mether, Calvin E. *Audiovisual Fundamentals: Basic Equipment Operation, Simple Materials Production.* 3d ed. (Dubuque, Iowa: Wm. C. Brown, 1984).

The Equipment Directory of Audio-Visual, Computer and Video Products. (Fairfax, VA.: International Communications Industries Assn., annual).

Johnson, Warren. "Resources for Hardware Selection." *Audiovisual Instruction* (April 1978), pp. 46–47

Kerstetter, John P. "Designing Classrooms for the Use of Instructional Media: A Planning and Specification Checklist." *Media Management Journal* (Fall 1986), pp. 25–28.

Knirk, Frederick G. *Designing Productive Learning Environments.* (Englewood Cliffs, N.J.: Educational Technology Publications, 1979).

Kodak Projection Calculator and Seating Guide (S-16). (Rochester, N.Y.: Eastman Kodak, 1979).

Lord, Kenniston W., Jr. *The Design of the Industrial Classroom.* (Reading, Mass.: Addison-Wesley, 1977).

McVey, Gerald F. "Environments for Effective Media Utilization: Some Design Considerations." *Viewpoints* (September 1975), pp. 59–77.

Magee, John L. "Before You Call for Service, Try These Simple AV Repairs." *American School and University* (May 1981), pp. 126–129.

Meisel, Susan Lee. "A Hard Look at Audiovisual Equipment." *Media and Methods* (October 1983), pp. 9–11, 48.

Minimum Specifications for 16-mm Sound Film Projectors. (The Hague, Netherlands: International Council for Educational Media, 1982).

Minimum Specifications for Slide Projectors. (The Hague, Netherlands: International Council for Educational Media, 1980).

Rosenberg, Kenyon C. *Dictionary of Library and Educational Technology.* 2d ed. (Littleton, Colo.: Libraries Unlimited, 1983).

Rowat, Robert W. "A Guide to the Use of the Overhead Projector." ERIC, 1982. ED 211109.

Sakovich, Vladimir, and Costello, William. "Work Horses or White Elephants: A Guide to Selecting AV Equipment." *Media and Methods* (January 1980), pp. 26–29, 60–61.

Schroeder, Don, and Lare, Gary. *Audiovisual Equipment and Materials: A Basic Repair and Maintenance Manual.* (Metuchen, N.J.: Scarecrow Press, 1979).

Stafford, Carl W. "Standardize Your Adapters." *Instructional Innovator* (May 1980), pp. 26–28.

Sturken, Marita. "Video Systems for Libraries." *Sightlines* (Spring 1983), pp. 25–26.

Sullivan, Sam, and Baker, Bryan. *A Handbook of Operating Information and Simplified Maintenance Instructions for Commonly Used Audio-visual Equipment.* Rev. ed. (Huntsville, Tex.: KBS, Inc., 1982).

Teague, Fred A.; Newhouse, Barbara S.; and Streit, Les D. *Instructional Media Basics.* (Dubuque, Iowa: Kendall/Hunt, 1982).

Wadsworth, Raymond H. *Basics of Audio and Visual Systems Design.* (Indianapolis: Howard W. Sams, 1983).

Waggener, Joe, and Kraft, Tim. "Video Troubleshooting for the Technically Butterfingered." *Audiovisual Instruction* (January 1979), pp. 44–45.

Wilkinson, Gene L. "Projection Variables and Performance." *AV Communication Review* (Winter 1976), pp. 413–436.

Wilshusen, John. "How to Prevent Equipment Failures." *Instructional Innovator* (March 1980), pp. 35–36.

Wyman, Raymond. *Mediaware: Selection, Operation, and Maintenance.* 2d ed. (Dubuque, Iowa: Wm. C. Brown, 1976).

Yeamans, George T. *Projectionists' Primer.* (Pullman, Wash.: Information Futures, 1979).

Audiovisual References

The following are all videotapes on basic operation and care of equipment. All are in color and are five to eight minutes long. Available from Audiovisual Center Marketing, C215 Seashore Hall, University of Iowa, Iowa City, IA 52242.

General Operating Principles for AV Equipment

Portable Audio Cassette Recorder

Overhead Projector

35-mm Slide Projector

Sound Filmstrip Projector

Opaque Projector

Portable Tripod Screen

16-mm Projector

Organizations

EPIE (Educational Products Information Exchange) Institute, P.O. Box 839, Water Mill, NY 11976

EPIE is a nonprofit, consumer-supported agency functioning like a "consumer's union" and providing analytical information about instructional materials and equipment. EPIE conducts workshops on analyzing instructional materials and publishes *EPIE Reports* bimonthly and a newsletter, *EPIEgram*.

International Communications Industries Association, 3150 Spring Street, Fairfax, VA 22031

Trade association for producers and distributors of audiovisual equipment and materials. Publishes annually *The Equipment Directory of Audio-Visual, Computer and Video Products.*

Possible Projects

10-A. Demonstrate the proper setup, operation, and disassembly of the following pieces of equipment: tape recorder, record player, overhead projector, slide projector, filmstrip projector, opaque projector, 16-mm film projector, and videotape recorder.

10-B. Given a piece of equipment from the list in project 10-A with a "problem," troubleshoot and correct the problem.

10-C. Demonstrate proper care and maintenance for each piece of equipment listed in project 10-A.

10-D. Set up (or diagram the setup) for a given instructional situation requiring audio, projection, and/or video.

10-E. Demonstrate the proper procedures for replacing lamps in the following types of projectors: overhead, slide, filmstrip, opaque, and film. You will be evaluated on selecting the correct replacement lamp and on handling it properly.

10-F. Procure catalogs illustrating projection tables and carts, identify examples from each of the functions described in the chapter, and compare the examples in terms of versatility of use, advantages, limitations, and cost.

10-G. Synchronize a set of slides and an audiotape. You may use existing slides, but you must record the narrative on the tape and incorporate the advance pulses into the system.

10-H. Evaluate a piece of audiovisual equipment using the "Appraisal Checklist: Equipment" in the chapter.

11
Technologies of Instruction

Outline

The Roots of Today's Technologies of
    Instruction
  Basic Concepts of Reinforcement
    Theory
  Emergence of Programmed
    Instruction
Programmed Instruction
  What It Is
  Programmed Instruction as a
    Technology of Instruction
  Applications of Programmed
    Instruction
  Utilization of Programmed
    Instruction
Programmed Tutoring
  What It Is
  Programmed Tutoring as a
    Technology of Instruction
  Applications and Utilization of
    Programmed Tutoring

Personalized System of Instruction
  What It Is
  PSI as a Technology of Instruction
  Applications and Utilization of PSI
Audio-Tutorial Systems
  What They Are
  Audio-Tutorial Systems as a
    Technology of Instruction
  Applications and Utilization of
    Audio-Tutorial Systems
Cognitive Psychology and
    Technologies of Instruction
Cooperative Learning
    Technologies of Instruction based
      on Cooperative Learning
Simulation and Games
  What They Are
  Simulation/Gaming as a
    Technology of Instruction
Computer-Assisted Instruction
Summary

Objectives

After studying this chapter, you
should be able to:

1. Define *technologies of instruction* and identify five of their characteristics.

2. Identify five examples of technologies of instruction.

3. Discuss the basic application of
reinforcement theory, including a definition of *reinforcer*.

4. Describe the relationship
between "teaching machines" and
programmed instruction.

5. Identify five attributes of today's
programmed instruction and distinguish programmed instruction from
other forms of instruction.

6. Distinguish between "linear"
and "branching" formats of programmed instruction.

7. Describe an appropriate application of programmed instruction in an instructional setting.

8. Generate five guidelines for using programmed instruction in the classroom.

9. Describe *programmed tutoring,* indicating what it is, how it is used, and an instructional situation in which it could be applied.

10. Discuss why the *Personalized System of Instruction* is a technology for *managing* instruction and compare and contrast PSI with the other technologies of instruction.

11. List the three types of sessions used in the *Audio-Tutorial System* and briefly describe the purpose of each.

12. Describe how *cognitive psychology* distinguishes between knowledge and behavior.

13. Discuss how *cooperative learning* can form the basis of technologies of instruction.

14. Explain why instructional *simulations* and *games* can be considered as technologies of instruction.

15. Explain why the computer itself is *not* a technology of instruction as defined in this chapter.

16. Synthesize an instructional situation in which *one* of the technologies of instruction could be used effectively. Your description should indicate both *how* and *when* you would use it.

Lexicon

reinforcement theory

programmed instruction

programmed tutoring

Personalized System of Instruction (PSI)

Audio-Tutorial System (A-T)

cognitive psychology

cooperative learning

simulation

game

computer-assisted instruction (CAI)

AMERICAN economist John Kenneth Galbraith defines *technology* as "the systematic application of scientific or other organized knowledge to practical tasks."* This view of the concept of technology correctly focuses on technology as a *process*, an approach to solving problems, rather than on the *products* of technology—computers, transistors, satellites, bionic devices, and the like. Unfortunately, the debate over the role of technology in education has too often been clouded by a tendency to concentrate on the role of artifacts such as audiovisual hardware, television transmission systems, "teaching machines," and so on. Advocates and critics alike have too often assumed that there is some sort of "magic" inherent in these artifacts. The only question seems to have been whether this "magic" was helpful or harmful to students, teachers, and educational institutions.

This is not to denigrate the educational value of the products of technology. Indeed, much of this book is devoted to helping you choose among these products and use them for more effective teaching and learning. But there is nothing magical about the hardware. The magic, if there is to be magic, stems from the selection of materials according to their usefulness in achieving specific learning objectives and their utilization in ways conducive to applying sound learning principles.

In this chapter, therefore, we highlight *technology as a process.* We will extend Galbraith's definition into the realm of education,

showing ways in which materials and activities can be combined to allow a "systematic application of scientific knowledge." These special arrangements we will refer to as *technologies of instruction.*

A Technology of Instruction: *a teaching/learning pattern designed to provide reliable, effective instruction to each learner through application of scientific principles of human learning.*

We use this term in the plural because many different arrangements could merit this label. The six examples of technologies of instruction explored in this chapter do not by any means constitute a full listing of all technologies of instruction; they are intended merely to be representative of some of the most common formats in widespread use today. Criterion-referenced instruction, competency-based education, and mastery learning are names given to instructional formats that could be classified as technologies of instruction. They share many features in common with each other and in common with the formats elaborated on in this chapter. Several formats are discussed in depth in this chapter. Two other technologies of instruction alluded to only briefly here are examined in detail in the two following chapters—simulation and gaming and computer-assisted instruction.

THE ROOTS OF TODAY'S TECHNOLOGIES OF INSTRUCTION

MANY of today's methods of instruction have roots in theories that are hundreds or even thousands of years old. Socrates,

Comenius, Pestalozzi, and Herbart would find many of their own ideas clearly reflected in contemporary classroom practices. But the body of theory that influenced most strongly the development of today's technologies of instruction is of much more recent origin. In fact, many regard an article published in 1954 in *Harvard Educational Review** as the catalyst that sparked a whole new movement in education. In that article, the author, psychologist B. F. Skinner, challenged educators to modify their traditional practices to put into effect new principles of learning that were emerging from studies in experimental psychology.

Basic Concepts of Reinforcement Theory

Skinner's body of theory, which he referred to as "operant conditioning" but is generally known as reinforcement theory, differs from earlier behaviorist theories in that it applies to voluntary behaviors. He claimed that earlier stimulus-response paradigms were adequate for explaining reflexive responses such as salivation, dilation of the pupil of the eye, the knee-jerk reflex, and the like. However, he was more interested in explaining responses that people emit voluntarily, such as driving a car, writing a letter, and balancing a checkbook.

The backbone of Skinner's theories was the concept of reinforcement. He hypothesized that the *consequences* of a response determine whether or not it will be learned. That is, a behavior that is followed by a satisfying

---

* John Kenneth Galbraith. *The New Industrial State.* Boston: Houghton-Mifflin, 1967, p. 12.

* B. F. Skinner. "The Science of Learning and the Art of Teaching." *Harvard Educational Review* (Spring 1954), pp. 86–97.

▲ *Figure 11.1*
Psychologist B. F. Skinner, whose theory of operant conditioning gave rise to the development of programmed instruction.

consequence is more likely to occur in the future. Giving such a satisfying consequence is referred to as *reinforcement.*

A reinforcer is any event or thing that increases the likelihood of a preceding behavior's being repeated: learned. This phrasing is intended to point out that a thing is a reinforcer only if it *works.* An object may be desirable or satisfying to one person at one time but not to another person or at another time. For instance, a chocolate bar might sound quite inviting to you right now, but not if you are a diabetic or are on a diet or have just finished eating a big box of candy.

Also fundamental to reinforcement theory is the notion that complex skills can be broken down into clusters of simpler behaviors. Each behavior bit can be learned one at a time through skillful arrangement for immediate reinforcement after each correct response. These simple behaviors then become links in a longer, more complex behavior

chain. Skinner was able to demonstrate this process dramatically by teaching a pigeon to turn a complete circle clockwise within just a single demonstration session. Closely observing the pigeon's behavior, he rewarded every partial movement of the head or feet toward the clockwise direction with a kernel of corn. Counterclockwise movements went unrewarded. Gradually, the pigeon's clockwise movements became less random, until, by the end of the session, counterclockwise movement ceased and the pigeon moved only in a clockwise direction.

Transferring these basic concepts (overt response, followed by reinforcement) to formal human learning requires adding another element to the formula—a *prompt.* Rather than waiting around for a desired response to occur spontaneously or randomly, the instructional material can be structured to hint at or prompt the desired response. The basic formula for applying reinforcement

theory to human learning, then, requires a prompt, an overt response, and a reinforcement. For example:

1. PROMPT (e.g., math problem)
   ↓
2. RESPONSE (e.g., student's answer)
   ↓
3. REINFORCEMENT (e.g., knowledge of correct response and/or praise)

Emergence of Programmed Instruction

In his 1954 article Skinner pointed out that the elements of his formula were not well represented in traditional classroom instruction. In large-group instruction, students spend much of their time listening, with little opportunity for overt response. Even if an overt response is given, the typical teacher, responsible for large numbers of students at once, has limited opportunity even to observe individual responses, much less to reinforce each one appropriately. How, then, could the principles of response/reinforcement be implemented in the classroom?

Skinner's initial solution to this problem was an innovative method of presenting instructional material printed in small bits or "frames," each of which included an item of information (prompt), an incomplete statement to be completed or question to be answered (response), and provision of the correct answer (reinforcement). A mechanical device—which later came to be referred to as a teaching machine—was used to control the logistics of the process.

This solution—programmed instruction—provided a mechanism for adapting lessons to an

▲ *Figure 11.2*
An early teaching machine of the type described by Skinner in his original article; the paper roll advanced only when the correct response was constructed.

consisting of a small box having on its top surface a window through which information printed on a paper roll could be read. The learner responded to a question or blank to be filled by selecting a multiple-choice answer. If the right one was chosen, the paper roll would advance to the next question when a knob was turned. Other early devices required written responses (see Figure 11.3).

Since reinforcement theory demanded that reinforcement be given only after a correct response, it was originally considered necessary to use a mechanical monitoring device to enforce this requirement. During the infancy of programmed instruction, much creative energy was invested in developing such "teaching machines" to automate the presentation of frames of information to the learner. Research and practical experience soon indicated, however, that students were quite capable of monitoring their own progress without

▲ *Figure 11.3*
By the mid-1960s the "machine" had shrunk, and most programs required written responses.

the help of a cumbersome and expensive page-turning machine. So, in many cases, the "teaching machines" were discarded, and their instructional contents were put into book formats. The earliest programmed instruction texts arranged the frames across the page in horizontal strips. The correct response for each question could be checked only by turning the page. Later, this method was relaxed, allowing the frames to be

individual's pace, thereby circumventing the large-group barrier. Further, it assured that students would be kept actively at work making frequent (and nearly always correct) responses, thus gaining frequent reinforcement. In short, programmed instruction appeared to be a feasible method for putting reinforcement theory into practice in all sorts of real-life classroom situations.

Reinforcement theory has been presented in some detail here not because it is the basis for *all* technologies of instruction but because of its historical primacy in stimulating the concept of a "technology of instruction." And it does lie at the heart of several of the techniques described in the rest of this chapter. The first to be examined in detail is programmed instruction itself.

PROGRAMMED INSTRUCTION

What It Is

Originally, the term *programmed instruction* was used in reference to a particular *format* for presenting printed learning materials to an individual learner. B. F. Skinner's 1954 article, previously mentioned, described a mechanical device

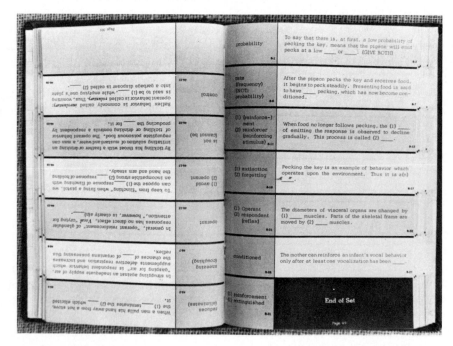

▲ *Figure 11.4*
An early programmed textbook was *The Analysis of Behavior* by James B. Holland and B. F. Skinner (1961); note the "zebra stripe" arrangement of the pages, requiring the reader to turn the page to see the correct answer.

arranged vertically, just as in conventional printed pages. These programmed texts were meant to be read with a piece of paper covering the rest of the page while a frame was being read. After writing an answer in the blank on the first frame, for example, the user moved the cover down to see the confirmation (correct answer) printed in the box to the left of the second frame. You will have a better idea of how programmed instruction works if you go through the following example.

	An Example of Linear Programming
	1. Psychologists differ in their explanations about what learning is and precisely how it occurs. The series of statements or "frames" presented here deal with one particular explanation of the process of _____.
learning	2. We cannot observe learning directly, but we can infer that it has occurred when a person consistently makes a *response* that he or she previously was unable to make. For example, if a student says "nine" when asked "What is three times three?" she is making a _____ that was probably learned through practice in school.
response	3. If you reply "kappa" when asked "What Greek letter is represented by K?" you are making a _____ that you learned through some prior experience.
response	4. The word or picture or other sensory stimulation that causes you to make a response is a *stimulus* (plural: stimuli). Therefore, if "kappa" is your response, "What Greek letter is represented by K?" would be the _____.
stimulus	5. To the stimulus "good," the student of Spanish responds "bueno"; the student of Arabic responds "gayid." To the stimulus "silver," the student of Spanish responds "plata"; the student of Arabic responds "fida." They are responding to English words which are serving as _____.
stimuli	6. In these frames the written statements are the stimuli to which you are writing _____ in the blanks.
responses	7. We learn to connect certain verbal responses to certain stimuli through the process of forming *associations*. We say that the student associates "nine" with "three times three"; he learns to associate "kappa" with "K"; and he _____ "plata" with "silver."
associates	8. Much verbal learning seems to be based on the formation of associations between _____ and responses.
stimuli	Etc.

Programmed Instruction as a Technology of Instruction

It is clear that programmed instruction was developed very consciously as a specific pattern of activities designed to put scientific principles of learning into practice. As such, it fits our definition of a technology of instruction. However, the translation from the laboratory into the classroom was quite direct and unadorned. By the early 1960s an orthodoxy had developed around the construction of programmed instruction. The elements of this orthodoxy were summarized by Wilbur Schramm as follows:

(a) an ordered sequence of stimulus items,

(b) to each of which a student responds *in some specified way,*

(c) his response being reinforced *by immediate knowledge of results,*

(d) so that he moves by small steps,

(e) therefore making few errors *and practicing mostly correct responses,*

(f) from what he knows, by a process of successively closer approximations, *toward what he is supposed to learn from the program.* *

Although many of the materials that incorporated these elements were found to be successful with students, in a good number of controlled studies the programmed materials failed to live up to the claims made by their adherents. In some experiments it was found that "large steps" worked better than "small steps." Delayed rather than immediate knowledge of results sometimes yielded just as good results. At times, even scrambling the order of the frames produced better learning than "an ordered sequence." In addition, it was found that some students considered the repetitious pattern of small, easy steps tedious and boring.

Further doubts were raised when Norman Crowder* challenged the programmed instruction orthodoxy with a competing technique of program writing—one that ignored all psychological theory and attempted instead simply to present information to readers in a more efficient, individualized form. He called this technique "intrinsic programming." Its basic method was to present a large block of information followed by multiple-choice questions requiring application of the facts or principles presented.

Each choice of answer directed the reader to a different page. If the correct choice was made, the learner skipped ahead to new frames of information. Incorrect choices led to explanations of the correct response and to fresh questions. If the learner had additional difficulty, he or she was routed to sequences of remedial instruction. At each step the learner encountered questions testing mastery of the subject matter and was directed onward to new material only after demonstrating a grasp of the prerequisite skills. Because Crowder's pattern of frames resembled the branches of a tree, this programming technique became known as the branching format. The original Skinnerian format is referred to as linear. The two patterns are compared in Figure 11.5. The major advantage of branching over linear programming is that students who catch on quickly can move through the material much more efficiently, following the "prime path." In the linear format, all learners are expected to go through all the steps.

By the late 1960s it had become clear that programmed instruction was not to be confined to the precise formats originally worked out by Skinner. The initial form of programmed instruction was seen to be too literal an application of reinforcement theory to formal learning. For one thing, it was apparent that *knowledge of results* was not consistently reinforcing to all learners all of the time. Its potential for being reinforcing varies with the situation, as is the case with other potential reinforcers such as food, sex, praise, money, and the like. In addition, programmed materials, like any other instructional materials, needed to be made varied and interesting, a need that could not be met by rigid adherence to any single stereotyped "recipe."

In recent years the basic concepts underlying programmed instruction have found expression in a multitude of forms; programmed tutoring, the Personalized System of Instruction, and computer-assisted instruction are three concepts that we will be examining more closely. And printed programs are still being produced and used. In fact, today they are more widely used than ever before. But they are not necessarily labeled as "programmed instruction" and they hardly ever follow the rigid formula of earlier linear programming. Note, for example, the variety of programming formats illustrated in Figures 11.6 and 11.7.

---

* Wilbur Schramm. *Programmed Instruction: Today and Tomorrow.* New York: Fund for the Advancement of Education, 1962.

* Norman Crowder. "On the Differences between Linear and Intrinsic Programming." *Phi Delta Kappan* (March 1963), pp. 250–254.

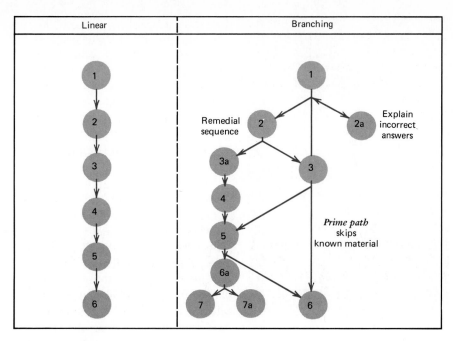

Linear	Branching

▲ **Figure 11.5**
Comparison of linear and branching formats of programmed instruction

The most comprehensive listing of commercially available programmed materials is *Programmed Learning and Individually Paced Instruction—Bibliography* compiled by Carl Hendershot, 5th ed. (Bay City, Mich.: Hendershot Bibliography, 1983).

Despite the great diversity of styles and formats evident among programmed materials, there are still a number of features shared in common among them. These include performance objectives stated in advance, clear sequence of activities, frequent response (requiring thinking, not just copying), regular feedback, test items that are parallel to the stated objectives, and validation based on actual learner tryouts. Note that these features are among the

---

Every hue has a tone sequence from its lightest tints to its darkest shades. Through light/dark contrast, color can be controlled to exaggerate form toward three-dimensional effect or to suppress form toward a flattened effect.

Examples

When your hair becomes bleached by summer sun or peroxide, it becomes lighter in value than before. When the bleach grows out, the hair becomes darker in value.

When you roast a marshmallow, it changes in value from white to a very light brown to a darker value of brown. If you are not careful at this point, it will turn black—a still darker value.

Exercise

Indicate the contrasting tones associated with each of the following:

(a) Coffee stain on a white shirt
(b) New blue denim patch on faded denim jeans
(c) Tree shadow on a yellow house
(d) Teeth brushed with "Sparkle-brite" showing through lips with red lipstick

— — — — — — — — — — — — — — —

(a) Stain is darker in value than white fabric
(b) Patch is darker in value than the jeans
(c) Shadow area is darker in value than the yellow wall
(d) Teeth are lighter in value than lips

You may find it helpful to make a tonal scale of at least one hue. Using blue-colored ink or paint, place the undiluted blue in the center frame. Going to the right of center, add a little water or white paint to dilute the blue for each step of the frame, leaving white in the last frame. Going to the left, add a very little black for each step until you reach black for the last frame. You may even succeed in extending this value scale further than the steps in following the sketch. It is possible to make such a tonal scale for each hue.

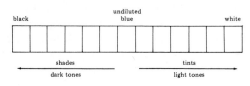

▲ **Figure 11.6**
A contemporary example of linear programmed instruction, with a book on art. This program calls for a variety of types of responses, including painting, as seen at the bottom of the page.

SELF-TEST

This self-test is designed to show you whether or not you have mastered the objectives of Chapter 2. Answer each question to the best of your ability, based on what you learned in this chapter. Correct answers are given following the test.

Read the following paragraph. Then answer the following questions that refer to the situation.

Mr. Cee, a sixth grade teacher, is concerned about Bill Boneau, a boy in his class. Bill, a natural leader, can command the respect of his fellow students. However, far too often, he uses this leadership ability to distract students from academics. In addition, he seldom pays attention to the teacher presentations or class discussions, and his homework is seldom done—all of which seem to be affecting his test scores. A notable exception to his lack of interest is science. Bill is interested in scientific projects, and he does well on them. His interest and leadership in this area have carried the entire class to levels of scientific inquiry and understanding far beyond those of any of Mr. Cee's previous classes.

1. List three inappropriate behaviors of Bill's which should be reduced in frequency.

   a. _____
   b. _____
   c. _____

2. List two appropriate behaviors to be encouraged.

   a. _____
   b. _____

3. List the rules for Bill that would be included in a behavioral contract.

   _____
   _____
   _____

▲ **Figure 11.7**
A review exercise in a programmed book. Previously learned principles are applied to the solving of a hypothetical problem.

criteria included here in the appraisal checklist for programmed materials.

Applications of Programmed Instruction

Programmed materials have been used successfully from the elementary school through the adult education levels and in almost every subject area. By itself or in conjunction with other strategies, a program can be used to teach an entire course or a segment of a course. Many teachers use short programmed units to teach simple principles and terminology. Programmed instruction is particularly useful as an enrichment activity. It can help provide highly motivated students with additional learning experiences that the teacher might ordinarily be unable to provide because of classroom time pressures. Programmed materials have proven to be very effective in remedial instruction. The program can function as a kind of tutor for slow learners in situations where more personalized attention may be virtually impossible (in overcrowded classrooms, for example). Such students may even take this particular tutor with them when they leave the classroom! One of the reasons for the success of programmed materials in remedial instruction is their "failure-proof" design. By being broken into small steps, by allowing the student to take as much time as needed for each step, and by being evaluated and revised carefully prior to publication, these materials are more likely to provide the slow learner with a successful experience. For some students it may be their first encounter with schoolwork that gives them an immediate and continued feeling of success.

Programmed instruction can be

▲ *Figure 11.8*
Through programmed instruction, trainees can begin study when ready, not just when a full class becomes available.

an effective means of providing classwide competencies in skills prerequisite to successful completion of a unit of study. For example, one high school physics teacher used a small programmed text to allow his students to teach themselves the power-of-ten notation, which is a prerequisite for solving physics problems. At the outset, some of the students were even more proficient with power-of-ten operations than their instructor; others had been introduced to the technique but had lost their competence in it because they had not been required to use the skill; still others had never even been introduced to it. The program on power-of-ten notation eliminated devoting class time to a subject that would have bored some and confused others. Instead, the students were allowed to consider the material on their own. Those who knew the technique could ignore the program; those who had previously learned the skill

but were a little rusty could use the program as a review; and those who had never been exposed to power-of-ten notation could master the necessary manipulations on their own and at their own pace. All students were subsequently required to pass a criterion test demonstrating mastery of this skill.

Programmed materials have a wide variety of other more or less specialized uses. They can, for example, be used for make-up instruction by students who have been absent from school for an extended period of time. They can be used to expand curricular offerings when it might be difficult or impossible otherwise to do so—because of too few interested students, for instance, or no qualified instructor. This could be an important consideration for smaller schools and for training programs in business/industry settings.

It is true that programmed materials are often more expensive than ordinary textbooks, mainly because of the time and effort spent in their careful development and in their validation testing. Their increased efficiency as learning tools, however, may compensate for their higher cost (especially in situations in which the cost of student time and failure is taken into account).

Programmed instruction is by its very nature individualized learning, in which the student advances at his or her own pace. However, as with other techniques for individualized instruction, this does not mean that students are always working alone. Group activities can and should be scheduled to supplement the programmed instruction and to meet other desired educational goals. In addition, as with other properly planned individualized activities, programs help release

Appraisal Checklist: Programmed Materials

Title _____

Series title _____

Source _____ Date _____ Cost _____

Length (completion time), Range: _____ to _____ minutes, Average _____ minutes

Subject area _____

Intended audience _____

Objectives (Stated or Implied):

Brief Description:

Entry Capabilities Required:

- Prior subject-matter knowledge/vocabulary
- Reading ability
- Mathematical ability
- Other

Rating	High		Medium		Low	Comments
Relevance to objectives	☐	☐	☐	☐	☐	
Accuracy of information	☐	☐	☐	☐	☐	
Likely to arouse/maintain interest	☐	☐	☐	☐	☐	
Exemplifies principles of programming (e.g., ''lean'' structure, responses require thought, relevant practice)	☐	☐	☐	☐	☐	
Test frames parallel to objectives	☐	☐	☐	☐	☐	
Feedback provides remedial branches	☐	☐	☐	☐	☐	
Appropriate vocabulary level	☐	☐	☐	☐	☐	
Evidence of effectiveness (validation data should describe tryout audience, time, outcomes)	☐	☐	☐	☐	☐	

Strong Points:

Weak Points:

Recommended action _____

Reviewer _____

Position _____

Date _____

teachers from routine classroom chores in order to interact personally with students and to provide them with human reinforcement.

Utilization of Programmed Instruction

Programmed instruction is basically learner centered. It focuses on the activities of the student rather than the activities of the teacher. The role of the teacher, however, is as important to the success of programmed instruction as it is to any other type of instruction. It is up to the instructor to arrange and maintain conditions conducive to achievement of the program's learning objectives. Be sure to familiarize yourself with the entire program before implementing it for class use so that you will be in a position to assist students to work through it when and if they need help. Familiarity with the program will also help you coordinate the programmed materials with other instructional activities—lectures, group discussions, and so forth.

The students' first exposure to programmed materials is particularly important. Be sure to explain the mechanics of using the materials so that the students will not get bogged down with them when they begin to work the program. For example, clarify whether answers are to be recorded directly on the materials or on separate sheets of paper. (Recording answers on separate sheets allows the materials to be used over and over again.) Once the mechanics of the program are understood, the student is free to concentrate on working the program and to experience the immediate success so important in initial exposure to new learning methods.

Because programmed materials often have the physical appearance of a test, the fact that the program is not a test should be emphasized. Carefully explain that even though the program confronts the student with a series of questions to be answered, users need not be fearful of making errors. If errors are made, the program automatically helps the learner correct them. Explain that students are never evaluated on the basis of their performance in working through the program. Evaluation is based upon student performance on criterion tests administered *after* using the program. Programs are for teaching, not for testing.

It should be established that students will be working at their own pace, neither pushed faster than they can efficiently perform nor held back if they wish to work rapidly. It would be counterproductive to assign a minimum amount of material to be covered in a single class period.

Students should be encouraged to ask questions about the material as they work, especially if they become confused. Confusion may indicate not only misunderstanding on the part of the student but also ambiguities and weaknesses in the program itself which you will want to record for future reference.

Stress the importance of being intellectually honest with oneself when working with programmed materials. Inform your students of the futility of peeking ahead in order to ascertain a correct response rather than thinking it out for themselves. Explain that there is nothing to gain by such actions and much to lose, namely, the opportunity to learn. Human nature being as it is, you will probably find some students unable to resist some initial peeking ahead. But this behavior will likely fade as students discover for themselves that there is no

advantage in it and that the program is designed to make certain they can work out the correct responses on their own.

PROGRAMMED TUTORING

What It Is

PROGRAMMED *tutoring* (also referred to as structured tutoring) is a one-to-one method of instruction in which the decisions to be made by the tutor are "programmed" in advance by means of carefully structured printed instructions. In a typical program the tutor and student sit down together to go through the lesson material. The "teacher's book" has the answers to the exercises; the "student's book" does not. An excerpt from a typical programmed tutoring teacher's book is shown on page 311. Note how the tutor's role in the program is set forth, step by step, to conform with learner response to the materials.

Because the tutor is continually choosing the next step on the basis of the learner's last response, programmed tutoring is a form of branching program-

▲ *Figure 11.9*
Psychologist Douglas G. Ellson, developer of programmed tutoring and low-cost learning systems.

ming. As such, it shares the basic advantage for which branching was originally developed: the fast learner may skip quickly through the material without tedious, unnecessary repetition.

Programmed tutoring uses what might be called "brightening," as opposed to the "fading" or gradual reduction of prompts used in conventional linear programmed instruction. In brightening, the

▲ *Figure 11.10*
A typical arrangement for a programmed tutoring lesson

item is first presented in a relatively difficult form. If the learner responds correctly, he or she is reinforced and goes on to a new item. If not, a series of increasingly clearer prompts or hints are given. For example, in teaching a beginning reader to follow written instructions, the student's book might say, "Point to your teacher." If the learner does not do so when first shown the instruction, the tutor might follow this sequence of brightening prompts:

1. "Read it again." (Wait for response.)
2. "What does it say?"
3. "What does it tell you to do?"
4. "Do what it tells you to do."

The sequence of prompts would continue until the learner gives an acceptable response. Then rein-

forcement would be given. The idea is to lead the student toward the solution with brightening hints but to avoid actually giving the correct answer.

Programmed Tutoring as a Technology of Instruction

Programmed tutoring shares with programmed instruction the characteristics of individualized pacing, active learner response, and immediate feedback. The use of a live tutor as a mediator adds immensely to the flexibility of the system, and it adds another major advantage over printed self-instructional material by employing *social reinforcers* in the form of praise ("That's great." "Oh, what a good answer." "You're really on the ball today.") rather than just simple knowledge of results. Administered flexibly and creatively by a live guide, this technology of instruction can overcome the monotonous pattern sometimes associated with other programmed formats.

Applications and Utilization of Programmed Tutoring

Programmed tutoring combines the qualities of programmed instruction with the warmth and personal attention that only a human tutor can add. The tutor may be a teacher aide, a parent, or another student ("peer tutoring"). Almost anyone can be trained as a tutor because the sequencing of the material and the tutor's responses are carefully programmed into the lesson by the designer. Thus, it is particularly attractive for areas in which qualified teachers are lacking. Douglas G. Ellson, a principal developer of programmed tutor-

---

STEP 1 Tell the student that this exercise will help him learn to sound out new words.

STEP 2 Point to the first word and ask the student to *sound* it out.
    a. If the student reads the word correctly, praise him; then go on to the next word.
    b. If the student is unable to read the word or reads it incorrectly, have him make the individual sounds in the word separately and then assist him in blending the sounds.

Example:
    Word: "THIN"

Tutor: Place your finger over the last two letters in the word and ask: "What sound does the *th* make?" If the student answers correctly, praise him and go to the next sound. If he answers incorrectly or fails to answer, tell him the sound and have him repeat it. Follow the same procedure for each sound in the word, and then show him how to blend the separate sounds.

STEP 3 Follow step 2 for each word on the sheet.

STEP 4 At the end of the session, praise the student.

STEP 5 Fill out your tutor log.

Source: Grant Von Harrison, *Beginning Reading 1: A Professional Guide for the Lay Tutor.* Provo, Utah: Brigham Young University Press, 1972, p. 101.

▲ *Figure 11.11*
The directions given in the tutor's guidebook structure the programmed tutoring lesson.

▲ *Figure 11.12*
Programs designed for small groups enable participants to learn from each other as well as from the program.

▲ *Figure 11.13*
Psychologist Fred S. Keller, originator of the Personalized System of Instruction, also referred to as the "Keller Plan"

ing, estimates that over a million young people in less-developed countries have learned to read by this method since its origins in 1960.

Reading and mathematics have been the most popular subject areas for application of tutoring. These subjects lend themselves to this method because of their high degree of structure. Also, being very basic skills, they are frequently the targets of remedial or compensatory education programs—the milieu in which volunteer tutoring projects are often mounted. Indeed, Ellson's tutoring program centered at Indiana University has been recognized by American Institutes for Research and the U.S. Education Department as one of the half dozen most effective compensatory education programs in the United States.

In preparing to utilize programmed tutoring, keep in mind that the research consistently indicates that tutors gain even more than their students. So give every-

one a chance to be a tutor, not just the most advanced students. In any case, ensure that the tutors are trained in and do use the correct procedures. The materials are validated for effectiveness only when they are used as directed.

A final utilization hint: Consider using the tutorial method to make productive use of high-absence days. Train those who are present to tutor absentees when they return. Tutors deepen their knowledge; the absentees catch up.

PERSONALIZED SYSTEM OF INSTRUCTION

What It Is

THE *Personalized System of Instruction (PSI)* could be described as a technology for *managing* instruction. It puts reinforcement theory into action as the overall framework for a whole course. In the PSI classroom students work individually

at their own pace using any of a variety of instructional materials—a chapter in a book, computer-assisted instruction, a videocassette, a sound filmstrip, a programmed booklet, and so on. The materials are arranged in sequential order, and the student must show *mastery* of each unit before being allowed to move on to the next.

Mastery is determined by means of a test taken whenever the student feels ready for it. The content and emphasis of the test should be no surprise because each unit is accompanied by a study guide that spells out the objective and most important points to be learned in that unit.

Study help and testing are handled by *proctors*—usually more advanced students who volunteer to help others. Proctors are a critical component of PSI for it is their one-to-one tutorial assistance that makes the system *personalized*. After scoring each test the proctor reviews it immediately with the student, asking questions to probe weak points and listening to defenses of alternative answers. If performance is below the specified mastery level, the student returns at another time to take a second form of the test.

Group meetings are rare, being used mainly for "inspirational" lectures, film showings, and review sessions. The instructor acts primarily as a planner, designer, manager, and guide to students and proctors.

PSI as a Technology of Instruction

Like programmed tutoring, PSI strives to implement the learning principles that programmed instruction originally envisioned: (a) the presentation of information appropriate to the student's current ability, (b) frequent opportunities to respond to the material, and (c) immediate feedback/correction. To these principles PSI adds the philosophy of mastery—the student may not tackle new material until the prior skills have been mastered—and the person-to-person contact with a proctor and instructor.

Unlike programmed tutoring and programmed instruction, PSI does not revolve around the design of specially structured materials; it manipulates the *framework* in which instruction occurs. It consciously puts into play a number of "generalized reinforcers," rewards that tend to work well with humans despite differences in preference or current need. These include grades, diplomas, and other similar tokens of achievement, personal attention, social approval, affection, and deferent behavior of others. The designers of PSI aimed to maximize rewards for conscientious study, minimize frustration, and eliminate the fear

connected with not knowing where one is going, how well one is doing, and what surprise the instructor is going to pull on the final exam.

Applications and Utilization of PSI

Since its origins in Fred S. Keller's psychology course at the University of Brasilia in the mid-1960s, PSI has been successfully used at all grade levels and in virtually every subject area. It is also widely known in military training and in business/industry education. The validity of the PSI approach has been attested to by extensive research. Kulik, Kulik, and Smith prepared a review of studies in which PSI had been compared with conventional instruction. Their conclusion was as follows:

In a typical published comparison, PSI and lecture means are separated by about two-thirds of a standard deviation. How large a difference is this? Let us take an average student, Mary Smith, who may take her introductory physics course, for example, by either a conventional method or by PSI. If she takes a typical lecture course, her achievement in physics will put her at the 50th percentile on a standardized test. She is an average student in an average course. If she takes the same course in PSI format, she will achieve at the 75th percentile on the standardized test. This increment is what PSI has to offer the individual student. . . . In our judgment, this is the most impressive record achieved by a teaching method in higher education. It stands in stark contrast to the inconclusive results of earlier comparisons of college teaching methods.*

Specific guidelines for setting up and running courses according to the PSI system can be found in the books and articles listed in the references section at the end of this chapter. A few cautions about implementing a PSI approach are in order. First, PSI involves a great deal of time in planning and developing supplementary materials. Even though less lecture time is involved, instructors should be prepared to spend about half again as many hours conducting a PSI course as conducting a conventional course. Second, a willingness and ability to state objectives specifically is prerequisite. Third, the "mastery" point-of-view built into PSI rejects norm-referenced grading (the "normal curve") and insists on complete mastery as the criterion of success. It aims to elevate all students to the "A" level.

▲ *Figure 11.14*
Interaction with the proctor "personalizes" the PSI approach.

---

* James A. Kulik, Chen-Lin Kulik, and Beverly B. Smith. "Research on the Personalized System of Instruction." *Programmed Learning and Educational Technology* (Spring 1976), pp. 13, 23–30.

In the fall of 1961, S. N. Postlethwait, a professor of botany at Purdue University, began preparing supplementary lectures on audio tape to provide an opportunity for students with inadequate academic backgrounds to keep up with his introductory botany class. Any student could listen to these recordings at the university audiovisual center. Soon Dr. Postlethwait decided that he could improve the effectiveness of these tapes by having the students bring their botany textbooks to the audiovisual center when they came to listen to the tapes. On the tapes he could refer them to the photographs, diagrams, and drawings in the text as he discussed the concepts and principles under study.

Later, the tapes included instructions that the students check views contained in the recorded lectures against views expressed in the text. Thus the author's point of view could be considered along with the lecturer's. Then Dr. Postlethwait decided to add a new dimension to his instructional approach. He placed plants in the audiovisual center so that students could observe and handle the plants when they were being discussed on the tapes. Ultimately, the students were instructed to bring their laboratory manuals to the center and conduct experiments in conjunction with study of their texts and listening to the tapes. Consciously or unconsciously, Dr. Postlethwait had moved his instructional technique from one focusing on abstract learning experiences (lectures) toward a multimedia system emphasizing concrete experiences—an integrated lecture-laboratory approach.

During the spring of 1962 an experimental group of thirty-six students was chosen to receive all of the instruction via the integrated lecture-laboratory approach. The experimental class met with Dr. Postlethwait only once each week, to take quizzes and for a general discussion of the week's subject matter. They were required to take the same examina-

AUDIO-TUTORIAL SYSTEMS

What They Are

THE term *Audio-Tutorial Systems* is used in the plural here to acknowledge that many variations have evolved from the original tape-controlled independent study method developed by S. N. Postlethwait at Purdue University in the early 1960s. Like PSI, this is a technology for *managing* instruction. But it springs from different roots and has a different emphasis from the preceding methods, which derive from programmed instruction.

As described in the accompanying "Flashback," the Audio-Tutorial System had its birth in expediency. It was an intuitive response to a felt problem. It later evolved into an identifiable, systematic method of instruction through years of experimentation and refinement by instructional developers.

The most visible aspect of most audio-tutorial (A-T) courses is the study carrel equipped with specially designed audiotapes that direct students to various learning activities. This component is known as the *independent study session.* The taped presentation is *not* a lecture but a tutorial conversation by the instructor, designed to facilitate effective communication. A live instructor is nearby to assist students when needed. Learners proceed at their own pace; sessions begin and end to suit students' schedules.

Because the students are proceeding individually, there seldom is more than one student at any given point in the study program. So, often only one or two pieces of equipment are necessary to accommodate many students in a laboratory situation.

tions given the conventionally taught group. At the end of the semester the experimental group scored just as well on the exam as the group that had received traditional instruction.

The students' reactions to the "supplementary" material were so positive that in the fall of 1962 Postlethwait decided that rather than carrying plants and other materials from the biology greenhouse to the audiovisual center each week, he would set up a botany learning center in the biology building. A conventional science laboratory was converted to a learning center with the addition of twenty-two learning carrels equipped with tape recorders. At this time, Postlethwait was covering the same content in his classroom lectures that was being presented on the tapes in the learning center. By the end of the semester most of the students were going to the learning center instead of coming to the lectures! In spite of the fact that Postlethwait missed their "sitting at his feet" to learn about botany, he candidly admitted that all the students missed by not coming to the lectures were his smiling face and West Virginia jokes.

Eventually, Postlethwait did away with his traditional lectures and restructured his Biology 108 course to give the students maximum freedom for independent study and to pace themselves according to their individual interests and capabilities. Students could come in at their convenience and spend as much time as necessary for them to master the material under study.

A significant aspect of Postlethwait's audio recordings was the conversational tone and relaxed atmosphere he deliberately cultivated. He would sit among the materials gathered for the particular lesson and speak into the recorder as if he were having a conversation with a friend whom he wished to tutor through a sequence of pleasant inquiries. Later, in their carrels, students would examine duplicates of the same materials while they listened to Postlethwait's chat.

Group meetings were later added to the program to supplement the independent study sessions. Students were brought together periodically in small groups (the "small assembly session") to discuss what they had learned in independent study and to present their own "lectures" on the current subject matter. Larger meetings (the "general assembly sessions") were scheduled for guest lectures, films, review sessions, and the like.

Serendipity is the faculty of making fortunate and unexpected discoveries by accident. Dr. Postlethwait turned out to be embarking on a serendipitous journey when he set out to tinker with the traditional format of his botany course. What began simply as audio tapes to supplement his classroom lectures eventually evolved into a full-scale technology of instruction—the Audio-Tutorial System.

Demonstration materials are set out at a central location; again, one set may be sufficient to serve a large class. Motion and color are provided when necessary by means of 8-mm film and/or videocassette. Instructions on how to perform a laboratory procedure, for instance, can be viewed coincident with handling the apparatus itself. The student can view the first step in a procedure, do that step, view the second step, turn the projector to "hold" while carrying out that step, and so on.

In addition to the independent study session, there are two other basic components in most A-T systems: a general assembly session and a small assembly session.

The *general assembly session* is a large-group meeting with no fixed format. It may include a presentation by a guest lecturer, a long film, an orientation to subject matter, an opportunity for review or emphasis of critical materials, help sessions, a major exam, or any other activity appropriate to a large-group setting.

During the *small assembly session,* six to ten students and an instructor meet for a modified seminar. Students are seated informally around a table with the instructor. The primary purpose of the session is to exploit the principle that one really learns a subject when one is required to teach it. For this session each student is expected to prepare a little lecture about each of the objectives being covered that session. Each student in turn is asked to discuss at least one of the objectives. The other students then have an opportunity to correct or add comments concerning any item. This session has proven to be an effective feedback mechanism for both the students and

▲ *Figure 11.15*
The independent-study carrel is the most visibly distinctive feature of the audio-tutorial approach.

the instructor. It lets the students know how they did and often provides clues to the instructor for improving the study program. The miniature seminar enables many students to see relationships and concepts which may not have been evident from the independent study session.

Audio-Tutorial Systems as a Technology of Instruction

Unlike programmed instruction, programmed tutoring, and PSI, A-T did not originate from a particular theory of learning. Its development was pragmatic. What worked was kept; what didn't work was pruned away. The resultant system, though, does fit our definition of a technology of instruction. It takes the form of an identifiable, unique pattern of teaching/learning. Its procedures provide consistent (replicable), effective instruction on an individ-

ualized basis. And, most importantly, A-T puts into action a number of principles of human learning:

1. The conversational audiotapes embody principles of communication theory (source credibility, personalization in the form of address, etc.).
2. The special emphasis on concrete media, such as slides, films, and realia applies what cognitive psychology advocates regarding realistic, meaningful messages.
3. Self-pacing and varied media alternatives cater to individual differences in learning style and rate.
4. The pervasive concern for individual success embodies the "whole person" emphasis of humanistic psychology.

These attributes differentiate A-T from the other systems discussed in this chapter. What unifies all of

these systems is their common technological approach, characterized by such qualities as modular units, requirement of active student participation, and provision of rapid feedback and correction.

Applications and Utilization of Audio-Tutorial Systems

The A-T approach is still most prevalent in science education, where it began. But during the two decades since its inception, it has also been successfully applied in many other areas, at many levels, and in both formal and non-formal educational settings. One indication of its widespread diffusion is the existence of a professional association, the International Society for Individualized Instruction, devoted to sharing ideas and research on Audio-Tutorial and other systems of individualized instruction.

As a result of these many and varied experiences with A-T, a number of generalizations can be

▲ *Figure 11.16*
Multisensory materials and varied activities help maintain student interest in audio-tutorial courses.

recommended to anyone considering implementing such a system. First, as is true of PSI, setting up an Audio-Tutorial System requires a great deal of preparation. However, A-T materials need not always be invented locally. Commercial publishers now offer sizable collections of packaged A-T materials.

Individualization and personalization are critical elements in this sort of system. Self-pacing and frequent corrective feedback must be designed into the system and vigilantly maintained. One aspect of personalization is the conversational tone of the audio materials; "lecture" style is not very appealing on a one-to-one basis.

Active participation by the learner is essential. A varied menu of activities—viewing films, manipulating real objects, field trips—helps keep interest high.

COGNITIVE PSYCHOLOGY AND TECHNOLOGIES OF INSTRUCTION

THE technologies of instruction described so far were influenced primarily by behaviorist principles, particularly reinforcement theory. But this branch of psychology is no longer the major contributor to new developments. Because of the limitations of behaviorism in dealing with higher mental processes and its failure to recognize cognitive developmental (mental growth) influences on learning, other theories of learning and development are shaping contemporary trends in technologies of instruction.

Cognitive psychology has become the more dominant learning theory. The name derives from its emphasis on cognitive processes—the mental operations we engage in when thinking. Because of many advances in understanding the physiology of the brain and the study of "artificial intelligence" through computer simulations of "thinking" behavior, cognitive psychologists are more willing than behaviorists to theorize about the kind of mental operations that may be involved in learning. Their insights are helping educators understand more clearly the role of media in learning and to develop new technologies of instruction, such as simulations, games, and computer-based instruction, as well as reshape older ones.*

Cognitivists make a distinction between knowledge and behavior. According to them, people acquire more knowledge from a learning situation than the required behavior might reveal. The accumulation of such knowledge, they believe, contributes to more complex responses to future learning situations. Media—film, video, still pictures, and so on—generally contain more information and sensory images than are needed to fulfill specific instructional objectives. This "excess" information is not wasted. To use the terms of the Swiss psychologist Jean Piaget, each learner will "assimilate" some aspects of the experience into existing mental structures. Eventually, especially when new influences challenge existing and simpler notions, more sophisticated mental structures are formed. As learners form more sophisticated thinking patterns, they become more adaptive—showing more complex and varied responses. For example, simulations and games, because they provide rich, often emotional experiences, extend the learner's repertoire beyond just a narrow set of "elicited behaviors."

Another implication is that learners should take a more active role in the learning process. Cognitive psychologists assert that learners develop individual "cognitive strategies" (methods of assimilating and processing information) by practicing those skills in a variety of situations, often self-initiated. Well-designed computer-based problem-solving activities and games allow learners to take more control over manipulating new experiences to fit in with and expand existing cognitive structures.

Under the influence of cognitivist psychology, newer technologies of instruction are emphasizing flexibility, looseness in structure, problem-solving processes, richness of stimuli, and learner control. Instruction designed with these guidelines in mind results in much higher learner motivation.

COOPERATIVE LEARNING

COGNITIVE psychology lends theoretical support to a movement in education and training referred to as cooperative learning. Rather than making learners competitors in the class or training environment, cooperative techniques make them helpers to each other. By having learners form small groups, and by, having the group rather than each individual work on the learning task, cooperative-learning methods result in increased motivation and higher individual achievement.† Each member of the group may be tested at the conclusion of the task, but the group works together to achieve objectives.

Technologies of instruction can benefit from the advantages of

---

* Thomas J. Shuell. "Cognitive Conceptions of Learning." *Review of Educational Research* (Winter 1986), pp. 311–336.

† Robert E. Slavin. *Cooperative Learning: Student Teams.* 2d ed. Washington, D.C.: National Education Association, 1987, pp. 18–25.

social interaction and reinforcement that characterize cooperative learning techniques. The opportunity to do so is more apparent with some technologies than with others. For example, games and simulations lend themselves readily to group participation. The Personalized System of Instruction, discussed earlier in this chapter, can be adapted to small study groups.

In 1971 Hartley reported on the effectiveness of designing programmed instruction for pairs of students.* As in the current research on cooperative learning, Hartley and his associates worked on the assumptions that group learning would reduce boredom and lead to better learning through interaction. Several studies have indicated that a small group using one terminal increases the economic efficiency of computer-based instruction plus benefitting from cooperative learning.† The laboratory experiments of the "Science: a Process Approach" program of the American Association for the Advancement of Science were designed as group activities.

Technologies of Instruction based on Cooperative Learning

The general concept of cooperative learning may be used as the basis for a specific technology of instruction. An example is Student

* James Hartley. "Factors Affecting the Efficiency of Learning from Programmed Instruction." *AV Communication Review* (Summer 1971), pp. 134–137.
† Joan Lieber and Melvin Semmel. "The Relationship between Group Size and Performance on a Microcomputer Problem-Solving Task for Learning Handicapped and Nonhandicapped Students." *Journal of Educational Computing Research* 3, no. 2 (1987), pp. 171–187.

Teams-Achievement Divisions (STAD) developed by Robert E. Slavin. STAD is a small-group format in which four-member groups, mixed in ability and background, work as a team to master lessons given by the instructor; they discuss problems, quiz each other, and tutor each other as required. At the end they take individual tests. Students' test scores are compared with their own past averages, and points are awarded based on equalling or surpassing past performance. These points are added to the team's score. As teams meet certain criteria they receive certificates or other rewards. STAD has been applied to a broad range of subjects from elementary through college level courses. Other variations, known as Teams-Games Tournament (TGT) and Team-Assisted Individualization (TAI), have also been developed.

STAD and each of its variations have several key factors in common: team rewards, individual accountability, and equal opportunities for success. Each can be seen as a technology of instruction in that it is a structured teaching/learning pattern aimed at improving individual learning while cultivating desirable social objectives through the application of psychological principles.

Potential social isolation is a legitimate criticism of some technologies of instruction. Incorporating cooperative-learning techniques into those technologies would be an effective way of dealing with that problem.

SIMULATION AND GAMES

What They Are

WE will not dwell long on defining simulation and games at this point. These concepts are described in detail in

Chapter 12. It will suffice to define *simulation* as any scaled-down representation of some real-life happening. A *game* is an activity in which participants follow prescribed rules that differ from those of reality as they strive to attain a challenging goal. As used in instruction, these two concepts can be applied separately, or together in the form of a *simulation game*. For present purposes the two will be grouped together to allow us to consider simulation/gaming (S/G) in general.

Simulation/Gaming as a Technology of Instruction

Recalling our basic definition of technology of instruction as a teaching/learning pattern that puts into effect scientific understandings about human learning, we find that simulations and games can embody a number of principles derived from both reinforcement theory and cognitive psychology.

Learner Control. In a typical simulation—for example, role

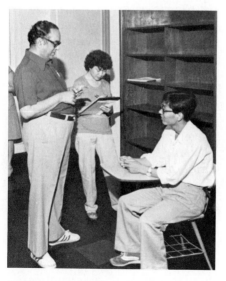

▲ *Figure 11.17*
Simulation exercises are widely used for developing communication skills.

playing—the participants generate their own stimuli (the dialog) and choose which direction to pursue and what strategies to try out.

Rich Stimuli. By placing the learner in a more or less realistic situation, simulations evoke in our imaginations the richness of real life.

Problem-Solving Orientation. Simulations, whether physical simulators such as airplane cockpits or social simulations such as role-plays for training supervisors, immerse the learners in problems typical of real life. They see problems in context, not as isolated bits of subject matter presented as facts or rules to be memorized.

Meaningful Organization of Subject Matter. By placing the learner in a more or less realistic setting, simulation presents the subject matter in context. Facts, principles, and problems are viewed in their interaction rather than presented singly as separate unrelated items.

Repetition. Repetition has always played a major role in school learning. The problem has been to maintain student interest in drill exercises. The game format, with its repetitive cycles of play (e.g., dealing out new hands in a card game), can direct learners through extensive drill-and-practice exercises while keeping interest high by means of variation in the pattern and the excitement of chance.

Reinforcement. S/G can be employed as a framework for reinforcement just as well as printed programmed materials. In a well-designed game the participants are required to make frequent responses related to the instructional objectives; for exam-

ple, classifying items, making value judgments, making decisions. Each of these responses can be connected with certain preordained consequences—favorable consequences for correct responses and unfavorable consequences for less correct actions. Through such trial-and-error patterns the participant's behavior can be "shaped" toward the desired learning goals. In addition, like programmed tutoring, S/G goes beyond just "knowledge of results" in its array of possible reinforcers. It capitalizes on the social context of game play to incorporate such generalized reinforcers as achievement, dominance, and social approval.

COMPUTER-ASSISTED INSTRUCTION

ANY discussion of technologies of instruction would be incomplete and woefully out of date if the revolution in computer applications were omitted. Because of the computer's impor-

tance, Chapter 13 will be devoted to this topic. Our purpose at this point is to call attention to the computer's unmatched ability to *manage information* with such speed and accuracy that teaching/learning interactions can be handled with much greater efficiency and effectiveness.

The computer *is not in itself a technology of instruction.* It is a physical tool that can be used to present programmed instruction, programmed tutoring, simulation/gaming, and other instructional formats on demand to individual learners without the necessity of a human helper being immediately present. Further, it can take such technologies of *managing* instruction as PSI and A-T and carry out their management functions far more efficiently than human paper shufflers and materials dispensers.

These functions, usually referred to as computer-assisted instruction and computer-managed instruction respectively, will be examined in detail in Chapter 13.

▲ *Figure 11.18*
Simulation of an economy allows these high schoolers to manipulate the economic concepts discussed in their textbooks. This interactive computer software series, "Income/Outcome$," was developed by the Agency for Instructional Technology, the Canadian Foundation for Economic Education, the Joint Council on Economic Education, and thirty state and provincial education agencies, with financial assistance from twelve foundations and corporations.

TABLE 11.1 Characteristics of Technologies of Instruction

	Programmed Instruction	Programmed Tutoring	Personalized System of Instruction	Audio-Tutorial Systems	Simulation and Gaming
A teaching/ learning *pattern*	Small units of information requiring practice, followed by feedback	Small units of information requiring practice, followed by feedback	Large units of information in sequential order; passing a test is required before proceeding (mastery)	Core of instruction is on audiotape, used in lab setting independently; small-group and large-group sessions are added	Small-group activity, may entail representation of reality and/or competition
designed to provide *reliable,*	Program recorded in printed form	Tutor follows directions; learner uses structured workbook	Course organization is clearly spelled out; based on print materials and standardized tests	Core material recorded on audiotape and other audiovisual materials	Procedures are enforced by means of game directions and play materials
effective instruction	Programs must be learner tested and revised during development process	Programs are learner tested and revised during development process	Materials themselves are not validated, but mastery is assured by testing/correction cycle	Materials themselves are not validated, but mastery is encouraged by small-group test/review sessions	May be learner tested for effectiveness
to *each* learner	Allows individual pacing	Allows individual pacing plus highly flexible, responsive branching via human tutor	Allows individual pacing plus one-to-one discussion of test errors and questions	Allows individual pacing in independent study portion of course	Usually group paced, with individuals assigned to compatible groups
through application of *scientific* principles of human learning	Reinforcement theory: verbal response followed by knowledge of results	Reinforcement theory: verbal or other overt response followed by knowledge of results plus social reinforcers Constant personalized human contact Variety	Rather frequent response to tests over content followed by immediate correction Occasional personalized human contact Mastery requirement ensures that learner is working at his or her level of comprehension	Conversational relationship with instructor via tape High use of audiovisual and other concrete media Occasional personalized human contact Active involvement in challenging tasks	Meaningful organization of content (in simulation) Frequent practice with immediate feedback Social interaction with small group Emotional involvement Repetition of drill-and-practice without tedium High motivation

SUMMARY

IN this chapter we have examined several teaching/learning formats, analyzing their differences in emphasis and their similarities as examples of technologies of instruction. These characteristics are summarized in Table 11.1. You can see how each of these formats fulfills the requirements of the definition given at the beginning of the chapter. In addition, it should now be clearer why other teaching/learning formats do not meet these requirements. A conventional lecture, for example, lacks reliability (it is not repeatable unless recorded), ordinarily lacks prior testing, does not accommodate individual differences, and allows little practice/feedback or other instructionally desirable traits. Much the same could be said of a sound-slide presentation or other multimedia show.

A computer or other machine in itself is not a technology of instruction although it can be a contributing element when coupled with a program with certain special qualities.

References

Print References

General

Gagne, Robert. *Instructional Technology: Foundations.* (Hillsdale, N.J.: Lawrence Erlbaum, 1987).

Hortin, John A. "Successful Examples of Instructional Technology." ERIC Document ED208726, 1981.

Programmed Instruction

Bullock, Donald H. *Programmed Instruction.* Volume 8, Instructional Design Library (Englewood Cliffs, N.J.: Educational Technology Publications, 1978).

Center for Vocational Education. *Employ Programmed Instruction.* (Athens, Ga.: American Association for Vocational Instructional Materials, 1977).

———. *Employ Reinforcement Techniques.* (Athens, Ga.: American Association for Vocational Instructional Materials, 1977).

Ellson, Douglas G. *Improving the Productivity of Teaching.* (Bloomington, Ind.: Phi Delta Kappa, 1986).

Hartley, James. "Programmed Instruction 1954–1974: A Review." *Programmed Learning and Educational Technology* (November 1974), pp. 278–291.

Kulik, Chen-Lin; Shwarb, B. J.; and Kulik, James A. "Programmed Instruction in Secondary Education." *Journal of Educational Research* (1982), pp. 133–138.

Programmed Tutoring

Cohen, P. A.; Kulik, James A.; and Kulik, Chen-Lin. "Educational Outcomes of Tutorings: A Meta-Analysis of Findings." *American Educational Research Journal* (1982), pp. 237–248.

Ellson, Douglas G. "Tutoring." In *The Psychology of Teaching Methods,* 75th yearbook of the National Society for the Study of Education. (Chicago: NSSE, 1976).

Harrison, Grant, and Guymon, Ronald. *Structured Tutoring.* Volume 34, Instructional Design Library. (Englewood Cliffs, N.J.: Educational Technology Publications, 1980).

Thiagarajan, Sivasailam. "Programming Tutorial Behavior: Another Application of the Programming Process." *Improving Human Performance Quarterly* (June 1972).

———. *Tutoraids.* Volume 20, Instructional Design Library. (Englewood Cliffs, N.J.: Educational Technology Publications, 1978).

Personalized System of Instruction

Coldeway, Annabel E., and Coldeway, Dan O. "An Extension of PSI through the Application of Instructional Systems Design Technology." *Canadian Journal of Educational Communications* (Fall 1987), pp. 279–293.

Freemantle, M. H. "Keller Plans in Chemistry Teaching." *Education in Chemistry* (March 1976), pp. 50–51.

Keller, Fred S. "Good-Bye, Teacher. . . ." *Journal of Applied Behavior Analysis* (Spring 1968), pp. 79–88.

Keller, Fred S. "Testimony of an Educational Reformer." *Engineering Education* (December 1985), pp. 144–148.

Keller, Fred S., and Sherman, J. Gilmour. *The Keller Plan Handbook.* (Menlo Park, Calif.: W. A. Benjamin, 1974).

Keller, Fred S., and Sherman, J. Gilmour. *The PSI Handbook: Essays on Personalized Instruction.* (Lawrence, Kans.: TRI Publications, 1982).

Kulik, J. A.; Kulik, C. C.; and Cohen, P. A. "Meta-analysis of Outcome Studies of Keller's Personalized System of Instruction." *American Psychologist* (April 1979), pp. 307–318.

Mathur, Rajeshwar N., and Prakash, Brahm. "Individually Guided System of Instruction: A Cooperative Learning Strategy." *Educational Technology* (February 1988), pp. 45–48.

"The Personalized System of Instruction (PSI)—Special Issue." *Educational Technology* (September 1977), pp. 5–60.

Reiser, Robert A. "Reducing Student Procrastination in a Personalized System of Instruction Course." *Educational Communications and Technology Journal* (Spring 1984), pp. 41–49.

Sherman, J. Gilmour, and Ruskin, Robert S. *The Personalized System of Instruction.* Volume 13, Instructional Design Library. (Englewood Cliffs, N.J.: Educational Technology Publications, 1978).

Cooperative Learning

Johnson, Joy. *Use of Groups in School.* (Lanham, Md.: University Press of America, 1977).

Male, Mary. "Cooperative Learning for Effective Mainstreaming." *Computing Teacher* (August–September 1986), pp. 35–37.

Slavin, Robert. *Cooperative Learning: Student Teams.* 2d. ed. (Washington, D.C.: National Education Association, 1987).

Audio-Tutorial Systems

Kalmbach, John A. "Successful Characteristics of Students in an Audio Tutorial College Course: A Descriptive Study." *NSPI Journal* (February 1980), pp. 43–46.

Postlethwait, S. N. "Principles behind the Audio-Tutorial System." *NSPI Journal* (May 1978), pp. 3, 4, 18.

———. "Using Science and Technology to Teach Science and Technology." *Engineering Education* (January 1984), pp. 204–209.

Postlethwait, S. N.; Novak, J.; and Murray, H. *The Audio-Tutorial Approach to Learning.* (Minneapolis, Minn.: Burgess Publishing Company, 1972).

Russell, James D. *The Audio-Tutorial System.* Volume 3, Instructional Design Library. (Englewood Cliffs, N.J.: Educational Technology Publications, 1978).

Audiovisual References

The Audio-Tutorial System—An Independent Study Approach. West Lafayette, Ind.: Purdue University, 1968. 16-mm film. 25 minutes.

Individualized Learning Using Instructional Modules. Englewood Cliffs, N.J.: Educational Technology Publications, undated. Set of 6 audio cassettes. 20 minutes each.

The Personalized System of Instruction. Washington, D.C.: Center for Personalized Instruction, 1974. 16-mm film. 20 minutes.

Programmed Instruction: The Development Process. Austin, Tex.: University of Texas, 1969. 16-mm film. 19 minutes.

PSI. Washington, D.C.: Center for Personalized Instruction, 1976. Sound-slide set (cassette), 80 slides, 20 minutes.

The Tutor's Guide. Los Angeles: UCLA Office of Instructional Development, 1987. Series of fourteen 15-minute videotaped programs on practical techniques of peer tutoring.

Periodicals

British Journal of Educational Technology (quarterly)
Council for Educational Technology
10 Queen Anne Street
London W1, England

Educational Technology (monthly)
Educational Technology Publications
720 Palisade Avenue
Englewood Cliffs, NJ 07632

Journal of Educational Technology Systems (quarterly)
Baywood Publishing Company
43 Central Drive
Farmingdale, NY 11735

Performance & Instruction (monthly)
National Society for Performance and Instruction (NSPI)
1126 Sixteenth Street, N.W.
Washington, DC 20036

Organizations

Center for Personalized Instruction
Loyola Hall, Room 29
Georgetown University
Washington, DC 20057

International Society for Individualized Instruction (ISII)
c/o Dr. Charles E. Wales
West Virginia University
Morgantown, WV 26506

National Society for Performance and Instruction (NSPI)
1126 Sixteenth Street, N.W.
Washington, DC 20036

Possible Projects

11-A. Appraise a commercially available program using the "Appraisal Checklist" in the chapter, one from another source, or of your own design.

11-B. Construct a short (ten- to fifteen-frame) program on a subject of your choice. Use either the linear or branching style of programming. Describe exactly how you would use your program and under what conditions.

11-C. Submit a bibliography of at least ten titles of commercially available programs which could be used in your subject field.

11-D. Observe a programmed tutoring session and write up your analysis of the session including strengths and weaknesses of the approach as you observed it being used.

11-E. Interview an instructor or students who have used the Personalized System of Instruction. Determine their reaction to using the system and ascertain what they perceive as the advantages and disadvantages of the approach.

11-F. Visit an Audio-Tutorial learning center. Interview students using A-T materials as well as the instructors. Prepare a report describing the center and the reactions of the students and the instructor(s).

11-G. Take some teaching/learning format not discussed in the chapter and analyze it according to the criteria shown in the summary table at the end of the chapter.

12 Simulation and Games

Objectives
After studying this chapter, you should be able to:

1. Define *game, simulation, simulation game,* and *instruction* and distinguish among examples of each.

2. Relate games to drill-and-practice learning.

3. Describe an instructional situation appropriate to game use; the description should include objectives, audience, and the nature of the game chosen.

4. Relate the special attributes of simulation to (a) discovery learning, (b) social interaction, and (c) physical skill learning.

5. Define *role-play* and discuss its applications.

6. Give at least two examples of simulators.

7. Describe an instructional situation appropriate to simulation use; the description should include objectives, audience, and nature of the simulation chosen.

8. Define *holistic learning* and relate it to simulation games.

9. Describe an instructional situation appropriate to simulation game use; the description should include objectives, audience, and nature of the simulation game chosen.

10. Identify at least four limitations of instructional games and simulations.

11. State at least three appraisal criteria that apply particularly to simulation/game materials.

12. Appraise one simulation/game using the "Appraisal Checklist" given in this chapter.

13. Name two general reference works most useful for locating simulation/game materials.

14. Define *frame game* and give two examples of adaptations of familiar game frames.

15. Outline the eight major steps in designing simulation/games.

16. Define *scenario, transaction,* and *consequence* in the context of simulation/game design.

17. Identify the utilization procedures that are emphasized in simulation/game use more than with other media.

18. Paraphrase the four major phases of the group debriefing process.

19. Discuss briefly the evaluation problems that are relatively unique to simulation/game use.

Lexicon
game
simulation
simulation game
drill-and-practice learning
inductive/deductive learning
discovery learning
role-play
simulator
holistic learning
frame game
scenario
transaction
consequence
debriefing

THE use of gaming and simulation techniques in instruction is by no means a new idea. The simulation of battlefield strategy in the form of games can be traced back to 3000 B.C. in China. Games such as chess and *go* are the residue of these ancient training exercises. Today's war gaming employs computers to digest vast volumes of data, and the application of gaming techniques to training and instruction has spread into business, higher education, and elementary/secondary education. Experience has shown that simulations and games can make a powerful contribution to learning if they are properly understood and properly used.

The reasons that simulation and game enthusiasts give to explain their interest in these methods are as varied as the kinds of simulation and game materials. Elementary educators emphasize the point that play is a natural and necessary component of young children's learning; play should be encouraged and melded with academic objectives. Some are concerned with avoiding the tedium too often associated with classrooms. In recent years there has been a movement toward more learner-centered instruction in the belief that it enhances motivation and learning. Methods in which learners are active and in control of their own learning processes also encourage independence and responsibility. Futurists, along with educational psychologists, cite the importance of learning to view problems as a whole. Adult educators and trainers are interested in simulation as a cost-effective method of practicing motor skills and interpersonal capabilities.

In any event, whether for these or other reasons, classroom activities based on simulation and gaming are popular at all educational

▲ *Figure 12.1*
Games appeal to all ages.

levels. The rapid spread of computers throughout educational systems in the 1980s gave fresh impetus to these methods, breathing new life into old formats and making them accessible to many more instructors and students.

BASIC CONCEPTS

BEFORE considering the instructional applications of games and simulations we must deal with the issue of terminology. The terms *game, simulation,* and *simulation game* are often confused with each other or used interchangeably. These terms actually refer to different concepts and so must first be examined one at a time. Later in the chapter, for example when discussing utilization techniques, the two concepts—game and simulation— will be addressed as one for the sake of convenience.

Game

A *game* is an *activity in which participants follow prescribed rules that differ from those of real-*

ity as they strive to attain a challenging goal.

The distinction between "play" and "reality" is what makes games entertaining. Most people seem to enjoy setting aside the logical rules of everyday life occasionally and entering an artificial environment with different dynamics. For example, in chess the markers each have arbitrarily different movement patterns based roughly on the military potentials of certain societal roles in some ancient time. Players capture each other's markers by observing elaborate rules of play, rather than simply reaching across the board to grab the marker.

Attaining the goal usually entails competition. The competition may be individual against individual, as in chess; group against group, as in basketball; or individual against a standard, as in golf (with "par" as the standard). In playing video games, players typically are competing against their own previous scores, and ultimately against the designer of the game as they approach mastery of the game.

To be challenging, goals should

have a probability of achievement of something in the range of 50 percent. A goal that is always attained or never attainable presents no real challenge; the outcome is too predictable. People exhibit most interest and motivation in a task when the challenge is in the intermediate range.

On the other hand, the "striving to attain a challenging goal" does not necessarily have to involve competition. Communication games, fantasy games, and "encounter" games exemplify a whole array of activities in which participants agree to suspend the normal rules of interpersonal communication in order to pursue such goals as self-awareness, empathy, sensitivity, and leadership development. These activities are considered games but they do not entail competition.

Simulation

A *simulation* is an *abstraction or simplification of some real-life situation or process.* In simulations, participants usually play a role that involves them in interactions with other people and/or with elements of the simulated environment. A business management simulation, for example, might put participants into the role of production manager of a mythical corporation, provide them with statistics about business conditions, and direct them to negotiate a new labor contract with the union bargaining team.

Simulations can vary greatly in the extent to which they fully reflect the realities of the situation they are intended to model. A simulation that incorporates too many details of a complex situation might be too complicated and time-consuming for the intended audience. On the other hand, if the model is oversimplified, it may fail completely to

communicate its intended point. A well-designed simulation provides a faithful model of those elements that are most salient to the immediate objective, and it informs the instructor and participants about elements that have been simplified or eliminated completely.

Simulation Game

A *simulation game combines the attributes of a simulation (role playing, a model of reality) with the attributes of a game (striving toward a goal, specific rules).* Like a simulation, it may be relatively high or low in its modeling of reality. Like a game, it may or may not entail competition.

Instruction

Any of the types of activities described so far may be designed to be *instructional,* that is, to *help someone learn new skills or values applicable beyond the game itself.* Most commercially developed games intend to provide diversion, not instruction. A person who plays *Clue* or *Thinking Man's Golf* enough times probably learns more and more about the game itself but little in the way of usable skills.

Admittedly, the attribute of being "instructional" is often a matter of degree. The stated intentions of the designer or user would have to be examined closely. For example, basketball—normally a noninstructional game—could be assigned by a football coach to his players as a means of developing agility and faster reflexes. In such a case basketball would be "instructional" for that situation.

Many game activities contain some modeling of reality, and the distinction between simulations and games is not always clear.

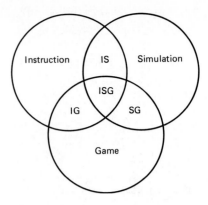

▲ *Figure 12.2*
"Game," "Simulation," and "Instruction" are each separate concepts. However, they do overlap, so a particular activity could be an instructional simulation (IS), instructional game (IG), or even an instructional simulation game (ISG).

Many role-playing exercises take on gamelike qualities as participants maneuver toward a good outcome for themselves. Yet the distinctions are worth making because they have significant implications for when and how these different types of materials are used. Figure 12.2 illustrates how the basic concepts of game, simulation, and instruction may overlap and interact; as shown, seven different classifications can be given. The following sections of the chapter will deal with the three classifications of most direct relevance to our interests: instructional games, instructional simulations, and instructional simulation games.

INSTRUCTIONAL GAMES

Play in Human Development

GAMES are, above all, a form of play. As such, they may be looked upon with suspicion by those who think learning and playing are incompatible. But as viewed by developmental psychologists, play can be a useful mechanism indeed; deprivation of play can impede an individual's cognitive and creative growth.

▲ *Figure 12.3*
Play is a natural and essential element of human development.

▲ *Figure 12.4*
A game format can be used to motivate children and adults to practice intellectual skills.

Anthropologists note that primitive societies often use the playing of games to acculturate their members and to teach survival skills. It is certainly reasonable to assume that play in more advanced societies serves similar functions. Freudian interpretations of play see it as a symbolic reenactment of a threatening event, a safety valve for relieving pressures placed on children by the childrearing practices of a culture. Child psychologist Jean Piaget views play as a manifestation of "assimilation," one of the mental processes fundamental to intellectual growth. All observers agree that play is an adaptive mechanism important for human development.

Games as Learning Frameworks

Games can provide attractive and instructionally effective frameworks for learning activities. They are attractive because they are fun! Children and adults alike tend to react positively to an invitation to play.

Of course, this is not true for every learner; no instructional method inspires universal acceptance. However, as a general principle, novelty reduces boredom for adults as well as for children. The pleasant, relaxed atmosphere fostered by games can be especially productive for those (such as low achievers) who avoid other types of structured learning activities.

The element of competition, though, can be a two-edged sword. It motivates some students and discourages others. For example, this factor appears to account for some of the differences between boys and girls in math achievement. Teachers often teach lower-level math skills through contests and games. Because males tend to be more competitive and aggressive, they have an advantage over females. In recent studies researchers*

---

* E. Fennema and P. L. Peterson. "Effective Teaching for Girls and Boys." In D. C. Berliner and B. Rosenshine, eds. *Talks to Teachers.* New York: Random House, 1987.

found that when boys participate in competitive games they improve their achievement in lower-level math. Such competitions seem to depress the achievement of girls because they tend to lose the games. Yet the teachers observed in these studies acted as though they believed that *all* children enjoyed the competitive games.

Because of these sorts of individual differences, the element of competition must be handled very thoughtfully in choosing and using instructional games. Individual-versus-individual competition can be a highly motivating device as long as the contenders are fairly matched and the conflict does not overshadow the educational objective. Group-versus-group competition entails the same cautions, but it has the added attraction of providing practice in cooperation and teamwork. When competitions are carefully organized to ensure fair matches, as in the case of Layman Allen's Thinkers League Tournament (described in the "Close-up"), highly successful and highly personalized learning can be fostered.

For instructional purposes, competition of the individual or team against a given standard is often the safest approach. It allows individualization, setting different standards for different players. In fact, one of the most effective standards can be the student's own past performance, the goal being to raise the level of aspirations continually.

In any event, in cases in which competition is an element, the scoring system provides a clue as to what type of competition is being fostered. Is one individual or team declared the "winner"? Or is it possible for all players to attain equally high scores, making everyone a winner? In fact, some

instructional games are designed to encourage players to decide among themselves what criteria to apply in determining success.

Gaming combines well with the *drill-and-practice method* of learning. This combination is employed with skills that require repetitive practice in order to be mastered. Multiplication table drills are an example of this. Drill-and-practice exercises can become tedious, leading to rapid burnout of interest. But putting this sort of practice into a game format makes it more palatable, thus keeping the learner "on task" for a longer time with greater satisfaction.

Of course, to be instructionally meaningful the game activity must provide actual practice of the intended academic skill. An instructionally fatal shortcoming of poorly designed games is that players spend a large proportion of their time exercising the "skill" of waiting for their turn, throwing dice, moving markers around a board, and similar trivial actions.

Applications of Instructional Games

Instructional games are particularly well suited to

- Attainment of cognitive objectives in general, particularly those involving recognition, discrimination, or drill and practice, such as grammar, phonics, spelling, arithmetic skills, formulas (chemistry, physics, logic), basic science concepts, place names, terminology, etc.
- Adding motivation to topics that ordinarily attract little student

▲ *Figure 12.5*
Card games can be used to exercise a wide range of basic intellectual skills.

MEDIA FILE:
"Tuf" Instructional Game

Content area: Mathematics
Age Level: Grade 3 through college

Players roll cubes containing numbers and mathematical symbols, and attempt to form these into equations. "Tuf" might be used throughout a whole course in algebra; it can be played at increasing levels of sophistication.

Source: Avalon Hill.

MEDIA FILE:
"On-Words" Instructional Game

Content area: Language arts, spelling
Age Level: Grade 4 through adult

In "On-Words" players roll letter and number cubes, then attempt to form words of a specified length. Intersecting words are formed, as in a crossword puzzle. Can be played at Basic, Advanced, or Adventurous levels, progressing from simple spelling and counting through word analysis.

Source: wff 'N Proof.

interest, for example, grammar rules, spelling, math drills.
- Small-group instruction; instructional games provide structured activities that students or trainees can conduct by themselves without close instructor supervision.
- Basic skills such as sequence, sense of direction, visual perception, number concepts, and following rules can be developed by means of card games. A leading advocate of the educational potential of card games is Margie Golick, a psychologist specializing in learning disabilities.*

---

* Margie Golick. *Deal Me In!* New York: Jeffrey Norton Publisher, 1973.

- Vocabulary building; a number of commercial games such as *Boggle, Fluster, Scrabble,* and *Probe* have been used successfully by teachers to expand spelling and vocabulary skills, although they were designed and are marketed primarily for recreational purposes.

INSTRUCTIONAL SIMULATIONS

Simulation and Discovery Learning

A particular value of simulation is that it provides a specific framework for implementing the *discovery method,* also referred to as *the inquiry approach, experi-*

ential learning, and other such terms denoting *inductive* teaching/learning strategies.

The conventional classroom teaching/learning approach based on lectures employs an *expository* (or *deductive*) strategy. It proceeds something like this:

Presentation of information
(The Point)
↓
Reference to particular examples
↓
Application of the knowledge to the student's experiences

The expository strategy is efficient and economical. One of its weaknesses, though, is its heavy dependence on language for transmission of information, which can be a real handicap for students with limited verbal skills. Another drawback to the expository strategy is the difficulty many students have in applying the abstract, usually verbal, concept ("The Point") to everyday experience. They may be able to pass a written test (knowledge on a verbal-symbolic level) but they cannot solve real-life problems.

In contrast, the *discovery* method proceeds more like this:

Immersion in a real or contrived problematic situation
↓
Development of hypotheses
↓
Testing of hypotheses
↓
Arrival at conclusion
(The Point)

In discovery learning the *learner is led toward "The Point" through trial-and-error grappling with a problem.* Cause-and-effect relationships are discovered by observing the actual conse-

quences of actions. This sort of immersion in a problem is the core of most simulations. Through simulations we can offer learners a laboratory in areas such as social sciences and human relations as well as in areas related to the physical sciences, where laboratories have long been taken for granted. True, it tends to be more time-consuming than the straightforward lecture approach, but the payoff is a higher level of comprehension that is likely to be retained longer.

The great advantage of this sort of firsthand immersion in a topic is that students are more likely to be able to apply to real life what they have practiced applying in simulated circumstances. This raises the issue of the degree of realism captured by a simulation. A common defect in poorly designed simulations is an overemphasis on *chance* factors in determining outcomes. Much of the reality is spoiled if "Chance Element" cards cause players to gain or lose great quantities of points or other resources regardless of their strategic decisions. An overemphasis on chance or an overly simplified representation of real relationships might end up

teaching lessons quite contrary to what was intended.

Role-Plays

Role-play refers to *one type of a simulation in which the dominant feature is relatively open-ended interaction among people.* In essence, a role-play asks someone to imagine that he or she is himself or herself, or another person, in a particular situation; he or she then behaves as that person would or the way the situation seems to demand. The purpose is to learn something about that sort of person or about the dynamics of that sort of situation. The role descriptions may be very general, leaving great latitude for the participant; for example, in *Action-alysis* (see "Media File") the person playing the role of "teacher" is given only a one-word description of the attitude he or she is supposed to be reflecting. The purpose here is to allow the person's own traits to emerge so that they may be discussed and possibly modified. In other simulations, such as historical recreations, highly detailed roles are described in order to project the realities of life in that period.

It is ironic that educational simulation/gaming, which is now prominently associated with the promotion of mutual understanding and cooperation, traces its ancestry to games designed to teach military tactics and strategies.

One of the earliest known examples of war gaming is *wei-chi* (meaning "encirclement"), the existence of which can be traced back to at least 2000 B.C. The game was introduced into Japan around the eighth century A.D. and survives throughout the world today in the popular game *go.* A variation of the encirclement game evolved in India as *chaturanga.* In this game, representations of foot soldiers, horsemen, chariots, and elephants faced each other on a board representing a battlefield. The Western version of *chaturanga,* chess, evolved into its current form during the Middle Ages. Although chess has long since lost its specific functions as a military training tool, tactics and strategic moves are still at its core, and the object of the game remains a "military" one: to capture (or checkmate) the opponent's king.

Franco-Prussian War troops on parade.

Following military defeats in the Napoleonic Wars, the Prussians throughout the nineteenth century invested great ingenuity in the refinement of war games that would allow greater latitude for experimentation at lower cost than actual military exercises. Terrain models of battlefields replaced checkered boards; rules for the value of movement of pieces were more realistically prescribed; teams of opposing forces replaced individual players; judges monitored the observance of rules. The resounding Prussian victory in the Franco–Prussian War of 1870 to 1871 and the subsequent Prussian reputation for military genius may be attributable in part to their preparedness born out of years of practice in *Kriegspiel.*

In the years immediately following the Franco–Prussian War, the competition began to catch up. War gaming took root in England and was introduced soon afterward at the United States Military Academy, where the data from the American Civil War added further precision to the components of war games.

By the early twentieth century, war gaming had spread to all the technologically advanced nations of the world. Germany and Japan raised war-gaming techniques to a high art as part of their preparations for World War II. At Japan's Total War Research Institute, for example, highly elaborate simulation games were used to plot both military and civilian strategies to be employed in the conflict which lay immediately ahead.

A breakthrough in war-gaming technique came toward the end of World War II with the advent of the electronic computer. The high-speed calculating power of the computer vastly increased designers' ability to deal with complexity. It became possible to include in the games, with a good deal of precision, social and political variables as well as military data. An important step in the evolution of war games toward educational games came with the development in the mid-1950s of so-called crisis games. Growing largely out of experimentation at the RAND Corporation to deal with potential Cold War problems, crisis games are simulations of hypothetical crisis situations, with participants trying to solve or alleviate the crises within a framework of rules structured to reflect the conditions of the simulated crisis situation.

Not long after the original RAND experiments, crisis games were in use at several universities. Gaming became a popular instructional technique in which students of international relations could adopt the roles of government decision makers and play out hypothetical crises.

Business Games

Since economists and business management theorists already possessed well-defined, quantitative models upon which simulation/gaming could be based, it is not surprising that business games were among the first academic games to be developed. The linkage of business games with military games is quite clear. In 1956 the American Management Association (AMA) launched a research project to consider the possibility of developing a simulation that would allow management trainees to experience the same kind of strategic decision-making practice as military officers were then experiencing. Its efforts culminated in the creation of the AMA Top Management Decision Simulation, a computer-assisted simulation game in which teams of players representing officers of companies make business decisions and receive "quarterly reports" on the outcomes of their decisions. Business executives and business educators reacted to the game with great enthusiasm.

By the end of 1959 variations of the AMA game had been developed at IBM and the University of California at Los Angeles, and within three years the development of over eighty-five such games had been noted in professional journals.

To a great extent, business games and crisis games were an extension of war games into new "battlefronts"—the marketplace and the diplomatic arena. Further development was needed to encourage the use of simulation/gaming for more "peaceful" academic purposes, that is, for the understanding and minimization of conflict rather than simply the achievement of supremacy within the conflict situation. This transition can perhaps best be illustrated by considering the career odyssey of one of the major figures in the development of classroom simulation games.

Clark C. Abt, a systems engineer, became involved in the 1950s with the design of computer simulations of air battles, space missions, disarmament inspection systems, and other military problems. He and his colleagues at the Missile Systems Division of the Raytheon Company began to apply war-gaming techniques to increasingly complex problems—problems that became more and more involved with human factors—the social, economic, and political causes and consequences of military actions.

Seeking to better understand these human factors, Abt returned to M.I.T. to earn a Ph.D. in the social sciences. He founded his own company, Abt Associates, in 1965.

Classroom Simulation Games

Within the next few years Abt Associates became a major fountainhead of classroom simulation games, some of the better-known examples being *Pollution, Neighborhood, Empire, Manchester, Colony,* and *Caribou Hunting Game.*

As Abt Associates was developing the techniques for classroom simulation/gaming, many educators, especially in the social studies, were becoming interested in inquiry-oriented approaches to teaching. Jerome Bruner and other instructional theorists, working in the same vein as John Dewey had a generation earlier, were advocating the importance of active student involvement in learning. Immersion in a problem, informed guessing, and hypothesis testing were the methods best calculated to promote discovery learning.

This theoretical viewpoint activated a number of reform-minded curriculum development projects. Bruner's own contribution was *Man: A Course of Study,* a total curriculum package incorporating the Abt Associates' *Caribou Hunting* and *Seal Hunting.* Other such projects, including the High School Geography Project and the Holt Social Studies Program, yielded several simulation games.

Another historical influence critical to the establishment of the academic respectability of simulation/gaming in the classroom was the Academic Games Program at Johns Hopkins University. Headed by eminent educational sociologist James S. Coleman from 1966 to 1973, the Johns Hopkins group developed a number of ground-breaking games (including *Life Career, Democracy, Generation Gap,* and *Ghetto*) and conducted many studies of game playing and the learning associated with it. Their general conclusions confirmed the advantages of simulation/gaming and also helped identify some of the problem areas in simulation/game utilization.

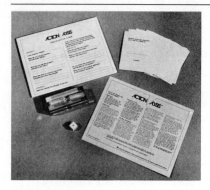

As a technology of instruction, the role-play simulation has proven to be a motivating and effective method of developing social skills, especially empathy—putting oneself in someone else's shoes. Our day-to-day social behavior tends to be governed by our assumptions about who we are, who our associates are, and *why* they act the way they do. A potent way of challenging—and thereby changing—these assumptions is to experience a slice of life from someone else's perspective.

The sorts of tasks that lend themselves especially well to role playing are counseling, interviewing, sales and customer services, supervision, and management. The settings most often simulated are committee meetings, negotiation sessions, public meetings, work teams, and one-to-one interviews.

Simulators

Competencies in the motor skill domain require practice under conditions of high feedback—giving the learner the feel of the action. Although it might be ideal to practice such skills under real-life conditions, some skills (for example, piloting an airplane or driving a car) can be practiced much more safely and conveniently by means of simulated conditions. The devices employed to represent physical systems in a scaled-down form are referred to as *simulators*.

One familiar example of a simulator is the flight trainer, a mock-up of the interior of the cockpit, complete with controls and gauges. Today the flight crews of most major airlines receive a large proportion of their training in flight simulators, which are often controlled by computers and offer highly realistic audiovisual effects. Besides eliminating the possibility of loss of life and aircraft, these simulators allow significant savings of energy—millions of gallons of fuel annually—and other costs.

One recent study estimated that in-air training costs about $4,000 per hour compared to only $400 per hour on the flight simulator, with no loss in effectiveness.

Another example, which more people have experienced personally, is the automobile driver-training simulator. One of the best known of such systems is the AEtna Drivotrainer, shown in Figure 12.7. This system typically consists of a number of simulated car-driving units complete with all the controls of a real automobile.

At the front of the room is a screen. At the rear are a film projector and audio console used to simulate the sights and sounds of actual driving conditions. Students "drive" on filmed streets and highways, and their individual responses to filmed driving conditions are recorded and scored. Since its inception in 1953, over 10 million students

▲ *Figure 12.6*
Physical simulators are used heavily in flight training such as here at Flight Safety International's Beechcraft Training Center.

▲ *Figure 12.7*
Students training on driver-education simulators learn to deal with potentially hazardous conditions in the safety of the classroom.

have sharpened their driving skills by means of this particular system.

Simpler simulators are in widespread use in areas such as training workers in a broad range of manual skills. A full discussion of such devices, including a number of examples, can be found in A. J. Romiszowski's *The Selection and Use of Instructional Media.**

---

* A. J. Romiszowski. *The Selection and Use of Instructional Media,* 2nd ed. New York: Nichols, 1988, pp. 273–284.

Applications of Instructional Simulation

Instructional simulations, including role-plays, are particularly well suited for:

- Training in motor skills, including athletic and work skills, and complex skills that might otherwise be too hazardous or expensive to practice in real-life settings.
- Instruction in social interaction and human relations, where empathy and coping with the motivations of other people are major goals.
- Development of decision-making skills (e.g., microteaching in teacher education, mock court in law school, management simulations in business administration).

INSTRUCTIONAL SIMULATION GAMES

Simulation Games and Holistic Learning

B ECAUSE they combine the characteristics of both simulations and games, instructional simulation games have advantages and applications in common with both formats. Thus, they exemplify one of the major rationales for the use of the simulation and gaming methods: the provision of *holistic learning.* That is, *through the modeling of reality* and through the players' interactions as they strive to succeed, *learners encounter a whole and dynamic view of the process being studied.* Conventional instruction tends to segment reality into separate packages (biology, mathematics, psychology, etc.), but that is not how the real world is organized. Through participation in simulation games we can see the whole process and its dynamic interrela-

As airplanes grew larger and faster, fuel costs rose, and the number of flights increased rapidly, the aviation industry underwent a revolution in training methods in the 1970s and 1980s. By now conventional training with its primitive simulators and in-flight practice has been replaced by methods employing state-of-the-art technologies of instruction.

Flight training is now closely geared to specific objectives, and self-instructional modules have largely replaced the former standard method—a class of fifteen to twenty pilots taught by a live instructor. Full-size models of cockpit controls are used to reinforce material learned in the modules. Flight maneuvers and emergency procedures can now be practiced more realistically and more safely than on an actual aircraft.

The new approach to pilot training has been outstandingly successful. Training times have been reduced substantially, and the expensive, fuel-consuming practice flying in real aircraft has been virtually eliminated while proficiency of crews has been upgraded. In most cases the cost of simulator training is about one-tenth that of in-flight training.

At the heart of most new aviation training systems is computer-based training. The systems are flexible and cost-effective, allowing the pilot trainees to proceed at their own pace and not confining them to a classroom or to specified training times. In addition, each student's error record, which is maintained by the computer program, can be reviewed by the instructors daily to identify student weaknesses and possible problems in the instructional procedures.

When the Boeing 767 made its debut in 1982, it was equipped with computer screens and push-button controls instead of the dozens of dials, levers, and gauges of an earlier era. The 767 is flown by two people instead of the usual three and represents a major advance in aviation technology. Likewise, new technologies of instruction were designed to train crews for the new aircraft. The first phase of study entails computer-based instruction—a random access 35-mm slide/tape unit that is controlled by a microcomputer; it allows branching to any part of the slide/tape presentation.

Pilot trainees spend an average of four hours per day in the study carrel. They then spend about 30 minutes at a cockpit instrument simulator in a briefing session with an instructor. After this they go to an enclosed cockpit mock-up with real switches, computers, and display screens for about two hours of practice. Here the trainees program the flight path the same way it is done in an actual 767. All of these preliminaries prepare the trainee to use the full-blown simulator. These flight simulators, costing millions of dollars, are so realistic that the Federal Aviation Authority has extended credit for landing maneuvers performed in them. In theory, the neophyte pilot with a commercial pilot's license and an instrument rating could progress all the way to being a qualified captain on a large jet transport without ever flying in the actual aircraft.

Source: Mary Condon. "Fly the Safe Skies—and Thank Training." *Training and Development Journal* (September 1984), pp. 25–32.

▲ *Figure 12.8*
Role-playing simulations help service personnel develop their "people" skills.

▲ *Figure 12.9*
A well-designed simulation game stirs emotional responses comparable to the reality being modeled.

tionships in action. In addition, our *emotions are allowed to get involved along with the thinking process.* Participants commonly experience excitement, elation, disappointment, even anger, as they struggle to succeed. This, of course, is how learning takes place in the world outside the classroom.

Applications of Instructional Simulation Games

As indicated earlier, instructional simulation games are found in curricular applications that require both the repetitive skill practice associated with games and the reality context associated with simulations. Societal processes (e.g., *Ghetto, Democracy*), cultural conflicts (e.g., *Bafa Bafa*), historical eras (e.g., *Empire, Manchester*), and ecological systems (e.g., *Extinction*) are popular topics.

In general, instructional simulation games are frequently used to provide an overview of a large, dynamic process. The excitement of play stimulates interest in the

---

MEDIA FILE:
"Stress Survival" Instructional Simulation Game

Content area: Management, supervision
Age Level: Adult

Players first determine their own stress threshold with a stress tolerance profile. The profile score becomes a "handicap" when dealing with simulated on-the-job stress situations, earning or losing points. Final score reflects the player's personal stress tolerance and ability to diffuse stress.

Source: Education Research.

MEDIA FILE:
"The Green Revolution Game" Instructional Simulation Game

Content area: Community development, social studies
Age Level: College and adult

The setting is a village in contemporary India. Players attempt to manage their limited resources to provide subsistence for their families. Pests, drought, crop failures, shortage of cash and credit, and deaths of family members are among the realistic variables with which each player must contend.

Source: Marginal Context Ltd.

---

subject matter, and the holistic treatment of the game gives students a feel for the total process before approaching parts of it in a more linear form.

Limitations of Instructional Games and Simulations

As with all of the instructional media, methods, and formats discussed earlier, simulations and games have their limitations as well as potential strengths. Any materials-based instruction is only as good as the materials themselves. The simulation/game format is not magical. The effectiveness of the learning depends on the quality of the particular material and its utilization. It also depends on the receptivity of the learners to these instructional methods. Not everyone responds enthusiastically to game playing or to role playing, where they may expose themselves to some psychological risks.

The use of simulation/game materials usually demands special grouping arrangements—pairing, for instance, or small groups. Some learners might not be able to exercise the responsibility and self-discipline necessary to assure the success of self-directed instruction.

Obtaining all the needed materials can be expensive and time-consuming. Sometimes costs can be kept down by making local modifications (e.g., altering the procedures so that consumable materials are not consumed). But effort will still be needed to get all the materials together and keep them together before, during, and after play.

Some simulation/game activities depend heavily on post-game discussion ("debriefing") for their full instructional effect. This debriefing must be skillfully planned and conducted. If the

instructor lacks discussion-leading skills, the whole learning experience is diminished.

Time can be a significant obstacle. Discovery learning is more time-consuming than straightforward lectures or reading assignments. A principle that can be stated in a single sentence might require an hour of play plus discussion to be conveyed experientially. You have to decide whether the added richness of the learning experience is worth the time.

As discussed earlier, some games entail competition in some form. A cultural setting that discourages competitiveness would not be a very compatible place for using competitive games. Likewise, a culture in which achievement is not valued might not provide the motivation required for students to get "into the spirit" of the game. On an individual level, there will be students for whom competition would be uncomfortable, unfair, or instructionally ineffective. This is true, of course, of every type of instructional treatment. It emphasizes the need to always be prepared to deal with individual differences.

Business Games/ Simulations

In addition to the physical simulators used for flight training and other motor skills, games and simulations are heavily used in business/industry for training in management skills. Usage begins at the preservice level in undergraduate schools of business, 95 percent of which reported in a 1987 survey that they use computer-mediated business simulations.* One out of six business instructors uses games/simula-

tions, with the average user devoting about one-quarter of class time to game/simulation use.

This pattern of rather heavy use continues within the businesses themselves, with Faria having found that among larger corporations (above 1,000 employees) 55 percent use games/simulations in their management training. The majority employ in-basket (simulations in which trainees sort through and make decisions about messages found in their "in" box) and role-playing exercises rather than the computer-based simulations that predominate in academic settings. Most common are simulations developed by outside agencies, such as *Looking Glass, Desert Survival Situation,* and *Strategic Management Game.* Because of their perceived effectiveness and high transfer value, such materials continue to grow in popularity in corporate settings.

SIMULATION/GAMING AND THE *ASSURE* MODEL

Plans for using simulations and games can be organized by turning once more to the ASSURE model. Again, it is assumed that you have analyzed the needs, interests, and learning characteristics of your audience and clearly specified your objectives. So we will begin here with the third element of the model: select media and materials. We will break this down into the three options of selecting off-the-shelf materials, modifying existing materials, or designing new ones.

Select Materials

Selection of any particular simulation or game involves the same considerations as selection of media materials in general. How does the material fit your curricu-

---

* A. J. Faria. "A Survey of the Use of Business Games in Academia and Business." *Simulation & Games* 18, no. 2 (June 1987), pp. 207–224.

This simulation places people in the midst of a plane crash in the desert. They must assess the salvaged items and determine their value for survival. Participants first work individually, then as a group, and finally compare their decisions to an expert's ranking. The Leader's Manual shares the expert's ranking and rationale and offers guidelines for facilitating group discussion.

Source: University Associates

lar objectives? Does it address those objectives in a way no other method can? Is the cost in money and time worth the benefit?

Other considerations that apply particularly to simulation and gaming are noted in the "Appraisal Checklist" included here. You will note that emphasis is placed on identifying whether the item really does provide *relevant practice of meaningful skills* within a *valid representation of reality.* These are aspects of simulation/game materials most likely to prove faulty.

Even more than with most other instructional materials, you will not be able to judge the appropriateness and effectiveness of simulation/gaming materials on the basis of superficial examination. You really can't judge a simulation/game by its "cover." A trial run-through by yourself or with friends is the only relatively sure way of determining how the game flows and what it teaches.

One discouraging aspect of simulation/gaming instruction is the difficulty of locating and acquiring simulation/gaming materials. Many such materials are marketed by their individual developers, so they do not get into regular trade distribution channels and are likely to be publicized only by word of mouth. Others are distributed by small

commercial houses that have an annoying tendency to move and/or go out of business very rapidly. Only a minority are sold through regular publishing outlets. So the prospective simulation/game user may need good detective skills and perseverance to obtain exactly the sort of material required. Fortunately, there are two reference aids that can help you in this task: *The Guide to Simulations/Games for Education and Training,* edited by Robert E. Horn and Ann Cleaves, and *Handbook of Simulation Gaming in Social Education,* edited by Ron Stadsklev. (Both books are described in detail in Appendix A.)

Modify Materials

Although the supply of commercially developed simulation and game materials is growing, you might find it necessary or desirable to *modify* some existing materials to fit your instructional objectives more closely.

Role-play and other less structured activities (e.g., communication games) can be modified easily by changing role descriptions, changing the setting of the activity, or simplifying the interaction pattern in the original activity.

Some games are designed for adaptation to varying age or grade

levels. Several of the games in the *Wff 'N Proof* series, such as *On-Words* and *Equations,* begin as simple spelling or arithmetic drills. The instruction manual contains directions for progressively raising the objectives and rules to higher cognitive levels, ending with games of transformational grammar and symbolic logic.

A more substantive type of modification is to take an existing game and change the subject matter while retaining the original game structure. The original game is referred to as a *frame game* because its framework lends itself to multiple adaptations. When one is modifying a frame game, the *underlying structure of a familiar game provides the basic procedures of play*—the dynamics of the process. The designer loads the desired content onto a convenient frame (see Stolovitch and Thiagarajan's *Frame Games* in the references at the end of this chapter).

Familiar parlor games such as tic-tac-toe, rummy, concentration, and bingo, which were intended for recreation rather than instruction nevertheless can be viewed as potential frameworks for carrying your own instructional content. Television game shows often have been modeled after such parlor games; they in turn suggest additional frameworks. Here are some sample adaptations:

Safety tic-tac-toe: A three-by-three grid is used; each row represents a place where safety rules pertain—home, school, street; each column represents the level of question difficulty. Teams take turns selecting and trying to answer safety-related questions, attempting to fill in three squares in a row.

Spelling rummy: Using alphabet cards instead of regular playing

Appraisal Checklist: Simulation/Game

Title _____

Source _____

Playing time _____ Date _____ Cost _____

Number of players _____

Special equipment/facilities needed: _____

Subject area _____

Format

☐ Has game features (e.g., competition, scoring)

☐ Has simulation features (e.g., role-playing, representation of real-world settings and problems)

Objectives (stated or implied):

Brief Description:

Entry Capabilities Required:

- Prior subject-matter knowledge/vocabulary
- Reading ability
- Mathematical ability
- Other:

Rating	High		Medium		Low	Comments
Relevance to objectives	☐	☐	☐	☐	☐	
Provides practice of relevant skills	☐	☐	☐	☐	☐	
Likely to arouse/maintain interest	☐	☐	☐	☐	☐	
Likely to be comprehended clearly	☐	☐	☐	☐	☐	
Technical quality (durable, attractive)	☐	☐	☐	☐	☐	
[Game] Winning dependent on player actions (rather than chance)	☐	☐	☐	☐	☐	
[Simulation] Validity of game model (realistic, accurate depiction)	☐	☐	☐	☐	☐	
Evidence of effectiveness (e.g., field-test results)	☐	☐	☐	☐	☐	
Clear directions for play	☐	☐	☐	☐	☐	
Effectiveness of debriefing guide	☐	☐	☐	☐	☐	

Strong Points:

Weak Points:

Reviewer _____

Position _____

Recommended action _____

Date _____

▲ *Figure 12.10*
Hollywood Squares is a television game show based on the familiar "frame" of tic-tac-toe.

cards, players attempt to spell short words following the general rules of rummy.

Reading concentration: This game uses about a dozen matched picture-word pairs of flash cards. Cards are placed face down. On each turn the player turns over two cards, seeking to match a pair. Both reading ability and memorization ability are exercised.

Word bingo: Each player's card has a five-by-five grid with a vocabulary word (possibly in a foreign language) in each square. The leader randomly selects words; players then seek the words on their boards, and if they are found, the square is marked. Winner is first player with five correctly marked squares in a row.

Design Materials

As just indicated, simple simulation/gaming materials may be adapted by an imaginative instructor with little more than pencil and paper. This does not mean, however, that designing simulation/gaming materials is a simple process. A great deal of careful

thought is required for the planning and development of *effective* materials. Good simulation/gaming materials do not just happen.

The accompanying "How To . . ." section presents a model for the design of simulation and game materials. As you can see, many individual steps are involved in the process, and the relationships between and among these steps can be quite complex.

Utilize Materials

For simulation/gaming, the utilization step of the ASSURE model entails procedures that are quite different at some points from those suggested earlier for other media.

Preview. Familiarize yourself with the materials, preferably going through a "dry run" with some friends or a few selected students. Acquaint yourself with the rules. Note individual phases of the simulation/game. Be sure you are aware of exactly when and where important instructional points are made. Practice any activities that the game director is responsible for (e.g., providing tokens, computing scores for each round).

Set a time schedule for use of the materials. Your first concern is to have enough time for a successful session. A "good" game squeezed into too short a time can become a "bad" game. Some games—*Starpower,* for example—cannot be broken down to fit into separate class periods; they must be played through continuously. If you have to divide play into separate periods, try to have the breaks come at natural stopping points.

Prepare the Environment.
Check over all the materials to be certain that everything is ready in

▲ *Figure 12.11*
Successful learning from simulation/gaming depends greatly on the instructor's utilization practices, especially on being well prepared.

sufficient quantities. Before the participants arrive, count everything again. If any audiovisual equipment is involved, give it a last minute checkout, too. As with any other kind of teaching, students will judge you harshly if they sense that *you* haven't done *your* homework.

Prepare the Audience. Inform your audience of the learning objectives of the simulation/game activities. Relate the simulation/game to previous studies. Announce the time schedule for completion of the activities. Run through the rules concisely and clearly. If the procedures are somewhat complex, walk the students through one initial round of activities. Resist the urge to lecture about content or to give hints about strategies. Get into the game as quickly as possible.

Present the Simulation/Game.
Once the simulation/game is rolling, your job is to keep the mood and the tempo upbeat. Stay in close touch with the action. Be

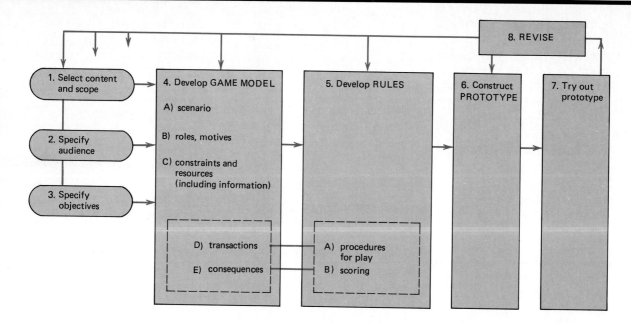

The process outlined in the above diagram will become clearer when considered step-by-step. Examples of each step are provided in the form of a rough prototype actually developed by participants in recent simulation/game design workshop.

Step 1. Select content and scope

Example: The general subject matter is ecology; more specifically, this activity will center on the sociopolitical conflicts involved in establishing a nature reserve, "Mountain Park Nature Reserve." Emphasis will be on developing the interpersonal skills to deal with such conflict situations. This activity will have both simulation *and* game characteristics. It should be playable within one session (approximately two to three hours). It will not deal with scientific or technical aspects of nature reserves.

Step 2. Specify audience

Example: "Mountain Park Nature Reserve" is meant to be played by environmental educators; that is, adults having previous formal background in some aspect(s) of ecology. The primary audience will be expected to have college level educational background.

Step 3. Specify objectives

Example: The general objectives are that participants will be able to: (a) describe the interactions

and conflicts among the social and political motivations of the major parties involved in establishing a nature reserve, and (b) anticipate and counter the objections raised by critics of the nature reserve.

Step 4. Develop Game Model

A. Create a scenario (for a simulation).

Example: A public hearing will be the setting for the action. This hearing has been set up to air the pros and cons of establishing the "Mountain Park Nature Reserve." The place is the capital city of a state or country with limited financial resources but a rather high degree of technological development. The time is the present.

B. Select roles to be represented and ascribe motives to those roles (for a simulation).

Example: The number of roles represented in the game can vary with the size of the playing group. Role descriptions will be written up for each of the following roles; each description will inform the player what his or her motives are—that is, what values he or she is seeking to promote. Possible roles include: representatives for concerned government agencies—Agriculture, Tourism, Industry, Conservation, etc.; residents of the impacted area; scientific experts; potential users; environmental activists; and others.

C. Describe constraints and resources.

Example: During the public hearing phase of the game, players will be able to address the total group only for specified limited amounts of time. During the prior "lobbying" phase their one-to-one contacts with other players will be limited according to how many "influence" chips they have accumulated. At the beginning of the game, players will have personal information only about those roles that are closely allied to their own positions.

D. Specify *transactions* to be carried out.

In order to achieve productive learning, players must be engaged in actions directly associated with the game's performance objectives. The transactions they carry out with other players or with the game materials should entail planning, discussing, choosing, testing hypotheses, gathering information, and the like. Players should *not* be spending most of their time waiting for turns, throwing dice, spinning spinners, or moving markers around a playing board.

Example: Since the second stated objective calls for countering the objections of critics, one of the main transactions will be listening critically to arguments, followed by the formulation of responses to those arguments. This means that one-to-one discussions will be one major transaction embedded in the game.

E. Arrange appropriate *consequences* for player actions.

Each action taken by the player should result in some feedback about the goodness or badness of that move. The designer wants to reinforce appropriate actions. This feedback can often be handled conveniently with a point system.

Example: Players will receive "influence points" depending on how they perform in each round of discussion in terms of: (a) presenting a logical argument consistent with their role, (b) using data to support their arguments, and (c) paraphrasing accurately the contrary arguments of others.

Step 5. Develop rules

A. Spell out procedures for play.

The aim here is to set up procedures and rules that will channel players into carrying out the sorts of transactions identified earlier. As mentioned previously, an existing game may serve as a "frame," supplying basic procedures for play.

Example: "Mountain Park Nature Reserve" will be played in two major phases—a series of small-group mini-debates and a public hearing that will conclude with a vote being taken. The debates will be carried out in triads consisting of two different roles plus an observer. (This "frame" is borrowed from *Actionalysis.*) The observer will award points to each role player depending on the criteria stated in Step 4E above. Each round of mini-debates lasts five minutes, after which everyone rotates into a new triad. Approximately six rounds will be allowed, after which the public hearing will afford various roles the opportunity to present testimony and to be questioned by others.

B. Devise scoring procedures (for a game).

A point system is often a convenient mechanism for delivering and keeping track of reinforcers.

Example: As described in Step 4E above, points will be allocated by the triad observers according to the given criteria. These "influence points" will be translated into political strength in the public hearing phase of the game. In the public hearing phase the scoring will be based on how many players vote for each position put forth.

Step 6. Construct prototype
At this point the designer constructs the needed player materials (e.g., role sheets and score cards) and a teacher's guide (including a debriefing outline).

Step 7. Try out prototype
The essence of the instructional technology approach is that materials are considered merely as prototypes until they have been tested in actual practice. Ideally, pilot testing would be conducted on a small sample group prior to use with the full group. Both the performance outcomes of the players and their emotional reactions to the prototype are observed and recorded to find clues to needed modifications.

Step 8. Revise
The tryout results may suggest revisions in any of the previous elements. There may be rough edges in the play procedures or scoring system. Playing time may run longer than desired. Additional roles may need to be added for increased realism. The original scope or objectives may even be reexamined.

The revised prototype would in turn be tested for effectiveness.

Individual Debriefing

In situations in which participants finish simulation or game activities at different times or in which the schedule prevents immediate group discussion, a form of individual debriefing may be used.

One method developed to help participants reflect on their feelings immediately after play uses a simple sentence-completion form to be filled out individually.* Each participant writes a completion to each of the following sentences:

1. I was _____. (the role you played in the game)
2. I did _____. (actions you performed)
3. I felt _____. (emotions you felt during play)
4. I wish _____. (open response)

The reactions captured on this form can either substitute for group discussion or can supplement the later discussion, with participants referring back to their sheets to remind themselves of their reactions.

Group Debriefing

It is usually preferable to have the debriefing conducted as a group discussion if time and conditions permit. This discussion will be most fruitful if pre-

*Theodore F. Smith " 'Was/Did/Felt/Wish' Bridges Gap When Debriefing Has to Be Delayed," *Simulation/Gaming*, January/February 1978, pp. 5–6.

ceded by careful planning, including formulating key questions in advance. The format suggested here is based on procedures recommended by Ron Stadsklev, an experienced simulation/game leader (see his *Handbook of Simulation Gaming in Social Education*).

Step 1. Releasing Emotions. Your first step in the group debriefing session should be to relieve any tensions that may have built up during the simulation/gaming activity. Some roles played by participants may engender conflict and anger. Players who feel they did not succeed very well in the game may be experiencing anxiety and feelings of inadequacy. In any event, learners are not likely to be able to think about your questions and concerns until these built-up feelings simmer down to a manageable level.

In order to release some of these pent-up feelings, start with some "safety valve" questions. In many cases the players will have attained some sort of score, so you can start simply by asking for and recording the scores. (You will find it useful to have a chalkboard handy so that you can write down the scores and other comments that participants make. The information on the chalkboard will help build up a "data base" you can refer to in subsequent portions of the debriefing.)

From tabulations of the scores you will be able to declare the winner of the game, if the game calls for winners and losers. Let the winner(s) show off a little

ready to intervene, but only when intervention is clearly called for.

Some participants in simulation/game activities may feel a bit confused in the initial stages and be hesitant to get into the swing of things. Reassure such students that initial confusion is not uncommon and that they will soon pick up on rules and procedures.

Watch for individuals or teams who have fallen behind in the activities or even dropped out of them. They may need additional help in mastering the game

mechanics. Withdrawal often signals some basic disagreement with the game's approach to the subject matter. Rather than stifling or suppressing the dissent, discuss the disagreement on a one-to-one basis. Ask the dropout to suspend criticism until the end of the activities.

Watch out for personality clashes; they may require switching of partners or teammates for successful completion of the activities.

Keep track of elapsed time. The excitement and fascination of sim-

ulation and game activities make it easy to forget that time is passing. If necessary, remind participants of time limitations. Resist the temptation to extend simulation/game play at the expense of debriefing time.

If announcements must be made during utilization, try not to interrupt the activities bluntly by shouting above the hubbub. Dimming room lights or flashing your message on the overhead projector can attract the attention you need.

Record significant participant

bit by asking them how they managed to score so highly. Then the lowest scorers should have a chance to explain their tale of woe—what went wrong for them?

At this point be sure to explain any hidden agendas or "dirty tricks" the designer may have built into the game to influence certain scores unfairly. In many simulations modeled on the social class structure, for instance, certain players start out as "disadvantaged" and are consistently impeded from advancing. Obviously, in simulations such as these the final scores are not meant to reflect player skills. Also, you may want to point out that chance plays some part in the scoring—as it does in real life—so that two players might have followed the same strategy and have come out with different scores.

To deal further with the emotional residue, ask one or two players how they felt while playing the game. Did anyone else feel that way too? Let all those who want to chime in freely.

Step 2. Description. The nature and purpose of the activity will, of course, have been explained before the beginning of play. But some students may not have fully appreciated or fully understood the symbolic intent of the activity at this initial stage. Others may have lost track of it in the heat of participation. For example, players of *Triangle Trade* might need to be reminded that they have simulated the experiences of British colonists of the seventeenth century. Make certain that all participants

are fully conscious of the real-world situation or experience that the activity was intended to represent or simulate. Ask basic questions such as "What real-life situation was represented in this activity?" "What real-life experiences?" "What was so-and-so or such and such intended to symbolize?"

Step 3. Transfer. Help the participants transfer the lessons learned in the game to reality. Encourage them to compare and contrast the activities of the simulation or game with the actual dynamics of the real-life situation or experience symbolized by the simulation game. Ask questions such as "How does the scoring system compare with real-world rewards?" "What elements of reality were missing from or muted in the simulation or game?" "Were some elements of reality given more weight than they would have in real life?" "Were some given less weight?"

Step 4. Drawing Generalizations. You are now ready to hit paydirt in your post-activity debriefing session. Get the participants to intellectualize and verbalize exactly what they have learned from the activity. Verbalization will reinforce what has been learned in the activity and strengthen insights that have been gained. Sample questions: "What conclusions can you draw from the simulation/game experience?" "What did you learn about what specific real-life problems?" "Did the simulation/game change any of your previous attitudes or opinions?"

reactions and comments for discussion during the debriefing period.

Require Learner Response

A unique attribute of simulations and games is that participants are continuously responding *throughout* the activity. Indeed, without response there can be no activity. Why, then, should we be concerned with the response element of our ASSURE model when dealing with simulations and games?

The truth is that attention to learner response is perhaps more important in simulations and games than in any other instructional method we have discussed in this book. The reason? Learner response in simulation/gaming is of a different order than is response in most other methods. During either the hurly-burly or the determined concentration of intense involvement in simulations and games, there is little opportunity to intellectualize or verbalize what one is learning or failing to learn from the activity.

The overlay of emotion inherent in simulation/gaming militates against cognitive awareness. Because conscious awareness of the main instructional points may be very low *during* play, it is doubly important to plan for a thorough discussion—a debriefing—*after* play. The debriefing to clarify the instructional goals may be conducted on either an individual or group basis, or a combination of both may be employed, as suggested in the accompanying "How To . . . Conduct Simulation/Game Debriefing."

◄ *Figure 12.12*
Avoid stifling student eagerness by dwelling too long on rules and play procedures; five minutes is a reasonable rule of thumb for rule explanations.

◄ *Figure 12.13*
For complex simulation/game activities, such as social and business simulations, the group debriefing is crucial for bringing out the main points of the experience.

Evaluate/Revise

The final element of the ASSURE model for teaching/learning is evaluation followed by revision. As we have pointed out throughout this text in connection with other instructional media and methods, although full evaluation must await completion of a learning activity, the process begins much earlier.

The notes made during utilization and the records kept of stu-

dent response to the simulation/ gaming materials used will contribute to your final evaluation. The debriefing session, however, will probably provide the most precise and useful data upon which your final evaluation will be based.

A frequent criticism of research and evaluation studies of simulation/game products is that paper-and-pencil tests are too often the primary instruments used to assess learning outcomes. Simula-

tions and games ordinarily emphasize different kinds of outcomes than conventional lecture/ textbook teaching. Their forte is the promotion of holistic learning, usually including appreciation of and insight into complex processes. These sorts of learnings do not lend themselves to measurement by means of typical multiple-choice tests or other verbal tests that dwell on cognitive— often low-level cognitive—outcomes.

A truer test of effectiveness would be the extent to which the simulation/game experience has changed the student's or trainee's approach to real-world problems. Short of following the learner out into the field, the next best means of evaluation would be performance on simulated problems with relatively open-ended opportunities to respond physically, mentally, and emotionally. If these are the goals of the material, logic requires that the method of evaluation be parallel.

References

Print References

General

Bell, Irene Wood. "Student Growth through Gaming in the Library Media Center." *School Library Media Activities Monthly* (February 1986), pp. 36–39.

Center for Vocational Education. *Employ Simulation Techniques.* (Athens, Ga.: American Association for Vocational Instructional Materials, 1977).

Coleman, James, et al. "The Hopkins Games Program: Conclusions from Seven Years of Research." *Educational Researcher* (August 1973), pp. 3–7.

Dalke, Connie. "Life-size Learning Games." *Teaching Exceptional Children* (Winter 1974), pp. 106–109.

Dormant, Diane. *Rolemaps.* (Englewood Cliffs, N.J.: Educational Technology Publications, 1980).

Dukes, Richard L., and Seidner, Constance J., eds. *Learning with Simulations and Games.* (Beverly Hills, Calif.: Sage Publications, 1978).

Evans, David R. *Games and Simulations in Literacy Training.* (Amersham, Buckinghamshire, England: Hulton Educational Publications, 1979).

Gardner, David. "Communications Games: Do We Know What We're Talking About?" *ELT Journal* (January 1987), pp. 19–24.

Glickman, Carl D. "Problem: Declining Achievement Scores, Solution: Let Them Play!" *Phi Delta Kappan* (February 1979), pp. 454–455.

Golas, Katharine C. "Separating Simulation from Instruction." *Training and Development Journal* (December 1983), pp. 72–73.

Greenblat, Cathy S., and Duke, Richard D. *Principles and Practices of Gaming/Simulation.* (Beverly Hills, Calif.: Sage Publications, 1981).

Heitzmann, William Ray. *Educational Games and Simulations.* Rev. ed. (Washington, D.C.: National Education Association, 1987).

Heyman, Mark. *Simulation Games for the Classroom.* (Bloomington, Ind.: Phi Delta Kappa, 1975).

Hoper, Claus, et al. *Awareness Games.* (New York: St. Martin's Press, 1975).

Jones, Ken. *Simulations: A Handbook for Teachers.* (New York: Nichols, 1980).

Julien, Don. "Adventure Games as a Continuing Education Exercise." *Library Software Review* (January–February 1986), pp. 16–20.

Krupar, Karen R. *Communication Games.* (New York: Free Press, 1973).

Malehorn, Hal. *Complete Book of Illustrated Learning Aids, Games, and Activities for the Early Childhood Teacher.* (Englewood Cliffs, N.J.: Parker, 1982).

Metzner, Seymour. *One-Minute Game Guide.* (Belmont, Calif.: Pitman Learning, 1968).

Michaelis, Bill, and Michaelis, Dolores. *Learning through Noncompetitive Activities and Play.* (Belmont, Calif.: Pitman Learning, 1977).

Molloy, William F. "Making Role Plays Pay Off in Training." *Training* (May 1981), pp. 59–63.

Pearson, Margot, and Smith, David. "Debriefing in Experience-Based Learning." *Simulation/Games for Learning* (December 1986), pp. 155–172.

Reiser, Robert A. "Increasing the Instructional Effectiveness of Simulation Games." *Instructional Innovator* (March 1981), pp. 36–37.

Saegesser, François. "The Introduction of Play in Schools: A Philosophical Analysis of Problems." *Simulation and Games* (March 1984), pp. 75–96.

Silverin, Steven B. "Classroom Use of Videogames." *Educational Research Quarterly* (1985–1986), pp. 10–16.

Stadsklev, Ron. *Handbook of Simulation Gaming in Social Education, Part One.* (Asheville, N.C.: University of North Carolina at Asheville, 1976).

Stolovitch, Harold D., and Thiagarajan, Sivasailam. *Frame Games.* (Englewood Cliffs, N.J.: Educational Technology Publications, 1980).

Tapson, Frank. "Organizing Games in the Classroom." *Mathematics in School* (January 1986), pp. 50–53.

Taylor, John, and Walford, Rex. *Learning and the Simulation Game.* (Beverly Hills, Calif.: Sage Publications, 1978).

Thatcher, Donald. "Promoting Learning through Games and Simulations." *Simulation/Games for Learning* (December 1986), pp. 144–154.

Thiagarajan, Sivasailam. "Keep That Delicate Balance." *Simulation/Gaming* (September–October 1977), pp. 4–8.

———, and Stolovitch, Harold D. *Instructional Simulation Games.* (Englewood Cliffs, N.J.: Educational Technology Publications, 1978).

van Ments, Morry. *The Effective Use of Role-Play: A Handbook for Teachers and Trainers.* (New York: Nichols, 1983).

Wiekert, Jeanne, and Bell, Irene Wood. *Media/Classroom Skills: Games for the Middle School.* (Littleton, Colo.: Libraries Unlimited, 1981).

Wohlking, Wallace, and Gill, Patricia J. *Role Playing.* (Englewood Cliffs, N.J.: Educational Technology Publications, 1980).

Curricular Applications

Barker, J. A. "Simulating and Gaming, without Computers, for School Biology Courses." *Journal of Biological Education* (Autumn 1982), pp. 187–196.

Calculator Activities and Games to Play at Home. (Washington, D.C.: National Council of Teachers of Mathematics, 1981).

Carstensen, Laurence W. "Teaching Map Reading through a Tournament." *Journal of Geography* (January–February 1987), pp. 30–31.

Creamer, Robert C.; Cohen, Richard B.; and Escamilla, Manuel. "Simulation: An Alternative Method for Bilingual-Bicultural Education." *Contemporary Education* (Winter 1977), pp. 90–91.

Dukes, Richard L. "Teaching Statistics with Nonsimulation Games." *Teaching Sociology* (April 1987), pp. 184–190.

Ellington, Henry; Addinall, Eric; and Percival, Fred. *Games and Simulations in Science Education.* (New York: Nichols, 1980).

Ernest, Paul. "Games: A Rationale for Their Use in the Teaching of Mathematics in Schools." *Mathematics in School* (January 1986), pp. 2–5.

Felder, B. Dell, and Hollis, Loye K. "Using Games to Teach Social Studies." *Georgia Social Science Journal* (Spring 1983), pp. 18–21.

Hoffman, Thomas R. "Training Games Corporations Play." *Audio-Visual Communication* (January 1977), pp. 32, 34.

Hotchkiss, Gwen, and Athey, Margaret. "Music Learning Grows with Games." *Music Educators Journal* (April 1978), pp. 48–51.

Jarchow, Elaine, and Montgomery, Janey. "Dare to Use Adventure Games in the Language Arts Classroom." *English Journal* (February 1985), pp. 104–196.

Krulik, Stephan, and Rudnick, Jesse A. "Strategy Gaming and Problem Solving—An Instructional Pair Whose Time Has Come." *Arithmetic Teacher* (December 1983), pp. 26–29.

Powers, Richard B. "The Commons Game: Teaching Students about Social Dilemmas." *Journal of Environmental Education* (Winter 1985–1986), pp. 4–10.

Rixon, Shelagh. "Language Teaching Games." *ELT Journal* (January 1986), pp. 62–67.

Sewall, Susan B. "Scientific Fun and Games." *Science and Children* (October 1986), pp. 10–12.

Solomon, Gwen. "Playing with History." *Electronic Learning* (May–June 1986), pp. 39–41.

Steiner, Karen. "Child's Play: Games to Teach Reading." *Reading Teacher* (January 1978), pp. 474–477.

Wertlieb, Ellen. "Games Little People Play." *Teaching Exceptional Children* (Fall 1976), pp. 24–25.

Design

Cryer, Patricia. "Designing an Educational Game, Simulation or Workshop: A 'Course Curriculum' Design Perspective." *Simulation/Games for Learning* (June 1987), pp. 51–59.

Ellington, Henry; Addinall, Eric; and Percival, Fred. *A Handbook of Game Design.* (New York: Nichols, 1982).

Gillespie, Perry. "A Model for the Design of Academic Games." In Loyda M. Shears and Eli M. Bower, eds., *Games in Education and Development.* (Springfield, Ill.: C. C. Thomas, 1974).

Greenblat, Cathy S. *Designing Games and Simulations.* (Newbury Park, Calif.: Sage Publications, 1987).

Maidment, Robert, and Bronstien, Russell H. *Simulation Games: Design and Implementation.* (Columbus, Ohio: Merrill, 1973).

Olmo, Barbara G. "Simulations—Do It Yourself." *Social Studies* (January–February 1976), pp. 10, 14.

Pausch, Erwin. "30,000 Ways to Invent Your Own Group Games." *Successful Meetings* (March 1976), pp. 533–536.

Audiovisual Reference

Finding Values through Simulation Games. Hollywood, Calif.: Media Five, 1977. 16-mm film. 20 minutes.

Periodicals

Journal of Experiential Learning and Simulation (quarterly)
Elsevier North-Holland, Inc.
52 Vanderbilt Avenue
New York, NY 10017

Simulation & Games: An International Journal of Theory, Design, and Research (quarterly)
Sage Publications, Inc.
P.O. Box 5084
Newbury Park, CA 91359

Organizations

International Simulation and Gaming Association (ISAGA)
% Dr. Cathy Stein Greenblat
Department of Sociology
Rutgers University
New Brunswick, NJ 08903

North American Simulation and Gaming Association (NASAGA)
% B. Farzanegan, Executive Director
University of North Carolina
at Asheville
Asheville, NC 28804

Possible Projects

12-A. Using the sources and references provided in the chapter, identify and describe three games and simulations that you could use for your own instructional objectives.

12-B. Appraise an instructional simulation/game using the "Appraisal Checklist" given in the chapter.

12-C. Play an instructional simulation/game and describe your own reaction to the experience; suggest objectives for which it might be appropriate.

12-D. Utilize an instructional simulation/game in an actual instructional situation. Describe the game, its objectives, and the actual results (performance outcomes and reactions) obtained with your group.

12-E. Design a simulation/game prototype. Include a description of the audience, objectives, the game materials (player materials and teacher's guide), and rules for play.

13 Computer-Based Instruction

Outline

Roles of Computers in Education and Training
  Object of Instruction
  Tool during Instruction
  Computer-Assisted Instruction
  Computer-Managed Instruction
  Computer Scheduling, Inventorying, and Budgeting
  Computer-Generated Materials
  Computer-Based Instructional Design
Background of Computers in Education and Training
Advantages of Computer-Based Instruction
Limitations of Computer-Based Instruction
Applications of Computer-Based Instruction
  Computer Literacy

  Computers and Individualized Instruction
  Computer Graphics
  Databases
  Computer Networks
Applications of the ASSURE Model
  Analyze Learners
  State Objectives
  Select Media and Materials
  Utilize Materials
  Require Learner Performance
  Evaluate/Revise
Computer Hardware
  Basic Computer Components
  Types of Computers
  Computer Languages
  Selecting Hardware

Objectives

After studying this chapter, you should be able to:

1. Distinguish between "computer-assisted instruction" (CAI) and "computer-managed instruction" (CMI).

2. Identify five instructional roles of computers in education and/or training other than CAI or CMI.

3. Generate examples of the use of the computer (a) as an object of instruction and (b) as a tool during instruction.

4. Compare and contrast the six methods of computer-assisted instruction in terms of the role of the teacher, the role of the computer, and the role of the learner, including a specific example of courseware in each mode.

5. Generate examples of the use of the computer for computer-managed instruction to (a) individualize learning, (b) provide computer-based testing, and (c) prescribe media, materials, and activities.

6. Describe the development of computer technology and its applications to instruction over the past four decades.

7. Discuss five advantages and five limitations of computers.

8. Discuss six different aspects of computer literacy as described in this chapter.

9. Explain how the modern computer can assist in the individualization of instruction, graphics, databases, and networking. Include in your explanation advantages, limitations, and applications of each.

10. Outline the process (steps) and materials needed to select computer-based materials.

11. Apply the "Appraisal Checklist" to a sample CAI program.

12. Identify and briefly describe the five common components of a computer system, given a generalized schematic diagram.

13. Distinguish between "ROM" and "RAM."

14. Suggest five criteria besides cost that might be important considerations in purchasing a computer for instructional purposes.

Lexicon

computer-assisted instruction (CAI)

computer-managed instruction (CMI)

microprocessor

computer literacy

database

courseware

software

hardware

peripherals

ROM (Read Only Memory)

RAM (Random Access Memory)

bit

byte

mainframe

THE computer with its virtually instantaneous response to student input, its extensive capacity to store and manipulate information, and its unmatched ability to serve many individual students simultaneously is widely used in instruction. The computer has the ability to control and manage a wide variety of media and learning material—films, filmstrips, video, slides, audiotapes, and printed information. The computer can also record, analyze, and react to student responses that are typed on a keyboard or indicated with a "light pen" on a screen. Some display screens even react to the touch of a student's finger.

There are two types of computer-based instruction: *computer-assisted instruction* (CAI) and *computer-managed instruction* (CMI). In CAI the student interacts directly with the computer which stores the instructional material and controls its sequence. In CMI the computer helps instructors administer and guide the instructional process. The student is not "on-line" (directly connected) with the computer system, and the instructional material is not stored in the computer. The computer does, however, store information about students and about relevant instructional materials that can be retrieved rapidly. The learner may be "on-line" to take tests. In addition, the computer can diagnose the learning needs of students and prescribe optimal sequences of instruction for them. We will take a closer look at each of these forms of computer-based instruction later in this chapter.

In addition, the computer can be an *object* of instruction, as in computer science and computer literacy. It also is a *tool* that can be used during instruction to do complex calculations, data manipulations, and word processing. Other educational and training roles will also be described.

ROLES OF COMPUTERS IN EDUCATION AND TRAINING

THE potential uses of computers in educational settings go far beyond the provision of direct instruction. There is the obvious administrative role of keeping school records, scheduling classes, making out paychecks, and the like. Guidance programs use computers to deliver career planning assistance. In the domain of instruction, though, there are seven broad classes of applications: computer as object of instruction; computer as tool; computer-assisted instruction; computer-managed instruction; computer scheduling, inventorying, and budgeting; computer-generated material; and computer-based instructional design.

Object of Instruction

The computer can itself be the *object* of instruction. For example, in computer literacy students learn "about" computers, and in vocational training trainees learn to use computers on the job for data processing and analysis purposes. In this role, the computer is treated like any other machine one is learning to use.

When a learner is studying computer programming, the computer and the associated software are the objects of instruction. The various programming languages and the techniques for constructing a program using these languages are beyond the scope of this book.

Tool during Instruction

The computer can also serve as a *tool* during instruction. It can be used by the learner to solve com-

▲ *Figure 13.1*
Computers have become pervasive in education and training. Most learners have access to and are influenced by computer-based instruction.

▲ *Figure 13.2*
Intense absorption is a common reaction to learning with a computer (CAI).

plex mathematical calculations as a slide rule or pocket calculator was once used, but with increased power and speed. Even a small microcomputer can analyze data, perform repeated calculations, or even gather data when hooked to laboratory equipment or subjects.

Today microcomputers are being used increasingly for word processing and composition. More and more students have access to computers with word processing programs upon which to do term papers and assignments. Some of the programs even check spelling, grammatical structure, and word use. Studies have shown that students are more willing to modify their original compositions when the papers do not have to be completely retyped. The students can devote more time to creative writing and less to the mechanics of "getting it on paper." In these roles the computer serves as a fancy calculator or typewriter.

Computer-Assisted Instruction

Computer systems can deliver instruction directly to students by allowing them to *interact with lessons programmed into the system;* this is referred to as *computer-assisted instruction (CAI).* The possibilities can best be discussed in terms of the various instructional methods described

in Chapter 1. Methods that the computer can facilitate most effectively are drill-and-practice, tutorial, gaming, simulation, discovery, and problem solving. Few programs represent just one of these categories.

Drill-and-Practice Method. The program leads the learner through a series of examples to increase dexterity and fluency in the skill. The computer cannot display impatience and goes ahead only when mastery is shown. Drill-and-practice is predominantly used for math drills, foreign language translating practice, vocabulary building exercises, and the like. Other drill-and-practice programs, such as *Sentences,* let the learners practice sentence constructions.

Drill-and-practice programs provide a variety of questions with varied formats. The trainee is usually given several tries before the computer presents the correct answer. Several levels of difficulty can be available within the same drill-and-practice program. Positive and negative feedback as well as reinforcement can be included.

Tutorial Method. In the tutorial role, the computer acts as the teacher. All interaction is between the computer and the learner. One example of the tutorial method is *Problem-Solving Strategies,* which guide learners through the application of three strategies, provides instruction, practice, and feedback based upon student response. Students are encouraged to guess, and the program provides feedback and does not penalize them for guessing (see "Media File," page 358).

In this method the pattern followed is basically that of branching programmed instruction (see Chapter 11); that is, information is presented in small units followed by a question. The student's response is analyzed by the computer (compared with responses plugged in by the author), and appropriate feedback is given. A complicated network of pathways or "branches" can be programmed. The more alternatives available to the computer, the more adaptive the tutorial can be to individual differences. The extent to which a skilled live tutor can be approximated depends on

MEDIA FILE:
"Wordwright" Drill-and-Practice Program

Wordwright is one of a series of courseware packages developed by The Encyclopaedia Britannica Corporation. The *Wordwright* package includes a drill-and-practice lesson on word definitions, as well as a range of other word games and tests. The vocabulary drill and practice lesson presents a sequence of ten vocabulary questions. If a student's answer is correct, the machine presents the next question. If a student's answer is incorrect, the machine responds with the correct definition as well as with examples of correct usage. After presenting the ten questions, the computer gives a summary of both the words defined correctly and the words incorrectly defined.

Source: Encyclopaedia Britannica.

the creativity of the program designer.

Gaming Method. In Chapter 12 we discussed the distinction between gaming and simulation. A game activity may or may not entail simulation elements. Likewise, a game may or may not be instructional. It depends on whether or not the skill practiced in the game is an academic or training one, that is, related to a specified instructional objective.

At the moment, recreational games can serve a useful purpose in building up computer literacy in an enjoyable, nonthreatening manner. But the ultimate goal of useful learning must be kept in mind. Instructors experienced in computer utilization recommend rationing purely recreational game use, using it as a reward for completing other assignments.

Simulation Method. The simulation method of instruction is described in detail in Chapter 12. In this method, the learner confronts a scaled-down approximation of a real-life situation. It allows realistic practice without the expense or risks otherwise involved.

The computer-based simulation *Operation: Frog* allows a student

to dissect and reconstruct a frog using the same "instruments" that would be used in a biology laboratory. The student must remove the twenty-three organs in sequence as in an actual dissection. "Help" screens and descriptive materials are available at the student's fingertips. (See "Blueprint" on page 382.)

A large number of civilian and military occupations involve the operation or maintenance of complex equipment such as aircraft, manufacturing machines, weapons systems, nuclear power plants, and oil rigs. Major airlines

and the military use computer-based simulators to reduce the amount of actual flying time required for training. The navy has reduced pilot training costs from $4,000 per hour to $400 per hour in one of its programs through the use of computer-based simulation.

A number of open-ended simulations that do not have stated objectives are available. Instructors and/or learners must determine their own objectives. Some of these simulations do not provide instruction within the programs. The instructor must provide this information before the simulation or let the learners discover the effect of changing certain variables for themselves. These simulations can be used in a variety of ways to suit the needs of the instructional situation.

Discovery Method. *Discovery* is a general term to describe activities using an inductive approach to learning; that is, presenting *problems* which the student solves through trial and error or systematic approaches. It approximates laboratory learning outside the classroom.

In CAI using the discovery

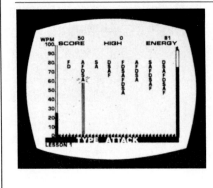

method the learner employs an information retrieval strategy to get information from a database. For example, a salesperson interested in learning about competitors' products can select from a set of critical product features, display them on the computer, and draw conclusions about the comparisons of the products.

Some discovery lessons such as *Inquir* analyze large databases of election information, population statistics, or other user-built databases. OIS (Occupational Information Systems) provides a large database of information about careers to assist the user with exploration of various careers.

Problem-Solving Method. Problem-solving programs fall into two categories, those the learner writes and those written by someone else to help the learner solve problems. In learner-written programs, the student defines a problem logically and writes a computer program to solve it. The computer will do the necessary calculations and/or manipulations to provide the answers. In this case the computer aids the learner in attaining problem-solv-

ing skills by doing complex calculations and manipulations.

In the second category, the computer is the problem solver. The computer makes the calculations while the student manipulates one or several variables. A learner may wish to factor a certain trinomial so that a mathematical problem involving rectangles can be solved. The issue is not

whether the learner can factor, but whether the learner can solve a problem involving rectangles. Factoring is a tedious task that can be done quickly by the computer. A previously written program can be used to factor as many trinomials as are supplied by the learner.

One commercially available problem-solving program is *Memory: A First Step in Problem Solving,* released by Sunburst Communications. It provides students in kindergarten through sixth grade with opportunities to practice the skill and strategies involved in problem solving. The program introduces a generic approach to problem solving across all subject areas as well as in common life situations. The goal is not to present a fixed problem-solving model but to promote the use of an individualized, systematic approach in which the student establishes a model that is appropriate to a specific problem, using strategies from a personal repetoire. The multimedia kit includes a chart showing a problem-solving skill matrix, classroom lessons, software summary

TABLE 13.1 Utilization of Various CAI Methods

Methods	Description	Role of Teacher	Role of Computer	Role of Student	Applications/ Examples
Drill-and-Practice	Content already taught Review basic facts and terminology Variety of questions in varied formats Question/answer drills repeated as necessary	Arranges for prior instruction Selects material Matches drill to student Checks progress	Asks questions "Evaluates" student response Provides immediate feedback Records student progress	Practices content already taught Responds to questions Receives confirmation and/or correction Chooses content and difficulty level	Parts of a microscope Completing balance sheets Vocabulary building Math facts Product knowledge
Tutorial	Presentation of new information Teaches concepts and principles Provides remedial instruction	Selects material Adapts instruction Monitors	Presents information Asks questions Monitors responses Provides remedial feedback Summarizes key points Keeps records	Interacts with computer Sees results Answers questions Asks questions	Clerical training Bank teller training Science Medical procedures Bible study
Gaming	Competitive Drill-and-practice in a motivational format Individual or small group	Sets limits Directs process Monitors results	Acts as competitor judge scorekeeper	Learns facts/strategies/ skills Evaluates choices Competes with computers	Fraction games Counting games Spelling games Typing (arcade-type) games
Simulation	Approximates real-life situations Based upon realistic models Individual or small group	Introduces subject Presents background Guides "debriefing"	Plays role(s) Delivers results of decisions Maintains the model and its database	Practices decision making Makes choices Receives results of decisions Evaluates decisions	Troubleshooting History Medical diagnosis Simulators (pilot/driver) Business management Laboratory experiments
Discovery	Inquiry into database Inductive approach Trial and error Tests hypotheses	Presents basic problem Monitors student progress	Presents student with source of information Stores data Permits search procedures	Makes hypotheses Tests guesses Develops principles/rules	Social science Science Food-intake analysis Career choices
Problem Solving	Works with data Systematizes information Performs rapid and accurate calculations	Assigns problems Checks results	Presents problem Manipulates data Maintains database Provides feedback	Defines the problem Sets up the solution Manipulates variables Trial and error	Business Creativity Troubleshooting Mathematics Computer programming

sheets, program descriptions for each computer disk, computer disks, and a hand puppet for use with younger students.

Computer-Managed Instruction

Computer-managed instruction (CMI) refers to the *use of a computer system to manage information about learner performance and learning resource options in order to prescribe and control individualized lessons.*

There is considerable impetus for using CMI these days because of the increasing emphasis being placed on individualized instruction. Both in formal education and in settings such as the military, business/industry, and government, there is recognition that greater efficiency, effectiveness, and equal opportunity can be reached in instruction only to the extent that teachers can accommodate the individual differences that cause each student to have different learning patterns.

Individualized instruction means that students will be moving through the checkpoints in

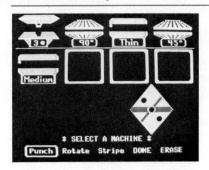

‡ SELECT A MACHINE ‡
Punch Rotate Stripe DONE ERASE

*T*he Factory focuses on several strategies used in problem solving: working backward, analyzing a process, determining a sequence, and applying creativity. The learners are given a square on the computer and three types of machines. The "punch" machine can punch squares or circles, with one, two, or three of each. The "rotation" machine can be programmed to rotate the square 45, 90, 135, or 180 degrees. And the "stripe" machine paints a thin, medium, or thick stripe.

The program has three types of activities. The learners can "test a machine" to see what each option does. They can "build a factory" composed of up to eight machines to make a product of their own design. The most difficult task is to assemble and program a variety of machines in the proper sequence to "duplicate a product" shown on the screen.

Source: Sunburst Communications.

▲ *Figure 13.3*
Educators are exploring ways to use computers to manage the data teachers need for sound decision making (CMI).

the educational process at different times via different paths. You can imagine the management problem this entails if you think of one teacher responsible for teaching five subjects or major topics, with twenty objectives in each subject, to thirty students. This adds up to a minimum of 3,000 checkpoints.

The computer can help solve this management problem by administering diagnostic tests, scoring them, prescribing appropriate next steps, monitoring the progress of the student all the way along the route, and keeping records. This is essentially what CMI does.

One of the largest CMI systems in use today was developed by the U.S. Navy.* This system manages the daily instruction of about 10,000 students in twenty-four courses in nine schools, and it represents about 28 percent of the

Navy technical training. The system generates detailed progress reports that indicate where each student currently is and how long it will be before he or she is finished.

Over the years a number of different CMI systems have been developed and tried out, among them PLAN developed by Westinghouse (in Iowa City schools), TIPS (at the University of Wisconsin), CISS (at New York Institute of Technology), Advanced Instructional System (for the U.S. Air Force), Plato Learning Management (Control Data Corp.), and TICCIT (developed by Mitre Corp. and Brigham Young University). Each of these systems is designed for a different environment, makes different assumptions about the instructional setting, and emphasizes different strengths. Finding the right match with your own institutional needs demands a careful analysis of the available products on a number of dimensions, including computer-system compatibility.

Whatever the merits of the various CMI systems, they generally

suffer from a lack of adequate instructional materials (referred to as "courseware"). CMI can be used most effectively with criterion-referenced materials. The instructional materials controlled by the CMI system may, of course, consist of standard textbooks or workbooks as well as CAI courseware. A notable exception to the general lack of courseware is Plato Learning Management. Because Plato began as a CAI system, it is rich in courseware. Time-sharing mainframe systems like Plato also tend to offer more courseware because the expense of developing such materials can be spread out over a larger number of users. The key, though, is that you can't have computer-managed instruction without *instruction* to manage.

Computer-Based Testing. Computers can be used to store and file banks of test items. The test items can be filed by subject content, objective measured, and/or level of difficulty. Items in the bank can be readily updated and modified, new items added, and old items deleted with minimal effort. From the pool of test items the instructor can choose the items to include on an examination, or the computer can be programmed to select the items,

---

* J. D. Davis. "The Navy CMI System: A Brief Overview." *Journal of Educational Technology Systems,* 2 (1978), pp. 143–150.

In 1960 University of Illinois administrators appointed a committee to suggest ways that the university's computer could be used for research in education, because the military no longer needed it to solve radar problems. The educators thought the engineers didn't know anything about teaching, and the engineers thought the educators didn't know anything about technology! Consequently, the committee came to the only possible conclusion under the circumstances; they could not agree on any projects worth funding.

One of the researchers in the computer lab who was not a member of the committee said, "That's crazy! Give me two weeks, and I will come back with a proposal." Within days the researcher prepared a proposal to develop a course in engineering—a subject with which he was familiar—with an eye to educational considerations. The course was to run on the computers already in the lab—which took care of the technical considerations.

The proposal was approved. The researcher hired a technician to build the hardware and a mathematician to help with the programming. Within one month they had developed an interactive video terminal connected to the computer to provide instruction. They developed programs for college-level computer science and high school mathematics. With the help of a friend, they soon added a program to teach French.

The system was built cheaply and hastily—but it worked! The keyboard had only sixteen keys. The video display was a cast-off television set that could no longer pick up broadcasts. It cost ten dollars. The system was the first to display slides and computer graphics. The slide-selection process was primitive—very primitive. A technician in another room picked them out and displayed them in front of the camera. He got pretty fast at it!

The researcher was Donald L. Bitzer. The system was PLATO—Programmed Logic for Automatic-

Early PLATO terminal

Teaching Operations. Primitive as it was, the original version had all of the elements that were to make PLATO unique: computerized instruction, an authoring system designed to make writing computerized instruction easy, and a learning management system that continually tested the student's understanding of the material and prescribed additional materials if the student needed more help.

Today more than 10,000 hours of PLATO courseware cover the span from kindergarten through graduate-school levels in every conceivable subject area including business/industry training. The course materials are available at individual terminals throughout the world, connected through telephone lines to a powerful mainframe computer at the University of Illinois. Control Data now sells PLATO materials for use on its 110 microcomputers—a long way from an indecisive committee and a ten-dollar television set!

either randomly or according to specified parameters. The computer can be programmed to select items based upon variables in each category used to classify test items.

The computer also can be used to print out a copy of the test in as many different forms as desired or to administer the test to the student who is sitting at the computer. In the latter case, the com-

puter can provide immediate feedback regarding right and wrong responses and keep a permanent record of the learner's achievement on the test.

Test scoring and analysis can be

computerized by typing the student responses at the keyboard, by using mark-sense sheets during the test that can be "read" by the computer, or by having the student take the test at the computer. The computer can display the number of students selecting each alternative, as well as the raw scores and standard scores of each student. In addition, group data such as means and standard deviations can be calculated.

Record Keeping. Records of student scores on tests can be stored by the computer. The student record can be updated each time a test is taken. The computer serves as an "electronic gradebook." At the end of the grading period, the scores can be manipulated (e.g., the lowest score can be dropped, the highest score doubled), the average calculated, the final grade determined, and the composite student performance printed out by the computer.

Computer Prescription of Media/Materials/Activities.
Based upon student data (background, interest, test scores, etc.) and instructor input (available materials, alternative sequences, time available, etc.), the computer (particularly a minicomputer or mainframe) can develop a learning prescription for each student or trainee. Often traditional instruction is lock-step because the teacher or trainer cannot keep all the alternatives as well as each student's characteristics and background in mind. The computer with its extensive storage capacity can perform the countless manipulations necessary to assign instructional activities and learning materials based on a wide variety of decision parameters programmed into it.

Computer Scheduling, Inventorying, and Budgeting

The scheduling of students, rooms, and instructional equipment (real objects, projectors, and carrels) is a greater logistical problem with individualized instruction, whether computer-based instruction is used or not. Depending upon how the program is written, the students, rooms, and equipment can be scheduled by the instructors or by administrators.

Schools and large training organizations have scheduling problems that are difficult to manage with paper-and-pencil records. However, a computer can accurately handle all of the factors (class size, equipment needed, room size, and so on) that need to be considered for efficient scheduling.

As instructional activities employ a wider variety of media and printed materials (other than full-length textbooks), the task of keeping track of the ever-increasing supply of materials becomes more demanding. Many courses of instruction in formal and especially nonformal education use booklets and worksheets. The computer can keep a record of the number of such items on hand and signal the operator when additional copies are necessary. In some cases the texts of the booklets and worksheets are stored in the computer and copies can be printed upon demand.

With increased concern for efficient allocation of limited funds and other resources, the computer is a handy tool for developing budgets and keeping records of expenditures. Many instructors store an expanding list of desired materials and equipment for purchase in the computer. If funds become available at the end of

the fiscal year, a request for these materials, along with necessary purchasing information, can be generated quickly.

Computer budgeting also facilitates the tracking of instructional expenses. Many organizations project a training/education budget based upon "best guesses" and past costs. When the instruction is conducted, costs for personnel, materials, equipment, and facilities are recorded in the computer in order to track the actual expenses.

Computer-Generated Materials

The computer can be used to generate materials. Computer-generated materials (CGM) are becoming more popular and commonly used. Such programs can produce one or more copies of a maze, a test (as described above), a puzzle, worksheet, illustration, diagram, or other instructor-developed items. With their increased graphics capabilities, microcomputers are being used to generate masters for overhead transparencies and slides.

Computer-Based Instructional Design

The computer can help with functions other than the delivery of course materials. It can be used to assist in the design and development of instructional materials and training programs. The computer can also manage course-development projects. These systems are *not* designed to be used exclusively for development of computer-based training materials, as the title may imply.

All instruction should be developed using a systematic process, and the computer can assist with these processes. As described earlier in this section, the computer can assist with the creation and editing of printed materials as well as the design and production of graphics, slides, overhead transparencies, and animated sequences. The computer can also be used during the analysis, design, development, implementation, and evaluation of complex instructional systems.

The computer provides word processing, checks spelling and sentence structure, and assists with editing and compilation of documents. The computer can also assist with decision making using algorithms. These computer-based systems utilize commercially available software for word processing, database management, spreadsheets, and project management.

Two current computer-based development systems include Courseware's Instructional Toolkit™* and Mountain Bell's Computer Managed Instruction Development project.† Although these systems can be used by individuals, they are designed to be used for large-scale projects involving a team of developers working together to produce a substantial amount of instructional materials. Under these conditions, standardization and communication of results from one task to another is very important. Computer-based instructional development saves time and money in both the initial design stage and in the revision of training materials. Course developers are able to produce course materials in a shorter time, at less

▲ *Figure 13.4*
Desk-top publishing systems allow teachers to produce their own instructional materials with minimum time and little expense.

cost, knowing that all appropriate instructional design strategies have been considered.

BACKGROUND OF COMPUTERS IN EDUCATION AND TRAINING

THE introduction of computers is considered by many to be the third revolution in education; the first was the printing of books, the second the introduction of libraries. The computers developed in the 1950s were awesome creations. Their vacuum tubes and miles of wiring filled several large rooms, dwarfing the sizable crew of attendants needed to keep them working. Not highly reliable but fabulously expensive, they were designed for carrying out complicated mathematical manipulations and did this very efficiently for those who were able to speak their highly specialized mathematical language.

The possibility of educational applications was mainly conjectural at that time, although important instructional experiments were conducted throughout the 1950s and 1960s. These experiments were spurred by the development of FORTRAN, a more easily learned computer language, and B. F. Skinner's research in programmed instruction. It was seen that the step-by-step format of linear programmed instruction lent itself well to the logical "mentality" of the computer. The factors of cost, hardware reliability, and the availability of adequate materials remained major barriers to the widespread adoption of computers for instruction.

The advent of the *microcomputer* in 1975 altered this picture dramatically. The microcomputer was made possible by the invention of the *microprocessor*, a tiny chip of silicon that contains within itself all the information-processing ability of those roomfuls of original computer circuitry. The development of the silicon

* Greg Kearsley. "Automated Instructional Development Using Personal Computers: Research Issues." *Journal of Instructional Development*, 9, no. 1 (1986), pp. 9–15.
† Charline Seyfer and James D. Russell. "Computer Managed Instruction Development." *Performance & Instruction*, 25, no. 9 (1986), pp. 5–8.

▲ *Figure 13.5*
The "mainframe" computer with its massive components was the norm before the advent of the microcomputer.

unusually rapid compared with other educational innovations. By 1987, figures compiled by Market Data Retrieval* indicated that almost 99 percent of the public senior high schools in the United States had one or more microcomputers for student instruction, more than doubling the number from five years earlier. Junior high schools were not far behind, with over 98 percent having at least one microcomputer, whereas only 25 percent had had microcomputers five years earlier. The biggest growth rate was in the elementary schools, from 11 percent to 94 percent in just five years. By 1988 there was one computer for every thirty students in U.S. schools. It was predicted that in the next five years there would be one computer for every five students.

chip reduced the cost of computers to a truly remarkable degree. The microcomputer was an immediate success in the marketplace, especially for use in small businesses and in the home.

The acceptance of microcomputers by the schools has been

* *Microcomputers in Schools, 1986–87: A Comprehensive Survey and Analysis.* Shelton, Conn.: Market Data Retrieval, 1987, p. 8.

▲ *Figure 13.6*
The tiny microprocessor fostered the microcomputer revolution. Chips like this one are used in home appliances, automobiles, toys, and hundreds of other devices, giving each a "brain" of its own.

▲ *Figure 13.7*
Innovative microcomputer systems such as the Macintosh have helped popularize the use of micros in business and homes.

ADVANTAGES OF COMPUTER-BASED INSTRUCTION

THE computer can be viewed generally as a tool for enhancing instruction (through CAI) and instructional management (through CMI). It is the *interactive* nature of computer-based instruction that underlies most of its advantages. As an active mode of instruction, it requires learner response (the *R* of the ASSURE model). Specific advantages are the following:

- Simply allowing students to learn at their own pace produces significant time savings over conventional classroom instruction. Computer-based instruction allows students some control over the rate and sequence of their learning (individualization).
- High-speed personalized responses to learner actions yield a high rate of reinforcement.
- The patient, personal manner that can be programmed provides a more positive affective

▲ *Figure 13.8*
Computers require the learner to interact with them and can promote interaction among students.

climate, especially for slower learners.
- Color, music, and animated graphics can add realism and appeal to drill exercises, laboratory activities, simulations, etc.
- The record-keeping ability of the computer makes individualized instruction feasible; individual prescriptions can be prepared for all students (particularly mainstreamed special students), and their progress can be monitored.
- Memory capacity allows students' past performance to be recorded and used in planning the next steps.
- Computers can provide coverage of a growing knowledge base associated with the information explosion. More information is put easily at the instructor's disposal. Computer-based instruction also provides a broad diversity of learning experiences. The types of learning experiences can utilize a variety of instructional methods and can be at the level of basic instruction, remedial, or enrichment.
- The computer provides reliable and consistent instruction from learner to learner, regardless of the teacher/trainer, the time of the day, or the location.
- Computer-based instruction can improve efficiency and effectiveness. *Effectiveness* refers to improved learner achievement, whereas *efficiency* means achieving objectives in less time or at lower cost. Efficiency is very important to business and industrial applications and is becoming increasingly important in educational settings. According to Kearsley,* the

---

* Greg Kearsley. *Computer-Based Training: A Guide to Selection and Implementation.* Reading, Mass.: Addison-Wesley, 1983.

"time savings (an average of 30 percent compared with conventional training) is almost completely due to the individualization of instruction, not the use of the computer itself. However, it is virtually impossible to run a large individualized instructional program without the use of a computer to manage the activity."
- One serendipitous effect of working with computers is that they literally force us to communicate with them in an orderly and logical way. The computer user must learn to communicate with explicit, exact instructions and responses. Any departure from precision is rejected by the computer. Observers who have watched the development of young people as they work with computers, particularly in computer programming, note a tendency for orderly, logical thinking to be carried over into other areas of the students' work. Deductive reasoning thus becomes the "hidden curriculum" or concomitant learning—an unintended but welcome side effect of contact with computers.
- Computer users learn keyboarding or typing skills. Now very young children as well as adults are developing these skills in order to communicate with computers.

LIMITATIONS OF COMPUTER-BASED INSTRUCTION

As we have seen with all the other media and technological innovations, there are always trade-offs to be made and limitations to consider. Some of the major limitations of computers in instruction are as follows:

- Despite the dramatic reduction in cost of computers and computer use, computerized instruction is still relatively expensive. Careful consideration must be given to the costs and benefits of computers in education and training. Maintenance can also be a major cost consideration, especially if equipment is subjected to heavy use.
- There is a lack of high-quality materials for use with computers. There is also a compatability problem. Software developed for one computer system usually cannot be used with another. The ease with which software can be duplicated without permission has inhibited some commercial publishers and private entrepreneurs from producing and marketing quality instructional software.
- Users, both learners and teachers, may have unrealistic expectations of computer-based instruction. They view computers as magical and expect learning to happen with little or no effort. Unfortunately, learners and teachers derive benefits proportional to their investments.
- A limited range of objectives can be taught by computers. Most computer-based instruction does not teach effectively in the affective, motor, or interpersonal skills domain. Even in the cognitive domain, programs tend to teach at the lower levels of knowledge and comprehension.
- Design of instructional materials for use with computers is a laborious task, even for instructors with courseware design skills. Consequently, quality computer-based instruction is expensive.
- Creativity may be stifled in computerized instruction. The computer is slavish in its adherence to its program. Creative or original learner responses will be ignored or even rebuked if the program's designer has not anticipated such possibilities.
- Computer-based instruction usually lacks socialization. Learners tend to work on their own at a computer, and there is little if any face-to-face interaction with teachers or other learners.
- Some learners, especially adult learners, may resist the linear, lock-step control of the learning process typical of computer instruction materials.
- The novelty associated with CAI in its earlier days seems to be decreasing. As learners become more familiar with computers in the home and the workplace, the newness of the stimulus wears off and has less motivational value.
- Design and production of computers specifically for instructional purposes has lagged behind design and production for other purposes.

APPLICATIONS OF COMPUTER-BASED INSTRUCTION

Computer Literacy

*L*ITERACY once implied exclusively the ability to read and write, i.e., verbal literacy. With the rapid spread of computer use in the late 1970s and early 1980s came an equally rapid flowering of public awareness of the emergent importance of computers in society. Out of this heightened popular awareness emerged yet another type of literacy—computer literacy—referring to the ability to understand and to use computers. Analogous to reading, the computer puts out messages that require interpretation by the user. Analogous to writing, the user generates messages that tell the computer what to do—*if* the "vocabulary," "grammar," and "sentence structure" are correct.

Our discussion thus far has focused on the two most fundamental aspects of computer literacy. However, computer literacy exists along a continuum from general awareness to the ability to write computer programs. Also involved are ethical issues related to how and when computers should be used. (See Figure 13.9) Most students start at the left of the continuum and move toward the right. Computer literacy involves knowledge, attitudes, and skills. Knowledge of hardware, software, and data-processing concepts is necessary as well as of the applications of computers. Attitudes include a willingness to use computers where appropriate in everyday situations without fear and an awareness of the social implications of abusive uses as well as beneficial uses. Skills include operating computers, modifying existing programs, and programming new applications.

The computer literacy of learners and instructors rose dramatically during the 1980s. More are now comfortable using computers, and fewer have to be taught how to use them.

Computers and Individualized Instruction

The recent emergence of computer technology coincides with a heightened awareness among educators of the importance of individualization. Research into new instructional methods consistently indicates that certain treatments work for certain people under certain conditions. There are no panaceas.

The great quest in the field of

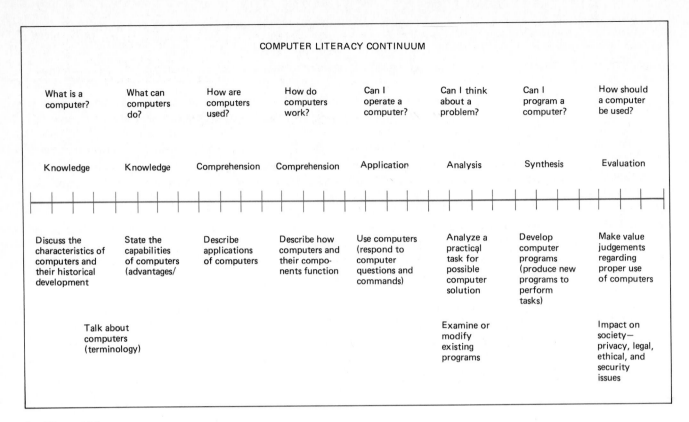

COMPUTER LITERACY CONTINUUM

What is a computer?	What can computers do?	How are computers used?	How do computers work?	Can I operate a computer?	Can I think about a problem?	Can I program a computer?	How should a computer be used?
Knowledge	Knowledge	Comprehension	Comprehension	Application	Analysis	Synthesis	Evaluation
Discuss the characteristics of computers and their historical development	State the capabilities of computers (advantages/	Describe applications of computers	Describe how computers and their components function	Use computers (respond to computer questions and commands)	Analyze a practical task for possible computer solution	Develop computer programs (produce new programs to perform tasks)	Make value judgements regarding proper use of computers
	Talk about computers (terminology)				Examine or modify existing programs		Impact on society— privacy, legal, ethical, and security issues

▲ *Figure 13.9*
The development of computer literacy can be laid out along a continuum.

Computer Graphics

media and technologies of instruction is to find ways of matching individual learners with the appropriate subject matter, pitched at the right level, and presented in a compatible medium at the optimal pace in the most meaningful sequence.

True individualization imposes a tremendous burden of decision making and resource management. One instructor might approach an ideal level of individualization with a handful of students. But when dealing with twenty, thirty, forty, or more students the logistics of individualization overwhelm any single teacher's capacity. The computer gives promise of overcoming these and other logistical barriers to individualization of instruction.

Computer Graphics

Recent advances in computer graphics can facilitate both learn-ing and teaching. The resolution (clarity) of the visuals has been increasing along with the variety of colors (up to 256) available. Any visual formerly limited to slides and filmstrips can now be reproduced on a computer screen.

The computer can be used to develop classroom visuals, flow-charts, diagrams, and drawings for viewing on the computer screen, projecting, or printing a hard copy. These computer-generated illustrations can enhance learning by providing more realistic visuals for instruction, especially simula-tions. They provide learners with opportunities to better understand the material being studied. Graphics can display mathemati-cal relationships and properties of mathematical functions in ways not previously possible. Users can produce a musical piece by arranging notes on the musical staff.

Students prefer high-quality color graphics for instruction. They can also learn from produc-ing graphics on the computer (visual literacy). The graphics tab-let is a device that facilitates the input of nontextual materials. The tablet is connected to the com-puter, and a special pen is used to draw whatever visual is needed. The tablet sends an electronic description of the visual to the computer, where it is displayed on the screen and can be stored for use later.

Graphics can be animated, and some programs will handle move-ment automatically within the parameters specified. Others require each frame of the anima-tion to be drawn as in film anima-tion.

Databases

Today's students need to learn to manage information; to define

There is at least one microcomputer in each of the 163 institutions in the Fairfax, Virginia public school system. As part of a coordinated computer literacy program, these machines are used to teach elementary students how computers will affect their lives, as well as how to use computers. The high school students use them in business and data processing courses. Word processing software is used to teach composition, and music synthesizers let students compose their own songs. Learning-disabled students use computers to improve their eye-hand coordination.

The program in Fairfax was cited in 1984 by AECT's Project BEST (Basic Education Skills through Technology) for exemplary use of computers "to enhance the efforts of teachers and stimulate student creativity."

Computer literacy focuses on integrating computers into the existing curriculum rather than using them as a stand-alone program. Now the program is extending into the uses of computers for instruction. For example, one foreign language teacher uses a program in which his students "visit" a French restaurant and must use French to order from the menu.

As the teachers' computer literacy expands, the computers are used more and more for the management of instruction. Teachers can call up questions from a test-item bank, have them printed, and administer them to students. The computer then collects the student answers through an optical scanner, analyzes the results, provides test scores, and updates student records.

---

problems clearly; to identify information needs; to retrieve, sort, and organize information; and to evaluate their findings. Students can use databases for inquiry and research. A *database* is a *collection of related information organized for quick access to specific data*. A telephone book is a printed database. Databases can also be stored in a computer; for example, a list of telephone numbers by name or company. A database is a versatile and easy-to-learn computer tool. It can be thought of as a file cabinet. In fact, one available database is *PFS: File*.

There are two types of databases. Classroom databases are created by students. Students can design information sheets and questionnaires, collect the data, input relevant facts, and then retrieve them in a variety of ways. The facts selected might include student information, book reports, or sample math problems.

Another type of database is the commercial database. Commercial databases are either purchased on diskettes or accessed via telephone hookup to a computer in another location. The Minnesota Educational Computing Corporation (MECC) sells a *Fifty States* database on diskette that contains information such as population, capital, area, major rivers, and state bird, flower, and tree for all the states. Several companies have developed database materials for use in the classroom (see the Database sources listed on page 386.) Other larger computer databases are available via telephone and contain medical information, historical data, census figures, and the like.

With databases students engage in higher levels of thinking and inquiry skills. They also learn to use databases for research.

Computer Networks

A computer network allows individual computers to share courseware, data, and peripheral devices such as printers. Common networks are AppleTalk, Omninet, and IBM's Classroom LAN. *LAN* is an acronym for "local area network," a term applied broadly even though the geographical size of such networks is constantly expanding.

Computer networks are of two basic types: hard disk and point-

---

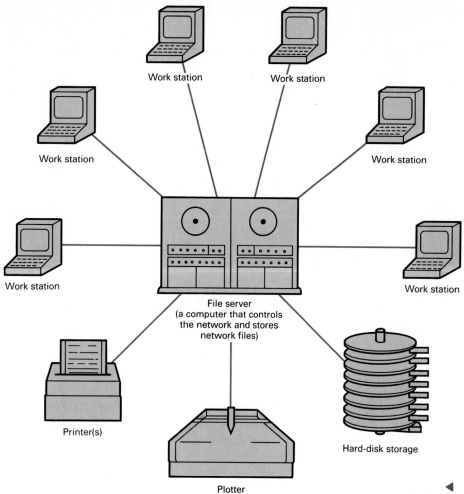

Work station

Work station

Work station

Work station

Work station

Work station

File server
(a computer that controls
the network and stores
network files)

Printer(s)

Plotter

Hard-disk storage

A hard-disk computer network configuration

◀ *Figure 13.10*
Computer networks expand the uses of
computer-based instruction in formal, group-
based learning.

to-point. As shown in Figure
13.10, the hard-disk computer
network is composed of a file
server, hard-disk storage, individual workstations, and peripherals
such as printers and plotters. The
file server is the computer that
controls the network. The hard-
disk storage, often included
within the file server, stores all
the network files. The individual
workstations are separate computers used by the learners for a variety of different tasks simultaneously. The peripherals can be
used by any of the individuals on
the network. When one person is
using the printer, the next per-

son's job is queued to be run as
soon as the first job is completed.
    The point-to-point networks
provide the same functions as the
hard-disk networks but also allow
each workstation on the network
to both receive data from and
send data to any other workstation
on the system. Such networks
often link microcomputers to
large computing environments
and databases.

Advantages. If an educational
organization has hundreds of different pieces of courseware and
curriculum packages available,

multiple copies for each computer can be very expensive.
Instead of purchasing twenty-five
courseware packages for twenty-
five individual computers, the
organization can buy one piece of
courseware and a site license
which allows the courseware to
be loaded onto the file server for
use at all twenty-five networked
computers.
    Updating is also less expensive.
The organization does not have a
significant investment in courseware on floppy disks. Instead, it
can purchase a new program and
a new site license. In addition,
instructional materials are now

being designed specifically for use on a network.

Networking relieves teachers of the burdensome task of distributing and collecting floppy disks. Some CAI courses may require a dozen floppy disks each. If the course is available at fifteen workstations, 180 diskettes are required for that program alone. In addition, the diskettes may get mixed up or misplaced.

Some instructional programs are designed to track individual learner progress. This is best done with a hard disk and is certainly facilitated with a network. Such data as lessons attempted, lessons completed, tests taken and retaken, and scores on tests can be recorded within the network for access by the instructor. For administrative purposes, the frequency and duration of computer workstation usage as well as use by individual students can be recorded.

Limitations. Initial costs of computer networks vary from several hundred dollars to tens of thousands of dollars. The user must determine if the cost savings previously described will more than offset the expense of the network.

Not all computer software can be used on a network because of its physical configuration. It is important to check software before purchase to determine if it will run on the network.

If there is a problem with the network, all computers on the network may be shut down. These problems can be very frustrating to the learners and particularly to the instructor. With stand-alone computers, only one student is frustrated by a machine failure.

Applications. In 1987 over one-third of the school districts and almost one-half of the universities in the United States had at least one networked computer lab.* These computer networks often integrate hardware, courseware, and a management system.

The networks can be used with most of the CAI and CMI applications described in this chapter. Some networked labs are used for individual subjects such as math, whereas other labs are used to teach multiple subjects. The content ranges from remedial math to advanced language arts and composition. The course management system may diagnose, reinforce, and enhance learning by individual students.

The computer network may be within an individual lab, or several labs can be interconnected in a larger network. Entire schools have been tied together for schoolwide electronic mail (messages for individual users) and electronic bulletin boards (messages for all users). The same is being done for school districts. Statewide networks are being developed that will connect all elementary and secondary schools in the state with each other and with the state of education department. The universities within the state can also be connected, along with postsecondary vocational and technical schools and community/junior colleges. In the future, schools throughout the nation—or even the world—may form a network.

APPLICATIONS OF THE *ASSURE* MODEL

Analyze Learners

As with all instructional materials and media, the attributes of the audience, both general characteristics and specific

---

* *Electronic Learning*, January 1988, p. 30.

▲ *Figure 13.11*
"We're getting a new computer in class today. I hope I'm the one it replaces."

entry competencies, need to be determined. With the use of computers in instruction, an important entry competency is usually keyboarding. Many applications of computers require the learner to be able to type. If the students cannot type, they may learn while using the computer, or they may use a computer game such as *Type Attack* (see the "Media File" on page 358) to learn and/or improve keyboarding skills. Other general characteristics, such as their attitudes toward computers, will also need to be taken into consideration.

State Objectives

The computer is *not* a toy, so there should be objectives for the use of the computer in the classroom. As described earlier in this chapter, the computer may be the *object of instruction*. The student may be learning to program or operate the computer. The computer may be a *tool* to meet other objectives, such as calculating or preparing reports (word processing). The computer can present the instruction and assist the student in meeting the objectives—*computer-assisted instruction*. In all of these applications, the purpose or objective needs to be stated in advance. Then and only then are you ready to select computer-based materials.

Select Media and Materials

In the context of computer-based materials, the term *software* refers in general to *any computer programs and their accompanying documentation.* It is customary to refer to *software that teaches the actual subject matter* as *courseware.*

As has happened before in the field of instructional media, the development of hardware for CAI has exceeded the pace of courseware development. It is clear that the ability to compose computer programs is not synonymous with the ability to design effective instruction. Reviewers who have had the opportunity to appraise critically a portion of the flood of CAI programs being offered in the marketplace dismiss a large percentage of them as "junk."

Search the sources, listings, and reviews to find the courseware that might meet your specific need. Students should be involved in choosing software. The teacher needs to get the learners' input about how long the software will hold student interest and how helpful it will be in helping them learn.

Preview the courseware using the "Appraisal Checklist." Finally, select the material that appears to meet your needs best.

Sources. There are numerous sources for educational and training courseware. They include educational institutions and consortia that develop new courseware, businesses that develop courseware to train their employees, software companies, and textbook publishers. In addition, clearinghouses such as CONDUIT and MECC are nonprofit organizations that sell courseware for minimal cost. CONDUIT, located at the University of Iowa, specializes in materials for higher education, whereas MECC, the Minnesota Educational Computing Corporation, provides courseware for elementary and secondary applications. Addresses for these organizations are given in the list of references at the end of this chapter.

Listings. In addition to catalogs from the sources just listed, there are numerous indices, on-line databases, and printed directories listing courseware available by subject headings. Several listings of computer courseware sources are included in Appendix A.

Reviews. Several agencies attempt to help teachers and trainers cope with the courseware selection task by conducting independent reviews and evaluations of materials. These include MicroSIFT at the Northwest Regional Education Lab and the EPIE Institute. Addresses for these and other review selection sources are included at the end of this chapter and in Appendix A. In addition, many educational magazines and training journals include courseware reviews. Numerous such periodicals are listed in the reference section at the end of this chapter. Additional review sources are given in Appendix A.

Previews. You can use the review and selection sources to identify those computer programs that might meet your educational and training needs. However, you should preview the materials yourself to see if they are likely to meet your specific needs. You should request a copy of the courseware from the distributor with return privileges. Some companies will provide preview/demo disks which include samples of a variety of their courseware. These disks allow you to preview the programs but avoid the possibility that the companies' programs will be illegally copied. There may be a clearinghouse or local site where you can preview materials. Many of these preview sites are operated by local school districts and universities. Some local computer stores sell instructional materials and will allow you to preview the courseware within the store. In all cases, use the "Appraisal Checklist: Computer-Based Instruction" when you preview courseware.

As we have pointed out in reference to the other media and technologies of instruction, each format of media/technology has particular attributes that contribute to a unique set of criteria by which to judge the associated materials. In the case of CAI materials, we find many of the same concerns that affect programmed instruction materials— active participation, remedial branches, and field-test data. To these we add criteria based on the special capabilities of computers—use of graphics, and clear and complete documentation. Finally, there are descriptive data related to the different physical variations among computer systems. For example, what size memory is required?

Modification is not possible with most commercial courseware. Even when it is possible to obtain a program listing, revising is a very difficult task and is usually against the copyright law. You can modify the *uses* of the courseware and the associated (adjunct) materials, such as handouts and study guides. For noncommercial programs that are obtained from other teachers and trainers the procedures for making modifications to meet specific needs are beyond the scope of this book; you should consult a textbook on

Appraisal Checklist: Computer-Based Instruction

Title _____ **Format**

Series title (if applicable) _____ disk size

Source _____ _____

Length (completion time), Range: _____ to _____ minutes, Average _____ minutes

Designed for what system? _____ Memory required? _____

Subject area _____

Intended audience _____

Objectives (stated or implied):

Brief Description:

Entry Capabilities Required:

- Prior subject-matter knowledge/vocabulary
- Reading ability
- Mathematical ability
- Other:

Rating	High		Medium		Low	Comments
Relevance to objectives	☐	☐	☐	☐	☐	
Accuracy of information	☐	☐	☐	☐	☐	
Likely to arouse/maintain interest	☐	☐	☐	☐	☐	
Ease of use ("user friendly")	☐	☐	☐	☐	☐	
Appropriate color, sound, graphics	☐	☐	☐	☐	☐	
Frequent, relevant practice (active participation)	☐	☐	☐	☐	☐	
Feedback provides remedial branches	☐	☐	☐	☐	☐	
Free of technical flaws (e.g., dead ends, infinite loops)	☐	☐	☐	☐	☐	
Clear, complete documentation	☐	☐	☐	☐	☐	
Evidence of effectiveness (e.g., field-test results)	☐	☐	☐	☐	☐	

Strong Points:

Weak Points:

Reviewer _____

Position _____

Recommended action _____ Date _____

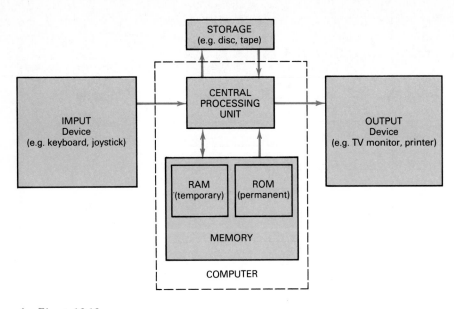

▲ *Figure 13.12*
Basic elements of a microcomputer system

the time and are interested. (See the references at the end of this chapter.)

Utilize Materials

Computers may be used individually by learners in the classroom, a learning center, the library, or at home. However, it is possible to use one computer with a classroom full of learners. Donald Shalvey* has suggested several classroom-tested tips for using a computer with elementary school classes. Some of the techniques may be used with learners of all ages.

- *Use keyboards of the paper, playground, and floor-mat kind.* For elementary-age learners keyboarding skills can begin

the programming language used to develop the courseware.

Some instructors *design* their own courseware. However, most teachers and trainers do not have the time or expertise to do so. It can take up to 300 hours to design, code (program), and "debug" (correct) one hour of computer-based instruction. There are books written on courseware design for those who have

* Donald H. Shalvey. "How to Get Comfortable with 32 Kids and One Computer." *Learning 87* 15, no. 9 (May–June 1987), pp. 33–36.

CLOSE-UP:
Classroom Use of a Single Computer

A high-school economics teacher uses a single computer with a class of twenty-four students. A computer projection device that sits on top of an overhead projector allows all students to see what is on the monitor.

The teacher uses prepared computer graphics instead of overhead transparencies for key points and illustrative graphs in the class. She can advance from one visual to the next as needed and can also reveal key words from the lecture with the touch of a key.

The biggest advantage of the computer in a large-group instructional situation is its usefulness in presenting "what if" results. For example, while presenting the concepts of supply and demand, the students can discuss the effect of an increase in availability of a product on its cost. Following the discussion the teacher can project the results. The teacher can also put student-suggested values into the computer, and the class can see the results immediately. Economics comes alive in the classroom when years of data can be manipulated within minutes for all to see.

by posting a large chart on the classroom wall and distributing 8″ × 10″ copies to each student. Students can work in pairs and provide drill-and-practice for each other. Some teachers have even painted keyboards on the playground blacktop and large indoor floor mats. The students then engage in hopping and "Simon says" games to learn the location of the various keys.

- *Use navigators and SWAT teams.* Use experienced students as "navigators" (assistants) for the novice users. One teacher called the helpers a SWAT (Support Workers at Terminals) team. As the SWAT team members and the computer neophytes communicate, they both get practice giving directions, following directions, and solving problems.
- *Try the tremendous "T" and the wonderful "Y".* Adapters (the T and Y types) can split the signal coming from the class computer and display it on a large monitor as well as on the computer screen. Computer projection using an overhead projector serves the same purpose. These two techniques allow the instructor to introduce new software or to demonstrate data analysis including graphs and charts to an entire class at one time.

Require Learner Performance

Getting students involved with learning is easy and natural with computers. The computer is not a passive medium. Good CAI materials provide active student involvement and branch on the basis of student responses. If the learners are not required to respond frequently and are doing a lot of reading, then perhaps that

particular software should be replaced by paper-and-pencil materials.

Some computer-assisted instruction programs are nothing more than "fancy page turners." These should be avoided. If all the learners are doing is reading and making simple responses, the use of these computer-based materials should be carefully reconsidered.

Evaluate/Revise

Many computer-based instructional materials include evaluations within the program itself. They often incorporate pretests, embedded self-checks, and post-tests. Branching within CAI is based upon the learner's performance—a consequence of evaluation. Mastery of the program content can also be measured by teacher-developed paper-and-pencil tests or by standardized tests.

Other types of evaluation should also be used with computer courseware. As part of the selection process an appraisal

checklist should be used. It may be applied again after use of the materials, and you may ask for student reactions to the material. Did they enjoy using the computer-based materials? Evaluation should be a continuous and on-going part of all instruction. Materials that don't achieve your objectives should be replaced.

COMPUTER HARDWARE

Basic Computer Components

REGARDLESS of the size of the computer or complexity of the system, computers have a number of standard components. The core element is the *central processing unit* (CPU). The other components needed for input, output, memory, and storage are referred to as *peripherals*. All of the *physical equipment of which the computer is composed* is referred to as the *hardware*. The basic hardware components are diagrammed in Figure 13.12.

MEDIA FILE:
Apple IIe Microcomputer

One of the most popular microcomputers used for instruction, the Apple IIe (for *expanded*) is built around a low-cost starter system that can be expanded by adding memory capacity and peripherals, such as a printer. The IIe comes with 128K bytes of memory with the possibility of adding an additional 64K.

The computer has a full ASCI keyboard with 63 keys (96 printable characters and special-purpose keys). Its major special features include built-in capability for color graphics and sound effects—from computer music to synthesized human speech.

The manufacturer, Apple Computer Inc., has shown a commitment to educational and training applications by funding an Apple Education Foundation and by publishing a sizable amount of supporting literature, including a newsletter, *Apple Education News*.

The Personal System/2 family is the second generation of IBM computers for education and training. The Model 25 is the lowest priced member of the family and is designed for student use. It features color graphics, animation, and sound. The Model 25 can be networked within classrooms, school districts, and beyond.

The Model 25 is designed for easy setup and portability. The disk drive, microprocessor, and monitor are built into a single unit with one power cord. One switch turns everything on. The separate keyboard has a generous cable. The Model 25 has 512K of RAM memory which can be expanded to 640K. The diskettes measure 3.5 inches by 3.5 inches and come in a hard plastic sleeve with built-in write protection and 720K of memory. The new machine is twice as fast as the first-generation PCs.

IBM offers a wide variety of business, communications, and educational programs.

Input. This is a means of getting information into the computer. The most commonly used input device is a typewriterlike keyboard. Other input devices include mice, track balls, joysticks, paddles, and graphics tablets. Joysticks and paddles are associated primarily with games. Graphics tablets can be used by students or teachers to incorporate drawings into their programs. Science laboratory monitoring devices can also be connected directly to a microcomputer with the proper interface device.

CPU (Central Processing Unit). This is the "brain" that carries out all the calculations and controls the total system. In a microcomputer the CPU is just one of the tiny chips inside the machine.

Memory. This stores information for manipulation by the CPU. The memory contains the *control* function, that is, the programs

(detailed sequential instructions) that are written to tell the CPU what to do in what order. Memory and CPU are part of the microcomputer and usually are built into the machine.

In microcomputers, control

instructions are stored in two types of memory.

ROM (Read Only Memory): control instructions that have been "wired" *permanently* into the memory. Usually stores instructions that the computer will need constantly, such as the programming language(s) and internal monitoring functions.

RAM (Random Access Memory): the flexible part of the memory. The particular program or set of data being manipulated by the user is *temporarily* stored in RAM, then erased to make way for the next program.

Storage. This is a way of keeping all the programs that you are not using. In microcomputers, the computer can process only one program at a time, so you need some place to store the other programs and sets of data for future use. These programs and data are stored outside the computer.

There are two types of disks and several sizes. The basic types are "floppy" (flexible) and "hard" (rigid). A floppy disk is a thin, circular piece of plastic with a mag-

The Mac II, as it is known, is compatible with the IBM PC software, which means that there are hundreds of software packages available for it. The monitor and computer are one unit with a movable keyboard. The 13-inch monitor is larger than most for microcomputers. The Mac II is best known for its graphics capability. Its color graphics are clearly shown on the monitor with near-photographic-quality images.

Inside the Mac II are 20, 40, or 80 megabytes of hard-disk storage plus several megabytes of random access memory (RAM). The large memory and quality graphics provide capabilities for desk-top publishing. The Mac II is more expensive than most student stations, but it is a valuable tool for the teacher or trainer.

large amount of information can be stored on a hard disk; and because they operate at very high speeds, the information can be accessed quickly.

Output. This is a means of displaying the results of your program. A television-type monitor, referred to as a CRT (cathode-ray tube), is the usual output device for a microcomputer. It may be built into the total package, or be a separate component.

Large computers and minicomputers commonly provide output in the form of data printed on paper sheets ("hard copy"). This option is also available on most microcomputer systems by adding a printer as a peripheral.

A permanent copy of computer output can be provided on paper by a printer. The most common use is for word processing. Printers have a variety of features, including the following:

- Impact and Nonimpact: The printerhead may come in contact with the paper (impact) or may never actually touch the paper (nonimpact). Impact printers include the ball type-head (used in typewriters), daisywheel (letters arranged around the edge of a disk, like petals on a daisy), and spin-writer (with the letters on pad-

netic recording surface, enclosed in a plastic or cardboard jacket for protection. The computer "reads" the information through an oval-shaped hole in the top of the jacket. The three standard sizes of disks are $3\frac{1}{2}$ inches, $5\frac{1}{4}$ inches, and 8 inches. The disk has the advantage of fast access to programs stored on different bands of the disk. The device that allows the computer to read information from and "write" information onto disks is called a disk drive.

Hard disks are similar to phonograph records, have the capacity to store more information, and usually are used with a network of many computers. They are made of aluminum and coated with a magnetic recording surface. A

▲ *Figure 13.13*
The "floppy" disk is one method of mass storage for microcomputers.

▲ *Figure 13.14*
A typical printer for use with microcomputers

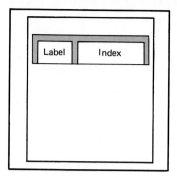

Keep disk in its protective envelope when not in use. [Protect disk from excessive heat and magnetized objects, including power cords which set up their own magnetic fields.]

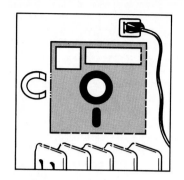

Disks should be stored vertically in their box, not laid flat, especially not with heavy objects set on them.

Marking on the disk label should be done only with felt-tip pen, not with sharp pencil or ballpoint pen. Avoid paper clips, which also could scratch the disk.

[Do not bend, fold, or warp by using rubber bands.]

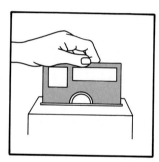

[Protect the delicate surface from fingerprints by grasping the disk only by the edge to place it into the disk drive.]

---

dles perpendicular to a wheel that spins). Some typewriters have been designed to connect directly to a microcomputer and serve as a printer. Nonimpact printers use heat, ink jets, lasers, and electricity to produce a character on the paper.

- Dot Matrix and Character: A dot matrix printer prints a series of dots in a 5-by-7 or 7-by-9 configuration to produce each letter.

The letters are the same size; however, the 7-by-9 dot matrix produces a higher quality letter because the dots are closer together. Full-character printers produce an entire character by striking the paper as a typewriter does.

- Printer Speed: Printer speeds range from 10 to 35 characters per second. Faster printers tend to be more expensive.

- Friction Feed, Bin Feed, and Pin Feed: There are three common ways to move the paper through the printer. With friction feed the paper is moved between two rubber rollers (as in a typewriter). Bin feed may move a single sheet into the printer with an automatic feed (as with a plain paper copier).

Floppy disks or diskettes	Size	Physical characteristics	Storage capacity	Machines using
	8″ diameter	thin, flexible paper case	800 K	not commonly used for instructional purposes
	5¼″ diameter	thin, flexible paper case	single-sided, double-density, approx. 140 K double-sided, double-density, 340 to 360 K double-sided, high density, 1 to 2 megabytes	commonly used with Apple II series, most PCs, and PC compatibles
	3½″ diameter	stiff plastic case	single-sided 400 K double-sided 700 to 800 K double-sided, high density 1.4 megabytes	commonly used with Macintosh, Amiga, Atari ST, IBM PS-2 series, and some PC compatibles
Hard disks				
	Varies—usually 5¼″ or 3½″	metal or metal-coated platters internal or external to the computer	20 to 40 megabytes most common up to 360 megabytes available for some machines	available for all personal computers

▲ *Figure 13.13*
The most common types of computer disks

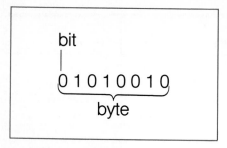

▲ *Figure 13.16*
Representation of the letter *A* in ASCII (American Standard Code for Information Interchange) code when 8 bits represent 1 byte.

Types of Computers

A *byte* is the number of bits required to store/represent one character of text (letter or number). A byte is most commonly, but not always, made up of eight bits in various combinations of 0s and 1s. See Figure 13.16 for the relationship between bits and bytes.

A computer's memory size is usually described in terms of how many bytes it can store at one time. A "kilobyte," usually abbreviated "K," refers to approximately 1,000 bytes (1,024 to be exact). Thus, if a computer can store 16,384 bytes, it is said to have a 16K memory capacity.

Note that the more powerful machines are capable of processing more bytes simultaneously, thus increasing their processing capacity. Most minicomputers have 32-bit microprocessor, double the 16-bit microprocessor of the microcomputer.

Computer Languages

As mentioned before, instructions are relayed to and throughout the computer via programs. Originally, since computers were used basically as high-powered calculators, the programs were written strictly in mathematical terms. But over the years, as a broader variety of business and educational applications have sprung up, new computer languages have been developed. Certain of these languages have incorporated terminology more and more resembling the English language. The most popular language for microcomputers is BASIC. A newer language, Pascal, is increasingly being used for

Single sheets may be hand fed into a printer. Special paper with perforated sets of holes on each side must be used for pin feed. As the pins are moved up, the paper is advanced. Pin-feed printers tend to be more expensive than friction-feed ones.

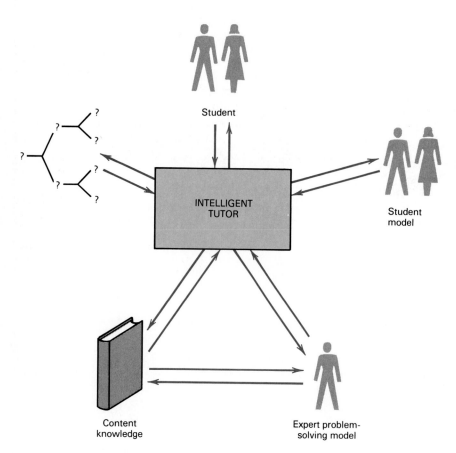

◄ *Figure 13.17*
Intelligent tutoring systems are computer systems that teach students on a one-to-one basis, similar to the manner in which a human tutor would. The computer uses artificial intelligence to integrate content, instructional techniques, teacher (or expert) skill, and is a model for student learning.

Appraisal Checklist: Microcomputers

Manufacturer _____

Model _____

Price _____

Memory size: RAM_____K, expandable to_____K; ROM_____K

Languages available _____

Peripherals available _____

Monitor: Size _____ ; Built-in yes _____ no _____; Color_____Green Screen _____.

Graphics available yes _____ no _____   Sound available yes _____ no _____

Rating	Excellent				Poor	Comments
Ease of operation	☐	☐	☐	☐	☐	
Durability/reliability	☐	☐	☐	☐	☐	
Availability of software	☐	☐	☐	☐	☐	
Video display quality	☐	☐	☐	☐	☐	
Keyboard layout and "touch"	☐	☐	☐	☐	☐	
Expandability	☐	☐	☐	☐	☐	
User documentation	☐	☐	☐	☐	☐	
Local service support	☐	☐	☐	☐	☐	
Portability	☐	☐	☐	☐	☐	

Other Features

Strong Points:

Weak Points:

Reviewer _____

Position _____

Recommended action _____   Date _____

Analyze Learners

General Characteristics. Robin Meadows's students are primarily sophomores in high school. It is their first biology course; however, they were introduced to biological principles in a general science course the previous year. In general science, the students did not study the frog, but they did dissect an earthworm. They represent a broad range of socioeconomic backgrounds, grade point averages, and reading levels. Some students have minor physical handicaps and others have low IQs. Because the school district has a computer literacy program that begins in the elementary schools, all students have keyboarding and computer skills.

Entry Competencies. Approximately 80 percent of the students are able to

1. Define/describe simple biological terms: *amphibian, anterior, artery, circulatory system, digestive system, dorsal, posterior, vein, ventral,* and *vertebrate.*
2. Measure an object within two millimeters using a metric ruler.
3. Convert from millimeters to centimeters and reverse the process.

Learning Style. Most students prefer visual learning and manipulation of materials, especially those students with low verbal skills. All students enjoy interacting with their peers, and a majority of them are motivated by using a computer to learn.

State Objectives

The teacher wants the students to learn a frog's anatomy and to practice dissection techniques. The specific objectives are to be able to:

1. Identify by name and function twenty common frog organs and locate these organs on a drawing.
2. Trace the blood flow in the circulatory system of the frog.
3. Describe the nature and function of the female and male urogenital systems of a frog and identify ten components of each system.
4. Demonstrate proper dissection techniques.

Select Media and Materials

The teacher considered the standard frog-dissection laboratory. A teacher in a neighboring school district mentioned a microcomputer simulation called *Operation: Frog* (developed by Interactive Picture Systems and distributed by Scholastic). The teacher previewed the simulation along with the teacher's handbook. The program is a simulated laboratory dissection of a frog. It features two stages: dissection and reconstruction. In the dissection stage, students use the computer to locate and remove organs and to investigate the frog's

---

instruction. The "C" language can provide high-level programming.

A popular programming language for use with elementary-aged children, LOGO, was developed by Seymour Papert at MIT. This visual language centers around commands to move a "turtle" around the screen and draw its path. Seeing the graphic change as the program runs helps children visualize and understand what their instructions to the computer (program) have done. The focus of learning LOGO is on the process of programming rather than the product. The process is discovered by the child rather than taught by the teacher.

Selecting Hardware

It is becoming increasingly common for instructors to be involved in the selection of instructionally related computer hardware for their institution. This section is meant to give you at least some general guidelines for participat-

body systems close up. In the reconstruction stage, students use the computer to reassemble the dissected frog.

In considering whether or not to use the simulation, the teacher listed the following strengths: (1) through computer simulation students are allowed an opportunity to see how several organs work in a live frog (which is not possible in an actual dissection), (2) a scoring feature adds an additional level of challenge for some students, (3) the reading level is low, and (4) the cost of enough copies is within the school's budget (computers are already available).

The drawbacks include the following: (1) students don't work with all of the frog's body parts, only twenty-three main organs (no bones are included and only one sample muscle), (2) body organs are unrealistically colored to make them easier to find, and (3) it isn't a substitute for actual dissection.

The teacher considered many variables and decided to remove objective 4 from the list and purchase *Operation: Frog* for use with the class.

Utilize the Materials

The teacher introduces the lesson by showing a short videotape on the life cycle of frogs. The students work in pairs. While one "performs" the dissection, the other records information from the screen on laboratory worksheets copied from the teacher's handbook.

The students use the same "instruments" they would use in an actual lab: dissecting scissors, a probe, forceps, and a magnifying lens. Diagrams and text screens offer detailed information about organs and body systems. A special "help" feature within the program provides prompts and guidance.

Students are instructed to observe the animated blood flow, to remove the common organs, and to explore the urogenital system in detail.

Require Learner Performance

The students are actively involved with both manipulating the dissecting instruments within the simulation and recording data. Following the lab they must complete the lab report and then go to the library to research the nature and function of the male and female urogenital system of frogs.

Evaluate/Revise

Evaluation of student achievement is based upon the laboratory report, the research paper on the frog urogenital system, and a paper-and-pencil test covering the common frog organs. The test includes a diagram upon which students must identify the common organs. On another diagram they are asked to trace the blood flow within the circulatory system.

---

ing intelligently in such a selection process.

The general rule of computer selection is to begin by specifying what you want the computer to do. Select the software in advance.

In comparing models, many different criteria may be considered. The "Appraisal Checklist: Microcomputers" includes the most important criteria for selecting microcomputers for instructional purposes. Which criteria will be most salient to you depends on the specifics of your situation. Certain of the rating criteria may need some further explanation:

- Expandability. Can additional output and input devices be added? Can internal memory be expanded? Can peripherals (add-on devices) such as a hard-copy printout device or a modulator/demodulator device (modem) that allows computer signals to be transmitted via telephones be added to the basic system?
- Local Service and Support. Does the supplier have a local representative to answer users' questions and to take care of maintenance problems?

References

Print References

Alessi, Stephen M., and Trollip, Stanley R. *Computer-Based Instruction: Methods and Development.* (Englewood Cliffs, N.J.: Prentice-Hall, 1985).

Baker, Justine. *Microcomputers in the Classroom.* (Bloomington, Ind.: Phi Delta Kappa, 1982).

Bitter, Gary G., and Camuse, Ruth A. *Using a Microcomputer in the Classroom.* 2d. ed. (Englewood Cliffs, N.J.: Prentice-Hall, 1988).

Bradley, Buff. "Let's Do More with Computers than Study Computers." *Learning* (October 1984), pp. 21–44.

Bullough, Robert, and Beatty, Lamond. *Classroom Applications of Microcomputers.* (Columbus, Ohio: Merrill, 1987).

Burnett, Tom, and Fiesen, Chuck. "Programming vs. Applications: Computer Curriculum for K-12." *T. H. E. Journal* (October 1986), pp. 84–87.

Cline, Hugh F., et al. *The Electronic Schoolhouse.* (Hillsdale, N.J.: Lawrence Erlbaum, 1986).

Coburn, Peter, et al. *Practical Guide to Computers in Education.* (Reading, Mass.: Addison-Wesley, 1982).

Connors, Eugene T., and Valesky, Thomas C. *Using Microcomputers in School Administration.* (Bloomington, Ind.: Phi Delta Kappa, 1986).

Crawford, Chris. *The Art of Computer Game Design.* (Berkeley, Calif.: Osborne/McGraw-Hill, 1984).

Dennis, J. Richard, and Kansky, Robert J. *Instructional Computing: An Action Guide for Educators.* (Glenview, Ill.: Scott Foresman, 1984).

DucQuy, N., and Covington, J. "The Microcomputer in Industry Training." *T. H. E. Journal* (March 1982), pp. 65–68.

Educational Products Information Exchange. *Microcomputer Courseware/Microcomputer Games.* (Water Mill, N.Y.: EPIE Institute, 1982).

———. *Microcomputer Hardware/Interactive Videosystems.* (Water Mill, N.Y.: EPIE Institute, 1982).

Fitzgerald, Patrica A., et al. "Computer-Assisted Instruction in Libraries: Guidelines for Effective Lesson Design." *Library Hi Tech* (Summer 1986), pp. 29–37.

A Framework for Assessing Computer Competence: Defining Objectives. (Princeton, N.J.: National Assessment of Educational Progress, no date.)

Frederick, Franz J. *Guide to Microcomputers.* (Washington, D.C.: Association for Educational Communications and Technology, 1980).

Grauer, Robert T., and Sugrue, Paul. *Microcomputer Applications.* (New York: McGraw-Hill, 1987).

A Guide to the Selection of Microcomputers. (London: Council for Educational Technology for the United Kingdom, 1980).

Harper, Dennis O., and Stewart, James H. *Run: Computer Education.* (Monterey, Calif: Brooks/Cole, 1983).

Hativa, Nira. "The Microcomputer as a Classroom Audio-Visual Device: The Concept and Prospects for Adoption." *Computers and Education* 10 (1986), pp. 359–367.

Hildebrandt, Darlene Myers. *Computer Information Directory.* 4th ed. (Federal Way, Wash.: Pedaro, 1987).

Hopper, Grace M., and Mandell, Steven L. *Understanding Computers.* (St. Paul, Minn.: West, 1984).

Judd, Dorothy H., and Judd, Robert C. *Mastering the Micro: Using the Microcomputer in the Elementary Classroom.* (Glenview, Ill.: Scott Foresman, 1984).

Kearsley, Greg. *Computer Based Training.* (Reading, Mass.: Addison-Wesley, 1983).

———; Hillelsohn, M. J.; and Seidel, R. J. "Microcomputer-Based Training in Business and Industry: Present Status and Future Prospects." *Journal of Educational Technology Systems* 10 (1981), pp. 101–108.

———; Hunter, B.; and Hillelsohn, M. J. "Computer Literacy in Business and Industry: Three Examples Using Microcomputers." *Educational Technology* (July 1982), pp. 9–14.

Kinzer, Charles K.; Sherwood, Robert D.; and Bransford, John D. *Computer Strategies for Education.* (Columbus, Ohio: Merrill, 1986).

McCreary, Elaine K., and Van Buren, Judith. "Educational Applications of Computer Conferencing." *Canadian Journal of Educational Communications* (Spring 1987), pp. 107–115.

Merrill, David. *TICCIT.* (Englewood Cliffs, N.J.: Educational Technology Publications, 1980).

Metzcus, Richard. *The PDK Guide: An Introduction to Microcomputer Literacy for Educators.* (Bloomington, Ind.: Phi Delta Kappa, 1983).

"Microcomputers." *Instructional Innovator* (September 1980).

Milner, Stuart D. "Teaching Teachers about Computers: A Necessity for Education." *Phi Delta Kappan* (April 1980), pp. 544–546.

Nickles, Herbert L., and Culp, George. *Instructional Computing with the TRS-80.* (Monterey, Calif.: Brooks/Cole, 1984).

Ohles, John F. "The Microcomputer: Don't Love It to Death." *T. H. E. Journal* (August 1985), pp. 49–53.

O'Neil, Harold F. *Computer-Based Education: A State-of-the-Art Assessment.* (New York: Academic Press, 1981).

Orlansky, J., and String, J. "Computer-Based Instruction for Military Training." *Defense Management Journal* (2d quarter 1981), pp. 46–54.

Radin, Stephen, and Lee, Fayvian. *Computers in the Classroom.* (Chicago: Science Research Associates, 1984).

Rahmlow, H.; Fratine, R.; and Ghesquiere, J. *PLATO.* (Englewood Cliffs, N.J.: Educational Technology Publications, 1980).

Reynolds, Andree, and Martin, Jeanette V. "Designing an Educational Computer Game: Guidelines That Work." *Educational Technology* (January 1988), pp. 45–47.

Richman, Ellen. *Spotlight on Computer Literacy.* (New York: Random House, 1982).

Roblyer, M. D. *Measuring the Impact of Computers in Instruction: A Nontechnical Review of Research for Educators.* (Washington, D.C.: Association for Educational Data Systems, 1985).

Seaman, J. "Microcomputers Invade the Executive Suite." *Computer Decisions* (February 1981), pp. 68–172.

Sleeman, D., and Brown, J. S. *Intelligent Tutoring Systems.* (New York: Academic Press, 1982).

Smith, C., ed. *Microcomputers in Education.* (Chicester, West Sussex, England: Elliss Horwood Limited, 1982).

Sniederman, B. *Software Psychology: Human Factors in Computer and Information Systems.* (Cambridge, Mass.: Winthrop Publishers, 1980).

Solomon, C. "Introducing Logo to Children." *Byte* 7 (1982), pp. 196–208.

Streibel, Michael J. "A Critical Analysis of the Use of Computers in Education." *Educational Communications and Technology Journal* (Fall 1986), pp. 137–161.

Terry, Colin, ed. *Using Microcomputers in Schools.* (New York: Nichols Publishing, 1984).

Troutner, Joanne. *The Media Specialist, the Microcomputer, and the Curriculum.* 2d ed. (Littleton, Colo.: Libraries Unlimited, 1988).

Vargas, Julie S. "Instructional Design Flaws in Computer-Assisted Instruction." *Phi Delta Kappan* (June 1986), pp. 738–744.

Vockell, Edward L., and Rivers, Robert H. *Instructional Computing for Today's Teachers.* (New York: Macmillan, 1984).

Watt, D. "Logo in the Schools." *Byte* (1982), pp. 116–134.

Williams, Frederick, and Williams, Victoria. *Microcomputers in Elementary Education: Perspectives on Implementation.* (Belmont, Calif.: Wadsworth, 1984).

Yeaman, Andrew R. J. "Microcomputer Learning Stations and Student Health and Safety: Planning, Evaluation, and Revision of Physical Arrangements." *Educational Technology* (December 1983), pp. 16–22.

Courseware Design

Burke, Robert L. *CAI Sourcebook.* (Englewood Cliffs, N.J.: Prentice-Hall, 1982).

Dean, Christopher, and Whitlock, Quentin. *A Handbook of Computer Based Training.* (New York: Nichols Publishing, 1983).

DeBloois, M. L. *Videodisc/Microcomputer Courseware Design.* (Englewood Cliffs, N.J.: Educational Technology Publications, 1982).

Galitz, W. *Handbook of Screen Format Design.* (Wellesley, Mass.: Q.E.D. Information Sciences, 1981).

Hannafin, Michael J., and Peck, Kyle L. *The Design, Development, and Evaluation of Instructional Software.* (New York: Macmillan, 1988).

Heines, Jesse M. *Screen Designs for Computer-Assisted Instruction.* (Bedford, Mass.: Digital Press, 1984).

Jenkin, J. "Some Principles of Screen Design and Software for Their Support." In P. R. Smith, ed., *Computer Assisted Learning.* (Oxford: Pergamon Press, 1981).

Nievergelt, J. "A Pragmatic Introduction to Courseware Design." *IEEE Computer* (September 1980), pp. 7–21.

Walker, Decker F., and Hess, Robert D. *Instructional Software: Principles and Perspectives for Design and Use.* (Belmont, Calif.: Wadsworth, 1984).

Audiovisual References

Adventures of the Mind. Bloomington, Ind.: Indiana University Audio-Visual Center, 1980. Series of 16-mm films (or videocassettes) about microcomputers. 20 minutes each. Individual titles are:
Data Processing Control Design
Extending Your Reach
For Better or For Worse
Hardware and Software
Speaking the Language

The Audio-Visual Library of Computer Education. Mill Valley, Calif.: Prismation Productions, 1983. 15-part, 345-minute series of materials dealing with computer literacy. Available as sound/filmstrip, sound/slide, or videocassette.

Computer Basics. Los Angeles: AV Systems, 1981. Series of 6 sound/filmstrips and computer diskette titled:
What Is a Computer?
Do You Need a Computer?
How to Use a Computer
How Do Computers Work?
How to Program a Computer
What Do Computers Mean?

Computer Hardware: What It Is and How It Works. Mount Kisco, N.Y.: Center for the Humanities, 1982. 2 sound filmstrips or sound/slide sets, also available on videocassette.

Computer History. Stamford, Conn.: Educational Dimensions Group, 1982. 4 sound filmstrips with teacher's guide.

Computer Literacy: The First Step. Stamford, Conn.: Educational Dimensions Group, 1982. 4 sound filmstrips with teacher's guide.

The Computer Programme. Wilmette, Ill.: Films, Inc., 1981. Films/videocassettes on the workings and applications of computers.

Computer Series 1: An Introduction to Computers. Bedford Hills, N.Y.: Educational Enrichment Materials, 1983. 5 sound filmstrips with teacher's guide.

Computer Software: What It Is and How It Works. Mount Kisco, N.Y.: Center for the Humanities, 1982. 2 sound filmstrips or sound/slide sets, also available on videocassette.

Computer-Rage. Morristown, N.J.: Creative Computing, 1980. Game.

Don't Bother Me, I'm Learning— Adventures in Computer Education. New York: CRM/McGraw-Hill, 1980. 16-mm film/videocassette on the use of computers in the classroom.

Don't Bother Me, I'm Learning— Computers in the Community. New York: CRM/McGraw-Hill, 1982. 16-mm film/videocassette on the use of computers in the community.

Making It Count: An Introduction to Computers. Seattle, Wash.: Boeing Aerospace, 1982. Videotape course on how computers work and their application.

Making the Most of the Micro. Wilmette, Ill.: Films, Inc., 1982. Series of 10 films or videocassettes produced by the British Broadcasting Company.

Microcomputer Courseware. Sioux Falls, S.D.: United Education and Software, 1983. Kit with 2 student workbooks, project kit, and computer diskette designed for personal or professional computer users.

Welcome to the Future: Computers in the Classroom. Wilmette, Ill.: Films, Inc., 1982. 16-mm film/videocassette. 28 min.

Computer Hardware Manufacturers

Apple Computer, Inc.
20525 Mariana Avenue
Cupertino, CA   95014

Atari, Inc.
P.O. Box 50047
60 E. Plumeria Drive
San Jose, CA   95150

Commodore
1200 Wilson Dr.
West Chester, PA   19380

Franklin Computer Corp.
7030 Colonial Highway
Pennsauken, NJ   08109

IBM Corporation
P.O. Box 2150
Atlanta, GA   30055

Kaypro Corporation
P.O. Box N
Del Mar, CA   92014

Plato/CDC
Control Data Corporation
8100 34th Avenue South
Minneapolis, MN   55440

Radio Shack
One Tandy Center
Fort Worth, TX   76102

Database Sources

Active Learning Systems
P.O. Box 1984
Midland, MI   48640

Minnesota Educational Computing Corporation (MECC)
3490 Lexington Avenue North
St. Paul, MN   55126

Newsweek
Educational Division
444 Madison Avenue
New York, NY   10022

Scholastic Software
P.O. Box 7502
Jefferson City, MO   65102

Organizations

International Association for Computing in Education (IACE)
1230 Seventeenth Street, N.W.
Washington, DC   20036
The most comprehensive of the organizations dedicated to the use of computers in education. Its emphasis is on the secondary school level, and its interests include both administrative and instructional uses of computers.

Association for the Development of Computer-Based Instructional Systems (ADCIS)
Miller Hall 409
Western Washington University
Bellingham, WA   98225
Organization for persons interested in research and development of computer-based instruction.

CONDUIT
University of Iowa
Oakdale Campus
Iowa City, IA   52244
Evaluates and distributes computer-based instructional materials and publishes a periodical, *Pipeline*.

EPIE (Education Products Information Exchange Institute)
Box 839
Water Mill, NY   11976
Publishes reviews of microcomputer courseware/hardware and procedures for their evaluation, including the *EPIE Annotated Courseware Provider List*.

International Council for Computers in Education
1787 Agate Street
University of Oregon
Eugene, OR   97403
Collects and distributes information concerning computer applications in elementary/secondary education and publishes *The Computing Teacher*.

Minnesota Educational Computing Corporation (MECC)
3490 Lexington Avenue North
St. Paul, MN   55126
Develops and disseminates courseware and computer-related materials, especially for elementary and secondary schools.

Northwest Regional Educational Laboratory
300 S.W. Sixth Avenue
Portland, OR   97204
Clearinghouse for catalogs and review guides, publishes evaluations of courseware including *Microcomputer Software Catalog List*.

Periodicals

A+: the Independent Guide for Apple Computing
Ziff-Davis Publishing Co.
One Park Avenue
New York, NY 10016
12 issues/year

AmigaWorld
CW Communications
80 Pine Street
Peterborough, NH 03458
6 issues/year

Classroom Computer Learning
Peter Li, Inc.
2451 East River Road
Dayton, OH 45439
10 issues/yr.

Collegiate Microcomputer
2706 Wilson Drive
Terre Haute, IN 47803
4 issues/year

The Computing Teacher
International Council for Computers
in Education
University of Oregon
1787 Agate St.
Eugene, OR 97403
9 issues/yr.

Education Computing News
951 Pershing Drive
Silver Spring, MD 20910
26 issues/year

Education & Computing
Elsevier Science Publishers
P.O. Box 211
Amsterdam, The Netherlands
4 issues/year

Electronic Education
Electronic Communications
Suite 220
1311 Executive Center Dr.
Tallahassee, FL 32301
8 issues/yr.

Electronic Learning: The Magazine for Educators of the 80s
Scholastic, Inc.
P.O. Box 644
Lyndhurst, NJ 07071
8 issues/yr.

Interface: the Computer Education Quarterly
Mitchell Publishing, Inc.
915 River Street
Santa Cruz, CA 95060
4 issues/year

Journal of Computer Based Instruction
Association for the Development
of Computer Based Instructional
Systems
Western Washington University
Miller Hall 409
Bellingham, WA 98225
4 issues/year

LOGO & Educational Computing Journal
Flower Field
St. James, NY 11780
6 issues/year

Microcomputers in Education
2539 Post Road
Darien, CT 06820
12 issues/year

Teaching and Computers: Scholastic's Magazine for Today's Elementary Classroom

Scholastic Magazine
P.O. Box 2040
Mahopac, NY 10541
12 issues/yr.

3-2-1 Contact
Children's Television Workshop
P.O. Box 2866
Boulder, CO 80322
10 issues/year

Possible Projects

13-A. Read and summarize an article on the use of computers in education or training.

13-B. Interview a student and/or instructor who has used computers for instruction. Report on how the computer was used, including the user's perceptions as to strengths and limitations.

13-C. Develop a list of topics you would include if you were to conduct a one-day computer literacy workshop for teachers/trainers in your subject area.

13-D. Describe how you could use a computer as an object of instruction or as a tool during instruction in your instructional field.

13-E. Synthesize a situation in which you could use computer-based materials. Include a description of the audience, the objectives, the role of the computer, and the expected outcomes (or advantages) of using the computer.

13-F. Locate computer programs suitable for your subject area using the information sources available to you.

13-G. Appraise an instructional computer program using the "Appraisal Checklist: Computer-Based Instruction" provided in the chapter.

13-H. Evaluate a microcomputer using the "Appraisal Checklist: Microcomputers" in the chapter.

14 Looking Ahead

Objectives

After studying this chapter, you should be able to:

1. Give two examples of the effect of miniaturization on instruction and explain how these increase access to learning.

2. Use the study *Visions 2000* to project how the broad adoption of new technology and associated software will affect distribution of teacher time by the year 2000.

3. Relate the multiplication of electronic delivery systems to the decentralization of education.

4. Describe how electronic networks can change the "global village" into the "global classroom."

5. Explain how digitization has made information more accessible to the learner.

6. Differentiate between CD-ROM, CD-WORM, and DVI.

7. Use an example of hypertext to illustrate its potential to help the learner.

8. Explain the relationship between learning styles and individualizing instruction.

9. Define "expert system" and explain the relationship between expert systems and artificial intelligence.

10. Assume the role of "knowledge engineer" and identify a topic that lends itself to expert system design.

11. List at least three information-processing skills that are exercised in pinball-type video games.

12. Discuss the instructional strengths and weaknesses of drill-and-practice games and hand-held microprocessor games.

13. Relate "altered states of consciousness" to improved learning.

14. Give two examples of how "bionic extensions of the brain" could in the future enhance communication and/or learning.

15. Critique the conventional self-contained classroom as an organizational arrangement for incorporating technology.

16. Critique the "craft approach" of public education as a system for incorporating technology.

17. Relate the accountability movement to the increased use of technology in education.

18. Relate the lifelong-learning movement to the increased use of technology in education.

19. Describe three areas of specialization within the educational technology career field.

20. Name at least three major professional associations in educational technology; characterize the membership of each.

21. Name at least three educational technology journals published by professional associations and one not published by an association; characterize the emphases of each.

Lexicon
biochip
microprocessor game
expert system
CD-ROM
CD-WORM
CD-I
DVI
hypertext
suggestive-accelerative learning and teaching
emgor
division of labor
low-cost learning technology
craft
accountability

The previous chapters of this book have focused on the various media and technologies of instruction—what they are, their advantages and limitations, and their potential applications to improving learning.

In this final chapter we attempt to give a broader perspective of how media and technology fit into the overall scheme of education and training. The emphasis is on change: what trends have brought us to where we are now, what new developments hold promise for improving learning productivity, what impediments limit the implementation of these developments, and what avenues may exist for getting around these impediments.

The field of instructional technology continues to grow, and so do the opportunities for professional employment. As media and the newer technologies of instruction have expanded into business, industry, and health and public service training programs, professional specializations have become more varied and more numerous. Because of the proliferation of computer-based instruction and other technologies in formal educational settings—historically the major employers of media professionals—schools, colleges, and universities have had to hire people trained in the new technologies. As state education departments and regional school service centers broaden the base of their support to the schools, more positions are created for professionals in instructional technology. This chapter will help you explore careers in this field.

The chapter concludes with consideration of the professional organizations and journals devoted to further implementation of media and technology in education and training, because these may be the tools by which you become further involved in the efforts of this field.

TRENDS IN MEDIA AND TECHNOLOGY

Two major trends in communications technology have paralleled each other over the past half century: (1) the miniaturization of the media of communication and (2) the multiplication of electronic delivery systems. Another two trends of more recent origin are "digitization" of media formats and what we will call "learning networks." The development of media formats that make print, images, and sounds randomly accessible in seconds began about ten years ago with the laser videodisc. Some people have referred to this trend as the "convergence" of all forms of communication caused by the "digitizing" of information.* (See the discussion in Chapter 6 on the compact disc.)

These trends have combined to increase our access to instructional media. As will be discussed later, however, the mere availability of media has not necessarily led to a proportionate increase in the *use* of these tools.

Miniaturization: Making Instruction Portable

Perhaps the most important single technological trend affecting the use of instructional media has been the movement toward miniaturization of mediaware formats and equipment. This trend has led to lower cost, increased ease of operation and portability of equipment, and hence to

_____
* Stewart Brand. *The Media Lab*. New York: Viking, 1987, p. 18.

increased availability of instructional media in the formal and nonformal learning situation.

16-mm Film Projectors. Even 16-mm film equipment has become more portable and easier to operate. For example, many such projectors now on the market feature automatic threading, whereas two decades ago all machines had to be manually threaded. The machines have become smaller because mechanical parts have become more reliable and smaller. Reduction in amplifier size has been made possible by the introduction of, first, transistors and printed circuits, and, more recently, integrated circuits. Many schools and colleges now use small-screen television viewers in individualized and small-group instructional situations, an impossibility two decades ago because small-screen television monitors for classroom use were not available.

Audiocassette Recorders/ Players. Very few technological innovations have been more quickly or universally adapted to instructional purposes than the cassette tape recorder. The advantages of the cassette were immediately obvious. First, the whole cassette is considerably smaller than a comparable reel-to-reel tape and its box. The principal reason for this reduction in size is that the tape itself is half the width of the standard $\frac{1}{4}$-inch recording tape. The next obvious difference between the cassette and reel-to-reel format is convenience of operation. No longer does the user have to thread the tape into the machine. Finally, the machine is considerably smaller than reel-to-reel tape recorders. The most widely sold form of cassette tape recorder today can be carried in one hand. This is a vast

▲ *Figure 14.1*
Miniaturization in audio can be seen in the progression from an early reel-to-reel tape recorder to a cassette recorder to a microcassette recorder.

change from the earlier 15- to 30-pound reel-to-reel tape recorders.

In the early days of cassette development, recording quality left a good deal to be desired. Even so, teachers were quite willing to trade quality for miniaturization. But, as the cassette format became widely adopted, making further technological improvements economically feasible for producers of cassettes, the quality of the recording improved. With today's high fidelity systems, it is difficult to tell the difference between the audio quality of a well-recorded cassette tape and a well-recorded reel-to-reel tape with similar quality speakers.

Video Recorders. Miniaturization of electronic components has today resulted in videotape recorders portable enough to be carried in the hand, a development that has contributed immensely to the use of videotaped materials for instructional purposes. Videotape itself also has been improved remarkably in recent years. When it was first introduced, the tape had to travel at a very high speed in order to record with any degree of fidelity. However, today's videotape recorders record at a relatively

slow speed, allowing much more recording time per standard reel. Today, videocassette machines can record up to six hours per reel. When videotape was originally introduced, the tape was 2 inches wide; today ½-inch tape is standard for school and home, with little discernible difference in quality.

Videodisc. The videodisc represents another step toward compressing the size of the software needed for the storage and playback of moving pictures. The collapse in 1984 of RCA's effort to market its line of videodisc equipment to the home consumer dictates caution in assuming that this new format will replace completely the existing means of magnetic tape recording. Many home and instructional users of video want a system on which they can record their own programming as well as play back mass-distributed programs. Until an erasable videodisc is proven feasible for general use, we can expect to see tape and disc continue to coexist. The fascinating potentials of laser videodiscs when combined with computer control—discussed in Chapter 7 under "Interactive Video" and later in this chapter—make this a most promising technology of the future.

Microfiche. Miniaturization has also had its effect on the print medium, making the printed word more easily and widely available for instructional and other purposes than the developers of movable type could have imagined. Perhaps the most universally used microform for reducing the size of the printed word so that it can be more widely disseminated is microfiche. In different microfiche formats, dozens, even hundreds, of

▲ *Figure 14.2*
The videodisc is a highly compact format for storage of still or motion pictures.

▲ *Figure 14.3*
One volume of a typical encyclopedia can be reduced to a small handful of microfiches.

pages of print can be recorded on a single piece of film. The contents of the entire *Encyclopaedia Britannica,* for example, can be reduced to a stack of microfiches small enough to be thrust into one's pocket.

Recent advances in the photographic quality of microfiche have raised the possibility of using microfiches as still-projection media. Microfiches containing color transparent images and the projectors to show them are now available, suggesting a new format for future packaging of filmstrips and slide sets. Up to ninety-eight images fit on one 4- by 6-inch fiche, making production, mailing, storing, and handling easier and less expensive than ever before.

▲ *Figure 14.4*
Microprocessor chips visible only under a magnifying glass are common components of today's computers.

Microprocessors and Computers.

Microprocessors have made possible the hand-held games that are so popular. The sophistication of these devices, because of the microchip, is even more impressive than their portability. We discuss the significance of microprocessor "toys" later in this chapter.

Another striking manifestation of miniaturization is seen in the area of computer technology. Mainly because of advances in microchip technology, computers, which were obtainable only in extremely cumbersome form and at extremely high cost, are now available in formats taking up no more space than a television set and costing about the same amount of money. The educational importance of this development was discussed in Chapter 13. Schools and small training organizations that only a few years ago could not have dreamed of using computer technology for administrative and instructional purposes are now finding this tool logistically and economically feasible. We can certainly expect that computer-based instruction will continue to grow rapidly in the years to come.

The degree of miniaturization that has evolved in the realm of microprocessors is truly staggering. The wiring in the integrated circuits of the pre-1980 era could be inspected with the naked eye. The next generation of integrated circuits required a magnifying glass. Today you need a microscope, or even an electron microscope. The tiny integrated circuits of today are etched in silicon using optical lithography or electron beams. The emerging development is to apply the techniques of genetic engineering—recombinant DNA—to construct tiny biological microprocessors of protein, or "biochips." Biochips measuring in the 10 to 25 nanometer range (a nanometer is *one-billionth* of a meter) would represent about two orders of magnitude smaller than the current silicon chips. Protein circuits as small as a single molecule are being envisioned. The implications of such biotechnology are discussed later in this chapter.

Multiplication of Electronic Delivery Systems

Another technological innovation that has already had an impact on education and undoubtedly will have an even greater impact in the future is the use of electronic systems for the delivery of instruction. Just a few years ago, the individual instructor was practically the sole "distributor of instruction" on the educational scene. Today we have instruction via open broadcast by radio and television stations, microwave systems, satellite, and closed-circuit systems such as cable television and the telephone.

Although instruction via open broadcast by radio and television, especially television, has been and will continue to be a significant force in education, there is presently a trend toward wider applications of closed distribution systems to the instructional situation. Closed distribution sys-

▲ *Figure 14.5*
A videotex home information system display

tems—microwave, closed-circuit, satellite—unlike open systems, have the advantage of being able to transmit a number of instructional programs simultaneously. In addition, they have the significant advantage of being able to overcome broadcast television's inherent limitation in coverage area. For example, satellite signals can be sent to virtually any spot on the face of the earth and, once received, can be carried by cable and/or microwave systems to any instructional setting, including the home. Direct reception of satellite transmissions by schools, business and industrial facilities, hospitals, or any other likely instructional setting is now a reality with the proper receiving equipment, eliminating the need for redistribution by cable. Satellite signals can now also be received and transmitted via telephones equipped with optical fibers capable of transmitting hundreds of messages simultaneously. Appropriate equipment attached to such telephones permits local display of the signals. A 1981 survey disclosed that telecommunications networks of the type described here are already in widespread use throughout the United States.* Looking only at educational networks within individual states, researchers found ninety-eight organizations operating networks in forty-four of the fifty states.

Computer technology is adding yet another dimension to electronic distribution of instruction. Along with the instructional capabilities of localized computers, we can expect the growing use of

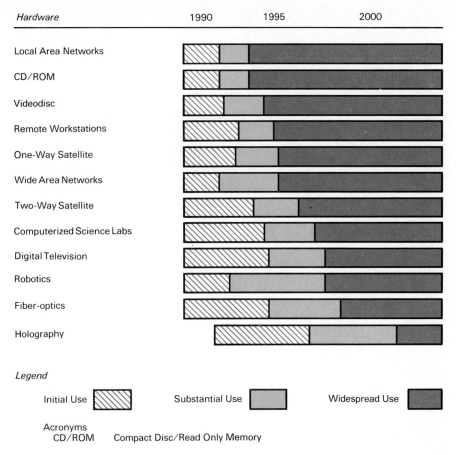

* Jerold Gruebel, W. Neal Robison, and Susan Rutledge. "Intrastate Educational Telecommunication Systems: A National Survey," *Educational Technology.* (April 1981), pp. 33–36.

Hardware	1990	1995	2000

Local Area Networks
CD/ROM
Videodisc
Remote Workstations
One-Way Satellite
Wide Area Networks
Two-Way Satellite
Computerized Science Labs
Digital Television
Robotics
Fiber-optics
Holography

Legend

Initial Use   Substantial Use   Widespread Use

Acronyms
CD/ROM   Compact Disc/Read Only Memory

▲ *Figure 14.6*
This is the province of Alberta's projection of the adoption and use of educational technology hardware through the year 2000. (*Source:* Alberta Education. *Visions 2000: A Vision of Educational Technology in Alberta by the Year 2000.* Edmonton: Alberta Education, Student Programs and Evaluation Division, 1987.)

large centralized computer facilities offering instructional programming to be used in "real time" or stored in microcomputer systems for delayed use.

State support of computer networks has been growing rapidly. A 1987 survey by the journal *Electronic Learning*† revealed the following: (1) twenty states distributed software through telecommunications systems; (2) thirty-one states maintained electronic bulletin boards; (3) thirty-five states were engaged in distance learning; and (4) thirty-seven states had centers for dis-

seminating telecommunications information. Inevitably, the state is going to become more deeply involved in statewide curriculum and instructional development.

The publication *Visions 2000*†† is a bold attempt by Alberta Province, Canada, to project the rate of adoption of new technologies in provincial schools by the year 2000. Alberta prides itself on its history of acceptance of technology and is determined to maintain its leadership. Figure 14.6 contains estimates of the rate of adoption of hardware from 1990 to 2000, and Figure 14.7 has esti-

† Reported in *Education Week,* October 14, 1987, pp. 1, 24.

†† *Visions 2000,* Edmonton, Alberta: Alberta Education, 1987.

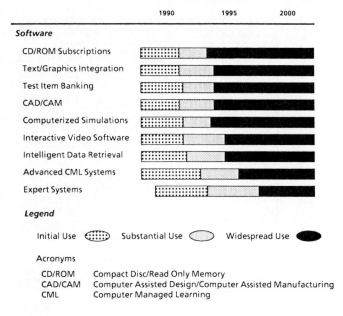

Software

	1990	1995	2000
CD/ROM Subscriptions			
Text/Graphics Integration			
Test Item Banking			
CAD/CAM			
Computerized Simulations			
Interactive Video Software			
Intelligent Data Retrieval			
Advanced CML Systems			
Expert Systems			

Legend

Initial Use   Substantial Use   Widespread Use

Acronyms

CD/ROM   Compact Disc/Read Only Memory
CAD/CAM Computer Assisted Design/Computer Assisted Manufacturing
CML   Computer Managed Learning

▲ *Figure 14.7*
Alberta's projection of the adoption and use of educational technology software through the year 2000.

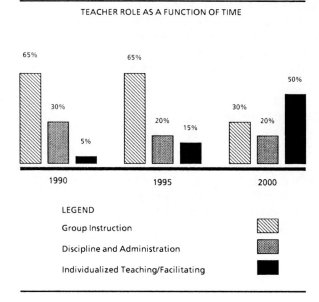

TEACHER ROLE AS A FUNCTION OF TIME

LEGEND

Group Instruction

Discipline and Administration

Individualized Teaching/Facilitating

▲ *Figure 14.8*
According to the Alberta projections, the amount of time teachers devote to group and individual instruction will change dramatically by the year 2000. This means that learners will become increasingly supported directly by software.

mates of the rate of adoption of software for the same period. The Alberta program is a very ambitious one.

The authors of *Visions 2000* anticipate that allocation of human resources will change as new technologies are adopted. Figure 14.8 shows their estimate of how teachers will shift their time through the decade of the 1990s. This projection implies a challenge to the leadership abilities of the administrators in the province; they are the keys to change.

Digitization of Print, Image, and Sound

Most of us had our first experience with "digitized" images in the late 1960s when we watched televised close-up pictures of the Moon sent back to Earth by U.S. astronauts. The images from their video cameras were converted into a digital code, a series of 1s

and 0s. The digitized information was transmitted to Earth, where it was converted back into pictures.

The combination of digitized images and laser technology resulted in the videodisc, the heart of interactive video. Shortly after the development of the videodisc, digitized sound, and then digitized print were incorporated into a new format—the compact disc (see Chapter 6). Now print, image, and sound are being combined in digitized formats for either storage or transmission.

Digitized information has decided advantages. In stored formats, such as videodisc and compact disc, information can be scanned and accessed with a speed and accuracy not possible in analog formats. Neither film nor videotape lends itself to rapid random access. Both videodisc and compact disc can store far more information than the analog formats. Finally, digitized still and

motion images can be intermixed with a degree of manipulation not possible in film or tape.

Transmission of digitized information is less cumbersome than transmission of analog information. Analog sound and image must be transmitted on separate wires, but digitized sound and image can be sent over the same line. An optical fiber line, no thicker than a thread, can transmit an incredible amount of information.

Digitization has led inevitably to the development of a number of systems for storage, retrieval, and transmission of information. It has also led to the "convergence" of media formats, with the potential for making older formats obsolete. For example, if still and motion images can be combined on one disc, and the same piece of equipment can display both, why have filmstrip and 16-mm projectors around? If laser discs are damage resistant and can store

▲ *Figure 14.9*
"A-V Online" compact disc. The complete NICEM indexes are on a single compact disc.

still and motion images, why maintain an inventory of fragile filmstrips and films? Let's look at some of the forms convergence is taking. Some have already been developed, and some are still in the design stage.

CD-ROM [Read Only Memory]. This format was described in Chapter 6. Entire encyclopedias, as well as many other reference works, are available on CD-ROM. There is a real possibility that CD-ROM will be the format of choice for reference material, especially in libraries. By being plugged into a word processor, a dictionary, thesaurus, zip code directory, and other important references can be accessed much more quickly than if the user had to reach for the printed work on a bookshelf.

CD-WORM [Write Once, Read Many Times]. This format attempts to get around the read only memory limitation of CD-ROM. The disc can be inscribed with the information of the user's choice—but only once.

Then the disc can be read many times. This is a useful format for anyone with a unique data bank that must be read often.

CD-I [Interactive]. In addition to verbal information, still images, graphics, audio, and computer software are to be incorporated into this format. It will be interactive. This format, if it survives, would be very useful in designing training programs.

DVI [Digital Video Interactive]. This format has all the features of CD-I with the addition of moving images. Seventy-two minutes of video with digital sound can be put on this version of the compact disc. RCA, the developer of DVI, has been able to do this by means of a compression system similar to that used on telephone transmissions.

Hypertext. This most futuristic format is best explained with an example. Suppose while you are reading an encyclopedia article on the presidency of John F. Kennedy, reference is made to the Cuban missile crisis. You are curious and want more information, so with a simple command up pops a summary of the confrontation

between Kennedy and Khrushchev. You want to see the observation photos of the missile sites, and another command displays the pictures. You want to listen to the informed opinions of prominent news analysts. A command allows you to hear their voices commenting on the crisis. You also want to read the *New York Times* coverage of the crucial day and up it pops—and so on.

Learning Networks

The fourth- and fifth-year students in Picton Primary School, New South Wales, Australia, and students in the West Pottsgrove Elementary School, Pennsylvania, are in constant touch with each other through electronic mail (E-mail). The students in each school compose their messages on their microcomputers, then send the messages through a modem to a satellite transmitting station. This project, now several years old, is an example of how telecommunication systems are linking students directly.

Of course, transworld linkages of schools are not as yet commonplace, but national networks are

▲ *Figure 14.10*
Pupils in West Pottsgrove, Pennsylvania, Elementary School are in constant touch with their peers in Picton Primary School in New South Wales, Australia, by means of electronic mail delivered by satellite.

becoming so. Regional and national networks of schools are increasing each year. However, until recently, telecommunications networks have been dedicated to delivering instructional programming to classrooms in traditionally structured education. There is now a rapidly growing trend to (1) link students with each other; (2) link students directly with distant program sources, usually through computer and modem; and (3) offer educational experiences and degrees outside the traditional institutions. Some networks provide information to teachers on program possibilities and also offer students the opportunity to interact. For example, the McGraw-Hill Information Exchange (MIX) provides services for teachers and is also used for on-line classroom projects for students.

In the future, continuing professional development is likely to be carried out through learning networks rather than on campuses. This has already occurred in advanced professional development of engineers. Telecommunications networks make possible large-scale collaborative efforts between industry and education. The National Technological University (NTU), subject of a "Close-Up" in Chapter 9, is an example of how such collaboration can create learning opportunities for practicing professionals beyond the traditional campus and degree programs. NTU delivers its programs by satellite.

The courses of the Electronic University Network are accessed by computer through phone lines. Unlike NTU, most of the Electronic University Network offerings are on the undergraduate level. Undergraduate degrees can be earned from Regents College of the State University of New

▲ *Figure 14.11*
New technologies can create new institutions. This distance learner is enrolled in the Electronic University Network.

York and Thomas A. Edison State College of New Jersey. A masters of business administration degree can be earned through the John F. Kennedy University in the San Francisco Bay area.

In the training arena, many companies are questioning the wisdom of transporting employees to large training centers when telecommunications can do the job more efficiently. When fuel prices go up, as they surely will, transportation costs will be one more argument, along with lost time, for using learning networks. AT&T, understandably, is leading the way.

The telephone is likely to be the most important general link to data services. AT&T's Integrated Services Digital Network (ISDN) will make possible multiple services while also carrying video and the usual audio signals. Based on the optical fiber, the system will be cheaper, more powerful, and of a higher quality than existing technology. With a hook-up to a TV set and a computer, ISDN would allow subscribers to talk on the phone, have their utilities metered, receive E-mail, and

watch television all at the same time. Because the phone is the most universal of all electronic instruments, ISDN services would become instantly available to virtually every home and business. The humble telephone, sending digitized information over optical fiber, could result in convergence of electronic delivery systems, including cable television.

Later in this chapter we discuss traditional barriers to the full acceptance of technologically based instruction in education. Telecommunications networks are most likely to break down those barriers by creating their own learning opportunities and even creating new institutions. The present system of education was built on the necessity of having the student come to the place where information is delivered; now information can be delivered directly to the student. We have the option to decentralize education whenever we so choose.

In the long run the development of electronic systems for the distribution of instruction will have a profound effect on the organization and administration of

▲ *Figure 14.12*
This Tennessee one-room schoolhouse of 1936 was designed primarily for lecture instruction but had to accommodate individual and small-group study for children of different grade levels.

We seem to be on the verge of making quantum leaps in surmounting some long-term barriers to learning.

Learning Styles and Individualized Instruction

True individualization—a different learning program for each student—has long been a goal of mass-education systems. In the United States systematic programs of individualized instruction go back at least to the "programmed" workbooks of the Winnetka Plan of the 1920s. The wave of innovation in the 1960s saw a resurgence of schemes for individualization such as Individually Prescribed Instruction (IPI), Individually Guided Education (IGE), and Program for Learning in Accordance with Needs (PLAN). For various reasons those innovations have not flourished, but we keep trying. Public Law 94-142, passed by Congress in 1975, mandates an Individualized Education Program (IEP) for each handicapped child in school. Mean-

our educational facilities. For the last half century educators and the public have been assuming that in order to increase access of each child to a full range of instruction, make better use of personnel, and increase cost efficiency, smaller schools had to be replaced by larger ones. However, advances in technology have now made it administratively and economically feasible to educate smaller groups of students in a larger number of instructional settings. Proponents of "decentralization" as a step toward greater public participation in the control of public education may well have found an unexpected and powerful ally in technological advances such as electronic systems for the distribution of instruction.

FUTURE TECHNOLOGIES OF INSTRUCTION

T HERE are many technological developments that could lead to major impacts on educa-

tion and training. For our purposes we will look at some promising work going on in learning styles, artificial intelligence and expert systems, learners and new information technologies, psychotechnology, and biotechnology.

▲ *Figure 14.13*
This Toronto classroom of the 1970s contains only one grade level but is easily adaptable to a variety of learning modes. The impact of technology is visible in terms of the role of instructional materials, the use of space, and the richness of stimuli.

while, research into the psychological processes of learning has underscored the importance of matching students to instructional treatments.

Learning style refers to the cluster of psychological traits that determine how an individual perceives, interacts with, and responds emotionally to learning environments. It is clear that certain traits affect dramatically our ability to learn effectively from different treatments. What is not so clear is *which* traits are the most important ones to pay attention to for practical purposes. The variables that are competing for attention in the marketplace of ideas can be grouped under perceptual preferences, information-processing habits, motivational factors, and physiological factors.

Perceptual Preferences/ Strengths.

Learners may vary regarding which sensory gateways they prefer using or are especially adept at using; the two are not necessarily synonymous, of course. The main choices are auditory, visual, tactile, and kinesthetic. Proponents of this variable claim that most students do *not* have a preference or strength for auditory reception, casting doubt on the widespread use of the lecture method. They find that slower learners tend to prefer tactile or kinesthetic experiences; sitting and listening are difficult for them. Dependence on the tactile and kinesthetic modalities decreases with maturity.

Information-Processing Habits.

This category includes a broad range of variables related to how individuals tend to approach the cognitive processing of information. Some of the contrasting traits include the following: analytical/global, focuser/nonfocuser, narrow/broad categorization, cogni-tive complexity/simplicity, reflective/impulsive, sharpener/leveler regarding memory processes, and tolerant/intolerant to incongruity.

Gregorc's Style Delineator groups learners according to concrete versus abstract and random versus sequential styles; it yields four categories: concrete sequential, concrete random, abstract sequential, and abstract random. "Concrete sequential" learners prefer direct, hands-on experiences presented in a logical order.* They learn best with workbooks, programmed instruction, demonstration, and structured laboratory exercises. "Concrete random" learners use a trial-and-error approach, quickly reaching conclusions from exploratory experiences. They prefer methods such as games, simulations, and independent-study projects. "Abstract sequential" learners decode verbal and symbolic messages adeptly, especially when presented in logical sequence. Reading and listening to lectures are preferred methods. "Abstract random" learners are distinguished by their capacity to draw meaning from human-mediated presentations; they respond to the tone and style of the speaker as well as the message. They do well with group discussion, lectures with question-and-answer periods, film, and television.

Motivational Factors.

A number of emotional factors have been found to influence what we pay attention to, how long we pay attention, how much effort we invest in learning, and how feelings may interfere with learning.

Anxiety, locus of control (internal/external), degree of structure, achievement motivation, social motivation, cautiousness, and competitiveness are variables that are frequently cited as critically involved in the learning process.

"Anxiety," according to Tobias, "is one of the learner characteristics of major importance for instructional concerns."† Tobias describes how anxiety can interfere with cognitive processing before, during, and after learning. He also cites research demonstrating that motivational differences can dramatically affect the effort that students invest in a task and thereby affect learning outcomes.

Physiological Factors.

Factors related to health, sex differences, and environmental conditions are among the most obvious influences on the effectiveness of learning. Hunger and illness clearly impede learning. Boys and girls respond differently to various school experiences. Temperature, noise, lighting, and time of day are everyday phenomena that affect our ability to concentrate and maintain attention. People have different preferences and ranges of tolerance regarding these factors.

Dunn has developed standardized instruments to measure learning styles and environmental preferences of adults which include these physiological factors among others.†† These instruments are among the best known and most widely used in school

---

* Anthony Gregorc. "Learning and Teaching Styles—Potent Forces behind Them." *Educational Leadership* (January 1979), pp. 234–236.

† Sigmund Tobias. "Learner Characteristics." In Robert M. Gagne, ed., *Instructional Technology: Foundations.* Hillsdale, N.J.: Lawrence Erlbaum, 1987.
†† Kenneth Dunn. "Measuring the Productivity Preferences of Adults." *Student Learning Styles and Brain Behavior.* Reston, Va.: National Association of Secondary School Principals, 1982.

applications. Teachers who have prescribed individual learning programs based on analysis of these factors feel that they have practical value in academic achievement, attitude, and discipline.

We have a long way to go before we can be confident of our theoretical base *and* before we have diagnostic tools of fully proven value in the realm of learning styles. But on another front, the work in "expert systems" may be addressing the equally important question of what technology is needed to make the connection between learning styles and instructional treatments.

Artificial Intelligence and Expert Systems

Almost immediately after electronic computers became a reality, scientists were intrigued by what they saw as parallels between the human brain and how the computer processes information. They asked if the computer could "learn" as well as retrieve and collate information. These experiments led to computers playing games such as checkers and chess with human experts . . . and winning. Then they asked, if the computer can learn the rules, strategies, and moves of a game, why couldn't it then enable an amateur to play on an equal footing with an expert? It certainly could. But, they reasoned, why limit this capability to playing games? Why not see if this "artificial intelligence" can be applied to more useful problems?

This line of experimentation led to the development of so-called *expert systems*. These are *software packages that allow the collective wisdom of experts in a given field to be brought to bear on a problem*. One of the first

such systems to be developed is called *MYCIN*. This is a program that helps train doctors to make accurate diagnoses of infectious diseases on the basis of tests and patient information fed into the computer. Expert systems are slowly making their way into education. Several programs have been developed to aid administrators, such as *The Negotiation Edge*. After feeding into the computer a series of adjectives that describe the adversary, the program offers advice on how to conduct a negotiating session. *SCHOLAR* is an expert system on the geography of South America. It is an example of a "mixed-initiative" system. The student and the system can ask questions of each other. *SCHOLAR* can adjust its instructional strategy according to the context of the student's inquiry. Scholastic Publications has developed a unique program that learns the rules of any game as it plays with its human partner. The student may play the game with self-chosen rules but must identify for the computer the criteria for winning the game. The computer absorbs the rules and eventually wins. Another expert system, *The Intelligent Catalog,* helps a student learn to use reference tools. Any learning task that requires problem-solving lends itself to an expert system, for example, qualitative analysis in chemistry.

An example closer to our concern with individualized learning is an expert system called *CLASS LD* developed at Utah State University. The program classifies learning disabilities by using an elaborate set of rules contributed by experts. In tests the program has proven to be at least as accurate as informed special education practitioners. The next step is to develop a software package that will design an Individualized

Education Program for a child diagnosed by *CLASS LD.* Because many learning-disabled children are in mainstreamed classes, the expert system would make manageable the classroom teacher's job of providing appropriate instruction. The school benefits from more effective and more efficient decision making.

But further down the road is an expert system that could truly individualize learning. Based on research on learning styles, we can imagine an expert system that learns all the important aptitudes and personality traits of an individual. When presented with a large body of material to be mastered, the learner uses the expert system as a guide to learning the content in the most effective manner. The program adjusts the content, instructional method, and medium to the learning style of the student. The learner is in charge of the program, not the experts. When this becomes possible, we will really have individualized learning.

A new professional specialty has emerged from the development of expert systems. The term *knowledge engineers* has been coined to describe the people who work with experts in a field to assemble and organize a body of knowledge and then design the software package that makes it possible to train someone to become skilled in the area or to enable anyone to call upon the skills of experts to solve a problem. Knowledge engineering is a logical extension of instructional design.

The Learner and New Information Technologies

Predicting the future is predictably unreliable. A chagrined futurist once remarked, "He who lives by the crystal ball learns to eat ground glass." We can safely forecast, however, that the successful citizen of tomorrow will be a manipulator of data stored and accessed in ways we are now only conceptualizing. This ability will be "in the bones" as surely as manipulating electronic toys and games are in the bones of today's children. And that's where it all starts.

The popularity of toys and games controlled by a microprocessor attests to the child's fascination with manipulating a source of information to achieve a goal. Maneuvering a vehicle with a remote control unit may be more than satisfying; it may also be making connections with the future world of robotics. Electronic games are not only fun; they may also be a link to future information technologies. We will take a closer look at electronic games from those for preschoolers to those in video arcades.

But as we do, let's keep in mind that the long-term effect is likely to be more important than our short-term evaluation of the instruction delivered by the games. How much content children learn from these games will be less important, in the long run, than *how* they learned. "The medium *is* the message," as Marshall McLuhan said.

Hand-Held Microprocessor Games.

A major class of "educational" games includes the inexpensive, limited-purpose, calculator-type toys such as *Speak and Spell, Talk and Teach,* and *Spelling Starter.* These are small hand-held instruments costing from fifteen to sixty dollars and sold primarily to the home market. In 1981 the EPIE Institute conducted field tests of the eight most widely distributed games. EPIE found that "the actual 'instructional' function of these games

▲ *Figure 14.14*
Drill-and-practice games such as *Math Blaster* borrow the "target-shooting" format to maintain interest in repetitive drills, such as multiplication tables.

was found to be nil."* In EPIE's judgment, the devices provided only for drill of previously learned skills. This is particularly true of the "drill-and-practice" games.

At the same time, there are other compact microprocessor-controlled educational game systems that hold considerably more promise. For example, Texas Instruments' *Touch & Tell* device adds two features that add immensely to its instructional potential: a voice synthesizer and a complex branching program. The compact *Touch & Tell* system consists of a flat touch-sensitive keyboard in a rugged plastic case that also holds the complete hardware and software. Different plastic templates can be placed on the keyboard to allow practice of many different alphabet, number, shape, and other visual discrimination skills. The voice synthesizer is employed to ask questions, to state correct answers, and to play lively musical salutes for a series of correct answers. The program keeps track of the correctness of responses and passage

---

* *Microcomputer Courseware/Microprocessor Games.* EPIE Materials Report 98/99m. Stony Brook, N.Y.: EPIE Institute, 1981, p. 42.

▲ *Figure 14.15*
Speak & Spell is another hand-held microprocessor game; it has several game modes, all based on spelling practice.

▲ *Figure 14.16*
Touch & Tell asks questions by means of a voice synthesizer and requires that the user press the correct square; it provides discrimination practice and builds literacy skills without the prerequisite of literacy.

of time, and it goes ahead to more challenging items or goes back to rehearse missed items depending on the child's response.

Because the mode of response is simply touching an image (letter, number, shape, picture, or the like) on a flat board, it is accessible to children of a very wide range of ages or handicapping conditions. The use of interchangeable overlays and plug-in command modules gives *Touch & Tell* great flexibility.

Pinball Games. Most visible because of their broad popularity are the pinball-type arcade games such as *Gauntlet* and *Highspeed.* But specific games are "used up" quickly. Unlike the mechanical pinball games of yesteryear, modular construction of the control units of the new machines makes insertion of a new game very simple. The player controls a joystick or paddle, making rapid hand movements in response to a moving pattern of threatening situations on a display screen. Successful play requires eye-hand coordination, quick reflexes, concentration, and visual perception skills. It is arguable to what extent these skills transfer to real-world utility. One realm of immediate application is military training. U.S. Air Force trainers feel that the rapid information-processing skills required in the pinball-type games are similar to those used by fighter pilots with video displays in their cockpits. Several commercial arcade games have been adapted for air force training and research purposes. The attention of U.S. Army trainers was caught by *Battlezone,* a shooting gallery game which uses realistic silhouettes of enemy tanks and helicopters as its targets. It, too, is being adapted for formal training use.

The rapid movement, visual and auditory stimulation, and immediate feedback aspects of the pinball-type games also hold great attraction for special education and remedial education. The eye-hand coordination practice, for instance, allows a brain-injured individual with a manual-dexterity handicap the chance to gain through practice capabilities that are "wired-in" from birth in normal, uninjured brains. For those

with sensory handicaps due to brain injury, games can be developed to target the specific auditory or visual skills for which they need practice. Experience to date indicates at least that novel computer games provide intrinsic motivation to persist at a learning task, increasing attention span as well as time on task.

For those with less dramatic learning disabilities, other adaptations of the animated graphics and interactivity of video games hold promise for remedial education. Neuro-Linguistic Programming, a technique of visualization for improving memory and learning in general, is the basis for *Spelling Strategy* and *Math Strategy.* Another game, *Speed Reader,* uses a moving cursor on the display screen to train for faster, smoother eye movements—one of the fundamental reading skills.

There is still not enough objective evidence available to make confident judgments about the overall effects of particular microprocessor-controlled games,

much less about these games as a whole. But some patterns have emerged and, interestingly, they parallel what educators have discovered about each of the previous waves of new technological marvels: that is, that the pedagogical merit varies with the features of the particular game. As stated in Chapter 1, seven decades of instructional media research have taught us to ask, What attributes are needed for proper communication of this idea, and does this material have those attributes?

The most relevant claim for this class of video games is that basic information-processing skills are flexed in solving these fast-moving puzzles. Concentrating, scanning the display for useful information, employing peripheral vision, separating relevant from irrelevant information, deciding, and acting must be integrated in order for the player to succeed. And the gradual improvement of most players' scores indicates that "something" is being learned along these lines. Whether that

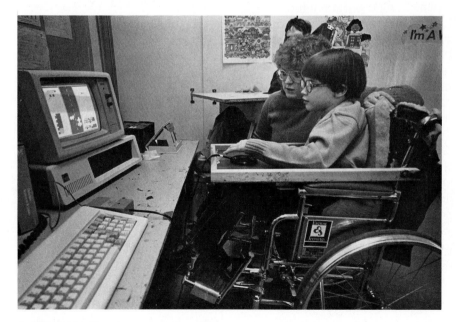

▲ *Figure 14.17*
Fast-action video games provide motivating practice in hand-eye coordination, especially valuable for those with motor handicaps.

"something" is a generic cognitive skill transferable to other situations has yet to be established.

These skills make a transition to the more demanding computer-based instructional programs in the schools and to the more serious uses of information technologies. Ironically, the tiny microprocessor may succeed where bulkier technologies have failed—it may catapult the school from the nineteenth into the twenty-first century.

Psychotechnology: Using Altered States of Consciousness

Shifting our attention from "technology as product" to "technology as process," we can recognize that new scientific understanding of human learning will also be contributing to changes in how instruction is carried out in the future. Conventional educational research and development have already yielded the sorts of technologies of instruction described in Chapter 11: programmed instruction, programmed tutoring, audio-tutorial methods, and the like. Looking into the future, though, breakthroughs in improved learning may well be coming from less conventional sources.

Meditation has long been associated with religious practices and religious training in India and the Orient. In the 1960s these religious influences began to attract popular attention in North America. Experimentation since that time has built up a sizable body of evidence that meditative techniques can have physiological and psychological effects on humans, and that these effects can have instructional consequences. For example, some studies have shown that meditation reduces

anxiety, thereby facilitating complex problem solving by groups under stress. Individuals often report that the relaxation and fresh perspective lent by meditation heighten their study abilities.

The meditative state and other "altered states of consciousness" are already being integrated into new teaching/learning approaches being developed in North America and elsewhere. One of the most advanced—known as "suggestive-accelerative learning and teaching"—is described in detail in volume 36 of the Instructional Design Library.* This approach has grown out of earlier research done by Georgi Lozanov in Bulgaria. Lozanov found that by inducing a state of conscious relaxation prior to a lesson, and by using special techniques involving music and drama during a lesson, adults could learn foreign languages with unusual ease and high rates of retention. Similarly impressive results have been reported by experimenters in Eastern and Western Europe, Canada, and the United States.

Typical of the early "mind-expanding" programs in the United States was EST, founded by Werner Erhard. He has formed a new company called Transformational Technologies, Inc. Erhard claims his "Forums" will give participants a "decisive edge" in their ability to achieve. Companies, government agencies, and even the Soviet Union have paid large fees to send managers through the program. What they hope to get out of the investment is reduced stress and anxiety in a management group that is, at the same time, more open to new

possibilities and more imaginative in their responses to the challenges of their environment.

Erhard, of course, is not alone in this movement sometimes referred to as "New Age" training. For example, Charles Krone has been successful (financially) with a program based on the teachings of the late Armenian mystic Georges Gurdjieff. Even Shirley MacLaine has gotten into the act with "Higher Self" seminars. (She supposedly has the advantage of being in personal touch with great gurus of the past.) Serious questions have been raised about these programs. Charges of "mind control" and "substitute religion" are not uncommon. Whether these programs have anything of lasting value to offer to education and training is certainly still open to question.†

Recently, a scholarly group from the National Research Council thoroughly studied a variety of psychotechnological techniques. In their final report†† they found no support for any parapsychological phenomena, such as mental telepathy. Biofeedback techniques did seem to have some potential benefit for individuals but did not seem promising for training programs. Interestingly, the report, although not supporting sleep learning, deemed it worthy of continued investigation. Under certain conditions, learning might take place during lighter periods of sleep. As established by research some years ago, mental practice was found to be useful, particularly in learning motor skills.

---

* Owen L. Caskey. *Suggestive-Accelerative Learning and Teaching.* Englewood Cliffs, N.J.: Educational Technology Publications, 1980.

† Ron Zemke. "What's New in the New Age?" *Training* (September, 1987), pp. 25-33.
†† Daniel Druckman and John A. Swets, eds. *Enhancing Human Performance: Issues, Theories, Techniques.* Washington, D.C.: National Academy Press, 1988.

Biotechnology: Bionic Extensions of the Brain

The possibility of constructing various sorts of electronic extensions of our brains and central nervous systems has advanced greatly in the past several years. One of the indications of a breakthrough in this area was the appearance in 1969 of the "Boston arm," an artificial limb that could be manipulated by signals from an individual's own nervous system. Nowadays a number of *emgors* (electro*my*ogram *s*ensors) are available. These prosthetic devices use the brain's own natural impulse, the myoelectric signal or electromyogram, to control electromechanical devices in the artificial limb.

These bionic developments moved closer to educational interests with the development of cerebellar stimulators or "brain pacemakers." These implanted devices are being used to regulate brain waves in patients whose afflictions are caused by irregular functioning of the brain's electrochemistry. Some success has been found in cases of severe depression, certain psychoses and neuroses, and cerebral palsy.

The convergence of developments such as these and the "biochips" mentioned earlier in the chapter raises the possibility of interfacing the brain with external electronic devices either indirectly, by detecting brain waves with external sensors, or directly, by employing implanted electrodes. The implications of these possibilities for instruction were explored in a paper by Glenn F. Cartwright.* He envisions as

---

* Glenn F. Cartwright. "Symbionic Technology and Education." Paper presented at the Annual Meeting of the American Educational Research Association, Montreal, April 1983.

aspects of the "symbionic mind":

- Memory enhancement by means of "add-on brains" to expand storage capacity.
- Controlling electronic appliances merely by thinking about them, employing "thought switches;" such appliances could help in monitoring or detecting blood alcohol levels, blood sugar levels, stress factors, and impending heart attacks.
- Plugging into the telephone network without phones; carrying on long-distance conversations in a seemingly telepathic fashion. It has been reported that the U.S. Air Force has trained subjects to control their alpha waves in order to send Morse code messages that could be picked up by a scalp-monitoring machine and fed into a computer.
- Artificial senses, replacing or simply bypassing damaged receptor organs such as the eye or ear.

Cartwright sees these developments as contributing to the decentralization of education and as changing the role of conventional teachers and trainers.

ORGANIZATIONAL IMPEDIMENTS

ANY casual observer of the daily goings-on in schools, higher education institutions, corporate training sites, and other organized instructional settings will notice that the tools and techniques discussed throughout this book are not actually employed to any extent remotely resembling the extent to which they are talked about and advocated by

bystanders. Of course, there is considerable variance. Some corporations make extensive use of advanced media and technology systems, but fewer schools and colleges do. Why is the adoption rate of technology so low, especially among public formal education systems?

The 1983 report of the National Commission on Excellence in Education pointed out a number of shortcomings in the American public education system, among them: inadequate academic content, low standards and expectations, insufficient time spent on learning, poor quality of teaching, and lack of leadership. Similar observations could be made regarding the situation in higher education as well. Many feel that such shortcomings are symptoms of a more fundamental problem— the very structure of public educational institutions. The case is stated succinctly by Charles Reigeluth:

Just as the one-room school- house, which was so appropri- ate for an agricultural society, proved to be inadequate for an industrial society, so our pres- ent system is proving to be inadequate for an information society. It is the fundamental structure of our educational system that is at the heart of our current problems. For example, it is our group-based, lock- stepped, graded, and time-ori- ented system that has the dubious distinction of effec- tively destroying the inherent desire to learn in all but a small percent of our children. Also, microcomputers are accelerating the trend toward increased use of nonhuman resources in the education of our children, but the current structure of our educational system cannot adequately

---

▲ *Figure 14.18*
The lecture and textbook, not the newer media and technologies, still dominate formal education.

accommodate the effective use of these powerful tools.

The sorts of structural problems that Reigeluth is referring to exist at two levels: (1) the structure of the classroom as a learning environment, and (2) the organizational structure of the school, college, or corporation attempting to deliver instruction. We will look at these two levels separately.

Structure of the Classroom

The typical setup of the classroom—almost everywhere in the Western world and at virtually every level—has the fundamental weakness of being organized around a single adult who attempts to orchestrate more or less diverse activities for a generally large group of learners. This

one person typically is expected to be responsible for selecting and organizing the content of lessons; designing materials; producing materials; diagnosing individual needs; developing tests; delivering instruction orally to the

group and/or through other media individually or in different groupings; administering, scoring, and interpreting tests; prescribing remedial activities; and coordinating the numberless logistical details that hold the whole enterprise together. Other sectors of society have long since recognized that improvements in effectiveness and productivity require division of labor, but this concept has not yet been accepted in the preindustrial world of formal education.

An example of a profession in which division of labor has been accepted is that of medicine. Physicians have tended toward the practice of specializations, enabling each to keep better abreast of innovations in practice. Second, physicians have adopted differentiated staffing within their offices and clinics so that less critical functions can be delegated to paraprofessionals and technicians, reserving to the physicians the function of diagnosing and treat-

* Charles M. Reigeluth. "Restructuring: The Key to a Better Educational System for an Information Society." IDD&E Working Paper No. 16. Syracuse, N.Y.: School of Education, Syracuse University, September 1983, p. 1.

▲ *Figure 14.19*
How can one teacher provide individualized instruction *and* take care of the thousand-and-one details of classroom management?

ing conditions that merit their attention. Physicians have an incentive to accept this restructuring in those societies in which there exists a free marketplace for their services. In this environment, embracing a division of labor increases their profits. Educators work in a very different environment—but there will be more about those factors a bit later.

Alternative classroom structures do exist and, in fact, have been adopted in many places. In Chapter 11 you encountered programmed tutoring, PSI, and Audio-Tutorial Systems, each of which provides a total and radically different pattern for setting up a learning environment.

More recently, a plan that incorporates virtually all of the technologies of instruction but centers on the notion of division of labor has been field tested in a number of countries, among them Indonesia, Liberia, and the Philippines. The classroom teacher, who may not be a fully certified teacher-training institution graduate, uses materials that are centrally designed and rather fully "scripted" to lead participatory lessons. Parents, volunteers, and student tutors share other teaching and logistical tasks. Thus, there is a division of labor both for the design and for the implementation of instruction. The plan takes a somewhat different shape in each locale and is known by a different name in each country, but the generic name and concept is "low-cost learning technology."* It is essentially a systematic method for implementing a variety of managerial and instructional innovations; it focuses on

---

* Daryl G. Nichols. "Low-Cost Learning Systems: The General Concept and Specific Examples." *NSPI Journal* (September 1982), pp. 4–8.

▲ *Figure 14.20*
Division of labor has helped extend health care without a proportionate increase in the number of physicians.

improving student learning outcomes while reducing overall costs, especially labor costs (hence the name "low-cost"). This concept has shown sufficient promise that the U.S. Agency for International Development (AID) has made a major commitment to implementing it in some thirty additional countries.

▲ *Figure 14.21*
The low-cost learning project in Indonesia, Project PAMONG, makes extensive use of students as peer-group teachers.

Structure of the Organization

The underlying reason why teachers and trainers teach the way they do, embracing the methods they do—however inefficient or ineffective they may be—is that they are following the "rules of the game" that their daily environment reinforces. A useful way of analyzing this situation is to compare teaching as a *craft* with instruction as a *technology*.* In a craft activity the emphasis is on the use of tools by the skilled craftsman. In a technology the emphasis is on the design of tools that produce replicable, reliable results. In a craft, ad-hoc decision making is valued, whereas in a technology value is placed on incorporating those decisions into the design of the tools themselves (e.g., the "scripted" lesson plan used in low-cost learning technology).

The organizational structures that evolve because of craft thinking are fundamentally different from those that evolve from engineering or technological thinking. Because a craft makes a virtue of the use of tools, the power and the discretion of a craftsperson in any given situation are very high, whereas the power and the discretion of management in the same situation are relatively low. However, in an engineering operation, the power and discretion of the individual operator are low, whereas the power and discretion of the team designing the required tools are extremely high. It is inadvisable to attempt to place the products developed by

▲ *Figure 14.22*
The approach of technology is to develop well-designed modules that can be used independently by the learner.

an engineering team into the organizational structure of a craft. The craftspeople will have a natural tendency to modify arbitrarily the engineered products.

This is precisely what happens in traditional education and training. The organizational structures are built around a craft model, a model that gives considerable discretion to each instructor in the classroom. When engineered products (e.g., fully "scripted" lesson plans) are placed in this environment, the individual instructor constantly second-guesses decisions that have already been built into the instructional system. The instructor tends to reduce such systematic products to separate bits of material to be used at his or her own discretion.

The craft tradition of education leads to a structure that stops short of developing specific instructional products centrally because it assumes that such specific decisions are made by the person in face-to-face contact with

learners. It is expected that any products that are developed may be used or ignored by the instructor in the classroom. In this structure, technological products represent an *added cost,* serving only to aid the teacher when he or she deems it appropriate. Solutions that increase overall costs besides demanding special effort to produce and implement are not likely to flourish.

If this analysis is correct, if the "rules of the game" do determine how educators act, reforms must be made in the rules of the game. History shows that changes in performance do follow changes in the rules. Consider the following rule changes in public education: *Brown* vs. *Topeka Board of Education* (racial desegregation of schools), the inclusion of questions on "new math" in the national college entrance exams (adoption of "new math" into the curriculum), and state-legislated consolidation of schools (reforms in school organization and curriculum).

---

* Robert Heinich. "Instructional Technology and the Structure of Education." *Educational Communication and Technology Journal* (Spring 1985).

FORCES TENDING TOWARD CHANGE

THE preceding argument leads to the conclusion that major restructuring of education both at the classroom level and at the highest organizational level will be required in order for media and technology to deliver the benefits on a massive basis that they already deliver on a piecemeal basis and in selected cases. This is a long-term process and one not sure of success. However, there are forces working in the direction of change.

Accountability in Education and Instruction

For almost two decades there has been a trend in education toward what has come to be referred to as *accountability*. Basically, accountability is a demand for some form of public demonstration that schools do what they are supposed to do and do it effectively. But beyond that, each teacher is accountable for the progress or lack of progress in his or her class.

Much of the impetus toward accountability has come from increasing competition for the tax dollar of the public—a general social and political phenomenon certain to continue in the foreseeable future. Taxpayers hard pressed for money to support schools want to be assured that their taxes are being well spent. They are concerned both with the cost–benefit ratio of instruction (whether or not we are getting the right kinds of benefit from instruction for the money that is being spent on it) and with the cost-effectiveness of instruction (whether or not these benefits are being achieved as effectively as

▲ *Figure 14.23*
Technology makes instruction visible. As parents and other community members get involved in the schools as reading tutors, volunteer aides, and the like, structured materials make their help more effective. By the same token, teachers gain credibility in the eyes of the general public by using well-designed materials.

possible at the lowest possible cost).

Not only a large segment of the public but also many educators support the idea that the schools should be held accountable for the learning progress of students. These educators claim that some teachers are too easily diverted from concentration on the learning tasks at hand to unnecessary and unrelated class activities. Some educators further claim that society has asked the schools to

do so many jobs that the main purpose, instruction, is lost, or at least diluted, in the process.

This demand by the public and by concerned educators for some sort of accountability seems reasonable. Accountability has, however, met with considerable resistance from many members of the education profession. They argue that the really vital outcomes of the educational process cannot be quantified or measured, that the only learning outcomes that can be measured are trivial ones—dates, names of historical personages, rules of grammar, multiplication tables, etc. They further argue that accountability requires rigid determination of goals in advance of instruction, thus ruling out serendipitous opportunities that arise during instruction to teach material not specifically covered by predetermined goals. Opponents also claim that accountability will lead to public onus being put upon dedicated teachers working with low-ability students who will naturally have far greater difficulty achieving specific predetermined objectives than will high-ability students.

These and other objections to accountability have a certain validity, and we hope the concept will develop in such a manner that legitimate qualms will be allayed. In any case, it seems reasonable to assume that the educational establishment, and individual teachers within the establishment, will become more and more publicly accountable for the outcome of the educational enterprise.

Perhaps the most widely known and highly publicized manifestation of the trend toward accountability has been the National Assessment of Educational Progress (NAEP) program. Under this program, general achievement tests are given periodically at various grade levels throughout the U.S. The tests are intended for long-range comparisons between groups of students at various periods of time. They compare how well students do on standard measures of learning in different parts of the country and in various kinds of schools. So far the results have been used simply to determine whether the schools in general are achieving what they are supposed to achieve. No attempt has yet been made to use NAEP to compare specific schools for instructional effectiveness, but many educators are naturally apprehensive that the program may in the future come to be used for this purpose. Despite opposition from the organized teaching profession, some form of national assessment is likely to continue on the educational scene.

A number of states have developed similar assessment mechanisms. In 1977, for example, California inaugurated its own educational assessment program. In March 1977, all students at designated grade levels took the same achievement tests in reading, arithmetic, social science, and science. The reports were processed and distributed in April 1977, not only to the schools and school districts but also to the parents of each child taking the test. Parents received a computer printout that indicated where their children stood in relation to other members of their grade levels throughout the state of California. Although, again, this assessment movement was resisted by professional educators in California, parents of California school children responded favorably to the program. A number of other states have established assessment programs.

Other states have developed minimum competency tests to determine promotion from one cluster of grades to another and/or graduation from high school. Although some of these efforts have been challenged in the courts (most notably in Florida), the assessment and minimum competency movements will probably continue to gain strength.

During the National Forum on Excellence in Education, held in 1983, many states revealed plans requiring accountability of teachers and schools. Many planned to use merit pay as an incentive to teachers to change their practices.

The trend toward accountability and public disclosure of educational achievement will result in closer ties between the general public and the educational enterprise. Educators will be called upon to explain their selection of instructional methods and materials in terms of attainment of instructional objectives. They will also be called upon to defend their selections in terms of cost–benefit ratios and cost-effectiveness. Education and evaluation of education will become public processes rather than purely private ones between teachers and students. It behooves all instructors, then, to be prepared to defend their choices of materials and methods. If they are not prepared to do so, they run the increasing risk that those materials and methods will be publicly judged as dispensable frills.

Fortunately for those particularly concerned with the use of media in the schools, instructional technology allows instructors to construct flexible yet structured designs for achievement of specific educational objectives that can be laid out for public inspection. As pointed out throughout this text, such designs, when properly planned and adhered to, can be demonstrated to result in consistent and readily apparent learning advances—readily apparent to the teacher, the student, and the public. Accountability need not necessarily make us apprehensive. We can, rather, look upon it as an opportunity to further the trend toward partnership between home and school in the educational enterprise, a trend that innovative technology itself has done so much to foster.

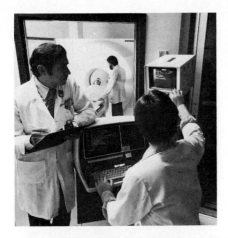

▲ *Figure 14.24*
Jobs at all societal levels, from neurosurgery to police work to auto mechanics, are being affected by technological advances. People will have to change as jobs change; lifelong learning becomes a practical necessity, not just a utopian ideal.

Lifelong-Learning Systems

Lifelong learning has long been an ideal of professional educators. Advances in the products and processes of instructional technology have brought us to the verge of making that ideal attainable for millions of our citizens. Indeed, we might say that in this respect, at least, our society has "lucked out." Never before in our development as a people have we had a greater need for lifelong learning.

Fifty years ago, it was possible for a doctor, a teacher, a scientist, or, for that matter, an electrician or a typewriter repairperson to be trained in a field and remain reasonably competent in it with little or no updating for the rest of his or her life. However, scientific and technological knowledge is increasing at such a rapid pace that this is no longer possible. Indeed, for millions of us, life-long education is something more than an ideal—it has become a necessity.

In our mobile society today, many people switch from the field in which they were trained to another, or to several others, during their working lives. Early retirement systems in some professions and businesses have contributed to this trend, and many people in our present-day economic system become what economists call "structurally unemployed" and must seek new jobs and careers outside the fields of their expertise and/or training. For all these people, access to an educational system geared to lifelong education is virtually a necessity.

Then there are the rest of our people—millions of ordinary members of our society who wish to keep up with a rapidly changing world, many of whom are beyond the age of formal schooling. These people, too, will more and more be demanding access to lifelong learning; and, indeed, there will be more and more such people as the average age of the population continues to climb.

Obviously, the products and processes of instructional technology are destined to play a major role in the development of lifelong-learning systems. Audio- and videocassettes and discs, electronic learning devices, electronic systems for delivery of instruction to wherever the lifelong learner may be (the formal learning institution, the factory, the business office, the community center, the home), and numerous other kinds of instructional technology will necessarily be in the forefront in society's efforts to establish such systems. Without the products and processes of instructional technology, lifelong learning would likely be destined to remain an ideal. With them, we at least have reason to hope that it will soon become a reality for the millions of people who need and desire it.

PROFESSIONAL CAREERS IN EDUCATIONAL TECHNOLOGY

Tʜɪs book has been dedicated to helping you become a more effective instructor (manager of instruction, if you will) through application of instructional media and technology to your teaching tasks. You may, however, wish to specialize in this fascinating and fast-growing field. (A directory of graduate programs in instructional technology is published by the Association for Educational Communications and Technology.*) If so, what opportunities for professional employment are likely to be open to you? Unlike some education areas, instructional technology is becoming more and more pervasive in formal and nonformal education with each passing year, and, correspondingly, an ever larger number of people are being employed in this specialty.

Traditionally, the areas in which the growth of instructional technology have created career opportunities are the various media programs at school, district, regional, and state levels. At all of those levels, media professionals are employed to run programs and, depending on the size of the organization, produce materials for use in schools. As school districts and regional media centers have built up their collections of audiovisual materials for distribution, they have employed instructional media professionals as

selectors of these materials. In formal education, media selection specialists determine not only what materials will be added to collections but also how well collections of materials are serving the curricular and instructional needs of the institution. In training programs, media specialists frequently evaluate the effectiveness of the programs as well as determine the materials to be used in them. Another major career area at all education levels is the professional management—classification, storage, and distribution—of media collections.

Instructional product design—the development of validated and reliable instructional materials—has been an important specialty in the field of instructional technology for some time. Publishers and producers of instructional materials, along with school districts, community colleges, and colleges and universities, are constantly on the alert for specialists trained in the skills of product design. Computer-assisted instruction, interactive video, and other emerging forms of individualized instruction constitute an important growth area within the instructional product design field.

And we must not overlook organizations other than schools that require specialists in educational technology. Health-care institutions, for example, are heavily involved with instructional technology and have been employing an increasing number of professionals to help develop the instruction used in those programs. Industrial training also presents a growing area of employment. In this area, skills in developing instructional materials are very advantageous. As service industries have increased in importance in our economy, training programs for service personnel have correspondingly

▲ *Figure 14.25*
The field of educational technology offers many and varied career opportunities in activities such as managing media centers; designing and producing film, television, and computerized programs; evaluating and selecting audiovisual materials; and implementing innovative programs with groups of learners.

---

* Donald P. Ely, ed. *Educational Media and Technology Yearbook, 1988*. Englewood, Colo.: Libraries Unlimited, 1988.

increased. Aside from employment opportunities within such industries, organizations that design programs for training service personnel employ, both on a permanent and a freelance basis, people skilled in designing instructional media.

Training programs in business and industry have need for a variety of professionals. Some of these specialties are

Training Coordinator: enrolls participants, schedules courses, orders class materials and media, and handles other administrative matters.

Trainer: presents information, leads discussions, and manages learning experiences.

Instructional Designer: translates training needs into training programs, determines media to be used, designs course materials.

Training Specialist: assesses training needs, designs overall programs.

Training Manager: plans and organizes training programs, hires staff, prepares and manages budgets.

Many if not most training programs rely heavily on instructional media. Consequently, specialists in instructional technology are in considerable demand in these programs.

PROFESSIONAL ORGANIZATIONS IN EDUCATIONAL TECHNOLOGY

W HETHER your interest in instructional technology is general or whether you intend to specialize in this area of education, you should be familiar with some of the major organizations dedicated to its advancement.

▲ *Figure 14.26*
Professional conventions, such as those sponsored by AECT, help practitioners keep in touch with new developments.

The Association for Educational Communications and Technology (AECT)

AECT is an umbrella organization intended to encompass all the substantive areas of educational technology. These various areas are expressed as divisions within the organizational structure of the association. For example, the Division of Educational Media Management is concerned with the administration of media programs and media collections. The Industrial Training and Education Division is concerned with the application of instructional technology to training programs. The Division of Instructional Development is concerned with analysis of instructional problems and the design of effective solutions. The Division of Telecommunications is concerned with instruction delivered via radio, television, and other telecommunications media. Other divisions of AECT reflect other professional con-

cerns within instructional technology. AECT publishes a monthly journal, *TechTrends,* and a research quarterly, *Educational Technology Research and Development.* Its annual convention features a major exhibition of audiovisual hardware and software in addition to a broad-ranging program of educational seminars and workshops. (**Address:** 1126 Sixteenth Street, NW, Washington, DC 20036)

American Library Association (ALA)

The ALA is an organization of professionals concerned with the organization, classification, storage and retrieval, and distribution of print and nonprint materials. The ALA has divisions for particular interests. The American Association of School Librarians, for example, is concerned with management of materials collections at the school level. (**Address:** 50

▲ *Figure 14.27*
Many national organizations have local chapters. Here members of a local chapter of the National Society for Performance and Instruction are building and maintaining a network of professional associates.

East Huron Street, Chicago, IL 60611)

American Society for Training and Development (ASTD)

ASTD is an association composed primarily of professionals engaged in training programs in business and industry.

ASTD is by far the largest association for people working in training and management development programs in business, industry, government, and similar institutions. In 1964 the original name, American Society of Training Directors, was changed to reflect the broadened base of interests of its members. Between 1970 and 1989 its membership grew fourfold to more than 23,000 individuals. The society publishes a monthly journal, *Training and Development Journal;* sponsors studies of problems in the training field; and conducts an annual convention that includes a varied and significant educational pro-

gram. ASTD is organized into divisions, including one on Instructional Technology. (**Address:** Box 1443, 1630 Duke Street, Alexandria, VA 22313)

National Society for Performance and Instruction (NSPI)

This organization originally was called the National Society for Programmed Instruction, but its name was changed to reflect broadened interests. NSPI members are interested in the study and application of performance and instructional technologies. NSPI membership of some 2500 includes a mixture of people in business, industry, the military, allied health professions, government, and formal education. The society publishes a monthly journal, *Performance and Instruction,* and a research quarterly, *Performance Improvement Quarterly.* (**Address:** 1126 Sixteenth Street, NW, Washington, DC 20036)

Association for the Development of Computer-Based Instructional Systems (ADCIS)

The general scope of this relatively recent organization is evident from its title. At present ADCIS has thirteen interest groups, for example, Computer-Based Training, Emerging Technologies, and Educators of the Handicapped. The annual conference of ADCIS features software and hardware exhibits as well as presentations on recent developments in this rapidly growing field. The organization publishes the *Journal of Computer-Based Instruction.* (**Address:** Miller Hall 409, Western Washington University, Bellingham, WA 98225)

International Interactive Communications Society (IICS)

This is another small organization spawned by new technology. It is an association of some 1400 communications industry professionals dedicated to the advancement of interactive video and related technologies. IICS provides a forum for users, manufacturers, and producers to share applications and techniques of electronic interactive media. Currently, IICS places emphasis on local activity by its chapters. The group's publication program includes a newsletter and a quarterly journal. (**Address:** 2120 Steiner Street, San Francisco, CA 94115)

State Organizations

Several of the national organizations just cited have state affiliates (e.g., AECT, ALA), or local chapters (e.g., NSPI, ASTD). By joining one or more of these, you will quickly be brought into contact with nearby professionals who share your particular concerns.

▲ *Figure 14.28*
A sampling of journals in educational technology

PROFESSIONAL JOURNALS IN EDUCATIONAL TECHNOLOGY

A LL of the organizations just cited publish journals of interest to their members. There are a number of other periodicals of special interest to teachers interested in using instructional media. *Media & Methods,* for example, highlights new software and hardware. *Booklist* will keep you current on the availability of new instructional materials.

Learning gives practical ideas for improving instruction. *Educational Technology* addresses both teachers and educational technologists with articles on a broad range of topics from the theoretical to the practical. For the business/industry setting, *Training* covers new developments in training techniques in a lively, popular style.

T. H. E. Journal (Technological Horizons in Education) Journal concentrates on technology in higher education. *E-ITV* keeps its readers abreast of the uses of television and video in training and education. The *Canadian Journal of Educational Communications* gives in-depth coverage of the broad field of educational technology.

The computer area has spawned a large number of journals, some of which are no longer published. *Electronic Learning, The Computing Teacher,* and *Journal of Computer-Based Instruction* are journals likely to continue publication.

By this time we hope that you have made the acquaintance of all these journals—and many more. But if you haven't, take the opportunity to browse through them in the periodical room of your university or public library. It will be time well spent.

As you work with instructional media and technology and as you gain experience in whatever instructional position you find yourself, you may want to explore the possibility of deepening your professional interest in one of the specialties in instructional technology. Through regular reading of one or more of the journals in the field, you will be kept informed about developments in instructional technology. You will find it a fascinating area within education and one with exciting career possibilities.

References

Print References

Adams, Dennis M., and Hamm, Mary. "Artificial Intelligence and Instruction: Thinking Tools for Education." *T. H. E. Journal* (August 1987), pp. 59–62.

Baldwin, Lionel. *High Technology and the Future of Education.* (Columbus, Ohio: National Center for Research in Vocational Education, 1986).

Bensen, M. James. "High Tech Comes to Instruction." *Vocational Education Journal* (September 1986), pp. 26–27.

Brand, Stewart. *The Media Lab.* (New York: Viking, 1987).

Breivik, Patricia S. *Managing Programs for Learning Outside the Classroom.* (San Francisco: Jossey-Bass, 1986).

Carnegie Commission on Higher Education. *The Fourth Revolution: Instructional Technology in Higher Education.* (New York: McGraw-Hill, 1972).

Caskey, Owen L. *Suggestive-Accelerative Learning and Teaching.* Volume 36, Instructional Design Library. (Englewood Cliffs, N.J.: Educational Technology Publications, 1980).

Comcowich, William J. "Expert Systems: A New Era in Videodiscs." *E-ITV* (August 1987), pp. 23–25.

Communications Tomorrow: The Coming Information Society. (Bethesda, Md.: World Future Society, 1982).

Daniel, John S. "Independence and Interaction in Distance Education: New Technologies for Home Instruction." *Programmed Learning and Educational Technology* (August 1983), pp. 155–160.

Gardner, Dwayne E. "School Buildings of the Future." *Council of Educational Facilities Planners Journal* (March–April 1987), pp. 24–27.

Halff, Henry M. "Instructional Applications of Artificial Intelligence." *Educational Leadership* (March 1986), pp. 24–31.

Hawkins-Sager, Susan. "The 'School without Schools': What It Really Taught Us." In *National Conference on Professional Development and Educational Technology Proceedings.* (Washington, D.C.: Association for Educational Communications and Technology, 1980).

Hawthorne, Elizabeth M.; Libby, Patricia A.; and Nash, Nancy S. "The Emergence of Corporate Colleges." *Journal of Continuing Higher Education* (Fall 1983).

Heinich, Robert. "Instructional Technology and Decision Making." *Educational Considerations* (Spring 1983), pp. 25–26.

———. "The Proper Study of Educational Technology." *Educational Communication and Technology Journal* (Summer 1984), pp. 67–87.

Helgerson, Linda W. "Optical Discs: New Storage Media for Education." *T. H. E. Journal* (March 1987), pp. 50–52.

Hodgkinson, Harold. "Today's Curriculum: How Appropriate Will It Be in Year 2000?" *NASSP Bulletin* (April 1987), pp. 2–4, 6, 7.

Holmberg, Borje. *Growth and Structure of Distance Education.* (London: Croom Helm, 1987).

Information Technology and Its Impact on American Education. (Congress of the United States, Office of Technology Assessment, Washington, D.C., 1982).

Knapper, Christopher K., ed. *Expanding Learning through New Communication Technologies.* (San Francisco: Jossey-Bass, 1982).

Lazar, Ellen A., ed. *The Teleconferencing Handbook: A Guide to Cost Effective Communication.* (White Plains, N.Y.: Knowledge Industries, 1983).

Lozanov, Georgi. *Suggestology and the Outlines of Suggestopedy.* (New York: Gordon and Breach Science Publishers, 1978).

McGinty, Tony. "Three Trailblazing Technologies for Schools." *Electronic Learning* (September 1987), pp. 26–30.

Mecklenberger, James A. "Expert Systems: The Next Technology Breakthrough for Education." *Electronic Learning* (September 1987), p. 6.

New Information Technologies: A Challenge for Education. (Paris: Organization for Economic Cooperation and Development, 1986).

Nichols, Daryl G. "Low-Cost Learning Systems: The General Concept and Specific Examples." *NSPI Journal* (September 1982), pp. 4–8.

Oettinger, Anthony G., and Zapol, Nikki. "Will Information Technology Help Learning?" *Teachers College Record* (September 1972), pp. 116–126.

Pool, Ithiel de Sola. *Technologies of Freedom: On Free Speech in an Electronic Age.* (Cambridge, Mass.: Harvard University Press, 1983).

Romberg, Thomas A. *Toward Effective Schooling: The IGE Experience.* (Lanham, Md.: University Press of America, 1985).

Van Horn, Royal W. "Environmental Psychology: Hints of a New Technology?" *Phi Delta Kappan* (June 1980), pp. 696–697.

Wedemeyer, Dan J. "The New Age of Telecommunication: Setting the Context for Education." *Educational Technology* (October 1986), pp. 7–13.

Wilcox, John. "A Campus Tour of Corporate Colleges." *Training and Development Journal* (May 1987), pp. 51–56.

Williams, Frederick. *The Communications Revolution.* Rev. ed. (Beverly Hills, Calif.: Sage Publications, 1984).

Zemke, Ron. "What's New in the New Age?" *Training* (September 1987), pp. 25–33.

Zukowski, Angela A. "Vision or Fear? Teacher Response to Educational Technology." *Momentum* (February 1986), pp. 13–16.

Audiovisual References

CD-ROM: The New Papyrus. Seattle: Intermedia, 1986. Videocassette. 22 minutes.

High Technology: How It Works. Educational Dimensions Group, 1983. Filmstrips. "Holography," $21\frac{1}{2}$ minutes; "Television," $20\frac{1}{2}$ minutes; "Fiber Optics," $17\frac{1}{2}$ minutes; "Videodisc," 20 minutes.

Tyler, Ralph. *The Development and Use of Technology in Education.* Bloomington, Ind.: Phi Delta Kappa, 1985. Videocassette. 20 minutes.

————. *Have Educational Reforms since 1950 Created Quality Education?* Bloomington, Ind.: Patten Foundation Lectures, 1974. Audiocassette. 70 minutes.

Possible Projects

14-A. For one week collect reports of new developments in electronic media from newspapers, news magazines, and other popular media sources. Write a two- to three-page report describing potential educational impacts of these new developments.

14-B. Play several different types of computer-based games at a video arcade or on a microcomputer. Compare and contrast their possible educational uses.

14-C. Compile your own list of trends in the uses of media and technology in instruction. In your two- to three-page report be specific about what learning tasks could be facilitated by which developments.

14-D. Replicate the Alberta Province "Delphi" study using students or trainees in classes or groups other than your own. Compare the results with those in *Visions 2000.*

14-E. If you work in a school or other organization offering instruction, analyze the structural/organizational factors that impede your full use of media/technology.

14-F. Prepare a documented profile on the status of your state or province in regard to the enforcement of accountability in public education.

14-G. Compile the copy for a brochure that would explain to newcomers to your community the nonformal educational opportunities (lifelong learning) available locally.

14-H. Interview two or more professionals working in educational technology; compare and contrast their duties in a two- to three-page written report or five-minute cassette recording.

14-I. Survey the content of several different educational technology journals and write a one- to two-page report summarizing the types of articles and information covered in each.

APPENDIX A

Information Sources

INSTRUCTORS ordinarily begin their search for needed audiovisual materials in the media collection at their own facility. School personnel would turn next to the catalogs of media collections housed at the school district or regional educational service center. But where can you turn beyond your own organization? And where can your organization obtain the materials that you need? This appendix will help you gain access to the wealth of audiovisual resources available for rental or purchase from commercial and noncommercial sources. (Appendix B focuses on sources that give away or loan materials free or for a nominal cost.)

COMPREHENSIVE INFORMATION SOURCES

ASSUMING that you had identified an instructional need for which audiovisual materials were not available within your organization or from a free loan source, where might you begin searching for another supplier? The most comprehensive information source is the set of indexes published by the National Information Center for Educational Media (NICEM). NICEM provides indexes for each media format and for several popular subject areas plus a producer/distributor index. All are revised periodically and are updated by a supplement service. Arranged by subject as well as by title, these annotated indexes give a comprehensive view of what is available in the marketplace. However, they are usually several years out of date and must often be used in conjunction with sources of more current information.

In 1984, NICEM was acquired in a joint venture by the Association for Educational Communications and Technology (AECT) and Access Innovations, Inc. The new address is: NICEM, P.O. Box 40130, Albuquerque, NM 87196.

The on-line version of the NICEM database is called A-V On-line. A-V On-line can be accessed through computerized search services such as Lockheed's DIALOG. Any library subscribing to such a search service would have a terminal by means of which you could sift through the NICEM references on line. You may also obtain a printout of the results of your search. An on-line search allows you to search key words and phrases as well as subject headings.

NICEM indexes covering still-picture formats are

Index to Educational Overhead Transparencies
Index to Educational Slides
Index to 35-mm Educational Filmstrips

Audio materials are indexed in

Index to Educational Audio Tapes
Index to Educational Records

Films and videotapes are covered by

Film and Video Finder. 3 volumes. First edition, 1987. These volumes replace the *Index to 16-mm Educational Film* and the *Index to Educational Video Tapes.*

NICEM indexes covering multiple types of media on a given topic are

Index to Environmental Studies
Index to Health and Safety Education
Index to Producers and Distributors
Index to Vocational and Technical Education
NICEM Index to Non-Print Special Education Materials: Multimedia (Learner Volume)
NICEM Index to Non-Print Special Education Materials: Multimedia (Professional Volume)

The University of Southern California maintains the nation's largest and most comprehensive bibliographic information retrieval system for special education, the National Information Center for Special Education Materials (NICSEM). NICSEM provides information on the content of materials and their applicability to specific handicaps. The NICSEM publications are helpful in the construction of individualized programs for handicapped children. Current publications include the following:

NICSEM Master Index to Special Education Materials
NICSEM Mini-Index to Special Education Materials: Family Life and Sex Education
NICSEM Mini-Index to Special Education Materials: Functional Communication Skills
NICSEM Mini-Index to Special Education Materials: High Interest, Controlled Vocabulary Supplementary Reading Materials for Adolescents and Young Adults
NICSEM Mini-Index to Special Education Materials: Independent Living Skills for Moderately and Severely Handicapped Students
NICSEM Mini-Index to Special Education Materials: Personal and Social Development for Moderately and Severely Handicapped Students
NICSEM Source Directory
NICSEM Special Education Thesaurus
Special Education Index to Assessment Materials
Special Education Index to Parent Materials

Other reference works covering a broad range of media and content areas are

Brown, Lucy Gregor. *Core Media Collection for Elementary Schools.* 2d ed. (New York: R. R. Bowker, 1978).
———. *Core Media Collection for Secondary Schools.* 2d ed. (New York: R. R. Bowker, 1979).
Hunt, Mary Alice, ed. *A Multimedia Approach to Children's Literature: A Selective List of Films (and Videocassettes), Filmstrips, and Recordings Based on Children's Books.* 3d ed. (Chicago: American Library Association, 1983).
Media Resource Catalog from the National AudioVisual Center, 1986, and *Supplement, 1988.* (Capitol Heights, Md.: National AudioVisual Center).
Winkel, Lois, ed. *Elementary School Collection: A Guide to Books and Other Media.* Annual. (Williamsport, Pa.: Bro-Dart Foundation).

SPECIALIZED INFORMATION SOURCES

MANY information sources are restricted to a particular media format, content area, or audience.

Filmstrip

Educational Sound Filmstrip Directory. Annual. (St. Charles, Ill.: Dukane Corporation, Audiovisual Division).

Audio

McKee, Gerald. *Directory of Spoken-Word Audio Cassettes.* (New York: Jeffrey Norton, 1983).
On Cassette: A Comprehensive Bibliography of Spoken Word Audio Cassettes. (New York: R. R. Bowker, 1985).
Schwann Record and Tape Guide. Monthly. (Boston: ABC Schwann Publications). Available from many record and tape stores.

Film

AAAS Science Film Catalog. (Washington, D.C.: American Association for the Advancement of Science, 1975). Updated in the review source *Science Books and Films.*
American Folklore Films and Videotapes: A Catalog. 2d ed. (New York: R. R. Bowker, 1982).
Artel, Linda, and Wengraf, Susan, eds. *Positive Images: A Guide to 400 Non-Sexist Films for Young People.* (San Francisco: Booklegger Press, 1976).
Collier, Marilyn. *Films for 3 to 5's.* (Berkeley: California University Department of Education, Instructional Laboratories, 1975). Cover title: *Films for Children Ages 3 to 5.*
Documentary Film Classics. 2nd ed. (Capitol Heights, Md.: National AudioVisual Center).
Film Resources for Sex Education. (New York: Sex Information and Education Council of the United

States, distributed by Human Sciences Press, 1976).
Films for Children: A Selected List. 4th ed. (New York: Children's and Young Adult Section of the New York Library Association, 1977).
Gaffney, Maureen, ed. *More Films Kids Like.* (Chicago: American Library Association, 1977).
Hitchens, Howard, ed. *America on Film and Tape: A Topical Catalog of Audiovisual Resources for the Study of United States History, Society, and Culture.* (Westport, Conn.: Greenwood Press, 1985).
Limbacher, James, ed. *Feature Films on 16-mm and Videotape Available for Rental, Sale and Lease.* 8th ed. (New York: R. R. Bowker, 1985).
May, Jill P. *Films and Filmstrips for Language Arts: An Annual Bibliography.* (Urbana, Ill.: National Council of Teachers of English, 1981).
Parlato, Salvatore J. *Films Too Good for Words: A Directory of Non-Narrated Films.* (New York: R. R. Bowker, 1973).
———. *Films Ex Libris: Literature in 16-mm and Video.* (Jefferson, N.C.: McFarland, 1980).
Sullivan, Kay. *Films For, By, and About Women. Series II.* (Metuchen, N.J.: Scarecrow, 1985).
Zornow, Edith, and Goldstein, Ruth M., eds. *Movies for Kids: A Guide for Parents and Teachers on the Entertainment Film for Children.* (New York: Frederick Ungar, 1980).

Video

Boyle, Deirdre. *Video Classics: A Guide to Video Art and Documentary Tapes.* (Phoenix, Ariz.: Oryx Press, 1986).
T.H.E. Catalog, Televised Higher Education: Catalog of Resources. (Boulder, Colo.: Western Interstate Commission for Higher Education, 1984).
Videolog. Three volumes: "Programs for Business and Industry," "Programs for General Interest and Entertainment," "Programs for the Health Sciences" (Guilford, Conn.: Jeffrey Norton). Program information on over 15,000 videotapes and

videocassettes in a broad range of categories.

Video Source Book. Annual. (Syosset, N.Y.: National Video Clearinghouse). Computer-generated catalog of 18,000 video programs, encompassing entertainment, sports, fine arts, business/industry, and education.

Programmed Instruction

Programmed Learning and Individually Paced Instruction Bibliography. 2 volumes. 5th ed. Includes Supplements 1–6. Compiled by Carl H. Hendershot. (Bay City, Mich.: Hendershot Bibliography, 1985). Supplements are issued irregularly.

Simulations and Games

Horn, Robert E., and Cleaves, Anne, eds. *The Guide to Simulations/Games for Education and Training*. 4th ed. (Beverly Hills, Calif.: Sage, 1980). Aims for comprehensive coverage of formal education and the business/industry training sector. All listings carry full descriptions, and some include evaluations and/or testimonials of users.

Stadsklev, Ron, ed. *Handbook of Simulation Gaming in Social Education*. 2d ed. (Tuscaloosa, Ala.: Institute of Higher Education Research and Service, University of Alabama, 1979). Published in two volumes—the first an introductory textbook on simulation/gaming, particularly as it relates to objectives in the social sciences, and the second a directory of individual materials with extensive descriptive annotations. Coverage is limited to "social education," interpreted broadly.

Computer Courseware

Apple Education Software Directory. Annual. (Chicago: WIDL Video).

EPIE Annotated Courseware Provider List. Annual. (Water Mill, N.Y.: EPIE Institute).

International Microcomputer Software Directory. Annual. (Fort Collins, Colo.: Imprint Software).

Microcomputer Index. Annual. (Santa Clara, Calif.: Microcomputer Information Services).

Microcomputer Market Place. Annual. (New York: R. R. Bowker).

Microcomputer Software Catalog List. Annual. (Portland, Oreg.: Northwest Regional Laboratory).

Micro Software Solutions. Annual. (Chatsworth, Calif.: Career Aids, Inc.).

Swift Directory. Annual. (Austin, Tex.: Sterling Swift).

RENTAL SOURCES

THE media formats that are generally available for rental are 16-mm films and videocassettes. Producers and distributors who sell films and videocassettes usually rent the materials that they sell. However, their rental prices are high compared to noncommercial sources. Several universities maintain large libraries of educational films and videocassettes. Indiana University, the University of Illinois, Syracuse University, and the University of Southern California are among these universities. University film-library rental prices are much lower than those charged by the producer or distributor. Each university publishes a catalog of titles available and their rental prices. But there is one "umbrella" publication that compiles rental as well as purchase information on each of the films and videocassettes available from these university film libraries:

The Educational Film/Video Locator of the Consortium of University Film Centers and R. R. Bowker Company. 3d ed. 2 volumes. (New York: R. R. Bowker, 1986).

COMMERCIAL INFORMATION SOURCES

COMMERCIAL producers and distributors of audiovisual materials publish promotional catalogs of their wares. Companies often assemble a special "school and library" catalog, arranged by subject or medium, to display their offerings more effectively. When you use these catalogs, keep in mind the bias of the seller. The descriptions given and the claims made do not pretend to be objective. Any purchases should be guided by objective evidence such as field-test results, published reviews, and local appraisals based on previews.

A sampling of major audiovisual producers and distributors follows. The alphabetical lists of companies are grouped roughly according to the media format(s) with which they are identified.

Nonprojected Visuals

Educational Insights
150 W. Carob Street
Compton, CA   90220

Encyclopaedia Britannica Educational Corporation
425 North Michigan Avenue
Chicago, IL   60611

Silver Burdett Company
250 James Street
Morristown, NJ   07690

Society for Visual Education (SVE), Inc.
1345 Diversey Parkway
Chicago, IL   60614

Overhead Transparencies

Allyn & Bacon
AV Dept.
7 Wells Avenue
Newton, MA   02159

Denoyer-Geppert Audiovisuals
5235 Ravenswood Avenue
Chicago, IL   60640

Encyclopaedia Britannica Educational
Corporation
425 North Michigan Avenue
Chicago, IL   60611

Hammond, Inc.
515 Valley Street
Maplewood, NJ   07040

Instructo Products Company/
McGraw-Hill
18 Great Valley Parkway
Malvern, PA   19355

Lansford Publishing Company
P.O. Box 8711
San Jose, CA   95155

McGraw-Hill Film Division
674 Via de la Valle
P.O. Box 641
Del Mar, CA   92014

Milliken Publishing
1100 Research Boulevard
St. Louis, MO   63132

Rand McNally
P.O. Box 7500
Chicago, IL   60657

3M Audio Visual
Building 225-3NE
3M Center
St. Paul, MN   55144

United Transparencies
P.O. Box 688
Binghamton, NY   13902

Filmstrips

Ambrose Publishing Company
381 Park Avenue
Suite 1601
New York, NY   10016

Argus Communications
7440 Natchez Avenue
Niles, IL   60648

Audio Visual Narrative Arts, Inc.
Box 9
Pleasantville, NY   10570

BFA Educational Media
468 Park Avenue South
New York, NY   10016

Communacad, The Communications
Academy
31 Center Street
P.O. Box 541
Wilton, CT   06897

Coronet/MTI
108 Wilmot Avenue
Deerfield, IL   60015

Denoyer-Geppert Audiovisuals
5235 Ravenswood Avenue
Chicago, IL   60640

EMC Productions
300 York Avenue
St. Paul, MN   55101

Educational Images
P.O. Box 367
Lyons Falls, NY   13368

Encyclopaedia Britannica Educational
Corporation
425 North Michigan Avenue
Chicago, IL   60611

Eye Gate Media
3333 Elston Avenue
Chicago, IL   60611

International Film Bureau
332 South Michigan Avenue
Chicago, IL   60604

January Productions
124 Rhea Avenue
Hawthorne, NJ   07506

McGraw-Hill Film Division
674 Via de la Valle
Box 641
Del Mar, CA   92014

National Film Board of Canada
1251 Avenue of the Americas
New York, NY   10020

The Reading Laboratory, Inc.
P.O. Box 28
Georgetown, CT   06829

Society for Visual Education (SVE),
Inc.
1345 Diversey Parkway
Chicago, IL   60614

Sunburst Communications
39 Washington Avenue
Pleasantville, NY   10570

Time-Life Multimedia: See Ambrose
Publishing Company.

Weston Woods Studio
389 Newton Turnpike
Weston, CT   06883

Slides

American Museum of Natural History
Central Park West at 79th Street
New York, NY   10024

Art Now, Inc.
144 North 14 Street
Kenilworth, NJ   07033

The Center for Humanities, Inc.
Communications Park, Box 1000
Mt. Kisco, NY   10549

Clay-Adams
141 East 25th Street
New York, NY   10010

Harcourt Brace Jovanovich
757 Third Avenue
New York, NY   10017

Harper & Row Media
2350 Virginia Avenue
Hagerstown, MD   21740

Hester and Associates
11422 Harry Hines Boulevard
Suite 212
Dallas, TX   75229

Instructional Resources Corp.
351 East 50th Street
New York, NY   10022

Metropolitan Museum of Art
Educational Marketing
6 East 82d Street
New York, NY   10028

Museum of Modern Art
11 West 53d Street
New York, NY   10019

National Audubon Society
950 Third Avenue
New York, NY   10022

National Geographic Educational
Services
17th and M Streets
Washington, DC   20036

Sandak, Inc.
180 Harvard Avenue
Stamford, CT   06902

Society for Visual Education (SVE),
Inc.
1345 Diversey Parkway
Chicago, IL   60614

United Scientific Company
215 South Jefferson Street
Chicago, IL   60606

Ward's Natural Science
Establishment, Inc.
P.O. Box 92912
Rochester, NY   14692

Wilson/Lund, Inc.
1830 Sixth Avenue
Moline, IL   61265

Audio Materials

American Audio Prose Library
915 E. Broadway
Columbus, MO   65201

Audio Book Company
Box 7111
Pasadena, CA   91109

Bilingual Educational Services, Inc.
2514 South Grand Avenue
Los Angeles, CA   90007

Books on Tape
P.O. Box 7900
Newport Beach, CA   92060

Bowmar Records
4563 Colorado Boulevard
Los Angeles, CA   90039

Broadcasting Foundation of America
52 Vanderbilt Avenue
New York, NY   10017

Caedmon
1995 Broadway
New York, NY   10023

Capitol Records
1750 North Vine
Hollywood, CA   90028

Columbia Records
51 West 52d Street
New York, NY   10019

Coronet/MTI Instructional Media
108 Wilmot Road
Deerfield, IL   60015

Decca Records
445 Park Avenue
New York, NY   10022

Educational Corp. of America/
Rand McNally
P.O. Box 7600
Chicago, IL   60680

Effective Learning Systems
5221 Edina Industrial Boulevard
Edina, MN   55435

Grolier Educational Corp.
Sherman Turnpike
Danbury, CT   06816

G. K. Hall Audio Publishers
70 Lincoln Street
Boston, MA   02111

Imperial International Learning
Box 548
Kankakee, IL   60901

Information Management Institute
The Hill
Portsmouth, NH   03801

Language Master System
Bell & Howell
7100 N. McCormick Road
Chicago, IL   60645

Listening Library, Inc.
1 Park Avenue
Old Greenwich, CT   06870

Miller-Brody Productions
342 Madison Avenue
New York, NY   10017

National Public Radio
2025 M Street, N.W.
Washington, D.C.   20036

Pacifica Foundation
5316 Venice Boulevard
Los Angeles, CA   90010

RCA Educational Division
Front and Cooper Streets
Camden, NJ   08102

Scholastic Records
730 Broadway
New York, NY   10003

Science Research Associates (SRA)
155 North Wacker Drive
Chicago, IL   60606

Society for Visual Education (SVE),
Inc.
1345 Diversey Parkway
Chicago, IL   60614

The Soundworks
911 N. Fillmore Street
Arlington, VA   22201

Spoken Arts
310 North Avenue
New Rochelle, NY   10801

3M Company
3M Center
St. Paul, MN   55144

Tuto/Tape
107 France Street
Toms River, NJ   08753

Variable Speech Control
(VSC) Corporation
185 Berry Street
San Francisco, CA   94107

Watershed Tapes
P.O. Box 50145
Washington, DC   20004

Films

Ambrose Publishing Company
381 Park Avenue
Suite 1601
New York, NY   10016

American Management Association
135 West 50th Street
New York, NY   10020

BFA Educational Media
468 Park Avenue South
New York, NY   10016

Barr Films
3490 East Foothill Boulevard
Pasadena, CA   91107

Benchmark Films
145 Scarborough Road
Briarcliff Manor, NY   10510

Bullfrog Films
Olney, PA   19547

CRM/McGraw-Hill Films
Box 641
Del Mar, CA   92014

Churchill Films
662 North Robertson Boulevard
Los Angeles, CA   90069

Cinema Guild
1697 Broadway
New York, NY   10019

Coronet/MTI Film and Video
108 Wilmot Road
Deerfield, IL   60015

Educational Dimensions Group
P.O. Box 126
Stamford, CT   06907

Encyclopaedia Britannica
Educational Corporation
425 North Michigan Avenue
Chicago, IL   60611

Filmmakers Library
133 East 58th Street
Suite 307
New York, NY   10022

Filmic Archives
The Cinema Center
Botsford, CT   06404

Films for the Humanities
P.O. Box 2053
Princeton, NJ   08543

Films, Incorporated
733 Green Bay Road
Wilmette, IL   60091

Icarus Films
200 Park Avenue South
Suite 1319
New York, NY 10003

Indiana University
Field Services
Audio-Visual Center
Bloomington, IN 47405

International Film Bureau
332 South Michigan Avenue
Chicago, IL 60604

Learning Corporation of America
1350 Avenue of the Americas
New York, NY 10019

Modern Learning Aids
P.O. Box 1712
Rochester, NY 14603

National Audiovisual Center
8700 Edgeworth Drive
Capitol Heights, MD 20743

National Film Board of Canada
1251 Avenue of the Americas
New York, NY 10020

New Day Films
22 Riverview Drive
Wayne, NJ 07470

Phoenix Films: *See* BFA Educational
Media.

Pyramid Films and Video
P.O. Box 496
Media, PA 19063

Time-Life Films and Video: *See*
Ambrose Publishing Company.

Video

AIMS Media
6901 Woodley Avenue
Van Nuys, CA 91406

Agency for Instructional Technology
(AIT)
P.O. Box A
Bloomington, IN 47402

Ambrose Publishing Company
381 Park Avenue
Suite 1601
New York, NY 10016

The Annenberg/CPB Collection
733 Green Bay Road
Wilmette, IL 60091

CEL Educational Resources
515 Madison Avenue
New York, NY 10022

Catticus Corporation
2600 10th Street
Berkeley, CA 94710

Center for Southern Folklore
1216 Peabody Avenue
P.O. Box 40105
Memphis, TN 38104

Central Educational Network (CEN)
4300 West Paterson
Chicago, IL 60646

Coast Telecourses
11460 Warner Avenue
Fountain Valley, CA 92708

Dallas Community College District
Center for Telecommunications
4343 North Highway 67
Mesquite, TX 75150

Direct Cinema Ltd.
P.O. Box 69589
Los Angeles, CA 90069

Eastern Educational Network (EEN)
120 Boylston Street
Boston, MA 02116

Electronic Arts/Intermix
84 Fifth Avenue
New York, NY 10011

Evergreen Video Society
213 West 35th Street, Second Floor
New York, NY 10001

Facets Video
1517 W. Fullerton
Chicago, IL 60614

Great Plains National Instructional
Television Library (GPN)
Box 80669
Lincoln, NE 68501

International Historic Films
P.O. Box 29035
Chicago, IL 60629

The Kentucky Network (KET)
2230 Richmond Road
Suite 213
Lexington, KY 40502

Maryland Center for Public
Broadcasting
11767 Bonita Avenue
Owings Mills, MD 21117

National Geographic Society
17th and M Streets, N.W.
Washington, DC 20036

National Video Clearinghouse, Inc.
(NVC)
100 Lafayette Drive
Syosset, NY 11791

Pacific Mountain Network (PMN)
Suite 170-13
248 West 26th Avenue
Denver, CO 80211

PBS Video (Public Broadcasting
Service)
1320 Braddock Place
Alexandria, VA 22314

Polyglot Productions
P.O. Box 668
Cambridge, MA 02238

Southern Educational Communica-
tions Association (SECA)
P.O. Box 5966
Columbia, SC 29250

Speedimpex USA, Inc.
45-45 39th Street
Long Island City, NY 11104

Tamarelle's International Films
110 Cohasset Stage Road
Chico, CA 95926

Time-Life Video: *See* Ambrose
Publishing Company.

TVOntario
U.S. Sales Office
Suite 206
143 West Franklin Street
Chapel Hill, NC 27514

Video Data Bank
School of the Art Institute of Chicago
Columbus Drive at Jackson Boulevard
Chicago, IL 60603

Video-Forum, Division of Jeffrey
Norton Publishers
145 East 49th Street
New York, NY 10017

Voyage Company
888 Seventh Avenue, Fourth Floor
New York, NY 10106

Western Instructional Television,
Inc. (WIT)
1438 North Gower Street
Los Angeles, CA 90028

World Video
P.O. Box 30469
Knoxville, TN 37930

Simulations and Games

Avalon Hill Company
4517 Harford Road
Baltimore, MD 21214

Denoyer Geppert Co.
5215 N. Ravenswood Avenue
Chicago, IL 60640

Didactic Systems, Inc.
P.O. Box 457
Cranford, NJ 07016

Educational Research
P.O. Box 4205
Warren, NJ 07060

Edu-Game
P.O. Box 1144
Sun Valley, CA 91352

Houghton-Mifflin
2 Park Street
Boston, MA 02107

Interact Company
P.O. Box 262
Lakeside, CA 92040

Management Research Systems, Ltd.
Suite 201, Executive Center
P.O. Box 1585
Ponte Vedra Beach, FL 32082

Marginal Context Ltd.
35 St. Andrew's Road
Cambridge CB4 1DL
England

Harvey Mette
School of Education
Long Island University
Greenvale, NY 11548

Simile II
P.O. Box 910
Del Mar, CA 92014

Simulations Publications, Inc.
44 East 23d Street
New York, NY 10010

Teaching Aids Company
925 South 300 West
Salt Lake City, UT 84101

Wff 'N Proof
1490-TZ South Boulevard
Ann Arbor, MI 48104

John Wiley & Sons, Inc.
605 Third Avenue
New York, NY 10158

Computer Courseware

Atari, Inc.
1312 Crossman Avenue
P.O. Box 61657
Sunnyvale, CA 94086

Avalon Hill Microcomputer Games
4517 Harford Road
Baltimore, MD 21214

C-4 Computer Company
115 North Neil Street
P.O. Box 1408
Champaign, IL 61820

Classroom Consortia Media
One Edgewater Plaza, Suite 209
Staten Island, NY 10305

COMPress
Division of Van Nostrand Reinhold
P.O. Box 102
Wentworth, NH 03282

CONDUIT
The University of Iowa,
Oakdale Campus
Iowa City, IA 55242

Harcourt Brace Jovanovich
1250 Sixth Avenue
San Diego, CA 92101

Houghton-Mifflin
P.O. Box 683
Hanover, NH 03755

IBM, Electronic Communications,
Inc.
Suite 220
1311 Executive Center Drive
Tallahassee, FL 32301

Instructional Software
131 Clarendon Street
Boston, MA 02116

Intellectual Software
798 North Avenue
Bridgeport, CT 06606

Milliken Publishing Company
1100 Research Boulevard
P.O. Box 21579
St. Louis, MO 63132

Minnesota Educational Computing
Corporation (MECC)
3490 Lexington Avenue North
St. Paul, MN 55126

Opportunities for Learning, Inc.
20417 Nordhoff Street
Reseda, CA 91335

Plato Educational Courseware
Control Data Corporation
P.O. Box 0
Minneapolis, MN 55440

Scholastic, Inc.
P.O. Box 7502
Jefferson City, MO 65102

Society for Visual Education,
Inc. (SVE)
1345 W. Diversey Parkway
Chicago, IL 60614

Softswap
San Mateo County Office of Education
333 Main Street
Redwood, CA 94063

Sunburst Communications
39 Washington Avenue
P.O. Box 40
Pleasantville, NY 10570

John Wiley & Sons, Inc.
605 Third Avenue
New York, NY 10158

REVIEW SOURCES

Booklist. American Library Association, 50 East Huron Street, Chicago,
IL 60611. Reviews all levels of
audiovisual materials. Most materials included are recommended.

Choice. Association of College and
Research Libraries, 100 Riverview
Center, Middletown, CT 06457.
Reviews college-level instructional
materials.

AFVA Evaluations. American Film and
Video Association (AFVA), 920
Barnsdale Road, Suite 152,
La Grange, IL 60525

EPIE Reports. EPIE (Educational Products Information Exchange) Institute, P.O. Box 839, Water Mill, NY
11976. Publishes several series of
evaluative reports on instructional
materials. Those covering conventional audiovisual and print materials are:

- *Textbook PRO/FILES* (biennial,
  K–12 textbooks)
- *EPIEgram: Materials* (monthly,
  K–12 textbooks and related mate-
  rials)
- *EPIE Report: Materials* (biennial,
  trends in instructional materials)
- *A-V/V PRO/FILES* (biennial,
  audiovisual and video products)
- *EPIEgram: Equipment* (monthly,
  audiovisual and video equip-
  ment)

- *EPIE Report: Equipment* (biennial, trends in media and microcomputer hardware)

Film Library Quarterly. See *Sightlines.*

Film and Video News. 70 Elm Place, Red Bank, NJ 07701

Media & Methods. Wagman Publishers, 1429 Walnut Street, Philadelphia, PA 19102

Media Review. Key Productions, 346 Ethan Allen Highway, Ridgefield, CT 06877. Monthly; carries objective reviews of all types of audiovisual materials; available in three editions: K–College complete, K–Grade 8, Grade 9–College.

Library Journal. R. R. Bowker, 205 East 42d Street, New York, NY 10017

School Library Journal. R. R. Bowker, 205 East 42d Street, New York, NY 10017

School Library Media Quarterly. American Association of School Librarians, American Library Association, 50 East Huron Street, Chicago, IL 60611

Science Books and Films. [Variant title: AAAS Science Books and Films.] American Association for the Advancement of Science, 1776 Massachusetts Avenue, N.W., Washington, DC 20036

Sightlines. Incorporates *Film Library Quarterly.* American Film and Video Association (AFVA), 920 Barnsdale Road, Suite 152, La Grange, IL 60525

Courseware

Courseware Report Card. 150 West Carob Street, Compton, CA 90220

EPIE Reports. EPIE (Educational Product Information Exchange) Institute, P.O. Box 839, Water Mill, NY 11976. Publishes several series of evaluative reports on instructional materials. Those covering computer software are:

- *MICROgram* (monthly, educational computing products)
- *Micro PRO/FILES* (bimonthly, indepth analyses of microcomputer hardware and software)
- *The Educational Software Selector—TESS* (definitive information source on availability of all types of microcomputer educational software, including many evaluative comments; published jointly with Teachers College Press, Columbia University)

Journal of Courseware Review. Apple Education Foundation, 20525 Mariani Avenue, Cupertino, CA 95014

Microcomputers in Education. Queue, Inc., 5 Chapel Hill Drive, Fairfield, CT 06432

Micro-Scope. JEM Research, Discovery Park, University of Victoria, P.O. Box 1700, Victoria, BC V8W 2Y2, Canada

MicroSIFT. Northwest Regional Educational Lab, 300 SW Sixth Street, Portland, OR 97204

Pipeline. Conduit Clearinghouse, University of Iowa, Oakdale Campus, Iowa City, IA 55242

Purser's Magazine. P.O. Box 266, El Dorado, CA 95623

School Microware Reviews. Dresden Associates, P.O. Box 246, Dresden, ME 04342

Software Review. Meckler Publishing, 520 Riverside Avenue, Westport, CT 06880

OTHER REFERENCE TOOLS

For more extensive, annotated guides to media reviews or descriptions or other audiovisual information sources, consult the following:

Chisholm, Margaret E. *Media Indexes and Review Sources.* (College Park, Md.: School of Library and Information Services, University of Maryland, 1972).

Hart, Thomas L.; Hunt, Mary A.; and Woolls, Blanche, eds. *Multi-Media Indexes, Lists and Review Sources: A Bibliographic Guide.* (New York: Marcel Dekker, 1975).

Media Review Digest. Annual. (Ann Arbor, Mich.: Pierian Press).

Rufsvold, Margaret I. *Guides to Educational Media.* 4th ed. (Chicago: American Library Association, 1977).

Sive, Mary Robinson. *Selecting Instructional Media.* 3d ed. (Littleton, Colo.: Libraries Unlimited, 1983).

Free and Inexpensive Materials

WITH the ever-increasing costs of instructional materials, teachers and trainers should be aware of the wide variety of materials that can be obtained for classroom use at little or no cost. These free and inexpensive materials can supplement instruction in many subjects, or they can even be the main source of instruction on certain topics. For example, many films are available for loan without a rental fee; the only expense is the return postage. By definition, any material that you can borrow or acquire permanently for instructional purposes without a significant cost (usually less than a couple of dollars) can be referred to as "free and inexpensive."

The types of free and inexpensive materials are almost endless. The more commonly available items include posters, games, pamphlets, brochures, reports, charts, maps, books, filmstrips, audiotapes, films, videotapes, multimedia kits, and realia. The more costly items, such as films and videotapes, are usually sent only on a free-loan basis and must be returned to the supplier after use. In some instances, single copies of audiocassettes, filmstrips, and videocassettes will be donated to your organization to be shared among many users.

ADVANTAGES

FREE and inexpensive materials can provide up-to-date information that is not contained in textbooks or other commercially available media. In addition, they often provide more in-depth treatment of a topic. If classroom quantities are available, printed materials can be read and discussed by the learners as textbook material would be. If quantities are limited, they can be placed in a learning center for independent or small-group study. Audiovisual materials lend themselves to classroom presentation by the instructor. Individual students who want to explore a subject of interest can use the audiovisual materials for self-study or for presentation to the class. Posters, charts, and maps can be combined to create topical displays. These can be motivational, as in the case of a safety poster, or can be used for direct instruction, as in studying the solar system. Materials that do not have to be returned can be modified and adapted for varied instructional or display purposes.

Materials that are expendable have the extra advantage of allowing learners to get actively involved with them. Students can cut out pictures for notebooks and displays. They can assemble printed information and visuals in scrapbooks as reports of group projects. Of course, when treating free materials as raw materials for student projects, you will have to develop your own objectives and plan appropriate learning activities to go along with the materials.

LIMITATIONS

SEVERAL potential limitations of free and inexpensive materials must be taken into consideration. First, many free and inexpensive materials can be described as sponsored materials because their production and distribution are sponsored by particular organizations. These organizations—whether private corporations, nonprofit associations, or government agencies—often have a message to convey. That message might be in the form of outright advertising. If so, you will have to be aware of your own organization's policies on the use of advertising matter. You may consider covering or removing the advertisement, but that, too, raises ethical questions in view of the effort and expense that the sponsor has incurred in providing the materials to you. In addition, you are removing the identification of the source of the material, and that prevents disclosure of any vested interests by which one might judge the information presented.

What may be even more troublesome to deal with is sponsored material that does not contain outright advertising but does promote some special interest in a less obvious way. For example, a "fun in the sun" poster may subtly promote the eating of junk food without including the name or logo of any manufacturer. As discussed in Chapter 8 in regard to sponsored films, a recent study by the Center for the Study of Responsive Law* disclosed a persistent tendency for privately sponsored materials to convey self-serving messages. Propagandistic or more subtly biased materials can thus enter the curriculum through the "back door." Careful previewing and caution are advisable when you consider sponsored materials. Teachers should solicit informational materials on the same subject from several points of view. Thereby, students are afforded a balance and diversity of opinions.

The Center for Study of Responsive Law (P.O. Box 19367, Washington, D.C. 20036) provides a free annotated bibliography, *Alternative Resources for Curriculum Balance,* upon receipt of a self-addressed, stamped envelope. It lists selected informational and educational resources in subject areas predominant in corporate educational efforts. The intent is to help provide a balance of resources and perspectives on controversial issues.

The final potential limitation is a logistical one. With the increas-

ing expense of producing both printed and audiovisual materials, your supplier may have to impose limits on the quantities of items available at one time. You may not be able to obtain a copy of the material for every student in the class.

LOCAL SOURCES

Many local government agencies, community groups, and private businesses provide informational materials on free loan. Public libraries often make films, prints, and filmstrips available. Even libraries in small communities may have access to films through a statewide network. These materials usually can be loaned to local organizations. However, public library collections are often entertainment oriented, as would be expected in a service designed for the general public, so you will probably not find in them a great many strictly instructional materials. Other government agencies, such as the Cooperative Extension Service, public health departments, and parks departments, make materials available for use in schools, churches, hospitals, and companies.

Community organizations such as the Red Cross, the League of Women Voters, medical societies, and the like welcome opportunities to spread information about their special interests. Films, slide-tapes, printed material, and guest speakers are frequently offered.

Among business organizations, utilities—telephone, electric, gas, and water companies—are most likely to employ education specialists who can inform you about what instructional services they offer. Chambers of commerce often can suggest private corpora-

tions that might supply materials of interest to you.

NATIONAL AND INTERNATIONAL SOURCES

Nationally, one of the most prolific sources of free and inexpensive materials is the federal government. In the United States, two federal agencies offer special access to materials—the U.S. Government Printing Office and the National Audiovisual Center. Your key to the tremendous wealth of posters, charts, brochures, books, and other printed government documents that are available to the general public is "Selected U.S. Government Publications," a monthly catalog of all new listings. You can have your name added to the free mailing list by sending a request to: Superintendent of Documents, U.S. Government Printing Office, Washington, DC 20402.

The National Audiovisual Center is the central clearinghouse for all federal government–produced audiovisual materials. Its catalog, *Selected Audiovisual Materials Produced by the United States Government,* is issued every four years, with a supplement every two years. It lists more than 12,000 titles of films, videotapes, slide sets, audiotapes, and multimedia kits that have been produced by or for government agencies. All are available for purchase; the 16-mm films (constituting 80 percent of the collection) can be rented; some of the materials are made available for free loan from regional sources. For further information, write to: National Audiovisual Center, Information Services/RN, General Services Administration, Washington DC 20409.

Trade associations and professional associations also aim to

_____
* Sheila Harty. *Hucksters in the Classroom: A Review of Industry Propaganda in the Schools.* Washington, D.C.: Center for Study of Responsive Law, 1980.

acquaint the general public with their own fields of interest and the causes they promote. Some examples are the American Society of Civil Engineers, the National Dairy Council, the American Petroleum Institute, National Wildlife Federation, American Heart Association, and National Association for the Advancement of Colored People.

Private corporations that operate on the national or even international basis offer sponsored materials, as discussed earlier in this appendix. Examples of these businesses include Goodyear Tire and Rubber Company, Exxon, and AT&T.

Most foreign governments disseminate information about their countries to promote trade, tourism, and international understanding. They typically offer free posters, maps, and informational booklets plus films on a free-loan basis. To find out what is available for any particular country, write to the embassy of that country in Washington, D.C. International organizations such as the Organization of American States (OAS), United Nations, and the North Atlantic Treaty Organization (NATO) also operate information offices. Popular sources of posters of foreign countries are the airline and cruise ship companies. Consult your local travel agent for possible materials and addresses.

COMPREHENSIVE INFORMATION SOURCES

I T would be impractical to list here all the thousands of suppliers of free and inexpensive materials, much less to offer up-to-date addresses. Instead, we recommend that you consult one of the many books and catalogs devoted specifically to free and

inexpensive materials. They are updated regularly and contain full name, address, and cost information.

The most comprehensive information source on free and inexpensive materials is the series of guides published by Educators Progress Service, 214 Center Street, Randolph, WI 53956. There is a cost for the guides themselves; the materials listed in the guides are free and inexpensive. Revised annually, the titles in this series include:

Educators Index of Free Materials

Educators Guide to Free Films

Educators Guide to Free Filmstrips and Slides

Educators Guide to Free Teaching Aids

Educators Guide to Free Audio and Video Materials

Educators Guide to Free Social Studies Materials

Educators Guide to Free Science Materials

Educators Guide to Free Guidance Materials

Educators Guide to Free Health, Physical Education and Recreation Materials

Educators Guide to Free Home Economics Materials

Elementary Teachers Guide to Free Curriculum Materials

Guide to Free Computer Materials

Books that list sources of free and inexpensive materials are:

Aubrey, Ruth H. *Selected Free Materials for Classroom Teachers.* (Belmont, CA: Pitman Learning). Updated periodically.

Cardozo, Peter. *The Third Whole Kids Catalog.* (New York: Bantam Books, 1981).

Feinman, Jeffrey. *Freebies for Kids.* (New York: Wanderer Books, 1979).

Free Stuff Editors. *Free Stuff for Kids.* (Deephaven, MN: Meadowbrook Press, 1984).

Moore, Norman R., ed. *Free and Inexpensive Learning Materials.* (Nashville: George Peabody College; Incentive Publishers, Inc., distributor). Updated biennially.

Weisinger, Thelma. *1001 Valuable Things You Can Get Free.* (New York: Bantam Books). Updated periodically.

National-level services for free-loan films are:

Association-Sterling Films, which provides free-loan films from its twelve offices in the United States and Canada.

Modern Talking Picture Service (5000 Park Street North, St. Petersburg, FL 33709), which provides sponsored films for free loan from its twenty-two offices in major cities throughout the United States and Canada.

HOW TO OBTAIN FREE AND INEXPENSIVE MATERIALS

W HEN you have determined what you can use and where you can obtain it, correspond on school or company stationery; some agencies will not supply free and inexpensive materials unless you do. For classroom quantities (when they are available), send just one letter. Do not have each student write individually. If a single student is requesting one copy of something for a class project, the student can write the letter, but you should also sign it. We recommend that you request a preview copy of the material before requesting multiple copies. Don't send a request for "anything you have"! Be specific and at least specify the subject area and the grade level. Only ask for what you need. Don't stockpile materials or take advantage of a "free" offer. Somebody is paying for those materials, so don't waste them. Follow up with a thank-you note to the supplier, and let them know how you used the materials and what the students' reaction was to them. Be courteous, but be honest. Many suppliers attempt to improve free and inexpensive materials on the basis of user comments.

APPRAISING FREE AND INEXPENSIVE MATERIALS

As with any other type of material, appraise the educational value of these materials critically. Some are very "slick" (technically well presented) but are not educationally sound. The "Appraisal Checklist: Free and Inexpensive Materials" is intended to help you make these judgments.

Appraisal Checklist: Free and Inexpensive Materials

Topic _____ **Type of Material** _____
(booklet, filmstrip, tape, film, etc.)

Source _____

Cost _____ **Date** _____

Objectives (stated or implied):

Brief Description:

Rating	High		Medium		Low	Comments
Free from undesirable advertising and/or bias	☐	☐	☐	☐	☐	
Accurate, honest, and up-to-date	☐	☐	☐	☐	☐	
Useful in meeting objectives	☐	☐	☐	☐	☐	
Appropriate level for the audience	☐	☐	☐	☐	☐	
Potential uses (alone or with other media)	☐	☐	☐	☐	☐	
Readability	☐	☐	☐	☐	☐	
Illustration quality (well done and eye-catching)	☐	☐	☐	☐	☐	
Durability (if to be reused)	☐	☐	☐	☐	☐	

Strong Points:

Weak Points:

Reviewer _____

Position _____

Recommended action _____   **Date** _____

APPENDIX C

Copyright Guidelines

BACKGROUND: COPYRIGHT LAW

To protect the financial interests of the creators, producers, and distributors of original works of information and/or art, nations adopt what are referred to as copyright laws. These laws set the conditions under which anyone can copy, in whole or in part, original works transmittable in any medium. Without copyright laws, writers, artists, filmmakers, and the like would not "receive the encouragement they need to create and the remuneration they fairly deserve for their creations" (from the legislative 1976 Omnibus Copyright Revision Act). The flow of creative work would be reduced to a trickle, and we would all be the losers.

The first copyright law in the United States was passed by Congress in 1790. In 1976, Congress enacted the latest copyright law, taking into consideration technological developments that had occurred since the passage of the previous Copyright Act of 1909. For example, in 1909, anyone who wanted to make a single copy of a literary work for personal use had to do so by hand. The very process imposed a limitation on the quantity copied. Today, a photocopier can do the work in seconds; the limitation has disappeared. Nor did the 1909

law provide full protection for films and sound recordings, nor anticipate the need to protect radio and television. As a result, violations of the law, and abuses of the intent of the law, have made serious inroads on the financial rewards of authors and artists. We are all aware (and probably guilty) of photocopy abuse, but did you know that more than one out of three cassettes of pop music sold in the open market is a pirated copy of the original production? Or that under-the-counter videotapes of new feature films are available *before* general distribution of the films to theaters takes place? Abuses such as these were not even contemplated in the 1909 law. Clearly, corrections were in order. The 1976 Copyright Act has not prevented these abuses fully, but it has clarified the legal rights of the injured parties and given them an avenue for redress.

More than a decade has gone by since the act was passed. During that time, the act has been amended to include computer software, and guidelines have been adopted for fair use of television broadcasts. These changes have cleared up much of the confusion and conflict that followed in the wake of the 1976 legislation.

However, we must remember that the fine points of the law will

have to be decided by the courts and by acceptable common practice over an extended period of time. As these decisions and agreements are made, we can modify our behavior accordingly. As of now, then, we need to interpret the law and its guidelines as accurately as we can, and to act in a fair, judicious manner.

INTERPRETING THE COPYRIGHT ACT

ALTHOUGH detailed examination of the law is beyond the scope of this text, here we describe the basic framework of the law and present examples of violations and examples of reasonable interpretation of "fair use" to help guide you in the decisions you need to make about copying protected works for class use. The law sets forth in section 107 four basic criteria for determining the principle of fair use:

1. The purpose and character of the use, including whether such use is of a commercial nature or is for nonprofit educational purposes
2. The nature of the copyrighted work
3. The amount and substantiality of the portion used in relation to the copyrighted work as a whole

4. The effect of the use on the potential market for or value of the copyrighted work

The following interpretations are based on several sets of guidelines issued to spell out the criteria in section 107.

For educational use, an instructor may make a single copy of a chapter from a book; an article from a periodical or newspaper; a short story, short essay, or short poem, whether or not from a collective work; an illustration from a book, periodical, or newspaper. The context in which the term *teacher* is used seems to be broad enough to include support personnel working with teachers.

The guidelines further stipulate the amount of material that may be copied and the special circumstances that permit multiple copies. Fair use is defined as one illustration per book or periodical, 250 words from a poem, and 10 percent of a prose work up to 1,000 words. Multiple copies cannot exceed the number of students in a class, nor can there be more than nine instances of multiple copying for one course during one class term. No more than one short poem, article, story, essay, or two excerpts may be copied from the same author. The limitations of nine instances and one item or two excerpts do not apply to current news periodicals, newspapers, and current news sections of other periodicals.

However, multiple copies must meet a "spontaneity" test. The copying must be initiated by the individual teacher, not directed or suggested by any other authority. The decision to use the work, *and* the "inspiration" for its use, must be close enough to the moment of use to preclude waiting for permission from the copyright holder. This means, of

course, that the same "inspiration" cannot occur the same time next term.

The last guideline, market value, means that copying must not substitute for purchase of the original, or create or replace an anthology or a compilation of works protected by copyright. It also prohibits copying works intended to be consumable, for example, workbooks or standardized tests.

If a work is "out of print," that is, no longer available from the copyright holder, then you are not affecting the market value of the work by copying it. The market-value guideline can act in favor of the user, as we will see from the following examples.

Unfortunately, neither the law nor the guidelines spell out fair use of media other than print. Eventually, fair-use criteria, therefore, may evolve more out of acceptable common practice than out of the law and guidelines.

As for music, the new copyright law protects the performance of the work as well as the work itself. For example, Beethoven's Fifth Symphony may be in the public domain, but the recorded performance by the Chicago Symphony Orchestra is protected.

The term, or period of time, of the copyright has been changed by the new act. For an individual author, the copyright term continues for his or her life and for 50 years after death. If a work is made for hire, that is, by an employee or by someone commissioned to do so, the term is 100 years from the year of creation or 75 years from the year of first publication or distribution, whichever comes first. Works copyrighted prior to January 1, 1978, are protected for 28 years and then may have their copyrights renewed. The renewal will

protect them for a term of 75 years after their original copyright date.

Computer Software and Copyright

In December 1980, Congress amended the copyright act to clear up questions of fair use of copyrighted computer programs. The changes defined *computer program* for copyright purposes and set forth permissible and nonpermissible use of copyrighted computer programs. According to the amended law, you may

- Make one back-up or archival copy of a computer program;
- Adapt a computer program from one language to another if the program is not available in that language;
- Add features to a copyrighted program in order to make better use of the program;
- Adapt a copyrighted program to meet local needs.

Without the copyright owner's permission, you may not

- Make multiple copies of a copyrighted program;
- Make replacement copies from an archival or back-up copy;
- Make copies of copyrighted programs to be sold, leased, loaned, transmitted, or given away;
- Sell a locally produced adaptation of a copyrighted program;
- Make multiple copies of an adaptation of a copyrighted program, even for use within a school or school district;
- Make any use of the printed copyrighted software documentation that is not allowed by the copyrighted program.

These guidelines would seem to be reasonable while still

protecting the proprietary rights of copyright holders. In fact, the guidelines seem to be more liberal than those affecting the repurposing of audiovisual materials.

Off-Air Videotaping

The Copyright Act of 1976 did not cover educational uses of video-taped copies of copyrighted broadcasts. A negotiating committee composed of representatives from industry, education, and government agreed on a set of guidelines for videorecording of broadcasts for educational use. According to these guidelines, you may

- Ask a media center to record the program for you if you cannot or if you lack the equipment;
- Retain a videotaped copy of a broadcast (including cable transmission) for a period of forty-five calendar days, after which the program must be erased;
- Use the program in class once during the first ten school days of the forty-five calendar days, and a second time if instruction needs to be reinforced;
- Have professional staff view the program several times for evaluation purposes during the full forty-five-day period;
- Make a limited number of copies to meet legitimate needs, but these copies must be erased when the original videotape is erased;
- Use only a part of the program if instructional needs warrant (but see the next list);
- Enter into a licensing agreement with the copyright holder to continue use of the program.

You, or a media center, may not

- Videotape premium cable services such as HBO without express permission;
- Alter the original content of the program;
- Exclude the copyright notice on the program;
- Videorecord in anticipation of a request for use—the request to record must come from an instructor;
- Retain the program, and any copies, after forty-five days.

Remember that these guidelines are not part of the copyright act but are, rather, a "gentleman's agreement" between producers and educators. You may accept them as guidelines in good faith.

As stated before, final interpretation of the provisions of the 1976 Copyright Act will have to wait for future court decisions to define the language and to resolve internal contradictions or conflicts in the law. For example, under the 1976 law, a suit was brought against Sony to prohibit the company from stating in its ads that videotape recorders may be used to record television programs for future viewing. In 1984 the Supreme Court decided that the copyright law does not prohibit an individual from videotaping a television program for personal viewing at a later time.

Until the courts decide otherwise, it would seem reasonable that teachers (and media professionals) can use the fair-use criteria to copy materials that would seem otherwise to be protected. Some examples follow:

1. If the school media center subscribes to a journal or magazine to which you refer students and you want to make slides of several graphics or photos to help students understand an article, it would seem

that this is fair use based on the following:

   a. The nature of the work is general, its audience (and market) is not predominantly the educational community.
   b. The character of use is non-profit.
   c. The amount copied is small.
   d. There is no intent to replace the original, only to make it more useful in a class in conjunction with the copyrighted words.

2. If *you* subscribe to a journal and want to include several pictures from it in a presentation in class, it would seem reasonable to do so for the same reasons.

3. Suppose a film you frequently use drops out of the distributor's catalog; it is "out of print." To protect the print you have, it would seem reasonable, after unsuccessful attempts to reach the copyright owner to get permission, to videotape the film and use the videotape in class. If, at a later date, the film is put back on the market by the same or another distributor, you must go back to using the film. This is not uncommon. For example, *Pacific 231,* an effective film to demonstrate editing, was originally distributed by Young America Films. After Young America Films was purchased by another company, *Pacific 231* was dropped from the catalog. It was not available for almost twenty years. Then Pyramid Films secured the distribution rights and it is now available for purchase. During the long period of unavailability, it would have been reasonable to use a videotape copy.

4. From experience you know that recordings of literary works put out by major record labels may disappear from their catalogs in a few years. For example, RCA Victor once made available a recording of Shakespeare's *Midsummer Night's Dream* with Mendelsohn's incidental music inserted at the appropriate place. It is no longer available. If you had taped the records, put the tapes on the shelf as a contingency, and used the records in class, you would at least now have the tape available if your records were damaged. You would not have intended to deprive anyone of income; you would simply have used the technology to guarantee availability to yourself.

5. You have rented a film for a specific date, but circumstances beyond your control prevent your using it before it is due back. It would seem reasonable, after requesting permission (a telephone call could clear it), to videotape the film, use the videotape, and then erase the tape after use. Again, you have not deprived anyone of income. (This should **never** be done if the film is in on a preview basis!)

With the cited exceptions of broadcast programs and computer software, there aren't any guidelines for fair use of nonprint materials. Until the courts decide otherwise, it would seem reasonable to extend the print guidelines to nonprint materials in a judicious fashion.

We are not advocating deliberate violation of the law. On the contrary, we support the intent of the copyright law to protect the financial interests of copyright holders. What we are saying is that the proper balance in the application of the guidelines eventually has to be decided by the courts and by accepted common practice. In the meantime, reasonable interpretations of fair use may permit you to do copying that might seem on the face of it to be prohibited.

Primacy of First Sale

Have you ever wondered why public libraries, book rental businesses, and video rental clubs are not in violation of the copyright law when they do not pay royalties to copyright owners on the items they circulate or rent? They come under the protection of what is referred to as the *primacy of first sale.* This means that the purchaser of a copyrighted work may loan or rent the work without having to pay a second royalty. At the present time, great pressure is being brought to bear on Congress to amend the law to require anyone who rents a copyrighted work to pay a royalty to the copyright owner. As you might expect, the television and motion picture industries are putting on the pressure, and video rental agencies are resisting the change.

Although it is not likely that *free* circulation of material from public libraries and regional media centers will be affected by a change such as this, college and university *rental* of films and videotapes certainly will be. Educators need to keep on the alert for any possible changes in the first-sale doctrine that could adversely affect access to materials.

SEEKING PERMISSION FOR USE OF COPYRIGHTED MATERIALS

Aside from staying within the guidelines that limit but recognize our legal right to free use of copyrighted materials, what else can we do to assure our students access to these materials? We can, obviously, seek permission from the copyright owners and, if required, pay a fee for their use. Certain requests will ordinarily be granted without payment of fee—transcripts for the blind, for example, or material to be tried out once in an experimental program. (Use of materials in the public domain—materials on which copyright protection has run out, for instance, or materials produced by federal government employees in the course of their regular work—need no permission.)

In seeking permission to use copyrighted materials, it is generally best to contact the producer or publisher of the material rather than its creator. Whether or not the creator is the holder of the copyright, the producer or publisher generally handles permission requests and sets fees. The address of the producer (if not given on the material) can be obtained from various reference sources, including the *Literary Market Place,* the *Audio-Visual Market Place,* and *Ulrich's International Periodicals Directory.*

Be as specific as possible in your request for permission. Give the page numbers and exact amount of print material you wish to copy. (If possible, send along a photocopy of the material.) Describe nonprint material fully. State how you intend to use the material, where you intend to use it, how you intend to reproduce it, your purpose in using it, and the number of copies you wish to make.

Remember that fees for reproduction of copyrighted materials are sometimes negotiable. If the fee seems to you to be too high or otherwise beyond your budget, do not be hesitant about asking that it be lowered.

If for *any* reason you decide not to use the requested material, make this fact known to the publisher or producer. Without this formal notice it is likely to be assumed that you have in fact used it as requested, and you may be dunned for a fee you do not in fact owe.

Keep copies of all your correspondence and records of all other contacts that you made relevant to seeking permission for use of copyrighted instructional materials.

THE TEACHER AND VIOLATION OF THE COPYRIGHT LAW

WHAT happens if an educator knowingly and deliberately violates the copyright law? The 1976 act contains both criminal and civil sanctions. The criminal penalty can be a fine up to $1,000 and a year in jail. Copyright owners may recover up to $50,000 in civil court for loss of royalties due to infringement. Furthermore, in any infringement lawsuit, the employing institution can be held liable along with the instructor.

The producers of materials for the education market are just as serious about seeing the copyright act enforced as are the companies serving the general public. In 1982 a high school home economics teacher in San Diego was brought into court by a publisher for copying substantially more than 10 percent of a copyrighted book. This really was a test of the legality of the guidelines. Because the guidelines are not part of the law, and the law treats fair use only in general terms, the courts are not required to consider them. The district court agreed with the teacher but was overruled by the appellate court, and the teacher was found guilty. Unfortunately, the case was not carried to the Supreme Court by the teacher, so we do not have as definitive a ruling as we do in the video case that follows.[*]

A Board of Cooperative Educational Services was taken to court and found guilty of distributing videotapes of copyrighted material. The media personnel in this case flagrantly violated the law.[†] Punitive damages aside, in a profession devoted to promoting ethical behavior, deliberate violation of the copyright law is unacceptable.

REFERENCES

WE have concentrated here on the problem of copying copyrighted materials for educational purposes and on the guidelines set up under the 1976 act to help assure that such duplication does not violate the law or otherwise infringe on copyright ownership. The act itself contains hundreds of these provisions covering all aspects of copyright law and ownership. Some of these other provisions are of particular interest to educators—provisions covering copying by libraries, for example, or use of copyrighted materials for instruction of the visually handicapped and the hearing impaired. Other provisions may be of interest to those who have authored or plan someday to author or produce instructional materials. In any case, it behooves each of us to be familiar at least with those aspects of the law likely to affect our own special activities and interests.

---

[*] "Appeals Court Cites 'Fair Use' Guidelines in Copyright Ruling." *Chronicle of Higher Education* (February 9, 1983), p. 28.
[†] Encyclopaedia Britannica Educational Corporation vs. The Board of Cooperative Educational Services (BOCES).

Print References

"Copyright Law and the Classroom." *Journal of Law and Education* (Spring 1986), pp. 229–236.

Explaining the New Copyright Law. (Washington, D.C.: Association of American Publishers, 1977).

Helm, Virginia M. *What Educators Should Know about Copyright.* (Bloomington, Ind.: Phi Delta Kappa, 1986).

Johnson, Beda. *How to Acquire Legal Copies of Video Programs.* (San Diego, Calif.: Video Resources Enterprise, 1986).

Miller, Jerome. *Using Copyrighted Videocassettes in Classrooms, Libraries and Training Centers.* (Friday Harbor, Wash.: Copyright Information Services, 1987).

Reed, Mary H. *The Copyright Primer for Librarians and Educators.* (Washington, D.C.: National Education Association, 1987.)

Sinofsky, Esther R. *Off-Air Videotaping in Education.* (New York: R. R. Bowker, 1986).

Talab, Rosemary Sturdevant. "Copyright, Fair Use, and the School Microcomputer Lab." *Educational Technology* (February 1984), pp. 30–32.

Troost, F. William. "Students—The Forgotten People in Copyright Considerations." *Educational-Industrial Television* (June 1983), pp. 70–74.

The Visual Artist's Guide to the New Copyright Law. (New York: Graphic Artists Guild, 1978).

Vlcek, Charles W. *Copyright Policy Development: A Resource Book for Educators.* (Friday Harbor, Wash.: Copyright Information Services, 1987).

Voegel, George H. "Copyrights Revisited." In G. H. Voegel, ed. *Advances in Instructional Technology.* New Directions for Community Colleges, no. 55. (San Francisco: Jossey-Bass, 1986).

Audiovisual References

Computer/Copyright Seminar, 1987. Friday Harbor, Wash.: Copyright

Information Services, 1987. Audio-cassette and documents.

Copyright Law. Produced by the Office of Instructional Technology, South Carolina Department of Education and South Carolina ETV Network. Lincoln, Nebr.: Great Plains

National Instructional Television Library, 1986. Videocassette. 20 minutes.

Copyright Law: What Every School, College and Public Library Should Know. Skokie, Ill.: Association for

Information Media and Equipment, 1987. Videotape.

Video/Copyright Seminar, 1987. Friday Harbor, Wash.: Copyright Information Services, 1987. Audiocassette and documents.

APPENDIX D

Glossary

accommodation. The cognitive process of modifying a schema or creating new schemata.

accountability. The idea that a person or agency should be able to demonstrate publicly the worth of the activities carried out.

acetate. A transparent plastic sheet, associated with overhead projection.

ad hoc network. An electronic distribution system that is rented by the user and set up for one-time use, for example, for a teleconference.

advance organizer. Outlines, "previews," and other such pre-instructional cues used to promote retention of verbal material, as proposed by David Ausubel. Also referred to as preinstructional strategies.

adventure game. An arcade video game that combines a visualized fantasy story stored on videodisc with microprocessor-controlled interaction with the player.

affective domain. The domain of human learning that involves changes in interests, attitudes, and values, and the development of appreciations and adequate adjustment.

animation. A film technique in which the artist gives motion to still images by creating and juxtaposing a series of pictures with small incremental changes from one to the next.

aperture. The lens opening that determines the amount of light that enters a camera. Also, the opening through which light travels from the lamp to the lens in a projector.

arrangement. The pattern or shape into which the elements of a visual display are organized.

articulation. The highest level of motor skill learning. The learner who has reached this level is performing unconsciously, efficiently, and harmoniously, incorporating coordination of skills. See *motor skills domain.*

aspect ratio. Length/width proportions or format of an audiovisual material, such as 3 × 4 for a filmstrip or motion picture frame.

assimilation. The cognitive process by which a learner integrates new information into an existing schema.

audio-card reader. A device for recording and reproducing sound on a card with a magnetic strip. The card may contain verbal and/or pictorial information. Separate tracks may provide for a protected master and erasable student responses.

audioconference. A teleconference involving transmission of voices only; the voices are amplified at each end by a speaker system.

audiographic conference. A teleconference involving voice plus graphic display capability; the graphics may be transmitted by a facsimile machine or elec-

tronically by means of an electronic blackboard or electronic tablet.

audio head. A magnetic element in a tape recorder that records or plays back sound.

Audio-Tutorial System. A technology for managing instruction that employs a study carrel equipped with specially designed audiotapes that direct students to various learning activities. This component is known as an independent study session. Large-group and small-group assemblies are also major components of this system.

automatic level control (ALC) (audio recorders). A circuit used to control the volume or level of the recorded signal automatically to provide uniform level without distortion due to overloading. Sometimes called automatic gain control (AGC) or automatic volume control (AVC).

automatic programmer. See *programmer.*

balance. The sense of equilibrium that is achieved when the elements of a visual display are arranged in such a way that the "weight" is distributed relatively equally.

bar graph. A type of graph in which the height of the bar is the measure of the quantity being represented.

bass. See *frequency.*

Beta (video). A $\frac{1}{2}$-inch videocassette format not compatible with the VHS format, which is also ½-inch but differs electronically.

bidirectional. A microphone that picks up sound in front of and behind itself and rejects sound from the sides.

biochip. A (hypothetical) miniature microprocessor constructed of organic matter, such as a protein molecule.

bit. An acronym for *binary digit*. The smallest unit of digital information. The bit can be thought of as a one or a zero—a circuit on or off.

broadcasting. Transmission of signals to many receivers simultaneously via electromagnetic waves.

byte. The number of bits required to store/represent one character of text (a letter or number). Most commonly, but not always, made up of eight bits in various combinations of zeros and ones.

cable television. A television distribution system consisting of a closed-circuit, usually wired, network for transmitting signals from an origination point (see *head-end*) to members of the network. Typically, the origination point receives and retransmits broadcast programs, adding recorded programs and/or some live originations.

capstan. A rotating shaft or spindle that moves the tape at a constant speed during recording or playback in tape recorders.

cardioid microphone. A microphone that picks up sound primarily in the direction it is pointed, rejecting sounds at the rear of microphone; a undirectional microphone.

carrel. A partially enclosed booth that serves as a clearly identifiable enclosure for learning-center activities.

cassette. A self-contained reel-to-reel magnetic tape system with the two reels permanently intalled in a rugged plastic case.

cathode-ray tube (CRT). The video display tube used in video monitors and receivers, radar displays, and computer terminals.

CCTV. See *closed circuit*.

CD-I (interactive). Incorporates a computer program as well as graphics, audio, and print information.

CD-ROM (read only memory). Digitally encoded information permanently recorded on a compact disc (see *compact disc*). Information can be accessed very quickly.

CD-WORM (write once, read many times). A compact disc on which the user may record information digitally one time, then access it many times.

characterization. The highest level of affective learning. The learner who has reached this level will demonstrate an internally consistent value system, developing a characteristic lifestyle based upon a value or value system. See *affective domain*.

cinéma vérité. A film-making technique in which the camera becomes either an intimate observer of or a direct participant in the events being documented.

circle graph. A graphic form in which a circle or "pie" is divided into segments, each representing a part or percentage of the whole.

closed circuit (system). Any technology that transmits signals through self-contained pathways (such as cable) rather than via broadcasting.

close-up. In motion or still photography, a shot in which the camera concentrates on the subject or a part of it, excluding everything else from view.

cognitive domain. The domain of human learning involving intellectual skills, such as assimilation of information or knowledge.

cognitive psychology. A branch of psychology devoted to the study of how individuals acquire, process, and use information.

communication model. A mathematical or verbal representation of the key elements in the communication process.

compact disc (CD). A 4.72-inch disc on which a laser has recorded digital information.

composition. The creative process of manipulating a camera to frame a picture to suit some contemplated purpose.

comprehension. The level of cognitive learning that refers to the intellectual skill of "understanding"; this includes translating, interpreting, paraphrasing, and summarizing. See *cognitive domain*.

computer-assisted instruction. Instruction delivered directly to learners by allowing them to interact with lessons programmed into the computer system.

computer literacy. The ability to understand and to use computers, parallelling reading and writing in verbal literacy. Actual computer literacy exists along a continuum from general awareness to the ability to create computer programs.

computer-managed instruction. The use of a computer system to manage information about learner performance and learning-resources options in order to prescribe and control individual lessons.

concrete–abstract continuum. The arrangement of various teaching methods in a hierarchy of greater and greater abstraction, beginning with "the total situation" and culminating with "word" at the top of the hierarchy. In 1946 Edgar Dale used the same construct to develop his "Cone of Experience."

condenser lens. Lens(es) between the projection lamp and slide or film aperture to concentrate light in the film and lens apertures.

condenser microphone (also referred to as electrostatic or capacitor). A microphone with a conductive diaphragm that varies a high-voltage electric field to generate a signal. May be any pattern (uni-, bi-, or omnidirectional). Requires a miniaturized amplifier and power supply.

consequence. In psychology, the result of a particular behavior. Learning may be facilitated by arranging positive consequences to follow desired behaviors.

cooperative learning. An instructional configuration involving small groups of learners working together on learning tasks rather than competitively as individuals.

copy stand. A vertical or horizontal stand for accurately positioning a camera when photographing flat subjects.

courseware. Lessons delivered via computer, consisting of content conveyed according to an instructional design controlled by programmed software.

covert response. A learner response that is not outwardly observable. See *overt response*.

craft. In a craft approach to problem solving the emphasis is on the use of tools by a skilled craftsman. Such ad hoc decision making contrasts with the approach of technology.

criterion. As part of a performance objective, the standard by which acceptable performance will be judged; may include a time limit, accuracy tolerance, proportion of correct responses required, and/or qualitative standards.

database. A collection of related information organized for quick access to specific items of information.

debriefing. Discussion conducted among simulation/game participants after play in order to elucidate what has been learned.

decoder. In electronics, the device in a synchronizer or programmer that reads the encoded signal or pulse and turns it into some form of control. In human communication, the element that translates any signal into a form decipherable by the receiver.

dedicated network. An electronic distribution system, for example for teleconferencing, that is owned and operated by the user.

deductive learning. See *expository learning*.

degausser. See *head demagnitizer or eraser*.

depth of field (photography). The region of acceptably sharp focus around the subject position, extending toward the camera and away from it. Varies with the distance of the camera from the subject, the focal length of the lens, and the F/stop.

digital recording. Advanced method of recording that involves a sequence of pulses or on-off signals rather than a continuously variable or analog signal.

digital video interactive (DVI). Similar to compact disc interactive (CDI) but with the addition of moving images. The DVI format can accommodate seventy-two minutes of digitized audio and video.

diorama. A static display employing a flat background and three-dimensional foreground to achieve a lifelike effect.

discovery learning. A teaching strategy that proceeds as follows: immersion in a real or contrived problematic situation, development of hypotheses, testing of hypotheses, arrival at conclusion (the main point).

dissolve. An optical effect in film and video involving a change from one scene to another in which the outgoing and incoming visual images are superimposed or blended together for a discernible period of time as one scene fades out while the other fades in. Also applicable to sequential slides.

dissolve control. A device that controls the illumination from one, two, or more projectors in such a manner that the images fade from one into another at a fixed or variable rate.

division of labor. In economics, the reorganization of a job so that some tasks are performed by one person or system and other tasks by others for purposes of increased efficiency and/or effectiveness.

documentary film. A film that deals with fact, not fiction or fictionalized versions of fact.

dolly. The movement of a camera toward or away from the subject while shooting.

downlink. The reception end of a satellite transmission; entails a satellite dish with a decoder and a display screen.

drill-and-practice game. A game format that provides repetitive drill exercises in an interactive method and that has game-type motivational elements.

drill-and-practice learning. A method of learning that presents a lengthy series of items to be rehearsed; employed with skills that require repetitive practice for mastery.

dry mounting. A method of mounting visuals on cardboard or similar sheet materials in which a special tissue impregnated with a heat-sensitive adhesive is placed between the visual and mount board and is softened by the heat of a dry-mounting press to effect the bond.

DVI. See *digital video interactive*.

economy of scale. In economics, the principle that certain functions decline in cost as they are expanded to encompass a larger population.

EIAJ standards. Electronic equipment standards, notably involving videotape recorders, promoted by the Electronic Industry Association of Japan; they allow for the compatibility of the equipment of all affected manufacturers.

electronic blackboard. A transmission system in which images drawn on a special surface are transmitted over telephone lines and reproduced on a video screen at the reception end.

electrostatic copying (xerography). A method of making overhead transparencies. Similar to the thermal process, this process requires specially treated film that is electrically charged and light sensitive.

emgor. An acronym for *electromyogram sensor*. A prosthetic device that uses the brain's own natural impulse, called the myoelectric signal or electromyogram, to control electromechanical devices in an artificial limb.

encoder. In electronics, a device used with a tape recorder or other information-storage device to produce the synchronizing signals or pulses for later decoding required to operate combinations of devices (projectors) in synchronization. In human communication, the element that converts the thoughts of the source into visible or audible messages.

exciter lamp. The small lamp that projects its single-coil illumination through the optical sound

track on 16-mm film; the varying light intensity is "read" by the projector's photoelectric cell, which converts the light impulses into electronic signals amplified and made audible by a loudspeaker (or earphones).

exhibit. A display incorporating various media formats (e.g., realia, still pictures, models, graphics) forming an integrated whole intended for instructional purposes.

expert system. A computer program, assembled by a team of content experts and programmers, that teaches a learner how to solve complex tasks by applying the appropriate knowledge from the content area.

expository learning. The typical classroom teaching approach that proceeds as follows: presentation of information (the main point), reference to particular examples, application of the knowledge to the students' experiences.

facsimile ("fax"). A transmission system in which images of printed text, diagrams, or hand lettering are sent via telephone lines to another site where the images are mechanically reproduced on paper.

fade in/out. In motion pictures and video, an optical effect in which a scene gradually appears out of blackness or disappears into blackness.

feedback. 1. In electronics, the regeneration of sound caused by a system's microphonic pickup of output from its own speakers causing a ringing sound or squeal. 2. In communication, signals sent from the destination back to the source that provide information about the reception of the original message.

fiber optics. A transmission medium using spun silicon shaped into threads as thin as

human hairs; it transmits more signals with higher quality than metal cables.

film, motion picture. Photographic images stored on celluloid; when projected at twenty-four frames per second, the still images give the illusion of motion.

filmstrip. A roll of 35-mm film containing a series of related still pictures intended for showing one at a time in sequence.

flip chart. A pad of large-sized paper fastened together at the top and mounted on an easel.

F/number. See *lens speed*.

focal length. Loosely, the focal distance when the lens is focused on infinity; more accurately, the distance from the focal point of the lens to the image plane when the lens is focused on infinity.

format. The physical form in which a medium is incorporated and displayed. For example, motion pictures are available in 35-mm, 16-mm, and 8-mm formats.

frame. 1. An individual picture in a filmstrip or motion picture. 2. The useful area and shape of a film image. 3. A complete television picture of 525 horizontal lines. 4. In programmed instruction, one unit in a series of prompt-response-reinforcement units; a block of verbal/visual information.

frame game. An existing game that lends its structure to new subject matter.

freeze frame. A film technique in which a filmmaker selects an image in a motion sequence and prints that image over and over again, so that one moment is held frozen on the screen.

freeze-frame video. A single, still image held on a video screen.

frequency. The rate of repetition in cycles per second (Hertz) of musical pitch or electrical signals. Low frequencies are bass; high frequencies are treble.

fresnel lens. A flat glass or acrylic lens in which the curvature of a normal lens surface is collapsed into small steps in an almost flat plane, resulting in concentric circle forms impressed or engraved on the lens surface. Because of lower cost, less weight, and compactness, it is often used for the condenser lens in overhead projectors and in studio lights.

front-screen projection. An image projected on the "audience side" of a light-reflecting screen.

f/stop. Numerical description of the relative size of the aperture that determines the amount of light entering a camera.

full-motion video. A normal, moving video image; the familiar illusion of normal motion is achieved by projecting thirty frames—each slightly different—every second.

game. An activity in which participants follow prescribed rules that differ from those of reality as they strive to attain a challenging goal.

geosynchronous satellite. A communications satellite traveling at such a speed that it appears to hover steadily over the same spot on the earth.

Gestalt learning. A theory of learning based on analysis of the unified whole, suggesting that the understanding of an entire process is better than the study of individual parts or sequences of the whole.

goal. A desired instructional outcome that is broad in scope and general with regard to criteria and performance indicators.

gothic lettering. A style of lettering with even width of strokes and without serifs (the tiny cross strokes on the ends of a letter).

graphics. Two-dimensional, nonphotographic materials designed to communicate a specific message to the viewer.

hardware. Mechanical/electronic components that make up a computer; the physical equipment that makes up a computer system. By extension, any audiovisual equipment.

head demagnetizer (degausser). A device that provides an alternating magnetic field used during routine maintenance to remove the residual magnetism from recording or playback heads.

head-end. The origination point of a cable television system.

headphone. A device consisting of one or two electro-acoustic receivers attached to a headband for private listening to audio sources; sometimes called earphone.

hearing. A physiological process in which sound waves entering the outer ear are transmitted to the eardrum, converted into mechanical vibrations in the middle ear, and changed in the inner ear into nerve impulses that travel to the brain.

Hertz (Hz). The frequency of an alternating signal. Formerly called *cycles per second* (cps).

holistic learning. In the modeling of reality learners encounter a whole and dynamic view of the process being studied. Emotions are involved along with the thinking process.

hypertext. A computer program that enables the user to access continually a large information base whenever additional information on a subject is needed.

Hz. See *Hertz*.

iconic. Pertaining to an image that resembles a real object.

inductive learning. See *discovery learning*.

input. Information or a stimulus that enters a system.

instruction. Deliberate arrangement of experience(s) to help a learner achieve a desirable change in performance; the management of learning, which in education and training is primarily the function of the instructor.

instructional development. The process of analyzing needs, determining what content must be mastered, establishing educational goals, designing materials to help reach the objectives, and trying out and revising the program in terms of learner achievement.

instructional module. A freestanding instructional unit, usually used for independent study. Typical components are (1) rationale, (2) objective, (3) pretest, (4) learning activities, (5) self-test, and (6) posttest.

instructional technology. "A complex, integrated process involving people, procedures, ideas, devices, and organization, for analyzing problems and devising, implementing, evaluating, and managing solutions to those problems in situations in which learning is purposive and controlled."*

instructional television. Any planned use of video programs to meet specific instructional goals regardless of the source of the programs (including commercial broadcasts) or the setting in which they are used (e.g., including business/industry training).

interactive media. Media formats that allow or require some level of physical activity from the user, which in some way alters the sequence of presentation.

internalization. The degree to which an attitude or value has become part of an individual. The

---

* Association for Educational Communications and Technology (AECT). *The Definition of Educational Technology.* Washington, D.C.: AECT, 1977.

affective domain is organized according to the degree of internalization. See *affective domain*.

interpersonal skills. The domain of learning that has to do with interaction among people; the ability to relate effectively with others.

IPS. Inches per second; more properly written in/s. Standard method for measuring the speed of tape movement.

ITFS. Instructional Television Fixed Service; a portion of the microwave frequency spectrum (2500–2690 mHz) reserved by law in the United States for educational use.

ITV. See *instructional television*.

jack. Receptacle for a plug connector for the input or output circuits of an audio or video device. There are several common sizes and formats of plugs, including:

	diameter
Standard Phone	0.25″ or 6.35 mm
Small Phone	0.206″ or 5.23 mm
Mini	0.140″ or 3.6 mm
Micro	0.097″ or 2.5 mm

keystone effect. The distortion (usually of a wide top and narrow bottom effect) of a projected image caused when the projector is not aligned at right angles to the screen.

lamination. A technique for preserving visuals that provides them with protection from wear and tear by covering them with clear plastic or similar substances.

lantern slide. A once common slide format of $3\frac{1}{4} \times 4$ inch dimensions.

lavalier mike. A small microphone worn around the neck.

learning. A general term for a relatively lasting change in performance caused directly by experience; also, the process or processes whereby such change is brought about. Learning is inferred from performance.

learning center. An individualized environment designed to encourage the student to use a variety of instructional media, to engage in diversified learning activities, and to assume major responsibility for his or her own learning.

lens speed. Refers to the ability of a lens to pass light expressed as a ratio—the focal length of the lens divided by the (effective) diameter. A fast lens (which passes more light) might be rated f/1.1 or 1.2; a much slower lens (which passes less light) might be designated f/3.5.

$$f/\# \text{ or } F/number = \frac{focal\ length}{aperture}$$

line graph. The most precise and complex of all graphs based on two scales at right angles. Each point has a value on the vertical scale and on the horizontal scale. Lines (or curves) are drawn to connect the points.

line of sight. A transmission path between two points that is uninhibited by any physical barriers such as hills or tall buildings; microwave transmission requires a clear line of sight between the transmitter and receiver.

listening. A psychological process that begins with someone's awareness of and attention to sounds or speech patterns, proceeds through identification and recognition of specific auditory signals, and ends in comprehension.

low-cost learning technology. An approach to implementing instructional technology in formal education featuring systematic selection and implementation of a variety of managerial, instructional, motivational, and resource-utilization strategies to increase student learning outcomes while decreasing or maintaining at a constant level the recurrent educational costs.

mainframe computer. A high-speed, multiple-purpose computer intended primarily for business and scientific computing; designed for processing huge amounts of numerical data.

material. An item of a medium format; in the plural, a collection of items of a medium format or of several media formats.

medium (pl. media). A means of communication. Derived from the Latin *medium*, "between," the term refers to anything that carries information between a source and a receiver.

message. Any information to be communicated.

method. A procedure of instruction selected to help learners achieve the objective or to internalize the message.

microfiche. A sheet of microfilm (usually 4″ × 6″) containing multiple micro-images in a grid pattern. It usually contains a title that can be read without magnification.

microfilm. A film in which each frame is a miniaturized image of a printed page or photograph. May be 16-, 35-, 70-, or 105-mm.

microform. Any materials, film or paper, printed or photographic, containing micro-images that are units of information, such as a page of text or drawing, too small to be read without magnification.

micro/minicassette. One of several audiocassettes much smaller than the compact cassette; used principally for note taking and dictation.

microphone. A device that converts sound into electrical signals usable by other pieces of audio equipment. Microphones vary in

sound quality, generating system used, directional patterns, and impedance.

microprocessor. The brain of the microcomputer; the electronic chip (circuit) that does all the calculations and control of data. In larger machines, it is called the Central Processing Unit (CPU).

microprocessor game. Inexpensive, limited-purpose calculator-type toy, such as *Dataman, Little Professor, Speak & Spell,* and *Teach & Tell.* Marketed primarily to the mass home market for arithmetic, spelling, or discrimination practice.

microwave transmission. A television distribution system using the ultra-high-and super-high-frequency ranges (2,000–13,000 mHz). Includes ITFS in the United States (2,500–2,690 mHz).

modem. An acronym for *mo*dulator/*dem*odulator; an electronic device that translates digital information for transmission over telephone lines; it also translates analog information to digital.

module. A free-standing, self-contained component of an instructional system.

monitor. A TV set without broadcast-receiving circuitry that is used primarily to display video signals.

motor skill domain. The category of human learning that involves athletic, manual, and other physical action skills.

multi-image. The use of two or more separate images, usually projected simultaneously in a presentation. Multiple images are often projected on adjacent multiple screens.

multimedia. Sequential or simultaneous use of a variety of media formats in a given presentation or self-study program.

multimedia kit. A collection of teaching/learning materials involving more than one type of medium and organized around a single topic.

multimedia system. A combination of audio and visual media integrated into a structured, systematic presentation.

multipurpose board. A board with a smooth white plastic surface with which special marking pens rather than chalk are used. Sometimes called "visual aid panels," these usually have a steel backing and can be used as a magnetic board for display of visuals. May also be used as a screen for projected visuals.

multiscreen. The use of more than one screen in a single presentation. Multiple images are often projected on adjacent multiple screens.

networking. The interconnecting of multiple sites via electronic means in order to send and receive signals between locations.

noise. 1. In audio systems, electrical interference or any unwanted sound. 2. In video, it refers to random spurts of electrical energy or interference. In some cases it will produce a "salt-and-pepper" pattern over the televised picture. 3. In communication, any distortion of the signal as it passes through the channel.

nonformal education. Purposeful learning that takes place outside the boundaries of formal educational institutions.

omnidirectional. A microphone that picks up sound from all directions.

opaque projection. A method for projecting opaque (nontransparent) visuals by reflecting light off the material rather than transmitting light through it.

open reel. Audio- or videotape or film mounted on a reel that is not enclosed in a cartridge or cassette.

optical sound. Sound that is recorded by photographic means on motion picture film. The sound is reproduced by projecting a narrow beam of light from an exciter lamp through the sound track into a photoelectric cell which converts it to electrical impulses for amplification.

oral history. Historical documentation of a time, place, or event by means of recording the spoken recollections of participant(s) in those events.

output. In electronics, the signal delivered from any audio or video device; also a jack, connector, or circuit that feeds the signal to another piece of equipment such as a speaker or headphones. In communication, information or a stimulus leaving a system.

overhead projection. Projection by means of a device that produces an image on a screen by transmitting light through transparent acetate or similar medium on the stage of the projector. The lens and mirror arrangement in an elevated housing creates a bright projected image cast over the head or shoulder of the operator.

overlay. One or more additional transparent sheets with lettering or other information that can be placed over a base transparency.

overt response. A learner response that is outwardly observable (e.g., writing or speaking). See *covert response.*

patch cord. An electrical wire used to connect two pieces of sound equipment (e.g., tape recorders and record players) so that electrical impulses can be transferred between the two units in order to make a recording.

performance objective. A statement of the new capability the learner should possess at the completion of instruction. A well-stated objective names the intended audience, then specifies:

(1) the performance or capability to be learned, (2) the conditions under which the performance is to be demonstrated, and (3) the criterion or standard of acceptable performance.

peripheral.   A device, such as a printer, mass storage unit, or keyboard, that is an accessory to a microprocessor and that transfers information to and from the microprocessor.

persistence of vision.   The psychophysiological phenomenon that occurs when an image falls on the retina of the eye and is conveyed to the brain via the optic nerve; the brain continues to "see" the image for a fraction of a second after the image is cut off.

Personalized System of Instruction (PSI).   A technology for managing instruction that puts reinforcement theory into action as the overall framework for a whole course. Students work individually at their own pace using a variety of instructional materials. The materials are arranged in sequential order, and the student must show mastery of each unit before being allowed to move on to the next.

pictorial graph.   An alternate form of the bar graph, in which a series of simple drawings is used to represent the value.

pinball-type game.   A microprocessor-controlled arcade game in which the player controls a joystick or paddle and makes rapid hand movements in response to a moving pattern of threatening situations on a display screen.

playback.   A device to reproduce a previously recorded program for hearing and/or viewing.

programmed instruction.   A method of presenting instructional material printed in small bits or "frames," each of which includes an item of information (prompt), an incomplete sentence to be completed or a question to be answered (response), and provision of the correct answer (reinforcement).

programmed tutoring.   A one-to-one method of instruction in which the decisions to be made by the tutor are "programmed" in advance by means of carefully structured printed instructions.

programmer.   A multichannel, multifunction device used with a tape recorder or microprocessor to perform certain predetermined functions when called upon to do so by the synchronizer. In addition to controlling projectors, dissolve controls, etc., it can be arranged to perform other functions (often via interfaces) such as operating a motorized screen, turning on room lights, etc. It may contain the functions of a synchronizer and/or a dissolve control.

projected visual.   Media formats in which still images are projected onto a screen.

projection lens.   A convex lens or system of lenses that recreates an enlarged image of the transparency, object, or film on a screen.

RAM.   See *random access memory.*

random access.   The ability to retrieve in any sequence slides, filmstrip frames, or information on audio- or videotapes or videodiscs regardless of original sequence.

random access memory (RAM).   The flexible part of the computer memory. The particular program or set of data being manipulated by the user is temporarily stored in RAM, then erased to make way for the next program.

range-finder camera.   A camera featuring a built-in, optical range finder, usually incorporated into the viewfinder and linked mechanically with the focusing mount of the lens so that bringing the range-finder images into coincidence also focuses the lens.

rate-controlled audio playback. An audiotape system that can play back recorded speech either at a faster or slower rate than the rate at which it was recorded—without loss of intelligibility. See *speech compression and expansion.*

read only memory (ROM). Control instructions that have been "wired" permanently into the memory of a computer. Usually stores instructions that the computer will need constantly, such as the programming language(s) and internal monitoring functions.

realia.   Real things; objects such as coins, tools, artifacts, plants, animals, etc.

rear screen.   A translucent screen of glass or plastic with a specially formulated coating on which the image is transmitted through the screen for individual or group viewing. The screen is between the projector and the viewer.

reel-to-reel.   Film or tape transport in which separate supply and take-up reels are used; they may be open or enclosed.

referent.   That which is referred to.

reinforcement theory.   A body of psychological theory revolving around the role of reinforcement (consequences that follow responses) in learning.

resolution.   Describes the quality of a video image in terms of the sharpness of detail.

responder.   A device used with some audiovisual equipment to allow a student to respond to the program; e.g., by answering multiple-choice questions.

role-play.   A simulation in

which the dominant feature is a relatively open-ended interaction among people.

ROM. See *read only memory.*

roman lettering. A style of lettering resembling ancient Roman stone-carved lettering: vertical strokes are broad and horizontal strokes are narrower; curved strokes become narrower as they turn toward the horizontal.

rule of thirds. A principle of photographic and graphic composition: divide an area into thirds both vertically and horizontally; the center(s) of interest should be near the intersections of the lines.

saturation. The strength or purity of a color.

scenario. Literally, a written description of the plot of a play. In simulation/game design, it refers to a description of the setting and events to be represented in a simulation.

schema (pl. **schemata**). A mental structure by which the individual organizes perceptions of the environment.

sequencing. Arranging ideas in logical order.

shot. The basic element of which motion pictures are made: each separate length of motion picture footage exposed in one "take."

showmanship. Techniques that an instructor can use to direct and hold attention during presentations.

shutter. The part of a camera (or projector) that controls the amount of light being permitted to pass through the lens.

simulation. An abstraction or simplification of some real-life situation or process.

simulation game. An instructional format that combines the attributes of simulation (role playing, model of reality) with the

attributes of a game (striving toward a goal, specific rules).

simulator. A device that represents a real physical system in a scaled-down form; it allows the user to experience the salient aspects of the real-life process.

single-lens reflex (SLR) camera. A camera in which the view-finder image is formed by the camera lens and reflected to a top-mounted viewing screen by a hinged mirror normally inclined behind the camera lens. During exposure of the film, the mirror flips up, allowing light to pass through onto the film.

slide. A small-format (e.g., 35-mm) photographic transparency individually mounted for one-at-a-time projection.

slow motion. A film technique that expands time by photographing rapid events at high speeds (many exposures per second) and then projecting the film at normal speed.

software. Computer program control instructions and accompanying documentation; stored on diskettes or cassettes when not being used in the computer. By extension, refers to any audiovisual materials.

speech compression and expansion. A method of maintaining intelligibility of normally recorded speech when it is played back at speeds greater than (compression) or less than (expansion) normal; the effect is attained by electronically correcting the pitch to approximate the pitch of normal speech. Variable speeds of playback may be set, from 50 percent of normal to 250 percent of normal speed.

spirit duplicating. An inexpensive duplicating/printing process using master sheets that release color through type indentations when a colorless alcohol fluid ("spirits") is applied; images can

be imprinted on paper, card stock, or acetate.

sponsored film. A film produced by a private corporation, association, or government agency, usually with the purpose of presenting a message of interest to the sponsor for general public consumption.

storyboard(ing). An audiovisual production/planning technique in which sketches of the proposed visuals and/or verbal messages are put on individual cards; the cards then are arranged into the desired sequence on a display surface.

study print. A photographic enlargement printed in a durable form for individual or group examination.

stylus. The "needle" assembly of a phonograph cartridge.

suggestive-accelerative learning and teaching (SALT). A U.S. adaptation of suggestopedy as proposed by Lozanov; major features are conscious relaxation, visual imagery, positive suggestions, multisensory inputs, and presentation of information to be learned in meaningful units, often to musical accompaniment.

synchronizer. A single-function device that, together with a tape recorder or other type of playback, operates other equipment, for example, signalling slide changes.

tacking iron. A small thermostatically controlled heating tool used to tack or attach dry-mounting tissue to the back of a print or to the mount board, so as to hold it in place while the print is trimmed and heated in the dry-mount press.

take-up reel. The reel that accumulates the tape or film as it is recorded or played.

technology. 1. A process—"the systematic application of scientific or other organized knowledge to practical tasks"; the process of devising reliable and repeatable solutions to tasks. 2. A product—the hardware and software that result from the application of technological processes. 3. A mix of process and product—used in instances where (a) the context refers to the combination of technological processes and resultant products; (b) process is inseparable from product.

technology of instruction. A teaching/learning pattern designed to provide reliable, effective instruction to each learner through application of scientific principles of human learning.

teleconference. A communications configuration using electronic transmission technologies (audio and/or video) to hold live meetings among geographically dispersed people.

telelecture. An instructional technique in which an individual, typically a content specialist or a well-known authority, addresses a group listening by means of a telephone amplifier; the listeners may ask questions of the resource person, with the entire group able to hear the response.

teletext. Print information transmitted on a broadcast television signal using the "vertical blanking interval," a portion of the signal not used to carry visual or auditory information.

teletraining. The process of using teleconferences for instructional purposes.

thermal film. Specially treated acetate used to make overhead transparencies. In this process infrared light passes through the film onto a prepared master underneath. An image is "burned into" the film wherever it contacts carbonaceous markings.

threading. Inserting or directing a film or tape through a projector or recorder mechanism.

tilt. The swivelling of a motion picture or video camera upward or downward.

time-lapse. A film technique that compresses the time that it takes for an event to occur. A long process is photographed frame by frame, at long intervals, then projected at normal speed.

transaction. In simulation/game design, the specific actions and interactions carried out by the players as they engage in the activity.

transparency. The large-format (typically 8- by 10-inch) film used with the overhead projector.

treble. See *frequency*.

"2-by-6 rule." A general rule of thumb for determining screen size: No viewer should be seated closer to the screen than two screen widths or farther away than six screen widths.

UHF (ultra high frequency). Television transmission on channels 14 through 83 (300–3,000 mHz).

ultra violet (UV). Rays just beyond (shorter than) the visible spectrum; ordinarily filtered or blocked to prevent eye damage and dye fading.

U-matic. A particular videocassette system offered by several manufacturers in which $\frac{3}{4}$-inch tape moves at $7\frac{1}{2}$ ips between two enclosed hubs.

unidirectional microphone. See *cardioid microphone*.

uplink. A ground station that transmits a signal to a satellite for retransmission to other ground stations.

user-friendly. A subjective measure of how easy an item of hardware or software is to use.

VHF (very high frequency). Television transmission on channels 2 through 13 (30–300 mHz).

VHS. A $\frac{1}{2}$-inch videocassette format. Not compatible with the Beta format, which is also $\frac{1}{2}$ inch but differs electronically.

video. The storage of visuals and their display on a television-type screen.

videocassette. Videotape that has been enclosed in a plastic case. Available in one $\frac{3}{4}$-inch format (U-matic) and two $\frac{1}{2}$-inch formats, Beta and VHS (Video Home System).

videoconference. A teleconference involving a television-type picture as well as voice transmission; the video image may be freeze-frame or full-motion video.

videodisc. A video recording and storage system in which audiovisual signals are recorded on plastic discs, rather than on magnetic tape.

videotex. Two-way, interactive transmission of text and graphics linking the user to a computer database.

view finder. The part of a camera, usually some type of lens, that allows the user to frame the subject being photographed.

visual literacy. The learned ability to interpret visual messages accurately and to create such messages.

volume unit meter (VU-meter). A device to indicate the relative levels of the various sounds being recorded or played. Usually calibrated to show a point of maximum recording level to avoid tape saturation and limit distortion.

wide-angle lens. A camera lens that permits a wider view of a subject and its surroundings than would be obtained by a normal lens from the same position.

Photo Credits

P. 263 (bottom): Purdue University
P. 265 (top): John Soudah
Fig. 9.13: Milt Hamburger, Instructional Television Service, Indiana University
Fig. 9.14: AT&T
P. 267: Northern Illinois University
Fig. 9.16: Andy McGuire

Chapter 10

Fig. 10.1: Andy McGuire
Fig. 10.3: John Soudah
Fig. 10.4: John Soudah
Fig. 10.6: Eastman Kodak Company
Fig. 10.7: John Soudah
Fig. 10.8: Indiana University Audio-Visual Center
Fig. 10.14: John Soudah
Fig. 10.15: Andy McGuire
Fig. 10.18: Michael Neff
Fig. 10.20: John Soudah
P. 293: John Soudah
Fig. 10.21: International Communications Industries Association
Fig. 10.22: John Soudah
Fig. 10.25: Kalart Victor
Fig. 10.28: Andy McGuire

Chapter 11

Fig. 11.1: Kathy Bendo
Fig. 11.2: Association for Educational Communications & Technology
Fig. 11.3: Indiana University Audio-Visual Center
Fig. 11.4: John Soudah
Fig. 11.8: Elyse Rieder
Fig. 11.9: Andy McGuire
Fig. 11.10: Michael Neff
Fig. 11.12: Andy McGuire
Fig. 11.13: J. S. Keller
Fig. 11.14: Donald Dietz/Stock Boston
P. 318: Dennis Short
Fig. 11.15: Dennis Short
Fig. 11.16: Hugh Rogers/Monkmeyer
Fig. 11.17: John Soudah
Fig. 11.18: AIT

Chapter 12

Fig. 12.1: Owen Franken/Stock Boston

Fig. 12.3: Alan Carey/The Image Works
Fig. 12.4: Richard Hutchings/Photo Researchers
P. 333: Richard Sobol/Stock Boston
P. 334 (top): Deane Dayton
P. 334 (middle): Deane Dayton
Fig. 12.5: Michael Molenda
P. 335: Thomas Cecere
P. 336: The Bettmann Archive
Fig. 12.6: Andy McGuire
Fig. 12.7: Doron Precision Systems, Inc., Drivotrainer System
P. 340: Link Flight Simulation
Fig. 12.8: Bell Labs
Fig. 12.9: John Soudah
P. 341 (middle): Arthur Tress/Photo Researchers
P. 341 (bottom): Houghton Mifflin
P. 343: Michael Molenda
Fig. 12.10: National Broadcasting Company, Inc.
Fig. 12.11: Thomas Cecere
Fig. 12.12: Rick Friedman/The Picture Cube
Fig. 12.13: Donald Dietz/Stock Boston

Chapter 13

Fig. 13.1: David Strickler/The Picture Cube
Fig. 13.2: Deane Dayton
P. 357 (bottom): Encyclopaedia Britannica Educational Corporation
P. 358 (top): John Soudah
P. 358 (bottom): Sirius Software
P. 359 (top): Apple Computer Inc.
P. 359 (bottom): Eric Neurath/Stock Boston
P. 361 (left): Sunburst Communications
Fig. 13.3: New York University Education Quarterly
P. 362: Computer-based Education Research Laboratory
Fig. 13.4: Andy McGuire
Fig. 13.5: Deane Dayton
Fig. 13.6: Michael Neff
Fig. 13.7: John Soudah
P. 369: Fairfax County Public Schools
P. 374: Andy McGuire
Fig. 13.14: Deane Dayton
Fig. 13.15: Andy McGuire
P. 375: Andy McGuire
P. 376: IBM

P. 376: Andy McGuire
P. 377: Radio Shack

Chapter 14

Fig. 14.1: The University of Iowa
Fig. 14.2: North America Philips Corporation
Fig. 14.3: Michael Neff
Fig. 14.4: RCA Corporation
Fig. 14.5: AT&T
Fig. 14.9: Andy McGuire
Fig. 14.10: Pottsgrove School District
Fig. 14.11: Electronic University Network
Fig. 14.12: The Bettmann Archive
Fig. 14.13: George S. Zimbel/Photo Researchers
Fig. 14.14: Davidson & Associates
Fig. 14.15: Texas Instruments Inc.
Fig. 14.16: John Soudah
Fig. 14.17: Alan Carey/The Image Works
Fig. 14.18: Spencer Grant/Stock Boston
Fig. 14.19: Laimute E. Druskis/Taurus Photo
Fig. 14.20: Mike Kelly/Picture Group
Fig. 14.21: Russ Dilts/Institute for International Research
Fig. 14.22: Andy McGuire
Fig. 14.23a: Michael Heron/Woodfin Camp
Fig. 14.23b: Agency for Instructional Technology
Fig. 14.23c: Bell & Howell Company
Fig. 14.24a: AECT Archives
Fig. 14.24b: AECT Archives
Fig. 14.24c: AECT Archives
Fig. 14.25a: Perry Ruben/Monkmeyer
Fig. 14.25b: Spencer Grant/Stock Boston
Fig. 14.25c: Jerry Berndt/Stock Boston
Fig. 14.25d: Mimi Forsyth/Monkmeyer
Fig. 14.26: R. Milko/AECT
Fig. 14.27: Andy McGuire
Fig. 14.28: Andy McGuire

Index

Berliner, Emile, 178
Beta, 236, **435**
Bidirectional microphone, **436**
Biochip, 392, **436**
Biotechnology, 403
Bit, 381, **436**
Bloom, Benjamin S., 42
Broadcasting, **436**
Brooker, Floyde, 215
Bruner, Jerome, 11
Bulletin boards, 89, 93, 120–122
  purposes of, 120–121
Byte, 381, **436**

C

Cable television, 258–260, **436**
  future view, 260
  innovative applications, 260
Camera
  parts of, 90
  selection of, 90–92
Capstan, **436**
Cardioid microphone, 175, **436**
Carlisle, Robert, 229
Carrels, 188–189, **436**
Cartoons, 86, 87, 110
Cartwright, Glenn F., 403
Cassette tape recorders
  battery tips, 275–276
  digital, 167
  operation of, 274
  troubleshooting, 275
Cassette tapes, 164–166, **436**
  accidental erasure prevention, 180
  advantages of, 164, 166
  applications of, 169, 170, 173
  attributes of, 164
  limitations of, 166
Cathode-ray tube (CRT), 378, **436**
CCTV. *See* Closed circuit television
CD I, 395, **436**
CD ROM, 167, 395, **436**
CD WORM, 395, **436**
Central processing unit (CPU), 376,
  378
Chalkboards, 118–119
  AV showmanship, 119
Characterization, 43, **436**
Charts, 107–108, 109
Cinéma vérite, 223, **436**
Circle (pie) graphs, 111, **436**
Classroom structure, 404–405
  alternative set-ups, 405
Closed-circuit television, 257–258,
  436
Close-up, 90, **436**
Cloth boards, 122–124
  making of, 123

Cognitive development, Piaget's theory, 11
Cognitive domain, 42–43, **436**
Cognitive psychology, **436**
  and technology of instruction, 321
Coleman, James S., 337
Color preferences, 68
Comenius, Johannes Amos, 74–75
Communication models, 4–6, **436**
  Shannon-Schramm model, 4–5
  Shannon-Weaver model, 4
  transactional model, 6
Compact discs (CD), 166–167, **436**
  advantages of, 167
  attributes of, 166–167
  as database, CD-ROM, 167
  limitations of, 167
Composition, 94, **436**
Comprehension, **436**
Computer-assisted instruction, 323,
  436
  discovery method, 358–359
  drill-and-practice method, 357
  gaming/simulation, 358
  problem-solving method, 359–360,
    361
  tutorial method, 357
  utilization of methods, 360
Computer-based instruction
  advantages of, 366
  and ASSURE model, 371–372, 375
  and computer literacy, 367, 368,
    369
  development systems, 364
  evaluation of, 376
  individualized instruction, 367–368
  limitations of, 366–367
Computer-based materials
  modification of, 373
  selection of, 372–373
Computer-generated masters, overhead
  transparencies, 142
Computer-generated slides, 147, 150
Computer graphics, 368
Computer hardware, 376–379, **439**
  central processing unit (CPU), 376,
    378
  disks, 377, 379
  memory, 378, 381
  printers, 378–379
  selection of, 382–383
  storage, 378
Computer languages, 381
Computer literacy, 368–369, **436**
Computer-managed instruction, 360–
  361, **436**
  types of systems, 361
Computer networks, 369–371
  advantages of, 370

applications of, 371
  hard disk, 369–370
  learning networks, 395–396
  limitations of, 371
  point-to-point, 369, 370
Computers
  computer-based testing, 361–363
  computer-generated materials, 363
  databases, 368–369
  design computer screen, 88
  development of, 364–365
  future trends, 392
  as object of instruction, 356
  overhead projection and, 137
  prescription of media/materials/
    activities, 363
  record-keeping and, 363
  scheduling and, 363
  as tool of instruction, 356–357
  types of, 381
Computers in education, 365
  utilization of computer, 373, 375–
    376
Computer software
  selection of, 372–373
  sources of information, 372, 419,
    423, 424
Concrete-abstract continuum, 11–12,
  436
Condenser lens, **437**
Condenser microphone, 175, **437**
Consequence, 347, **437**
Continental classroom, 254–255
Cooperative learning, 321–322, **437**
  characteristics of, 321–322
Copyright guidelines, 429–434
Copy stand, **437**
Courseware, 372–373, **437**
  sources of information, 419, 423,
    424
Covert response, 56, **437**
Craft, 406, **437**
Criterion, **437**
Crowder, Norman, 310
Cultural understanding, and films,
  225–226
Cut mode, 195

D

Dale, Edgar, 13
Dale's Cone of Experience, 12, 13,
  100
Databases, **437**
  CD-ROM programs, 167
  classroom type, 369
  commercial type, 369
  sources of, 167
  videotext services, 268–269

L

Lamination, nonprojected visuals, 115, 118, **440**
Lantern slide, **440**
Lashley, K. S., 22
Lavalier mike, 242, **440**
Learner analysis, 36–37
Learner performance, 53, 56–57
  evaluation of, 57–58
Learning, **440**
Learning centers, 188–191, **440**
  advantages of, 189
  applications of, 189
  carrels, 188–189
  design aspects, 189–190
  evaluation of, 190
  limitations of, 189
  management of, 190–191
Learning networks, 395–396
Learning styles
  information-processing habits, 398
  motivational factors, 398
  perceptual factors, 397
  physiological factors, 398–399
Lenses, projectors, 290
Lens speed, 90, **440**
Lenticular screen, 287
Lettering, in visuals, 81–82
Line graphs, 111, **440**
Line of sight, **440**
Listening, **440**
  See also Hearing/listening.
Local area network (LAN), 369
Low-cost learning technology, 405, **440**

M

Mager, Robert, 45, 58
Magnetic boards, 123–124
Mainframe computer, 365, **440**
Mainstreaming, 16
Material, **440**
Matte white screen, 287
Media comparison studies, 22–23
Meditation, 402
Medium/media, 6–7, **440**
  in distance education, 15
  in instruction, 12–14
  post-lesson evaluation, 59–60
  in special education, 15–16
  in training, 17, 20–22
  trends in, 390–396
Memory, computer hardware, 378, 381
Merriman, H. R., 179
Message, **440**

Method, **440**
Microfiche, 391, **440**
Microfilm, **440**
Microform, 391, **440**
Micro/minicassette, 165, **440**
Microphones, 174–175, **440**
  acoustics and placement of, 174
  feedback problems, 279
  function of, 172
  parts of, 174
  pick-up patterns, 175
  and tape recorders, 174–175
  types of, 175
  and video production, 242
Microprocessor, 364–365, **441**
Microprocessor games, 400, **441**
Microwave (ITFS) transmission, 260–261, **441**
Miniaturization, 390–392
  cassette tape recording, 390
  computer technology, 392
  film equipment, 390
  print medium, 390
  videodiscs, 390
  videotape recorders, 390
Mock-ups, 101–102
Models, 101–102
Modem, **441**
Modifying media, 49–50
Modules, 187–188, **441**
  components of, 187–188
  design of, 188
Monitor, 242–243, **441**
Motor skills domain, 43, **441**
Mounting nonprojected visuals, 111–115
  dry mounting, 115, 116
  with iron, 117
  rubber cement mounting, 113–115
Multi-image presentations, 197–200, **441**
Multi-image systems
  advantages of, 199
  application of, 199–200
  automatic programmers, 198
  dissolve units, 197–198
  limitations of, 199
Multimedia, **441**
Multimedia kits, 184–186, **441**
  advantages of, 186
  applications of, 186–187
  commercial kits, 185
  limitations of, 186
  teacher-made kits, 185–186, 187
Multimedia systems, **441**
  attributes of, 184
  development chart in, 196
  interactive video, 200–209
  learning centers, 188–191

  modules, 187–188
  multi-image presentations, 197–200
  multimedia kits, 184–186
  sound-slide combinations, 191–193, 194–195
  storyboarding, 193, 196
Multipurpose boards, 119, **441**
Multi-screen, 197, **441**

N

NAPLPS, 269
National Assessment of Educational Progress (NAEP) program, 408
National Information Center for Educational Media (NICEM), 47, 417
National Information Center for Special Education Materials (NICSEM), 48, 417–418
National Society for Performance and Instruction (NSPI), 412
National Technology University (NTU), 263, 396
National University Teleconferencing Network (NUTN), 266
Networking, **441**
  computer networks, 369–371
  learning networks, 395–396
New Age training, 402
Noise, **441**
Nonformal education, **441**
Nonprojected visuals
  ASSURE model application, 129
  display methods, 117–127
  field trips, 102–103, 104
  film and storing, 115–117
  graphic materials, 105–111
  laminating, 115, 118
  models, 101–102
  mounting, 111–115
  realia, 100–101, 102
  sources of information, 419
  still pictures, 103–105, 107

O

Objectives, 37–46
  classification of, 41–42
  domains of learning and, 42–44
  individual differences and, 44, 46
  origins of, 45
  rationale for, 37
  requirements of, 38–40
Omnidirectional, 175, **441**
Opaque projection, 153–155, **441**
  advantages of, 153–154
  applications of, 154–155

AV showmanship, 155
   limitations of, 154
Opaque projectors, 194, 283–284
   operating problems, 283–284
   operation of, 284
   troubleshooting, 286
Open reel tape, 164, 235, **441**
Optical sound, 214, **441**
Oral history, **441**
Output, 378, **441**
Overhead projection, 134–142, **441**
   advantages of, 135–136
   applications of, 137
   AV showmanship, 138
   limitations of, 136–137
Overhead projectors, 134, 279–280
   cleaning of, 279
   operation of, 280
   troubleshooting, 281
Overhead transparencies
   computer-generated masters, 142
   design elements, 142
   direct drawing method, 138–139
   electrostatic film process, 140
   Fryeon process, 141
   sources of information, 135–136,
      419–420
   spirit-duplicated process, 140, 142
   thermal film process, 139–140
   uses of, 134–135
Overlay, **441**
Overt response, 56, **441**

P

Patch cord, 177, **441**
Pegboards, 119
Performance objective, **441**
Peripheral, 376, **442**
Persistence of vision, 214, **442**
Personalized System of Instruction
   (PSI), 269, 316–317, **442**
   applications of, 317
   characteristics of, 316–317
   as technology of instruction, 317
Phonograph records, 163–164
   advantages of, 163–164
   attributes of, 163
   limitations of, 164
   sources of, 164
   types of, 276
Photography, 86, 90–92
   camera, parts of, 90
   composition tips, 94–95
   elements of, 90
   selection of camera, 90–92
   selection of film, 92

Piaget, Jean, 11, 74, 321
Pictorial graphs, 111, **442**
Picture preferences of learners, 67–68
Pinball games, 401–402, **442**
PLATO Learning Management, 361,
   362
Playback, **442**
Porta-pak, 241
Posters, 108, 110
Postlethwait, S. N., 318
Presentation method, 8
Previewing media, 51
Printed materials, design elements,
   84–85
Printers, computer, 378–379
Problem-solving method, 11
   and computers, 359–360, 361
   and films, 225
Professional journals, 413
Professional organizations, 411–412
Programmed instruction, 19, 307–314,
   442
   application of, 312
   development of, 310
   elements of, 310
   objectives in, 45
   sources of information, 311, 419
   as technology of instruction, 310
   utilization of, 314
Programmed tutoring, 314–316, **442**
   applications of, 315–316
   characteristics of, 314–315
   as technology of instruction, 315
Programmer, multimedia, 198, **442**
Projected visuals, 134–153, **442**
   filmstrips, 150–153
   opaque projection, 153–155
   overhead projection, 134–142
   selection criteria, 155
   slides, 142–150
Projection lamps
   coding of, 289
   handling of, 290
   replacement of, 290
   types of, 289
Projection lens, 290, **442**
Projection setups, 284–294
   equipment carts, 292–294
   lenses, 290
   projector lamps, 289–290
   projector placement, 290–292
   screen placement, 288–289
   screen size, 286–287
   screen surfaces, 287–288
   seating arrangement, 284, 286
Psychotechnology, altered states of
   consciousness, 402
Public television stations, 256

R

Radio, 250–251
   broadcast radio, 250–251
   interactive radio, 251
RAM. *See* Random access memory
Random access, **442**
Random access memory (RAM), 378,
   442
Range-finder camera, 91, **442**
Rate-controlled audio playback, 177,
   180, **442**
Read only memory (ROM), 378, **442**
Realia, 100–101, 102, **442**
Realism, in visuals, 66–67
Rear screen, **442**
Record players, 276–277
   operation of, 277
   stylus, 276
   troubleshooting, 277
Reel-to-reel, **442**
Referent, **442**
Reigeluth, Charles, 403
Reinforcement theory, 306–307, **442**
Reiser, Robert M., 46
Research
   applied to practice, 23–24
   media comparison studies, 22–23
Resolution, **442**
Responder, **442**
Review sources, 423–424
Role-play, 335, 338, **442**
Roman lettering, 81, **443**
Romiszowski, A. J., 339
ROM. *See* Read only memory
Rubber cement mounting, 113–115
Rule of thirds, 94, **443**

S

Satellite communication, 261–263
   direct home/school reception, 262
   networks, 262, 263
Saturation, **443**
Scenario, **443**
Schema/schemata, 11, **443**
Schramm, Wilbur, 4, 310
Screen
   placement, 288–289
   size, 286–287
   surfaces, 287–288
Selection of media/materials, 23–24,
   46–49
   media format, choosing, 46
   selection criteria, 23–24, 48, 155
   sources of materials, 47–48
Sequencing, 69, **443**